Siree Guru Granth Sahib
(Sikh Religion Scriptures 2)

Siree Guru Granth Sahib
(Sikh Religion Scriptures 2)

Gurmukhi to English Translation

Swarn Singh Bains

Book 2 of 2 Original pages (711-1430)
Book pages (710-1448)

By the grace of guru the God
Translated by:
    Swarn Singh Bains
    3 Shakespeare Road,
    Dundas on
    L9H 7R5, Canada
    Ph 905 627 0625

Originally from
    Vill: Kishan pura, distt Ropar
    Punjab India
    E mail; *bains_swarn@hotmail.com*
            bains_swarn@yahoo.com
    @ Author
    My family after me

Print information available on the last page.

Rev. date: 11/19/2020

To order additional copies of this book, contact:
Xlibris
844-714-8691
www.Xlibris.com
Orders@Xlibris.com
585087

wishes

God is limitless, unfathomable, beyond imagination and beyond comprehension. His praise and the way to attain salvation described in Siree Guru Granth Sahib is also beyond comprehension. To translate Siree Guru Granth Sahib is also beyond comprehension. Siree Guru Granth Sahib is the scripture of Sikh religion. It is the original writings of Sikh Masters (guru) and Hindu and Muslim saints. It is a divine book. It has no stories. It is written Gurmukhi (Punjabi) alphabets. Written in 31 Indian classical tunes and fully balanced book. It does not differentiate between religion gender creed and race. People have the longing to know about God and to become divine. Therefore the devotees try to interpret Siree Guru Granth Sahib depending upon their knowledge and devotion. By the grace of guru the God; Swarn Singh Bains has attempted with devotion and best intentions and completed the translation of Siree Guru Granth Sahib in English to the best of his humble ability with the help of Mahaan Kosh and borrowing some English words from computer programme. What I learned during my effort? The guru is God. Worshipping guru the God devotionally attains salvation. I hope the learned masters; the scholars and the Godly people will accept his humble attempt. Names of tunes, lunar dates, name of days, letter of alphabets used in certain places cannot be changed or translated. The original page numbers and stanza numbers are kept for reference purpose.

Swarn Singh Bains

GOD IS ONE. It is true. He is the Creator. He is carefree. He has no enemy. He is immortal. He does not take birth. He came into existence on His own. He is realized by guru's grace.

Tune Todee, Chau-Padas, Fourth Master, First House: My mind cannot survive without God. O God love of my life, unite me with my guru so that I do not take birth again in the world. ||1||Pause|| My mind yearns for God. I want to see my beloved God with my eyes. The merciful guru taught me God's name and the way to realize God. ||1|| I got imbued with God's name and realized God the Lord of the universe. Enshrining God in the mind tastes sweet to my mind body and mouth. I am lucky. ||2|| Those enticed by useless greed, forgot the good God. They are self-willed ignorant. They are unfortunate. ||3|| I obtained the discerning intellect from the guru. Guru's wisdom is same as God. Servant Nanak has obtained God's name from the guru. It was written in my fate from destiny. ||4||1|| Todee, Fifth Master, First House, Du-Padas: God is one. He is realized by guru's grace. The saints do not know anyone else. They became carefree forever dyed with God's love. God is on their side. ||Pause|| Your canopy is very high, O Lord; no one else has a tent with so high canopy. The devotees found an

710

immortal Lord. They attained divine wisdom through love. ||1|| Disease, sorrow, pain, old age and death do not come close to them They become carefree in love of one Lord; O Nanak, they have surrendered their minds to the Lord. ||2||1|| Todee, Fifth Master: Forgetting the Lord, one is ruined forever. Anyone who has Your support cannot be deceived. ||Pause|| Page 712 Without reciting God the life is burning like the life of a snake. One may rule over the whole world. But in the end he will lose and depart. ||1|| One, who is blessed by God, sings His praises. He is at peace, and his birth is blessed; Nanak praises him. ||2||2|| Todee, Fifth Master, Second House, Chau-Padas: God is one. He is realized by guru's grace. The mind wanders in ten directions. It is intoxicated by the worldly greed. God has deluded him. ||Pause|| He does not focus his mind even for a moment on God's sermon or His praises in the company of devotees. He is excited seeing the temporary colour of the safflower and goes to rob other's house. ||1|| He does not love God's lotus feet and he does not please the true Lord. He wanders around in many ways like an ox around the oil mill. ||2|| He does not recite God's name, does not give awns, and does not bathe at shrines. He does not sing God's praises at all. He enjoys doing false deeds. He does not realize himself. ||3|| He never does good for others; he does not serve or worship the guru. He is entangled in the company of five thieves and takes their advice. He is intoxicated by the worldly wealth. ||4|| I pray in devotee's congregation; hearing that God is the love of devotees. Nanak runs after God and pleads; protect the honour of Your own. ||5||1||3|| Todee, Fifth Master: O mortal, without realizing God; coming into the world is useless. He puts on various ornaments and many decorations, but it is like dressing the dead. ||Pause|| Going all over and working hard the miser collects wealth. He does not give awns or shows generosity, he does not serve the saints; his wealth does not do him any good. ||1|| The soul-bride imagines, puts on ornaments makes her bed. She does not obtain the company of her Husband Lord; she feels pain seeing it. ||2|| The man works all day threshing the husks with the pestle. He feels pain working for nothing. It is not of any use to him. ||3|| Those, whom God is kind, enshrine God's name in the mind. Following devotees company, servant Nanak obtained God's sublime taste. ||4||2||4|| Todee, Fifth

Master: O Lord, ocean of mercy, please live in my heart forever. Please bestow such an intellect that I fall in love with God. ||Pause|| May I obtain the dust of Your servants and apply to my forehead. Singing Gods praises the worst sinners become sacred. ||1|| Page 713 Your command appeals to me and I do what pleases You. Whatever You give satisfies me; I do not go anywhere else. ||2|| Know that God is close and be the dust of everybody's feet. Finding the company of devotees I shall find God. ||3|| I am Your child forever; You are my God, my King. Nanak is Your child; You are my mother and father; Your name is milk to my mouth. ||4||3||5|| Todee, Fifth Master, Second House, Du-Padas: God is one. He is realized by guru's grace. I beg for the gift of Your name, O Lord. Nothing else shall go with me. Be kind that I sing Your praises. ||1||Pause|| Power, wealth, various pleasures and enjoyments, all are like the shadow of a tree. He runs around in many directions, but all of his pursuits are useless. ||1|| If I long for anything other than God; it appears that everything is temporary. Says Nanak, I beg for the dust of saint's feet so that my mind may find peace. ||2||1||6|| Todee, Fifth Master: The name of the dear Lord is the Support of my mind. My mind finds happiness in my soul and life doing so. ||1||Pause|| God's name is my caste, my honour and my family. God's name is my companion; it is always with me. God's name bestows salvation to me. ||1|| Sensual pleasures are talked about a lot, but nothing goes with You in the end. God's name is Nanak's companion of the same congregation. God's name is my treasure. ||2||2||7|| Todee, Fifth Master: Singing the sublime praises of the Lord eradicates your disease. Your face will become happy and mind pure. You will find your company here and hereafter. ||1||Pause|| I wash guru's feet and serve Him; I offer my mind to him. Renounce self-conceit, negativity and ego and accept what happens. ||1|| He, on whose forehead such destiny is written serves the saints. Says Nanak, other than one God there is no other able to do so. ||2||3||8|| Todee, Fifth Master: O true guru, I have come to Your sanctuary. Grant me the peace and glory of God's name and remove my worry. ||1||Pause|| I cannot see any other place of shelter; got tired and I came to Your door. I can be saved only by ignoring my account. I am worthless, please, save me! ||1|| You are always forgiving and kind; You give food to all. Slave Nanak follows the saints; save him this time O Lord; ||2||4||9|| Todee, Fifth Master: My tongue sings the praises of the Lord of the world, the ocean of virtues. Peace, contentment and joy welled up in my mind, all sorrows departed. ||1||Pause|| Page 714 Whatever I ask for, I receive; I serve God's feet the source of nectar. I am released from birth and death and crossed over the terrifying world-ocean. ||1|| I realized the reality by searching; slave of the Lord of the universe became pure. O Nanak, If you want salvation; recite God forever. ||2||5||10|| Todee, Fifth Master: The slanderer stopped slandering by guru's grace. The supreme Lord became kind; Shiva's arrow changed his thinking. ||1||Pause|| He who follows truthful path cannot be caught by the net or the noose of death. He earned the wealth, the jewel of God's name; it does not decrease by eating and spending. ||1|| In an instant, he is reduced to ashes; he received the rewards of his doing. Servant Nanak speaks the truth of the scriptures; see it o whole world; ||2||6||11|| Todee, Fifth Master: O miser, your body and mind are full of sin. Recite God in the company of devotees. Only God can cover your sins. ||1||Pause|| When many holes appear in your boat, you cannot plug them with your hands. Worship the one who owns the boat; He saves the counterfeit with the genuine. ||1|| People want to lift the mountain with words, but it stays there. Nanak has no strength; O God, please protect me in Your sanctuary. ||2||7||12|| Todee, Fifth Master: Recite the lotus feet of the Lord in your mind. Lord destroys the false with an axe. God's name is the medicine. ||1||Pause|| Lord removes the three fevers; He destroys the pain and attains peace. No obstacle blocks the path of one who prays to God. ||1|| By the grace of the saints, God is my doctor; God is the doer the cause of causes. He is the giver of peace to the innocent-minded people; O Nanak, God is the support. ||2||8||13|| Todee, Fifth Master: Recite God's name forever. By His grace the supreme Lord has made me a permanent resident. ||1||Pause|| He who owns me took care of me; my sorrows and sufferings are eradicated. He gave His hand and saved me, God is my mother and father. ||1|| All beings became kind to me by God's grace. Nanak seeks the sanctuary of the destroyer of pain; His glory is great! ||2||9||14|| Todee, Fifth Master: O Lord I seek the sanctuary of Your court. O destroyer of millions of sins; other than You, who else can save me? ||1||Pause|| I searched many ways and contemplated every means. Salvation attains in devotee's company. Enticed by worldly wealth loses the game. ||1|| Page 715 My mind is in love with God's lotus feet; I met the beloved, noble, hero. Nanak celebrates reciting God, all sickness has been cured. ||2||10||15|| Todee, Fifth Master, Third House, Chau-Padas: God is one. He is realized by guru's grace. O ignorant; you are attached to worldly wealth. It is never enough. That, which you think is yours, is not yours. ||Pause|| You do not remember your Lord, even for an instant. That, which belongs to others; you believe it as your own; ||1|| God's name is your companion. You do not enshrine in the mind. You are attached to what is going to leave you; ||2|| You collect that which will bring you only hunger and thirst. You have not obtained the supplies of the sacred name. ||3|| You have fallen into the pit of lust, anger and emotional attachment. By guru's grace, O Nanak, a few are saved. ||4||1||16|| Todee, Fifth Master: I have one Lord. I do not recognize any other. ||Pause|| By good fortune, I found my guru. The guru implanted the name of the Lord in me. ||1|| The name of the Lord is my meditation, austerity, fasting and daily religious practice. Reciting God's name I found total joy and bliss. ||2|| The praises of the Lord are my good conduct, occupation and social class. Listening to the singing of Lord's praises, I am happy. ||3|| Says Nanak, those who realize God; Everything comes to their home. ||4||2||17|| Todee, Fifth Master, Fourth House, Du-Padas: God is one. He is realized by guru's grace. My beautiful mind longs for the love of the Lord. By mere words, Lord's love does not well up. ||Pause|| I search to visualize Him, looking in each and every street. Meeting the guru, my doubts have been dispelled. ||1|| I obtained this wisdom hearing from devotees. It was written on my forehead from destiny. In this way, Nanak has seen the Lord with his eyes. ||2||1||18|| Todee, Fifth Master: My ignorant heart is full of pride. By the will of God o mother; it swallowed me like a vulture. ||Pause|| Everyone wants more. Cannot attain anything without effort? I am attached and sing God's praises. The unlucky is engulfed by fire. ||1|| Listen, O mind to the teachings of devotees, all your sins shall be erased. One who is destined to receive God's blessing, O servant Nanak, shall not be cast into the womb again. ||2||2||19|| Page 716 Todee, Fifth Master, Fifth House, Du-Padas: God is one. He is realized by guru's grace. God blessed me with such wisdom. He banished the five evils and the illness of ego from my body. ||Pause|| Breaking my bonds and releasing me from bad deeds, He enshrined guru's teachings in my mind. He did not consider my beauty or ugliness; He embraced me with love. I am drenched with His love. ||1|| I saw my beloved eliminating the curtain in between. My mind is happy, pleased and satisfied. My house is His; He is my God. Nanak is obedient to His Lord. ||2||1||20|| Todee, Fifth Master: O my mother, my mind is in love. This is my luck and faith and recitation. Reciting God is a good omen. ||Pause|| Visualizing God everyday is the support of my life. On the road, and on the river, these supplies are with me. I made my beloved my companion. ||1|| By the grace of the saints, my mind became pure. He made me His own by His grace. Nanak found peace reciting God the friend of His devotees from beginning through the ages. ||2||2||21|| Todee, Fifth Master: O dear God, please meet me; You are my life. Do not let me forget You from my heart; bestow Your devotee with the gift of perfect knowledge. ||Pause|| Eliminate my doubt and save me, O my beloved, all-knowing searcher of hearts. The wealth of God's name is worth millions of kingdoms to me; O God, please bless me by Your grace. ||1|| Twenty-four hours a day, I sing Your praises. It satisfies my ears O all-powerful Lord. I seek Your sanctuary, O giver of life; Nanak praises You forever. ||2||3||22|| Todee, Fifth Master: O God, I am the dust of Your feet. O merciful to the meek, beloved, enticing Lord, be kind and fulfill my yearning. ||Pause|| People praise You in ten directions O inner-knower. You are ever-present. Those who sing Your praises, O Creator, those beings never die in sorrow. ||1|| The worldly affairs and entanglements of worldly wealth and sorrows disappear in the company of devotees. The comforts of wealth and the enjoyments of soul O Nanak are false without the Lord. ||2||4||23|| Todee, Fifth Master: O my mother, my mind is thirsty. I cannot survive even for a moment without my beloved. My mind hopes to visualize him. ||Pause|| I recite God's name O Creator, that the sins may leave my mind and body. The perfect supreme Lord giver of peace is immortal; praising Him makes pure. ||1|| By saint's grace my desire got fulfilled by singing your praises by Your grace. Page 717 Peace, contentment and happiness well up. It gives as much light as million suns O Nanak. ||2||5||24||

Todee, Fifth Master: The Lord is the purifier of sinners; He is the bestowal of soul, life, honour and happiness. The inner-knower pleases my mind. ||Pause|| He is beautiful wise intelligent and with discriminating wisdom. He dwells in the hearts of His slaves. His devotees sing His praises. He is beautiful pure and incomparable Lord. You eat what you sow ||1|| I am amazed by His wonders. There is no other like Him. I live by reciting Him and singing His praises. Servant Nanak praises Him forever. ||2||6||25|| Todee, Fifth Master: O mother, the worldly wealth is deceiving. Without worshipping God; everything is like a straw on fire, cloudy shade and flood of water. ||Pause|| Renounce smartness and clever tricks; with your palms pressed together, follow the path of God's devotees. Recite the inner knower God. This is real purpose of human body. ||1|| The devotees preach Vedas but the unfortunate ignorant do not understand them. Servant Nanak is absorbed in loving worship; reciting God removes filth. ||2||7||26|| Todee, Fifth Master: O mother, guru's feet taste sweet to me. The transcendent Lord blesses the fortunate. Seeing the guru attains millions of rewards. ||Pause|| Singing the praises of immortal Lord; lust, anger and stubborn pride vanish. Those imbued with God's love become immortal; birth and death do not grind them anymore. ||1|| Without worshipping God, all joys and pleasures known to the kind saint are false. Servant Nanak found the jewel God's name; without it everyone gets robbed. ||2||8||27|| Todee, Fifth Master: I Recite God's name in the company of devotees. I am peaceful and content day and night; the seeds of my destiny have sprouted. ||Pause|| I the fortunate met the true guru. He has no end or limits. Taking by the hand He took me out of the poisonous world ocean. ||1|| My birth and death have ended through guru's teachings; I no longer have to suffer. Nanak took to God's refuge; he humbly bows to Him forever. ||2||9||28|| Todee, Fifth Master: O my mother, my mind is at peace. I enjoy millions of princely joy and pleasures; all sufferings departed reciting God. ||1||Pause|| The sins of millions of lifes are erased; reciting God finds peace of mind and body. Seeing God's beauty, my hopes are fulfilled; visualizing Him eliminated my hunger. ||1|| God bestows the four great blessings, the eight powers of mystics, Elysian cow and ever fruiting tree. O Nanak, taking to the refuge of the ocean of peace. You shall not suffer the pains of birth and death and get smoked in pregnancy. ||2||10||29|| Page 718 Todee, Fifth Master: I have enshrined God's feet in my heart. Reciting my Lord the guru, all my affairs have been resolved. ||1||Pause|| Reciting God obtains all, such as giving awns, do good or worship. Singing the praises of immortal and infinite God attains immeasurable peace. ||1|| Those, whom God made His own; He does not check their account anymore. I live by hearing and reciting the jewel God's name. God dwells in Nanak's throat. ||2||11||30|| Todee, Ninth Master: God is one. He is realized by guru's grace. What can I say about my low life? I am entangled in love of gold and women, I do not sing God's praises. ||1||Pause|| I fell in love with the false world thinking it to be true. I never worshipped the friend of the poor who is always with me and helps. ||1|| I am intoxicated by worldly wealth night and day; filth of my mind does not leave. Says Nanak, without God's refuge the salvation is not possible any other way. ||2||1||31|| Tune Todee; the word of devotees: God is one. He is realized by guru's grace. Some say God is near, others say, He is far. The fish that lives in water climbs the date tree. ||1|| Why do you speak nonsense? One, who finds God, hides it. ||1||Pause|| The religious scholars, recite the Vedas. Ignorant Naam Dev knows the Lord. ||2||1|| Tell me; whose blemishes remain reciting God's name? Sinners become pure saying God; ||1||Pause|| Naam Dev said to himself that he is going to say God God; Why do you keep fast on eleventh lunar day and go to pilgrimage? ||1|| Says Naam Dev, I have become a man of good deeds and good thoughts. Tell me; who did not go to heaven through guru's teachings saying God? ||2||2|| Here is a verse with a three-fold play on words. ||1||Pause|| In the potter's home there are pots, in the king's home there are elephants. Veda's in the Brahmin's home. Pots, elephants and Veda's have similar feeling. ||1|| Asafetida in grocer's home and horns on buffalo's head; Lingam in Shiva's temple; Asafetida, horns and Lingam are same. ||2|| In the house of the oil-presser there is oil; in the forest there are vines. Bananas in the gardener's home; Oil, vine and bananas are same. ||3|| The Lord of the universe abides in His saints; as Lord Krishna in Gokal. God abides in Naam Dev. God, Krishna and Lord of the universe is same. ||4||3|| Page 719 Tune Bairaaree, Fourth Master, First House, Du-Padas:

God is one. He is realized by guru's grace.

LISTEN, O MIND, to the unspoken Speech of Lord's name. Riches, wisdom, powers of mystics and peace are obtained, by saying God God; through guru's teachings. ||1||Pause|| Preaching of Puraanas and six Shaastras, sing the sublime Praises of God. Shiva and millions of gods sing praises but do not know how to realize God. ||1|| The gods, Heroes and the celestial singers and the whole creation sing His praises. O Nanak, those whom God bestows His kindness, become the good saints reciting God. ||2||1|| Bairaaree, Fourth Master: O mind; sing God's praises in the company of saints. The gift of God's name the priceless jewel is given by the guru. ||1||Pause|| I offer my mind, body and everything to the humble being who recites God's name. I offer my wealth and reputation to him; who unites me with my friend God. ||1|| When God becomes kind a little bit; I sing God's praises. Surrendering to God the master; Nanak's disease of ego is cured. ||2||2|| Bairaaree, Fourth Master: Lord's humble servant sings the praises of God's name. If someone slanders God's humble servant, he does not gain respect. ||1||Pause|| God does everything. He gets the credit for it. God teaches us. He makes us speak. ||1|| Page 720 God created the creation combining five elements. He puts the elements in it. O servant Nanak, God unites us with the guru and resolves the conflict. ||2||3|| Bairaaree, Fourth Master: O mind, recite God's name and attain salvation. God eliminates millions of sins and carries us across the terrifying world ocean. ||1||Pause|| God lives in the body. He is carefree, enemyless and formless. God lives close by but unseen. He is realized contemplating guru's teachings. ||1|| God is the banker, appraiser, diamond and pearl. He created everything. O Nanak, one whom God blesses, deals in God's name. He is a true banker and a dealer. ||2||4|| Bairaaree, Fourth Master: O mind, recite bodiless and formless Lord. Recite God the bestowal of peace forever. There is no limit to His creation. ||1||Pause|| In the fiery pit of the womb, you are attuned to God. God protects in the womb. Serve such a Lord, O my mind; who will free you in the end. ||1|| Those who have God enshrined in the mind; I bow down in respect to him. Realize God by God's grace by reciting His name, the bestowal of salvation O Nanak. ||2||5|| Bairaaree, Fourth Master: O my mind, recite God's name forever. Obtain the reward of your choice. The sufferings do not touch again. ||1||Pause|| Falling in love with God obtains meditation, austerity fast and worship. Without God's love any other love is false. It is forgotten in a moment. ||1|| You are infinite perfect in every way. Your value cannot be described. Nanak has come to Your sanctuary, O God; save him as You please. ||2||6|| Tune Bairaaree, Fifth Master, First House: God is one. He is realized by guru's grace. Meeting with the humble saints, sing the praises of the Lord. The pains of millions of lifes shall be eradicated. ||1||Pause|| You receive the reward of your choice. By His Kindness, the Lord blesses us with His name. ||1|| All happiness obtains praising Lord's name. By guru's grace, Nanak obtained this understanding. ||2||1||7||

Page 721 Tune Tilang, First Master, First House:

God is one. It is true. He is the Creator. He is carefree. He has no enemy. He is immortal. He does not take birth. He came into existence on His own. He is realized by guru's grace.

I offer this one prayer to You; please listen to it, O Creator. You are true, great, merciful and spotless, O cherisher Lord. ||1|| The world is a transitory place of mortality; know this in your mind definitely. The messenger of death caught me by the hair of my head, yet I do not know it in my mind. ||1||Pause|| Spouse, children, parents and siblings, none of them will be there to hold my hand. Finally when I die there will be no one to say my final prayer. ||2|| Night and day, I wandered around in greed with evil thoughts in my mind. I never did good deeds; this is my condition. ||3|| I am unfortunate, miser, negligent, shameless and without the fear of God. Says Nanak, I am Your humble servant, the dust of the feet of Your slaves. ||4||1|| Tilang, First Master, Second House: God is one. He is realized by guru's grace. Your love is marijuana and my mind is the leather pouch to hold it. I am detached by being intoxicated. My hands are my begging bowl; I am hungry to visualize You. I beg at Your door, day after day. ||1|| I long to visualize You. I am a beggar at Your door, please give me awns. ||1||Pause|| Saffron, flowers, musk oil and gold beautify the body. Lord's devotees are like sandalwood, which imparts fragrance to everyone. ||2|| No one says that butter or silk are polluted. This is how God's devotee looks like. Those who bow in respect to Your name and remain absorbed in it. Nanak begs for charity at their door. ||3||1||2|| Tilang, First Master, Third House: God is one. He is realized by guru's grace. This body is treated with worldly wealth O beloved; and dyed with greed. Page 722 My Husband Lord does not like my clothes, O beloved; how can the soul-bride go to His bed? ||1|| I praise You, O dear merciful Lord; I praise You. I praise those who recite Your name. Those who recite Your name, I praise them forever. ||1||Pause|| If the body is dyed O beloved, it dyes with the deep red colour. If God dyes with His colour; His colour is such that has never been seen before! ||2|| Those whose shawls are dyed deep red, O beloved; their Husband Lord is with them. May I get the dust of their feet; that is Nanak's prayer. ||3|| He creates and imbues us by His grace. O Nanak, if the soul-bride pleases her Husband Lord, He will enjoy with her. ||4||1||3|| Tilang, First Master: O childish soul-bride, why are you so proud? Why do not you enjoy the love of the Lord? Your Husband Lord is very near, O ignorant; why do you search for Him outside? Make God's love the brush to apply mascara and devotion is the makeup. You will be a happy soul bride when your Husband Lord loves you. ||1|| What can the young bride do if she is not pleasing to her Husband Lord? She may plead in pain a lot; still, she does not reach the destiny. Nothing is achieved without luck, no matter how much you try? She is intoxicated with greed, pride and ego and engrossed in worldly wealth. She cannot obtain her Husband Lord this way; the young bride is ignorant! ||2|| Go and ask the happy soul-brides, how did they obtain their Husband Lord? Whatever God does, accept it with love; do not order or find faults. By His love, you obtain the priceless merchandise; put your mind to His lotus feet. Do as the husband says, surrender your mind and body by applying such fragrance. So speaks the happy soul-bride, O sister; in this way the Husband Lord is obtained. ||3|| Lord is realized by eliminating ego; no other clever trick works. When the Husband Lord looks at the soul-bride with love, that day is counted and the bride obtains the priceless treasure. She, who is loved by her Husband Lord, is the true soul-bride; O Nanak, she is the queen of all. Imbued with His love, intoxicated with joy; she is absorbed in His love forever. She is beautiful, glorious and smart; she is called truly wise. ||4||2||4|| Tilang, First Master: As the word of the Lord's sermon comes to me, so I express O Lalo. Brought the sinful marriage party from Kabul, he demands gifts by force. Modesty and faith both have vanished and falsehood is the leader O Lalo. The Qazis and Brahmins have lost their role; the evil reads the marriage vows O Lalo. The Muslim women read Quran and call on God in pain O Lalo. The enemies and Hindu women are put in the same category, O Lalo. Page 723 The songs of murder are sung, O Nanak, blood is sprinkled instead of saffron, O Lalo. ||1|| Nanak sings God's praises in this body. One who created and attached everyone to pleasures, sits and watches. The Lord finds out the truth and does true justice on the case. The bodies will be cut into pieces and India will remember this. They came in 1578 Bikarmee era, they will depart in ninety-seven (after some years) and then another man will rise up. Nanak speaks the true sermon; he tells truth as it happens. ||2||3||5|| Tilang, Fourth Master, Second House: God is one. He is realized by guru's grace. Everyone comes by God's command. Everything happens by God's command. It is true, there is God. His creation is true. He is the Lord of all. ||1|| So praise the true Lord; the Lord is the master of all. No one is equal to Him; what am I worth? ||Pause|| Air, water, earth and sky; God abides all. He is pervading all O Nanak. There is no lie about it. ||2||1|| Tilang, Fourth Master: You do ill deeds everyday and earn bad credits. When you earn by lying and cheating, you think you conquered the world. ||1|| Such is the play of the world, they do not recite God's name. The false perishes in a moment O my mind recite God. ||Pause|| He does not think of the time, when the devil of death will come and consume him. O Nanak, the Lord saves those, in whose heart God dwells by His grace. ||2||2|| Tilang, Fifth Master, First House: God is one. He is realized by guru's grace. The Lord infused His Light into the dust and created the universe. The sky, the earth, the trees, and the water – God created all. ||1|| O human being, whatever you see with your eyes, shall perish. The lazy and greedy world eats the sinful food. ||Pause|| Hiding like animals they commit and eat the forbidden sinful food. God arrests them and punishes them to hell. ||2|| That is what happens in God's court o brother. When the devil of death arrests you; what use is crying then? ||3|| Pure Lord God knows your condition. O Nanak, say your prayer to the holy God. ||4||1|| Tilang, Second House, Fifth Master: There is no other than You O Lord. You are the Creator; whatever You do, happens. You are the strength, and You are the support of the mind. Forever O Nanak, recite the one. ||1|| The great giver is the supreme Lord over all. You are our support, You are our sustainer. ||Pause|| Page 724 You exist and You always will be. You are permanent, unfathomable, lofty and infinite. Those who serve You, are not concerned of any sufferings. By guru's grace, Nanak sings your praises. ||2|| Whatever is seen is Your form. You are the treasure of virtues, Lord of the universe and beautiful. O mortal say God God God. O Nanak, by His grace, we realize Him. ||3|| I admire those who say God God. The world attains salvation in his company. Says Nanak, fulfill my hope O God. I long for the dust of the feet of the saints. ||4||2|| Tilang, Fifth Master, Third House: My Lord is kind. My Lord is kind. He gives gifts to all beings. ||Pause|| Why do you waver, O mortal? The Creator will protect you. He, who created you, will give you to eat. ||1|| One, who created the world, takes care of it. He is the life of everybody the true protector. ||2|| His creative power cannot be known; He is the carefree Lord. O human being, pray to Him till you live. ||3|| O God, You are all-powerful, inexpressible and imperceptible; my soul and body are Yours. By Your mercy, may I find peace; this is Nanak's prayer forever. ||4||3|| Tilang, Fifth Master, Third House: O Creator, I am in love with You by Your grace. You are the Creator of the world, You are sacred of all. ||Pause|| In an instant, You create and destroy. Wonderful is Your form! Who can know Your play? You are the light in the darkness. ||1|| You are the master of Your creation, O merciful Lord; You are invisible. One who worships You day and night; why should he go to hell? ||2|| Devil of death is the friend of those who have Your support. Their addiction to sins is forgiven and Your devotees visualize You. ||3|| The world is not permanent. Reciting Your name attains true happiness. Meeting the guru, Nanak understands; He sings Your praises forever. ||4||4|| Tilang, Fifth Master: Think of the Lord in your mind, O wise one. Enshrine God's love in your mind and body. He frees you from bonds. ||1||Pause|| Visualizing God is priceless. You are the pure cherisher; You are the great and immeasurable Lord. ||1|| Give me Your help, O brave Lord; You are one and only one Lord. O God the Creator of creation; Nanak looks to Your support. ||2||5|| Tilang, First Master, Second House: God is one. He is realized by guru's grace. One who created the world looks after it; what more can we say, O brother? Page 725 He who created the creation knows and looks after it. ||1|| Savor the story of the beloved Lord, which brings a lasting peace. ||Pause|| She, who does not enjoy the love of her Husband Lord, shall repent in the end. She wrings her hands, and bangs her head, when the night has passed away. ||2|| Nothing gained by repenting, when everything is over. She shall enjoy her beloved when her turn comes again. ||3|| The happy soul-bride attains her Husband Lord; she is better than me. I do not have those virtues; whom should I blame? ||4|| I shall go and ask those friends who enjoy their Husband Lord. I touch their feet and ask them to show me the path. ||5|| She, who understands Lord's command, O Nanak, attains that fragrance. When she obtains virtues then she pleases the beloved. ||6|| The minds that are united remain united and are called united. You may say as much as you want. Mere words do not unite anyone. ||7|| As metal melts into metal, so does love melt into love? By guru's grace, this understanding is obtained and carefree Lord is realized. ||8|| He may have an orchard of betel nut trees in the garden, but the donkey does not appreciate its value. If someone savors the fragrance, he will appreciate the flower. ||9|| One, who drinks the nectar O Nanak, abandons his doubts and wanderings. Easily and intuitively, he merges with God and obtains the immortal status. ||10||1|| Tilang, Fourth Master: The guru, my friend, told me the stories, the discourse of the Lord. I praise my guru I owe Him; ||1|| Come join with me, O follower of the guru, and the beloved of my guru. ||Pause|| Praises of the Lord are pleasing to the Lord; I obtained them from the guru. I praise those who self surrender and obey guru's will. ||2|| I admire those who met the beloved guru. I admire those who serve the guru. ||3|| Your name, O Lord, is the destroyer of sufferings. The guru-willed attain salvation by serving the guru. ||4|| Those who recite God's name are accepted by God. Nanak is a sacrifice to them forever and owes them. ||5|| Praise that pleases God is His true praise. The guru-willed who serve the beloved God; reap the reward. ||6|| Those who love God are attached to God devotionally. They recite God's name and live by it. ||7|| I worship those guru-willed who worship the beloved God. They attain salvation and with their family and the whole world. ||8|| My guru serves the Lord with love. I admire the guru. The guru showed me God's path; the guru did the greatest service. ||9|| Page 726 The devotees who serve the guru perform good service indeed. Servant Nanak praises them forever. ||10|| God is pleased with the guru-willed companions and friends. God embraces and honours them in His court. ||11|| The guru-willed that recite God's name visualize God. I wash their feet and drink the dust of their feet dissolved in that water. ||12|| Those who eat betel nuts and betel leaf and cigarettes in their mouth. They never recited God. Devil of death arrested and took them away. ||13|| Those who recite God enshrining in the mind; The devil of death does not touch the beloved devotees of the guru. ||14|| Name of the Lord is a priceless treasure, only a few guru-willed know it; O Nanak, those who surrender to guru, enjoy peace and pleasure. ||15|| The guru who bestows his grace is called the great bestowal. I praise the guru forever who blessed me with God's name. ||16|| I praise the guru, who brings Lord's message. I am happy and enjoy seeing the guru in human body. ||17|| The guru says the sacred and beautiful word God with his tongue; Those who hear learn and follow the guru; their hunger departs. ||18|| Some speak of Lord's path; tell me, how can I follow it? O Lord, Your name is my supplies; I take with me to spend on the journey. ||19|| The guru-willed who recite God, are dealers of priceless merchandise. I praise my guru forever and I am absorbed in guru's teachings. ||20|| You are the master, my Lord; You are my ruler as well. Your worship pleases You. You are a pile of virtues. ||21|| God is one. He is manifested in many forms. Whatever pleases Him, O Nanak, is a good deed? ||22||2|| Tilang, Ninth Master, Kaafee: God is one. He is realized by guru's grace. It is time to miss God if you want o mortal; The life is going every moment like water from a cracked pitcher. ||1||Pause|| Why do not you sing the praises of the Lord o ignorant fools? You are attached to false greed, you do not think of death. ||1|| No harm has been done yet if you sing God's praises. Says Nanak, repeating His name you shall obtain immortal state. ||2||1|| Tilang, Ninth Master: Wake up, O mind! Wake up! O lazy; why are you sleeping? That body you were born with; shall not go with you in the end. ||1||Pause|| Mother, father, children and relatives whom you love; Will throw your body in the fire when your soul departs from it; ||1|| Page 727 The world deals with the living; know that. O Nanak, sing praises of the Lord; everything is like a dream. ||2||2|| Tilang, Ninth Master: Sing Lord's praises, O mind; He is your true companion. Your time is passing by; listen carefully to what I say. ||1||Pause|| You are in love with property, chariots, wealth and power. When the noose of death is put around your neck, nothing will belong to you. ||1|| Knowingly O ignorant – you have ruined your affairs. You did not restrain yourself from committing sins, you did not give up your ego. ||2|| So listen to the teachings imparted by the guru, O brother. Says Nanak openly; seek refuge of the Lord. ||3||3|| Tilang, the word of devotee Kabeer Jee: God is one. He is realized by guru's grace. The Vedas and Quran are false if the worry of the mind is not removed. If you intently miss God for a moment; You will visualize God. ||1|| O mortal search your soul all the time, you will not get in trouble anymore. This world is just a magic show; no one is your helper. ||1||Pause|| Reading the imaginary things people are happy; they say nonsense in ignorance. The true Creator is in the creation; He is not the dark-skinned Krishna. ||2|| The stream of nectar flows in the sky; take bath in it. Serve the Lord forever with love and see Him ever-present everywhere. ||3|| The Lord is the purest of the pure; doubt it only if there is another one. O Kabeer, whoever does the kind deeds, knows it. ||4||1|| Naam Dev Jee: Your name is the support of this blind O Lord. I am poor humble. Your name is my support. ||1||Pause|| O kind merciful Lord. You are unseen God. You are ever-present everywhere. I worship You. ||1|| You are the river of life, You are the giver of all; You are great O Lord. You give, You take away; there is no other like You. ||2|| You are wise, You are giver; what can I the poor do; O Naam Dev's master. Be kind to me. ||3||1||2|| Hello, my friend; listen to this news; I praise dedicated and devoted to God. Your slavery is good and your name is great. ||1||Pause|| Where did you come from? Where are You now and where you are going. Tell me if it is the city of Dwaarkaa. ||1|| How handsome is your turban! And how sweet is your talk. Why are the Mugals in the holy city of Dwaarkaa? ||2|| You alone are the Lord of thousands of worlds. You are my Lord King, like the dark-skinned Krishna. ||3|| You are the Lord of the sun, Lord Indra and Lord Brahma, the King of men. You are the Lord of Naam Dev, the King the liberator of all.||4||2||3|| Page728

God is one. It is true. He is the Creator. He is carefree. He has no enemy. He is immortal. He does not take birth. He came into existence on his own. He is realized by guru`s grace.

Tune Soohee, First Master, Chau-Padas, First House: Wash the vessel and anoint it with fragrance; then, go to get milk. Add culture to make yoghurt to purify further. ||1|| Same way, recite God to purify you. All other actions are fruitless. ||1||Pause|| Make your mind the churning wheel and churn it continuously with intent. If you churn God this way with your tongue then you obtain the nectar. ||2|| Bathe your mind again and again in the pool of truth and attune your mind to it. The devotee prays to God devotionally by reciting God with every breath; then merges with God. ||3|| People talk and talk and die but no one equals You. Servant Nanak, lacking worship says this: may I sing God`s praises. ||4||1|| Soohee, First Master, Second House: God is one He is realized by guru`s grace. God lives in the mind. He does not go out. Giving up the nectar, why are you eating poison? ||1|| Recite such divine words o my mind; And become the slave of the true Lord. ||1||Pause|| Everyone speaks of wisdom and meditation; But the whole world wanders bound by bonds. ||2|| One who serves the Lord is His servant. The Lord is pervading everywhere in water and land as well. ||3|| I am not good; no one is bad. Prays Nanak, God saves us! ||4||1||2|| Page 729 Soohee, First Master, Sixth House: God is one. He is realized by guru's grace. What is that shine which becomes black by rubbing or mixing? The impurity is not removed by washing even if you wash hundred times. ||1|| They are my friends, who will go with me when I go. Where the account is asked for; they are there. ||1||Pause|| The houses, mansions and temples are closed from all four sides. When demolished they are of no use, they are empty inside. ||2|| They wear white clean clothes and go to pilgrimage. They kill and eat the living beings, how can they call themselves clean white. ||3|| The body is like the simbal tree; people are mistaken like the parrots. Its fruits are useless; same qualities are in the body. ||4|| The blind carries a heavy load and long journey through high mountains. My eyes can see, but how can I climb up and cross over the mountain? ||5|| What good does it do to serve, and be good, and be clever? O Nanak, recite God's name, it will free you from chains. ||6||1||3|| Soohee, First Master: Build the raft of meditation and self-discipline, to carry you across the river. There is no ocean no tides; this is how comfortable your path shall be. ||1|| My body and mind is dyed by Your deep red permanent colour O beloved. ||1||Pause|| My friends have departed; how will they unite with God? If they have virtues in their bag, God will unite them with Him. ||2|| Once united; will not be separated if they are truly united. True Lord brings their comings and goings to an end. ||3|| He, who eradicates the ego and then sews his robe with love; The deaf receives God's sacred reward through guru's teachings. ||4|| Says Nanak, O soul-brides, our Husband Lord is very dear! We are the maid servants of the Lord; He is our true Lord and master. ||5||2||4|| Soohee, First Master: God looks Those, whose minds are filled with love of the Lord, after. They are blessed with peace and their pains are forgotten. There is no doubt that God will certainly save them. ||1|| The guru comes to meet those with pre-ordained destiny. He gives them the awns of God's sacred name. Those who follow guru's will; do not go begging. ||2|| One who has visualized God; why should he bow down to anyone else? The gate-keeper at Lord's gate shall not stop him to ask any questions. One, who is blessed by God; his words save others. ||3|| God sends and recalls; no one advises Him. He demolishes constructs and creates; He knows everything. O Nanak, the gift of God's name is obtained by God's grace. ||4||3||5|| Page 730 Soohee, First Master: That vessel which is pleasing to God, is pure. The filthiest vessel does not become pure just by washing. The realization comes through guru's refuge. By washing at guru's refuge it becomes pure. The Lord sets the standards of dirty and the pure. Do not think that you will automatically find a place of rest hereafter. According to the actions one committed, so he becomes. He bestows the sacred name of the Lord. He departs purifying his life, the divine music plays. What to say of poor mortals? It will be heard in the whole universe. O Nanak, he attains contentment and saves his dynasty. ||1||4||6|| Soohee, First Master: The Yogi practices yoga, and the pleasure-seeker practices pleasure. The austere practice austerities bathing and rubbing at sacred shrines; ||1|| Your invitation will be heard o brother if some tells it. ||1||Pause|| As one plants so he harvests; whatever he earns, he eats. In the world hereafter, his account is not called for, if he goes with God's insignia. ||2|| As one acts, so is he proclaimed? Any breath that does not recite God is a waste. ||3|| I will sell this body, if someone buys it. O Nanak, the body that does not recite God; is of no use. ||4||5||7|| Soohee, First Master, Seventh House: God is one. He is realized by guru's grace. Yoga is not the patched coat, the walking stick or smearing the body with ashes. Yoga is not the ear rings, the shaved head or the blowing the horn. Remain attached to God in the world. This is the yoga way. ||1|| By mere words, Yoga is not performed. One, who sees everything with one eye, is a yogi. ||1||Pause|| Yoga is not wandering to the tombs of the dead; Yoga is not sitting in trance. Yoga is not wandering through foreign lands and bathing at shrines. Remain attached to God in the world. This is yoga way. ||2|| Meeting with the guru, dispels the doubt and the wandering mind is restrained. Nectar rains down, celestial music plays and wisdom is obtained at home. Remain attached to God in the world. This is the yoga way. ||3|| O Nanak, remain dead while yet alive, practice such Yoga. The horn resounds without blowing; then one attains the immortal state. Remain attached to God in the world. This is the Yoga way. ||4||1||8|| Soohee, First Master: What scale, what weights, and what goldsmith shall I call for You? From what guru should I receive lesson? By whom should I have You appraised? ||1|| Page 731 O my beloved Lord, Your limits are not known. You abide all including water and land; You are all-pervading. ||1||Pause|| Mind is the scale, soul the weights and serving You is the appraising. I weigh my Lord in myself that is how I focus my mind. ||2|| You are the balance, the weights and the scale; You are the weighed. You see and understand and You are the trader. ||3|| The blind, low class wandering soul, comes for a moment, and departs in an instant. Nanak lives in that company; how can the ignorant realize the Lord? ||4||2||9|| Tune Soohee, Fourth Master, First House: God is one. He is realized by guru's grace. I recite God's name through guru's teachings. All desires of my mind and body are fulfilled; all fear of death dispelled. ||1|| O my mind, sing the praises of Lord's name. The honourable guru guided my mind. I drink God's essence with love. ||1||Pause|| Guru's congregation is sacred that sings God's praises. O God; unite me with devotee's company, I will wash their feet. ||2|| God's name is everything. It is enjoyed through guru's teachings. I found the nectar the divine water of God's name. My thirst for it quenched. ||3|| The guru is my social status and honour; I sold my head to the guru. Servant Nanak is the disciple of the guru; O guru, save the honour of Your servant. ||4||1|| Soohee, Fourth Master: I recite supreme God's name and all my problems are solved. The fear of birth and death is erased through guru's teachings; serving the unmoving, unchanging Lord I attained peace. ||1|| O my mind, recite the name of the beloved God. I offered my mind and body to the guru; I sold my head for a high price. ||1||Pause|| The kings enjoy pleasures. Without God's name they are caught by the devil of death. The justice of destiny hits them over the head, they repent spreading their hands. ||2|| O God the cherisher; save your humble servant; I am at your refuge. O saint; may I see you and attain peace. O God; fulfill the hope of Your servant; ||3|| You are all-powerful, great, primal, my Lord. Please bless me with the gift of humility. Servant Nanak obtained peace reciting God's name. I praise God's name forever. ||4||2|| Soohee, Fourth Master: Reciting Lord's name is Lord's love. Lord's love is permanent colour. The contented guru dyed me with God's colour. It shall never fade. ||1|| Page 732 O my mind; dye yourself with the love of God's name. The honourable guru taught me God's love and I surrendered to God without hesitation. ||1||Pause|| The self-willed the ignorant bride, will keep coming and going forever. She never missed God. She was always enticed by duality. ||2|| I the evil minded am full of filth. O God; embrace and save me. The guru bathed me in the pool of nectar. All my sins washed away. ||3|| O Lord; kind to the meek, please unite me with devotee's company. Joining devotee's company servant Nanak obtained God's love. My mind and body are dyed with it. ||4||3|| Soohee, Fourth Master: One; who says God God, yet does evil deed; the mind does not cleanse this way. He performs all sorts of rituals night and day but he will not find peace, even in dreams. ||1|| O wise, you cannot worship God without guru. The untreated cloth does not dye, no matter how much one wants. ||1||Pause|| He meditates, does austerity, self-discipline, fasts and worship, but his sickness of self-wellness does not go away. He is sick with too much pride; he is ruined in love of duality. ||2|| Outwardly, he is religious and wise, but his mind wanders in ten directions. Engrossed in ego, he does not contemplate guru's teachings. He will be born again and again. ||3|| O Nanak, the mortal blessed by God realizes it and recites God's name. He realizes one and merges with one by guru's grace. ||4||4|| Soohee, Fourth Master, Second House: God is one. He is realized by guru's grace. I searched my soul through guru's teachings. I obtained the priceless God's name through it. ||1|| Saying God God; my mind became peaceful. The fire of desire extinguished in an instant. Meeting the guru my hunger vanished. ||1||Pause|| I live by singing the praises of the Lord O mother. I recite God's name through the kindness of the virtuous guru; ||2|| I search for my beloved God. Joining the company of devotees I enjoy God's sublime essence. ||3|| By the pre-ordained destiny inscribed on my forehead, I found God. O Nanak, the honourable guru unites us with God. ||4||1||5|| Soohee, Fourth Master: By God's grace; the mind dyes with God's love. The guru-willed merges with God saying God God. ||1|| Imbued with Lord's love, the mind enjoys the pleasure of His love. He is happy forever following perfect guru's teachings day and night. ||1||Pause|| Everyone longs for Lord's love; The guru-willed are dyed with deep red colour of love. ||2|| The ignorant, self-willed without culture cannot be dyed. Page 733 Even if he thinks hundred times, he does not obtain Lord's love. ||3|| One meets the guru by God's grace. O Nanak, he merges with God's love through God's sublime essence. ||4||2||6|| Soohee, Fourth Master: My tongue is satisfied with the subtle essence of the Lord. The guru-willed drinks and merges in peace. ||1|| If you taste the subtle essence of the Lord O brother; Then, how can you be enticed by other tastes? ||1||Pause|| Enshrine God's love in your mind through guru's teachings. And get intoxicated with God's subtle taste. ||2|| The self-willed cannot enjoy this taste. He acts in ego and suffers terrible punishment. ||3|| God's subtle essence is obtained by God's grace. O Nanak, sing God's praise and enjoy the taste. ||4||3||7|| Soohee, Fourth Master, Sixth House: God is one. He is realized by guru's grace. People of low caste attain high status by reciting God. Go and ask Bidar, the son of a maid; Krishna stayed in his house. ||1|| Listen to God's unexplainable sermon O humble brothers. Listening to it eliminates worries, sufferings and hunger etc. ||1||Pause|| Ravi Daas, a shoe maker praised God and sang God's praises a little bit. The Low caste became divine. All four castes touched his feet. ||2|| Naam Dev loved the Lord; people called him the seamster. God embraced Naam dev and turned away from high caste people. ||3|| All devotees the servants of God get ceremonial mark applied to their forehead equal to the pilgrimage at sixty-eight shrines. Servant Nanak shall touch their feet night and day, if God is graceful. ||4||1||8|| Soohee, Fourth Master: Those with preordained destiny enshrine and recite God in the mind. How can anyone think ill of those; who have God on their side? ||1|| O my mind, recite God. Reciting God eliminates the pain of many lifes. ||1||Pause|| God bestows the treasure of worship to His devotees from destiny. Whoever competes with them is a ignorant; his face is blackened here and hereafter. ||2|| Those, who love God's name, are God's devotees and servants. Serving them realizes God. Ashes thrown on the head of the slanderers; ||3|| He who experiences, knows it. Ask world guru Nanak and contemplate. Throughout four ages from beginning and for ages; nobody realized God by slandering. Salvation attains by serving God's devotees. ||4||2||9|| Soohee, Fourth Master: Wherever God is worshipped, there the Lord becomes one's friend and helper. Page 734 By guru's grace, God dwells in the mind; He cannot be realized any other way. ||1|| So gather God's wealth, O brother. God helps them here and the next world. ||1||Pause|| Earn Godly wealth in devotee's company. Godly wealth cannot be earned any other place or any other way. The dealer of God the Jewel trades in the priceless jewel. By the words of cheap traders, God's wealth cannot be obtained. ||2|| God's wealth is priceless jewels, gems and rubies. Worshipping God with love anytime is the right time and sacred. Seeding God's name at the right time does not fall short; eaten, spent by God's devotees. In this world and the next, the devotees obtain honour with Godly wealth. ||3|| The wealth of carefree

God is eternal and true. It cannot be destroyed by fire, theft, water and the devil of death. Thieves do not come close to Lord's wealth; devil of death cannot tax it. ||4|| The faithless commit sins and collect evil wealth. It does not go with them at all. The faithless suffer here. It falls from their hand. The faithless find no place to rest in the next world. ||5|| God is the banker of God's wealth O saints. Whoever he gives, load and go away. God's wealth never falls short. Guru made servant Nanak, realize this. ||6||3||10|| Soothe, Fourth Master: Whomever God is pleased with sings God's praises, becomes His approved devotee. One who has God enshrined in his mind, his glory cannot be described. ||1|| Sing God's praise devotionally enshrining guru in the mind. ||1||Pause|| He is the guru. His service is rewarding, through him we obtain the highest treasure. The faithless in love of duality with self interest serve the useless filth. That is fruitless and ignorant. ||2|| One who has faith. His singing is approved. He is honoured in God's court. The faithless close their eyes, pretending and faking devotion, but their pride of false pretences soon fades away. ||3|| All beings are Yours. You are the inner knower primal Lord. Says Nanak the servant of servants! As You ask so I explain; ||4||4||11|| Page 735 Soohee, Fourth Master, Seventh House: God is one. He is realized by guru's grace. O Lord the treasure of virtues. Which of Your virtues should I recount and sing? I cannot express Your glory. You my master are lofty my Lord. ||1|| The Name of the Lord is my only support. Keep me as You pleases O my Lord; I have no other but You. ||1||Pause|| You are my strength and my destiny O my Lord; I pray to You. There is no other place where I can offer my prayer; I can tell my pains and pleasures only to You. ||2|| Water is locked in the earth, and fire is locked in wood. You keep sheep and the lion in the same place; O mortal recite God and eliminate your doubts and concerns. ||3|| Watch God's greatness O saints; the Lord blesses the dishonoured with honour. As earth comes on top from below the feet O Nanak, so the whole world falls at God's devotee's feet. ||4||1||12|| Soohee, Fourth Master: You O Creator know everything; what can I tell You? You know all bad and the good; as we do, so are we rewarded. ||1|| O my Lord, You know the state of my inner being. You know all bad and good; as it pleases You, so You make us speak. ||1||Pause||

God infused the attachment of worldly wealth in everyone. In the same body God makes us worship Him as well. You unite some with the guru and bless them with peace; while others, the self-willed are engrossed in worldly affairs. ||2|| All belong to You, You belong to all, O Creator; You wrote the destiny on the forehead of everyone. As You bless, so one becomes; nothing happens without Your grace. ||3|| You alone know Your greatness; everyone constantly recites Your name. Whoever pleases You unites with You and attains destiny says Nanak. ||4||2||13|| Soohee, Fourth Master: Those who enshrine God in the mind, their all sicknesses are eliminated. Those who recite God's name attain salvation and supreme status. ||1|| O my Lord, Lord's humble servants become healthy. Those who recite God through guru's teachings, their sickness of ego departs. ||1||Pause|| Brahma, Vishnu and Shiva suffer from the disease of the three worldly qualities because they do their deeds in ego. The ignorant do not remember the Creator. The guru-willed realize God. ||2|| The entire world is afflicted by the disease of ego. They suffer the terrible pain of birth and death. Page 736 By guru's grace, a few are saved; I admire those humble beings. ||3|| The one who created the universe knows. His beauty is incomparable. O Nanak, God watches and enjoys it. The guru-willed thinks of God. ||4||3||14|| Soohee, Fourth Master: Everything happens by God's will. We will do if we can; Nothing happens by our doing. God keeps us as He pleases. ||1|| O my dear Lord, everything is in Your power. I have no power to do anything. Keep me as You wish. ||1||Pause|| You bless us with soul, body and everything. You cause us to act. We act by Your command that You wrote in our destiny. ||2|| You created the universe combining five elements; if anyone can create, it will be the sixth element. You unite some with the guru and cause them to understand, while others, the self-willed do their deeds and cry. ||3|| I cannot describe God's greatness. I am ignorant, thoughtless and lowly. O my Lord save servant Nanak; the innocent is at Your refuge. ||4||4||15||24|| Tune Soohee, Fifth Master, First House: God is one. He is realized by guru's grace. As the juggler sets his play; He plays his play in many different costumes. But when the play ends, he takes off the costumes. Then there is only the Lord. ||1|| How many forms and images appeared and disappeared? Where did they go? Where did they come from? ||1||Pause|| Countless waves rise from water. Many ornaments are created from gold. I sowed all kinds of seeds. When the fruit ripens, the same seeds are in it; ||2|| One sky reflects in thousands of bodies of water. But when the body breaks, only the sky remains. Doubt, greed and emotional attachment to worldly wealth are all useless; Freed from doubt, one realizes God. ||3|| He is imperishable; He will never vanish. He does not come, He does not go. The perfect guru has washed away the filth of ego. Says Nanak, I have obtained the supreme status. ||4||1|| Soohee, Fifth Master: Whatever God wills, that happens; Without You, there is no other at all. The humble being who serves Him; his works are successful. O Lord, please preserve the honour of Your slave. ||1|| I seek Your sanctuary, O perfect, kind Lord. Without You, who will care for me? ||1||Pause|| He is permeating and pervading water land and sky. God dwells close by; He is not far away. Nothing is achieved by worshipping others. When someone is attached to the true Lord, his ego goes away. ||2|| Page 737 He is attached to God whom the Lord attaches. The jewel of divine wisdom is awakened inside. Evil-mindedness is eradicated, and the supreme status is attained. By guru's grace, he recites God's name. ||3|| Pressing my palms together, I offer my prayer; If it pleases You O Lord, then my deeds will be fulfilled by Your grace. Be kind and bless me with Your worship. Servant Nanak recites God forever. ||4||2|| Soohee, Fifth Master: Blessed is the soul-bride, who realizes God. She obeys God's command and abandons self-conceit. Imbued with her beloved, she is happy. ||1|| Listen, O my companions, this is the way to realize God. Surrender your mind and body to Him; stop worrying about other's talks. ||1||Pause|| One soul-bride counsels others. You do what pleases God. Such a soul-bride merges in God. ||2|| The egotistic does not realize Him. She repents, when her life-night passes away. The unfortunate self-willed suffer in pain. ||3|| I pray to God, if I think Him far away. God is imperishable; He is pervading and permeating everywhere. Servant Nanak sings His praises; sees Him ever-present everywhere. ||4||3|| Soohee, Fifth Master: I control my house through the guru because I am the lady of the house. My Husband Lord has made the ten senses my slaves; I gathered all requirements of this house. I am thirsty with desire and longing for my Husband Lord. ||1|| What virtues of my beloved Husband Lord should I describe? He is intelligent beautiful and kind; He is the destroyer of ego. ||1||Pause|| I am adorned with truth and I have applied the mascara of God's love to my eyes. I chew the betel-leaf of God's name. My bracelets, robes and ornaments look beautifully on me. The soul-bride becomes happy, when her Husband Lord comes to her home. ||2|| By charming virtues, I enticed my Husband Lord. He is under my control; the guru has dispelled my doubts. My mansion is the highest of all. Renouncing all other brides, my beloved has become my lover. ||3|| The sun has risen and its light enlightens my soul. I prepared my bed with unlimited devotion. My darling beloved is new and fresh; He has come to my bed to enjoy with me. O Servant Nanak, my Husband Lord found peace meeting the soul bride. ||4||4|| Soohee, Fifth Master: My mind is yearning to meet God. I have gone out searching to find my beloved Husband Lord. Hearing news of my beloved, I spread my bed in my home. Wandering all around, I came, but I did not see Him. ||1|| How can this poor heart be comforted? Come and meet me, O friend; I am a sacrifice to You. ||1||Pause|| One bed is spread for both the bride and her Husband Lord. The bride is asleep, while her Husband Lord is always awake. The bride drank liquor and got intoxicated. The soul-bride wakes up when her Husband Lord calls her. ||2|| She has lost hope; many days have passed. I travelled through all lands and countries. Page 738 I cannot survive for a moment without touching the feet of my beloved. O God; be kind and unite me with You. ||3|| God became kind and united me with the company of devotees. My inner fire is extinguished. I realized my beloved at home. I look beautiful with makeup. Says Nanak, the guru has dispelled my doubt. ||4|| Wherever I look, I see my Husband Lord, O brother. My mind opened up then my mind stabilized. ||1|| Second Pause||5|| Soohee, Fifth Master: O bestowal of this virtueless; what virtues of Your can I cherish and follow. You bought me, I belong to You; what clever tricks can I try? O my darling, blissful enticing beloved, I yearn to visualize You. |||1||Pause| O God, You are the giver, I am a poor beggar; You do good forever. I cannot do anything, O my immovable and infinite Lord. ||2|| What service can I do? How should I engage you?

How can I visualize You? Cannot find Your extent and limits. My mind longs to touch Your feet. ||3|| I beg persistently for this gift that the dust of the saints touch my face. Guru became kind to servant Nanak. God took me by the hand and took across. ||4||6|| Soohee, Fifth Master, Third House: God is one. He is realized by guru's grace. His service is less but his demands are more. He does not obtain destiny, but he says that he has. ||1|| He competes with those who have been accepted by the beloved Lord. This is the stubbornness of the false ignorant. ||1||Pause|| He imitates but he does not practice truth. He says that he attained destiny but he cannot even get near it. ||2|| He says that he is unattached, but he is intoxicated with worldly wealth. There is no love in his mind, and yet he says that he is imbued with the Lord. ||3|| Says Nanak, hear my prayer O God: I am silly, stubborn and filled with lust. Please, liberate me! ||4|| I admire the greatness of visualizing You; You are the giver of peace, loving primal being intuitively; ||1||Second Pause||1||7|| Soohee, Fifth Master: He is ready to do evil deeds. When the time to recite God's name came; he slept in. ||1|| The ignorant does not take advantage of the opportunity. He is attached to worldly wealth and worldly delights. ||1||Pause|| He is happy with the waves of greed and feels proud of it. He does not see the face of God's devotees. ||2|| The ignorant fools will never understand. Again and again, he is entangled in worldly deeds. ||1||Pause|| He listens to the sounds of sin and he is pleased with it. His is lazy to listen to the praises of the Lord. ||3|| Cannot you see with your eyes o blind! You shall leave all these false deeds behind. ||1||Pause|| Says Nanak, please bless me O God. Page 739 Be kind and bless me with the company of devotees.||4|| When one becomes humble then only he can achieve something. Whoever God makes to understand; recite God's name. ||1||Pause||2||8|| Soohee, Fifth Master: God is in you but cannot be seen. But you hang a stone around your neck. ||1|| The faithless wanders around deluded by doubt. He churns water and wasting his life away. ||1||Pause|| That stone, which he calls his god. That stone pulls him down and drowns him. ||2|| O sinner, you are faithless to yourself; The boat of stone will not carry you across. ||3|| Meeting the guru, O Nanak, realizes God. The perfect architect of destiny is pervading in water land and the middle. ||4||3||9||

Soohee, Fifth Master: How have you enjoyed your dear beloved? O friend, please teach me the way. ||1|| You look beautiful dark red. You are dyed with the love of your beloved. ||1||Pause|| I wash Your feet with my eyelashes. Wherever You send me, I go. ||2|| I will do meditation, austerity, self-discipline and celibacy. If, you could unite me with the Lord of my life; I will eradicate self-conceit, power and arrogant intellect. O Nanak, she is the true soul-bride. ||4||4||10|| Soohee, Fifth Master: You are my life, the support of my life. Visualizing you, my mind is soothed and comforted. ||1|| You are my friend, You are my beloved. I shall never forget You. ||1||Pause|| I am Your bought slave. You are my great Lord the treasure of virtues. ||2|| There are millions of servants in Your court. You live with them forever. ||3|| I am nothing; everything is Yours. You abide with Nanak in good and bad. ||4||5||11|| Soohee, Fifth Master: His mansions are comfortable with high gates. Your devotees live there. ||1|| The natural discourse of God is very sweet. Only a few have seen with their own eyes. ||1||Pause|| In that arena the divine music and celestial sound plays. There, the saints celebrate with their Lord. ||2|| There is no birth or death, pain or pleasure there. The nectar of the true name rains down there. ||3|| This mysterious story is learned from the guru. Nanak speaks the sermon of the Lord. ||4||6||12|| Soohee, Fifth Master: Visualizing Him eliminates millions of sins. Meeting with him this terrifying world-ocean is crossed over. ||1|| He is my companions and dear friend. Who inspires me to miss Lord's name? ||1||Pause|| Listening to his teachings all peace attains. Serving Him, the devil of death is driven away. ||2|| His determination soothes and supports my mind. Reciting his name my face becomes happy. ||3|| God embellishes and supports His servants. Nanak seeks his sanctuary; he is forever a sacrifice to him. ||4||7||13|| Page 740 Soohee, Fifth Master: The gods heroes or Demy-gods do not live forever. The silent sages and humble servants also depart. ||1|| Those, who recite God, live forever. They realize God in the company of devotees. ||1||Pause|| Kings, emperors and merchants all die. Whoever is seen shall be consumed by death. ||2|| Mortal beings are clinging to false worldly attachments. When they leave them behind, then they regret. ||3|| O Lord, treasure of mercy, please bless Nanak. That he recites your name day and night.

||4||8||14|| Soohee, Fifth Master: You dwell in each and every being. The entire universe is strung on Your thread. ||1|| You are my beloved the support of my life. My mind becomes happy seeing you. ||1||Pause|| I am tired of wandering in different lifes. Now I took refuge of devotee's company. ||2|| You are hard to find, incomprehensible, invisible and infinite. Nanak recites your name day and night. ||3||9||15|| Soohee, Fifth Master: What is the use of glory of worldly wealth? It disappears in no time. ||1|| This is a dream, but the sleeping does not know it. In his unconscious state, he clings to it. ||1||Pause|| The poor ignorant is enticed by the attachments of the world. Watching them, he gets up and departs. ||2|| God's court is the highest of all. He creates and destroys countless beings. ||3|| There never was and there never will be anyone like him. O Nanak, recite One God. ||4||10||16|| Soohee, Fifth Master: I live by reciting his name. I wash Your lotus feet and drink the washed water. ||1|| He is my Lord, the inner-knower. He is with his devotees all the time. ||1||Pause|| Listening to his praises I recite his sacred name. Twenty-four hours a day, I sing Your praises. ||2|| Seeing Your divine play, my mind is happy. Your virtues are infinite, O God, Lord of supreme joy. ||3|| Nothing bothers when one recites his name. Nanak recites God forever. ||4||11||17|| Soohee, Fifth Master: I enshrine him in my mind through guru's teachings. With my tongue, I recite the recitation of the Lord. ||1|| Visualizing his image is fruitful; I am a sacrifice to it. His lotus feet are the support of the mind and life. ||1||Pause|| The birth and death is eliminated in the company of devotees. By listening to immortal sermon intently; ||2|| I renounced lust, anger, greed and emotional attachment. Reciting His name is the true cleansing bath. ||3|| Says Nanak, by witnessing the reality. Reciting God's name carries across the world ocean. ||4||12||18|| Soohee, Fifth Master: The sinner is absorbed in greed and emotional attachment. Page 741 He does not perform any service to the Creator. ||1|| O God, Your name is the purifier of sinners. I am worthless; please save me! ||1||Pause|| O God, You are the great giver, the inner-knower. The body of the egotistic human is not ripe. ||2|| He tastes, pleasures, conflicts, jealousy and intoxication of the worldly wealth; Attached to these, the jewel of human life is wasted. ||3|| The sovereign Lord is the destroyer of pain; He is the life of the world. Forsaking everything,

Nanak has entered His sanctuary. ||4||13||19|| Soohee, Fifth Master: He sees and tastes but he is blind; he hears but makes it unheard. God lives close but he thinks Him far. The sinner commits sins. ||1|| Do something that you can get free o mortal. Say God God and recite the sacred sermon. ||1||Pause|| You are forever imbued with the love of horses and mansions. Nothing shall go with you. ||2|| You may clean the pot of clay. It is filthy; it will suffer the punishment of the devil of death. ||3|| You are bound by lust, anger, greed and emotional attachment. You are sinking into the great pit. ||4|| Hear this prayer of Nanak, O Lord; I am a stone, sinking – please, save me! ||5||14||20|| Soohee, Fifth Master: One who dies (humble) while yet alive realizes God. That humble being achieved what was written in his fate. ||1|| Listen, O friend, this is how to cross over the terrifying world-ocean. Meet with devotees and recite God's name. ||1||Pause|| Do not think of anyone else but God. And recognize the supreme Lord in each and every heart. ||2|| Whatever He does, accept that as good. You will know the value from the beginning to the end. ||3|| Says Nanak, I admire that humble being. In whose heart Lord dwells. ||4||15||21|| Soohee, Fifth Master: The guru is the transcendent Lord the Creator. He gives His support to the entire universe. ||1|| Recite in your mind the lotus feet of the guru. Pain and suffering shall leave this body. ||1||Pause|| The guru saves the being from drowning in the terrifying world-ocean. He reunites those separated for countless lifes. ||2|| Serve the guru, day and night. You will find peace contentment and happiness in your mind. ||3|| The fortunate obtains the dust of the feet of the true guru. O Nanak, praise the true guru forever. ||4||16||22|| Soohee, Fifth Master: I praise my true guru. Twenty-four hours a day, I sing the praises of the Lord. ||1|| Recite the name of God the master. He is the inner-knower of all hearts. ||1||Pause|| Love Lord's lotus feet. This is true complete and pure way. ||2|| By the grace of the saint, enshrine God in the mind. The sins of countless lifes will be eradicated. ||3|| Please be kind O God, merciful to the meek. Nanak begs for the dust of the saints. ||4||17||23|| Page 742 Soohee, Fifth Master: I live by seeing my guru. This is my perfect destiny O God. ||1|| Please, listen to this prayer, O my God. Please bless your devotee with Your name. ||1||Pause|| Please keep me in your refuge O kind Lord. By guru's grace, only a few realize You. ||2|| Please hear my prayer, O God, my friend. May Your lotus feet enshrine in my mind; ||3|| Nanak makes one prayer: May I never forget You O treasure of virtues? ||4||18||24|| Soohee, Fifth Master: He is my friend, companion, child, relative and sibling. Wherever I look, I see the Lord with me. ||1|| Lord's name is my social status, honour and wealth. He is my pleasure, poise, bliss and peace. ||1||Pause|| I have tied myself with the recitation of the supreme Lord. Millions of weapons cannot pierce it. ||2|| The sanctuary of Lord's feet is the wall around me. The pinch of the devil of death cannot demolish it. ||3|| Slave Nanak is forever a sacrifice The devotee saint the king God; the destroyer of ego of his devotees. ||4||19||25|| Soohee, Fifth Master: Sing praises of the Lord of the world continuously. Enjoy happiness and peace there. ||1|| Come, O my companions, let us go and enjoy God. Let us fall at the feet of God`s devotees. ||1||Pause|| I pray for the dust of the feet of the humble. It shall wash away the sins of countless lifes. ||2|| I offer my mind, body, life and soul to God. Reciting God I eradicate pride and worldly attachments. ||3|| O Lord, merciful to the meek, please encourage me. So that slave Nanak may merge in Your sanctuary. ||4||20||26|| Soohee, Fifth Master: The place where the saints live is heaven. They enshrine the lotus feet of God in their heart. ||1|| Listen, O my mind and body, and let me show you the way to find peace. You may eat and enjoy the various delicacies of the Lord; ||1||Pause|| Digest God`s sacred name in your mind. Its taste is wonderful. It cannot be described. ||2|| Your greed shall die and your thirst shall quench. If you seek God`s refuge o mortal. ||3|| The Lord dispels the fears and attachments of countless lifes. God has showered His grace on slave Nanak. ||4||21||27|| Soohee, Fifth Master: God covers the many shortcomings of His slaves. By His kindness God makes them His own. ||1|| You liberated Your humble servant. He was entangled in the net of the worldly dream. ||1||Pause|| Even mountain of sin and corruption Are removed in an instant by the merciful Lord; ||2|| Sorrow, disease and the most terrible calamities are removed by reciting the name of the Lord; ||3|| By His kindness He attaches us to the hem of His robe. Page 743 O Nanak, touch God`s feet in His refuge. ||4||22||28|| Soohee, Fifth Master: One who withdraws from God's path and attaches to the world. Is known a sinner in both worlds; ||1|| He approves who pleases Him. He knows His creative power. ||1||Pause|| One who practices truth, righteous living, charity and good deeds! With supplies for God's path, the worldly success shall not fail him. ||2|| God abides in all. As He makes us do, so we do. ||3|| You are inaccessible and unfathomable my true Lord; Nanak speaks as You inspire him to speak. ||4||23||29|| Soohee, Fifth Master: Recite God's name in the morning. It helps here and hereafter. ||1|| Recite God's name forever. Desires of mind are fulfilled. ||1||Pause|| Sing the praises of the imperishable God, night and day. Dieing while living attains eternal place; ||2|| Serve the sovereign Lord, you shall never lack anything. While eating and consuming, you shall live your life in peace. ||3|| The life of the world, primal being is realized in the company of devotees. By guru's grace, O Nanak, recite God's name. ||4||24||30|| Soohee, Fifth Master: When the perfect guru becomes kind; Pain departs and the efforts are rewarded. ||1|| I live by visualizing you. I praise Your lotus feet. Without You my Lord; I have nobody. ||1||Pause|| I have fallen in love with the company of devotees. I obtained what was written in my fate from destiny. ||2|| Reciting God's name, wonderful things happen by his grace. The three worldly fevers cannot consume it. ||3|| May I never forget Lord's feet, even for an instant. Nanak begs for this gift, O my Beloved. ||4||25||31|| Soohee, Fifth Master: May there be such an auspicious time, O beloved. The time when, I recite God's name with my tongue. ||1|| Hear my prayer, O God, merciful to the meek. May the saints ever sing God's praises. ||1||Pause|| Reciting your name is the essence of life. You dwell near those upon whom You bestow kindness. ||2|| Your name is the food to satisfy the hunger of Your humble servants. You are the giver, O Lord. ||3|| The saints attain peace saying God. O Nanak, the Lord the great giver, knows all. ||4||26||32|| Soohee, Fifth Master: Your life is slipping away but you never notice it. You are constantly entangled in false attachments and imaginary ideas. ||1|| Recite God day and night forever. Conquer your priceless life seeking God's refuge. ||1||Pause|| You commit sins and forget. You do not enshrine the jewel God's name in your mind at all. ||2|| You waste your life feeding and pampering your body. Page 744 You do not know the state of the great Lord of the universe. ||3|| Enter the sanctuary of the all-powerful, unfathomable Lord. O God, the inner knower, please, save Nanak! ||4||27||33|| Soohee, Fifth Master: Cross over the terrifying world-ocean in the company of devotees. By reciting the jewel of God`s name. ||1|| I live by reciting God. All pain, disease and suffering and sins are eradicated meeting the perfect guru. ||1||Pause|| The immortal status is obtained through the name of the Lord; The mind and body become pure, which is the true purpose of life. ||2|| Twenty-four hours a day, recite God. It is obtained by pre-ordained destiny. ||3|| Recite the merciful God in His refuge. Nanak longs for the dust of the saints. ||4||28||34|| Soohee, Fifth Master: The beautiful does not know the work of his home. The ignorant is engrossed in false attachments. ||1|| As You attach us, so we attach; When You bless us with Your name, we recite. ||1||Pause|| Lord's slaves are imbued with the love of the Lord. They are intoxicated with reciting God, night and day. ||2|| Taking by the arm God took me out. Separated for countless lifes, we are united with Him again. ||3|| Save me, O God, my Lord by your grace. Slave Nanak seeks your sanctuary at Your door, O Lord. ||4||29||35|| Soohee, Fifth Master: By the grace of the saints, I found my eternal home. I found total peace and I shall not waver again. ||1|| Reciting the guru I found God in my mind. In this way, the Creator made me immortal. ||1||Pause|| I sing praises of the unchanging, eternal Lord. And the noose of death is snapped. ||2|| By His grace He attached me to Him. In constant bliss, Nanak sings His praises. ||3||30||36|| Soohee, Fifth Master: Teachings of God's devotees are sacred. Whoever recites God's name all the time attains salvation. ||1||Pause|| The sufferings of today's age are erased. When one name abides in the mind; ||1|| I apply the dust of the feet of God's devotees to my face and forehead. Nanak has been saved, in the sanctuary of the guru, the God. ||2||31||37|| Soohee, Fifth Master: Third House: Sing praises of the merciful Lord of the universe. Please, bless me with Your realization O perfect, compassionate Lord. ||Pause|| Please, grant Your grace o merciful Lord. My soul and body are all Your property. ||1|| Recitation of God's sacred name goes with you. Nanak begs for the dust of the saints. ||2||32||38|| Soohee, Fifth Master: Without Him, there is no other at all. True Lord is our protector. ||1||

Name of the Lord is my resolve. The Creator, the cause of causes, is all-powerful and infinite. ||1||Pause|| He eradicates all illness, and heals us. O Nanak, He is my saviour. ||2||33||39|| Page 745 Soohee, Fifth Master: Everyone longs to visualize God. By perfect destiny, He is visualized. ||Pause|| Forsaking the beautiful Lord, how can they sleep? The great enticer worldly pleasure led them down the path of sin. ||1|| Separation of love is in my eyes. This merciless shows no mercy to the poor beings. ||2|| Countless lifes have passed away, wandering aimlessly. The terrible worldly pleasure does not allow them to live in their home. ||3|| Day and night, they receive the rewards of their actions. Don't blame anyone else; your own actions lead you astray. ||4|| Listen, O friend, saint, humble and my brother: In the sanctuary of Lord's feet, Nanak found salvation. ||5||34||40|| Tune Soohee, Fifth Master, Fourth House: God is one. He is realized by guru's grace. Even a grass hut is beautiful, if the Lord's praises are sung there. Those mansions where the Lord is forgotten are useless. ||1||Pause|| Humility and joy attains in the company of devotees where God is missed. May the self-praise and entanglement of the worldly burn; ||1|| I grind flour, cover myself with a blanket and find peace and contentment. The empire that does not give satisfaction is of no use. ||2|| Some wander naked, but one who loves God obtains honour. Silk clothes are worthless, if they lead to greed. ||3|| Everything is in Your Hands O God. You do and cause others do. May Nanak receive the gift of reciting God with every breath? ||4||1||41|| Soohee, Fifth Master: Lord's saint is my life and wealth. I am his water-carrier. He is dearer to me than all my siblings, friends and children. ||1||Pause|| I make my hair into a fan, and wave it over the saint. I bow my head to touch his feet and apply his dust to my face. ||1|| I offer my prayer with sweet words in humility. Renouncing ego I enter His sanctuary and obtain the treasure of God's virtues. ||2|| I search for visualizing God's servants again and again. I rehearse the sacred teachings enshrining in my mind again and again. ||3|| In my mind, I wish, hope and beg for the company of God's devotees. O God; be kind to Nanak that I touch the feet of Your servants. ||4||2||42|| Soohee, Fifth Master: She has enticed the worlds and solar systems; I have fallen into her clutches. O Lord, please save this corrupt soul; please bless me with Your

Name. ||1||Pause|| One that does not bring peace to anyone; still I chase after her. She leaves everyone; still I cling to her, again and again. ||1|| Be kind O Lord that I sing God's praises. This is Nanak's prayer, O Lord that he merges with devotee's company. ||2||3||43|| Page 746 Tune Soohee, Fifth Master, Fifth House, Partaal: God is one. He is realized by guru's grace. O beloved, love your guru. Recite God in your mind. Nothing else is of any use. Enshrine the saint in your mind and forget the falsehood and duality. ||1||Pause|| The Lord is absolute. The world is manifest. There are many chambers and He hums in them many ways. There are many chambers in the mind. God's temple is there. He enjoys there. He does not die or burn. ||1|| He engages in His activities, wandering around in various ways. He is realized by giving up duality. The world is engaged in bad deeds. Now I joined the company of devotees. I stand in front of God's door. I see Him. O Nanak, meeting the guru; He shall not wander anymore. ||2||1||44|| Soohee, Fifth Master: God made this world a stage; He created the entire creation. ||1||Pause|| He created it in many ways and shapes. He watches, enjoys and never gets tired of it. He enjoys everything, still remains detached from it. ||1|| He has no colour, no sign, no mouth and no moustache. Cannot say anything about our creation. Nanak is the dust of the feet of the saints. ||2||2||45|| Soohee, Fifth Master: I came to You. I came to Your sanctuary. I came with faith in You and by Your grace. Guru sent me on this path. Keep me as You please. ||1||Pause|| The worldly pleasure is very difficult to go through. It is like a windstorm. ||1|| I am afraid to hear that Justice of destiny is very strict. ||2|| The world is a deep, dark pit; it is all on fire. ||3|| I took shelter of Your devotees. Nanak recites God. Now, I found the perfect Lord. ||4||3||46|| Tune Soohee, Fifth Master, Sixth House: God is one. He is realized by guru's grace. I pray to the guru, to bless me with the shelter of God's name. When the true King is pleased, the world gets rid of its diseases. ||1|| You are the support of Your devotees and saints, O true Creator. ||1||Pause|| True is Your creation and true is Your court. True are Your treasures, and true is Your expanse. ||2|| Your form is inaccessible, and You are beautiful. I admire Your servants; those who love Your name, O Lord. ||3|| Page 747 All desires are fulfilled, when the inaccessible and infinite Lord is realized.

Nanak met the guru O Lord; he is a sacrifice to Your feet. ||4||1||47|| Tune Soohee, Fifth Master, Seventh House: God is one. He is realized by guru's grace. He obeys Your will, O Lord, to whom You are kind. He who pleases You is Your devotee. You take care of everybody. ||1|| O my sovereign Lord, You are the support of the saints. Whatever pleases You, they accept. You are the support of their minds and bodies. ||1||Pause|| You the treasure of mercy; You are kind and concerned the fulfiller of our hopes. You are the life of Your devotees, the beloved of Your devotees. ||2|| You are unfathomable, infinite, lofty and exalted. There is no one like You. This is my prayer, O my Lord; may I never forget You, O peace giving Lord. ||3|| Day and night, I sing your praises with every breath, if it pleases You. Nanak begs for peace by reciting Your name, O Lord; may I obtain it if it pleases You. ||4||1||48|| Soohee, Fifth Master: Where is the place, where You are never forgotten, O Lord? May I recite You twenty-four hours a day there, and my body becomes pure. ||1|| O my Lord, I came searching for that place. After searching, I found devotee's company and sought their refuge. ||1||Pause|| Reading the Vedas, Brahma got tired, he did not realize anything. The seekers and mystics wander crying; they too are enticed by the worldly pleasure. ||2|| There were ten prophets kings and then there was Shiva the renunciate. They did not find Your limits either; they grew weary of applying ashes to their bodies. ||3|| Peace, poise and bliss are found in the essence of God's name. Lord's saints sing the songs of joy. When Nanak saw the guru in person, then he recited God with love. ||4||2||49|| Soohee, Fifth Master: Those who do imitating deeds and religious rituals are robbed by the devil of death with their eyes open. Sing the praises of God that saves reciting God for a moment. ||1|| O saints, cross over the world-ocean. Whoever practices saint's teachings is carried across by guru's grace. ||1||Pause|| Millions of baths at sacred shrines fill the body with filth in today's age. One who sings God's praises in devotee's company will cleanse the body. ||2|| Reading Vedas, Quran, Simritees and Shaastras, do not liberate anyone. One Word (God) that the guru-willed recites, his thinking becomes pure. ||3|| The divine lesson of all four castes is the same. Page 748 The guru-willed who recites God's name attains salvation in today's age. God abides in everybody. ||4||3||50|| Soohee,

Fifth Master: Those dyed with God's name; God accepts their deeds. Those who fall at the feet of God are respected everywhere. ||1|| O my Lord, no one is as great as Lord's saints. The devotees are in harmony with their God; He abides in water, land and the sky. ||1||Pause|| Millions of sinners are saved in devotee's company; the devil of death does not approach them. Those separated from God for many lifes are reunited with God again. ||2|| Attachment to worldly wealth, doubt and fear are eradicated coming to saint's refuge. Whatever devotion one serves the saints with, obtains the reward from them. ||3|| Who can I say God's servant's glory to? Those who please their God; Says Nanak those who meet the guru become purest of all; ||4||4||51|| Soohee, Fifth Master: Those who seek Your refuge, You save them from burning fire by giving Your hand. I respect and honour You in my mind. I gave up any other desire. ||1|| O my sovereign Lord, missing You attains salvation. You are my support. I count on You. I am saved reciting Your name. ||1||Pause|| You pulled me out of the deep, dark pit by Your kindness. You care for me, and bless me with total peace and cherish me. ||2|| The transcendent Lord blessed me with His grace; He freed me breaking my bonds. God inspires me to worship Him; He inspires me to serve Him. ||3|| My doubts, fears, false attachments and sorrows are gone. O Nanak, God became kind and I met with the perfect guru. ||4||5||52|| Soohee, Fifth Master: When nothing existed, what deeds were being done? What good deeds you did in order to take birth? The Lord sets His play in motion and watches. He created the creation. ||1|| O my sovereign Lord, I cannot do anything. He is the Creator, He is the cause. He pervades all. ||1||Pause|| Nobody is saved just by talking. This body is unripe and ignorant. Be kind O bestowal God; Your gifts are unique. ||2|| You created all beings. Everyone worships You. You know Your way and limits; Your creation is priceless. ||3|| I am worthless, ignorant, thoughtless and ignorant. I know nothing about good actions and faith. Be kind that Nanak sings Your praises and Your will tastes sweet. ||4||6||53|| Soohee, Fifth Master: Page 749 Your saints are fortunate; they have wealth of God's name in their homes. Their birth is approved, and their actions are fruitful. ||1|| O my Lord, I am a sacrifice to the humble servants of the Lord. I make my hair into a fan, and wave over them; I apply the dust of their feet to my face. ||1||Pause|| Those generous, humble beings are beyond both birth and death. They worship God by offering themselves to Him and unite with God. ||2|| They become immortal; their domain is true and they are imbued with true God. True is their happiness, and honour. They know whom they belong. ||3|| I wave fan over them, carry water and grind flour for God's humble servants. Nanak prays to God; may I go to meet your devotees. ||4||7||54|| Soohee, Fifth Master: The guru is the transcendent supreme Lord and does everything. Your servant begs for the dust of Your feet. I admire visualizing You. ||1|| O my sovereign Lord, as You keep me, so I live. When it pleases You, I recite Your name and attain peace by Your grace. ||1||Pause|| Serving You is the way and cause to salvation. Whom You inspire serve You. Where devotees sing Your praises that is heaven. You instil devotion. ||2|| I live by reciting Your name and attain peace and contentment. I wash Your lotus feet and drink this water, O my guru kind to the poor; ||3|| I am a sacrifice to the wonderful time when I came to Your door. God became kind to Nanak, I found the perfect guru. ||4||8||55|| Soohee, Fifth Master: Those who miss You are very happy; those who forget die in pain. Whoever God is kind to, recites Your name forever. ||1|| You are my support O master of the humble; I pray to God; may I live listening to your sermon. ||1||Pause|| May I become the dust of Your devotee's feet. I admire seeing You. Enshrining the sacred word in the mind I met devotee's company by Your grace. ||2|| You know the state of my mind. No one is as great as You. Whoever You inspire worships You and becomes Your devotee. ||3|| With my palms pressed together, I beg for one gift; may I realize You O God. Nanak recites Your name with every breath singing Your praises twenty-four hours a day. ||4||9||56|| Soohee, Fifth Master: Those whom You protect, do not suffer any pain. Intoxicated by the worldly wealth, he cannot even speak. He does not think of death. ||1|| O my Lord, You belong to the saints, saints belong to You. Page 750 Your servant has no concern. The devil of death does not come close to him. ||1||Pause|| Those imbued by Your love O Lord; their pain of birth and death goes away. No one can erase Your blessings; the guru assured me. ||2|| Those who recite Your name twenty-four hours a day obtain peace. In Your sanctuary, with Your support, they subdue the five evils. ||3|| I do not know about wisdom, concentration and good deeds; I do not know about You. O Nanak, guru is the greatest of all, who saved my honour. ||4||10||57|| Soohee, Fifth Master: Renouncing everything, I came to gurus refuge; save me, O my saviour! Whatever You make me do, that I do; what can this poor creature do? ||1|| O my dear Lord, You know everything my God; O guru, be kind that I sing God`s praises day and night. ||1||Pause|| Recite God twenty-four hours a day, devotion comes by guru`s grace. Renounce ego and become humble; this is called dead while living. ||2|| Those who recite God in devotee's company; their life is fruitful. Their deeds are fulfilled; whom God bestows His grace. ||3|| O merciful to the meek, Kind Lord, I seek Your sanctuary. Be kind and bless me with Your name. Nanak is the dust of devotee's feet. ||4||11||58|| Tune Soohee, Ashtapadee, First Master, First House: God is one. He is realized by guru`s grace. I am full of sins; I have no virtue. How can I meet my Husband Lord? ||1|| I have no beauty, no enticing eyes. I do not have a noble family, good manners or a sweet voice. ||1||Pause|| The soul-bride adorns her with peace and poise. She is a happy soul-bride, if she pleases her Husband Lord. ||2|| He has no form or feature; At the last moment, God cannot be recited. ||3|| I have no understanding, intellect or cleverness. Be kind to me O God and attach me to Your feet. ||4|| She may be very clever, but this does not please her Husband Lord. Attached to worldly wealth she is deluded by doubt. ||5|| But if she gets rid of her ego, then she merges in her Husband Lord. Only then can the soul-bride obtain the nine treasures of her beloved. ||6|| Separated for many lifes, I suffered in pain. Please take my hand, O my beloved sovereign Lord. ||7|| Says Nanak, there is God and shall always be. She enjoys the beloved when she pleases Him. ||8||1|| Page 751 Soohee, First Master, Ninth House: God is one. He is realized by guru`s grace. The colour of safflower is transitory; it lasts for only a few days. Without God`s name, the false is deluded by doubt and cheated by cheats. Those who are attuned to the true Lord, do not take birth again. ||1|| How one dyed in Lord's love; be dyed by any other colour? Serve God the dyer; focusing your mind to the true Lord. ||1||Pause|| You may wander in the four directions; you cannot become rich without luck. If you are robbed by sins; You are like a prisoner who has no place to go. Those protected by guru are saved; They are attuned to guru's teachings. ||2|| They wear white clothes, but they are filthy and stonehearted. They do not say God from the mouth. They are robbed by duality. They do not realize their origin; they are like animals! ||3|| They enjoy themselves and beg for happiness forever. They do not miss God and suffer again and again. Those who enshrine God the bestowal of pain and pleasure in the mind, do not feel hungry anymore. ||4|| One with debt is summoned, and the devil of death smashes his head. He audits his account and asks for the loan to be paid up. Those attuned to truth are saved by the grace of God. ||5|| If you make any other friend than God, you will become dirt after death. He is lost seeing many colours. He keeps coming and going being lost. We are saved by God's grace. We unite with Him by His grace. ||6|| The careless lacks wisdom; cannot obtain divine wisdom without the guru. He is ruined bothered by indecision. Good and bad both are with him. Without guru's teachings and God's love, everyone is robbed by devil of death. ||7|| He, who created the creation, gives sustenance to all. Why should you forget Him; who gives to everyone forever. O Nanak never forget God's name, the support of the unsupported. ||8||1||2|| Soohee, First Master, Kaafee, Tenth House: God is one. He is realized by guru's grace. The guru-willed obtained difficult to obtain human birth. The mind and body get dyed in God's love if it pleases the guru. ||1|| He departs improving his life taking with the merchandise of the true name. He is honoured in God's court, through guru's teachings. ||1||Pause|| He praises the true Lord with his mind and body; truth pleases God. Page 752 Attuning to God the mind became happy. I found the perfect guru. ||2|| I live, by cherishing Your Virtues; You dwell in me. You dwell in my mind, and slowly sink in my mind. ||3|| I teach my ignorant mind again and again. The guru-willed sings God's praises dyed by His love. ||4|| Recite the beloved God in your mind all the time. If you take virtues with you, the pain shall never afflict you. ||5|| The self-willed is deluded by doubt; he is not dyed by God's love. He is in love of worldly pleasure; his mind and body are ruined. ||6|| Serving the guru, you go home with a profit. Through guru's sermon and teachings, one attains salvation. ||7|| Nanak makes one prayer: if it pleases You. Bless me to enshrine God`s name, and my mind and sing God`s praises. ||8||1||3|| Soohee, First Master: As iron is melted in the foundry and re-shaped. Same way the faithless spends his life aimlessly. ||1|| Without realizing God everything is a suffering and earns more suffering. In ego, he comes and goes deluded by doubt. ||1||Pause|| You save those guru-willed who recite Your name O Lord. Those who follow guru`s teachings, unite with You by Your grace. ||2|| You create and watch; whatever You give, we receive. You create and destroy; You keep an eye on it. ||3|| The body will turn to dust and flown away by the wind. Where is the place to rest if one does not attain the destiny; ||4|| He is robbed in broad daylight; what a darkness! Pride is robbing their homes like a thief; who should we complain to; ||5|| The thief does not break into devotee's home; if he is awake reciting God`s name. Guru`s teachings extinguished the fire and the soul lights it. ||6|| God`s name is a jewel, a ruby; the guru taught me that. One who follows guru's teachings remains free of desire forever. ||7|| Night and day, enshrine Lord's name in your mind. Please unite Nanak with You, if it is pleasing to Your will. ||8||2||4|| Soohee, First Master: Never forget God`s name from your mind; recite him day and night. As You keep me by Your grace, so I live and find peace. ||1|| I am blind; Lord's name is my cane. I take God`s support. Worldly wealth does not entice me. ||1||Pause|| Wherever I look I see him with me by guru`s grace. I see Him inside and out through guru`s teachings. ||2|| Recite the name of the formless God serving the guru by his will. If it pleases You, the fear of doubt disappears by Your will. ||3|| Taking birth is painful, yet the death has to come. Birth and death are accepted by singing God`s praises. ||4|| When You are; I am not. You created me. Page 753 You establish and disestablish; You are realized through guru`s teachings. ||5|| When the body becomes dust, no one knows where it goes. He abides in everything; that is the strange thing. ||6|| You are not far away O God; You know everything. The guru-willed sees You close; You are in the body. ||7|| Please, enshrine Your name in me so that I become peaceful. May slave Nanak sing Your praises; O guru, teach me this; ||8||3||5|| Tune Soohee, Third Master, First House, Ashtapadees: God is one. He is realized by guru`s grace.

Everything is created by reciting the name. God`s name cannot be recited without the guru. Guru`s teachings are very sweet. Cannot find taste without tasting. He wastes his life in exchange for a shell; he does not search his soul. The guru-willed knows only one God. Pain of ego does not bother him. ||1|| I praise my guru who is attuned to the true Lord. Following guru`s teachings, he is enlightened and attains peace. ||1||Pause|| The guru-willed sings, realizes and contemplates guru`s teachings. Body and soul originate from the guru. The deeds of guru-willed are resolved. The blind self-willed acts blindly and earns poison in this world. Enticed by the worldly pleasure he loves and suffers in it without the beloved guru. ||2|| One who serves and follows guru`s will is the real devotee. Following guru`s teachings is praising God and enshrines God in the mind. The guru-willed speaks the true sermon that eliminates ego. He is the bestowal and does true deeds. He teaches the true teachings. ||3|| The guru-willed works, earns and inspires others to recite God`s name. He is forever unattached, imbued with God`s love through the guru intuitively. The self-willed always tells lies; he seeds poison, and eats poison. He is bound by the devil of death and burns in the fire of desire; no one can save him other than the guru. ||4|| Where one bathes in truth is a sacred shrine. The guru-willed knows it. Guru's teachings attain as much as bathing at sixty-eight shrines. Bathing there the inner filth eliminates. Guru`s true teachings are pure. Filth does not attach to them. True praise is obtained from the perfect guru. ||5|| Body, mind, everything belongs to God; cannot say anything bad about it. One becomes pure by God`s command and the ego departs Intuitively tasting guru's teachings extinguishes the fire of greed. Imbued and intoxicated by guru`s teachings, one attains peace. ||6|| Page 754 One who believes in God`s name, falls in love with it through guru`s will. True honour is obtained from the guru, through the love of true name. One God abides in all. Only a few think about it. Lord unites us with Him and blesses us; He saves us through devotional worship. ||7|| Truth pervades everywhere. The guru-willed realize it. Birth and death occur by His command; the guru-willed understands him. He who recites God`s name pleases the guru. He obtains the choice reward. O Nanak, one who eradicates ego, fulfills his deeds. ||8||1|| Soohee, Third Master: The body-bride is very beautiful; her Husband Lord lives with her. She is always a happy soul-bride by following guru`s teachings. Imbued by God`s worship, burns away the ego from inside. ||1|| Guru's teaching is admirable. It wells up from the perfect guru and merges with truth. ||1||Pause|| Everything abides in the body, the continents, worlds and the underworld. The bestowal of life lives in the mind. He looks after everyone. The body-bride is ever content; the guru-willed recite God's name. ||2|| God lives in the body; He is invisible cannot be seen. The ignorant self-willed does not understand; he searches God outside. Serving the guru attains eternal peace and visualizes the invisible. ||3|| The treasure of priceless jewels of worship are in the body. In this body is the whole world; its markets, cities and streets. In this body, one realizes the nine treasures of God's name through guru's teachings. ||4|| In the body, the Lord weighs everything; He is the one who weighs all. This mind is the jewel, the gem, the diamond; it is absolutely priceless. God's name cannot be bought. God's name is obtained from the guru. ||5|| The guru-willed searches his soul. All others are lost in doubt. Whomever God gives, he gets it. No other trick works. True love of God abides in the body. It is realized by guru's grace. ||6|| In the body, are Brahma, Vishnu and Shiva, from whom the whole world emanated? The Lord set His play of coming and going in the world. The perfect guru showed that salvation attains by reciting God's name. ||7|| That body, which serves the guru, is embellished by the true Lord. Without the name, the mortal finds no place of rest in God's court. The devil of death tortures them. O Nanak, those blessed by God are honoured. ||8||2|| Page 755 Tune Soohee, Third Master, Tenth House: God is one. He is realized by guru's grace. Do not praise the world; it shall pass away. Do not praise other people; they shall die and turn to dust. ||1|| I praise my Lord. O guru-willed; always praise the carefree true Lord. ||1||Pause|| Making worldly friendships, the self-willed die and get burnt. In the city of death, they are bound and beaten; time never returns. ||2|| The lives of the guru-willed are fruitful following guru's teachings. Their souls are illuminated and they dwell in peace with ease. ||3|| Those who forget guru's teachings; they are engrossed in love of duality. Their hunger and thirst never ends, they burn night and day. ||4|| They make friends with enemies and enemy with saints. They drown with their families and their dynasty. ||5|| It is not good to slander anyone, but the ignorant, self-willed still do it. The faces of the slanderers are blackened and they go to hell. ||6|| O mind, as good as you do; so you get and keep doing similar deeds. Whatever you sow, so you reap; nothing can be done to it. ||7|| The words of the divine people attain salvation. They are filled with nectar and they are not greedy at all. ||8|| The virtuous accumulate virtues and teach others. Those who meet them are lucky; night and day, they recite God's name. ||9|| He, who created the universe, gives sustenance to all. One Lord alone is the great giver the true master. ||10|| That true Lord is with you o guru-willed. He blesses you by His grace. He blesses you and unites with Him. Recite God forever. ||11|| The mind is impure; the true Lord is pure. How can it merge with Him? God unites you with him by His grace by eliminating ego through guru's teachings. ||12|| Cursed is the life of those who forget their Husband Lord in this world. She does not forget Him by His grace contemplating guru's teachings. ||13|| When guru wants, she unites with Him and enshrines truth in her mind. Once united with guru through love, does not separate again. ||14|| I praise my Husband Lord, contemplating guru's teachings. Meeting with the beloved she attains peace. She is a praiseworthy bride. ||15|| The mind of the self-willed does not soften; they are filthy and stone hearted. Even if you feed milk to a snake! It is still filled with poison. ||16|| He does all. Who else should I say? He is the bestowal. The filth washes with guru's teachings and she looks adorable. ||17|| Page 756 True is the banker, True are His traders. The false cannot stay there. They do not believe in truth, their pain consumes them. ||18|| The world wanders in the filth of ego; it dies, and re-born, again and again. He acts according to pre-ordained destiny, no one can erase. ||19|| Joining the society of saints, he embraces love for the true Lord. Praising the true Lord with truthful mind, he proves true in God's court. ||20|| The teachings of the perfect guru are perfect; recite God's name forever. Ego and possessiveness are terrible diseases; it is a hindrance to life. ||21|| I praise my guru; bowing down to Him again and again, I fall at His feet. I offer my body and mind to Him, eradicating ego from within. ||22|| Indecision leads to ruin; focus your mind on one Lord. Renounce ego and possessiveness and merge in truth. ||23|| Those who meet the guru are my brothers; they follow guru's teachings. Those who merge with the true Lord do not separate again; they are judged to be true in the court of the Lord. ||24|| Those who worship the true Lord are my friends and brothers. Sell the demerits cheap and enter into partnership of virtues. ||25|| The virtuous attains peace and he does true worship. They deal in truth through guru's teachings and earn profit of God's name. ||26|| You collect gold and silver through sins, but it does not go with you on departure. Nothing goes with you other than God's name; all are plundered by the devil of death. ||27|| Lord's name is the food of the mind; enshrine it in your heart. This food is inexhaustible; it stays with the guru-willed. ||28|| O mind, you forgot your origin, you shall depart losing your honour. The world is troubled by the love of duality; recite God through guru's teachings. ||29|| God's value cannot be estimated; God's praises cannot be written. When one attunes to God devotionally through guru's teachings; merges with God. ||30|| My Husband Lord is playful; He imbued me with His love with ease. The soul-bride imbues with His love, when she embraces her Husband Lord. ||31|| Those who serve the guru reunite with God separated for a long time. They are filled with treasure of God's name. It does not exhaust by eating or spending. They intuitively praise God. ||32|| They are not born, they do not die; they do not suffer pain. Those protected by the guru are saved. They celebrate with the Lord. ||33|| The friends united with the Lord do not separate again; night and day, they remain united with Him. There are only a few who are truthful in the world. ||34||1||3|| Soohee, Third Master: God is sacred and inaccessible; how can we meet Him? The doubt dispels through guru's teachings and the carefree God dwells in the mind. ||1|| The guru-willed recite God's name. Page 757 I admire those who sing God's praises all the time. ||1||Pause|| The guru is like Lake Mansarovar; the fortunate find Him. The guru-willed servants find the guru; the swan-souls feed on God's name. ||2|| The guru-willed recite God's name with love enshrining in the mind. If it is pre-ordained, they accept the will of the guru. ||3|| The fortune searched his soul and found the treasure of God's name.

The perfect guru showed me the way; I realized the supreme Lord. ||4|| There is one God of all; no other. By guru's grace, God abides in the mind; He is revealed in the heart. ||5|| God is the inner-knower of all hearts; God dwells in every place. Who should we call evil? Search guru's teachings with love and find out. ||6|| He calls others bad and good, as long as he is in duality. The guru-willed realizes one God and merges with Him. ||7|| That is selfless service, which pleases God, and approved by God. Servant Nanak worships God focusing his mind to guru's feet. ||8||2||4||9|| Tune Soohee, Ashtapadees, Fourth Master, Second House: God is one. He is realized by guru's grace. If someone unites me with my beloved; I will sell myself to him. ||1|| So that I can visualize God; We meet the guru by God's grace and recite God's name. ||1||Pause|| I recite Your name in pain and pleasure. ||2|| If You give me hunger, I will still feel satisfied; I am joyful, even in sorrow. ||3|| I will cut my mind and body in pieces, and offer to You; I will burn myself in fire. ||4|| I wave fan over You, and carry water for You; I eat what You give. ||5|| Poor Nanak has fallen at Your door; O Lord, unite me with You. ||6|| I take out my eyes and place them at Your feet; I realized this wandering all over the world. ||7|| If You seat me near You I worship You. If You beat and drive me out, I will still recite Your name. ||8|| If people praise me, it is your praise. If they slander me, I will not leave You. ||9|| If You are on my side, let anyone say anything. If I forget You, I will die. ||10|| I praise my guru; I fall at his feet and console with the saint. ||11|| Poor Nanak is lost in love to visualize You. ||12|| Even in storm and torrential rain, I go out to see my guru. ||13|| If the ocean is very salty but still the devotees cross it to see the guru. ||14|| As the human dies without water; similarly the devotee dies without guru. ||15|| Page 758 As the earth enjoys rain, so does the devotee meeting the guru. ||16|| God's servant consults other servants. They humbly talk to each other. ||17|| Nanak prays to God, that he meets the guru, and finds peace. ||18|| You are the guru, the disciple; I recite You through the guru.||19|| Those who serve You, become You. You preserve their honour. ||20|| O Lord, Your treasure of worship is full. You give whomever You want. ||21|| Whomever You give they obtain it. All other clever tricks are fruitless. ||22|| Worshipping my guru, my mind woke up. ||23|| Poor Nanak begs for this gift, that he becomes slave of Your slaves. ||24|| Even if the guru rebukes me, it feels very sweet to me. If he forgives me, that is guru's greatness. ||25|| What the guru-willed says is approved. What the self-willed says is not. ||26|| Even in cold, frost and the snowfall, the devotee goes to see his guru. ||27|| All day and night, I see my guru; I put guru's feet in my eyes. ||28|| I do everything for the guru; whatever pleases Him is approved. ||29|| Night and day, I worship guru's feet; be kind to me o my master. ||30|| Guru is Nanak's body and soul, he is satisfied and fulfilled seeing Him. ||31|| Nanak's God is all pervading. Wherever I see; he is there. ||32||1|| Tune Soohee, Fourth Master, Ashtapadees, Tenth House: God is one. He is realized by guru's grace. I am in love with my beloved. My body and soul become content when I see my guru in front of me. ||1|| I have faith in God's name. I obtained the inaccessible and unfathomable nectar from the perfect guru. ||1||Pause|| I enjoy seeing the guru; I am in love with God's name. He united me with Him by His grace. I attained salvation. ||2|| The guru loves God's name. I offer my body and mind to Him if I meet Him. If it is pre-ordained, then I shall drink the nectar intuitively. ||3|| Praise the guru while asleep and recite guru when you are awake. If I meet such a guru-willed; I will wash his feet. ||4|| I long for such a friend; that will unite me with my beloved. Meeting the true guru is meeting God. I found Him with ease. ||5|| Page 759 Guru is the ocean of virtues of God's name. I yearn to see Him! Without Him, I cannot live for an instant. If I do not see Him, I will die. ||6|| As the fish cannot survive without water; The saint cannot live without God. Without Lord's name, he dies. ||7|| I am in love with my guru! How can I live without guru, O my mother? Guru's sermon is my support. I live by following guru's teachings. ||8|| God's name is a jewel; the honourable guru gave it to me, O my mother. True name is my support. I remain lovingly absorbed in Lord's name. ||9|| Guru's sermon is the treasure of God's name. He teaches God's name. He who falls at guru's feet obtains it. ||10|| May some beloved come and tell me the untold story of love? I offer my mind to him. I bow down and touch his feet. ||11|| You are my only friend O all-knowing Lord. You united me with my friend guru. You are my support forever. ||12|| My true guru is ever-present. He does not come or go. He is immortal; He is permeating and pervading all. ||13|| I gathered the wealth of God's name. It is my property and wealth. O Nanak, I am approved in God's Court by guru's grace. ||14||1||2||11|| Tune Soohee, Ashtapadees, Fifth Master, First House: God is one. He is realized by guru's grace. He is entangled in sinful acts. His mind is troubled by many different ideas. ||1|| O my mind, how can I find the unapproachable and incomprehensible perfect Lord? ||1||Pause|| He remains entangled in the intoxication of worldly love. His excessive greed never ends. ||2|| Anger and wickedness live in the body. He is in the dark of ignorance, he does not understand anything. ||3|| He wanders in a burning door. He cannot go to God's court. ||4|| The mortal is bothered by hope and worry. He cannot find destiny. He wanders in other's places. ||5|| He wanders lost like a hunter. He wanders thirsty like a fish out of water. ||6|| I have no intelligence or anything to say. You are my only hope, O my Lord. ||7|| I offer this prayer to the saints Prays Nanak, to unite him with You. ||8|| By God's grace I joined the company of devotee's. Nanak is satisfied, finding the perfect Lord. ||1||Second Pause||1|| Page 760 Tune Soohee, Fifth Master, Third House: God is one. He is realized by guru's grace. Emotional attachment is temporary. It is an ocean of fire and pain. O God; save me by Your grace. ||1|| I seek the sanctuary of the lotus feet of the Lord. He is the master of the meek, the support of His devotees. ||1||Pause|| He is the master of orphans and destroyer of devotee's fear. In the company of devotees, the devil of death cannot touch them. ||2|| The merciful Lord is incomparably beautiful, embodiment of life. Singing His praises cuts the net of the devil of death. ||3|| One who constantly recites God's sacred name. The disease and beauty of the worldly pleasure does not bother him. ||4|| He attains salvation along with his companions. The five thieves will not affect him. ||5|| He, who devotionally recites God; He obtains the reward of it. ||6|| Showering His mercy, God made me His own; He blessed me with the worship of His name. ||7|| God was in the beginning, in the middle, and will be in the end. O Nanak, without Him, there is no one else. ||8||1||2|| Tune Soohee, Fifth Master, Ashtapadees, Ninth House: God is one. He is realized by guru's grace. Why do you meet those that make you unhappy? The mind satisfies meeting the saint friends. They dye you with God's love. My love for them shall never die; it shall never be broken. ||1|| O supreme Lord; be kind that I sing Your praises forever. May I meet my friend saints and recite God's name with them. ||1||Pause|| He does not see, hear or understand. The blind is enticed by the worldly pleasure. His false body will perish. Still he does false deeds. Those who have relation with the perfect guru recite God's name. ||2|| By God's order, they come into the world and leave by God's order. By His command the universe is created. By His command they enjoy everything. One, who forgets the Creator; suffers the pain of separation; ||3|| One, who pleases God, goes to His court with honour. One who recites God's name obtains peace and happiness here. The supreme Lord confers honour on those who serve the guru with love. ||4|| He abides in all places and places of importance and looks after all beings. I gathered the true treasure of wealth and riches of one name; I shall never forget Him from my mind when He is kind to me. ||5|| Page 761 My coming and going ended; the formless Lord dwells in my mind. His limits cannot be found; He is lofty and exalted, inaccessible and infinite. One who forgets God, shall die and reborn millions of times; ||6|| Those who love God enshrine Him in the mind. Those who share those values get together and recite God all the time. Those dyed in God's love; their worries go away. ||7|| You are the Creator, the cause of causes; You are the one and all. You are all-powerful, omnipresent; You have the discerning intellect. O Nanak, reciting God's name is the resolve of the devotees; ||8||1||3|| Tune Soohee, Fifth Master, Ashtapadees, Tenth House, Kaafee: God is one. He is realized by guru's grace. Even though I make mistakes by mistake; I am still Yours O Lord. Those who love others, die repenting. ||1|| I will never leave my Husband Lord's company. My beloved is always adorable. He is my hope and inspiration. ||1||Pause|| You are my friend my relative. I am proud of You. When You dwell in me, I am at peace. You are the honour of the humble. ||2|| If You are pleased with me, O treasure of mercy; may I not see any other. Please bless me that I forever enshrine and miss You in my mind. ||3|| I will come to you so that I can see you. I will listen to your stories from the guru by his grace. ||4|| O beloved, millions of other love; do not come close to You. You are the King of kings; I cannot describe Your praises. ||5|| O beloved; You have millions; better than me. May I visualize you even for a moment and enjoy by your grace. ||6|| Seeing Him, my mind is at peace and my sins go away. Why should I forget Him, O my mother? He is omnipresent. ||7|| In humility, I bowed down to Him and He met me intuitively. I obtained my pre-ordained destiny by saint's grace O Nanak. ||8||1||4|| Soohee, Fifth Master: The Simritees, the Vedas, the Puraanas and the other scriptures proclaim That, without God's name everything is false and worthless; ||1|| The infinite treasure of God's name abides in the minds of devotees. Birth death attachment and suffering are erased in devotee's company. ||1||Pause|| Those indulged in attachment, conflict and ego shall cry. Those without God's name never find peace. ||2|| People are engrossed by possessiveness. Entangled in worldly pleasure leads to heaven and hell. ||3|| Practicing cleansing and contemplating I came to a conclusion. Without God's name there is no peace, the mortal will surely lose. ||4|| Page 762 Many come and go; they die and reborn again and again. Without realizing, everything is a conflict. They wander in reincarnations. ||5|| Whoever God is kind to; join the company of devotees. They recite God's sacred name. ||6|| Billions and billions search for Him. Whom he makes to understand; they get close to him. ||7|| May I never forget You o bestowal. Bless me with Your name. May I sing Your praises day and night – O Nanak, this is my heart-felt desire. ||8||2||5||16|| Tune Soohee, First Master, Kuchajee ~ The Ungraceful Bride: God is one. He is realized by guru's grace. I am virtueless and full of faults. How can I enjoy my Husband Lord? Each of His soul-brides is better than the next; who knows my name? Those brides who enjoy their Husband Lord are sacred. I do not have their virtues; whom can I blame for this? Which of Your virtues, O Lord, should I say? Which of Your names should I say? I cannot even find one of Your virtues. I admire You forever. Gold, silver, pearls and rubies are pleasing. My Husband Lord gave me these things, I love them. Palaces are built of brick mud and stones; I am lost in searching in these; I do not sit near my Husband Lord. The cranes shriek in the sky, and the herons have come to rest. The bride is going to her in-law's house; what face she will show there? She kept sleeping as the day dawned; she forgot all about her journey. She is separated from her Husband Lord, and now she suffers. You are virtuous; I am without a virtue. This is Nanak's only prayer: All are virtuous soul-brides. I am unfortunate, how do I spend my night? ||1|| Soohee, First Master, Suchajee ~ The Noble And Graceful Bride: When I have You, I have everything. O Lord, You are my wealth. With You in my mind I live in peace; I admire You in me. By Your will, You bestow thrones and greatness. By Your will, You make us beggars and wanderers. By Your will, the ocean flows in the desert and lotus blossoms in the sky. By Your will, one cross over the terrifying world-ocean; by Your will, he drowns in the middle. By Your will, I have my Husband Lord and I am imbued with His praises. By Your will, I am afraid of my Husband Lord, I keep coming and going. You, O my Lord, are inaccessible and immeasurable; I fall to Your feet saying so. What should I beg for? What should I say and hear? I am hungry and thirsty for visualizing You. May I find my Lord through guru's teachings; this is Nanak's prayer. ||2|| Page 763 Soohee, Fifth Master, Gunvantee ~ The Virtuous Bride: If I see guru's devotee, I humbly bow and fall at his feet. I tell him the state of my mind and beg to unite me with the guru. I ask him for the lesson that my mind shall not go anywhere else. I surrender this mind to you. Please, show me the path to God. I came from far away to seek Your sanctuary. I hope in my mind that you will eliminate all my sufferings. Walk this path O brother; do whatever guru tells you to do. Abandon the intellectual pursuits of the mind, and forget the love of duality. This way, you visualize God and nothing should stop you. I do not say anything on my own. I say what God told me to say. God blesses the treasure of worship; guru spreads it O Nanak. I shall never again feel greedy; I am satisfied and fulfilled. If I see guru's devotee, I humbly bow and fall at his feet. ||3|| Tune Soohee, Chhant, First Master, First House: God is one. He is realized by guru's grace. I am fully grown with youth. I am a guest at my parent's home O Lord. I am filthy polluted in my mind. Virtues do not come without guru O Lord. I do not know the value of virtues; I am lost in doubt. I waste my youth in vain. I do not know my Husband, the way to his home or visualize him. I do not attain love of my Lord. I did not ask and follow guru's path. I spent the life sleeping. O Nanak, in the prime of my youth, I am a widow; without my Husband Lord, the soul-bride is withering away. ||1|| O elder; bless me with God as my husband. God pleases me O Lord. He, whose sermon is universal, pervades throughout the four ages O Lord. The whole universe recites the husband Lord. The virtueless does not. As we hope, so we desire, the all-pervading Lord fulfills it. Lord's bride is forever happy and virtuous; she will never be a dirty widow. O Nanak, I love my true Husband Lord; I love Him forever. ||2|| O elder; find the auspicious moment that I too go to my in-laws O Lord. Time of marriage is set by God's will; His will does not change O Lord. God writes in your fate what you do; nobody can change it. Only God's name is the marriage party. He pervades the universe. The worldly wealth cries and leaves, seeing the bride and groom in love. O Nanak, touching guru's feet following his teachings attains peace and destiny by reciting God's name. ||3|| Page 764 My father got me married far away, I cannot return to my parents' home O Lord. I am delighted to see my Husband Lord; this is where I belong, O Lord. God united me with my beloved and gave me control of my destiny. By good destiny I met Him in a peaceful place; I became virtuous through guru's teachings. I have truth and contentment in my lap; I speak truth by Lord's will. O Nanak, I shall not suffer the pain of separation; may I merge with Him through guru's teachings. ||4||1|| Tune Soohee, First Master, Chhant, Second House: God is one. He is realized by guru's grace. My friend has come to my home. The true Lord united me with him. If it pleases God, He unites us. I attained peace meeting the guru-willed. I obtained the merchandise, which I wanted. Meeting him my mind is happy forever and I look adorable. The infinite divine music of the guru-willed plays; I came to my beloved's home. ||1|| So come, my beloved friends, sing the songs of joy, O ladies. Sing the true songs of joy and God will be pleased. You shall sing throughout the four ages. My Husband Lord came into my home, my place looks beautiful. My affairs are resolved through guru's teachings. Applying the ointment, the supreme essence of divine wisdom to my eyes, I see Lord throughout the universe. Join me, my friends, sing the songs of joy; my friend came to my home. ||2|| My mind and body are drenched with nectar; I am in love with the jewel Lord. The invaluable jewel is in me the highest of all realities. You the great bestowal are in the disguise of a human being. You the Lord are all knowing; You created the creation. Listen, O my friends; my beloved enticed my mind. My body and mind are drenched with nectar. ||3|| O supreme soul of the world. Your play is true. Your play is true, O inaccessible and infinite Lord; without You, who will make me understand? There are millions of mystics and wise, without You no one is anyone? Death is hovering over the head; the guru keeps my mind in its place. O Nanak, guru's teachings burn the ill deeds; virtuous realize God. ||4||1||2|| Tune Soohee, First Master, Third House: God is one. He is realized by guru's grace. Come, my beloved I want to see your face O Lord. I stand in my doorway, watching You; my mind is filled with joy. My mind is filled with joy; hear me, O God. I believe in You. Visualizing You, I do not need anyone's help. My pain of birth death is gone. Page 765 I know that You are in everyone; I realized this by Your grace. O Nanak, I admire my beloved; He met me in my house. ||1|| When her beloved came to her home, the bride was happy O Lord. She is fascinated by guru's teachings; she is happy to see her Lord. She is filled with virtues and pleased, when she recites God with love. Her demerits eradicated, she built the house of virtues by the grace of the perfect Lord, the architect of destiny. Killing the thieves, she became one of five judges. She bestows true justice. O Nanak, salvation attains reciting God's name through guru's teachings. ||2|| The young bride found her Husband Lord; her hopes are fulfilled. She recites the beloved through guru's teachings. God is inside not far away. God is not far; He is in each and every heart. All are His brides. He is the essence and enjoys the way he thinks right. He is imperishable, immovable, invaluable and infinite, realized through the guru. O Nanak, He unites us with Him by His grace by missing Him lovingly. ||3|| My Husband Lord lives in the highest shrine. He is the Lord of the universe. I am amazed seeing His place; the divine music plays there O God. I worship Him through guru's teachings reciting God's name, his symbol. Counterfeit have no place to go without God's name. Even he is accepted through jewel of God's name. Perfect is His honour, intellect and identity. He never comes or goes. O Nanak, the guru-willed realizes himself and becomes immortal like God. ||4||1||3|| God is one. He is realized by guru's grace. Tune Soohee, Chhant, First Master, Fourth House: One, who created the world, looks after and puts them to work. Your grace illuminates the body. The body shines like moonlight. The body moon glows by God`s grace, the darkness of suffering is gone. The groom looks adorable in the marriage party; the enchanting bride sees him. The wedding performed with honour playing divine music. One, who created the world, looks after and put them to work; ||1|| I admire my beloved who is free of sins. This body is attached to him and we consult each other. We consult each other; how can I forget him? Seeing him brings joy to my heart; I embrace Him with my heart. Attained all merits; no demerit left forever. I admire my beloved who is free of sins. ||2|| One who has nose for merits can smell the fragrance. If you have virtues; share with the beloved; Page 766 Share the merits and forget the demerits. Wear silk clothes and set up the show in your arena. Wish well wherever you go, mix and drink nectar. One, who has the nose for virtues; can smell the fragrance; ||3|| He does everything; who else do we say; No one else can do anything. You can tell the one who makes a mistake. If he makes a mistake, we can tell him; how can God make a mistake? He sees and hears. He bestows gifts without asking or begging. The great giver, the architect of the universe, gives His gifts. O Nanak, He is the true Lord. He does everything; unto whom should we complain? No one else can do anything. ||4||1||4|| Soohee, First Master: My mind is imbued and sings His praises; He is pleasing to my mind. True is the ladder of the guru; climbing it attains divinity. Real peace comes through the truth. How could the true teachings even be erased? He the bestowal of cleansing bath and divine wisdom; He cannot be cheated; By fraud, attachment and corruption falsehood, hypocrisy and duality; My mind is imbued and sings His praises; He is pleasing to my mind. ||1|| So praise the Lord, who created the creation. Filth sticks to the filthy mind; it does not affect those who drink nectar. Churn and drink the nectar and give the mind to the guru to evaluate. I intuitively realized my God, when I linked my mind to the true Lord. I sing God`s praises with love, if it pleases Him; how could I meet Him being a stranger? So praise the Lord, who created the creation. ||2|| When He came, what else remains behind? Why should he go then; My mind has reconciled with the beloved. My mind is imbued with God. One imbued with

God`s love becomes truthful to God who created this body. He is the master of the five elements; He created the true creation. I am worthless; hear me O my beloved! Whatever pleases You is true. One, who realizes truth does not come and go anymore. ||3|| Apply such an ointment to your eyes, which is pleasing to your beloved. We realize, understand and know Him, if He makes us know Him. He shows the way, and He conquers our mind. He causes us to do good or bad deeds; who can know his value; I know nothing of tantric spells magical words and hypocritical rituals; I enshrined God in my mind and attained satisfaction. The ointment of God`s name is realized by those who realize truth through guru`s teachings. ||4|| Why should my beloved go to someone else's home! My beloved is imbued with truth. He is in my mind. In my mind, my beloved enjoys including good deeds and faith. Believing in God`s name is equal to bathing at sixty-eight shrines. Page 767 He creates and tests the way he thinks it right. My beloved dyed me in his deep red colour. ||5|| If a blind man is the leader, how will he know the way? He is impaired, has no realization; how will he know the right way? How can he follow the path and reach the destination. The blind thinks blind. Without Lord's name he does not understand. The blind drowns in filth. Enshrining guru`s teachings in the mind creates passion for the light of day and night. With palms pressed together he prays to the guru to show him the way. ||6|| If the mind becomes a stranger, then the whole world becomes stranger. Who do I open up to; everyone is suffering in pain. The whole world is suffering; who will know my plight; Coming and going is scary; it never ends. Without God`s name they are half empty and sad; they never follow guru`s teachings. If the mind becomes stranger, then the whole world becomes stranger. ||7|| One, who enshrines the guru in his mind, becomes content. The devotee serves the guru if he believes in his true teachings. He believes in guru`s teachings and merges in it and reaches the destiny. The Creator creates and he abides in it without any doubt. Following guru`s teachings attains peace and the divine music plays. One, who enshrines the guru in his mind, becomes content. ||8|| How can we praise His deeds? He creates and looks after. His value cannot be estimated, no matter how much one may think. He who creates knows the value. He never forgets his doing. If you please him; He honours you through priceless guru`s teachings. I the lowly and humble pray to you; do not forget the Lord O brother. O Nanak, One who did so; only he can teach. ||9||2||5|| Tune Soohee, Chhant, Third Master, Second House: God is one. He is realized by guru`s grace. Recite God and obtain peace and contentment. O guru-willed; receive the divine reward. O guru-willed; recite God and reap the reward. It eliminates the pain of many lives. I praise my guru who settled all my affairs. Recite God by God`s grace; o mortal attain peace in return. Says Nanak, listen O brother: reciting God attains peace and joy. ||1|| Listening to God`s praises; I am imbued to Him intuitively. I recite God`s name following guru`s teachings. Those with pre-ordained destiny meet the guru, their fear of birth and death goes away. Page 768 Whoever eliminates evil-deeds and duality from within; attunes to God with love. Those blessed by God, sing God's praises all the time. Hearing God's praises the mind gets drenched intuitively. ||2|| God's name attains salvation in today's age. Such thinking originates from guru's teachings. Contemplating guru's teachings creates love for God's name by God's grace. He sings God's praises intuitively, all his sins are eradicated. All are Yours, You belong to all. I am Yours and You are mine. God's name attains salvation in any age. ||3|| The beloved has graciously come to my home. Singing the praises of the Lord, one gets satisfied and fulfilled. Singing God's praises satisfies forever and never feels hungry again. Those who recite God's name are worshipped all over. O Nanak, God unites and separates by His grace. No one else can do it. My beloved has graciously come to my home. ||4||1|| God is one. He is realized by guru's grace. Tune Soohee, Third Master, Third House: God protects His devotees in all ages. The guru-willed who eliminate ego through guru's teachings are God's devotees. Eliminating ego pleases God. His sermon is true. The guru-willed do true worship and tell others as well. Devotee's lifestyle is true and pure; the true name pleases them. O Nanak, devotees who practice truth look adorable in God's court. ||1|| God is the caste and honour of His devotees. The devotees enshrine God's name in the mind. They worship and eliminate ego; they differentiate between virtues and vice. They realize merits and demerits through God's name; God's worship tastes sweet to them. They worship God forever. They are detached from the world living at home. Imbued with worship, their minds become pure forever; they see God with them all the time. O Nanak, those who recite God's name forever, are honoured at God's court. ||2|| The self-willed recite God without the guru. It cannot be done without the guru. They are troubled by the sickness of ego. They bear the pain of birth and death. They suffer the pain of birth and death deluded by duality. The reality cannot be understood without the guru. Without God's worship, the whole world is lost and regrets in the end. Page 769 Only a few among millions realize, that God's name is the essence. O Nanak, honour attains reciting God's name. Honour is lost in love of duality. ||3|| God's devotees praise God in their home, that is the true deed. God bestows the treasure of worship. They merge with God eliminating the fear of death. Conquering the thorny pain of death, they merge with God; they obtain the treasure of God's name; that pleases God. God bestowed this gift with ease, which is always full never falls short. God's devotees are honoured and adored forever through guru's teachings. O Nanak, He unites us with Him by His grace and honours forever. ||4||1||2|| Soohee, Third Master: Where devotees talk about God through guru's teachings by singing God's praises, attains truth O God. Enshrining truth in the mind eliminates ego and sins O God. Enshrining God in the mind takes across the terrible world ocean; you do not have to do it again. True guru teaches true sermon. He truly reveals God. Praising God merges with God. He sees God everywhere. O Nanak, it is true that there is God. Reciting His name attains salvation. ||1|| True guru reveals the true Lord; the true Lord preserves our honour O God. God's love is devotee's true food; God's true name attains peace. God's name attains peace; no one dies again and never goes through the pregnancy. The souls merge, truth merges. Enlightenment attains reciting God's name. Those who know the truth are true; night and day, they recite the truth. O Nanak, those who enshrine true name in the mind; do not suffer the pain of separation. ||2|| They sing God's praises through true teachings and enjoy singing O God. Singing praises of the pure God makes the mind and body pure and God dwells in them O God. They practice truth speak truth. Whatever the truthful does that happens. Wherever I look, I see the true Lord pervading; there is no other. Those who practice truth, merge with truth. The others take birth and die. O Nanak, God is everything. He makes us do everything. ||3|| True devotees are honoured in His court. Truth prevails there. True sermon is in the body. The truthful realize the truth. Self-realization realizes the truth. The truthful know the truth. Guru's true teachings are truly admirable. Realizing truth attains happiness. Imbued with truth, the devotees love God; they do not love any other. O Nanak, one with pre-ordained destiny realizes the true Lord. ||4||2||3|| Soohee, Third Master: The soul-bride may wander through the four ages. Without the true guru, she will not find her true Husband Lord. Page 770 God's rule is eternal. No one is beyond it O God. No one is beyond it, it is true. There is only one God. That soul-bride, who accepts guru's teachings, meets her Husband Lord. Meeting the guru, she finds the Lord; cannot attain salvation without God's name. O Nanak, the soul-bride ravishes her Husband Lord; her mind accepts Him and she finds peace. ||1|| Serve the true guru, O innocent bride; you shall obtain the husband Lord. You shall be a happy bride forever; you shall never be dirty again. You will never be dirty again; only a few guru-willed realize it by eliminating ego. Do good deeds and merge with guru's teachings and know one God in the mind. The guru-willed recites God, day and night, and obtains true honour. O Nanak, the soul-bride recites her beloved; God pervades everywhere. ||2|| Serve the guru, O innocent soul-bride; he will unite you with your Husband Lord. The bride is imbued with God's love; meeting with her beloved, she finds peace. Meeting her beloved, she finds peace and merges in the true Lord; True Lord abides everywhere. The bride adores herself with truth day and night, she merges with truth. God the bestowal of happiness is realized through guru's teachings. The soul bride embraces God. O Nanak, the bride realizes the destiny; she realizes God through guru's teachings. ||3|| Lord unites His young and innocent bride with Him. Through guru's teachings, she is enlightened; God is omnipresent. God is omnipresent; He dwells in her mind. She realizes her pre-ordained destiny. On her cozy bed, she is pleasing to my God; she wears truth as her makeup. The bride became pure by eliminating the filth of ego and she merged with God through guru's teachings. O Nanak, the Creator united her with Him through the treasure of God's name. ||4||3||4|| Soohee, Third Master: The guru-willed realize God by singing God's praises. Night and day, recite God through guru's teachings. The infinite divine music will play. God came to my home; the infinite divine music plays; O ladies sing God's praises. That soul-bride who worships God through guru's teachings; becomes the beloved of her Husband Lord! Those who enshrine guru's teachings in the mind, enjoy guru's teachings. O Nanak, they sing God's praises forever because God graciously came to their home. ||1|| The devotees are joyous in the mind by attuning to God's name with love O God. Reciting pure God's praises; the mind of the guru-willed became pure O God. Sing pure praises through God's sacred sermon enshrining God's name in the mind. Those who enshrine God in the mind attain salvation. God abides in everyone and realized through guru's teachings. Page 771 Singing Your praises attains peace. Guru's teachings realize God. O Nanak, those whom guru leads on God's path their birth is fruitful. ||2|| Joining the company of devotees they lovingly recite God's name O God. Through guru's teachings, they attain salvation and become immortal by lovingly attuning to God's name O God. Meeting the guru they enshrine God's name in the mind. Their mind is imbued with God. They realize God the bestowal of happiness reciting God all the time by eliminating false attachment. Imbued with guru's teachings, they become peaceful enshrining God's name in the mind. O Nanak, those who serve the guru with love are happy forever. ||3|| Without the guru, the world is deluded by doubt; they do not attain salvation O God. Reciting God the guru-willed realize God; their sufferings depart O God. Their pains depart when God is pleasing to their mind; they sing God's praises imbued with it. Lord's devotees are pure forever; they are respected forever in all ages. Through true worship they find the destiny the abode of the Lord. O Nanak, reciting God's sermon through guru's teachings brings joy and peace. ||4||4||5|| Soohee, Third Master: If you long for your Husband Lord, O innocent bride; focus your mind to guru's feet. You shall be a happy soul bride forever; He (God) does not die or leave. God does not die or leave. He is realized through the guru with ease and the soul bride becomes the love of the Lord Husband. Through truth and self-control, she is forever pure; she is embellished with guru's teachings. My true God is true forever. He created Him on His own. O Nanak, she who focuses her mind to guru's feet, enjoys her Husband Lord. ||1|| The innocent bride finds her Husband Lord; she enjoys him with love forever. Those who enjoy guru's teachings; the filth does not attach to their body. Those attuned to God; filth does not attach to their body. God unites them with Him. Night and day, she recites God and eliminates ego from inside. Through guru's teachings, she easily finds Him. She is imbued with her beloved. O Nanak, honour attains through God's name. She misses God dyed in His love. ||2|| Those who miss God dyed by His love; attain destiny O God. Those who self-surrender, recite the purest merciful God O God. She eliminates false attachment; she pleases God when she is pleasing to him. Night and day, she sings God's praises; she speaks the unspoken story. One God abides throughout the four ages. No one realizes Him without the guru. Page 772 O Nanak, She attaches her mind to God and enjoys imbued in love. ||3|| The soul bride is happy meeting the beloved Husband Lord O God. Through guru's teachings, her mind becomes pure; she enshrines the Lord in her heart. Enshrining God in the mind she fulfills deeds. She realizes God through guru's teachings. My beloved enticed my mind; so I realized God the architect of destiny. Serving the guru, she finds lasting peace; God the destroyer of pride, dwells in her mind. O Nanak, she is united with her guru. She became divine through guru's teachings. ||4||5||6|| Hymn, Third Master: The song of joy of God's name is realized through guru's teachings O God. The mind and body of the guru-willed is drenched with God the beloved Lord. Reciting God's name with love, he and his ancestry attain salvation. Coming and going ended, peace attained and the divine music plays. Reciting God I found God by His grace O Nanak. The song of God's name is sung contemplating guru's teachings. ||1|| I am lowly, God is very high. How will I meet Him O God? I met the guru by God's grace and found God through guru's teachings intuitively. Through guru's teachings my ego departed and I am happy. I enjoy my bed, since I became pleasing to God enshrining God in the mind.

O Nanak, the soul bride who follows God's will is fortunate. I am lowly, God is very high. How will I meet Him O God? ||2|| God abides in everyone and he is the Lord of everyone. God is far from some, but He is the support of some other's mind. The Creator is the support of some. The fortunate find the guru. One God the master abides in all. The guru-willed realize Him. The mind agreed and became content, O Nanak, contemplating God. God abides in everybody. He is the lord of everyone. ||3|| Serving guru the bestowal; God's name enshrines in the mind O God. O Lord, bless me with the dust of the feet of the perfect guru, so that I the sinner, may be liberated. Even sinners are liberated, by eradicating the ego; they obtain their destiny. I spent the night listening to the discerning wisdom; God's name enshrined in my mind through guru's teachings. Reciting God attains eternal peace O Nanak, God's name tastes sweet. Those who serve the guru enshrine God's name in the mind. ||4||6||7||5||7||12|| Page 773 Tune Soohee, Fourth Master, Chhant, First House: God is one. He is realized by guru's grace. Meeting the guru the sins depart and I enjoy virtues O God. I recite God's name through guru's teachings forever O God. Guru's teachings taste sweet and eliminate the useless sins. The disease of ego is gone, fear has left, and I am absorbed in peace. The body is at peace following guru's teachings and enjoys divine wisdom. Night and day, I continuously enjoy peace and pleasure. O Nanak, this is my pre-ordained destiny. ||1|| Truthful and content groom's father came to arrange the wedding. Inviting the saints for the ceremony, we sang guru's sermon. Singing guru's sermon I attained supreme status. I enjoyed their company. Anger and false attachment departed and the rituals and doubt eradicated. The pain of ego is gone, I found peace; my body has become healthy. By guru's grace, O Nanak, I realized God, the ocean of virtues. ||2|| The self-willed is separated, far away from God; she does not obtain the destiny and she burns in pain. She is filled with ego and falsehood. She deals in falsehood O Lord. Practicing fraud and falsehood she suffers in pain; without the guru, she does not find the way. The ignorant wanders on dismal path; she is pushed around all the time. God, the great giver leads her to meet the guru by His grace. Separated from many lives, God unites them with Him intuitively O Nanak. ||3|| The wedding time has come and the soul-bride is happy O God. The Pandits and astrologers have come to find the auspicious time. They checked the almanacs, and the bride's mind is happy, when she heard that her beloved has come home. The virtuous and wise men got together and decided to perform the marriage ceremony immediately. She has found her Husband, the inaccessible, unfathomable primal Lord, who is forever young and her friend from childhood. O Nanak, when God unites by His grace. She shall never be separated again. ||4||1|| Soohee, Fourth Master: God started the first round of the marriage ceremony by His grace. Recite the hymns of the Vedas of Brahma and eliminate sins O Lord. Recite God's name truthfully reading from scriptures. Recite and worship the perfect guru and eliminate your sins and sufferings. The fortunate attained peace and joy reciting God's sweet name. Page 774 Servant Nanak proclaims that the first round of the marriage ceremony has begun. ||1|| In the second round of marriage ceremony; the guru united me with the true spouse O Lord. My mind became peaceful and the filth of ego eliminated O Lord. I became carefree reciting God's praises and I realized God in me. God created the creation and he lives in everything. God is inside out. I sing songs of joy joining God's devotees. Servant Nanak proclaims; in the second round of the marriage ceremony, the infinite divine music started to play. ||2|| In the third round of the marriage ceremony my mind became detached O Lord. Meeting with God's humble saints I the fortunate found my Lord O God. I found the pure Lord, I sing God's praises. I recite God's sermon. I the fortunate found the saint and I spoke God's unspoken sermon. My mind started saying God God. I recite God due to my pre-ordained destiny. Servant Nanak proclaims the third round of the marriage ceremony; the mind is filled with divine love. ||3|| In the fourth round of the marriage ceremony, my mind became peaceful; I found my Lord O God; I found the guru-willed intuitively. He feels sweet to my mind and body O God; God`s sweetness pleases God. I am attuned to God's love forever. I obtained fruit of my choice O Lord; I received the blessing of God`s name. God completed the marriage ceremony; the soul-bride enjoys God's name in the mind. Servant Nanak proclaims the fourth round of marriage ceremony, I found the immortal God. ||4||2|| God is one. He is realized by guru's grace. Tune Soohee, Chhant, Fourth Master, Second House: The guru-willed sings God's praises. Sings from His mind and tongue; Singing God's praises; pleases God. I realized Him with ease. I recite God through guru's teachings forever. I enjoy and sleep peacefully. By good fortune, I found the perfect guru and recite God's name forever. In peace and poise, one meets God the life of the World O Nanak, and enters the absolute state. ||1|| Joining the society of the saints, I bathe in God's sacred pool. Bathing in sacred waters, my filth is removed, my body became sacred. The filth of ill will is removed, doubt is gone, and the pain of ego is dispelled. By God's grace, I found devotees company and I attained my destiny. Page 775 My tongue recites God's name and sings songs of joy O Nanak. ||2|| The guru-willed searches in his mind the jewel of God's name with love. Reciting God's name with love through guru's teachings eliminates ignorance. Bright divine wisdom burns inside. It illuminates the heart, and the body looks adorable. I humbly surrendered my mind and body to Him. It pleases my God. Whatever God says, I gladly do and Nanak merged with God. ||3|| The Lord arranged the marriage ceremony; The guru-willed came to marry me. He came to marry me; I the guru-willed realized God; now my Lord loves me. I sing songs of joy in the company of saints. God guided me. The gods, mortal beings, the heavenly singers came in the pre-ordained marriage party. O Nanak, I found my true Lord, who never dies or leaves. ||4||1||3|| Tune Soohee, Chhant, Fourth Master, Third House: God is one. He is realized by guru's grace. Come, humble saints and sing praises of the Lord of the universe. Let us get together o guru-willed and play the divine music O God. O God, the divine music is yours. You are omnipresent O Creator. I recite Your name all the time through guru's teachings with love. I remain intuitively attuned to Lord's love; Reciting God's name in the mind is your worship. O Nanak, the guru-willed thinks of one God not anyone else. ||1|| God the inner knower abides in everyone O God. One who recites guru's teachings; that is reciting God as well O God. My Lord the inner knower abides in all. Guru's teachings realize the truth and attain peace. God lives in everyone. I sing God's praises if it pleases Him. He unites us with Him by His grace. O Nanak, God is realized through guru's teachings by reciting His name forever. ||2|| This world is impassable; the self-willed cannot cross over. He is filled with ego, lust, anger and cleverness. Filled with cleverness does not attain destiny; the life goes waste. He suffers pain and disgrace on the path of death. He regrets in the end. There is no friend other than God's name; including children, family or relatives. O Nanak, worldly wealth and emotional attachments are entanglements. Nothing goes with you. ||3|| I ask my guru, the bestowal; how to cross the terrible world-ocean. Follow guru's will; this is called dead while living. Be humble and cross the terrible world ocean. The guru-willed enshrines God's name in the mind. Page 776 The fortunate realizes the perfect primal Lord reciting God's name with love. The intellect is enlightened and the mind is satisfied praising God's name. O Nanak, God is found through guru's teachings and the souls merged. ||4||1||4|| Soohee, Fourth Master, Fifth House: God is one. He is realized by guru's grace. O humble saints, I met my beloved guru; my desire is eradicated. I offer my mind and body to the guru that he may unite me with virtuous God. Blessed is the guru, the supreme being, who guides me to realize God. Fortunate servant realized God through reciting God with love O Nanak. ||1|| I met my beloved guru, who showed me the path to the Lord. I met my Husband Lord after a long separation through guru's teachings. Without You, I am sad like a fish out of water, I shall die. The fortunate recites God's name and merges with Him O Nanak. ||2|| Lost in doubt; the self-willed wanders around in ten directions. I think of different things in my mind every day. My mind is greedy. He buried unlimited amount of wealth in the ground; still searches for more. O servant Nanak, recite God's name; without God's name, you will rot in filth and die. ||3|| Meeting the beautiful and fascinating guru, I conquered my mind, loving God through his sermon. I gave up thinking of other things. My desire and worries are forgotten. I have pain of love in my heart; seeing the guru my mind consoled. O God; may the fortunate realize you; servant Nanak praises You forever. ||4||1||5|| Soohee, Chhant, Fourth Master: O mortal; eradicate the ego which does not let you realize God. This priceless body has been ruined by ego. Attachment to worldly wealth is total darkness; the ignorant self-willed is attached to it. O servant Nanak, the guru-willed is saved. Ego is eliminated through guru's teachings. ||1|| O mortal, control your mind. The mind wanders like the day. Mortal's life-night passes painfully in constant hope and desire. I found the guru, O humble saints; reciting God, my desires are fulfilled. O God; teach servant Nanak that he forgets desires and sleeps in peace. ||2|| The bride hopes in her mind, that her sovereign Lord will come to her bed. My Lord is very kind; O sovereign Lord. May He unite me with Him by His grace; Page 777 O Lord; my mind and body long to see the guru. I spread my bed of loving faith. O Lord; servant Nanak realized God with ease by His grace. ||3|| O Lord I am in bed with God; I realized God through guru's teachings. O Lord; my mind and body are filled with love and affection. Be kind and unite me with the guru. I praise my guru, O Lord; I surrender my soul to the guru. By guru's grace O Lord; servant Nanak realized God. ||4||2||6||5||7||6||18|| Tune Soohee, Chhant, Fifth Master, First House: God is one. He is realized by guru's grace. Listen o innocent: why do you forget after seeing! Listen, o innocent: you are in false love with safflower colour that will fade. He is lost seeing the false, which is not worth anything. God's name is permanent. You will become deep red contemplating guru's sweet teachings. You are attached to temporary false emotional attachment and falsehood. Poor Nanak seeks Your refuge O Lord the treasure of mercy. Please preserve the honour of Your devotee. ||1|| Listen o innocent: serve your Lord the master of your life. Listen o innocent: whoever comes, shall go. Listen, O stranger: everyone shall go; join the company of saints; Listen o renunciate: by good fortune one realizes God and remains attached to God's feet. Surrender your mind openly O guru-willed and give up your pride. O Lord the bestowal of salvation; what virtues of Yours, poor Nanak can say? ||2|| Listen o innocent; what good is false pride? Listen o innocent: all ego and pride shall disappear. Definitely all will go, the pride is temporary. Be the servant of Gods saints. Remain dead while still alive, you shall cross over the terrifying world-ocean, if it is your pre-ordained destiny. One who intuitively attunes to God; serves the guru and drinks nectar. Nanak seeks God's refuge at His door; I praise Him forever. ||3|| Listen o innocent: do not think that you have found God. Listen o innocent: those who worship God are humble. Those who recite God attain peace and the fortunate visualize God. I admire the humble servants who eliminated their ego. Those who realize God are really lucky. I will sell me to them. Humble Nanak, seeks your refuge O ocean of peace; preserve honour of Your own. ||4||1|| Soohee, Fifth Master: The guru gave me support of your lotus feet O my Lord. Page 778 God's treasures are full of nectar. He has everything O Lord. My father is all-powerful. God is the doer, the cause of causes. Reciting Him the pains do not bother. He takes us across the world ocean. He protects His devotees forever. I live by praising Him O Nanak, God's name is very sweet. I drink it wholeheartedly forever. ||1|| God unites us with Him by His grace; we shall never separate again O Lord. One who has Your support becomes immortal and lives forever O Lord. I take my support from You O true Creator. No one is without Him; such is my God. I sing songs of joy in the company of saints hoping to visualize God. Meeting the guru I realized my dream. Nanak praises him forever. ||2|| I realized the true place, received honour, greatness and truth O Lord. Meeting the kind guru, I sing the praises of immortal O Lord. Sing the praises of the Lord of the universe the master of life continuously. Good time has come; the inner-knower has embraced me. The divine music of truth and contentment plays with melody. Hearing the music of God the Creator, all my fears eradicated O Nanak. ||3|| The essence of God's divine wisdom has welled up in this world and the next O Lord. When one merges with God with devotion, no one can separate them O Lord. I am amazed by seeing and listening that I have realized the amazing Lord. The perfect Lord pervades in water land and the sky, in every heart. I have merged again in the one from whom I originated. The value of this cannot be described. O Nanak, miss Him whose ways cannot be explained? ||4||2|| Tune Soohee, Chhant, Fifth Master, Second House: God is one. He is realized by guru's grace. I sing praises of the Lord of the universe. I am awake, night and day, in God's love. Awake with Lord's love, my sins have left. I realized the beloved saint. Touching guru's feet the doubt disappeared. All my affairs are settled. Listening to guru's sermon attains peace by reciting God's name o fortunate. Prays

Nanak; I have entered my Lord's sanctuary. I offer my body and soul to God. ||1|| The infinite divine music pleases me. True joy comes singing God`s praises. Singing God's praises the sufferings go away and the mind becomes happy. Seeing him my mind and body became pure and I recite God's name. Page 779 When I recite God becoming the dust of devotee's feet; I please God. Prays Nanak, please be kind that I sing God's praises forever. Meeting the guru, I cross over the world-ocean. Worshipping Lord's feet, I am emancipated. Worshipping God's feet I obtained all rewards; coming and going ended. Reciting God, worshipping Him with love; is pleasing to God. Recite the unseen and infinite perfect Lord; No one is without him. Prays Nanak, the guru has eliminated my doubts; wherever I look, I see Him. ||3|| Lord's name is the purifier of sinners. It resolves the affairs of the humble saints. Meeting the saint the guru I recite God. My all desires are fulfilled. The fever of ego eliminated reciting God. I realized God after a long separation. My mind found peace and I am happy; may I never forget God from my mind. Prays Nanak, the true guru taught me to recite God all the time. ||4||1||3|| Tune Soohee, Chhant, Fifth Master, Third House: God is one. He is realized by guru's grace. You are unattached O Lord; the ignorant like me is Your maidservant O Lord. You are the ocean, full of jewels; I do not know Your reality O Lord. I do not know Your reality; You are the wisest; be kind to me O Lord. Be kind and bless me with such wisdom that I recite Your name twenty-four hours a day. O soul, don't be proud? Become the dust of all, and then you shall be saved. Nanak's Lord is the master of all; the ignorant like me is Your maidservant O Lord. ||1|| You are handsome, unfathomable, pearl; You are my Husband Lord and I am Your bride. You are the greatest of the great and highest of all; I am very small. I am nothing; You are everything. You are all knowing. I live by enjoying Your nectar O Lord and enjoy all Your pleasures. I the servant of servants, seek Your refuge that my mind and body rejuvenate. O Nanak, God is omnipresent. He does what He pleases. ||2|| You are my pride; You are my strength O Lord. You give me realization, intellect and cleverness by Your grace O Lord. Whom God blesses, knows and recognizes it. The self-willed trapped in worldly wealth wanders all over. One who pleases God is virtuous. She enjoys all pleasures. You are Nanak's support. You are Nanak's pride O Lord. ||3|| I praise You; You are the mountain my shelter O Lord. I admire Him forever, who lifted my veil of doubt O Lord. Page 780 The darkness eliminated, I gave up useless deeds and my mind reconciled with God. By God's grace I became humble and my life became fruitful and accepted. I became invaluable, very heavy to weigh. The door and the path of liberation opened. Says Nanak, I became carefree; God is my shelter. ||4||1||4|| Soohee, Fifth Master: Other than my beloved primal being perfect guru; I do not know anyone else. He is my mother, father, sibling, child, relative, soul and life. He is pleasing to my mind, O Lord. My body and soul are all His blessings. He is full of every virtue. My God the inner-knower is omnipresent. In His sanctuary, I obtain every pleasure. I am totally free. Nanak praises God with devotion forever. ||1|| The fortunate find such a guru; meeting Him it appears as if He is God. Bathing in the dust of the saints; sins of many lifes vanish O Lord. Bathe in God`s dust and recite God, you shall not be born again. Touching guru's feet the fear of doubt goes away and receive the reward of your choice. Sing God's praises. Reciting His name all the time the sorrow and worry do not bother again. O Nanak, God is the giver of all souls; His power is absolute. ||2|| Reciting and praising God with love; God comes under saint's control. Those who humbly touch saint's feet and serve the guru attain salvation O Lord. Eliminating ego attains salvation by God's grace. Their lives are fruitful, desires are dispelled and they surrender to God. He united with whom he belonged and the soul merged with supreme soul. O Nanak, recite the name of formless God and obtain peace meeting the guru. ||3|| Sing songs of joy o Godly beings. Your desires will be fulfilled O Lord. Attuned to God lovingly; one does not die or takes birth again. Reciting His name I realized the immortal God. All my deeds are fulfilled. My mind is attuned to guru's feet with peace and contentment. The immortal Lord abides everywhere including all high low places of importance. Says Nanak, my affairs are resolved focusing my mind to guru's feet. ||4||2||5|| Soohee, Fifth Master: Be kind O my beloved Lord; may I visualize you O Lord. O My beloved; bless me with millions tongues and I say your name with each tongue O Lord. Reciting God; the path of death is conquered and no pain shall bother. God pervades completely in water and land. Wherever I look I see God. Doubt, attachment and corruption are gone. God is the nearest of all. O God; be kind and bless Nanak that he visualizes You. ||1|| O beloved God; give me million ears that I listen to immortal's praises O Lord. Listening to it, this mind becomes pure and the noose of death is cut. The noose of death is cut reciting the immortal God and obtained happiness and wisdom. Recite God day and night with devotion. Reciting God eliminates sins and the ill will departs from mind. Says Nanak, O God; be kind that I listen to immortal God's praises. ||2|| Please give me million hands to serve You and walk on Godly path O Lord. Service to the Lord is the boat to carry us across the terrifying world-ocean. Reciting God takes one across the terrifying world ocean. All his deeds are fulfilled. All useless thoughts disappeared and the infinite divine music plays. All fruits of mind's desires are obtained; we are ignorant of Your virtues. Says Nanak, O God; be kind that my mind follows Your path. ||3|| This is the blessing and honour that makes this mortal fortunate. Attaching my mind to God's feet attains this joy and happiness. My mind is attached to God's feet in His refuge. He is the Creator, the cause of causes the cherisher of the world. Everything is Yours; You are my God; O my Lord merciful to the meek. I am worthless, O my beloved, ocean of peace. My mind woke up in saint's company. Says Nanak, by God's grace my mind is attached to His lotus feet. ||4||3||6|| Soohee, Fifth Master: Reciting God; the devotee saints created the temple to sing His praises O Lord. Reciting God's name all sins are eliminated. Singing God's praises attains high status listening to God's sacred sermon. God's sermon is very sweet and peaceful. It speaks the unspoken words. The time and the moment were auspicious and true, when the eternal foundation of this temple was placed. O servant Nanak, God became kind and He blessed me fully. ||1|| The joyful divine music plays continuously. God is enshrined in my mind. Doing so, the deeds of the guru-willed got fulfilled! The fear of falsehood and doubt eliminated O Lord. The guru-willed speaks the divine words. Listening to God's praises my mind and body rejuvenated. All pleasures are obtained by him, whom God makes His Own. Being dyed by God's name realizes the priceless treasure in the body. O Nanak, the fortunate never forget God. ||2|| God gave me shade under His canopy; all my burning desire is eliminated. The home of sorrow and sin is demolished and my affairs are resolved. When God commands, the misfortune is averted; the true faith flourishes. Page 782 Recite God when you sleep, sit or stand. The Lord the treasure of virtue, the ocean of peace pervades water land and sky. Servant Nanak has entered God's sanctuary; there is no other than Him. ||3|| My home, garden and pool are built; my sovereign Lord met me. My mind is adorned and my friends rejoice; I sing the songs of joy and praise the Lord. Singing the praises of the true Lord, all desires are fulfilled. Attached to guru's feet one remains awake forever and celebrates. My Lord the bestowal of happiness became kind and saved me here and hereafter. Prays Nanak, recite God's name who gave you life and soul; ||4||4||7|| Soohee, Fifth Master: Reciting God's name one will swim across the terrifying world ocean. I worship God's feet the boat that takes across the ocean meeting the guru. Attain salvation through guru's teachings and never die again. Coming and going ends. Whatever He does, I accept as good and my mind attains peace. Pain, hunger or disease, do not afflict me. I found peace in God's refuge. Reciting God; Nanak is dyed by God's love. His worries are eliminated. ||1|| The humble saints taught me God's sermon. God is under His beloved devotee's control O God. I offered my mind to Him and God blessed me with everything. He made me His maidservant; reaching God's abode I found peace and my sadness is dispelled. I recite true God with joy and happiness and I shall never separate from Him. She is fortunate and a true soul-bride, who finds the way to recite God's name. Says Nanak, I am imbued with His love, drenched in the supreme essence of His love. ||2|| I am in continuous happiness O my friend; I sing the songs of joy forever O Lord. God embellished her and she is the virtuous soul-bride O Lord. With natural ease, He became gracious. He did not consider merits or demerits. Enshrining God's name in the mind; God embraces His servant. Pride, emotional attachment and intoxication are eliminated. God freed me by His grace. Says Nanak, I crossed over the terrifying world-ocean and all my affairs are resolved. ||3|| Sing praises of the Lord of the world forever O my companions; all your wishes shall be granted O Lord. Meeting God's devotees, the life becomes fruitful by reciting one God O Lord. Recite God, who pervades the universe in many forms. God created the creation and he is visible everywhere. God fully abides in water land and sky. There is no place without Him. Page 783 Visualizing God, Nanak rejoices. God united Nanak with Him. ||4||5||8|| Soohee, Fifth Master: Permanent is the city of God the guru; I find peace reciting His name. God established the city, rewards of choice are received there O Lord. The Creator established it. I found total peace; my children, siblings and followers all rejoice there. Singing the praises of the perfect transcendent Lord, all affairs are resolved. God is my master, my protector, my father and mother. Says Nanak, I praise my guru, who fashioned this beautiful place. ||1|| Homes, mansions, stores and markets are beautiful where God's name abides. The saints and devotees worship God. Their noose of death is cut. The noose of death is cut reciting the immortal God's name. Everything is perfect for them and they obtain the fruit of their desire. The beloved saints enjoy peace and pleasure; their pain, suffering and doubts are dispelled. Perfect guru's teachings saved them. Nanak praises him forever. ||2|| Blessing of the Lord came true; it increases day by day. The supreme Lord made me His own. His greatness is great! God the protector of His worshippers became kind. All beings live in peace by God's doing by His grace. God's praises are sung in ten directions that are beyond imagination. Says Nanak; I praise my guru who poured the permanent foundation. ||3|| The spiritual wisdom and meditation of the perfect transcendent Lord and the sermon of the Lord is continuously heard there. Unlimited fascinations of the destroyer of fear of His devotees are heard in melody of divine music played there O Lord. Contemplation of the essence of the melody of divine music is discussed in the congregation of saints every day. Reciting God's name cuts all filth and eradicates all sins. There is no birth or death, no coming or going, and no entering into the womb for taking birth again. Nanak found the guru the transcendent Lord; by his grace his desires are fulfilled. ||4||6||9|| Soohee, Fifth Master: God has come to resolve His saint's affairs; He came to complete their tasks. The land is beautiful, the pool is beautiful and nectar is poured in it. Pouring nectar instead of water is a perfect deed and all desires are fulfilled. Admirations are pouring in from all over the world; all sins are eliminated. The Vedas and Puraanas sing praises of the perfect, unchanging, immortal primal Lord. The transcendent Lord kept His promise, Nanak recites God's name. ||1|| The Creator bestowed the nine treasures, wealth and mystic powers. There is no shortage of anything. Page 784 I attained peace by eating, spending and enjoying; God's gifts keep increasing. His gifts increase and shall never be exhausted and I found the inner-knower. Millions of obstacles are removed and pain does not approach me. I attained peace and contentment and my greed has vanished. Nanak sings praises of the master, whose greatness is amazing. ||2|| It was His job, and He did it; what can the mortal being do? The devotees are adorned, singing God's praises. They are honoured forever. Singing praises of the Lord of the universe, harmony wells up and we become friends with the company of devotees. He who worked to construct this sacred pool, how can I say His praises? The merits of the sixty-eight shrines of pilgrimage, charity and good deeds are realized in this sacred pool. It is God's way to purify the sinners through guru's teachings. ||3|| My Lord is the treasure of virtues. How can we praise Him? The saints pray to Lord; please bless them with sublime essence Your name O Lord. Bless us with the gift of Your name; may I never forget You even for a moment. Sing the praises of the Lord of the world with your tongue all the time. Those who love to recite God's name; their mind and bodies are drenched with nectar. Prays Nanak, my desires have been fulfilled visualizing my beloved. ||4||7||10|| Tune Soohee, Fifth Master, Chhant: God is one. He is realized by guru's grace. My dear Lord my beloved speaks very sweet. I have grown weary of testing Him, but he never speaks harsh to me. He does not know any bitter words; the perfect God does not consider my faults. God the purifier of sinners does His job. He does not delay His work. He dwells in every heart, pervading everywhere; He is the nearest of all. Slave Nanak seeks His sanctuary forever; the Lord is my sacred friend. ||1|| I am wonder-struck visualizing the infinite Lord. My beloved Lord is beautiful; I am the dust of Your lotus feet. Realizing God my mind is soothed. No one is as great as He. God is from the beginning, in the middle, water and land and sky, He pervades all. He will always be there. Worshipping His lotus feet, I have crossed over the terrifying world-ocean. Nanak seeks refuge of the perfect transcendent Lord; You have no end or limits O Lord. ||2|| I never forget Him. God my beloved is support of my life. The guru speaks of the true infinite Lord. I recite God in devotee's company and my pain of birth and death eliminated. I obtained peace contentment and joy and the knot of ego untied. Page 785 He is inside and out of all; He is untouched by love or hate. Slave Nanak seeks refuge of the Lord of the universe; the beloved God is the support of the mind. ||3|| I searched and found the immovable home of the Lord. I saw all transitory and perishable, and then I attached my mind to God's feet. God is immortal; I am His maidservant. He does not die or comes or goes. All good deeds are completed and I received the reward of my choice. The Vedas the Simritees the mystics and seekers sing God's praises. Nanak has entered Lord's refuge, the fortunate sings God's praises. ||4||1||11|| God is one. He is realized by guru's grace. Vaar Of Soohee, With Hymns Of The Third Master: Hymn, Third Master: Wearing enticing makeup the divorcee goes to enjoy other's spouses. She leaves her husband at home enticed by the love of duality. She eats it as sweet; the excessive taste only makes her sick. She divorced her sublime Husband Lord. Then she feels the pain of separation. She will revert back if she is a guru-willed. She will be imbued with God's love. She truly and peacefully recites God's name enshrining in the mind. She the obedient is a soul bride forever; God united her with Him. O Nanak, she who realized her beloved Lord is a happy soul-bride forever. ||1|| Third Master: O beautiful the humble; always recite your husband Lord. O Nanak, you along with your dynasty will be saved. ||2|| Ladder: He established His throne, in the sky and the underworld. By His command, He created the earth, the true place of faith. He creates and destroys; He is the true Lord of the poor. You give sustenance to all; Your command is unique. You are all pervading; You look after everyone. ||1|| Hymn, Third Master: The beautiful is a happy soul-bride, only when she believes in true name. She consoles with her guru and becomes more beautiful. There is no place like this.

Wear such a makeup that never gets dirty; and love the Lord forever. O Nanak, what is the sign of a happy soul-bride? Truthful, happy and merged in her Husband Lord; ||1|| Third Master: O people: I look beautiful dressed in a red robe. Husband Lord is not obtained by makeup; I am tired of wearing makeup. O Nanak, those who listen to guru's lesson realize the Husband Lord. Obey whatever pleases Him. The Husband Lord is realized this way. ||2|| Page 786 Ladder: By His command, He created the creation in many ways in the universe. I do not know how great Your command is, O unseen infinite true Lord. You unite some with you through guru's teachings. Those imbued with truth become pure eliminating the ego and corruption. Whoever You unite, unites with You and becomes truthful. ||2|| Hymn, Third Master: O beautiful, the whole world entices them who dwell in duality and do evil deeds. In an instant, the falsehood vanishes like the shade of a tree. The guru-willed who is dyed by the true permanent Love is the most beautiful. Enshrining God's sacred name in the mind the worldly power comes under control. O Nanak, praise your guru; meeting him, I sing God's praises. ||1|| Third Master: The deep red makeup is useless if she cannot realize the Husband Lord. This colour does not take long to fade; she, who loves duality, ends up a widow. She who loves to wear her red dress is ignorant and double-minded. Guru's teachings dye her red if she adores him with love. O Nanak, she is a happy soul-bride forever, who follows, gurus will. ||2|| Ladder: He created Him and He knows His value. His limits cannot be known; He is realized through guru's teachings. Worldly attachment is like a whirlwind. It deludes with duality. The self-willed find no place to rest; they continue coming and going. Whatever pleases Him happens. Everything happens by His will. ||3|| Hymn, Third Master: The red-robed bride is vicious; she forsakes God and falls in love with someone else. She is not humble or self-disciplined; the self-willed constantly tells lies, she is ruined by bad deeds. One with pre-ordained destiny meets the guru as her husband Lord. She discards all her red dresses and wears the ornaments of forgiveness. In this world and the next, she is honoured and the whole world worships her. She who enjoys with the Creator Lord does not mix with the crowd. O Nanak, the guru-willed is the happy soul-bride forever; she has the imperishable Lord as her husband. ||1|| First Master: The red colour is like a dream at night; it is like a necklace without a string. The guru-willed takes on the permanent colour contemplating the Lord. O Nanak, God's love is the essence, all sins are like ashes. ||2|| Ladder: He created this world by playing the amazing play. In the body of five elements, He infused attachment, falsehood and pride. The ignorant self-willed keep on coming and going in life; He teaches some guru-willed the divine knowledge. He blesses them with the treasure of worship of God's sacred name. ||4|| Hymn, Third Master: O red-robed woman, discard your deep red makeup, then you can love your Husband Lord. Page 787 No one attains divinity through red shining makeup. The ignorant self-willed burns to death; Meeting the guru eliminates the red shining makeup by eliminating ego. Her mind and body are imbued with the deep red colour of love, and her tongue is imbued with singing the essence the divine virtues. She who wears the makeup of guru's teachings in her mind becomes a happy soul-bride forever. O Nanak, she attains destiny by God's grace enshrining God in the mind. ||1|| Third Master: O innocent bride, forsake your red dress and wear the makeup of the beloved Lord. Your coming and going shall be forgotten contemplating guru's teachings. The soul-bride looks beautiful that is content with her Husband Lord at home. O Nanak, both the bride and her husband Lord enjoy each other. ||2|| Ladder: The ignorant, self-willed is engrossed in false attachment of the family. They die engrossed in ego and possessiveness, yet they take nothing with them. They do not realize that death hovers over them. They dwell in duality. The opportunity does not come again; devil of death will catch him. He acts according to his pre-ordained destiny. ||5|| Hymn Third Master Do not call them 'satee', (immolate) who burn themselves on their husband's pyre. O Nanak, those who die of pain of separation are the real immolate. ||1|| Third Master: They are also known as 'satee', those who live in peace and contentment. They serve their Lord; get up in the morning and recite His name. ||2|| Third Master: They burn in the fire of love of their husband Lord. If they truly love their husbands; then they will bear the pain. O Nanak, if they do not love their husbands; why should they burn themselves? Whether they live or die or go away seeing from far. ||3|| Ladder: You take pain and pleasure with you; the Creator in your fate writes it. There is no other gift as great as God's name; it has no form or sign. God's name is inexhaustible treasure enshrined in guru-willed's mind. When God bestows His name by his grace then they are not written in your fate. Through service they meet those devotees who recite God's name. ||6|| Hymn, Second Master: Those who know the process; why should they tell others. Those who do not know the process; how can they solve the problem; ||1|| Second Master: He accumulates wealth for the night, in the morning he has to leave; O Nanak, it does not go with you; then you repent. ||2|| Second Master: Paying a fine under pressure, does not bring merit or goodness. That what is done in happiness O Nanak fulfills the deeds. ||3|| Second Master: You cannot find the destiny by force; you may try your best. Those with true intentions find the destiny O Nanak, contemplating guru's teachings; ||4|| Ladder: The Creator, who created the world, knows it. He created the universe and He shall destroy it. Page 788 People got tired of wandering throughout the four ages, but no one knows God. The guru visualized me the one Lord, my mind and body are at peace. The guru-willed praises God forever; whatever he does happens. ||7|| Hymn, Second Master: Those who love God have no concern of falling out. Nothing scares them. O Nanak, this document is revealed at the court of the Lord. ||1|| Second Master: Walking meets the walking, the flying meets the flying. The living meets the living, and the dead meets the dead. O Nanak, praise the one who created all this. ||2|| Ladder: Those who recite the true Lord become true contemplating guru's teachings. They purify their minds subduing their ego and enshrine God's name in the mind. The ignorant are attached to their homes, mansions and shrines. The self-willed do not realize the Creator. They are in the dark. Whom He makes to realize, understands! What can mortals do? ||8|| Hymn, Third Master: O bride, decorate yourself, after consoling with your Husband Lord. May be that the Husband Lord does not come to your bed? When bride and Husband console with each other that is the real makeup. When your Husband Lord loves you then your makeup is accepted. Make your Husband's love the makeup, the joy of betel nuts chewing and love of your food. Surrender your body and mind to your Husband Lord, O Nanak, then He will enjoy you. ||1|| Third Master: The bride uses black eyelashes, flowers and fragrance of betel as makeup. Her Husband Lord does not come to her bed, all her efforts go waste. ||2|| Third Master: They are not said to be husband and wife, who merely sit together. Two souls merged into one soul though have two bodies, are real husband and wife. ||3|| Ladder: Without devotion there is no worship, love does not well up for God's name. Love wells up meeting with the guru. Love imbues one with God's love. Mind and body imbued with God's love eliminates ego and greed. The mind and body become pure and adorable surrendering to the Lord. Intuitive love belongs to God; He abides in the world. ||9|| Hymn, First Master: O Lord, You are great who created all of us. You created oceans, waves, seas, pools, plants, calendars and prophets. You look after everything what you create. The guru-willed's service is approved and attains salvation by doing so intently. Earn by begging at God's door that is entered in your fate. O Nanak, Going to carefree God's door; the true carefree does not come empty ||1|| First Master: The beautiful teeth shine like diamonds lay with jewels. O Nanak, the age is the enemy of those who die of old age. ||2|| Page 789 Ladder: I praise the Lord forever; I offer my body and mind to Him. Through guru's teachings I realized the unfathomable true Lord. The Lord, the jewel of jewels abides in my mind, body and heart. The pains of birth and death are gone; I shall never be born again. O Nanak, praise God's name the ocean of excellence. ||10|| Hymn, First Master: O Nanak, burn this body; this burnt body forgot God's name. The dirt is piling up behind; hand does not reach there in the deep pool. ||1|| First Master: O Nanak, you do so many bad deeds that cannot be counted. How to get rid of fear? When God blesses then there is no fear. ||2|| Ladder: God started the true faith through true command. The all-knowing God pervades everywhere forever. He is realized by guru's grace by serving him through guru's teachings. Guru made the perfect place to worship; enjoy it through guru's teachings. He is immortal, inaccessible and unexplainable; know that o guru-willed; ||11|| Hymn, First Master: O Nanak, the bags of wealth are brought in. The counterfeit and genuine are identified in God's court. ||1|| First

Master: They go to bathe at sacred shrines, but their minds are evil, bodies are thieves. Bathing washes some filth away, but they accumulate twice as much. They wash the body outside but inside is full of pure poison. The devotees are better without bathing, the thieves are still thieves. ||2|| Ladder: He issues His orders and puts the world to work. He puts some to worship him. They obtain peace through the guru. The mind runs around in ten directions; the guru stabilizes it. Everyone longs for God's name; it is realized through guru's teachings. Your pre-ordained destiny, written by God cannot be erased. ||12|| Hymn, First Master: There are two lamps to light the fourteen shops. All beings trade there. The shops open and trading are done. Whoever comes there is bound to depart. The Righteous brokers make the deals. O Nanak, those who earn the profit of God's name; are accepted there. When they return home, they are greeted with cheers; They obtain the greatness of the true name. ||1|| First Master: Even when the night is dark, the white paint still looks white. Even when the day is bright and hot, still the black deeds look black. The blind ignorant without intellect; are still blind of divine wisdom. O Nanak, without Lord's grace, they will never receive honour. ||2|| Ladder: The true Lord created the body-fortress. Some are ruined through the love of duality engrossed in ego. This human life is difficult to obtain; it troubles the self-willed. Whom He teaches, realizes blessed by the guru. He created the entire world. He is pervading all. ||13|| Page 790 Thieves, adulterers, prostitutes and pimps, make friendships with the faithless, and eat faithlessly. They do not know the value of God's praises, and live with the devil. If you put sandalwood on the forehead of a donkey, he still loves to roll in the dirt. O Nanak, if you spin false then you weave false. If you think false. Then your clothes and honour is also false. ||1|| First Master: The prayer callers, the flute-players, the horn-blowers, enjoy themselves Some give, some beg, but they are acceptable only through Your name. O Nanak, I admire those, who believe by listening to your name. ||2|| Ladder: Attachment to worldly wealth is totally false, false makes false. Ego creates fight and fight kills the world. The guru-willed do not fight and see God in all. Those who realize God, their souls cross over the terrible world ocean. Enshrining God's name in the mind the soul merges with supreme soul. ||14|| Hymn: First Master: O true guru, bless me with the awns O all-powerful bestowal. May I eliminate ego arrogance lust, anger and pride? May I burn greed, and get the support of God's name. God's name is ever new and pure. It never gets dirty. O Nanak, liberation obtains this way and obtains peace by Your grace. ||1|| First Master: There is only one Husband Lord of all, whoever stands at His door. O Nanak, they ask for news of their Husband Lord, from those who are imbued with His love. ||2|| First Master: All are imbued with love for their Husband Lord; I am a discarded bride. What good am I? My body is filled with many faults; my Lord and master does not even turn His thoughts to me. ||3|| First Master: I admire those who praise God from their mouth. All are happy soul-brides at night; I am a discarded bride at night; ||4|| Ladder: I beg at Your door for awns. O God, be kind and give me awns. Please unite the guru-willed with You, so that the humble can obtain Your name. The infinite divine music plays when the soul merges with soul. I sing God's praises in my mind and enjoy God through guru's teachings. God pervades the world; fall in love with God; ||15|| Hymn, First Master: Those who do not enjoy the taste of love cannot enjoy God. They are like guests in an empty house; they leave as they came. ||1|| First Master: He receives hundreds and thousands of reprimands, day and night; The swan is eating the corpse leaving the lobster. Cursed is that life, in which one eats only to fatten his belly. O Nanak, without the true name, all friends become enemies. ||2|| Ladder: The minstrel sings God's praises all the time and obtains salvation. The guru-willed serves and praises God enshrining in the mind. Page 791 He obtains his destiny reciting God's name O beloved. The guru-willed obtaine||16|| Hymn, First Master: When the lamp is lit, the darkness disappears. Reading the scriptures, sinful thinking is destroyed. When the sun rises, the moon is not visible. Wherever spiritual wisdom appears, ignorance disappears. Reading the scriptures is the ritual of the world. The scholars read and contemplate them. Without understanding, all are ruined. O Nanak, the guru-willed attains salvation. ||1|| First Master: Those who do not enjoy guru's teachings; cannot love God's name; They speak bland words and are continuously disgraced. O Nanak, they act according to the pre-ordained destiny. No one can erase it. ||2|| Ladder: One, who praises God, receives honour. He eliminates ego and enshrines truth in the mind. He speaks the true sermon and attains eternal peace. He is united with God after a long separation by guru's grace. In this way, his filthy mind is purified, reciting God's name. ||17|| Hymn, First Master: The body is a fresh branch and virtue is a bunch of flowers. Worship God with these flowers. Why search for another branch. ||1|| Second Master O Nanak, it is springtime for those, whose husband Lord lives at home. Whose Husband Lord is far away, she burns in pain forever. ||2|| Ladder: God bestows His kindness through guru's teachings. Night and day, I serve the true Lord truthfully. My God is infinite; no one knows His limits. Falling at guru's feet I recite God's name all the time. You shall obtain the fruit of your desires in your home. ||18|| Hymn, First Master: Spring brings the first blossom, but the Lord is already blossomed. By His blossoming, everything blossoms; no one causes Him to blossom. ||1|| Second Master: Contemplate the one who is already blossomed. O Nanak, praise the one who gives to all. ||2|| Second Master: You cannot unite with God on your own. You unite with Him by pre-ordained destiny. One whose soul merges with supreme soul is really united. ||3|| Ladder: Praise the name of God, this is the true service. Attached to other deeds, one takes birth again and again; Attuned to God's name, one realizes the name, and praises God through God's name. Praise God through guru's teachings and enshrine God's name in the mind. Service to the guru is fruitful; serving Him realizes the fruit. ||19|| Hymn, Second Master: Some people have others, but I the humble have you O Lord. Page 792 If I forget You O God; why shall I not die crying? ||1|| Second Master: I recite God in pleasure and pain. Says Nanak, O wise bride, this is how you unite with your Husband Lord. ||2|| Ladder: I am a worm, how can I praise You, O Lord; Your greatness is great! You are immovable, kind and beyond comprehension. You unite us with you by Your grace. I have no other friend but You; you are my support in the end. You save those who enter Your sanctuary. O Nanak, He is carefree; He has no greed at all. ||20||1|| Tune Soohee, the word of Kabeer Jee, and other devotees. Of Kabeer God is one. He is realized by guru's grace. Since your birth, what have you done? You have never recited God's name. ||1|| You do not recite God; what do you do otherwise? O son of an ignorant mother; what are you doing o unfortunate? ||1||Pause|| Through pain and pleasure, you have taken care of your family. But at the time of death, you shall have to suffer alone. ||2|| When you are caught by the neck, then you cry; Says Kabeer, why didn't you think of it before? ||3||1|| Soohee, Kabeer Jee: The innocent young bride trembles and shakes. I do not know how my Husband Lord will deal with me. ||1|| The night is gone; may the day not pass away? My black hair turned grey. ||1||Pause|| Water does not remain in the unbaked clay pot; When the soul-swan departs, the body withers away. ||2|| It is like a young girl wearing makeup; How can she enjoy without her Husband Lord? ||3|| My arm is tired of driving away the crows. Says Kabeer, this is the way the story of life ends. ||4||2|| Soohee, Kabeer Jee: You have to pay for what you did. The tough devil of death has come to take you away. What did you earn, and what did you lose? Come immediately! You are summoned to His court! ||1|| Let us go; you have been summoned to God's court. The order has come from the court of the Lord. ||1||Pause|| I pray to him that I still have some business to take care. I will do it tonight; I will pay your expenses. Let me say my morning prayer at home? ||2|| Those who are attuned to God's love in devotee's company are admirable and fortunate. They are content here and hereafter. They win the priceless treasure of this human life. ||3|| He is asleep while awake; he wastes his life away. The property and wealth he accumulated no longer belongs to him. Says Kabeer, those people are lost. Who forget their Husband Lord and rot in the dust. ||4||3|| Page 793 Soohee, Kabeer Jee, Lallit: My eyes are tired, my ears are tired of hearing; my beautiful body is tired. Due to old age, all my senses are tired; but my attachment to worldly wealth is not tired. ||1|| O ignorant, you did not think of spiritual wisdom. You have wasted this human life. ||1||Pause|| O mortal, serve the Lord, as long as you live. When the body goes, your love for the Lord shall not go; you shall dwell at the feet of the Lord. ||2|| One who enshrines guru's teachings in the mind has no greed. Obey God's command and play chess playing in the mind. ||3|| Those who intuitively worship the immortal God become immortal. Says Kabeer; those who know the game of chess never lose. ||4||4|| Soohee, Lalit, Kabeer Jee: There are five rulers in my body. All demand tax. I have not seeded anyone's land, why are they troubling me? ||1|| O Godly people, the tax collector is constantly torturing me! Raising my arms high, I complained to my guru. He saved me. ||1||Pause|| The nine tax-assessors and the ten magistrates go out; they do not let their subjects live in peace. They do not measure with a full tape, and they take huge bribes. ||2|| One Lord is contained in the seventy-two chambers of the body, He wrote off my account. The records of the justice of destiny are searched; I owe nothing. ||3|| Do not slender the saint. Saint and God is the same. Says Kabeer, I have found that guru, who thinks of everything. ||4||5|| Tune Soohee, the word of Sree Ravi Daas Jee: God is one. He is realized by guru's grace. The happy soul-bride knows the essence of her Husband Lord. Renouncing pride, she enjoys peace and pleasure. She surrenders her body and mind to Him, she does not hide anything. She does not see or hear, or speak to another. ||1|| How can anyone know the pain of other's? If he has not felt pain; ||1||Pause|| The discarded bride is miserable and loses in both worlds; She, who does not worship her Husband Lord; The bridge to pray is hard to cross. No one will accompany you there; you will have to go alone. ||2|| Suffering in pain, I have come to Your door, O compassionate Lord. I am very thirsty, but You do not answer me. Says Ravi Daas, I seek Your sanctuary O God; Save me as You please; ||3||1|| Soohee: The day, which dawns, has to end. You have to go; nothing remains forever. My companions are leaving, I also have to leave. We have to go far away. Death is imminent. ||1|| Page 794 Why are you asleep? Wake up, o ignorant! You thought that your life in the world is forever. ||1||Pause|| One who gave you life shall also provide you with food. In each and every heart, He runs His shop. Worship God and give up ego and possessiveness. Recite God's name in the mind. ||2|| Your life is passing away, do something for the journey. Evening has set in and soon there will be dark all over. Says Ravi Daas, O ignorant self-willed. Don't you realize that this world is the house of death?! ||3||2|| Soohee: You may have lofty mansions, halls and kitchens. But you cannot stay there even for an instant, after death. ||1|| This body is like a straw hut.

When it is burnt, it mixes with dust. ||1||Pause|| Even relatives, family and friends begin to say, "Take his body out, immediately!"||2|| Your wife is also gone. She ran away, saying ghost! ghost! ||3|| Says Ravi Daas, the whole world has been robbed. But I escaped, reciting the name of one God. ||4||3|| God is one. He is realized by guru's grace. Tune Soohee, the word of Sheikh Fareed Jee: Burning and writhing in pain, I wring my hands. I have gone insane, seeking my Husband Lord. O my Husband Lord; You are angry with me in Your mind. The fault is with me, not with my Husband Lord. ||1|| O my Lord, I do not know Your real meaning. Having wasted my youth, now I regret. ||1||Pause|| O black songbird, what made you black? "I have been burnt by the separation from my beloved!" Without her Husband Lord, how can the soul-bride ever find peace? When He becomes kind, then God unites us with Him. ||2|| The lonely soul-bride suffers in the deep well of the worldly. She has no companions and no friends. O God; unite me with the company of devotees. Then, when I look, I see God my friend. ||3|| The journey is full of sorrows. It is sharper than a two-edged sword, and very narrow. That is where my path lies. O Sheikh Fareed; it is time to find your way. ||4||1|| Soohee, Lalit: You could not build the boat, when there was time; When the pool is full and over-flowing, then it is very difficult to swim. ||1|| Do not touch the thorny safflower; it will burn, my dear. ||1||Pause|| First, the bride is ignorant and then, her Husband Lord is deaf. She is not humble; how can she unite with him? ||2|| Says Fareed; O my companions; say God God God. When the soul departs, the body returns to dust. ||3||2||

Page 795. *God is one. It is true. He is the Creator. He is carefree. He has no enemy. He is immortal. He does not take birth. He came into existence on his own. He is realized by guru's grace.*

Tune Bilaaval, First Master, Chau-Padas, First House: You are the emperor; who am I! What is your greatness? As You bestow, so I say O Lord; I am ignorant, I do not know how to say anything? ||1|| Tell me; how to sing Your praises; So that I merge with truth. ||1||Pause|| Whatever happened; happened by Your grace O friend. I do not know Your limits O Lord. I the ignorant have no wisdom. ||2|| What should I say and think? I do not know what and how to say the unexplainable. As it pleases You, so I speak; it is by a little bit of Your grace. ||3|| Among so many dogs, I belong to none; I bark for my belly. If Nanak does not worship; he does not know master's name. ||4||1|| Bilaawal, First Master: Making my mind the temple, body the magician; I take sacred bath in it. Guru's teaching is enshrined in my mind; so I shall not take birth again. ||1|| My mind is pierced by the merciful Lord, O my mother! Who can know the pain of another? I do not worry about anyone else. ||1||Pause||O Lord, inaccessible, unfathomable, invisible and infinite: please, take care of me! You fully abide in water and land. Your light shines in every being. ||2|| All teachings, instructions and understandings are Yours; I worship You. I know no one but You O Lord. I sing Your praises all the time. ||3|| All beings are in Your protection; You worry about all. Whatever pleases you is good. This is Nanak's prayer. ||4||2|| Bilaawal, First Master: You are the teachings and you are the destiny. You are the listener, You are the knower. You create and test for quality by Your creative power. You are the bestowal; You are realized by reciting your name. ||1|| Page 796 Such is the name of the formless Lord. I am a beggar; You are invisible and unknowable. ||1||Pause|| Love of worldly wealth is like a cursed woman, ugly, dirty and promiscuous. Power and beauty are false; and last for only a few days. When one obtains God's name, the dark inside is illuminated. ||2|| I tasted the worldly and gave up. Now, I have no doubts. One, whose father is known, cannot be illegitimate. One, who belongs to one Lord, has no worry. The Creator acts, and causes all to act. ||3|| One who is devoted to guru's teachings conquers his mind through his mind. Enshrining God in the mind, one meets no obstruction. He does not think anything else; he praises the guru. O Nanak, attuned to God's name attains salvation. ||4||3|| Bilaaval, First Master: Through guru's teachings the mind attains peace. Imbued with Lord's love, the mind is satisfied. The self-willed deluded by doubt are insane. How can you survive without God; He is realized through guru's teachings. ||1|| How can I live without visualizing God O my mother? I cannot survive without God o guru; please make me realize! ||1||Pause|| Forgetting my God, I die in pain. With each breath and morsel of food, I recite God and seek Him. I became content reciting God's name and detached from the world forever. Now, the guru-willed realizes God with me. ||2|| The unspoken speech is spoken, by the will of the guru. He the unapproachable and unfathomable; God makes us visualize. Without the guru, what should we practice, what should we do? Eradicate the ego and enshrine guru's teachings in the mind. ||3|| The self-willed are separated from God due to bad deeds. The guru-willed are honoured reciting God's name. The Lord showered His mercy on me the servant of servants. Name of the Lord is the wealth and resolve of servant Nanak. ||4||4|| Bilaaval, Third Master, First House: God is one. He is realized by guru's grace. Cursed are; the food, sleep and the clothes worn on the body. Cursed are the body, family and friends, if one cannot find his Lord. Missing the step of the ladder cannot catch again; his life is wasted, uselessly. ||1|| Love of duality does not allow him to lovingly focus his attention on the Lord; he who forsakes the feet of the Lord. O bestowal of life of the World you eradicate the sorrows of your humble servants. ||1||Pause|| You are kind O bestowal of kindness; what can these poor beings do? It is said they all obtain salvation by Your grace. Only the guru-willed obtain salvation; the self-willed are tied in bonds. ||2|| Those, who enshrine God in the mind and remain attuned to Him forever. Their devotion cannot be described. God looks after them. Page 797 Those lost in doubt are self-willed. They are neither this side nor the other side. ||3|| Whom God blesses realizes this through guru's teachings. In the midst of the worldly wealth, Lord's servant is emancipated. O Nanak, one with pre-ordained destiny scares away the devil of death. ||4||1|| Bilaaval, Third Master: How can the unweighable be weighed? If there is anyone else so great, then he can understand the Lord. There is no other than Him. How can His value be estimated? ||1|| By guru's grace, He comes and enshrines in the mind. One realizes Him when duality departs. ||1||Pause|| He is the assessor, applying the touchstone to test it. He analyzes the coin, and approves it as currency. Whatever He weighs is a perfect weight. He the true Lord knows all. ||2|| All forms of worldly wealth emanate from Him. He becomes pure whom He unites with Him. He attaches to Him, whom the Lord attaches. When truth is revealed to him, then he merges in the true Lord. ||3|| He is the devotion, he is the essence. He teaches the

way and he recites God. He is the true guru, and He is His teaching.
O Nanak, He speaks and teaches. ||4||2|| Bilaaval, Third Master: God
is a devotee; the devotees become God by serving Him. What excuse
anyone has? You set such play. You abide in all equally. ||1|| God's
name enshrines in the mind through guru's teachings. One with
pre-ordained destiny meets the guru and attunes to Him with love
forever. ||1||Pause|| How can I serve You? How can I be proud of this?
When You withdraw Your Light, O Lord, then tell me what happens?
||2|| You are the guru and the disciple; You are the treasure of virtues.
As You cause, so we do; as it pleases You O Lord. ||3|| Says Nanak,
You are the true Lord; who can know Your actions? You bless some
with Your grace and some wander in doubt and pride. ||4||3|| Bilaaval,
Third Master: The perfect Lord created the perfect creation. He looks
after everyone equally. In this worldly play God's name is supreme.
Do not be proud of you? ||1|| One, who realizes guru's teachings;
merges with the guru; One who understands this sermon; God's
name dwells in him. ||1||Pause|| This is the reality of four ages. Human
beings realize this treasure. Celibacy, self-discipline and pilgrimages
were the faith in past ages; but in today's age; singing God's praises is
the faith. ||2|| Every age has its faith; study the scriptures and find out.
The guru-willed who says God God God; attains salvation. ||3|| Page
798 Says Nanak, loving the true Lord eliminates ego. Those who say
or listen to God's name attain eternal peace. ||4||4|| Bilaaval, Third
Master: The Lord attaches the guru-willed to His love; Happiness
prevails in his home, who adores guru's teachings. O women, come
and sing the songs of joy. Meeting with the beloved, lasting peace is
obtained. ||1|| I admire those, who enshrine God in the mind. Meeting
with God's humble servant obtains peace, they sing God's praises
intuitively. ||1||Pause|| They are always imbued with Your love joyfully;
God dwells in their mind. They obtain eternal glory. The guru-willed
are united with God by His grace. ||2|| The guru-willed are dyed in
God's love through guru's teaching. They attain destiny singing God's
praises. They are dyed in the deep crimson colour by God's grace.
This dye never fades away; it is permanent. ||3|| Enshrining guru's
teachings in the mind, the darkness of ignorance disappears. God is
realized through guru's divine teachings. Those attuned to the true

Lord; do not take birth again. O Nanak, my perfect guru implanted God's name in me. ||4||5|| Bilaaval, Third Master: From the perfect guru, I obtained God's grace. The name of the carefree Lord abides in my mind. Guru's teachings eliminated my ego of the worldly wealth. Through the guru, I have obtained honour in the court of the Lord. ||1|| I serve the Lord of the universe; I have nothing else to do. May I the guru-willed be happy forever; I beg for the blessing of Your name. ||1||Pause|| From the mind, mental faith is obtained. Through guru's teachings, I realized Him. Only a few think birth and death the same way. He does not die again and he does not face the devil of death. All priceless treasures are in the mind. True guru has revealed this to me, and my egotistical pride is gone. I am intuitively absorbed in God's worship forever. Night and day, I sing one name. ||3|| In today's age, one obtains honour; Reciting God's name through guru's teachings; Wherever I look, I see the Lord permeating and pervading. He is forever the giver of peace; His worth cannot be estimated. ||4|| By perfect destiny, I have found the perfect guru. He revealed the treasure of God's name in my mind. Guru's teachings taste very sweet to me. O Nanak, my greed vanished, my mind and body became peaceful. 5||6||4||6||10|| Tune Bilaaval, Fourth Master, Third House: God is one. He is realized by guru's grace. Effort and intelligence come by God's grace, do as He guides you. As the magician plays string instrument, so does the Lord play the living beings. ||1|| Page 799 O my mind, recite God's name. According to the pre-ordained destiny I found the guru. God abides in my mind. ||1||Pause|| Entangled in worldly wealth, the mortal wanders around. Save Your humble servant, O Lord, As you saved Prahlaad from the clutches of Harnaakash; God protects in His sanctuary. ||2|| What can I say about those, who have been saved; God changes the sinners to sacred. Ravi Daas, the leather-worker, who worked with hides and carried dead animals was saved, by entering Lord's sanctuary. ||3|| O God, merciful to the meek, bestowal of salvation to His devotees; please preserve my honour of the sinner. O Lord, make me the slave of slaves; servant Nanak is the slave of Your slaves. ||4||1|| Bilaaval, Fourth Master: I am ignorant, idiot and ignorant; I seek Your sanctuary, O primal being, Lord; Be kind and save me O Lord. I am a virtueless stone. ||1|| O my mind, recite God's name. Obtain God's sublime essence through guru's teachings and give up useless deeds. ||1||Pause|| God saves His devotees. I sing Your praises, please save the virtueless. I have none but You O my Lord. I the fortunate recite God. ||2|| The life of the self-willed is cursed. They suffer severe pain. The unfortunate with bad deeds, take birth again and again. ||3|| God's name is the support of His servants. It is pre-ordained due to good deeds. The guru implanted God's name in servant Nanak. His life is fruitful. ||4||2|| Bilaaval, Fourth Master: My mind is filled with greed, false attachment and ill will. I cannot serve You, O God; I am ignorant; how can I swim across? ||1|| O my mind, recite the name of God the Lord of men. The mortal met the guru by God's grace and attained salvation. ||1||Pause|| O my father, my Lord and master, please bless me that I sing Your praises. Those who are attached to You are saved, like iron floats with wood. ||2|| Those who do not serve God are faithless, ignorant with low intellect. They are unlucky bad character. They keep taking birth and death again and again. ||3|| Whom You unite with You O Lord; bathe in guru's pool and become content. The filth of ill will departs reciting God and attains salvation O Nanak. ||4||3|| Bilaaval, Fourth Master: Come, O saints my brothers. Let us speak the sermon of the Lord. God's name is the boat in today's age; that saves through the boatman guru's teachings. ||1|| O my mind, praise God by saying God God. Page 800 Due to pre-ordained destiny, sing God's praises in devotee's company and attain salvation. ||1||Pause|| God's sublime essence is in the body; it is realized through guru's teachings. Serving the true guru visualizes God, drink nectar in his refuge. ||2|| Reciting God's name is very sweet. Taste it O saints; God's sublime essence tastes sweet through guru's teachings. All other tastes are eliminated attaining God's taste. ||3|| Reciting God's name attains Godly taste. Serve the Lord O saints. The four great blessings are obtained through guru's teachings reciting God O Nanak. ||4||4|| Bilaaval, Fourth Master: Anyone, from any class – Kashaatriya, Brahman, Soodra or Vaishya – can say the mantra to recite God. Worship the guru as the supreme Lord; serve Him day and night. ||1|| O humble servants of the Lord, see the true guru with your eyes. Obtain the reward of your choice by saying God through guru's teachings. ||1||Pause|| We may think various ways, but only happens what has to happen. Everyone longs for his good. He who does it, we do not even imagine. ||2|| So renounce the clever thinking O godly person; that is hard to do. Recite God's name day and night through guru's teachings. ||3|| Good or bad thinking is in Your control O Lord. You are the Lord of us mortals. O God, O Creator Lord of servant Nanak, as You wish, so I speak. ||4||5|| Bilaaval, Fourth Master: I worship the source of joy, the sublime primal being all the time with love. The justice of destiny and devil of death have no control over me. ||1|| O mind, recite the name of the Lord of the universe. The fortunate found the guru and sings God's praises with love. ||1||Pause|| The ignorant faithless are the slaves of the worldly wealth. They wander engrossed in worldly wealth. They wander burning in greed like an ox around the oil mill. ||2|| The guru-willed attain salvation by serving. The fortunate do the service. Those who recite God, attain the reward. Their worldly bonds are broken. ||3|| God is master, the servant and the Lord of the universe. O servant Nanak, everything happens by God's grace. He keeps us as he pleases. ||4||6|| God is one. He is realized by guru's grace. Tune Bilaaval, Fourth Master, Partaal, Thirteenth House: O brother, say God's name; the saviour of the sinners. The Lord emancipates his saints and devotees. Page 801 God is omnipresent. He abides in water and land. Sing His praises all the time, it will eliminate your sufferings. ||1||Pause|| God has made my life fruitful. I recite God the dispeller of pain. I surrendered to the guru the bestowal of salvation. The Lord has made my life's journey rewarding. Joining the holy congregation, I sing praises of the Lord. ||1|| O mortal, place your hopes in the name of the Lord. Your love of duality shall vanish. He who is hopeful and detached; Meeting such a person realizes God. Those who sing the praises of God's name; Servant Nanak falls at their feet. ||2||1||7||4||6||7||17|| Tune Bilaaval, Fifth Master, Chau-Padas, First House: God is one. He is realized by guru's grace. He is attached to what he sees. How can I meet You, O imperishable God? Have mercy on me, and show me the way. Please unite me in the company of devotees. ||1|| How can I cross over the poisonous world-ocean? True guru is the boat to carry us across. ||1||Pause|| The worldly wealth shakes us like wind blowing. But Lord's devotees remain ever stable.

They remain unaffected by pleasure and pain. The guru is the protector over their heads. ||2|| The worldly wealth coils around like a poisonous snake. The moth burns to death in ego of seeing the light. God cannot be realized by doing all kind of makeup. When God is kind, He unites us with the guru. ||3|| I wander around sad, seeking one priceless jewel. This priceless jewel cannot be obtained by any efforts. That jewel is in the temple of the Lord. The guru lifted my veil and I became content by seeing. ||4|| Whoever tasted it enjoys the flavour; He is like the mute, who enjoys but cannot say. I saw the joyful beautiful Lord. Servant Nanak merged with Him singing His praises. ||5||1|| Bilaaval, Fifth Master: The divine guru blessed me with eternal happiness. He linked His servant to His service. No obstacles block my path, reciting the name of unexplainable incomprehensible Lord. ||1|| The soil has been sanctified, singing His praises. The sins are eradicated, reciting the name of the Lord. ||1||Pause|| He is pervading everywhere; From the very beginning, and throughout the ages, His glory has been honourably manifest. By guru's grace, sorrow does not touch me. ||2|| Guru's feet seem sweet to my mind. He is present everywhere without any difficulty. I found total peace, when the guru was pleased. ||3|| The supreme Lord has become my saviour. Wherever I look, I see Him with me. O Nanak, the Lord the master protects and cherishes His slaves. ||4||2|| Bilaaval, Fifth Master: You are the treasure of peace, O my beloved God. Page 802 O Lord Your virtues are unlimited. I am an orphan, seeking Your sanctuary. Be kind that I worship Your feet. ||1|| Be kind and dwell in my mind. I am worthless; please attach me to You. ||1||Pause|| When one misses God; all his sufferings are eliminated. Lord's servant does not suffer pain of devil of death. All pains are eliminated by reciting God' name; In whose heart God abides. ||2|| Name of God is the support of my mind and body. Forgetting God's name, the body shall be reduced to ashes. When I miss God; all my deeds are fulfilled. Forgetting the Lord, one begs from everyone. ||3|| I am in love with the lotus feet of the Lord. I got rid of all evil ways. God's name is in my mind and body. O Nanak, eternal bliss fills the home of Lord's devotees. ||4||3|| Tune Bilaaval, Fifth Master, Second House, sung to the tune of Yaan-Rey: God is one. He is realized by guru's grace. You are the support of my mind, O my beloved; All other clever tricks are useless, O beloved; You alone are my protector. ||1||Pause|| Meeting the perfect guru, O beloved, one becomes content. He, who God is kind to, serves the guru. Fruitful is to visualize guru the master, who has all the virtues. O Nanak, guru is the supreme, the transcendent Lord; He is always with you. ||1|| I live by hearing the praises of those who know their God. They recite and teach God's name. They are attuned to God's name. I the servant beg to serve Your humble servants. I will serve them to the best of my ability. This is Nanak's prayer: O my Lord. May I visualize Your humble servants. ||2|| They are said to be fortunate, O beloved, who enjoy the true congregation. Reciting God's sacred name the mind becomes pure. The pains of birth and death are eradicated, O beloved, and the fear of the devil of death is ended. O Nanak, those who obey God's will; visualize Him. ||3|| O my lofty, incomparable and infinite Lord, who can know Your virtues? Those who sing and those who listen to your praises are saved and all sins are erased. You save the beasts, demons and ignorant, and even stones are carried across. Slave Nanak seeks Your refuge; he praises You forever. ||4||1||4|| Bilaaval, Fifth Master: Renounce the tasteless water of corruption, O my companion, and drink essence of God's name. Without tasting the nectar, all have drowned; their souls did not find happiness. You have no honour, glory or power; become the slave of devotees. Page 803 O Nanak, those approved by God; are admired. ||1|| Seeing worldly wealth deludes the mind, O my friend; like the deer seeing the mirage or the transitory shade of a tree. Worldly pleasure is fickle, it does not go with you, O my companion; in the end, it will leave you. Enjoyment of extreme pleasures and beauty, no one finds peace this way. Blessed are the humble devotees O friend O Nanak who recite God's name. ||2|| O my fortunate companion: go and join the company of the saints. There, the pain, hunger or disease will not afflict you; attune to the love of Lord's lotus feet. There is no birth or death, no coming or going in reincarnation, when you enter the sanctuary of the eternal Lord. Love, separation or worldly attachments do not trouble you, O Nanak, when you recite one Lord. ||3|| God pierces your mind by His grace o beloved, you intuitively are imbued by His love. My bed is embellished, meeting with my beloved; I sing His praises in joy. O my friends and companions, I am imbued with Lord's love; the desires of my mind and body are fulfilled. O Nanak, the amazing merged with amazing. What can anyone say about it? ||4||2||5|| Tune Bilaaval, Fifth Master, Fourth House: God is one. He is realized by guru's grace. The entire universe is the form of one Lord. He is the trade, and He is the trader. ||1|| Only a few obtain such wisdom. Wherever I go, I see Him there. ||1||Pause|| He is manifested in many forms, yet absolute in one form. He is water and the waves. ||2|| He is the temple, He is the worship service. He is the worshipper, He is the idol. ||3|| He is Yoga; He is the process. Nanak's God is forever liberated. ||4||1||6|| Bilaaval, Fifth Master: He creates, He supports. He causes all to act; yet He takes no blame. ||1|| He is the teaching, He is the teacher. He is the wealth, He is the enjoyer. ||1||Pause|| He is silent, He is the speaker. He cannot be cheated; He is beyond cheating. ||2|| He is hidden, He is manifest. He abides in everyone yet hidden. ||3|| He is absolute, He is with the universe. Says Nanak, all are beggars of God. ||4||2||7|| Bilaaval, Fifth Master: He shows the path to the lost. Such a guru is found by good fortune. ||1|| O my mind recite God's name in your mind. The beloved feet of the guru abide in my heart. ||1||Pause|| Page 804 The mind is engrossed in lust, anger, greed and emotional attachment. Breaking my bonds, the guru has liberated me. ||2|| Experiencing pain and pleasure, one is born, only to die again. Lotus feet of the guru bring peace and shelter. ||3|| The world is drowning in the ocean of fire. O Nanak, holding me by the arm, the guru has saved me. ||4||3||8|| Bilaaval, Fifth Master: I offer my body, mind, wealth and everything to my Lord. What is the wisdom, by which I recite God's name. ||1|| With this hope, I have come to beg from God. Seeing you my yard becomes admirable. ||1||Pause|| Trying several methods, I reflect deeply on the Lord. In the company of devotees, this mind is saved. ||2|| I have no intelligence, wisdom, common sense or cleverness. I meet You, only by Your grace. ||3|| My eyes are content, visualizing my Lord. Says Nanak, such a life is fruitful. ||4||4||9|| Bilaaval, Fifth Master: Mother, father, children and wealth, will not go with you. All sufferings are eradicated in the company of devotees. ||1|| God is pervading and permeating all. Recite God with your tongue, the sufferings will not trouble you. ||1||Pause|| One who is afflicted by the terrible fire of thirst and desire? Become soothed by saying God God God. ||2|| By millions of efforts, peace is not obtained; The mind is satisfied by singing the praises of the Lord. ||3|| Please bless me with worship, O God, O searcher of hearts. This is Nanak's prayer, O Lord. ||4||5||10|| Bilaaval, Fifth Master: By good fortune, the perfect guru is found. Meeting with the devotees, recite God's name. ||1|| O supreme Lord, I seek Your sanctuary. Meditating on guru's feet, sinful acts are erased. ||1||Pause|| All other rituals are just worldly affairs; Joining the company of devotees, one is saved. ||2|| One may contemplate the Simritees, Shaastras and Vedas; But only reciting God's name attains salvation. ||3|| Be kind to servant Nanak, O God, Bless him with the dust of the feet of devotees, that he may be saved. ||4||6||11|| Bilaaval, Fifth Master: I contemplate guru's teachings in my heart; All my hopes and desires are fulfilled. ||1|| The faces of the humble saints are radiant and bright. By His grace God bestowed His name on them. ||1||Pause|| He took them out of the deep dark hole. They are admired in the whole world. ||2|| He elevates the lowly and fills the empty. They receive the supreme, sublime essence of God's name. ||3|| The mind and body become pure and the sins are burnt to ashes. Says Nanak, God is pleased with me. ||4||7||12|| Bilaaval, Fifth Master: All desires are fulfilled, O my friend, Page 805 Lovingly attaching your mind to Lord's lotus feet; ||1|| I praise those who recite God. The fire of desire is quenched, singing the praises of the Lord. ||1||Pause|| The life of the fortunate becomes fruitful. Those, who are attuned to God through devotee's company; ||2|| Wisdom, honour, wealth, peace and celestial bliss are attained, if one does not forget the Lord of supreme joy, even for an instant. ||3|| My mind is very thirsty for visualizing God. Says Nanak, O God, I seek Your sanctuary. ||4||8||13|| Bilaaval, Fifth Master: I am worthless, lacking all virtues. Bless me with Your grace and make me Your Own. ||1|| My mind and body are embellished by the Lord of the world. By His grace, God has come into my heart. ||1||Pause|| He is the life and protector of His devotees, the destroyer of fear. Now, I have been carried across the world-ocean. ||2|| It is God's way to purify sinners, say the Vedas. I have seen the supreme Lord with my eyes. ||3|| In the company of devotees, the Lord has become manifest. O slave Nanak, all pains are relieved. ||4||9||14|| Bilaaval, Fifth Master: Who can know the value of serving You O God? God is imperishable, invisible and incomprehensible. ||1|| His virtues are infinite; God is profound and unfathomable. The mansion of God, my Lord my Master, is lofty and high. You are unlimited, O my Lord and Master. ||1||Pause|| There is no other than One God. You alone know Your worship. ||2|| No one can do anything, O brother. Whom God blesses obtains His name. ||3|| Says Nanak, that humble being who pleases God; He finds God, the treasure of virtues. ||4||10||15|| Bilaaval, Fifth Master: He protects in mother's womb by His grace. Forgetting the sublime essence of the Lord, you taste a poisonous fruit. ||1|| Worship the Lord of the universe and renounce all entanglements. When the devil of death comes to kill you, O ignorant, then your body will be destroyed and disgraced. ||1||Pause|| You think your body, mind and wealth are your. You never recite the name of the Creator at all. ||2|| You have fallen into the deep dark pit of worldly attachments. Caught in the illusion of worldly wealth and forgot the supreme Lord. ||3|| The fortunate sing God's praises. In the society of saints, they find God O Nanak. ||4||11||16|| Bilaaval, Fifth Master: Mother, father, children, relatives and siblings O Nanak, only the supreme Lord is our support. ||1|| He blesses us with peace, contentment and joy. The perfect guru, whose sermon is perfect; has many virtues that cannot be counted. ||1||Pause|| God makes all arrangements. Reciting God, all desires are fulfilled. ||2|| He is the bestowal of wealth, faith, pleasure and liberation. Page 806 Reciting the name of the Lord of destiny, my desire is fulfilled. ||3|| In the company of devotees, Nanak enjoys Lord's love. He returned home, with the perfect guru. ||4||12||17|| Bilaaval, Fifth Master: All treasures come from the perfect guru. ||1||Pause|| The mortal lives by reciting God's name. The faithless dies in shame and misery. ||1|| Name of the Lord is my protector. The faithless talks nonsense. ||2|| Slandering others, many have been ruined. Their necks, heads and feet are tied by death's noose. ||3|| Says Nanak, the humble devotees recite God's name; Devil of death does not approach them. ||4||13||18|| Tune Bilaaval, Fifth Master, Fourth House, Du-Padas: God is one. He is realized by guru's grace. What cause will lead me to meet my God?

Each and every moment I recite God. ||1|| I recite continuously the lotus feet of God. What wisdom will lead me to realize my beloved? ||1||Pause|| Please, bless me with such blessing, O my God, That Nanak may never forget You. ||2||1||19|| Bilaaval, Fifth Master: In my heart, I recite Lord's lotus feet. Disease is gone, I found total peace. ||1|| The guru relieved my sufferings by his grace. My birth became fruitful, and my life approved. ||1||Pause|| God's sacred unexplainable sermon is realized. Says Nanak the divine persons live by reciting God. ||2||2||20|| Bilaaval, Fifth Master: I obtained peace by the grace of the perfect guru. Peace and joy have welled up, and divine music plays. ||1||Pause|| Sufferings, sins and worries have been dispelled. Reciting God all sins departed. ||1|| Join together, O beautiful soul-brides, celebrate and be happy. Guru saved my honour O Nanak. ||2||3||21|| Bilaaval, Fifth Master: Intoxication of attachments, love of worldly wealth and enmity are all useless. Day by day, his life is winding down; practicing sin and corruption, the noose of death traps him. ||1|| I seek Your sanctuary, O God, merciful to the meek. I have crossed over the terrible world-ocean, with the dust of devotees in their company. ||1||Pause|| O God, giver of peace, all-powerful Lord, my soul, body and wealth are Yours. Please, break my bonds of doubt, O transcendent Lord, forever kind God of Nanak. ||2||4||22|| Bilaaval, Fifth Master: The transcendent Lord brought bliss to all; He confirmed His Natural way. He became kind to the humble devotees, the whole family became happy. ||1|| The true guru resolved my affairs. Page 807 May God live forever who confirmed peace, joy and salvation? ||1||Pause|| The forests, meadows and the universe have blossomed. The whole creation is taken care of. Nanak obtained the fruit of his desire; his desires are fulfilled. ||2||5||23|| Bilaaval, Fifth Master: One who is blessed by the Lord? Reciting God eliminates death. ||1||Pause|| Worship God in the company of devotees. Singing praises of the Lord, the trap of the devil of death is broken. ||1|| He is the true guru, and He is the caretaker. Nanak begs for the dust of the feet of devotees. ||2||6||24|| Bilaaval, Fifth Master: Water your mind with the name of the Lord. Night and day, sing the praises of the Lord. ||1|| Be in such love, O my mind; Realize God close by twenty-four hours a day; ||1||Pause|| Says Nanak, one who has such pure destiny His mind is attached to Lord's feet. ||2||7||25|| Bilaaval, Fifth Master: The disease is gone; God eliminated it. I sleep in peace, I am content. ||1||Pause|| Eat your fill, O my brother. Recite God's sacred name in your mind. ||1|| Nanak has entered the sanctuary of the perfect guru; He who preserved the honour of His name; ||2||8||26|| Bilaaval, Fifth Master: The guru made my home and property permanent. ||Pause|| Whoever slanders these homes; is pre-destined by the Creator to be destroyed. ||1|| Slave Nanak seeks God's refuge; His teachings are eternal and infinite. ||2||9||27|| Bilaaval, Fifth Master: The sickness of fever and worry are eradicated. The supreme Lord has blessed you, so enjoy the happiness o saints. ||Pause|| All joy wells up in your society; your mind and body are healthy. So sing God's praise forever. This is the way of worship. ||1|| Go and live in such a place where good deeds take you. O Nanak, God is pleased with you; your time of separation ended. ||2||10||28|| Bilaaval, Fifth Master: Nothing goes with you. The worldly wealth is useless entanglement. Even the emperors have to die; that is what the saints think; ||Pause|| To eliminate the ill will is the protecting shield of destiny. Those who do useless sinful deeds are born in many life's, only to die again. ||1|| God's devotee speaks the truth; worship God; Reciting God's name with love attains salvation O Nanak. ||2||11||29|| Bilaaval, Fifth Master: The perfect guru blessed me with peace and thinking in trance. God is always my helper and companion; I contemplate His sacred virtues. ||Pause|| Page 808 Everyone in the world yearns for honour. When the guru the God is pleased, no hindrance comes on the way. ||1|| One who has the Lord on his side; everyone becomes his slave. O Nanak, the guru bestows honour forever. ||2||12||30|| Tune Bilaaval, Fifth Master, Fifth House, Chau-Padas: God is one. He is realized by guru's grace. The world is created like building a house of sand. It does not take long to destroy it, like the drop of water on the paper. ||1|| Listen o my intelligent mind; contemplate the truth! The mystics, the seekers, householders and Yogis have gone leaving their homes behind. ||1||Pause|| This world is like a dream in the night. Whatever you see shall parish. O ignorant, why do you attach to it? ||2|| Where are your brothers and friends? Open your eyes and see! Some have gone; some will go; everyone must take his turn. ||3|| Those who serve the perfect guru, become immortal in God's court. Servant Nanak is God's slave; preserve his honour, O Lord. ||4||1||31|| Bilaaval, Fifth Master: Burn away the praises of others. When you meet your beloved; talk to him. ||1|| When God becomes kind, one starts worshipping Him. My mind clings to worldly desires; meet the guru and eliminate it. ||1||Pause|| I pray sincerely and offer this soul to Him. I will sacrifice all other riches, for a moment's union with my beloved. ||2|| Through the guru, I got rid of the five thieves, pain and other involvement. I have been enlightened. I remain awake day and night. ||3|| The blessed soul-bride with a pre-ordained destiny seeks His sanctuary. Says Nanak, One who realizes God attains peace. ||4||2||32|| Bilaaval, Fifth Master: The fortunate one is dyed in the colour of Lord's love. This colour never gets dirty or stained. ||1|| The fortunate realizes God with ease. He obtains celestial peace, which never leaves him. ||1||Pause|| Old age and death cannot touch him, and he shall not suffer pain again. Drinking the nectar, he is satisfied; the guru makes him immortal. ||2|| He who tastes the invaluable God's name knows it. Its value cannot be estimated; what can I say? ||3|| O supreme Lord; visualizing you is fruitful and your sermon is full of virtues. Page 809 May I be blessed with the dust of the feet of Your slaves; Nanak admires You. ||4||3||33|| Bilaaval, Fifth Master: Keep me in your refuge by your grace O God; I do not know how to serve You; I am a low-life ignorant. ||1|| I take pride in You, O my beloved. I the sinner continuously make mistakes; You are the forgiver. ||1||Pause|| I make many mistakes daily. You are without mistakes. I associate with the servants instead of the master; this is my fate! ||2|| You bless me with everything by your grace, I am thankless. I am attached to Your gifts, but I do not even think of you. ||3|| There is none other than You, O Lord, destroyer of other affects. Says Nanak, I have come to Your sanctuary, O merciful guru; please save the ignorant. ||4||4||34|| Bilaaval, Fifth Master: Don't blame anyone else; recite God's name; Serving Him, unlimited peace is obtained; O mind, sing His praises. ||1|| O beloved, other than You, who else should I say? You are my merciful Lord; I am filled with faults. ||1||Pause|| As You keep so I remain; there is no other way. You are the support of the unsupported; Your name is my only support. ||2|| One who accepts Your doing at face value is liberated. The entire creation is Yours; all are subject to Your ways. ||3|| I wash Your feet and serve You, if it pleases You, O Lord; Be kind, O merciful God that Nanak sings Your praises. ||4||5||35|| Bilaaval, Fifth Master: Death hovers over his head, but the animal does not understand. Entangled in conflict, pleasure and ego, he does not think of death. ||1|| Serve your guru; why wander around O unfortunate? Seeing the temporary colour of safflower; why are you attached to it? ||1||Pause|| You commit sins again and again, to gather wealth to spend. But dust shall mix with dust; you shall depart naked. ||2|| Those, who you work for; will become your enemies; They will leave you in the end and let you burn in anger. ||3|| Those, with pre-ordained destiny become servants of servants. Says Nanak, they are free of bonds in guru's refuge. ||4||6||36|| Bilaaval, Fifth Master: The cripple crosses over the mountain the ignorant becomes wise. The blind can see the universe by surrendering to the sacred guru. ||1|| This is the glory of company of devotees; listen, O my friends. Filth is washed away, millions of sins are eliminated and the mind becomes pure. ||1||Pause|| Such is the worship of the Lord of the universe; an ant can defeat the elephant. Whoever the Lord makes His own, is blessed with a gift of eternity. ||2|| The lion becomes a cat, and the mountain looks like a mole. Page 810 Those who worked for half a shell become rich. ||3|| What greatness of Yours can I describe, O Lord of infinite virtues? Please be kind and bless me with Your name; Nanak is at Your door. ||4||7||37|| Bilaaval, Fifth Master: He proudly slanders others and is greedy. He deceives, steals from other's house and does other bad deeds. ||1|| I have seen this with my eyes, by the grace of the perfect guru. Power, property, wealth and youth are useless, without God's name. ||1||Pause|| Beauty, incense, scented oils, beautiful clothes and foods When they come in contact with the body of the sinner, they stink. ||2|| Wandering around, he took birth as a human for a moment. Losing this opportunity, he must wander through countless lifes. ||3|| By God's grace, he meets the guru; contemplating God, he is amazed. He is blessed with peace, poise and bliss, O Nanak, his words come true. ||4||8||38|| Bilaaval, Fifth Master: The feet of the saints are the boat, to cross over the world-ocean. The guru shows the way and the lost finds the way in the forest. ||1|| Saying God God God in love of

God; While standing, sitting and sleeping, say God God God. ||1||Pause|| The five thieves run away, when one joins the company of devotees. His investment is intact, he earns large profits; he goes home with honour. ||2|| He becomes eternal, his anxiety is ended and he wavers no more. Visualizing God his doubt and ignorance disappeared. ||3|| The virtues of our virtuous Lord are profound; how many of them can I say? Nanak obtained the nectar of the Lord in devotee's company. ||4||9||39|| Bilaaval, Fifth Master: Life without the company of devotees is useless. Joining their congregation, all doubts are dispelled, and I am emancipated. ||1|| I am grateful to the day, when I met the devotees; I offer my body mind and soul to them forever. ||1||Pause|| They made me renounce the ego for good. This mind has become the dust of all and my worldly attachment erased. ||2|| In an instant, I burnt away the ideas of slander and ill will towards others. I see, consideration, compassion close by not far. ||3|| My body and mind are soothed, and now, I am liberated from the world. Love, soul, life, wealth and everything are realized O Nanak. ||4||10||40|| Bilaaval, Fifth Master: I serve Your slave and wipe his feet with my hair O Lord. I offer my mind to him, and listen to the praises of the enjoyable Lord. ||1|| Meeting You, my mind will be rejuvenated, please meet me, O Merciful Lord. I am happy reciting the kind God. ||1||Pause|| Page 811 God's devotees are the saviours of the world, touch their feet. Bless me, O God, with the gift of the dust of the feet of the saints. ||2|| I have no skill or wisdom, nor any service to my credit. Please, protect me from doubt, fear and emotional attachment, and cut away the noose of death from my neck. ||3|| I pray O Lord of mercy, my father! I sing Your praises in the company of devotee's O giver of peace. ||4||11||41|| Bilaaval, Fifth Master: Whatever You wish, You do. Without You, there is nothing. Seeing Your blessing, the devil of death leaves and goes away. ||1|| By Your grace, one is emancipated, and ego is dispelled. You are omnipotent, all powerful O God the guru. ||1||Pause|| Searching, I found that everything is false other than God's name. Devotee's company attains all pleasures of life; fulfill my desire O Lord. ||2|| Whoever You attach to you, so he does. All other clever ideas are useless! You are pervading everywhere, O my Lord, merciful to the meek. ||3|| I ask for everything from You, but only the fortunate obtain it. This is Nanak's prayer, O God; I live by singing Your praises. ||4||12||42|| Bilaaval, Fifth Master: Dwelling in devotee's company, all sins are erased. Attuned to God with love one does not cast in the womb again. ||1|| Saying the name of the Lord of the universe, the tongue becomes pure. The mind and body become pure by rehearsing guru's teachings. ||1||Pause|| Tasting God's subtle essence one is satisfied; he enjoys doing so. The intellect is brightened and illuminated; turning away from the world, the heart-lotus blossoms. ||2|| He is soothed, peaceful and content; all his thirst is quenched. Wandering in ten directions is stopped, and one becomes pure. ||3|| The saviour Lord saves him, and his doubts are burnt to ashes. Reciting God and seeing God's devotees attains peace O Nanak. ||4||13||43|| Bilaaval, Fifth Master: Carrying water, waving fan over him and grinding flour for His devotee I am happy; Burn in the fire, your power property and authority; ||1|| Touch the feet of the servant of the humble saints. Renounce and abandon the wealthy and the kings. ||1||Pause|| The dry bread of the saints is equal to all treasures. The thirty-six course food of the faithless is like poison. ||2|| Wearing the old blankets of the humble devotees, one is never naked. Even wearing the silk robes the faithless loses his honour. ||3|| Friendship with the faithless breaks down mid-way; But whoever serves God's humble servants, is saved here and hereafter. ||4|| Everything comes from You, O Lord; You created the creation. In the company God's devotees, Nanak sings God's praises. ||5||14||44|| Page 812 Bilaaval, Fifth Master: With my ears, I listen to word God and sing his praises. I place my head on the feet of the saints, and say God's name. ||1|| Be kind to me, O merciful God and bless me with this wealth and success. I apply the dust of saint's feet to my forehead. ||1||Pause|| Being the lowest of the low; I offer my humble prayer. I rub their feet renouncing my ego; I merge in saint's congregation. ||2|| I never forget to recite God with any breath; I never go to any other. Meeting the guru is rewarding; it eliminates ego and attachment. ||3|| I am embellished with truth, contentment, compassion and faith. My spiritual marriage is fruitful, O Nanak, I am pleasing to my God. ||4||15||45|| Bilaaval, Fifth Master: The eternal words of devotees are apparent in everyone. The humble being that joins the devotees; meets the sovereign Lord;

||1|| This faith in the Lord of the universe attains peace reciting God. People say that they brought the guru home. ||1||Pause|| He undoubtedly preserves the honour of those who seek His sanctuary. Seed God's name in your mind the land of destiny. ||2|| God the inner-knower does and causes others to do by His will. He purifies many sinners; this is the natural way of the Lord. ||3|| Don't be fooled, O mortal being, by the illusion of worldly pleasure. O Nanak, God saves the honour of those, whom He approves. ||4||16||46|| Bilaaval, Fifth Master: He fashioned you from clay and made your priceless body. He covers your faults and makes you look adorable. ||1|| Why do you forget God from your mind, who has all these virtues? One who forsakes God and joins others, blends with dust. ||1||Pause|| Recite God with each breath; do not delay. Renounce worldly enticement and false love; recite God! ||2|| He who created one and all is that God; So serve the supreme Lord learning from the guru. ||3|| God is the highest and greatest of all. He abides in all. O God; make Nanak the servant of your servants. ||4||17||47|| Bilaaval, Fifth Master: The Lord of the universe is my only support. I renounced all other hopes. God is all-powerful and above all; He is the perfect treasure of virtues. ||1|| God's name is the support of all beings. So fall at His feet. The saints take support of the transcendent Lord in the mind. ||1||Pause|| He preserves, He gives and he takes care of all. Page 813 O God; merciful to the meek, the treasure of mercy, I recite Your name with every breath. ||2|| Whatever the Creator does is great. Through guru's teachings and God's will, one attains peace. ||3|| Those who obey God's will renounce anxiety, worries and calculations. He does not ignore or leave those dyed by His love O Nanak. ||4||18||48|| Bilaaval, Fifth Master: Meeting Him the burning fire extinguishes and sins run away. I fell into the deep dark pit; giving His Hand, He pulled me out. ||1|| He is my beloved; I am the dust of His feet. Meeting with Him attains peace; He bestows the gift of life. ||1||Pause|| I now received my pre-ordained destiny. Living with Lord's devotees, my hopes are fulfilled. ||2|| The fear of the worldly is dispelled and I found peace with ease. The all-powerful guru became kind and God's name entered in my mind. ||3|| O God, You are the anchor and support of Nanak. He is the doer, the cause of causes, the

all-powerful Lord is inaccessible and infinite. ||4||19||49|| Bilaaval, Fifth Master: One who forgets God is filthy, poor and low. The ignorant does not think of God the doer, instead he thinks himself the doer. ||1|| Pain comes forgetting God. Peace comes when one remembers God. The saints are happy singing God's praises all the time. ||1||Pause|| He changes the high to low, and elevates the low in an instant. The value of God's blessing cannot be estimated. ||2|| Watching the worldly plays beauty and joys, the day of departure has come. The dream became dream. What you earned goes with you. ||3|| God is all-powerful, the cause of causes; I seek Your sanctuary. Day and night, Nanak recites Your name and praises forever. ||4||20||50|| Bilaaval, Fifth Master: I carry water on my head; with my hands I wash their feet. I praise him forever and I live by seeing him. ||1|| Whatever I think in my mind; I receive from God. I sweep the homes of God's devotees and wave fan over them. ||1||Pause|| The saints speak the sacred words; I listen and enshrine in my mind. The sublime essence soothes and satisfies me and extinguishes the fire of sin. ||2|| When saint's group worships God; I join them and sing God's praises. I bow in respect to God's devotees and apply the dust of their feet to my face. ||3|| Sitting and standing I recite God's name. This is my work! This is Nanak's prayer to God that he may merge in Lord's sanctuary. ||4||21||51|| Bilaaval, Fifth Master: He, who praises God; swims across the world-ocean; He who dwells in devotee's company; the fortunate realizes God. ||1|| Page 814 Your slave lives by hearing the words spoken by your devotees. The guru is revealed in the universe; He saves the honour of His servant. ||1||Pause|| God pulled me out of the ocean of fire and quenched my burning thirst. The guru sprinkled God's sacred name on me and saved me. ||2|| The pains of birth and death are removed and I obtained eternal peace. The noose of doubt and emotional attachment has been cut and I became pleasing to my God. ||3|| Let no one think any other way. Everything is in God's hand. O Nanak, eternal peace is obtained in the company of saints. ||4||22||52|| Bilaaval, Fifth Master: God became kind and cut my bonds. The supreme Lord is kind to the meek; I am saved by His grace. ||1|| The guru was graceful to eliminate my sufferings. Reciting the worthy God soothes my mind and body. ||1||Pause|| God's name is the medicine to cure the sickness. Dwell in devotee's company with love, the pain will not bother you. ||2|| Say God God from your mind lovingly. Sins are erased and one gets purified in devotee's refuge. ||3|| Listening and reciting God's praises drives the ill deeds away. Nanak says the greatest word (God). That is God's praise. ||4||23||53|| Bilaaval, Fifth Master: From devotion wells up worship and the soul becomes peaceful. Reciting God's name the Lord of the universe erases doubt and delusions. ||1|| One, who meets the perfect guru attains peace. Renounce your ideas and listen to guru's teachings. ||1||Pause|| Recite forever the name of the primal Lord the great bestowal. May I never forget that primal, infinite Lord from my mind. ||2|| I have enshrined love for the lotus feet of the amazing guru. One whom You bless O God, commits to Your service. ||3|| I drink nectar, the treasure of wealth; my mind and body are happy. O Nanak, never forget God the Lord of supreme joy. ||4||24||54|| Bilaaval, Fifth Master: The greed and false attachment disappeared. The affect of doubt went away. I have found peace and joy; the guru blessed me with faith. ||1|| Worshipping the perfect guru, my anguish is eradicated. My body and mind are soothed; I found peace, O brother. ||1||Pause|| I woke up reciting God and I was amazed. Drinking the nectar, I am satisfied. Its taste is beyond imagination. ||2|| I am liberated along with my companions my family and dynasty. Service to the guru is recognized in God's sacred court. ||3|| I am lowly, orphan, ignorant, worthless and without a virtue. Page 815 God blessed Nanak. God made him His servant. ||4||25||55|| Bilaaval, Fifth Master: God is the shelter of His devotees. They have nowhere else to go. O God, Your name is my power, realm, family and riches. ||1|| By his grace, God saves His servants. The slanderers rot slandering others; they are swallowed by devil of death. ||1||Pause|| The saints recite only one God's name, not anyone else. They offer their prayers to one Lord, who is pervading all places. ||2|| I have heard this old story spoken by the devotees. That, God cuts the wicked into pieces and honours His devotees. ||3|| Nanak speaks the true words, which are known to all. God's servants are under God's Protection. They have no fear. ||4||26||56|| Bilaaval, Fifth Master: God, who has all the power, cuts the worldly bonds. No other action will save me, O my Lord. Protect me by Your grace. ||1||

I have entered Your sanctuary, O perfect Lord of mercy. Those whom You protect, O Lord of the universe, are saved from the worldly trap. ||1||Pause|| He is enticed by Hope, doubt, corruption and emotional attachment. The false materialistic world abides in his mind. He forgot the supreme Lord. ||2|| O perfect Lord the supreme soul, all beings belong to You. As You keep us, so we live, O infinite, inaccessible God. ||3|| O Lord the cause of causes and all-powerful, please bless me with Your name. O Nanak, praising God in devotee's company attains salvation. ||4||27||57|| Bilaaval, Fifth Master: Is there anyone who has not attained salvation praising God? You are enticed by the great worldly enticer. This is the way to hell! ||1|| O vicious mind, you cannot be believe. You are totally intoxicated. The donkey's leash is removed after putting the load on his back. ||1||Pause|| You destroy the value of chanting, meditation and self-discipline; you shall suffer the beating of devil of death. Those who do not recite God suffer! They speak shameless words. ||2|| God is with you and a friend. You have differences with Him. You are in love with the five thieves; this brings terrible pain. ||3|| Nanak seeks the sanctuary of the saints who have conquered their mind. He offers his body, wealth and everything to God's servants. ||4||28||58|| Bilaaval, Fifth Master: Making an effort obtains joy and reciting God obtains eternal peace. Reciting the name of the Lord of the universe realizes divine wisdom. ||1|| I live by worshipping the lotus feet of the guru and reciting God. Worshipping the supreme Lord I drink the nectar. ||1||Pause|| All beings dwell in peace, the minds of all yearn for the Lord. Those who do good deeds all the time; nobody talks ill of them. ||2|| Page 816 The place where God's name is recited is admirable and blooms with fragrance. Hearing the sermon and God's praises brings peace, contentment and joy. ||3|| May I never forget the master of the orphans from my mind? Nanak seeks God's refuge. He has everything in His hand. ||4||29||59|| Bilaaval, Fifth Master: He who arrested and freed you offered you eternal peace. Contemplate His lotus feet forever and you shall be soothed. ||1|| In life or death, you are of no use. He created this creation, but only a few are dyed with His love. ||1||Pause|| O mortal, the Creator made summer and winter; He saves you from heat. From an ant, He makes an elephant. He reconnects the broken.

||2|| Eggs, wombs, sweat and earth – these are God's ways of creation. It brings full reward by reciting God with love forever. ||3|| I cannot do anything; O God, I seek the sanctuary of devotees. O guru; pull Nanak out of the enticing false love. ||4||30||60|| Bilaaval, Fifth Master: I searched all over including the forest for God. He is undeceived, imperishable, and inscrutable; such is my Lord. ||1|| When can I lovingly see my God? Seeing God in a dream is better than not seeing Him while awake. ||1||Pause|| Listen about God in shrines and Shaastras. But I yearn to see him. He has no form or outline. He is not made of five elements. He is immortal. ||2|| Some of God's devotees say the same thing. God meets them by His grace. God is admirable. ||3|| They know that He is inside and outside as well, their doubts are dispelled. O Nanak, those with good deeds realize God. ||4||31||61|| Bilaaval, Fifth Master: All beings are pleased seeing God's power and blessings. The true guru has paid off my debt on his own. ||1|| God is realized through guru's teachings to eat and spend. It never runs short. His gifts are plentiful. It never runs short. ||1||Pause|| Recite God the unfathomable and infinite treasure in the company of devotees. He does not hesitate to bless with faith, wealth, work and liberation. ||2|| The devotees worship the Lord of the universe single-mindedly. They gather the wealth of Lord's name, which cannot be estimated. ||3|| O God, I seek your sanctuary by your greatness. O Nanak, His limits cannot be found. The Lord is infinite. ||4||32||62|| Bilaaval, Fifth Master: Reciting the perfect Lord, my deeds are fulfilled. The Creator dwells in Kartaar pur (Godly town) with the saints. ||1||Pause|| Those who pray to the guru, face no hindrance. God the Lord of the universe is the saviour and the wealth of His devotees. ||1|| Page 817 There is never any shortage; Lord's treasures are always full. The lotus feet of immortal, infinite Lord are enshrined in my mind. ||2|| All those who work for Him dwell in peace. They do not lack anything. By the grace of the saints, I met God, the Lord of the universe. ||3|| Everyone celebrates there in the beautiful true home of the Lord. O Nanak, reciting priceless God's name through the guru attains peace. ||4||33||63|| Bilaaval, Fifth Master: Worship and adore the Lord and you shall be free of disease. This is Lord's healing stick, which eradicates all disease. ||1||Pause|| Worship God through

the perfect guru continuously and enjoy. Serving the company of devotees I realized God intuitively. ||1|| Contemplating Him, peace is obtained, and separation is ended. O Nanak, seek God's refuge, the all-powerful, the cause of causes. ||2||34||64|| Tune Bilaaval, Fifth Master, Du-Padas, Fifth House: God is one. He is realized by guru's grace. I abandoned all other efforts and took God's name as a cure. Fever, sins and all diseases are eradicated and my mind is soothed. ||1|| Worshipping the perfect guru, all pains are dispelled. The saviour saved me by His grace. ||1||Pause|| Taking me by the arm He took me out and accepted me on His own. Reciting God, my mind and body became happy and carefree. ||2||1||65|| Bilaaval, Fifth Master: Placing His Hand on my forehead, God bestowed me with His name. Serving the supreme lord is rewarding and never suffers any loss. ||1|| God saves the honour of His devotees. Whatever God's devotees want, He gives it. ||1||Pause|| God's servants seek the refuge at His lotus feet. They are God's love of life. O Nanak, they intuitively realize God and merge with Him. ||2||2||66|| Bilaaval, Fifth Master: God gave them the shelter of His lotus feet. God's servants seek His sanctuary by His grace. ||1|| The infinite God is the saviour, serving Him is rewarding. The guru built justifying village where the devotees live. ||1||Pause|| Recite God forever; hindrance will not come your way. O Nanak, praising God's name the enemies run away. ||2||3||67|| Bilaaval, Fifth Master: Worship God in your mind and body in the company of devotees. Saying the praises of the Lord of the universe the devil of death runs away seeing from a distance. ||1|| One who recites God's name remains awake forever. Page 818 He is not affected by charms and ritualistic stunts, they do not come close to him. ||1||Pause|| Lust, anger, intoxication of ego and emotional attachment are dispelled, by loving devotion. Those attuned to God with love in God's refuge, enjoy His essence. ||2||4||68|| Bilaaval, Fifth Master: The living creatures and their ways are in God's power. They do what He says. When the Lord of the universe is pleased, there is nothing to worry. ||1|| Missing God, the pain shall never afflict you. The pain of the devil of death does not come close to the beloved devotees of the Lord. ||1||Pause|| All-powerful Lord is the cause of causes; there is no other. O Nanak, put your mind devotionally to God's refuge. ||2||5||69|| Bilaaval, Fifth

Master: Reciting God, the sufferings ran away quickly. I attained peace joining devotee's company. I shall not wander anymore. ||1|| I praise my guru. I praise His feet. I am blessed with peace and happiness. I sing his praises as soon as I see him. ||1||Pause|| This is my life's purpose to talk and sing his praises in tunes with love. O Nanak, When God is happy, you obtain the fruit of your choice. ||2||6||70|| Bilaaval, Fifth Master: This is the prayer of Your slave, please enlighten me. By Your grace, O supreme Lord, please erase my sins. ||1|| I take shelter of Your lotus feet, O God, primal Lord, treasure of virtue. Sing praises and recite God's name as long as you live. ||1||Pause|| You are my mother, father and a relative; You abide in everyone. Nanak seeks God's refuge, praising Him purifies. ||2||7||71|| Bilaaval, Fifth Master: Reciting God obtains all mystic powers. Everyone wishes him well. Everyone calls him God's devotee. Hearing of him, God's devotees come to meet him. ||1|| The perfect guru blesses him with peace, poise, salvation and happiness. All living beings become kind to him and they recite God. ||1||Pause|| He is permeating and pervading everywhere. God is the ocean of virtue. O Nanak, the devotees are happy seeing God's support. ||2||8||72|| Bilaaval, Fifth Master: God, the great giver, became kind. He has listened to my prayer. He saved His servant and disgraced the slanderers. ||1|| You are God's servant O friend. No one will rob you. The supreme Lord protects you by His grace. ||1||Pause|| One Lord is the giver of all beings; there is no other; Nanak prays, You are my only strength O God. ||2||9||73|| Bilaaval, Fifth Master: The Lord of the universe has saved my friends and companions. The slanderers have died, so do not worry! ||1||Pause|| God fulfilled all hopes and desires. I met my guru. Page 819 God is celebrated all over the world, serving Him is rewarding. ||1|| God is Lofty, infinite and immeasurable. All beings are in His control. Nanak seeks His refuge. He is with me forever. ||2||10||74|| Bilaaval, Fifth Master: I worship the perfect guru. He became kind to me. The saint showed me the way and the noose of death is cut. ||1|| Singing God's name, my pain hunger and doubt have been dispelled. I attained contentment peace and joy All my deeds are fulfilled. ||1||Pause|| The fire of desire is extinguished and I became soothed. God protected me. O Nanak, seek His refuge. His blessing is great! ||2||11||75||

Bilaaval, Fifth Master: The place where it happens is beautiful and rewarding. My affairs are resolved. Reciting God's name my desire and doubt have departed. ||1|| Dwelling with the Holy people, one finds peace, poise and tranquility. When one recites God's name is the auspicious time. ||1||Pause|| They have become famous throughout the world. they walk with this honour. O Nanak, seek His refuge, who abides in every being. ||2||12||76|| Bilaaval, Fifth Master: God eradicated the disease. Peace and tranquility have welled up. The Lord blessed me with the gifts of greatness and amazing beauty. ||1|| The guru, the Lord of the universe became kind and preserved my honour o brother. I am under His protection. He is always my help and support. ||1||Pause|| The prayer of Lord's humble servant never goes in vain. Nanak is united with the Lord of the universe by His grace. ||2||13||77|| Bilaaval, Fifth Master: Those who forget the giver of life, die and reborn again and again. Those who worship Lord night and day remain imbued with His love. ||1|| They find peace contentment and great joy. Their desires are fulfilled. I found peace in devotee's company and praise the virtuous God. ||1||Pause|| O Lord the inner knower the master; please listen to Your servant's prayer. Nanak's Lord is pervading all high low places of interest. ||2||14||78|| Bilaaval, Fifth Master: No harm touches you in the refuge of the supreme Lord. I have God's protection circling around me. No pain will bother me O brother. ||1|| I have met the perfect true guru, who has done this deed. He gave me medicine of God's name and I enshrine God's love in my mind. ||1||Pause|| The saviour Lord has saved me and eradicated all my wandering around. Says Nanak, God became graceful and helped me. ||2||15||79|| Bilaaval, Fifth Master: The supreme Lord, my guru protected me his child by his grace. I obtained peace, contentment and happiness; my service is rewarded. ||1||Pause|| Page 820 God heard the prayers of His humble devotee. He eliminated my disease and rejuvenated me by His blessing. ||1|| He has forgiven my sins by exercising His power. He gave me the fruit of my choice. Nanak praises Him. ||2||16||80|| Tune Bilaaval, Fifth Master, Chau-Padas And Du-Padas, Sixth House: God is one. He is realized by guru's grace. O my beloved Lord; let me not listen to the faithless singing his songs and tunes saying useless words. ||1||Pause||

I serve God's devotees. I do this forever. I obtained the priceless gift from the primal Lord that I sing His praises in the company of devotees. ||1|| My tongue is imbued with God's praises forever. My eyes are focused on seeing Him with love. Be kind to the poor O destroyer of pain that I enshrine Your lotus feet in my heart. ||2|| I am the lowest of low, that is how I feel. Through guru's teachings my ego and pride are eradicated. ||3|| God the merciful and love of His devotees is immeasurable; cannot be weighed. Whoever enters the sanctuary of the guru O Nanak, is blessed with the gifts of fearlessness and peace. ||4||||1||81|| Bilaaval, Fifth Master: O dear God, You are the support of my life. I bow in humility and reverence to You. I am a sacrifice forever. ||1||Pause|| Sitting, standing, sleeping and waking, this mind thinks of You. I tell You my pleasure and pain, and the state of my mind. ||1|| You are my shelter, power, intellect and wealth. You are my family. Whatever You do, is good for me. Observing this Nanak is at peace in your refuge. ||2||2||82|| Bilaaval, Fifth Master: I have heard that God is the saviour of all. You make us forget the intoxication of worldly attachment and the company of sinners. ||1||Pause|| He collects poison and hoards it. He forgot the nectar from his mind. He is imbued with lust, anger, greed and slander; he has abandoned truth and contentment. ||1|| Pull me out of these, O my Lord. I have entered Your sanctuary. Nanak prays to God; please give the poor the company of devotees and save him. ||2||3||83|| Bilaaval, Fifth Master: I heard about God from the saints. Singing of God's sermon, praises and the songs of joy give happiness there day and night. ||1||Pause|| God made me his own by His grace and bestowed His name on me. Singing God's praise all day eliminates lust and anger from the body. ||1||Page 821 I am satisfied and satiated visualizing God. I eat and drink God's nectar with love. Nanak seeks Your refuge O God; be kind and unite me in devotee's company. ||2||4||84|| Bilaaval, Fifth Master: He has saved His humble servant. By His grace he bestowed His name on me. My sorrows and worries are eliminated. ||1||Pause|| Sing the praises of the Lord of the universe, O all humble servants of the Lord; sing the priceless songs of the Lord with your tongue. The desires of millions of lives, are eliminated reciting God with love. ||1|| I fell at the feet of the bestowal of peace and recite God through guru's teachings. Says Nanak; by God's blessing I have crossed over the world-ocean, and my doubt and fear are dispelled. ||2||5||85|| Bilaaval, Fifth Master: Through the guru the Creator; Lord has eliminated the fever. I praise my guru, who saved the honour of the whole world. ||1||Pause|| Placing His hand on child's forehead, He saved him. God blessed me with the supreme, sublime essence of God's name. ||1|| The merciful Lord saves the honour of His slave. O Nanak, guru's words are honoured in the court of the Lord. ||2||6||86|| Tune Bilaaval, Fifth Master, Chau-Padas And Du-Padas, Seventh House: God is one. He is realized by guru's grace. Guru's teachings are a lamp of enlightenment. It dispels the darkness from the body and opens the beautiful vault of jewels. ||1||Pause|| I was amazed seeing it; I cannot describe its greatness. I am intoxicated and enraptured with it and I am wrapped in it forever. ||1|| No worldly entanglements or traps can catch me, I have no ego. You are the highest of high, no curtain separates us; I am Yours, and You are mine. ||2|| One God, one creation and one infinite and unlimited God; One Lord fully pervades all; He is the support of every life. ||3|| He is pure, truly the purest of all. He has no end or limits; He is forever unlimited. Says Nanak, He is the highest of high. ||4||1||87|| Bilaaval, Fifth Master: Without the Lord, nothing is of any use. One you are attached to is the greatest enticer. ||1||Pause|| You shall leave your gold, woman and your beautiful bed behind and depart in an instant. You are entangled in joy of senses; you are cheated by sins. ||1|| You built, furnished and decorated a palace of straw; it will burn with fire. You sit in it with pride. What can you attain by bragging about it? ||2|| The five thieves hover over your head. They will catch you from your hair and take you away. Page 822 You do not see, you blind and ignorant; intoxicated with ego, you just keep sleeping. ||3|| As the birds are enticed by bait and get caught in the net. Says Nanak, I worship the primal being guru to cut my bonds. ||4||2||88|| Bilaaval, Fifth Master: Name of the Lord is infinite and priceless. He is the love of my life and support of my mind; I miss him as the betel leaf chewer remembers the betel leaf. ||1||Pause|| I obtained peace through guru's teachings and I am dyed by God's love. I the fortunate love my beloved Lord; my marriage is eternal. ||1|| I do not need any image, incense, perfume or lamps; I am glowing with love. Says Nanak, the soul bride is enlightened by husband Lord's love. My desires are fulfilled. ||2||3||89|| Bilaaval, Fifth Master: I say God God God by His grace. Since I met the kind devotees, my ill will disappeared. ||1||Pause|| The cool, calm, peaceful and kind Lord pervades everywhere. Lust, anger, greed and pride; all eradicated from my body. ||1|| Truth, contentment, compassion, faith and purity! I have received these from the teachings of the saints. Says Nanak, one who realizes this in his mind, achieves total understanding. ||2||4||90|| Bilaaval, Fifth Master: What are we the poor beings? We cannot describe anything about God. Even Brahma, Shiva, mystics, sages and kings, know nothing about You. ||1|| What can I tell? I am unable to tell anything. Wherever I look, I see the Lord pervading. ||1||Pause|| Where the pain of devil of death is heard; You are the support there O God. I seek Your refuge to hold Your feet O God. The guru taught this to Nanak. ||2||5||91|| Bilaaval, Fifth Master: O immovable, beautiful, imperishable Lord, purifier of sinners; may I worship You for a moment. I realized the amazing Lord by surrendering to the saint and enshrining his sacred feet in my mind! ||1|| In what way, and by what discipline, He is realized? Tell me, O wise man, by what means can we recite Him? ||1||Pause|| If one person serves another person, the one served stands by him. Nanak seeks Your refuge and protection, the ocean of peace; He seeks the shelter of Your name. ||2||6||92|| Bilaaval, Fifth Master: I serve the saint in his refuge. I got rid of all worldly concerns, bonds, entanglements and other affairs. ||1||Pause|| I obtained peace, poise and great bliss by obtaining God's name from the guru. Page 823 Such is the sublime essence of the Lord, that I cannot describe it. The perfect guru has turned me away from the world. ||1|| I see the beloved with everyone. No one is without Him. He pervades all. The perfect Lord, the treasure of mercy, abides everywhere. Says Nanak, my deeds are fulfilled. ||2||7||93|| Bilaaval, Fifth Master: My mind says something else and I say something else. You are wise, all-knowing, O God; what can I say to You? ||1||Pause|| You know even the unspoken, whatever is in the mind. O mind, why and how long will you cheat? God is with you; He sees and hears everything. ||1|| Knowing this, my mind has become blissful; I do not see anyone other than the Creator. Says Nanak, the guru became kind to me; my love for the Lord shall never wear off. ||2||8||94|| Bilaaval, Fifth Master: The slanderer falls like this. This is the sign. Listen, O brother: he collapses like a wall of mud. ||1||Pause|| Seeing badly; the slanderer enjoys. He feels pain seeing something good. Twenty-four hours a day, he plots, but nothing works. The evil man dies, constantly making evil plans. ||1|| The slanderer forgets God, death approaches him and he keeps arguing with the humble servant of the Lord. God is Nanak's protector. What can any ignorant man do to him? ||2||9||95|| Bilaaval, Fifth Master: Why do you wander lost like this? You act and incite others to act, and then deny it. God is always with you; He sees and hears everything. ||1||Pause|| You purchase glass, discard gold; you love your enemy and renounce your real friends. That which exists, seems bitter; that which does not exist, seems sweet to you. Occupied in corruption, you are burning! ||1|| The mortal has fallen in the deep, dark pit; he is entangled in the darkness of doubt and emotional attachment. Says Nanak, when God becomes kind; one meets with the guru, who takes him by the arm and pulls him out. ||2||10||96|| Bilaaval, Fifth Master: With my mind, body and tongue, I remember the Lord. I am happy, my anxieties are dispelled; the guru has blessed me with total peace. ||1||Pause|| By God's grace I the ignorant became wise. Giving His Hand, He saved me, now no one can harm me. ||1|| I praise seeing God's devotees; I recite God's name by his grace. Says Nanak, believing in God I do not believe anyone else at all. ||2||11||97|| Bilaaval, Fifth Master: The perfect guru saved my honour. He enshrined God's sacred name in my mind; my filth of many a life is washed away. ||1||Pause|| The demons and wicked enemies are driven away by reciting guru's teachings. Page 824 What can any creature do to me? God blessed me by His grace! ||1|| I attained peace reciting God enshrining His lotus feet in my mind. Slave Nanak has entered His sanctuary; no one is above Him. ||2||12||98|| Bilaaval, Fifth Master: Recite God's name forever. The pains of old age and death shall not afflict you; in God's court, your affairs will be settled easily. ||1||Pause| Forsake your ego and fall at guru's feet; receive this treasure from him. The noose of birth and death is cut; this is the sign of true court. ||1|| Whatever You do, I accept as good. I have eradicated pride from my mind. Says Nanak, I seek His protection that created the universe. ||2||13||99|| Bilaaval, Fifth Master: God dwells in my mind and body. One who continuously sings God's praises and does well for others; his tongue is priceless. ||1||Pause|| His dynasty is saved in an instant, and the filth of countless incarnations is washed away. Reciting God he passes blissfully through the forest of poison. ||1|| I have obtained the boat of God's feet and crossed the terrifying world-ocean. The saints, servants and devotees belong to God; Nanak's mind is attached to Him. ||2||14||100|| Bilaaval, Fifth Master I am satisfied seeing your amazing play. You are my Lord the inner-knower; You live with the devotees. ||1||Pause|| In an instant, the Lord establishes and blesses. From a lowly worm He makes a king. ||1|| May I never forget You from my heart; slave Nanak prays for this blessing. ||2||15||101|| Bilaaval, Fifth Master: The imperishable Lord is worthy of worship. I offer my mind and body to God, who looks after all beings. ||1||Pause|| His refuge is worthwhile, He is all-powerful; He is indescribable and bestowal of peace, the ocean of mercy and kindness. He embraces His devotees; no evil can touch them. ||1|| The merciful Lord is wealth, property and everything to His humble saints. Nanak the seeker begs for visualizing God and the dust of the feet of saints. ||2||16||102|| Bilaaval, Fifth Master: Reciting God is equal to millions of other efforts. He sings God's praises in devotee's company; devil of death does not scare him. ||1||Pause|| To enshrine God's feet in the mind and body attains everything you work for. Coming and going, doubt and fear have run away, and the sins of countless incarnations are burnt away. ||1|| Be free and worship the Lord of the universe. The fortunate attains this gift. Page 825 Be kind O perfect God the great giver, that slave Nanak may sing Your immaculate praises. ||2||17||103|| Bilaaval, Fifth Master: The Lord saved me from the demon. The demon did not succeed in his plot, he died in disgrace. ||1||Pause|| The Lord raised His axe and cut his head; in an instant, he was reduced to dust. ||1|| One who thinks bad of others, is destroyed by the bad thinking. The Creator pushes him there. Of his sons, friends and wealth, no one helped him; he departed, leaving behind all his brothers and relatives. Says Nanak, I praise God, who fulfilled the word of His slave. ||2||18||104|| Bilaaval, Fifth Master: Perfect is service of the perfect guru. Our Lord does everything. My guru resolved all my affairs. ||1||Pause|| God is from the beginning, in the middle and in the end. He created the creation. He saves His servant. Great is the blessing of my God! ||1|| The guru is supreme transcendent Lord; all beings are in His power. Nanak seeks the sanctuary of His lotus feet and recites God's name the pure sermon. ||2||19||105|| Bilaaval, Fifth Master: He protects me from suffering and sin. Falling at guru's feet, I am soothed; I recite God's name in my mind. ||1||Pause|| By His kindness God extended His Hand and saved the entire world by His power. My pain has been dispelled, and peace and pleasure have come; my greed extinguished, my mind and body are truly satisfied. ||1|| He is the master of orphans, all-powerful to protect in His sanctuary. He is the mother and father of the whole universe. He is the love of His devotees, the destroyer of fear; Nanak sings praises of his Lord lovingly. ||2||20||106|| Bilaaval, Fifth Master: Realize the One, from whom You originated. Reciting the supreme transcendent Lord, I found peace, pleasure and salvation. ||1||Pause|| I fortunately met the perfect guru the inner-knower wise the all-knowing Lord. He saved me by giving His Hand and made me His own. He is absolutely all-powerful, the honour of the dishonoured. ||1|| Doubt and fear have been dispelled in an instant; the light is lit in the dark. Nanak recites God with every breath. He praises Him forever. ||2||21||107|| Bilaaval, Fifth Master: Both here and hereafter, the mighty guru protects me. God looks after here and the next world. My affairs are settled. ||1||Pause|| Reciting God's name and bathing in the dust of devotee's feet attains peace and contentment. Coming and going have ended and I became immortal; the pains of birth and death are eradicated. ||1|| I crossed over the ocean of doubt and fear. The fear of death is gone; One God abides in every heart. Page 826 Nanak has entered the sanctuary of the destroyer of pain; I see Him in and outside as well. ||2||22||108|| Bilaaval, Fifth Master: Seeing his face the sufferings went away. Please, never be far from my eyes; You are always in my mind. ||1||Pause|| My beloved Lord the master is the support of life. God, the inner-knower, is all pervading. ||1|| Which of Your virtues should I contemplate and worship? With each and every breath, O God, I miss You. ||2|| God is the ocean of mercy, kind to the meek; He cherishes all beings. ||3|| Twenty-four hours a day, Your humble servant recites Your name. God inspired Nanak to love Him. ||4||23||109|| Bilaaval, Fifth Master: Body, wealth and youth are passing by. You did not recite God, did useless deeds and the time of death has come. ||1||Pause|| You eat many type of food daily, your face tired and teeth are worn out. Deluded by possessiveness o ignorant you commit sins, never show mercy. ||1|| O ignorant, you have fallen in the terrible ocean of sufferings. Nanak took God's refuge; He took me by the arm and pulled me out. ||2||24||110|| Bilaaval, Fifth Master: I miss my God. My enemies and evil people are tired of talking nonsense but I am at peace o brother my friend. ||1||Pause|| The disease and misfortunes have departed by God's grace. I found peace, comfort and total bliss, enshrining my beloved's Name in the mind. ||1|| My soul, body and wealth are all Yours O God, You are my all-powerful Lord. You are the protector of Your slaves; slave Nanak is Your slave forever. ||2||25||111|| Bilaaval, Fifth Master: Reciting God's name I am saved. Suffering eradicated, peace obtained by reciting the inner knower. ||1||Pause|| He made all beings comfortable. He is the strength of His devotees. He preserves His servant's honour. The servant is proud of the destroyer of fear. ||1|| I found friendship, erased ill will. God screened out the evil. Nanak obtained comfort contentment and eternal bliss. He lives by singing God's praises. ||2||26||112|| Bilaaval, Fifth Master: The supreme Lord has become kind. The guru completed all affairs. The devotees are happy reciting God. ||1||Pause|| God protected me; all enemies are reduced to dust. He embraces His devotees and bestows salvation attaching them to Him. ||1||Page 827 I returned home safe and sound. Faces of the slanderers are painted black. Says Nanak, my guru is perfect; by guru's grace I am happy O God; ||2||27||113|| Bilaaval, Fifth Master: I have fallen in love with my beloved Lord. ||Pause|| It cannot be cut or released O Lord; I am tied so much by love; ||1|| Day and night, He lives in my mind O God by Your grace. ||2|| I admire the beloved Lord by hearing His untold sermon. ||3|| Says Nanak the servant of servants; be kind to me O God. ||4||28||114|| Bilaaval, Fifth Master: I praise and worship God's feet. My guru is the supreme transcendent Lord; I enshrine Him in my heart. ||1||Pause|| Recite the name of bestowal of peace, who created the whole world. Say God from your tongue and attain honour in true court. ||1|| Those who join devotee's company find this treasure. Nanak sing's God's praises all the time; O Lord; be kind to me. ||2||29||115|| Bilaaval, Fifth Master: The guru saved me in his refuge. I am applauded throughout the world that my Lord saved me. ||1||Pause|| The caretaker Lord, giver of peace, fulfills the deeds of the whole world. He perfectly abides everywhere including places of importance. I touch His feet with admiration. ||1|| The ways of all beings are in Your power, O all powerful Lord the cause of causes. God saves from the beginning from ages. Fear does not bother reciting God O Nanak. ||2||30||116|| Tune Bilaaval, Fifth Master, Du-Padas, Eighth House: God is one. He is realized by guru's grace. I am nothing; everything is Yours O God; You are absolute here and manifest in the world after. My Lord enjoys both worlds. ||1||Pause|| He is in and out of the body as well. He is omnipresent. He is the king and the subjects, master and the disciple as well. ||1|| He plays hide and seek, wherever I look he is close by. Nanak surrendered to God's devotee and merged with him like water in water. ||2||1||117|| Bilaaval, Fifth Master: Page 828 You are all-powerful and cause of causes. Please cover my sins O Lord of the universe my guru; I am a sinner. I humbly seek your refuge. ||1||Pause|| Whatever we do, You see and know; there is no chance to deny. I hear a lot about Your blessing. Reciting Your name eradicates all sins. ||1|| It is my nature to make mistakes; it is Your nature to save the sinners. You are the embodiment of kindness, the treasure of compassion, O kind Lord, bestowal of life; may Nanak visualize You. ||2||2||118|| Bilaaval, Fifth Master: Bless me with such kindness O Lord; May I see the saint and put my head at his feet and body in his dust. ||1||Pause|| May I enshrine God's name in my mind through guru's teachings. May I scare the five thieves and burn away all doubts O God; ||1|| Whatever You do, I accept as good; may my duality go away. You are Nanak's God, save me in devotee's company O Lord; ||2||3||119|| Bilaaval, Fifth Master: I beg for such awns from Your humble servants. May I miss You with love. May I be with You and serve You. ||1||Pause|| May I serve your servants intuitively and stay with them forever. I apply the dust of the feet of His humble servants to my forehead; my hopes, and many waves of desire, are fulfilled. ||1|| Praising God's devotees makes one pure; touching his feet is as good as bathing million times in river Ganges. Nanak bathes in the dust of the feet of His humble servants; the sins of many a life are eliminated. ||2||4||120|| Bilaaval, Fifth Master: Keep me as You please O kind Lord. O guru the supreme transcendent Lord, I am your child, You are my father. ||1||Pause|| I am worthless; I have no virtue. I cannot understand Your actions. You only know Your state and extent. My soul, body and property are all Yours. ||1|| You the inner-knower the primal Lord; know all unspoken words. My body and mind are soothed O Nanak, by God's grace. ||2||5||121|| Bilaaval, Fifth Master: Keep me with You forever, O God. You are my beloved the enticer; without You my life is useless. ||1||Pause|| In an instant, You make a beggar to a king. My God is the master of orphans. You save Your servants from the burning fire; You protect them by Your grace. ||1|| Reciting God attains peace of mind and contentment and all struggles end. O Nanak, serve the treasure of divine wealth and give up all smart ideas. ||2||6||122||Page 829 Bilaaval, Fifth Master: May you never forget Your servant, O Lord? May I embrace You O Lord and talk about our previous love. ||1||Pause|| It is Your nature to save the sinners; please do not remember my sins. You are my life, wealth and happiness; burn my curtain of ego. ||1|| How can a fish live without water and a child without milk? Servant Nanak longs for Lord's lotus feet; seeing You attains peace O Lord. ||2||7||123|| Bilaaval, Fifth Master: I see happiness here, and hereafter. The perfect guru performed his deed and saved me by God's grace. ||1||Pause|| The Lord, my beloved, abides in my mind and body; all my pain and sufferings are eradicated. I sing His praises in peace, contentment and bliss, my evil enemies are destroyed. ||1|| God did not consider my merits and demerits; He made me His own by His grace. God's greatness is beyond measure, He is immovable and imperishable; Nanak says hail to the Lord; ||2||8||124|| Bilaaval, Fifth Master: How can one attain salvation without love and worship? Be kind O saviour of sinners; protect me by believing in me. ||1||Pause|| I do not know how to worship you, I am intoxicated with liquor and deluded by filth like a dog. My life is going by, attached more and more to the worldly wealth I commit sins, I am drowning. ||1|| I seek the refuge of the destroyer of sufferings the formless Lord. I recite Your name as the devotees do in the congregation. O Lord the destroyer of serious sufferings, Nanak lives by visualizing You. ||2||9||125|| Tune Bilaaval, Fifth Master, Du-Padas, Ninth House: God is one. He is realized by guru's grace. He unites us with Him by His grace. Since I came to Your sanctuary, my sins vanished. ||1||Pause|| Renouncing self – pride and other anxieties, I sought devotee's refuge. Reciting Your name O beloved, my sickness is eradicated. ||1|| Even utterly ignorant and thoughtless persons have been saved by the Kind Lord. Says Nanak; surrendering to the perfect guru, my coming and going ended; ||2||1||126|| Bilaaval, Fifth Master: I live by listening to Your name. When the perfect guru became pleased, then my hopes were fulfilled. ||1||Pause|| Pain is gone, my mind is comforted; the music of harmony fascinates me. The yearning to meet my beloved God has welled up. I cannot live without Him, even for an instant. ||1||Page 830 You saved many devotees and humble servants; many sages worship You. O Nanak, singing God's praises the blind gets support, the poor gets wealth. ||2||2||127|| Tune Bilaaval, Fifth Master, Thirteenth House, Partaal: God is one. He is realized by guru's grace. O beloved I cannot sleep; I sigh. I wear necklaces, beautiful clothes ornaments and make-up. I am sad, sad and sadder. When will You come home? ||1||Pause|| I seek refuge of the happy soul-bride and I place my head on her feet. Unite me with my beloved; When will He come home? ||1|| She says listen my friend; I tell you the way to meet the beloved! Eradicate ego; then you shall find your beloved Lord in your heart. Then, in delight, you sing the songs of joy and praise. Recite God the embodiment of bliss. Nanak came to Lord's door; Then I found my beloved. ||2|| The enticing Lord has revealed His beauty to me. Now, sleep seems sweet to me. My thirst is quenched; Now, I am absorbed in peace. The story of my Husband Lord is sweet. I have found my beloved, enticing Lord. ||Second Pause||1||128|| Bilaaval, Fifth Master: My ego is gone by visualizing Him. I am absorbed in my Lord the help and support of the saints. Now, I have fallen to His feet. ||1||Pause|| My mind does not think anything else but to live at His feet. I am entangled like the bumblebee with flowers for honey. I do not desire any other taste; I seek only one Lord. ||1|| I broke away from others, my coming and going ended. O mind, tie God's sublime essence in devotee's company and change; There is no other, other than God. O Nanak, touch and love the feet of the Lord. ||2||2||129|| Tune Bilaaval, Ninth Master, Du-Padas: God is one. He is realized by guru's grace. The name of the Lord is the dispeller of sorrow, know this; Reciting God, even Ajaamal the sinner and Ganakaa the prostitute were liberated; let your soul know this. ||1||Pause|| The elephant's thirst vanished in an instant, as soon as he said God. Says Naarad; listen O child Dhroo; get absorbed in God's worship. ||1|| He obtained the immovable, immortal and eternal state; the world was amazed. Says Nanak; the Lord the protector of His devotees is very close. ||2||1|| Bilaaval, Ninth Master: Without the name of God, you shall suffer in pain. Without worship, doubt is not dispelled; the guru reveals this secret. ||1||Pause|| What use are pilgrimages and fasting without seeking God's refuge? Page 831 Yoga and sacrificial feasts are fruitless if one forgets the praises of God. ||1|| Renounce pride and worldly attachment and sing God's praises. Says Nanak, one who does this attains salvation. ||2||2|| Bilaaval, Ninth Master: Those who do not worship God; They waste their life uselessly; keep this in mind. ||1||Pause|| He goes to pilgrimage and keeps fast but his mind is out of control. That faith is useless; I speak the truth. It's like a stone kept in water; still, the water does not penetrate it. The person who is without God's worship; think him the same. ||2|| In today's age the salvation attains by reciting God's name. Guru explains the secret. Says Nanak, he who sings God's praises is a great man. ||3||3|| Bilaaval, Ashtapadees, First Master, Tenth House: God is one. He is realized by guru's grace. He lives close by and sees all. Only a few guru-willed realize this. Without the fear of God, His worship cannot be performed. Imbued with guru's teachings attains peace forever. ||1|| Such is the wisdom of reciting priceless God's name. The guru-willed attains honour by reciting God with love. ||1||Pause|| Everyone talks about divine wisdom. They keep arguing by talking and suffer in pain. No one stops talking and discussing. Without being imbued with the subtle essence, there is no liberation. ||2|| Spiritual wisdom and contemplation all come from the guru. Through true practice the mind becomes true. The self-willed talks about it, but does not practice it. Forgetting God's name, he finds no place of rest. ||3|| The worldly pleasure has caught the mind in a trap of the whirlpool. Each and every heart is trapped by the poison and sin. Whoever has come is subject to death. Your affairs shall be resolved by enshrining God in the mind. ||4|| He who is attuned to guru's teachings is a learned one. The self-willed, egotistic loses his honour. The Creator inspires us to His worship. He bestows honour to the guru-willed. ||5|| The night is dark, the divine light is pure. Those without God's name are lowly and unworthy of dealing with. The Vedas preach sermons of devotional worship. Listening hearing and believing, one gets enlightened. ||6|| The Shaastras and Simritees speak of reciting God's name. The guru-willed attain peace doing this sacred deed. The self-willed suffers the pains of rebirth. His bonds are broken, enshrining God's name in the mind. ||7|| Believing in God's name is the true honourable worship. Who should I see? There is none other than the Lord. I see and I say that He is pleasing to my mind. Says Nanak, there is no other as such. ||8||1|| Page 832 Bilaaval, First Master: The mind says and human does. This mind talks about good and bad. Intoxicated with worldly pleasure does not attain satisfaction. Satisfaction and liberation require the truthful mind. ||1|| He is proud seeing the body wealth and family. But other than God's name nothing goes with you. ||1||Pause|| He enjoys tastes, pleasures and joys in his mind. The wealth will pass on to others and body will be reduced to ashes. The entire creation shall mix with dust. Without guru's teachings the filth does not go away. ||2|| The various songs, tunes and rhythms are false. Created in the three qualities, people go far away after death. In duality, the pain of evil-deeds does not leave them. But the guru-willed are saved taking medicine of singing God's praises. ||3|| He wears a clean loincloth, applies mark on the forehead, and wears a rosary around his neck; He is full of anger and yet performs like a juggler. Forgetting God's name, he is intoxicated by worldly pleasure. Without worshipping the guru, there is no peace. ||4|| He is like a pig, a dog, a donkey, a cat; He is like a beast, a filthy, lowly and wicked. He who turns away from the guru wanders in different lifes. Bound in bonds, he comes and goes. ||5|| Serving the guru, the treasure is found. Enshrining God's name in the mind is always rewarding; Nobody questions him in God's court.

One, who obeys Lord's command, is approved at Lord's door. ||6|| Meeting the true guru, one realizes the Lord. Obeying God's will, one realizes His command. Realizing God's command he dwells in the court of the true Lord. Through guru's teachings, death and birth are ended. ||7|| He knows that everything belongs to God. He offers his body and mind to the one who owns them. He does not come, he does not go. O Nanak, the truthful merges in the true Lord. ||8||2|| Bilaaval, Third Master, Ashtapadees, Tenth House: God is one. He is realized by guru's grace. The world is like a crow; with its beak, it croaks divine wisdom. He is filled with greed, falsehood and pride. Without God's name, your secret will be known. ||1|| Serving the guru, God's name dwells in the mind. Meeting the guru, God's name comes to mind. Without the name, other love is false. ||1||Pause|| Do what the guru tells you to do. Contemplating guru's teachings attains peace. Through the true name, you shall obtain honour. ||2|| He does not understand yet preaches others. He is mentally blind, and does blind acts. How can he find home, a place of rest, and reach the destiny? ||3|| Serve the dear Lord, the inner-knower; His light shines in everyone. Why should anyone follow the disgraced? ||4|| Page 833 The true name is realized through true guru's teachings. Realizing God eliminates ego and pride. The guru-willed always recite God's name. ||5|| Serving the true guru, duality and evil-will goes away. Guilty deeds are eradicated and the sinful intellect is erased. The priceless body and soul merge with supreme soul. ||6|| Meeting with the guru, attains great honour. Pain is taken away by enshrining God's name in the mind. Imbued with God's name attains eternal peace. ||7|| Obeying guru's teachings is essence of all good deeds. Obeying guru's teachings obtains salvation. O Nanak, obeying guru's teachings saves the family as well. ||8||1||3|| Bilaaval, Fourth Master, Ashtapadees, Eleventh House: God is one. He is realized by guru's grace. Self-surrendering eliminates ego, the devotee sings God's praises forever. The guru-willed understands the priceless body; his soul merges with carefree divine soul. ||1|| God's name is my support and resolve. The guru-willed cannot live without God's name. I say God God. ||1||Pause|| That house has ten doors and the thieves always keep stealing. They steal the entire true wealth. The blind self-willed cannot see. ||2|| The golden body is full of jewels. It is realized through divine wisdom and love. The thieves and robbers hide in the body; they are arrested through guru`s teachings. ||3|| God`s name is the ship the boat. Guru`s teachings is the oars to take across. The tax collector devil of death does not come close; the thieves do not steal. ||4|| I sing God`s praises continuously day and night. I just keep singing. The mind of the guru-willed goes to God`s home; meeting the Lord the minstrel declares by beating the drum. ||5|| Seeing his face and listening to guru`s lesson my mind gets satisfied. Listening and reciting with joy my beloved Lord is delighted. ||6|| The universal worldly pleasure is enticing. The guru-willed eliminate the worldly virtues. Seeing everything with one eye, the devotee sees the whole creation. ||7|| God`s name abides in every soul. God does this by his grace. O Nanak, the merciful God became kind to the humble and the devotee merged with God`s name through devotional worship. ||8||1||4|| Bilaaval, Fourth Master: Recite God`s soothing name. God is full of scent like sandalwood. Page 834 Joining devotee's congregation attains supreme status. I am just a castor-oil tree, made fragrant by their association. ||1|| By reciting the name of the Lord the master, the Lord of the creation; Those humble beings who seek Lord's sanctuary are saved like Prahlaad; they are emancipated and merge with the Lord. ||1||Pause|| Of all plants, the sandalwood tree is the most sublime. Everything near the sandalwood tree becomes fragrant like sandalwood. The false faithless and egotistic are dried up; the proud are separated from God and go far from God. ||2|| Only the Creator knows His state and wisdom; he is the Creator. One who meets the true guru is transformed. The pre-ordained destiny cannot be erased. ||3|| Through guru`s teachings the treasure of jewels is found in the ocean and the treasure of divine worship opens. One feeling originated in guru`s refuge that I am not fulfilled saying God`s praises. ||4|| Reciting God all the time the mind is detached forever. I say God`s praises with love. I say God every moment but God does not take me across. I am still far away. ||5|| The Shaastras, the Vedas and the Puraanas advise faith and good deeds. The hypocrites, self-willed are ruined by doubt; in the waves of greed, their boat is heavily loaded, and sinks. ||6|| Reciting God`s name attains salvation.

The scriptures say so. Eradicating ego one becomes pure. The guru-willed attains salvation through divine wisdom. ||7|| This world is Your colour and form. As You ask us, so we do. O Nanak, the mortal play as they are played. What pleases God; we follow. ||8||2||5|| Bilaaval, Fourth Master: The guru-willed recites the inaccessible, unfathomable Lord. I admire the true guru the true primal being. He brought God`s name in my life; I am absorbed in God`s name through guru`s teachings. ||1|| Name of the Lord is the only support of His humble servant. I followed the guru and by his grace I found God`s door. ||1||Pause|| The body is the field of deeds; the guru-willed churn and take out the essence. The priceless jewel is realized through God`s name. It is found through intuitive love. ||2|| God`s worshippers become the slave of slaves. I offer my mind and body to the guru. I realized the unknown by guru`s grace. ||3|| The self-willed is troubled by love of worldly pleasure. His mind burns in thirst of greed. I obtained the sacred water through guru`s teachings. Guru`s teachings extinguished the fire of greed. ||4|| My mind dances in front of the guru to the tune of divine music. Page 835 I praise God day and night, moving my feet to God's beat. ||5|| Imbued with the Lord's love, my mind sings His praises joyfully through guru's teachings. The sacred stream flows there, whoever drinks finds happiness. ||6|| The egotistic does stubborn deeds like a child building a sand castle. When ocean waves come, destroy the sand castle in a moment. ||7|| God is the pool the ocean. He set this worldly play. As the wave merges in water again, O Nanak, so does he merge in Him. ||8||3||6|| Bilaaval, Fourth Master: My mind wears the earrings of guru's wisdom. Guru's teachings eliminate the filth of the body. I became immortal in devotee's company. Birth and death are eliminated. ||1|| O my mind; remain united with devotee's company. Be kind O Lord; may I wash Your devotee's feet all the time. ||1||Pause|| Abandoning family life he lives in the forest, but his mind does not remain at rest, even for an instant. Wandering mind then returns home and falls at God's devotee's feet. ||2|| The, renunciate abandoned his children but the hope of mind became prominent. Hope does not end with more hope, but through guru's teachings one finds joy of detachment. ||3|| When he feels, he removes clothes and becomes renunciate but mind wanders in ten directions. He wanders around, but greed does not end. Meeting the company of devotees he became kind. ||4|| He learned many mystic postures because he wants mystic powers; Satisfaction, contentment and tranquility do not come close to him. Meeting God's devotees reciting God's name is the reality. ||5|| Life is born from the egg, womb, sweat and earth; God created the beings of all colours and forms. One who seeks devotee's refuge attains salvation belonging to any caste; ||6|| The likes of Naam Dev, Jai Dev, Kabeer, Trilochan and Ravi Daas the leather-worker; all low caste; Whoever joins devotee's company like Dhanna Jaat and Sain obtained God's blessing. ||7|| God protects His saint's honour! This is His natural way of saving. Nanak has entered the sanctuary of the Lord, the life of the world, who showered His kindness and saved him. ||8||||4||7|| Bilaaval, Fourth Master: The thirst for God has welled up in me; listening to guru`s teachings my mind is pierced by his arrow. Page 836 Only the mind knows the state of mind. No one knows the pain of others. ||1|| The Lord, the guru, the enticer, has enticed my mind. Seeing the guru amazes me. I am enjoying it the utmost. ||1||Pause|| I wander all over the world, I yearn to see God. I sacrifice my mind and body to the guru, who has shown me the way to God. ||2|| If someone brings me news of God; He looks sweet to my heart, mind and body. I cut my head and place it under his feet, who unites me with God. ||3|| Let us go, my friend and find God; singing his praises realizes Him. He is called the love of His devotees; let us follow in the footsteps of those who seek God's sanctuary. ||4|| God bestows kindness; the mind gets enlightened by guru's teachings. One who enjoys God with love; I offer him every piece of my body and mind. ||5|| I made God my necklace; I wear God as ornament in my mind with love. I spread my bed in God's love. I cannot abandon Him, He pleases me a lot. ||6|| God says one thing, I do another thing; All makeup is a waste in argument. She adorns her to meet God but God takes only the virtuous as a bride and virtueless is spat upon. ||7|| I am Your devotee and You are inaccessible Lord. What can I do; I am under Your control. O kind Lord to the meek, save me; Nanak has entered the sanctuary of the Lord the guru. ||8||5||8|| Bilaaval, Fourth Master: My mind and body are filled with love of immortal

God. My mind bows in respect to Him every moment. Meeting the guru my hope is fulfilled like the rain bird stops crying when a drop of rain falls in his mouth. ||1|| Join with me O my friend and teach me the sermon of the Lord. By gurus grace one meets God. I will cut and put my head in front of him. ||1||Pause|| In every pour of my body I have this pain; I cannot sleep without seeing God. The doctors and healers are wonderstruck; God's love is the pain of my mind and body. ||2|| I cannot live for a moment without my beloved like an addict without the drug. Those who thirst for God; Other than God nothing else pleases them. ||3|| If someone would come and unite me with God; I will admire him forever. After being separated for many a life I am united with God when I truly entered guru's refuge. ||4|| Page 837 The soul-bride and the Lord share the same bed; the self-willed is lost in doubt. If one seeks His refuge saying guru guru; is united with God in no time. ||5|| Some do rituals to impress others. They are evil and greedy. When a son is born to a prostitute, what is his father's name? ||6|| Because of worship in previous life, I worship God by guru's grace. Worshipping by enshrining God's name in the mind I realized God. ||7|| God came and ground the henna and applied it to my hands and feet. O Nanak, those whom God is kind; he pulls them out taking by the arm. ||8||6||9||2||1||6||9|| Tune Bilaaval, Fifth Master, Ashtapadees, Twelfth House: God is one. He is realized by guru's grace. I cannot express the praises of my God. I have abandoned all others and took to His refuge. ||1||Pause|| God's lotus feet are infinite. I praise them forever. My mind is in love with them. I do not leave and go anywhere else. ||1|| I say God's name with my tongue. Filth of my sins and evil deeds is burnt away. Boarding the boat of the saints, I am saved. I have been carried across the terrifying world-ocean. ||2|| My mind is tied to the Lord with the string of love and devotion. This is the real way of the saints. They forsake sin and corruption. They met the formless God. ||3|| Visualizing God, I am wonderstruck. By tasting the perfect flavour; I do not waver here or there. God abides in my mind. ||4|| Those who recite Your virtues O God; do not go to hell. Those enticed by the divine music; do not have to see the devil of death. ||5|| I seek the sanctuary of the Lord, the brave Lord of the world. The merciful Lord is under the control of His devotees.

Vedas do not know the mystery of the Lord. The sages constantly serve Him. ||6|| He is the destroyer of pains and sorrows of the poor. It is very difficult to serve Him. No one knows His limits. He is pervading the water, the land and the sky. ||7|| Pray and bow to Him millions of times. I am tired and finally came to God's court. O God, make me the dust of the feet of devotees. Please fulfill this Nanak's wish. ||8||1|| Bilaaval, Fifth Master: O God, please release me from birth and death. Finally I am at Your door. I humbly joined the company of devotees. The love of the Lord is sweet to my mind. Page 838 Be kind and attach me to Your lap. O Nanak, recite God's name. ||1|| O merciful master of the meek, You are my Lord O master. I yearn for the dust of the feet of the saints. ||1||Pause|| The world is a pit of poison; It is filled with greed ignorance and emotional attachment. Please take my hand, and save me, O dear God. Please bless me with Your name; Without You O God, I have no place to go. O Nanak, admire Him with love. ||2|| The human body is gripped by greed and attachment. Without God's worship, it will be reduced to ashes. The messenger of death is scary. The secretive accountant knows your deeds. Day and night, they tell God's stories. O Nanak, seek the sanctuary of the Lord. ||3|| O Lord, destroyer of fear and ego; Be merciful and save the sinner. My sins cannot be counted. Without the Lord, where can I hide them? I took Your support O Lord. Please, give Nanak Your hand and save him! ||4|| The Lord, the treasure of virtue, the Lord of the world; Looks after all beings; My mind is in love and thirsty of visualizing You. O Lord of the universe, please, fulfills my hopes. I cannot survive without You even for a moment. By great fortune, Nanak has found the Lord. ||5|| I have none without You O God. My mind loves You, as the Greek – partridge loves the moon; As fish loves water; As the bee and the lotus cannot be separated; As the chakvi (duck) bird longs for the sun; So does Nanak, thirsty for Lord's feet. ||6|| As the young bride is the love of husband's life. As the greedy looks for the gift of wealth; As milk mixes with water; As food to the hungry; As the mother loves her son; So does Nanak constantly recite God all the time; ||7|| As the moth dies burning by the lamp; As the thief steals without hesitation; As the elephant is trapped by lust; As the sinner is caught in sins; As the gambler's addiction does not leave him; So does Nanak attach his mind to God; ||8|| As the deer loves the sound; As the rain bird longs for rain; As Lord's humble servant lives in the society of saints; They recite God with love. My tongue says the name of the Lord. Please bless Nanak with the gift of visualizing You; ||9|| One who sings the praises of the Lord and writes them by hearing. Receives all fruits from the Lord; He saves his entire dynasty and crosses over the world-ocean; Lord's feet are the boat to carry him across. Join the company of devotees and sing the praises of the Lord. The Lord protects his honour. Nanak seeks the sanctuary of Lord's door. ||10||2|| Bilaaval, First Master, T'hitee ~ The Lunar Days, Tenth House, Beat Jati: God is one. He is realized by guru's grace. The first day: One universal Creator is unique; Immortal, beyond birth, social class or any involvement; He is forever and unfathomable, with no form or feature. By searching, I saw Him in each and every heart. Page 839 I admire those who see God and visualize God to me. By guru's grace, I have obtained the supreme status. ||1|| Who else can I worship but the Lord of the universe? I see the destiny through guru's teachings. ||1||Pause|| Those attached to duality repent in the end; They are tied up at death's door and continue coming and going. What can anyone bring or take with them? The devil of death hovers over their head and they are beaten. No one is freed without guru's teachings. Practicing hypocrisy, no one finds liberation. ||2|| The true Lord created the universe, combining the elements together. Breaking the egg, He unites and separates. He made the earth and the sky the place to live. He created day and night with intent. One, who created the creation, also watches over it. There is no other Creator. ||3|| The third day: He created Brahma, Vishnu and Shiva; The gods, goddesses in many forms; Their creeds and forms cannot be counted. One, who fashioned them, knows their value. He evaluates and totally pervades all. Who is close or far away? ||4|| The fourth day: He created the four Vedas; The four sources of creation and distinct forms of sermon. He created the eighteen Puraanas, six Shaastras and the three qualities. Whom the Lord causes to understand; realizes it; The world is enticed by three qualities but salvation comes in fourth state. Prays Nanak, I am his slave; ||5|| The fifth day: the five passions are demons. God is forever and detached. Some are gripped by doubt, hunger, emotional attachment and desire. Some taste the sublime essence of guru's teachings and are satisfied. Some are imbued with Lord's love, while some die and reduced to dust. Some attain the destiny and visualize God. ||6|| The false has no honour, fame or name; Like the black crow, he never becomes pure. He is like the bird, kept in a cage; Walking back and forth in the cage does not attain liberation. He is liberated when the master liberates him. He attains liberation through guru's teachings by worshipping God. ||7|| The sixth day: God organized the six systems of worship. The divine music plays there uniquely. If God wills then one is summoned to His palace. One who contemplates guru's teachings obtains honour. Those who make false pretences burn, and are ruined. The truthful merge in the true Lord. ||8|| The seventh day: When the body is imbued with truth and contentment; The seven seas are filled with pure water. Bathing in peace contemplating the true Lord in the heart; Everyone attains salvation through guru's teachings. When the mind is true the truth comes out of the mouth. The truthful meets no hindrance. ||9|| The eighth day: The eight mystic powers are subdued. He does good deeds. Forgets the affect of wind, water and fire; Formless Lord's name dwells there. The devotee's mind merges with it lovingly. Prays Nanak, that he will not be consumed by death; ||10|| The ninth day: God's praise abides in nine continents. Almighty God abides in everyone. Page 840 This whole world is sacred. Listen to God's discourse that protects all forever. He was in the beginning, for ages, now and will always be. He is beyond comprehension and capable of doing everything. ||11|| The tenth day: recite God, give awns and take purifying bath. Night and day, bathe in spiritual wisdom and virtues of the true Lord. Truth cannot be polluted; doubt and fear run away from it. The flimsy thread breaks in an instant. Know that the world is just like the thread. Be content and enjoy the love of God. ||12|| The eleventh day: Enshrine God in your heart. Eradicate cruelty, ego and emotional attachment. Earn the fruitful rewards, by observing the fast of knowing yourself. Engrossed in hypocrisy, does not realize the truth. The Lord is flawless, self-sustaining and unattached. The pure, true Lord cannot be polluted. ||13|| Wherever I look, I see one God;

He created the other beings in many forms and shapes. Eating the fruits finishes the fruit. Eating all kind of delicacies one loses the true taste. In fraud and greed, people are absorbed and entangled. The guru-willed is liberated by practicing truth. ||14|| The twelfth day: eliminate the useless deeds. Remain awake day and night, never sleep. He remains awake lovingly attuned to God. With faith in the guru, he is not consumed by death. Those who become detached, conquer the five enemies Prays Nanak, they are lovingly absorbed in the Lord. ||15|| The twelfth day: be kind and give awns. One, you think is outside; realize Him inside. Observe the fast of remaining free of desire. Recite God's recital with your mouth. Know that there is one God in the universe. Realize purity contentment and truth. ||16|| The Thirteenth Day: He is like a tree on the seashore. The roots are nectar and the top attuned to love attains salvation. One, who is fearful of God, does not drown; The fearless of God drown and lose honour. He, who fears in the mind, realizes God in the mind. Enshrining true Lord in the mind attains salvation. ||17|| Fourteenth Day: One enters the fourth state; Eliminates the greed and ego and merges in truth. Then the sun enlightens the moon. One realizes the value of the process of worship. He pervades the fourteen worlds, underworld, galaxies and universe. ||18|| On fifteenth day; the new moon day! Moon hides in the sky. O wise man; realize God contemplating guru's teachings. The moon in the sky illuminates the three worlds. Creating the creation, the Creator tests it for quality. Seeing guru sees God. The self-willed are lost and keep coming and going. ||19|| God builds the house and the door and looks adorable in it. One who realizes him meets the guru. Where there is hope, there is destruction and desolation. The bowl of duality and selfishness breaks. Prays Nanak, I am their servant who burn away the false attachment and become detached. ||20||1|| Page 841 Bilaaval, Third Master, The Seven Days, Tenth House: God is one. He is realized by guru's grace. On Sunday: First the Lord the Primal Being came into existence. He is all pervading Lord; no other. Through and through, He is woven into the fabric of the world. Whatever the Creator does, happens. Imbued with His name attains eternal happiness. Only a few guru-willed realize Him. ||1|| Make your mind the rosary and recite God's virtues with it. God is forever, unfathomable and unlimited. Be the servant of servants and recite God. ||1||Pause|| Monday: The true Lord is permeating and pervading all. His value cannot be described. Many have said this focusing their mind. Whom God gives, realizes this. The immortal God cannot be described. Through guru's teachings, one merges with God. ||2|| Tuesday: The Lord created the worldly love and worldly wealth. He put everyone to their deeds. He understands; whom the Lord causes to understand. Through guru's teachings, one realizes destiny. He worships the Lord in loving worship. His ego and worldly attachment are eliminated through guru's teachings. ||3|| Wednesday: He bestows supreme wisdom. The guru-willed attains it contemplating guru's teachings. Imbued with God's love the mind becomes pure. He sings God's praises and washes away the filth of ego. In the court of the true Lord, he obtains lasting honour. Imbued with God's name and adorned by guru's teachings. ||4|| The profit of God's name is obtained at guru's refuge. The great giver gives it. I admire him who gives it. By guru's grace, ego is eradicated. O Nanak, enshrine God's name in the mind. Celebrate the Lord, the giver. ||5|| Thursday: The mortal is deluded by doubt. All demons and ghosts are attached to duality. God created everything and looks after all. O Creator, You are the support of all. The beings are under Your protection. He unites with You, whom You unite. ||6|| Friday: God is permeating and pervading everywhere. He creates all and appraises all. One who becomes a guru-willed contemplates the Lord. He practices truth and self-restraint. Keeping fast and religious rituals are love of duality without realizing God. ||7|| Saturday: contemplate good omens and Shaastras; The world is wandering in ego and possessiveness. The blind, self-willed is engrossed in the love of duality. Tied up at the door of death he is beaten and punished. By guru's grace, one finds lasting peace. He practices truth focusing on truth. ||8|| Those who serve the true guru are fortunate. Conquering their ego, they embrace love of the true Lord. They are intuitively imbued with God's love. Page 842 You the giver of peace unite them with You. Everything comes from One God, not anyone else. The guru-willed realizes this and understands. ||9|| These are the fifteen lunar days and seven days of the week; The months and seasons come over and over again; The world comes and goes like day and night. The Creator creates coming and going. The true Lord remains forever by His power. O Nanak, only a few guru-willed; realize God through guru's teachings. ||10||1|| Bilaaval, Third Master: The primal Lord created the universe. The beings are engrossed in worldly attachment. In love of duality, they are attached to the material world. The unfortunate die, and continue to come and go. Meeting the true guru, this understanding is obtained. The illusion of the material world is shattered and one merges in truth. ||1|| One who has pre-ordained destiny written on his forehead; God dwells in his mind. ||1||Pause|| He created the universe, and looks after as well. No one can erase what He wrote in your account. If someone calls him a mystic or a seeker; Deluded by doubt, he will continue coming and going. The humble being that serves the true guru understands this. Conquering the ego, he finds Lord's door. ||2|| From one God, everything was created. One Lord is pervading everywhere; none else. Renouncing duality, if one contemplates one God. Through guru's teachings, God's door becomes his destiny. Meeting the true guru, one finds the Lord. By eliminating duality; ||3|| One who's Lord is all-powerful; No one can kill him. Lord's servant remains in Lord's refuge; Lord blesses him with honour. There is none higher than Him. Why should he be afraid? Who should he be afraid of? ||4|| Through guru's teachings, peace abides in the body. Contemplating guru's teachings eliminates suffering. You shall not have to come or go, or suffer. Imbued with God's love merges in peace. O Nanak, the guru-willed sees God close by. My God is always fully pervading everywhere. ||5|| Some are selfless servants, while others wander, deluded by doubt. The Lord does and causes everything to be done. One Lord is all pervading; there is no other. The mortal may complain, if there were any other; Serving the true guru is the essence of everything. In the court of the true Lord, you shall be judged true. ||6|| All the lunar and weekdays are beautiful, if one contemplates guru's teachings. If one serves the true guru, he obtains the reward. The lunar days and weekdays all come and go. Following guru's teachings, one becomes eternal and merges with true Lord. The days are auspicious, when one is imbued with truth. Without God's name, all are false and wander in doubt; ||7|| The self-willed die and find no place to rest after death. They do not remember one Lord; they are deluded by duality. The human body is unconscious, ignorant and blind. Without guru's teachings, how can they go across? The Creator created Him. By contemplating guru's teachings; ||8|| The religious fanatics perform all sorts of rituals. They wander and wander like the false dice on the board. They find no peace, here or hereafter. Page 843 The self-willed waste away their life serving the guru eliminates doubt. They find destiny in the heart. ||9|| Whatever the perfect Lord does happens. These are lunar and weekdays, any other is duality. Without the true guru, there is pitch dark. The ignorant worship lunar and weekdays. O Nanak, the guru-willed realizes and obtains understanding; He remains forever absorbed in one name. ||10||2|| Bilaaval, First Master, Chhant, Dakhnee: God is one. He is realized by guru's grace. The young, innocent soul-bride has come to the pasturelands O God. Putting the pitcher down, she lovingly attunes to her Lord. She remains lovingly absorbed in God's pastureland, adorned by guru's teachings intuitively. With her palms pressed together, she prays to the guru, to unite her with her beloved Lord. In true love for the beloved Lord the bride eliminates lust and anger. O Nanak, seeing the young beautiful bride her Lord Husband comforts her. ||1|| The young soul-bride is truly beautiful O God. She does not come or go anywhere; stays with her Husband Lord O God. In the company of my beloved Lord I enjoy God's worship. The unknown and unspoken is realized intuitively singing God's praises. Through God's name she enjoys the true beloved Lord. The guru bestowed his teachings on poor Nanak. ||2|| Fascinated by the supreme Lord, she sleeps with her Husband Lord. Following guru's teachings, she merges with true Lord O God. Imbued with love she merges with God along with her friends and companions. Through His love, God dwells in her mind and she meets the guru. Day and night, with every breath I recite the formless God and never forget Him. Guru's teachings the destroyer of fear, and lit the lamp in me, O Nanak. ||3|| O soul-bride, the Lord's light pervades the universe O God. The invisible and infinite Lord is pervading each and every heart. The true Lord is invisible and infinite; He is realized by self-surrendering. Guru's teachings burn away the filth of ego false attachment and greed. By His grace I go to His door and see Him and beg for salvation from the bestowal. Tasting the nectar of God's name, I am satisfied O Nanak and enshrine Him in my mind. ||4||1|| Bilaaval, First Master: My mind is filled with joy; I am truly happy O God. I am enticed by the love of my Husband immortal Lord O God. The unknowable Lord is the master of masters. Whatever He wills, happens. O Great giver, kind and compassionate Lord; You live in all beings O beloved. Page 844 I have no other spiritual wisdom, meditation or worship; God's name dwells in my mind. I do not know about pilgrimage or fanaticism; Nanak says the truth. ||1|| The night is beautiful drenched with dew and the day is delightful; She sleeps in her home and her Husband Lord wakes her up O God. She obtains new company, new wealth awakened by guru's teachings and she is pleasing to her Husband Lord. Renouncing falsehood, fraud and love of duality she became a public servant. God's name is my necklace, and guru's teaching is my symbol. With his palms pressed together, Nanak begs for the gift of the true name; please, bless me with Your grace by Your will. ||2|| Wake up O beautiful bride and recite guru's sermon. Listen to that o self-centred and speak the unspoken story. The unspoken Speech, the state of salvation; only a few guru-willed realize. Merging in guru's teachings eliminates ego and realizes the universe. Remaining detached, imbued with infinite Lord, the mind realizes the true essence of virtues. He is pervading all places; O Nanak, enshrine Him in the heart. ||3|| God is realized through devotional worship O God. Following guru's teachings with love, the desires are fulfilled O God. Conquer your mind and follow guru's teachings with love; you shall realize the Lord of the universe. Her mind shall not waver or wander, when she realizes her Husband Lord. You are my support O Lord; You are my strength and anchor. Truth is forever pure O Nanak. Guru's teachings settled the issue. ||4||2|| Chhant, Bilaaval, Fourth Master, Mangal ~ The Song Of Joy: God is one. He is realized by guru's grace. My God has come to my bed, my mind merged in peace O God. By guru's grace I realized God and I am enjoying it O God. O fortunate happy soul-bride, God is my pride and joy O God. God is Nanak's Husband Lord. He pleases him O God. ||1|| The Lord is the honour of the humble. God is God O

God. The guru-willed eradicates ego; she recites God forever O God. Whatever pleases my God, he does it, imbued in love O God. Servant Nanak attains peace enjoying God's Love O God. ||2|| The human life attains by God's grace. Now is the time to worship Him. The guru-willed happy soul-bride meets Him and their love blossoms. Those who did not attain human life are unlucky O God. O my God; save Nanak, he is Your humble servant O God. ||3|| The guru taught God's immortal sermon. My mind and body got drenched with love O God. Page 845 God's name is the life of devotees. The guru-willed realize God O God. They do not survive without God's name like the fish without water. Realizing God, the life is fulfilled by God's grace O Nanak. ||4||1||3|| Bilaaval, Fourth Master, Hymn: Seek the beloved Lord and enshrine in your mind o fortunate; The guru revealed God to me through devotion O Nanak, ||1|| Chhant: The soul-bride has come to enjoy with her Lord, after erasing poisonous ego. Following guru's teachings, she eliminated her ego; she is lovingly attuned to God. The lotus blossomed inside. She woke up through guru's teachings O God. Servant Nanak has found God by good fortune O God. ||1|| The Lord pleases me and I am honoured to recite God's name O God. Through the perfect guru, she realized God; she is lovingly focused on Him. The darkness of ignorance is dispelled, the divine light is lit. God's name is Nanak's resolve and he merged with Him. ||2|| The soul-bride enjoys her beloved Lord when it pleases God. My eyes are drawn to His love, like the cat to the meat. The perfect guru united me with God; I am satisfied by God's essence. Servant Nanak is happy with God's name and is attuned to God. ||3|| By God's grace He united me the ignorant with Him. The soul bride praises the guru who eliminated the ego. Those fortunate are lucky that enshrine God in the mind. O servant Nanak, praise God's name and admire His name. ||4||2||4|| Bilaaval, Fifth Master, Chhant: God is one. He is realized by guru's grace. Joy of singing has welled up; I sing praises of God. I heard of my immortal Husband Lord, happiness fills my mind. Fortunately my mind is in love with Him; when will I meet perfect Lord? O my friend, teach me how to realize God and attain peace. Day and night, I serve my God. How can I realize Him? Prays Nanak, be kind and attach me to You O Lord; ||1|| I am happy that I purchased the jewel of Lord O God. By searching, I found it with the saints. By God's grace I met the saints and contemplate the unspoken sermon. I recite God my master single mindedly with love. With my palms pressed together, I pray to God, to bless me with the profit of Lord's praise. Prays Nanak, I am Your slave O my inaccessible and unfathomable God; ||2|| Page 846 The date for my wedding is set by perfect stars O God. I am totally at peace, my sorrow has ended O God. The saints recited God; surprisingly they came in the marriage party. Driven by happiness they got together; my mind is filled with love. Souls merged with souls and all enjoy reciting God's name. Prays Nanak, God the cause of causes united me with all saints. ||3|| Beautiful is my home, and fortunate is the land. God has come to my home; I touch guru's feet. Touching guru's feet I became content, all my desires are fulfilled. My hopes are fulfilled by saint's dust. I met my husband God after a long separation. Divine music plays with joy. My egotistic thinking is gone away. Prays Nanak, I attained my Lord's refuge by attuning to Him in saint's company. ||4||1|| Bilaaval, Fifth Master: God my husband Lord is virtuous. The infinite divine music with divine tune plays in His court O God. Night and day, the joyous divine music plays and I enjoy it. In God's realm the disease, sorrow and suffering do not bother. There is no birth or death there. There are treasures of wealth and mystic power and store full of sacred worship. Prays Nanak, I praise the supreme Lord the support of my life. ||1|| Listen, O my companions and friends, let's join and sing the songs of joy. Let us love and enjoy our Lord with mind body and soul. Lovingly enjoying Him pleases Him. Do not stop even for a moment; Do not be ashamed to embrace Him with love. Touch the dust of His feet to your mind. He cheated me by enticing with His worship. I do not go anywhere anymore. Prays Nanak, meeting with my beloved Lord I became immortal. ||2|| I am wonder-struck and amazed seeing the virtues of immortal Lord. By His grace He took me by the arm. My noose of death is cut O God. Holding by the arm He made me His slave and love sprouted in me. The filth and worldly attachment eliminated and good time has come. By His grace through love all evil thinking departed; Prays Nanak, I became pure by realizing the immortal God. ||3|| Like the rays of sun merge with sun, and water merges with water. My soul merged with supreme soul and became one. I see God, hear God, and speak of the one and only God. God is the Creator of the creation, none else. He is the Creator, and the enjoyer. He created the creation. Prays Nanak, One who drinks God's sublime nectar realizes this. ||4||2|| Page 847 Bilaaval, Fifth Master, Chhant: God is one. He is realized by guru's grace. Join with me O my friends; let us sing our beloved's song of joy. Renounce your pride, O my friends, then only you please your beloved. Renounce pride, emotional attachment, corruption and duality and serve the formless God. Touch the feet of the kind beloved the destroyer of sins in His refuge. Be the slave of His slaves, forsake sorrow and do not bother with other ways. Prays Nanak, O Lord, please be kind that I sing Your praises. ||1|| The name of my beloved is sacred. It is the guiding stick of the blind. The beautiful bride entices many ways. This enticer is amazing and childlike. She entices in many ways. She is stubborn and pleasing to mind but she does not recite God's name. She robs at home, in the forest, while fasting, worshipping and walking and at riverbanks. Prays Nanak; be kind and be my walking stick of the blind; ||2|| O my beloved Lord; keep me the orphan as you please. I have no wisdom or cleverness; what should I say to please You? I am not clever, skilful or wise; I the worthless have no virtue at all. I have no beauty or pleasing smell, no beautiful eyes. Keep me as You please. I recite His name and praise the Lord. How can I realize His virtues? Prays Nanak, I am the servant of Your servants; keep me as You please. ||3|| I am the fish, You are the water; how can I live without You? I am the rain bird, You are the raindrop; I get satisfaction when the drop falls in my mouth. When it falls in my mouth, my thirst is quenched o Lord the love of my life. You are the love of everyone O beloved; may I realize You and be liberated. I think in my mind for the darkness to go like the chakvi duck longs for sunrise. Prays Nanak; unite me with my beloved like the fish does not separate from water. ||4|| I am a blessed soul bride that my beloved Husband Lord came home. The door to my mansion looks beautiful and my mind has blossomed. My peace-giving Lord rejuvenated me, and blessed me with joy, bliss and love. My new Husband Lord is eternal and young, how will I sing His praises? My bed is beautiful;

He is with me. My worry and suffering departed. Prays Nanak, my hopes are fulfilled meeting my infinite Lord. ||5||1||3|| Bilaaval, Fifth Master, Chhant, Mangal ~ The Song Of Joy: God is one. He is realized by guru's grace. Hymn: God is beautiful, peaceful and merciful; He is the treasure of eternal peace. Page 848 Meeting with God, the ocean of peace, O Nanak, this soul is happy. ||1|| Chhant: One finds God, the ocean of peace, when it is pre-ordained. Give up self-pride and touch God's feet by God's grace. Renounce cleverness and tricks, and forsake your evil-minded intellect. O Nanak, seek God's refuge and your marriage will be eternal. ||1|| Why forsake God and worship someone else? I will die without Him. The ignorant does not feel shame; she enjoys the company of bad persons. Where can I rest abandoning God the purifier of sinners O God? O Nanak, worship the kind Lord with love and attain eternal state. ||2|| May the vicious tongue that does not recite the name of the Lord of the world be burnt. One who does not serve God the love of His devotees, shall be eaten by crows. Enticed by doubt, does not understand the pain it brings; he wanders through millions of life's. O Nanak, those who love anyone other than God will rot in filth like worms. ||3|| Fall in love with God and feel the sorrow of separation. Stop applying sandalwood on the forehead, scent and enjoyment. Give up the poison of ego O God; Do not waver this way or that way and remain awake in God's service. O Nanak, she who has realized her God, is a happy soul-bride forever. ||4||1||4|| Bilaaval, Fifth Master: Seek God O fortunate joining the company of devotees O God. Sing the praises of the Lord of the universe forever, imbued with love of the supreme Lord. Serving God forever, you shall obtain the reward you desire. O Nanak, seek God's refuge and sing His praises with utmost love. ||1|| May I never forget God who gave me everything O God? The fortunate guru-willed; searched and united with God. Holding me by the arm, He lifted me out of darkness and made me his own. Nanak lives by reciting God's name; his mind and heart are soothed. ||2|| What virtues of Yours can I speak, O God the inner-knower? Reciting God, I have crossed over to the other shore. Singing the praises of the Lord of the universe, all my desires are fulfilled. Nanak is saved, reciting God the Lord of all. ||3|| The eyes that are drenched with the love of the Lord are joyous. I realized my beloved God and my desires are fulfilled. I obtained the nectar of God's love, now the taste of bad deeds is bland. O Nanak, as water merges with water, my soul merged in supreme soul. ||4||2||5||9|| Page 849 Vaar Of Bilaaval, Fourth Master: God is one. He is realized by guru's grace. Hymn, Fourth Master: I sing of the sacred Lord, the God, in the melody of perfect tune. I listen and follow guru's teachings, I am fortunate from destiny. All day and night, I say God's praises enshrining God in my mind. My body and mind are revived; the garden of my mind has blossomed. The darkness of ignorance is erased with the light of the lamp of guru's wisdom. Nanak lives to visualize God even for a moment. ||1|| Third Master: When you say God from the mouth that is the perfect tune to sing; When you focus on guru's teachings, then singing tunes is pleasing. Worship God, forgetting singing and sounds and attain honour in God's court. O Nanak the guru-willed; contemplate God; your ego will be eliminated. ||2|| Ladder: O God, You are inaccessible; You created everything. You are totally pervading the entire universe. You sit in trance and sing Your praises. O devotees, recite God day and night; He shall save you in the end. Those who serve God find peace; they are absorbed in God's name. ||1|| Hymn, Third Master: In love of duality, the perfect singing is impossible. The self-willed find no place to rest. Through imitation God's worship is impossible; God is not realized this way. No one can accomplish anything through stubborn deeds. O Nanak, the guru-willed searches his soul and eliminates ego. God is the supreme Lord; the supreme Lord dwells in my mind. Birth and death are erased and my soul merges with supreme soul. ||1|| Third Master: Sing the perfect tune o beloved, attuning Your mind to one God. Getting absorbed in true Lord erases the pain of birth and death. Singing the perfect tune is joyful if one follows guru's teachings. Sit in saint's congregation with devotion and sing God's praises with love. O Nanak, those who unite with God by His grace look adorable. ||2|| Ladder: God abides in all beings but He befriends with His devotees. Everyone is under God's control, His devotees are happy. God unites all of His devotees with Him and they rest in peace. God is the master of all. Those who miss Him with love are His devotees. No one can equal You. Those who try, struggle and die in frustration. ||2|| Page 850 Hymn, Third Master: Those who contemplate God are divine if they follow guru's will. God dwells in their mind and eliminates the sickness of ego. He sings God's virtues, gathers virtues, his soul merges with divine soul. In today's age there are very few wise persons who worship God with love. Third Master: One who does not serve the guru and does not love guru's teachings. Earns the painful disease of ego; he is engrossed with ego. Acting stubborn-mindedly, he takes birth over and over. The birth of the guru-willed is fruitful. God unites him with Him. O Nanak, when God is gracious, then only God's name dwells in the mind. ||2|| Ladder: The greatness is in God's name. O guru-willed recite God. Enshrining God's name in the mind fulfills the desires of mind. When one opens his mind to the guru, attains eternal peace. When the perfect guru delivers God's lesson; the hunger departs forever. One with pre-ordained destiny sings God's praises. ||3|| Hymn, Third Master: No one goes empty-handed from the guru; He unites you with God. Fruitful is visualizing the guru. What you earn you get; Guru's teaching is nectar. It eliminates all thirst and hunger. Drinking God's sublime essence attains contentment and truth dwells in the mind. Reciting God attains immortal state and infinite divine music plays. God pervades in all ten directions; he is realized through the guru intuitively. O Nanak, those filled with truth do not remain hidden. ||1|| Third Master: Serving the guru, one realizes God by His grace. Human beings become gods, when God blesses them with true worship. Conquering ego they unite with God truly through guru's teachings. O Nanak, they intuitively unite with God reciting God's name. ||2|| Ladder: Guru has the greatness of God's name; God blessed him with it. His devotees and followers are amazed by witnessing. It pleases them. The slanderers and evil cannot believe it. They do not wish others well. What can they do or talk when one is lovingly attuned to God; Whatever pleases God flourishes day by day; while others talk nonsense? ||4|| Hymn, Third Master: Cursed is the hope in love of duality; that ties to worldly love and pleasure. One, who forsakes the peace of God in exchange for straw, forgets God's name and suffers. Page 851 The ignorant self-willed are blind. They are born and die again and again. Their affairs are not resolved.

In the end, they depart repenting. One, blessed by God, meets the guru and recites God's name. Imbued with God's name one attains peace. Servant Nanak praises him. ||1|| Third Master: Hope of mind entices the world; it entices the whole universe. The entire creation is subject to death. The devil of death catches by God's order. Those blessed by God are saved. O Nanak, The mind is saved by guru's grace, if it gives up arrogance. Conquer hope of mind and remain unattached through guru's teaching. ||2|| Ladder: Wherever I go in this world, I see God. In the world after, everything happens by God's will. He bestows true justice. The faces of the false are cursed, the true devotees are honoured. God bestows true justice and the slanderers are disgraced. Servant Nanak worships the true Lord; the guru-willed finds peace. ||5|| Hymn, Third Master: By perfect destiny one finds the guru, if the Lord grants His grace. This is the best effort of all to obtain God's name. It brings soothing and peace inside and mind becomes ever peaceful. He eats and wears nectar O Nanak, he obtains honour reciting God's name. ||1|| Third Master: O mind, listening to guru's teachings realizes the treasure of virtues. The giver of peace dwells in your mind; your ego and pride disappear. O Nanak, by God's grace, one obtains sacred treasure of virtues. ||2|| Ladder: God creates all the kings, emperors, rulers, lords, nobles and chiefs. Whatever God makes them do, they do; they are all indebted to God. Such God the Lord of all is on guru's side; He enslaves all castes, the four sources of creation, the whole universe and offers them to guru to work for him. See the honour of serving God O saints; He destroys all evil from the body. God became kind to the devotees and saved them by His grace. ||6|| Hymn, Third Master: Fraud in the mind gives pain forever. The self-willed cannot concentrate. They do painful deeds and receive pain in the next world. By luck one meets the guru; then he attunes to God's name. O Nanak, he realizes peace with ease; and doubt disappears. ||1|| Third Master: The guru-willed is dyed by God's love forever. God's name pleases him. Page 852 The guru-willed sees and says God. He finds peace reciting God's name. O Nanak, the guru-willed is enlightened by divine wisdom. His pitch-dark ignorance is eliminated. ||2|| Third Master: The self-willed are filthy and ignorant. The guru-willed become pure by enshrining God in the mind. Says

Nanak, listen O brother; Serving the true guru eliminates the filth of ego. He is bothered by the pain of worry. He is beating his head with worldly deeds. Asleep in love of duality, they never wake up; they are attached to the love of the worldly pleasure. They do not recite God's name, do not contemplate guru's teachings; this is the nature of the self-willed. They do not love God's name, they waste their life away O Nanak, the devil of death kills them in disgrace. ||3|| Ladder: He whom God blesses with His worship is a true banker. People beg from him; the priceless merchandise is not available in other shops, they do not believe them either. Those who befriends with God's devotees obtain God's essence, those who turn away from devotees collect dust. God's devotees are the dealers of God's name. The tax collector, devil of death do not come close to them. O Nanak those who loaded the wealth of God's name are carefree forever. ||7|| Hymn, Third Master: In this age, the devotee earns Godly wealth. Rest of the world wanders in doubt. By guru's grace, God's name dwells in his mind. He recites God's name forever. In the midst of sins he remains detached; guru's teaching burns away the ego. He is saved along with ancestors. Blessed is the mother who gave birth to him. Attuning to God with love he attains peace and contentment. Brahma, Vishnu and Shiva wander in the three qualities. They are engrossed with ego and worldly attachments. The religious scholars are lost by reading and being quiet lose the silent sages. They are deluded by duality. The Yogis, Bhairo's followers and those wandering in forest are deluded; without the guru, they do not find the reality. The miserable self-willed are deluded by doubt. They waste their life away. O Nanak, those imbued with God's name are worthy. God unites them with Him by His grace. Third Master: O Nanak, praise Him, who has control over everything. Worship Him devotionally O mortals. No one is without Him. The guru-willed enshrine Him in the mind and attain eternal peace. ||2|| Ladder: Those who do not earn the wealth of God's name are bankrupt forever. They wander begging all over the world No one even spits in their face. They lose their honour slandering others. They help to write this in their fate. That wealth, for which they slander others, does not come in their hands, no matter where they go. Page 853 The guru-willed earns Godly wealth through worship.

The unlucky cannot get it without worship. God's wealth is not found anywhere else. ||8|| Hymn, Third Master: The guru-willed have no worry. Worry leaves them. Whatever happens; let it be. Cannot say anything about it; O Nanak, the Lord listens to what they say if he accepts it. ||1|| Third Master: He conquers death and desire and enshrines God's name in the heart. Night and day, he remains awake never sleeps and drinks nectar with love. He speaks sweet sacred words and sings God's praises forever. He is adorned by God's love; realizing God he obtains peace. ||2|| Ladder: Godly wealth is priceless jewels. God bestows that wealth through the guru. If anyone can see, will beg for it. Other party will give if he wants; it cannot be acquired by force. Whom God attaches to the guru with love, obtains God's wealth that has it pre-ordained in his destiny. There is no equal to God's wealth. Recommendation does not help. It is not tied to somebody's waste. Whoever talks bad of Godly wealth; God paints his face black in all four directions. Power or ill talk does not help to obtain God's blessing. Whoever God blesses, His grace, increases day by day. ||9|| Hymn, Third Master: O God; save the world from burning by Your grace. Take it to the door of salvation and save. The guru bestows happiness through his teachings. Nanak knows no other than God, who can bestow his blessing? ||1|| Third Master: Ego and worldly pleasure is enticing, it attracts towards duality. It cannot be killed, it does not die, and it is not sold in a store. It is burnt through guru's teachings; then it leaves you. The body and mind become pure and God's name dwells in the mind. O Nanak, guru's teaching is the destroyer of worldly wealth; the guru-willed obtain it. ||2|| Ladder: Praising guru is pre-ordained from destiny, realized by obeying his will. He tested His sons, nephews, sons-in-law and relatives, and subdued the egotistic pride of all. Wherever anyone looks, my guru is there; God blesses the whole world. One, who meets and believes the guru, is rewarded. One who turns away from the guru wanders around cursed. Page 854 The beloved divine God; took servant Nanak's side. Seeing this, everyone fell at guru's feet and their ego erased. ||10|| Hymn, First Master: One plants, another harvests, yet another takes out the grain from the chaff. O Nanak, it is not known, who will ultimately eat the grain. ||1|||| | | First Master: He who has

God enshrined in the mind attains salvation. O Nanak, what pleases God; happens. ||2|| Ladder: The kind supreme Lord carried me across the world-ocean. The perfect guru eradicated my fear of doubt by his grace. Lust, anger, other useless deeds and the enemies all lost. I enshrined the treasure of God's sacred name in the mind. O Nanak, in devotee's company the birth and death is eliminated. ||11|| Hymn, Third Master: Those who forget God's name are false, also judged false. The five thieves plunder their homes, the ego breaks in. The faithless are defrauded by ill will. They do not taste God's sublime essence. Those who lose the nectar through doubt, remain engrossed in evil deeds. They make friends with the wicked, and fight with God's devotees. O Nanak, the faithless go to hell tied by the devil of death and suffer; They get what they earn; they live as God keeps them. ||1|| Third Master: Those who serve the guru become humble. They recite God in the mind with every breath and morsel of food. Devil of death cannot rob them. They enjoy God's name in the mind. Worldly wealth worships them. One, who becomes the slave of Lord's slaves, obtains the greatest treasure. O Nanak, I praise him forever, who has God dwelling in the mind and body. One with pre-ordained destiny obtains the sublime essence from saints. ||2|| Ladder: Whatever the perfect guru says, the transcendent Lord listens. That happens in the world and everybody talks about it. God's virtues are unlimited that cannot be counted. Truth, contentment and joy are with the guru. Guru's lesson is true. O Nanak, the supreme Lord looks after the saints as He pleases. ||12|| Hymn, Third Master: He does not understand him; he believes God to be far away. He forgets to serve the guru; how can his mind feel God's presence? The self-willed wastes away his life in worthless greed and falsehood. O Nanak, by God's grace he is united with God through guru's teachings. ||1|| Third Master: The guru-willed sings true God's praises reciting the name of the Lord of the universe. He praises God's name all the time and becomes peaceful. The fortunate realizes God the perfect embodiment of supreme bliss. O Nanak, praising God's name the mind and body will never suffer again. ||2|| Page 855 Ladder: If someone slanders the guru, and then seeks his refuge; Guru forgives his past sins and unites him with the congregation. When it rains, the water drains from ponds to streams to sacred rivers and becomes cleansed. Same greatness is in the guru with no ill feelings. Meeting him the thirst and hunger are eliminated and peace dwells. O Nanak, this is the greatness of my true Lord; whoever obeys the guru pleases everyone. ||13||1|| declaration|| Bilaaval, The word of the devotees. Of Kabeer Jee: God is one. It is true. He is the Creator. He is realized by guru's grace. This world is a play; no one can remain here forever. Walk the straight path; otherwise, you will be pushed around. ||1||Pause|| The devil of death will take away the children, young and old O brother. The devil of death eats the poor human, like a cat eats a mouse. ||1|| It gives no special consideration to either the rich or the poor. The king and his subjects are treated equal; so great is the death. ||2|| Those who please God are His devotees. Their story is different. They do not come or go, they never die; they remain with God. ||3|| Know that by renouncing your children, spouse, wealth and property. Says Kabeer, listen, O saints; then you unite with the Lord of the universe. ||4||1|| Bilaaval: I do not read and I do not argue or discuss. I have gone insane, saying and hearing to the praises of the Lord. ||1|| O elder, I am insane and the rest of the public is wise. I am spoiled; let no one else be spoiled like me. ||1||Pause|| I am not insane on my own; the Lord made me insane. The guru has burnt away my doubt. ||2|| I am spoiled; I have lost my intellect. Let no one follow me and go insane. ||3|| He who does not recognize him is insane. When he understands himself, then he knows one Lord. ||4|| One who is not intoxicated now, will never be intoxicated. Says Kabeer, I am imbued with Lord's love. ||5||2|| Bilaaval: Leave your house and go to the forest. Pick roots and eat. Even now he does not give up the useless deeds. He is an evil sinner. ||1|| How can he be saved? How can he cross over the terrifying world-ocean? Save me O my Lord! Your humble servant seeks Your sanctuary. ||1||Pause|| The smell of committing sins cannot be eliminated. Make all efforts to give it up; still it does not leave you. ||2|| Page 856 Youth and old age have passed, I haven't done any good. This priceless soul is not worth a shell. ||3|| Says Kabeer, O my Lord, You are omnipresent. No one is as kind as You and none as sinful as I am. ||4||3|| Bilaaval: Every day he cleans his body bringing water in a fresh clay pot. He does not think of worldly deeds; he is absorbed in God's subtle essence. ||1|| Who in our family ever recited the name of God? Since the idiot took to rosary; there is no happiness. ||1||Pause|| Listen, O my sisters-in-law, a strange thing has happened! This boy has ruined our weaving business. Why didn't he die? ||2|| God is the bestowal of all happiness; the guru bestows His name. He preserved the honour of Prahlaad, and destroyed Harnaakhash with his nails. ||3|| He gave up worshipping gods and ancestors, he follows guru's teachings. Says Kabeer, God the destroyer of all sins saves His saints. ||4||4|| Bilaaval: There is no king equal to God. They are kings for a few days. They wear false silk robes. ||1||Pause|| Your humble servant never wavers. He is known in the whole universe. No one raises a hand or says anything against God's servant. ||1|| Missing the formless God O my ignorant mind; divine music plays; Says Kabeer, my worry and doubt are gone. I am honoured like Dhroo and Prahlaad. ||2||5|| Bilaaval: Save me! I am bad. I am not humble or religious, I do not meditate or worship. I am full of ego and do bad deeds. ||1||Pause|| I look after this body thinking it immortal but it is temporary like a clay pot. He who created and looked after me; I forgot Him and follow others. ||1|| I am a thief not Your devotee; I seek Your refuge to follow Your path O God. Says Kabeer, please listen to my prayer; do not tell the devil of death. ||2||6|| Bilaaval: I humbly stand at Your door. Who else other than you will care for me? Please open the door that I may visualize You. ||1||Pause|| You are the richest of the rich, generous and unattached. I only listen to Your praises. What can I beg from the miser? You only can save me. ||1|| You blessed Jai Dev, Naam Dev and Sudaamaa by Your grace. Says Kabeer, You are all-powerful bestowal O Lord. It takes only a moment for You to bestow four priceless gifts. ||2||7|| Bilaaval: He has a walking stick, earrings, a patched coat and a begging bowl. He is an imitator full of duality. ||1|| Page 857 Stop doing Yoga and breathing exercises, O ignorant. Renounce fraud and worship God O ignorant. ||1||Pause|| That who you beg from enjoys the worldly pleasure. Says Kabeer, what good is the worldly Yogi. ||2||8|| Bilaaval: In worldly attachment they forgot Your refuge O God; Not a bit love wells up to them; what can the ignorant do? ||1||Pause|| Cursed are the body, wealth and the worldly pleasures. Cursed is their intellect and thinking; Those who worship the worldly pleasure are stuck in their own deeds. ||1|| What good is farming and trading? They are entangled in false pride. Says Kabeer, in the end, they are ruined; death will take them away. ||2||9|| Bilaaval: In the middle of the body pool is a beautiful lotus flower. That is the supreme soul God, who has no form or feature. ||1|| O my mind, eliminate doubt and recite God the life of the world. ||1||Pause|| Nothing is seen coming into the world, and nothing is seen going. Whoever is born has to die like the leaves at the end of life? ||2|| Give up the transitory worldly pleasure, contemplate divine wisdom and attain peace and contentment. Says Kabeer, worship God the destroyer of demons in your mind; ||3||10|| Bilaaval: The illusion of birth and death is gone by attuning to God with love. Attain the absolute state while living through guru's teachings. ||1||Pause|| The sound comes out of bronze and absorbs in bronze. When the bronze breaks o scholar, where does the sound go? ||1|| I found the secret of the world. Only body can rejuvenate itself. Such an intellect is in the body O renunciate; ||2|| I have come to know myself; my light has merged in supreme Light. Says Kabeer, now I know the Lord of the universe and my mind is satisfied. ||3||11|| Bilaaval: When Your lotus feet dwell in one's heart, why should he waver, O God? Know that all comforts, nine treasures and peace come to him, who sings God's praises intuitively. ||Pause|| When God opens the secret, then one obtains such realization and sees God in all. He stays away from the worldly please forever; God weighs everything. ||1|| Then he finds peace everywhere, worldly wealth does not entice him. Says Kabeer, my mind believes now; God's love made me so. ||2||12|| Bilaaval, the word of devotee Naam Dev Jee: God is one. He is realized by guru's grace. The guru made my life fruitful. Page 858 My pain is forgotten, I have found peace in me. ||1|| The guru has blessed me with the ointment of divine wisdom. Without Lord's name, life is mindless. ||1||Pause|| Reciting God, Naam Dev has realized God. His soul has merged with God, the life of the world. ||2||1|| Bilaaval, the word of devotee Ravi Daas: God is one. He is realized by guru's grace. Seeing my poverty, everyone laughs. Such is my condition. I hold eighteen mystic powers in the palm of my hand by Your grace. ||1|| You know that I am nothing, O Lord, the destroyer of sins. All beings seek Your sanctuary, O God fulfiller of all affairs. ||1||Pause|| Whoever enters Your sanctuary is relieved of sins. You have saved the high and the low from the shameless world. ||2|| Says Ravi Daas, what more can I say about the unspoken speech? You are, what You are; how can anything compare with You? ||3||1|| Bilaaval: The family, into which a devotee is born; Whether high or low class, rich or poor, shall have its pure fragrance spread all over the world. ||1||Pause|| Whether he is a Brahmin, a Vaishya, a Soodra, or a Kashaatriya; whether he is an outcaste, a wicked or thankless; He becomes pure worshipping God. God saves him and his families. ||1|| Blessed is the village, the place, the family and the whole world. One who drinks God's sublime essence and abandons other tastes; intoxicated with divine essence, he discards sin and corruption. ||2|| The scholars, warriors and kings, none of them equals God's devotee. As the leaves of the water lily remain in water, says Ravi Daas, so are God's devotees in the world. ||3||2|| The Word of Sadhana, Tune Bilaaval: God is one. He is realized by guru's grace. Seeing your beautiful dance I disguised myself and followed you. Whether I had lust or selfishness but you preserved my honour. ||1|| What good is praising You, O world guru if You do not erase my past deeds? Why do you go close to a lion; he is going to eat you O jackal? ||1||Pause|| For the sake of a single raindrop, the rain bird suffers in pain. What use is to obtain ocean after death. ||2|| I have grown old, how can I find peace? If I drown and die, then a boat comes along; tell me how can I go aboard? ||3|| I am nothing, I have nothing and nothing belongs to me. O God; it is time to protect my honour; Sadhana is Your humble servant. ||4||1||

Page 859 *God is one. It is true. He is the Creator. He is carefree. He has no enemy. He is immortal. He does not take birth. He came into existence on His own. He is realized by guru's grace.*

Tune Gond, Chau-Padas, Fourth Master, First House: If one believes in God; he obtains all fruits of his choice. God knows what is in your mind. He does not lose whatever one earns. O my mind put your hope on God, who abides in all. ||1|| O my mind, place your hope in Lord the master of the universe. Your hope for any other than God is useless; it goes waste. ||1||Pause|| All that you see is the enticement of worldly wealth and family; you waste your life attaching to it. Nothing is in their hand; what can the poor do? They cannot do anything. O my mind; place your hope in the beloved God, who shall carry you across and save your whole family as well. ||2|| If you place your hope in any other than God; you will know that it is of no use. To place your hope other than God is the love of duality. This false hope shall vanish in an instant. O my mind; place your hope in the beloved God; who shall reward you for all your efforts. ||3|| Hope and desire are all Yours O Lord. As You inspire so we hope. Page 860 My guru told me that no one has anything in their hand O my master, You know servant Nanak's desire that visualizing God I get satisfied. ||4||1|| Gond, Fourth Master: Serve and worship such a Lord, who destroys all sins in a moment. If one forsakes God and places his hopes in another, all his service goes waste. O my mind, serve God the giver of peace; serving Him, all your hunger shall depart. ||1|| O my mind; believe in God. Where I go, my Lord is with me. God saves His servant's honour. ||1||Pause|| If you tell your story to others, they tell it to everyone. If you tell your sorrows to God; He eliminates your sorrows quickly. If you tell your sorrows to any other than God; you should be ashamed; ||2|| The relatives, friends and siblings in the world you see, O my mind, all meet with you for their sake. When their self-interests are not served, they do not come near you. O my mind, serve God forever; He shall help you in good and bad times. ||3|| Why should you believe those O my mind; who cannot save you in the end? Recite God through guru's teachings; God saves those who love Him. Says Nanak: recite God forever O saints. This is the way to liberation. ||4||2|| Gond, Fourth Master: Reciting God attains happiness, eternal peace and soothing of mind. The sun gives harsh heat; seeing the moon the guru eliminates the heat. ||1|| O my mind, night and day, recite God's name like a rosary. God protects you everywhere; worship such God all the time. ||1||Pause|| O my mind; recite God the priceless treasure. O guru-willed, search for God the jewel. Those who worship find God. I massage the feet of God's servants. ||2|| Realizing guru's teachings attains divine taste. He is the greatest of all saints. God bestows him with greatness. No one can reduce it even a bit. ||3|| Page 861 He who gives you happiness o mind, pray Him with palms pressed together God; bless Nanak with one gift that I enshrine Your feet in my mind forever. ||4||3|| Gond, Fourth Master: All kings, emperors, nobles, lords and chiefs are false and transitory. They are engrossed in duality; know this well. The eternal Lord is permanent; recite Him o my mind and get accepted. ||1|| O my mind, recite God's name the bestowal of justice. One who realizes God through guru's teachings is the greatest of all. ||1||Pause|| All the wealthy, high class and property owners that you see, O my mind, shall vanish like the fading colour of the safflower. Serve the true Lord forever, O mind; you shall be honoured in God's court. ||2|| There are four castes and four way of worship; whoever worships God is the highest of all. As castor oil plant, near the sandalwood tree becomes fragrant; same way, the sinner is accepted in devotee's congregation. He is the highest and purest of all, in whose mind God dwells. Servant Nanak washes the feet of God's humble servant; may he be a low caste; ||4||4|| Gond, Fourth Master: The Lord, the inner-knower does everything. As He asks, so we do. Serve such Lord forever, O my mind, who protects you from everything. ||1|| O my mind; recite and read about God every day. Other than God, no one can kill and revive; why worry O my mind? ||1||Pause|| The Creator created the entire creation and infused His light in it. One Lord speaks. One Lord causes all to speak. The perfect guru reveals one Lord. ||2|| God is with you inside and out! Tell me O mind, how can You hide anything from Him? Serve the Lord whole-heartedly; then O mind, you shall find total peace. ||3|| Everything is under His control; He is the greatest of all. O my mind; worship Him forever. O Servant Nanak that Lord is always with you. Recite His name forever and he will free you. ||4||5|| Gond, Fourth Master: My mind yearns to visualize God as a thirsty is for water. ||1|| My mind is pierced by the arrow of Lord's love. God knows the state and the pain of my mind. ||1||Pause|| Whoever tells me the story of my beloved Lord, is my brother and a friend. ||2|| Page 862 Let us get together O friends and sing God's praises learning from the peaceful guru. ||3|| O God; fulfill Nanak's hope that he visualizes and becomes peaceful. ||4||6|| First set of six. || Tune Gond, Fifth Master, Chau-Padas, First House: God is one. He is realized by guru's grace. He is the

Creator; He is the enjoyer of all. ||1||Pause|| The Creator listens, and the Creator sees. The Creator is unseen, and the Creator is seen. The Creator creates and destroys. The Creator is everywhere and the Creator is hidden. ||1|| The Creator speaks and the Creator knows all. The Creator comes, and goes. The Creator is absolute; the Creator is manifest. By guru's grace O Nanak, He is realized. ||2||1|| Gond, Fifth Master: You are caught, like a fish and a monkey; you are entangled in the transitory world. You walk and breathe but you will attain salvation by singing God's praises. ||1|| O mind, reform yourself, and forsake your aimless wandering. You have no place to live; why do you teach others? ||1||Pause|| Like the elephant, driven by lust, you are attached to your family. The birds get together and separate! Reciting God in devotee's company you will not separate. ||2|| Like the fish gets caught driven by taste, you are robbed by greed. You have fallen prey to five thieves; you will be saved in God's refuge. ||3|| Be kind O destroyer of pains of the poor; all beings are Yours. May I be blessed to visualize You in the company of servant of servants O Nanak. ||4||2|| Tune Gond, Fifth Master, Chau-Padas, Second House: God is one. He is realized by guru's grace. He created the soul and life. He infused His light in the dust by His grace; He gives everything to all including food and joy. Where will you go leaving such a God? ||1|| Start serving the Lord. God is realized by guru's grace. ||1||Pause|| He created the creation in many forms and shapes. He creates and destroys in an instant; His divine wisdom cannot be described. Recite that God forever O my mind. ||2|| The permanent Lord does not come or go. His virtues are unlimited; how many of them can I count? Page 863 The store of treasure of His priceless name is full; He gives food to all beings. ||3|| His name is the true primal being; Singing a little bit of His praises eliminates millions of sins. The child like companion is the friend of His devotees. O Nanak, love the supporter of life whole-heartedly. ||4||1||3|| Gond, Fifth Master: I trade in the name of the Lord. God's name is the support of the mind. God's name is the shelter of my mind. Reciting God's name erases millions of sins. ||1|| God blessed me the wealth of one Lord's name. The true deed of mind is to attach to the guru. ||1||Pause|| God's name is the wealth of my soul. Wherever I go, God's name is with me. Reciting

God's name is sweet to my mind. God's sweet name abides in water land and sky. ||2|| Through God's name one attains happiness in God's court. Through God's name all attain salvation. Through God's name my affairs are resolved. My mind is greedy of God's name. ||3|| Through God's name I have become carefree. Through God's name my coming and going ended. The perfect guru united me with the Lord, the treasure of virtue. Says Nanak, I dwell in peace and contentment. ||4||2||4|| Gond, Fifth Master: He grants honour to the humble; He gives food to all the hungry; He protects in the terrible womb. So humbly bow forever to that Lord the master. ||1|| Recite such a God in your mind. He helps you everywhere, in good times and bad. ||1||Pause|| The beggar and the king are the same to Him. He looks after both the ant and an elephant. He does not ask for anyone's advice. Whatever He does, He does Himself. ||2|| No one knows His end. He is the formless Lord. He is formed and He is formless. He is in every heart and He is the support of all hearts. ||3|| Through the love of God's name, all are dyed deep red. Singing the praises of the Creator, the saints are forever happy. Through the love of God's name, Lord's humble servants are satisfied. Nanak falls at the feet of those humble servants of the Lord. ||4||3||5|| Gond, Fifth Master: Associating with them, the mind becomes pure. Associating with them, one recites God. Associating with them, all sins are erased. Associating with them, the heart is illumined. ||1|| Those saints of the Lord are my friends. They sing God's praises all the time. ||1||Pause|| Through their teachings, God enshrines in the mind. By their teachings, the desire of doubt is dispelled. Singing His praises is the essence of purity. The world longs for the dust of their feet. ||2|| Millions of sinners are saved by associating with them. They have the support of the name of one formless Lord. He knows the secrets of all beings; He is the treasure of mercy, the supreme Lord. ||3|| When the supreme Lord becomes merciful; Then one meets the kind guru. Page 864 Day and night, Nanak recites His name. Reciting God's name attains peace contentment and joy. ||4||4||6|| Gond, Fifth Master: Enshrine guru's picture in the mind. Through guru's teachings; enshrine his lesson in the mind. Enshrine guru's feet in your heart. Bow humbly forever before the guru the supreme Lord.

||1|| Let no one wander in doubt in the world. Without the guru, no one can cross over. ||1||Pause|| The guru shows the path to those who have wandered off. He leads them to renounce others and attaches them to God`s worship. He erases the fear of birth and death. The greatness of the perfect guru is endless. ||2|| By guru's grace, the inverted heart-lotus blossoms; The light shines in the darkness. Whoever realized God; did it through the guru. By guru's grace, the ignorant mind comes to believe. ||3|| The guru is the Creator; guru has the power to do everything. The guru is the transcendent Lord; He is, and always shall be. Says Nanak that God inspired me to know this; Without the guru, liberation is not obtained, O brother. ||4||5||7|| Gond, Fifth Master: Say guru, guru, guru, O my mind; I have no other than the guru. Take the support of the guru, day and night. No one can decrease His blessing. ||1|| Know that the guru and the transcendent Lord are one. Whatever pleases Him is approved. ||1||Pause|| One whose mind is attached to guru's feet; His pains, sufferings and doubts run away. Serving the guru, obtains honour. I praise the guru forever. ||2|| Visualizing the guru I am content. Efforts of the devotee of the guru are rewarded. Pain does not afflict guru's servant. Guru's servant is known in ten directions. ||3|| Guru's glory cannot be described. Guru is merged in the supreme Lord. Says Nanak, one who is lucky; His mind is attached to guru's feet. ||4||6||8|| Gond, Fifth Master: I worship my guru; the guru is the Lord of the universe. My guru is the supreme Lord; guru is God. My guru is divine, invisible and secretive. Everyone worships guru`s feet and serves him. ||1|| Without the guru, I have no other place to go. Night and day, I say guru guru guru. ||1||Pause|| Guru is my spiritual wisdom; the guru is in my heart. Guru is the Lord of the world, the primal Lord. With my palms pressed together, I remain in guru's sanctuary. Without the guru, I have no other; ||2|| The guru is the boat to cross over the terrifying world-ocean. Serving the guru, one is released from the devil of death. Guru`s lesson illuminates the dark. In guru`s company, all are saved. ||3|| The perfect guru is found, by good fortune. Serving the guru, pain does not afflict anyone. No one can erase guru`s teachings. O Nanak, Nanak is the guru and God. ||4||7||9||Page 865 Gond, Fifth Master: Make your habit to say God

God. God is the support of life. Sing the praises of the Lord. The Lord is ever-present, all-pervading. ||1|| Join the humble saints and recite God. This is the most sacred deed. ||1||Pause|| Gather the treasure of wealth of the Lord; Let word God be your food. Never forget the word God. The guru revealed this to me by his grace. ||2|| The Lord is always our help and support. Say God God God with love. Saying God God makes pure. The sins of countless lifes go away. ||3|| Reciting God eliminates birth and death cycle. Repeating Lord's name, one crosses over the terrifying world-ocean. The enlightenment is the highest of all. Night and day O servant Nanak; recite Him. ||4||8||10|| Gond, Fifth Master: My Lord protects them from obstructions. He eliminated the obstruction from His servants. They cannot find the destiny of Lord's devotee. Joining together, Lord's humble servants sing the songs of joy. ||1|| The five demons are the rulers of the whole world; They carry water for Lord's devotee. ||1||Pause|| They forcibly take gifts from the world; But they bow in respect to God's devotees. They plunder and dishonour the faithless. But they massage and wash the feet of God's devotees. ||2|| One mother gave birth to the five sons; The Creator created the creation this way; The world enjoys the three worldly qualities. God's devotees are above this. ||3|| He saves His humble servants by His grace. They belong to Him and He saves them from the five thieves. Says Nanak, devotion to God is the essence. Without worshipping God, all suffer; ||4||9||11|| Gond, Fifth Master: Sufferings and troubles are eradicated by reciting God's name. Pain is dispelled and peace takes its place. Reciting God's sacred name attains satisfaction. By the grace of the saints, I received all fruitful rewards. ||1|| Reciting God, His humble servant is carried across; Sins of countless lifes are taken away. ||1||Pause|| By enshrining guru's feet in the heart; One crosses over the ocean of fire. All painful diseases of birth and death have been eradicated. I am attached to God in peaceful trance. ||2|| In all high low places, One God pervades. He is the inner-knower of everything. Whom the Lord blesses with understanding, recites the name of God, twenty-four hours a day; ||3|| In whose mind dwells God? He is enlightened. With loving devotion, sing the praises of the Lord. Reciting the supreme Lord, O Nanak, you shall be saved.

||4||10||12|| Gond, Fifth Master: Page 866 Bow in humility to the lotus feet of the guru. Eliminate lust and anger from this body. Be the dust of all; See God in every one. ||1|| In this way, worship the Lord of the world, the Lord of the universe. My body and wealth belong to God; my soul belongs to God. ||1||Pause|| Twenty-four hours a day, sing praises of the Lord. This is the purpose of human life. Renounce your ego and pride and know that God is with you. By the grace of devotees, dye your mind with Lord's love. ||2|| Know the one; who created you; You will be honoured in God's court. Your mind and body will become pure and content. Recite the name of the Lord of the universe with your tongue. ||3|| Be kind O merciful to the humble. My mind begs for the dust of the feet of devotees. Be kind and bless me with this gift; That Nanak lives by reciting God's name. ||4||11||13|| Gond, Fifth Master: My service to the Lord is my service of incense and lamps. Time and again, I humbly bow to the Creator. I renounced everything and sought the refuge of God. By good fortune, the guru has become pleased with me. ||1|| Twenty-four hours a day, I sing praises of the Lord of the universe. My body and wealth and soul belong to God. ||1||Pause|| Singing the praises of the Lord, I am happy. The supreme Lord is the perfect bestowal. By His grace, He put His humble servants to His service. He eliminated their pain of birth and death and united them with Him. ||2|| This is the essence of good deeds, faith and wisdom. Recite God's name in the company of devotees. God's feet are the boat to cross over the world-ocean. God, the inner-knower, is the cause of causes. ||3|| By His grace, He saved me. The five demons have run away. I will not lose my life in a gamble. The Lord has taken Nanak's side. ||4||12||14|| Gond, Fifth Master: In His grace, He blessed me with peace and bliss. The guru has saved the child. God is kind and compassionate; He is the Lord of the universe. He bestows to all beings. ||1|| I seek Your sanctuary, O God, merciful to the meek. Reciting the name of the supreme Lord, I am content forever. ||1||Pause|| There is no other as kind as God. He abides in every soul. He takes care of His servant, here and hereafter. It is Your nature O God, to purify sinners. ||2|| Reciting God is the cure of all diseases. Reciting God is the only meditation or mantra. Illnesses and pains are dispelled, reciting God. The fruits

of mind's desire are realized. ||3|| He is the cause of causes, the all-powerful merciful Lord. Contemplating Him is the greatest of all treasures. God is forgiving O Nanak, Recite God forever. ||4||13||15|| Gond, Fifth Master: Recite God God God O my friend. Page 867 Your mind will become pure. All misfortunes of your mind and body shall be eliminated. All your pain and ignorance will be dispelled. ||1|| Singing God's praises crosses over the world-ocean. The fortunate realizes the infinite God. ||1||Pause|| One who sings Lord's praises; The devil of death cannot rob him. His coming into this world is approved; The guru-willed realizes his master. ||2|| He sings God's praises by the grace of a saint. His lust, anger and instability of mind are eradicated. He knows the Lord to be ever-present. This is the perfect teaching of the perfect guru. ||3|| He earns the treasure of Lord's wealth. Meeting the guru, all his affairs are resolved. He is awake in love of God's name; O Nanak, his mind is attached to Lord's feet. ||4||14||16|| Gond, Fifth Master: Lord's feet are the boat to cross over the terrifying world-ocean. Reciting God's name eliminates death. Singing God's praises eliminates the path of death. This is the greatest way to drive away the five thieves. ||1|| I have entered Your sanctuary, O perfect Lord; Please give Your hand to Your devotee. ||1||Pause|| The Simritees, Shaastras, Vedas and Puraanas (scriptures) explain about God. The Yogis, celibates, Vishnu's followers and servants of God also explain; But cannot find the limits of the eternal God; ||2|| Shiva and the gods lament and moan; They do not understand even a tiny bit of the unseen unknown Lord. One whom the Lord blesses with devotional worship, Are rare in the world; ||3|| I am worthless, with no virtue at all; All treasures are in Your vision. Poor Nanak begs for serving You. O guru, be kind and bless me with the service. ||4||15||17|| Gond, Fifth Master: One who is cursed by the saints is destroyed. The slanderer of the saints is dropped from the sky. Hold the saints close to your soul. The saints can save in a moment. ||1|| He who pleases God is a saint. The saint and God, have only one job. ||1||Pause|| God bestows the saint by His grace. He dwells with saints, day and night. He takes care of the saints forever. He takes the power away from the enemies of the saints. ||2|| Let no one slander the saints. Whoever slanders them, will be destroyed. One whom does the Lord protects? No one can harm him; no matter how much the whole world may try. ||3|| I place my faith in God. My soul and body all belong to Him. Nanak is honoured by doing so. The self-willed lose and the guru-willed win forever. ||4||16||18|| Gond, Fifth Master: Reciting God's name is like drinking the nectar. Reciting God's name eliminates sins. ||1||Pause|| Page 868 The Lord abides in everyone. The Lord illuminates each and every heart. Reciting Lord's name, one does not go to hell. Serving the Lord, all rewards are obtained. ||1|| Enshrine God in the mind; The Lord is the boat to cross over the world-ocean. Reciting Lord's name, the devil of death runs away. The Lord breaks the teeth of wicked witch. ||2|| The Lord is the bestowal forever. The Lord blesses us with peace and bliss. The Lord has revealed His power. The Lord is the mother and father of the saints. ||3|| God is devotee's company and devotee's company is God; Time and again, I sing God's praises. Meeting with the guru, I have realized the permanent Lord. Slave Nanak has taken the support of the Lord. ||4||17||19|| Gond, Fifth Master: One who is protected by the protector Lord! The formless Lord is on his side. ||1||Pause|| In mother's womb, the fire does not touch him. Lust, anger, greed and emotional attachment do not affect him. In devotee's company, he recites the formless Lord. Dust falls into the faces of the slanderers. ||1|| Lord's recitation is the protective shield of His devotees. The wicked and evil cannot touch him. Whoever is egotistic shall be destroyed. God is the sanctuary of His humble slave. ||2|| Whoever enters the sanctuary of the sovereign Lord! He saves that slave, holding him close in Him. Whoever is proud! In an instant, he will be mixed with dust; ||3|| It is true, there is God and shall always be. I praise Him forever. By His grace, He saves His slaves. God is the support of Nanak's life. ||4||18||20|| Gond, Fifth Master: Wonderful and beautiful is His discourse. And His beautiful face; ||Pause|| He is not old; He is not young. He does not suffer in pain; He is not caught in death's noose. He does not die; He does not go away. From the beginning, throughout ages, He abides everywhere. ||1|| He does not feel hot or cold. He has no enemy; He has no friend. He is not happy; He is not sad. Everything belongs to Him; He can do anything. ||2|| He has no father or mother. He is beyond imagination, always have been so. He is not affected by good or bad. He watches everything in everybody. ||3|| From the three qualities, one power was produced. That is the great worldly pleasure as a result. He is undeceivable, impenetrable, unfathomable and merciful. He is merciful to the meek and forever compassionate. His divine wisdom cannot be known. Nanak praises Him forever. ||4||19||21|| Page 869 Gond, Fifth Master: I praise the saints. I sing the praises of the Lord in the company of saints. By the grace of the saints, all sins are eliminated. The fortunate finds the sanctuary of saints. ||1|| Reciting God, no obstruction comes your way. By guru's grace, he recites God; ||1||Pause|| When the supreme Lord becomes kind; He makes me the dust of the feet of devotees. Lust and anger leave his body. God the jewel dwells in his mind. ||2|| Fruitful and approved is his life. He realizes God close to him. He sings God's praises in devotional worship. He wakes up from sleep of countless lifes; ||3|| Lord's lotus feet are the support of His humble servant. To sing praises of the Lord of the universe is the true trade. He fulfills the hopes of His devotees. Nanak finds peace in the dust of the feet of the humble. ||4||20||22||6||28|| Tune Gond, Ashtapadees, Fifth Master, Second House: God is one. He is realized by guru's grace. Humbly bow to the perfect guru. Fruitful is His image and fruitful is service to Him. He is the inner-knower the architect of destiny. Twenty-four hours a day, he is imbued with God's love. ||1|| Guru is the Lord of the universe, the Lord of the world. He is the saviour of His slaves. ||1||Pause|| He satisfies the kings, emperors and nobles. He destroys the egotistic and evil. He puts illness into the mouths of the slanderers. Everybody praises him. ||2|| Supreme bliss fills the minds of the saints. The saints worship guru the God. The faces of His companions become happy. The slanderers lose all places of rest. ||3|| With each and every breath, Lord's humble slaves praise Him. The supreme Lord the carefree guru. All fears are eradicated, in His sanctuary. Beating the slanderers, the Lord knocks them to the ground. ||4|| Let no one slander God's humble servants. Whoever does so, will be miserable; Twenty-four hours a day, Lord's humble servant recites one God. The devil of death does not come close to him. ||5|| Lord's humble servant has no enemy. The slanderer is proud. Lord's humble servant wishes well, the slanderer does bad deeds. Recite God through guru's teachings. Lord's humble servants are saved, the slanderer go to hell. ||6|| Listen, O my beloved friends and companions: Truth prevails in God's court. As you sow, so shall you reap? The proud will surely be uprooted. ||7|| O poor being; guru has a place for you. By Your grace; preserve the honour of your servant. Says Nanak I praise the guru. Reciting him attains honour. ||8||1||29||Page 870 Tune Gond, Word Of The Devotees. Kabeer Jee, First House: God is one. He is realized by guru's grace. When saints get together; they talk divine wisdom. When ignorant meet; they keep quiet. ||1|| O elder; what should I say? Speak such words, that you remain absorbed in God's name. ||1||Pause|| Speaking with the saints, one does good for others. Speaking with an ignorant is to babble uselessly. ||2|| By speaking and speaking, only argument increases. If they do not speak, what can the poor do? ||3|| Says Kabeer, the empty pitcher makes noise; Full vessel does not waver. ||4||1|| Gond: When a man dies, he is of no use to anyone. But when an animal dies, it is used in ten ways. ||1|| What do I know what good I am? What do I know O elder? ||1||Pause|| Bones burn, like a bundle of logs; the hair burn like a bale of grass. ||2|| Says Kabeer; then the man wakes up. When the devil of death hits him over the head with his club; ||3||2|| Gond: The sky, the underworld and everything in four directions are imaginary. God is the source of all; when one dies, he does not go into imaginary space. ||1|| I have become sad. Wondering where the soul comes from and where it goes. ||1||Pause|| The body is made of five elements; where do the elements come from? You say that the soul is tied to fate; but who gave the fate? ||2|| The body is God and God abides in the body. He is everywhere. Says Kabeer, do not give up God's name; may it be whatever happens! ||3||3|| Tune Gond, The Word Of Kabeer Jee, Second House: God is one. He is realized by guru's grace. They tied my arms, bundled me up, and threw me in front of an elephant. The elephant driver struck him on the head and infuriated him. But the elephant ran away, trumpeting; I praise this picture. ||1|| O my Lord, You are my help. The Qazi shouted at the driver to drive the elephant on. ||1||Pause|| He yelled, O driver, I will cut you in pieces. Hit him, and drive him on! But the elephant did not move; instead, he began to meditate. The Lord abides in his mind. ||2|| What sin has this saint committed? You put him in a bundle and thrown in front of an elephant? The elephant bows down in front of the bundle. The blind Qazi could not understand; ||3|| Three times, he tried to do it. Page 871 His stubborn mind did not soften yet. Says Kabeer, such is my Lord and master. The soul of His humble servant dwells in the fourth state. ||4||1||4|| Gond: It is not human, it is not god. It is not called celibate, or a worshipper of Shiva. It is not a Yogi, it is not a hermit. It has no mother; He is not anyone's son. ||1|| Then, who lives in this body? No one can find its limits. ||1||Pause|| It is not a householder; he is not a renunciate; It is not a king, it is not a beggar. It has nobody, no drop of blood. It is not a Brahmin it is not a Khshatriya. ||2|| It is not called a man of austere self-discipline, or a scholar. It does not live; it is not seen dieing. If someone cries over its death; that who cries loses his honour. ||3|| By guru's grace, I have found the path. Birth and death have both been erased. Says Kabeer, this is God's family; It is like the ink on the paper, which cannot be erased. ||4||2||5|| Gond: The threads are broken, and the starch ran out. The weaving sticks hang at the front door. The poor brushes are scattered in pieces. Death has overtaken this follower of Raamanand. ||1|| This devotee has wasted all his wealth. Coming and going has irritated him. ||1||Pause|| He has given up talk of his weaving equipment. His mind is attuned to Lord's name. His daughters and sons have nothing to eat; All Raamanand's followers go satisfied. ||2|| One or two are in the house, one or two more are on the way. We sleep on the grass, they sleep in the beds. They wish them well and carry prayer books in their belts. We get dry grains, while they get chapatti to eat. ||3|| All Raamaanand's followers are the same. They are the support of the drowning. Listen, O Loi (His wife). You are blind without the guru; Kabeer has taken shelter with these shaven-heads. ||4||3||6|| Gond: When her husband dies, the woman does not cry. Someone else takes care of her. When this protector dies; He enjoys here and goes to hell in the next world. ||1|| The world loves only one bride; She is the wife of all beings. ||1||Pause|| She looks adorable with a necklace around her neck. She is a poison to the saint, but the world is delighted with her. Adoring herself, she sits like a prostitute. Cursed by the saints, she wanders around. ||2|| She runs around, chasing after the saints. She is afraid that she will be hurt by guru's grace. She is the body, the life of the faithless. She appears to me like a blood-thirsty witch. ||3|| I know her secrets well; By God's grace one meets the guru. Says Kabeer; now I have thrown her out; She sits in the lap of the world. ||4||4||7|| Page 872 Gond: When someone is not respected at home. The guests go hungry. She is not gracious. But without a bride at home, he feels bad. ||1|| The soul bride is sacred. She entices the self-disciplined and renunciates. ||1||Pause|| This bride is the daughter of a miser. Abandoning Lord's servant, she sleeps with the world. She is standing at the door of devotees. I have come to your sanctuary; please save me! ||2|| This bride is very beautiful. The bells on her ankles make tinkling music. As long as one lives; she is with him. Then she goes away at a fast pace bare feet. ||3|| This bride has conquered the three worlds. The eighteen Puraanas and the shrines of pilgrimage love her; She pierced the hearts of Brahma, Shiva and Vishnu. She destroyed the great emperors and kings of the world. ||4|| This bride is neither this side nor the other. She is in collusion with the five thieves. Says Kabeer, by guru's mercy, one is freed then; ||5||5||8|| Gond: As the house will not stand when the beams are removed from inside; Same way; how can anyone go across the world ocean without God's name? Without the pitcher, the water is not contained; Same way without God's devotee the ill will does not leave. ||1|| One who does not remember the Lord, let him burn; His body and mind are absorbed in the worldly field. ||1||Pause|| As the land is not sowed without a farmer. Without a thread, how the beads are strung? Without a loop, how can the knot be tied? Just so, without God's devotee, the ill will does not depart. ||2|| As without a mother or father, the child is not born; Without suds, how can the clothes be washed? Without a horse, how can there be a rider? Without a devotee, one cannot reach the court of the Lord. ||3|| As without music, there is no dancing. The bride rejected by her husband is dishonoured. Says Kabeer; do this one thing: Become a guru-willed and you shall never die again. ||4||6||9|| Gond: Real beating is to beat your mind. Beating your mind frees from the devil of death! Beat your mind and appraise it. Such a beating attains eternal liberation. ||1|| Who do we beat; tell the world! In all aspect, one must carefully consider. ||1||Pause|| Best dance is to dance with your mind. The Lord is not satisfied with falsehood. He is pleased only with truth. So play the beat of the drum in the mind. The Lord is the protector of such a dancer. ||2|| He who wanders all over in the bazaar, eliminates the five passions and learns divine wisdom. He who embraces devotional worship of the Lord I accept such a wanderer as my guru. ||3|| He is a real thief, who does not envy and who uses his sense organs to God's name. Says Kabeer, these are the qualities of the one. My guru is admirable beautiful and a scholar. ||4||7||10|| Page 873 Gond: Blessed is the Lord of the world. Blessed is the guru. Blessed is the grain, which fills the hungry. Blessed are those saints, who know this. Meeting with them, one meets the Lord, the sustainer of the world. ||1|| This grain comes from the primal Lord. Recite God with taste like food. ||1||Pause|| Long for God as you long for food; Mixed with water, its taste becomes sublime. One, who abstains from food; Loses his honour in the universe; ||2|| One, who gives up food, is practicing hypocrisy. She is neither a happy soul-bride, nor a widow. Those who claim in this world that they live on milk alone; Secretly eat whole load of food. ||3|| It is hard to live without food. Giving up food one does not meet the Lord of the world. Says Kabeer, I know this. Blessed is the food, which brings faith in God. ||4||8||11|| Tune Gond, The Word Of Naam Dev Jee, First House: God is one. He is realized by guru's grace. They feed public free food with horsemeat. Giving awns of gold equal to one's weight. They bathe at Praag shrine; ||1|| Says Naam dev, doing all above does not equal to reciting God's name. O lazy mind recite God's name. ||1||Pause|| Some say that Lord of life lives in Gaya; God is realized in a river that flows by Banaras. Some say by reciting the four Vedas by heart; ||2|| Some say by following religion. Some say reciting guru's teachings by senses. Performing the six rituals; ||3|| Expounding on Shiva's power; O mind; give up all these rituals. Just recite the name of the Lord of the universe. Reciting God's name, you will swim across the world ocean. ||4||1|| Gond: As the deer is enticed by sound; It loses its life, but it cannot stop thinking about it. ||1|| The same way, I look at my Lord.

I will not abandon my Lord and turn my thoughts to another. ||1||Pause|| As the fisherman looks for fish; The goldsmith concentrates and shapes gold into ornaments; ||2|| As the wicked man looks upon another man's wife. As the gambler looks for throwing the dice. ||3|| Wherever Naam dev looks, sees God; Naam Dev recites continuously on the feet of the Lord. ||4||2|| Gond: Carry me across, O Lord, carry me across. I do not know how to swim; O my Lord; give Your hand. ||1||Pause|| It changes a mortal into a god in a moment; guru taught me this reality. Born of human being I have conquered the heavens; I took such medicine; ||1|| Please take me where You took Dhroo and Naarad, O my master. Naama realizes; reciting your name attains salvation in an instant. ||2||3|| Page 874 Gond: I am restless and unhappy. As the cow is lonely without the calf. ||1|| Without water, the fish writhes in pain. So is poor Naam Dev without Lord's name. ||1||Pause|| Like cow's calf, when let loose, sucks her udders and drinks milk. ||2|| Naam Dev found the Lord. Meeting the guru, I have seen the unseen Lord. ||3|| As the wicked man wants another man's wife, Same way Naam Dev loves the Lord; ||4|| As the earth burns with heat from sun So does poor Naam Dev burn without God's name. ||5||4|| Tune Gond, The Word Of Naam Dev Jee, Second House: God is one. He is realized by guru's grace. Saying God God eliminates doubts. Saying God's name is the highest religion. Saying God God rejuvenates the whole caste and ancestry. The Lord is the walking stick of the blind. ||1|| I bow to the Lord. I humbly bow to the Lord. Saying God God the fear of devil of death goes away. ||1||Pause|| The Lord took the life of Harnaakhash, Gave Ajaamal a place in heaven. Listening to parrot's word (God), the prostitute was saved. That Lord is the light of my eyes. ||2|| Saying God God, the child eater Pootna was saved. She the killer of children was full of sins. Reciting God, Dropadi was saved. Gautam's wife that was turned to stone was saved. ||3|| The Lord, who killed Kans dragging from the hair. Gave the gift of life to Kali. Prays Naam Dev, such is my Lord; Singing His praises, fear and suffering are dispelled. ||4||1||5|| Gond: Saint Bhairau, went after evil spirits and the goddess of small pox. Riding a donkey, he used to do nonsense rituals. ||1|| I only recite the name of one Lord. I gave up all other gods in exchange for

Him. ||1||Pause|| That man who says Shiva, Shiva; Riding a bull he plays a tambourine. ||2|| One who worships the great goddess? Will be born as a woman, not a man. ||3|| You are called the primal goddess. At the time of liberation, where did you hide? ||4|| Follow guru's teachings and recite God's name with love O friend. Thus prays Naam Dev and so says the Gita as well. ||5||2||6|| Bilaaval Gond: Today, Naam Dev saw the Lord, instructing the ignorant. ||Pause|| O religious scholar, your cow was grazing in farmer's fields. The farmer broke its leg with a stick and now it walks with a limp. ||1|| O scholar, I saw your great god Shiva, riding a white bull. In a merchant's house, food was prepared for him killing merchant's son. ||2|| Page 875 O scholar, I saw your Raam Chander coming too He lost his wife, and fought a war against Raawan. ||3|| The Hindu is blind; Muslim has only one eye. The spiritually wise is wiser than both; The Hindu worships at the temple, the Muslim at the mosque. Naam Dev serves that Lord, who has no temple or mosque. ||4||3||7|| Tune Gond, The Word Of Ravi Daas Jee, Second House: God is one. He is realized by guru's grace. O people; recite God the bestowal of salvation. Without reciting God the body shall be reduced to ashes. God is the giver of liberation. He is my father and mother. ||1|| Recite God while living; you shall meet Him after death. His servant is happy forever. ||1||Pause|| God is my life. One recites God due to pre-ordained destiny. Reciting God detaches the devotee. Reciting God the poor finds wealth. ||2|| When one liberator does a favour; What can the world do to me? Erasing my social status, I have entered His court. You, the bestowal, bestow salvation in all ages. ||3|| Spiritual wisdom has welled up, I have been enlightened. By His grace the Lord has made the worm His slave. Says Ravi Daas, now my greed is gone. Reciting God is God's worship. ||4||1|| Gond: He bathes at the sixty-eight sacred shrines. He worships idols on twelfth day of lunar calendar. He digs wells in the desert. But if he slanders others, all this is useless. ||1|| How can the slanderer of God's devotee be saved? Know for certain, that he shall go to hell. ||1||Pause|| Someone may mortgage the whole property. He may offer his wife along with her jewellery. May listen to all the Simritees; But if he slanders others, attains no reward. ||2|| Someone may offer sacred offerings; Donate land and builds splendid buildings; He may neglect his own affairs to work for others; But if he slanders others; will be born again and again. ||3|| Why do you slander others O people of the world? The words of the slanderer will be exposed soon. I contemplated and came at this conclusion. Says Ravi Daas that the sinner goes to hell; ||4||2||11||7||2||49|| Total|| Page 876 Raamkalee, First Master, First House, Chau-Padas:

God is one. It is true. He is the Creator. He is carefree. He has no enemy. He is immortal. He does not take birth. He came into existence on His own. He is realized by guru's grace.

Some read Sahaskrit scriptures, and some read Puraanas. Some recite God' name with a rosary in devotion; I know nothing now or ever. I recognize only Your one name. ||1|| I do not know O Lord, how I will get salvation. I am foolish and ignorant. I seek Your refuge O God. Please, save my honour and self-respect! ||1||Pause|| Sometimes, my mind flies in the sky, sometimes goes in the underworld. The greedy soul does not remain stable, it searches in the four directions. ||2|| With pre-determined death the soul comes into the world, mother gives birth. I see one going, O my Lord; the burning fire is coming closer! ||3|| No one is anyone's friend, brother, father or mother. Prays Nanak, whatever You give, helps in the end. ||4||1|| Raamkalee, First Master: Your Light is prevailing everywhere. Wherever I look, I see the Lord. ||1|| Please get rid of my desire to live, O my Lord; My mind is entangled in the deep dark pit of worldly pleasure. How can I cross over, O Lord? ||1||Pause|| He dwells inside; why not outside? Because God cares for those who recite Him in the mind; ||2|| He is near, He is far. He is omnipresent. Meeting the true guru eliminates the darkness. Page 877 Wherever I look, I see Him; ||3|| Worry inside; the worldly wealth outside; Your discourse pierces my eyes. Prays Nanak, the servant of servants O mortal; it will happen! ||4||2|| Raamkalee, First Master: What can I say where you live, who can search the door in the door. For the sake of that door, I wander sad; may somebody come from that door and tell me about it; ||1|| How can I cross over the world-ocean? If I do not die while living; ||1||Pause|| Pain is the door, anger is the guard; hope and anxiety are the two shutters. Worldly wealth is the moat filled with water; in the middle of this moat, He has built his home. The primal Lord sits there in the seat of truth. ||2|| I do not know how many names You have. There is no other equal to You. Do not say loud, say in the mind. God knows it. He will look after. ||3|| As long as there is hope and worry, how can anyone miss God? In the midst of hope, remain untouched by hope; then, O Nanak, you shall meet the Lord. ||4|| In this way, you shall cross over the world-ocean. This is the way to be dead while alive. ||1||Second Pause||3|| Raamkalee, First Master: I blow the horn of guru's teachings with love and everybody hears it. I carry my honour as my begging-bowl, I beg God's name as awns. ||1|| O elder, God is always awake. He who sustains the world is God. He created it in an instant. ||1||Pause|| He controls water, life and air. He gave two lamps to see like sun and moon. He gave the earth to live and die and you forgot all this! ||2|| There are many mystics, seekers, Yogis, wandering pilgrims, spiritual teachers and good people. If I meet them, I sing their praises and serve them. ||3|| Paper and salt, protected by oil, remain untouched by water, as the lotus remains unaffected in water. Meeting with such devotees, O Nanak, what can death do to me? ||4||4|| Raamkalee, First Master: Listen, Machhindra; what Nanak says. One who controls the five passions does not waver. This practice contemplates Yoga. He saves him and saves his dynasty. ||1|| One who attains such realization is a hermit. Day and night, he remains absorbed in deep trance. ||1||Pause|| He begs for love of the Lord and lives in the fear of God. He is satisfied, with the priceless gift of contentment. Becoming the embodiment of meditation, he attains the Yogic posture. He sits in trance of the true name. ||2|| Nanak speaks the sacred sermon. Listen, O Machhindra: this is the sign of the true hermit. One who in the midst of hope remains untouched by hope! Shall truly find Lord. ||3|| Prays Nanak and says further mystery! Eliminates the gap between the guru and His disciple. He eats the medicine of guru's blessing. Page 878 He obtains the knowledge of the six Shaastras. ||4||5|| Raamkalee, First Master: My boat is wobbly. It is filled with sins. It will sink with wind gust. The mystics have come to serve you. They are honouring you. ||1|| O guru the saviour; please save me. Bless me with worship of immortal God. I praise you! ||1||Pause|| Those who worship the mysterious, become mystics, yogi and bhairo. Those who say God and touch your feet, their deeds are fulfilled O God. ||2|| I know nothing of meditation, self-discipline, self-control or good deeds. I only recite Your name, O God. O Nanak, meeting guru the God, attains salvation through his teachings. ||3||6|| Raamkalee, First Master: Focus your soul to the supreme soul such a way! Like making a raft of your body to cross over. Love Him in your mind. That lamp burns forever. ||1|| Float such a lamp on water. This lamp will bring eternal knowledge. ||1||Pause|| Good clay makes a good pot. The lamp made of such clay is acceptable to the Lord. Shape this lamp on good deeds. It will accompany you here and hereafter. ||2|| When He grants His grace. Then; a few guru-willed will realize Him. In that heart, this lamp is permanently lit. It is not extinguished by water or wind. Such a lamp will carry you across the water. ||3|| Wind does not shake it or put it out. Its light reveals the divine throne. The Khshatriya, Brahmins, Soodras and Vaishyas Cannot find its value, even by thousands of calculations; if anyone lights such a lamp O Nanak, he is released. ||4||7|| Raamkalee, First Master: People bow down to You and believe in Your name. With an offering of truth, one finds a place to sit. If a prayer is offered with truth and contentment; You O Lord, will hear it and call him to sit close to You. ||1|| O Nanak, no one returns empty-hand. Such is the court of the true Lord. ||1||Pause|| Whatever I receive is my own doing. Please bless this humble beggar. I beg with love. What you put in a pot, same comes out. This comes from above after appraising. ||2|| One who created everything, does everything. He knows His value. The guru-willed realize God the sovereign Lord. He does not come, He does not go. ||3|| People curse the beggar. Begging does not bring honour. This happens at my Lord's court. He asked me to say, so I said. ||4||8|| Raamkalee, First Master: The drop is in the ocean, and the ocean fills with drops. Who knows the mystery? He created the creation searching Him, he knows the reality. ||1|| Page 879 If someone contemplates such wisdom; attains salvation doing so. The night after day, day after night, summer and winter come by his doing! No one knows His divine wisdom. Without guru, no one understands it. ||2|| The female in male, the male is in the female. Realize and tell me O wise man. With knowledge in the mind, realize God by thinking.

O guru-willed; tell me God's unspoken story. ||3|| The Light is in the mind, the light lights the mind controlling the five passions through guru's teachings O brother. Nanak admires those who intuitively say God through guru's teaching. ||4||9|| Raamkalee, First Master: When He showers His blessing. The ego is eliminated from the mind. That humble servant is very dear to the Lord. One, who contemplates guru's teachings. ||1|| That humble servant of the Lord is pleasing to God. He worships God day and night, erasing ego he sings God's praises. ||1||Pause|| The divine music plays loud. My mind is happy by the subtle essence of the Lord. Through the perfect guru, I am absorbed in truth. Through the guru, I have found the Lord, the primal being. ||2|| Guru's teaching is the enticing sound, the Vedas and everything. My mind is attuned to the Lord of the universe. He is my shrine of pilgrimage, fasting and austere self-discipline. Lord saves and carries across, those who meet the guru. ||3|| One, whose self-conceit and other concern is gone; That servant serves guru's feet. The true guru has eliminated my doubts. Says Nanak, I realized God through guru's teachings. ||4||10|| Raamkalee First Master He runs around, begging for clothes and food. He the evil minded burns with hunger and will suffer in the world after. He does not obey guru's teachings; through evil thinking he loses his honour. Through guru's teachings, only a few worship God. ||1|| The real way of the Yogi is to live in peace. He sees all equal. He becomes content through awns of guru's teachings. ||1||Pause|| The five bulls (elements) created the body the cart. It happens by God's grace. When the axle breaks, the wagon falls and crashes. It falls apart, under heavy load. ||2|| Contemplate guru's teachings O yogi. See pain and pleasure, sorrow and separation alike. Contemplate God's name through guru's teachings. You shall live forever by reciting the formless Lord. ||3|| Wear the loincloth of contentment and be free of entanglements. You shall get rid of lust and anger through guru's teachings. Let your mind be the ear rings and seek refuge of God the guru. O Nanak, worshipping God attains liberation. ||4||11|| Page 880 God is one. He is realized by guru's grace. Raamkalee, Third Master, First House: In first age (satyug), everyone spoke the truth. In each and every home, everyone worshipped God. In the first age (Golden Age), faith stood on four legs. Only a few guru-willed realize God by contemplating. ||1|| In all four ages, God's name is the essence. One who recites God's name attains salvation. No one obtains God's name without the guru. ||1||Pause|| In the second age (Traytaa), one leg was removed. Hypocrisy became prevalent and people thought God was far away. The guru-willed realize by contemplating. Enshrining God's name in the mind attains peace. In the third Age (Dwaapur), duality and double-mindedness arose. Deluded by doubt, they believed in duality. In the third age, faith stood on two feet. Those who became guru-willed recited God's name. ||3|| In today's age (Kalyug), faith stands on one foot. It walks on one foot enticed by the love of worldly pleasure. Love of worldly wealth and emotional attachment bring total darkness. Surrendering to the guru and reciting God's name attains salvation. ||4|| Throughout the ages, there is only the one God. Among all pervades one Lord no other. Praising the true Lord, true peace is attained. Only a few guru-willed recite God's name. ||5|| Through all ages, God's name is the highest of all. Only a few guru-willed realize this. One who recites God's name is God's humble devotee. O Nanak, in all ages God's name obtains honour. ||6||1|| Raamkalee, Fourth Master, First House: God is one. He is realized by guru's grace. If a fortunate is fortunate, he recites God's name. Reciting God's name he attains peace and merges in God reciting God. ||1|| O mortal guru-willed worship God. Enshrining God in the mind through guru's teachings, enlightens the mind through love. ||1||Pause|| The great giver is filled with diamonds, emeralds, rubies and pearls; The fortunate with preordained destiny takes them out through guru's teachings. ||2|| Lord's name is the jewel, the emerald, the ruby; the guru took out and showed me putting on his palm. The unfortunate, self-willed did not see; it was hidden behind a straw. ||3|| One with a pre-ordained destiny meets the guru and serves him. O Nanak, he obtains the jewel, the gem He obtains it through blessed guru's teachings. ||4||1|| Raamkalee, Fourth Master: Meeting with God's devotees I became happy listening to God's sermon. The filth of evil-will disappeared. I became enlightened meeting devotee's company. ||1|| Page 881 God's devotees say God God through guru's teachings. Whoever hears and says God is liberated and looks adorable. ||1||Pause|| If someone has pre-ordained destiny, God unites him with His devotees. O saint, be kind and visualize yourself to me that my poverty and pain go away. ||2|| Lord's people are good and sublime. They do not appeal to the unfortunate. More the divine people say God, more the slanderers slander them. ||3|| Cursed are the slanderers who do not like God's friends and companions. Those who do not admire the guru are thieves. They are turned away from God with black faces. ||4|| O God be kind, I the humble am at Your refuge. I am Your child, You are my father O God. Be kind and unite Nanak with You. ||5||2|| Raamkalee, Fourth Master: God's devotees are His friends and honourable. He protects them by His grace. The guru-willed devotees please God. He unites them with him by His grace. ||1|| O Lord, my mind longs to meet the humble servants of the Lord. The nectar of God's essence tastes sweet. One drinks it in saint's company. ||1||Pause|| God's people His devotees are sacred. Meeting them makes sacred. I am the slave of God's slaves. My Lord is pleased with me. ||2|| The devotees who serve God whole-heartedly with love are fortunate. One who talks too much without love is a liar, he obtains false rewards. ||3|| Be kind to me O life of the world. Please let me touch saint's feet. I cut my head and put it on the path, where saints walk. ||4||3|| Raamkalee, Fourth Master: If I am fortunate it does not take long to meet God's devotees. God's servants are the pools full of nectar. The fortunate bathes in it. ||1|| O Lord, let me work for the humble servants of the Lord. I carry water, wave fan and grind grain for them. I massage their feet and apply the dust of their feet to my forehead. ||1||Pause|| God's devotees are the greatest who lead me to meet the guru. No one is as great as the guru. Meeting the guru, I recite God. ||2|| Those who seek guru's refuge, realize God. My Lord preserves their honour. Some with their self-interest come and sit in front of the guru like a stork with eyes closed. ||3|| Associating with the low life like the stork and the crow is like feeding on a rotten corpse. O God, unite Nanak with Your devotees that I become a swan. ||4||4|| Page 882 Raamkalee, Fourth Master: O guru, be kind, and unite me with God my beloved, support of my life. I the slave fall at the guru's feet that showed me the way to realize God. ||1|| O God; God's name pleases my mind. I have no friend except God. God is my father mother and a friend.

||1||Pause|| I cannot live without my beloved even for a moment. I will die without seeing Him o mother. I the fortunate am blessed that I came to guru's refuge. Meeting the guru I visualized God. ||2|| I do not know or understand anyone else in my mind. I just recite God. Those without God's name are shameless. They cut their nose rubbing on the ground. ||3|| O life of the world, save me O my Lord. I enshrined Your name in my heart. Nanak is my perfect guru. I recite God's name in his congregation. ||4||5|| Raamkalee, Fourth Master: The guru the great giver is great primal being. Meeting Him, God dwells in the mind. The perfect guru gave me life. I recite God's sacred name. ||1|| O Lord, the guru taught me to recite God's name with love. I listen and enjoy God's discourse. I am fortunate. ||1||Pause|| Millions of gods recite God but they cannot find Him. With sexual urge in the heart, they beg for beautiful women, wealth and mystic powers spreading their hands. ||2|| Singing and reciting God's praises is a great deed O guru-willed; remember this. With good fortune one recites God. God takes across the world ocean. ||3|| God is close to His servant and His servant is close to Him. The servant enshrines God in his mind. O Nanak, God is my father and mother. God looks after his beloved child. ||4||6||18|| Tune Raamkalee, Fifth Master, First House: God is one. He is realized by guru's grace. O kind to the poor Lord; do not look for my merits and demerits. How can one wash the dirt O Lord? That is the state of a human being. ||1|| O my mind; serve the guru and attain peace. Whatever you desire you get. Pain shall not bother you anymore. ||1||Pause|| He creates and bestows honour on the earthen pots. His light abides inside. Whatever He wrote from destiny that is what I do. ||2|| He thinks that the body and mind is his, that keeps him coming and going. He does not miss God who gave him these. The blind is lost in emotional attachment. ||3|| Page 883 He, who created you knows how to reach the incomparable God's abode. I the servant Nanak worship and sing God's praise O God. ||4||1|| Raamkalee, Fifth Master: Put your palms under his feet, serve him this way. Think everyone better than you then you attain peace in God's court. ||1|| O saints, contemplate such a sermon. Reciting a little bit of God's sermon makes gods, human and demons sacred. ||1||Pause|| Give up ill planned ideas and stay home in peace but do

not lie. Meet the guru and obtain the priceless treasure. Churn the truth this way. ||2|| O guru-willed, eliminate doubt and search your soul with love O brother. Know that God is near and ever-present. How can you become an enemy with anyone? ||3|| The way to salvation is found through the guru and realize God with ease. Blessed are those who realize God in today's age. Servant Nanak admires them. ||4||2|| Raamkalee, Fifth Master: Coming does not please me, going does not bring me pain and any disease does not afflict my mind. I obtained eternal joy meeting the perfect guru and all my sorrows erased. ||1|| This is how my mind is attached to God's worship. Attachment, sorrow, disease and public opinion do not affect those, who enjoy saying God God God. ||1||Pause|| The heaven, the land of dead and the amazing underworld are sacred. Obeying God enjoys peace forever. Wherever I look, I see virtuous God; ||2|| There is no worldly power, no water or wind, no atmosphere or earth. Guru the yogi lives there, where unknowable and immortal God lives. ||3|| Body, mind and wealth all belong to God, how can I describe God's virtues? Says Nanak, the guru destroyed my ego. I merged with him like water in water. ||4||3|| Raamkalee, Fifth Master: It is beyond the three qualities. Mystics and seekers do not know her. The safe full of jewels and nectar is in guru's treasure. ||1|| It is amazing! It cannot be described. It is an unfathomable object, O brother! ||1||Pause|| Its value cannot be estimated. What can anyone say? I do not have the intellect to explain. One who realizes it knows it. ||2|| Only the Creator knows it. What can any poor creature do? Only He knows his divine power. God's stores are filled with it. ||3|| Tasting such nectar, the mind becomes satisfied and satiated. Says Nanak, my hopes are fulfilled in guru's refuge. ||4||4|| Page 884 Fifth Master: God made me His own and defeated all my enemies. Those enemies, who robbed the world, have been arrested. ||1|| The guru is my transcendent Lord. I enjoy countless pleasures of power and tasty delights by reciting Your name with my faith in You. ||1||Pause|| I do not think of anything else. God protects me. I am carefree with the support of God's name. ||2|| I have become perfect meeting with the giver of peace. I lack nothing at all. I really have obtained the highest state. It does not leave me anymore. ||3|| I cannot describe what You are, O true unseen, infinite Lord.

Immeasurable, unfathomable and unmoving Lord O Nanak, He is my Lord. ||4||5|| Raamkalee, Fifth Master: You are wise. You are unchanging. You are my social class and honour. You are unwavering. You never waver. Why do I worry? ||1|| You are the one and only Lord. You alone are the emperor. By Your grace, I found peace. ||1||Pause|| You are the ocean full of pearls and I am Your swan to pick them. You give without hesitation. I am fulfilled and content with it. ||2|| I am Your child, You are my father. You give me milk to drink. I play with You joyfully. You are forever the ocean of excellence. ||3|| You are perfect, perfectly all-pervading. I am fulfilled with You as well. I merged with You with ease. Nanak cannot describe it? ||4||6|| Raamkalee, Fifth Master: Make your hands the cymbals, your eyes the tambourines, and your forehead the guitar to play. Let the sweet flute music resound in your ears and with your tongue sing the tune. Dance with your mind, moving hand around and shake your ankle bracelets. ||1|| This is the dance of the Lord. The kind Lord watches all your makeup and jewellery. ||1||Pause|| The whole earth is the stage, sky is the canopy on top. The wind is the culture and life is created out of water. He created the puppet uniting five elements. You got what you earned. ||2|| The sun and the moon are the two lamps to give light in all four corners. The ten senses and five musicians are in one body. They all put on their own show and speak their unique words. ||3|| In each and every home there is dancing, day and night. In each and every home, they dance to the drumbeat. Some dance, some circle around, some come and some go reduced to dust. Says Nanak, one who meets the true guru, does not dance anymore. ||4||7|| Page 885 Raamkalee, Fifth Master: God is one. His tune is one and sings only one song. He lives in one place, there is only one way to go there. He alone lives there. Put your mind to one and serve one. He is realized through one guru. ||1|| Blessed is the singer, who sings His praises. He recites and sings the praises of the Lord. He gave up the entanglement and interest of the worldly pleasures. ||1||Pause|| He plays five instruments with seven tunes intuitively. He plays the instruments with ease and does not go out of tune. If he follows guru's teachings he does not wander in circle again. ||2|| He plays his pawns to realize God close by. He gives up the filthy sounding ankle bells.

He is in peace and content and appeals to all. Such a dancer does not take birth again. ||3|| If anyone is pleasing to his Lord. He sings God's praises among millions. He takes shelter of devotee's company. Says Nanak, he sings only God's praises. ||4||8|| Raamkalee, Fifth Master: Some say Raam Raam and some say Khuda. Some serve Him as the owner of the world others as 'Allaah'. ||1|| He is the cause of causes, the generous Lord. He showers His grace and mercy on us. ||1||Pause|| Some bathe at shrines and some make the pilgrimage to Mecca. Some perform worship services, some bow their heads in prayer. ||2|| Some read Vedas, and some Quran. Some wear blue robes and some wear white. ||3|| Some call themselves Muslim, some call themselves Hindu. Some yearn for paradise and others long for heaven. ||4|| Says Nanak, one who realizes God's command, finds the secret of his Lord. ||5||9|| Raamkalee, Fifth Master: The wind merges in the wind. The light blends in the light. The dust becomes dust with the dust. What is the fate of the one who cries without reason? ||1|| Who has died? O people, who has died? O all knowing people; sit together and contemplate that the poor soul has departed. ||1||Pause|| No one knows what happens after death. The one who is crying will also get up and depart. Mortal beings are bound by the bonds of doubt and attachment. When life becomes a dream, the blind man babbles and grieves in vain. ||2|| The Creator created this creation. Everyone comes and goes by God's infinite command. No one dies no one is capable of dieing. The soul does not perish. It is imperishable. ||3|| That which is known, does not exist. I praise the one who knows all. Says Nanak, the guru has dispelled my doubt. No one dies no one comes or goes. ||4||10|| Raamkalee, Fifth Master: Recite the name of the Lord of the universe, the Lord of the world. Reciting God's name you live forever. Death cannot consume you. ||1||Pause|| He came in this life wandering though millions of lifes. Page 886 By great fortune I found the company of devotees. ||1|| Without the perfect guru, no one is saved. Grandfather Nanak says this after reflecting. ||2||11|| Tune Raamkalee, Fifth Master, Second House: God is one. He is realized by guru's grace. The four Vedas proclaim it, but you don't believe them. The six Shaastras also say the same thing. The eighteen Puraanas all speak of one God. Even so, the Yogi does not understand this mystery. ||1|| The divine instrument plays the incomparable tune. He is intoxicated O yogi. ||1||Pause|| In the first age (satyug), He established the village of truth. In the second Age (Traytaa Yug), things began to decline. In the third age (Dwaapur Yug), half of it was gone. When one recites one God in today's age, he realizes God. ||2|| The beads are strung on one thread. With many knots in many ways. The beads of rosary are counted many ways with love. When the thread is pulled out, the beads fall in one pile. ||3|| Throughout the four ages, there is only one way to realize God. It is a difficult place, with several windows. Searching and searching, he comes to Lord's door. Then, O Nanak, the Yogi attains his destiny. ||4|| Thus, the divine instrument plays the incomparable tune. Listening to it, Yogi's mind enjoys it. ||1||Second Pause||1||12|| Raamkalee, Fifth Master: The body is a patchwork of threads. The muscles are stitched together with the needles of bones. The Lord has erected a pillar of water. O Yogi, what are you proud of? ||1|| Recite God day and night. The patched coat shall last for only a few days. ||1||Pause|| Smearing ashes on your body, you sit in a trance. You wear the earrings of yours and mine. You beg for bread, but you are not satisfied. Abandoning Lord, you beg from others. You should be ashamed. ||2|| Your mind is restless O Yogi, as you sit in your Yogic postures. You blow your horn, but still feel sad. You do not understand God the guru. Again and again, you will come and go. ||3|| Whoever God is kind to I offer my prayer to him the guru the Lord of the world. God's name is my patched coat and a robe. O servant Nanak, the Yogi became immortal. ||4|| One who recites God this way? Finds the guru, the Lord of the world, in this life! ||1||Second Pause||2||13|| Raamkalee, Fifth Master: He is the Creator, the cause of causes. I do not see any other at all. My Lord the master is wise and all knowing. The guru-willed finds and enjoys His love. ||1|| Such is the sweet, subtle essence of the Lord. Only a few guru-willed realize it. ||1||Pause|| God's light is pure and His name is sacred. Page 887 Drinking it one becomes immortal and free of desire. The body and mind are soothed and the fire is extinguished. The worldly being became joyful. ||2|| What can I offer You O Lord? Everything belongs to You. I praise You forever, hundreds of thousands of times. You created my body mind and soul. By guru's grace, this lowly being is honoured. ||3|| Opening the door, You called me to Your abode. As You are, so You revealed to me. Says Nanak, the veil is lifted. I am Yours and You are enshrined in my mind. ||4||3||14|| Raamkalee, Fifth Master: He put His servant to His service. God gave me the sacred name to recite. He eliminated all worries. I praise that guru forever. ||1|| The guru has perfectly resolved my affairs. The guru played the divine music. ||1||Pause|| His glory is profound and unfathomable. Whom He blesses, becomes content. Whoever's bonds God cuts. That person does not take birth again. ||2|| One who has God dwelling inside? Is not touched by pain and sorrow He has God the jewel the gem in his lap. He swims across the ocean world along with his family. ||3|| He has no doubt, double-mindedness or duality. He worships only one formless Lord. Wherever I look, I see the kind Lord. Says Nanak, I found the taste worthy God. ||4||4||15|| Raamkalee, Fifth Master: Ego is eliminated from my body. The will of God is dear to me. Whatever He does, tastes sweet to my mind. Then, I saw this amazing play. ||1|| Now, I know that my demons are gone. My thirst is quenched and my attachment is dispelled. The perfect guru taught me so. ||1||Pause|| By his grace the guru took me in his refuge. The guru has attached me to Lord's feet. When the mind is totally content; one sees the guru and the supreme Lord one and the same. ||2|| Whoever did so, I am his slave. My God dwells in all. I have no enemies, no adversaries. I walk hand in hand, like brothers, with all. ||3|| Whom the guru, the Lord, blesses with peace does not suffer pain anymore; He looks after everyone. Nanak is imbued with love of the Lord of the world. ||4||5||16|| Raamkalee, Fifth Master: You read the scriptures including translation. But you do not miss God devotionally. You preach others. But you do not practice what you preach. ||1|| O scholar; contemplate the Vedas. Eradicate anger from your mind, O scholar; ||1||Pause|| You place your stone god in front of you. Page 888 Your mind wanders in ten directions. You apply a ceremonial mark and touch its feet. You teach others but you do bad deeds. ||2|| You perform six religious rituals and sit wearing your loincloth. In the homes of the wealthy, you read the scriptures. You recite rosary and beg awns. No one has ever been saved this way O friend. ||3|| He who practices guru`s teachings is a scholar. The worldly wealth of the three qualities leaves him. Reciting God is as good as reciting four Vedas. Nanak seeks His sanctuary. ||4||6||17|| Raamkalee, Fifth Master: No trouble comes near him. The whole worldly wealth becomes his slave. All sins are his water-carriers. He is blessed by the Creator. ||1|| One who has Lord`s blessing. All his deeds are fulfilled. ||1||Pause|| One who is protected by the Creator; no one can harm him; Even an ant can conquer the whole world. His glory is endless; how can I describe it? I admire Him and touch his feet. ||2|| He performs worship, austerities and meditation. He gives awns to many in many ways. He who is approved by God in today`s age is the real devotee, whom God blesses with honour. ||3|| He is enlightened in devotee`s company. He finds peace and his desires are fulfilled. The perfect guru has blessed him with confidence. Nanak is the slave of His slaves. ||4||7||18|| Raamkalee, Fifth Master: Don't blame others. As you sow, so shall you reap? You are entangled by your actions. You come and go entangled in worldly wealth. ||1|| The saints know this reality. Enlightenment comes through guru`s teachings. ||1||Pause|| Body, wealth, spouse are all temporary. Horses and elephants will pass away. Power, pleasure and beauty are all false. Without God`s name, all will turn to dust. ||2|| The egotistic people are deluded by doubt. This entire creation does not go with you. Through pleasure and pain, the body grows old. The faithless spend their life this way. ||3|| God`s name is sacred in today`s age. This treasure is obtained from God`s devotees. O Nanak, whoever the guru is kind to. He sees God in everybody. ||4||8||19|| Raamkalee, Fifth Master: The divine wisdom is realized and divine music plays. The infinite divine music is amazingly joyful. The saintly people play there with the Lord. They remain totally detached, absorbed in the supreme Lord. ||1|| It is the place of peace and joy. They sing God`s praises in devotee's company. They suffer no disease, sorrow or birth and death. ||1||Pause|| Only God`s name is recited there. Only a few find that place to rest. Love is their food and singing God`s praises is their resolve. Page 889 They become immortal. ||2|| No one wavers, or goes anywhere. By guru's grace, only a few find this place. They are not touched by doubt, fear, attachment or worldly wealth. They get in trance by God's grace. ||3|| He has no end or limit of His creation. He is hidden and he is in the creation. One who enjoys the taste of reciting God? O Nanak, his amazing divine state cannot be explained. ||4||9||20|| Raamkalee, Fifth Master: Meeting with devotee's company, I recite God. I attain contentment in their company. I put my forehead on saint's feet. I humbly bow to the saints many times. ||1|| This mind praises the saints. I obtained peace in their refuge; they protected me by their grace. ||1||Pause|| I wash the feet of the saints and drink that water. I live by seeing saint's face. My mind rests its hopes in the saints. The saints are my true wealth. ||2|| The saints have covered my sins. By the grace of the saints, I am no longer bothered. The kind Lord blessed me with saint's congregation. The helpful saints became kind to me. ||3|| My thinking, intellect and wisdom have been enlightened. The Lord is profound, unfathomable, infinite, the treasure of virtue. He cherishes all beings. Nanak is content seeing the saints. ||4||10||21|| Raamkalee, Fifth Master: Power wealth and property are of no use to those who worship You. The corrupt worldly entanglements are of no use to those who worship You. Brothers of the same faith and friends all can be cheated. But God's name goes with you. ||1|| Sing the praises of God's name. Reciting God preserves your honour. Reciting God the devil of death does not touch you. ||1||Pause|| Without the Lord, all deeds are useless. Gold, silver and wealth are just dust. Reciting God's name attains happiness. Here and hereafter, you shall be happy. ||2|| All elder are tired of trying. Worldly wealth does not fulfill the hope of anyone in the end. Only a few recite God. Their desire is fulfilled. ||3|| God's name is the support of His devotees. The saints have conquered this priceless human life. Whatever the saint does, is accepted by God. Slave Nanak praises him. ||4||11||22|| Raamkalee, Fifth Master: You gather wealth by hurting others. It is of no use to you. It was meant for others. You blindly do egotistic deeds. You will be tied by the chains of the devil of death hereafter. ||1|| Give up your feeling bad of others, you ignorant! You only live here for a night, you ignorant! You are intoxicated with worldly wealth. You are going to go soon. You are seeing a dream. ||1||Pause|| In his childhood, the child is ignorant. In the full of youth, he commits sins. Page 890 In the third stage of life, he gathers the worldly wealth. When he grows old, he leaves all this behind and departs regretting. ||2||

Obtained this human life after a long time. Without God's name, it is reduced to dust. It is worse than an animal, a demon or an ignorant. It does not realize the one who made it. ||3|| Listen O man, the Creator, Lord of the universe, Lord of the world, merciful to the meek is always kind. If You free the human, then only his bonds will be broken. O Nanak, please unite me with You in the blind world. ||4||12||23|| Raamkalee, Fifth Master: He created this body by His grace. The ignorant fool is enticed by it. He cherishes it and constantly takes care of it. In the end he gets up and goes away. ||1|| O mortal, everything is false without God's name. He is involved with others, than worshipping God; worldly wealth is all false. ||1||Pause|| Bathing at shrines, does not wash away the filth. Religious rituals and good deeds are all just egotistic displays. Serving others does not attain salvation. Without God's name, they shall depart weeping. ||2|| Without Lord's name, the veil is not lifted. I have studied all Shaastras and Simritees. He whom God inspires; recites God's name. He obtains all fruits and merges in peace. ||3|| O saviour Lord, please save me! All peace and comforts are in Your Hand. As you attach me, so I do O Lord; O Nanak, the Lord knows all. ||4||13||24|| Raamkalee, Fifth Master: Whatever He does makes me happy. The ignorant mind is satisfied in the company of devotees. Now, it does not waver anymore; Truth has merged with truth. ||1|| Pain is gone and all illness is gone. I accepted God's will and obtained company of divine person. ||1||Pause|| All is pure; all is sacred. Whatever He does is good. Wherever He keeps me, is the place of liberation for me. God makes me to recite His name. ||2|| Where God's devotee goes is as good as going to sixty-eight shrines. Wherever one recites God is heaven. Visualizing him attains eternal peace. I sing and recite God's praises forever. ||3|| The Lord is pervading in each and every heart. The kind Lord is realized by His grace. His mind opens up and the doubt goes away. Nanak has met with the perfect guru. ||4||14||25|| Raamkalee, Fifth Master: Millions of meditations and austerities rest in him, along with wealth, wisdom, mysticism and divine knowledge. He enjoys various beautiful forms, pleasures and delicacies; The guru-willed enshrines God's name in the mind. ||1|| Such is the greatness of reciting the name of God. Its value cannot be described. ||1||Pause|| He is brave, patient and wise. Page 891 He is intuitively in trance, profound and unfathomable. He is liberated forever and all his affairs are resolved in whose mind abides God's name. ||2|| He is totally peaceful, blissful and healthy; He is impartial and completely detached. He does not come or go, he never wavers; God's name abides in his mind. ||3|| God is kind to the poor. He is the Lord of the world the Lord of the universe. O guru-willed reciting His name, your worries will depart. The guru has blessed Nanak with God's name. Serving the saints is the duty of the saints. ||4||15||26|| Raamkalee, Fifth Master: Sing God's praises through guru's teachings. The homeless find a place to live in the next world. Fall at the feet of the perfect guru. You will wake up from the sleep of many a life. ||1|| Recite God's name; say God God. By guru's grace, it enshrines in the mind. It shall take you across the world ocean. ||1||Pause|| Recite the treasure of immortal God's name in your mind. Then, the veil of worldly wealth will be lifted. Drink guru's sacred teachings. Your soul shall become pure. ||2|| Contemplating, I finally reached at this conclusion, that, without worshipping God, the liberation is not attained! Worship God in devotee's company. Dye your mind and body with God's love. ||3|| Renounce all your cleverness and trickery. O mind, without Lord's name, there is no place to rest. Lord of the universe, the Lord of the world, became kind to me. Nanak has taken the shelter and support of God's name. ||4||16||27|| Raamkalee, Fifth Master: In saint's congregation, play joyfully with God's love. You will not have to meet the devil of death hereafter. Your egotistic intellect shall be destroyed. The ill will is destroyed. ||1|| Sing the praises of Lord's name, O scholar! Religious rituals and ego are of no use. You shall go home happy O scholar; ||1||Pause|| I have earned the profit, the wealth of the Lord's praise. All my hopes have been fulfilled. Pain has left and peace has come to my home. By the grace of saints, my heart-lotus has blossomed. ||2|| One who is blessed with the gift of the jewel of God's name! Obtains all treasures. His mind becomes content, finding the perfect Lord. Why should he go begging again? ||3|| Hearing God's sermon, he becomes sacred. Reciting God he finds the way to salvation. He, who enshrines God's name in the mind, is approved; O Nanak: such a humble being is sacred O brother. ||4||17||28|| Raamkalee,

Fifth Master: No matter how hard you try to hold, it does not stay with you. The love you established here does not stay with you. Says Nanak, when you abandon it, then it falls at your feet. ||1|| Listen, O saints: this is the pure philosophy. Without God's name, there is no salvation. Meeting with the perfect guru, one is saved. ||1||Pause|| Page 892 When someone respects her; Then she becomes proud; When someone puts her out of his mind, then she serves him like a slave. ||2|| She assures you, but cheats at the end. She does not remain in any one place. She enticed many worlds. Lord's humble servants cut her into pieces. ||3|| Whoever begs from her remains hungry? Whoever is attached to her obtains nothing. Who renounces her and joins the society of the saints; O Nanak, the fortunate is saved. ||4||18||29|| Raamkalee, Fifth Master: See the Lord in everything. God absolutely pervades all. Realize that the priceless jewel is in your heart. It belongs to you, realize it ||1|| Drink the nectar by the grace of the saints. You get it if you are lucky. Cannot find taste without the tongue. ||1||Pause|| How can a deaf listen to eighteen Puraanas and Vedas? The blind cannot see even in million lights. An animal loves grass. One whom God does not inspire, does not realize Him. ||2|| God, the Knower, knows all. He is with His devotees, all the way. They sing His praises joyfully. O Nanak, devil of death does not come close to them. ||3||19||30|| Raamkalee, Fifth Master: Blessing me with His name, He purified me. God is my wealth and detached me from worldly wealth. Breaking my bonds, the Lord has linked me to His service. I am a devotee of the Lord and I sing the praises of the Lord. ||1|| The infinite divine music plays. The devotee sings God's praises with love by guru's grace. ||1||Pause|| My pre-ordained destiny has been realized. I have awakened from the sleep of countless incarnations. In the company of devotees, my hatred is gone. My mind and body are imbued with love of God. ||2|| The kind Lord has saved me. I have no service or work to my credit. God became kind to me by his grace. He took me out from drowning in the sufferings. ||3|| Listening to His praises, joy has welled up in my mind. Twenty-four hours a day, I sing praises of the Lord. Singing His praises, I have obtained supreme status. By guru's grace, Nanak is lovingly focused on the Lord. ||4||20||31|| Raamkalee, Fifth Master: In exchange for a shell, he gives up a jewel. He tries to get what he must leave. He collects the worthless things. Enticed by worldly wealth he is walking on a crooked path. ||1|| O unfortunate; have you no shame? You do not recite God the ocean of happiness the perfect Lord in your mind. ||1||Pause|| Nectar tastes bitter to you and poison tastes sweet. I have seen the condition of the faithless from close. You are fond of falsehood, fraud and ego. Page 893 Hearing God's name you say that he is stung by a scorpion. ||2|| You continuously ache for worldly wealth. The self-willed never praises God. God is carefree and formless. He is the great giver. But you do not love Him, you ignorant! ||3|| God is the emperor of emperors. He does not need anything. He is the perfect Lord? You are intoxicated by emotional attachment, entangled in doubt and family life. O Nanak: they are saved only by Your grace O Lord. ||4||21||32|| Raamkalee, Fifth Master: Night and day, recite God's name. Hereafter, I shall obtain a seat in the court of the Lord. I am in bliss forever. I have no sorrow. The disease of ego never afflicts me. ||1|| O saints; search for the all knowing God. You shall be amazed and attain salvation reciting God. ||1||Pause|| Calculate measure and think this. Without God's name, no one can go across. None of your efforts will go with you. You can cross over the terrifying world-ocean through the love of God. ||2|| By washing the body, the inner filth is not removed. Afflicted by ego; increases duality. One who eats the medicine of God's name? All his diseases are eradicated. ||3|| Be kind O merciful, supreme Lord; that I never forget You from my mind O Lord of the world. Let me be the dust of the feet of Your slaves. O God, please fulfill Nanak's wish; ||4||22||33|| Raamkalee, Fifth Master: You are my protection, O my perfect guru. I have no other but You. You are all-powerful, O perfect supreme Lord. Those with perfect deeds recite Your name. ||1|| Your name O God; is the boat to carry me across. I take your refuge in my mind. I have no other place but You. ||1||Pause|| I live by reciting Your name. I will find place in God's court. Pain and darkness are gone from my mind. Evil-mindedness is dispelled and I am absorbed in Lord's name. ||2|| I am in love with Lord's lotus feet. This is perfect guru's way. My concern is gone and I became carefree. My tongue continuously recites God's sacred name. ||3|| The noose of millions of lifes are cut. I have obtained the profit of the true wealth. This treasure is inexhaustible; it will never run out. O Nanak, the devotees look beautiful in the court of the Lord. ||4||23||34|| Raamkalee, Fifth Master: God's name is a jewel, a ruby. It brings truth, contentment and divine wisdom. God bestows the treasures of peace and contentment. God is in devotee's control. ||1|| The treasure of my Lord is such. Consuming and spending, it never falls short. There is no end to God's creation. ||1||Pause|| Singing God's praises is priceless. It is the ocean of bliss and virtue. God's divine sermon is my wealth. The saints hold the key to it. ||2|| Page 894 They sit there, in the cave in deep trance. Only God lives there. They converse with God through worship. There is no pleasure or pain, no birth or death there. ||3|| One whom the Lord blesses by His grace. They realize Godly wealth in devotee's company. Nanak prays to kind God; God is my merchandise and God is my capital. ||4||24||35|| Raamkalee, Fifth Master: The Vedas do not know His greatness. Brahma does not know His mystery. One who is born; does not know the end. The transcendent Lord, the supreme Lord is infinite. ||1|| Only He knows His divine state. Others speak of Him by hear say. ||1||Pause|| Shiva does not know the secret. The gods are tired of searching. The goddesses do not know the cure. Above all, is the inaccessible supreme Lord? ||2|| The Creator plays His plays. He separates and He unites. Some wander around, while others are linked to His devotional worship. He enlightens His devotees by his grace. ||3|| Listen to the true story of the saints. They say what they see with their eyes. He is not affected with virtue or vice. Nanak's God is everything. ||4||25||36|| Raamkalee, Fifth Master: I have not done anything wise. I have no knowledge, intelligence or spiritual wisdom. I have not practiced recitation, self-control, humility or faith. I know nothing of good deeds. ||1|| O my beloved God, my Lord; I have none but You; I make mistakes, still I am Yours. ||1||Pause|| I have no wealth, no intelligence, no mystic powers and no enlightenment. I live in the village of sins and sickness. O my one Creator Lord; Your name is the support of my mind. ||2|| Listening to Your name, my mind becomes at peace. Your name O God is the destroyer of sins. You, O Limitless Lord, are the bestowal of life. Whom You inspire; realizes You. ||3|| Whoever has been created; rests his hopes in You.

All worship and adore You O God the treasure of excellence. Slave Nanak is a sacrifice to You. My merciful Lord is infinite. ||4||26||37|| Raamkalee, Fifth Master: The saviour Lord is kind. He destroys millions of sins with one glance. All beings worship Him. He is realized through guru's teachings. ||1|| My God is the bestowal of life. The perfect transcendent Lord, my God abides in every being. ||1||Pause|| I took His support in my mind. It destroyed my bonds. Recite the name of bestowal of happiness in the mind. And enjoy in your mind. ||2|| Lord's sanctuary is the boat to carry us across. God's feet are the bestowal of life. Page 895 God is support of life of saints. God is infinite, the highest of high. ||3|| That mind is excellent and sublime, which recites God's name. God bestows it by His grace. Peace, contentment and joy come from reciting God's name. Meeting with the guru, Nanak recites God's name. ||4||27||38|| Raamkalee, Fifth Master: Abandon all your clever ideas. Become His servant and serve the Creator. Totally erase your ego. You shall obtain the fruit of your desire. ||1|| Be attentive to your guru. Your hopes and desires shall be fulfilled and you shall obtain all treasures from the guru. ||1||Pause|| None else can do it. Guru is the formless Lord. Do not believe that He is a mere human being; He bestows honour to the humble. ||2|| Take support of the guru the God. Give up all other hopes. Ask for the treasure of the name of the Lord. Then you shall be honoured in the court of the Lord. ||3|| Recite the word given by the guru to recite. This is the essence of worship. When the guru becomes merciful. Slave Nanak attains contentment. ||4||28||39|| Raamkalee, Fifth Master: Whatever happens, accept that as good. Leave your pride behind. Day and night, continuously sing the praises of the Lord. This is the perfect purpose of human life. ||1|| Enjoy reciting God's name O saint. Renounce your cleverness and tricks and become sacred reciting guru's word (mantra). ||1||Pause|| Place your hope in one Lord. Recite God's name and become pure. Bow down to guru's feet. And cross over the terrifying world-ocean. ||2|| God is the great giver. He has no end or limits. All treasures are in His home. He will be your saviour in the end O ignorant; ||3|| Nanak has obtained this treasure; Say God God God the sacred name. Whoever recites it is emancipated. O Nanak, you get what you earn. ||4||29||40||

Raamkalee, Fifth Master: Make this invaluable human life fruitful. You shall not lose when you go to God's court. In this world and the next, you shall obtain honour. In the end, He will save you. ||1|| Sing the praises of the Lord. In both worlds you will be content by reciting the amazing Lord. ||1||Pause|| While standing or sitting, recite God. All your troubles shall depart. All enemies will become friends. Your mind will become pure. ||2|| This is the most sacred deed. Of all faiths, this is the most sacred faith. Reciting God, you will be liberated. You shall get rid of the burden of countless births. ||3|| Your hopes shall be fulfilled. The chain of the devil of death will be cut. So listen to guru's teachings. O Nanak, you shall be absorbed in celestial peace. ||4||30||41|| Page 896 Raamkalee, Fifth Master: Respect all. Eradicate your pride. Whom you belong; all belong to Him as well. Worshipping Him attains eternal peace. ||1|| Why do you wander in doubt of others? Nothing is of use other than God's name. Many regret saying mine mine; ||1||Pause|| Whatever the Lord does, accept it as good. Without accepting, you shall merge with dust. His will tastes sweet. Only a few enjoy it by guru's grace. ||2|| He is carefree and inaccessible. Twenty-four hours a day, O mind, recite Him. Reciting Him the sufferings depart. Here and hereafter, you shall be happy. ||3|| Who knows, who and how many have been saved singing God's praises? They cannot be counted or evaluated. Even the sinking iron is saved in devotee's company O Nanak, who realizes His grace. ||4||31||42|| Raamkalee, Fifth Master: Recite God in your mind. This is the teaching given by the perfect guru. All fears and greed ends. Your hopes shall be fulfilled. ||1|| Service to the guru is fruitful. His value cannot be described; true Lord is unseen and mysterious. ||1||Pause|| He is the doer, cause of causes. Recite Him forever O my mind. Serve Him all the time. You shall attain, truth, contentment and happiness O friend; ||2|| My Lord the master is the greatest. In an instant, He establishes and disestablishes. There is no other than Him. He is the saviour of His servants. ||3|| Please be kind and listen to my prayer. Show Your face to Your devotee. Nanak recites guru's word like a rosary. His divine power is the highest of all. ||4||32||43|| Raamkalee, Fifth Master: Having faith in people is useless. O my Lord, You are my only support. I have discarded all other hopes. I have met with my carefree Lord the treasure of virtues. ||1|| O my mind; recite one name. Singing God's praises your hopes will be fulfilled. ||1||Pause|| You are the doer, the cause of causes. Your lotus feet O Lord, are my sanctuary. I recite God with my mind and body. Joyous God has revealed His form to me. ||2|| I seek His eternal support; He who created all beings; Reciting God; He bestows His blessing. He is the protector O innocent. ||3|| Be the dust of everybody's feet. Eradicating ego realizes God. Night and day, recite God's name. O Nanak, this is the most rewarding deed. ||4||33||44|| Raamkalee, Fifth Master: He is the doer; cause of causes the kind Lord. The kind Lord looks after all. The Lord is unseen and infinite. God is great and endless. ||1|| Page 897 I respectfully say God to the universal Lord the Lord of the world. The Creator Lord is all pervading. ||1||Pause|| He is the Lord of the universe, the life of the world. Recite Him in your mind eliminating other concerns. He is the head of devotees, Lord of the world, Lord of the universe. He the liberator is completely pervading everywhere. ||2|| You are kind and fulfiller of everyone's desires. You are the spiritual teacher, prophet and a scholar. Master of hearts calls you. That is more sacred than the Quran and other western scriptures. ||3|| The Lord is powerful and merciful. All-pervading God is the support of each and every heart. God is omnipresent. His play cannot be known. ||4|| Be kind and compassionate O God the creator, bless me with devotion and worship O Lord. Says Nanak, the guru has eliminated my doubt. God the bestowal of salvation is one. ||5||34||45|| Raamkalee, Fifth Master: The sins of millions of lifes are eradicated. Reciting God eliminates worry. When Lord's lotus feet are enshrined in the mind. All evils deeds go away from the body. ||1|| Sing the praise of the Lord of the world, O mortal. Speak the unspoken story of perfect Lord and merge with Him. ||1||Pause|| Hunger and thirst are totally quenched. By the grace of the saints, recite the immortal God. Night and day, serve God. This is the sign of realizing God. ||2|| By God's grace all worldly entanglements are eliminated. Seeing guru's face attains contentment. My previous deeds became my fate. With my tongue, I continuously sing God's praises. ||3|| The saints of the Lord are accepted forever. It is written in saint's fate. One who is blessed with the dust of the feet of God's slave? O Nanak, he obtains the supreme status. ||4||35||46||

Raamkalee, Fifth Master: Praise seeing God. Focus your mind to God's lotus feet. Apply the dust of the feet of the saints to your forehead. The filth of evil deeds of many lifes will go away. ||1|| Meeting Him, egotistic pride is eradicated. By God's grace the bestowal of salvation is realized. ||1||Pause|| Serve the guru and recite God's name. Worship the guru and sing God's praises forever. See God close by in your mind. Accept guru's teachings faithfully. ||2|| Through guru's teachings, see happiness and sorrow the same. Hunger and thirst shall never bother you. Mind becomes content and satisfied through guru's teachings. Recite God; it will cover your sins. ||3|| Guru is the supreme Lord the Lord of the universe. The guru is the great giver, kind and forgiving. One whose mind is attached to guru's feet; O slave Nanak; he is very lucky. ||4||36||47|| Page 898 Raamkalee, Fifth Master: Who supports you in the world? You ignorant fool, who is your companion? God is your companion; you do not think of Him. You look upon the five thieves as your friends. ||1|| Serve that home, which will save you, my friend. Sing God's praises day and night and love devotee's company. ||1||Pause|| This human life is passing away in ego and conflict. You are not satisfied with the taste of sins. Wandering and roaming around, you suffer terrible pain. You cannot cross over the impassable sea of worldly wealth. ||2|| You do the deeds which do not help you. As you sow so shall you reap? No one other than God will save you. You will be saved, only by God's grace. ||3|| Your name O God is the purifier of sinners. Please bless Your slave with this gift. Please be kind and liberate me. Nanak is at Your refuge O God. ||4||37||48|| Raamkalee, Fifth Master: I have found peace in this world. I will not have to appear before the justice of destiny. I will be respected in the court of the Lord. I will not have to enter the womb for birth again. ||1|| Now, I know the value of friendship with the saints. By his grace he bestowed God's name on me. I got what I earned. ||1||Pause|| My mind is attached to guru's feet. Blessed are the fortunate and the auspicious time. I have applied the dust of saint's feet to my forehead. All my sins and pains have been eradicated. ||2|| Performing true service to the devotees, the mind becomes pure O mortal. I have seen the fruitful vision of Lord's humble slave. God's name dwells in each and every heart. ||3|| All my troubles and sufferings have been erased. I have merged in one, from whom I originated. I realized the amazing Lord of the universe. O Nanak, God is perfect and forgiving. ||4||38||49|| Raamkalee, Fifth Master: The tiger grazes the cows. The shell is worth thousands. An elephant nurses the goat when God bestows His grace; ||1|| You are the treasure of kindness, O my beloved Lord. I cannot describe, Your virtues are too many. ||1||Pause|| The cat sees the meat, but does not eat. The great butcher throws away his knife. The Creator abides in the heart. The net holding the fish breaks apart. ||2|| The dry wood becomes green. In the high desert, the beautiful lotus flower blooms. The guru the God puts out the fire. He links His servant to His service. ||3|| He saves even the ungrateful. My God is forever kind. He is forever the support of the humble saints. Nanak has found the sanctuary of His lotus feet. ||4||39||50|| Raamkalee, Fifth Master: Page 899 God killed the five tigers. He has driven out the ten wolves. Wandering in three worldly qualities ended. In the company of devotees, coming and going ended. ||1|| I live by reciting God. The true merciful Lord saved His servant by His grace. ||1||Pause|| The mountain of sins is burnt to ground. Reciting God I worship God's feet. God, the embodiment of joy, becomes manifest everywhere. I worship God with love and attain eternal peace. ||2|| I have crossed over the world-ocean like chasing the footprints of stolen ox. I shall never endure suffering again. The ocean is contained in the pitcher. There is no surprise to God's deeds. ||3|| When I leave this world, I go to the underworld. When He pulls me out, then I am happy for His kindness. Vice and virtue are not under my control. Nanak sings God's praises with love. ||4||40||51|| Raamkalee, Fifth Master: Neither your body nor your mind belongs to you. Attracted by worldly wealth you are entangled in fraud. You play like a baby lamb. Suddenly, death will catch you in its net. ||1|| Seek the sanctuary of Lord's lotus feet, O my mind. Recite ever present and helper God's name O guru-willed, and obtain the true wealth. ||1||Pause|| Your unfinished worldly affairs will never be finished. You always yearn for sex, anger and pride. You do bad deeds for your soul. O ignorant; nothing goes with you. ||2|| You practice deception and know many cheating tricks. For the sake of pennies, you do filthy deeds. You never think of the one who gave you everything. The pain of false greed never leaves you. ||3|| When the supreme Lord becomes kind. This mind becomes the dust of the feet of devotees. With His gracious hands, He has attached me to His lap. Nanak truly merges in true God. ||4||41||52|| Raamkalee, Fifth Master: I seek the sanctuary of the sovereign Lord. I became carefree singing the praises of the Lord of the universe. In the company of devotees the pain goes away. ||1||Pause|| One, who has God dwelling in his mind. He does not have to go through the impassable world-ocean. All his affairs are resolved by reciting God's name with his tongue. ||1|| On whose forehead the guru places his hand. Why should that slave feel any worry? The fear of birth and death is eliminated. I praise the perfect guru. ||2|| I am happy meeting the guru, the transcendent Lord. He, whom God is kind; visualizes Him. One who is blessed by the supreme Lord? Crosses over the terrifying world-ocean in devotee's company; ||3|| Drink the nectar, O beloved God's devotees; you shall be happy in the true court. Give up all useless deeds and enjoy. O Nanak, recite God and cross over the world ocean. ||4||42||53|| Page 900 Raamkalee, Fifth Master: The fire runs away from the fuel. The water forsakes mud in ten directions. The feet are on top the sky is beneath. The ocean appears in the cup. ||1|| Such is the power of dear Lord. His devotees never forget Him, recite Him all day O my mind. ||1||Pause|| First comes the butter and milk later. The dirt cleans the soap. The fearless are afraid of fear. The living is killed by the dead. ||2|| The visible body is hidden, one without body is visible. The Lord of the world can do all these things. The cheat cheats the one who cannot be cheated. With no merchandise, the trader trades again and again. ||3|| Tell all this in saint's congregation. So say the Simritees, Shaastras, Vedas and Puraanas. Rare are those who contemplate and recite God. O Nanak, they attain salvation. ||4||43||54|| Raamkalee, Fifth Master: Whatever pleases Him happens. Be in God's refuge forever. Other than God nothing helps. ||1||Pause|| All that your children, spouse and wealth you see; nothing goes with you. Eating the poisonous medicine, you have gone astray. You will go leaving the worldly pleasure behind. ||1|| Slandering others, you are ruined. Because of your actions, you shall be sent to the womb for birth. Your past actions do not go away; devil of death will catch you.

||2|| You tell lies and do not practice what you preach. Your greed will not end. You are sick with an incurable disease slandering the saints; you will vanish. ||3|| He, who creates, honours and praises His saints. O Nanak, embrace Your servant by your grace O bestowal of salvation. ||4||44||55|| Raamkalee, Fifth Master: Such is the perfect guru my help and support. Reciting Him does not go waste. ||1||Pause|| Visualizing Him the devotee becomes happy. The dust of His feet cuts the net of death. His lotus feet dwell in my mind. He resolved all my affairs. ||1|| One, on whose forehead He places His hand. My God is the Lord of orphans. He is the saviour of sinners, the treasure of mercy. I praise Him forever. ||2|| One, who He blesses with His sacred lesson; renounces corruption. His egotistic pride is eliminated. Recite one God in devotee's company. Sins are erased, reciting God with love. ||3|| The guru, the transcendent Lord, dwells among all. God the treasure of virtue pervades each and every heart. I hope to visualize You O God. Nanak says the true prayer every day. ||4||45||56|| Page 901 Tune Raamkalee, Fifth Master, Second House, Du-Padas: God is one. He is realized by guru's grace. Sing the songs of praise of the Lord. Reciting God attains eternal peace. Coming and going ends. ||1||Pause|| Singing God's praises obtains enlightenment. Then you dwell in God's lotus feet. ||1|| In the society of saints, one is saved. O Nanak, he crosses over the terrifying world-ocean. ||2||1||57|| Raamkalee, Fifth Master: My guru is perfect. Reciting God's name attains contentment and all useless sickness disappears. ||1||Pause|| Worship true God. In His sanctuary, eternal peace is obtained. ||1|| One who feels hungry for God's name sleeps in peace? Reciting God all pain is eliminated. ||2|| Enjoy peace O my brother. The perfect guru has eradicated all anxiety. ||3|| Twenty-four hours a day, recite God's recitation. O Nanak, He shall save you. ||4||2||58|| Tune Raamkalee, Fifth Master, Partaal, Third House: God is one. He is realized by guru's grace. I pay respect to the Lord the Supreme Being. God is present in water, land, earth and the sky. ||1||Pause|| Over and over again, the Creator destroys, sustains and creates. He has no home. He does not eat. ||1|| He is deep, profound, jewel, high, great and infinite. He stages His plays. His virtues are priceless. Nanak praises Him. ||2||1||59|| Raamkalee, Fifth Master: You must abandon

your beauty, pleasures, fragrances, enjoyments, enticement of worldly wealth, gold and spousal love. ||1||Pause|| You are enticed by and enjoy the unlimited amount of worldly wealth. These pleasures will not go with you. ||1|| Entangled with children, spouse, siblings and friends, enticed by doubt; these will go away like the shadow of a tree. Nanak finds peace in saint's refuge. ||2||2||60|| God is one. He is realized by guru's grace. Tune Raamkalee, Ninth Master, Ti-Padas: O mind, take the shelter of God's name. Reciting Him the ill will disappears and attains salvation. ||1||Pause|| He who sings God's praises is fortunate. The sins of countless lives are washed off, and he goes to heaven. ||1|| Page 902 At the last moment, Ajaamal realized God; the salvation the yogi's long for; he attained in a moment. ||2|| The elephant had no virtue and no wisdom; what religious acts he performed? O Nanak that is God's way to bestow salvation. ||3||1|| Raamkalee, Ninth Master: O devotees: what should I do now? So that my evil-will disappears and my mind engages in God's worship. ||1||Pause|| My mind is entangled in worldly wealth; it does not know any divine wisdom. What name does the world recite that bestows salvation? ||1|| When the merciful saints became kind, they told me this! One, who sings God's praises, has realized the highest religion. ||2|| One who enshrines God's name in his mind night and day or even for an instant! His fear of death disappears and makes his life worthwhile. ||3||2|| Raamkalee, Ninth Master: O mortal, focus your thoughts on the Lord. Every moment, day and night, your life is decreasing and going in vain. ||1||Pause|| You wasted your youth in bad deeds and the childhood in ignorance. You have grown old, even now you do not realize. What evil deeds you are involved in? ||1|| Why did you forget the Lord; who blessed you with this human life? Reciting Him attains salvation; you do not praise Him at all. ||2|| Why are you intoxicated with wealth? It does not go with you. Says Nanak, think of God. He will help you in the end. ||3||3||81|| Raamkalee, First Master, Ashtapadees: God is one. He is realized by guru's grace. Same moon and same stars rise and same sun shines in the sky. Same earth, same wind blows. The life goes on forever. ||1|| Give up your attachment to life. The tyrants are accepted leaders; this is today's age; ||1||Pause|| No one knows where he lives or what shrine he visits?

Without God's blessing, he cannot build a mansion and live in it. ||2|| If someone practices truth, he is not accepted; self-discipline is not practiced in the home of self-willed. If someone recites God, he is scorned. These are the signs of today's age. ||3|| Whoever is the master is humiliated. The servants are not scared of him. When the master is put in chains? He dies at the hands of his servant. ||4|| Page 903 Praise the Lord; today's age (Kalyug) has come. The penance of the previous three ages is gone. One obtains virtue, if the Lord bestows it. ||1||Pause|| In this turbulent age of today's age (Kalyug), sharia law decides the cases, and the blue-robed Qazi is the judge. Brahma's sermon the Atharavan Veda is no more sung. ||5|| Worship without faith; self-discipline without truthfulness; the sacred thread without celibacy; what good are these? You may bathe and wash, and apply mark to the forehead, but without inner purity, the reality is not realized. ||6|| In today's age the Quran and other western scriptures are prevailing. The scriptures, Puraanaas and the scholars are no more. O Nanak, God's name now is Rehmaan, the merciful. Know that there is only one Creator of the creation. ||7|| O Nanak, reciting God's name is the highest reward. There is nothing more. If one goes begging for what he already has, he should be chastised. ||8||1|| Raamkalee, First Master: You preach the world and fill your belly. Abandoning Yogic postures of worship, how will you find the true Lord? You are attached to possessiveness and the love of sexual pleasure. You are neither renunciate nor a worldly person. ||1|| O Yogi, be stable, and the pain of duality will run away. You beg door to door, you don't feel ashamed. ||1||Pause|| You sing divine songs, but you do not search your soul. How will the burning fire be extinguished? The inner fire extinguishes through guru's teachings. And you will enjoy the awns of contentment. ||2|| You apply ashes to your body, it is hypocrisy. Attached to the worldly wealth, you will suffer the punishment of devil of death. When your skull breaks, begging will not please you. Bound by your deeds, you will come and go. ||3|| You do not control your lust, yet you claim to be a celibate. You beg for worldly wealth, greedy of worldly three qualities. Without kindness the enlightenment is not obtained. You are drowned in worldly entanglements. ||4|| You assume different disguise at different place. You play all sorts of false tricks, like a juggler. You are burning in the inner fire of worries. Without previous good deeds written in you fate, how can you cross over? ||5|| You wear all kind of earring. But liberation does not come without learning divine wisdom. You are enticed by the taste of tongue and other senses. You are an animal; your destiny cannot be erased. ||6|| People are entangled in three worldly modes. Yogis are entangled in the three yogic modes. Contemplating guru's teachings eliminates sorrows. Following guru's teachings make truly pure. One who contemplates the truthful way is a Yogi. ||7|| O God; You have the priceless treasure. You do everything. You establish and disestablish; whatever You do, happens. One who practices celibacy, truth, self-control, is truly a good hearted. O Nanak, that Yogi is the friend of the universe. ||8||2|| Raamkalee, First Master: There is yearning to learn in the mind in the body. Through guru's teachings the yearning and love wells up in the mind. The unlimited divine music plays and my mind enjoys it. Through guru's teachings, O my mind believe in God's name. ||1|| O mortal, through worship of God, peace is obtained. Saying God pleases the guru-willed and he merges in it. ||1||Pause|| Page 904 Eradicating attachment to the worldly wealth, one merges in the Lord. Meeting the guru, we unite with God. God's name is a priceless jewel a diamond. Attuned to it, my mind attains peace. ||2|| The diseases of ego and possessiveness do not afflict. Worshiping God the concern of devil of death runs away. Lock of the devil of death does not lock me. The pure name of the Lord illuminates my heart. ||3|| Contemplating guru's teachings I became immortal. Guru's teachings woke me up and I gave up the ill will. I am awake night and day, lovingly attuned to God. I realized the way of liberation in me. ||4|| In the secluded cave of my mind, I remain unattached. Through guru's teachings, I killed the five thieves. My mind does not waver or goes anywhere else. I remain intuitively absorbed in peace. ||5|| The guru-willed devotees (yogi) remain awake. I am woven in the essence of reality and detached forever. The world is asleep; it dies, and keeps coming and going. Realization does not come without guru's teachings. ||6|| The unlimited divine music plays day and night. The guru-willed realizes the way to immortality. It is realized through guru's teachings. God the bestowal abides in all. ||7|| My mind is absorbed in absolute state of contentment. Renouncing ego and greed, I realized God. When the disciple and guru's mind accept each other O Nanak, duality is eradicated and he merges in the Lord. ||8||3|| Raamkalee, First Master: You calculate the auspicious day, but you do not contemplate. God is above calculations. He, who meets the guru, understands the way. Following guru's teachings, one realizes God's command. ||1|| Do not tell lies, O preacher, speak the truth. Eliminate ego and attain destiny through guru's teachings. ||1||Pause|| Calculating and counting, the astrologer draws the horoscope. He reads to others but he does not know the reality. Following guru's teachings is the highest of all. Telling all other stories is useless. ||2|| You bathe, wash, and worship stones. But without being imbued with the Lord, you are the filthiest of all. Eliminating pride, you shall receive Godly wealth. Reciting God attains salvation. ||3|| You study and argue Vedas, but do not contemplate. You are drowning; how will you save your ancestors? God abides in all but only a few contemplate. When one meets the guru, then he understands. ||4|| Making calculations gives worry and pain to the mind. Seeking guru's refuge attains happiness. I sinned and made mistakes but now I seek Your refuge. Due to my past deeds I met the guru the God. ||5|| If one does not enter guru's sanctuary, God cannot be found. Deluded by doubt, one is born to die, and come back again. He is tied at death's door and dies uselessly. He does not follow guru's teachings or recites God's name; ||6|| Some call themselves sacred, religious scholars and spiritual teachers. Dyed by duality they do not attain destiny. Page 905 One who enshrines God's name in the mind through guru's grace. Such a person is one in millions. ||7|| One is bad, another is good, but God is always good. O wise man; realize this through guru's support. Only a few guru-willed realize God. His coming and going ends and he merges in the Lord. ||8|| Those who have the Lord enshrined in the heart. They obtain all virtues contemplating the true Lord. One who acts in harmony with guru's will O Nanak, he truly absorbs in the true Lord ||9||4|| Raamkalee, First Master: Practicing restraint, he wears the body down. The mind is not satisfied by fasting or austerities. Nothing equals reciting God's name. ||1|| Serve the guru, O mind and associate with God's devotees. Chains of devil of death or snake bite do not affect those who enjoy God's sublime essence. ||1||Pause|| The worldly singers enjoy reading and arguing. In the three worldly qualities and sins, they are born and die. Without God's name, they suffer in pain. ||2|| The Yogi draws the breath up high and reaches higher conscious level. He practices body cleansing and many rituals of purification. But without God's name, all this breathing is useless. ||3|| The fire of five passions burns inside; how can he be peaceful? The thief is inside; how can he enjoy the taste? The guru-willed sharpens his mind. ||4|| He is filled with filth and yet goes to shrines. His mind is not pure, what is the use of performing rituals? He obtains the reward of his doing; who else can he blame? ||5|| He does not eat food; he tortures his body. Without guru's divine wisdom, satisfaction is not possible. The self-willed is born to die, to be born again. ||6|| Go, and ask the guru and associate with God's humble servants. When your mind is imbued with God's love; you will not die and reborn again. Without Lord's name, what else should anyone do? ||7|| Why do you think bad of others? Recite God; this is the highest service. O Nanak, one recites God's name by His grace. ||8||5|| Raamkalee, First Master: God is the Creator, none else. God creates whatever exists. He is the true Lord throughout the ages. Creation and destruction do not come from anyone else. ||1|| Such is my Lord profound and unfathomable. Whoever recites Him obtains happiness. Reciting His name the arrow of devil of death does not pierce. ||1||Pause|| God's name is a priceless jewel a diamond. The true Lord is immortal and immeasurable. That tongue which recites God is pure. True Lord is inside; do not neglect and forget this. ||2|| Some sit in the forest, and some make their home in the mountains. Forgetting God's name they rot in egotistic pride. Other than God's name, there is no knowledge or meditation; ||3|| The guru-willed obtain honour in God's court. God is not realized through stubbornness or egotistic deeds. He reads and explains the scriptures to others. Page 906 Going to sacred shrines does not eliminate the disease. Without God's name, how can he find happiness? ||4|| He tries but his lust does not go away. His mind wavers, he goes to hell. He suffers punishment at the place of death. Without God's name his soul burns. ||5|| Many mystics, seekers, sages and demy-gods; practice stubbornness, they cannot find the mystery. One who contemplates guru's teachings and serves him. His mind and body become pure and eliminates ego. ||6|| Through pre-ordained destiny (previous deeds), he obtains God's name. I remain in Your sanctuary intuitively. Love for devotional worship has welled up by your grace. O guru-willed, recite God's name. ||7|| Your, self-pride and ego will depart and mind will fall in love with God. Practicing fraud and hypocrisy do not attain anything. Without guru's teachings there is no place to go. O Nanak the guru-willed; realize this essence. ||8||6|| Raamkalee, First Master: As you come, so you go, you ignorant as you are born, so will die. As you enjoy pleasures, so you will suffer. Forgetting God's name you are caught in the terrifying world-ocean. ||1|| Seeing the body and wealth you became proud. You fell in love with gold and spouse! Do you believe that you eliminated your doubt by forgetting God's name? ||1||Pause|| You do not practice truth, abstinence, self-discipline or humility; the ghost in your skeleton has turned to dead wood. You do not do good for others, no donations, cleansing baths or austerities. Without devotees company, your life goes in vain. ||2|| Enticed by greed you forgot God's name; wasted your life in coming and going. When the devil of death catches you from the hair; you lose your consciousness and engulfed by death. ||3|| Day and night, you are jealous and slander others; you do not have kindness or God's name in your heart. Salvation does not attain without guru's teachings; you go to hell without reciting God's name. ||4|| In an instant, you change various costumes like a juggler; you are entangled in emotional attachment and sin. Wherever you see worldly wealth, you are enticed and intoxicated by it. ||5|| You do all kind of useless deeds; without guru's teachings you doubt everything. You suffer the sickness of egotistic pride; this disease will depart through guru's teachings. ||6|| The faithless becomes happy and proud when he acquires wealth. Whom this body and wealth belong; takes it away; then you worry and feel pain. ||7|| Nothing goes with you in the end; whatever you see is God's grace. God is primal and infinite; enshrining His name in the mind attains salvation. ||8|| You weep for dead, who hears it? He is gone in the terrifying world ocean. Seeing the family, wealth and household the faithless is engaged in useless deeds. ||9|| Page 907 When God sends, we come and when he calls we go back; He does what He wants; the kind God bestows His blessings. ||10|| I seek the company of those who taste and enjoy reciting God. Wealth, mysticism, wisdom and knowledge attain from the guru. The priceless essence of salvation attains in his refuge. ||11|| The guru-willed realizes pleasure and pains the same and is freed from happiness and sorrow. Conquering ego, the guru-willed realizes God O Nanak, and merges in peace. ||12||7|| Raamkalee, Dakhanee (southern language), First Master: Abstinence, donations, self-control and truthfulness and God's love have welled up through guru's teachings. ||1|| My kind guru is permanently dyed by God's love. He is always attuned to God with love. He enjoys visualizing God. ||1||Pause|| He sees everything in the universe equal and is dyed by unlimited divine music. ||2|| Wearing the long loincloth of kindness, he is dyed by God's love and enjoys reciting His name. ||3|| He realizes God meeting the guru and enjoys reciting and thinking of God. ||4|| All are in the one, and one is in all. The guru saw and showed to me. ||5|| He who created the worlds, solar systems and galaxies. That God cannot be explained. ||6|| From God's light the universe is lit, He is merged in the universe. ||7|| Truth dwells in God's realm. God sits there in trance. ||8|| With no worldly attachment the yogi is detached and abides in everyone. ||9|| O Nanak, salvation attains in God's refuge through guru's teachings. ||10||8|| Raamkalee, First Master: He created earth and the sky enshrining God in the mind eradicating his ego. ||1|| The guru saved many through guru's teachings O saints; ||1||Pause|| He conquers attachment, and eradicates ego and sees Your divine Light pervading the universe O God; ||2|| He conquers desire, and enshrines God in the mind and contemplates guru's teachings. ||3|| The horn of consciousness plays unlimited; Your Light illuminates every heart. ||4|| He plays Godly flute in the mind and burn his status in the fire. ||5|| He lights the lamp in the five element body with his pure light. ||6|| Like sun and moon he plays his horn through guru's unique teachings. ||7|| The true hermit, invisible, inaccessible, infinite God sits in His realm. ||8|| The mind is the king of the city of the body; five senses contemplate in it. ||9|| The king recites guru's teachings sitting on his throne and bestows real justice. ||10|| What can poor death or birth say to him? Conquering his mind, he remains dead yet alive. ||11|| Page 908 Brahma, Vishnu and Shiva are image of God. He created them. ||12|| Purifying your body, crosses over the terrifying world-ocean realizing the essence of reality. ||13|| Serving the guru, obtains everlasting peace by reciting guru's teachings. ||14|| The virtuous God unites them with Him by eliminating ego and greed. ||15|| Eradicate the three qualities and dwell in the fourth state. This is the unique way of worship. ||16|| This is the Yoga of the guru-willed. He searches God in his mind through guru's teachings. ||17|| Dyed with guru's teachings the mind becomes stable. This is all there is; ||18|| O hermit; contemplating and arguing the scriptures are hypocrisy; the guru-willed contemplates guru's teachings. ||19|| The saint guru-willed practices this Yoga. He practices abstinence and truth through guru's teachings. ||20|| One who dies through guru's teachings O hermit; realizes the way to divinity. ||21|| Attachment of the worldly wealth is the terrifying world-ocean; one swims across through guru's teachings along with his dynasty. ||22|| Guru's teachings are the enlightenment in all four ages O hermit; the devotees contemplate guru's sermon. This mind is enticed by worldly wealth O hermit. Contemplating guru's teachings you shall be freed from it. ||24|| He unites us with him by his grace; Nanak is at Your refuge O God. ||25||9|| Raamkalee, Third Master, Ashtapadees: God is one. He is realized by guru's grace. Make humility your ear rings O Yogi, and compassion your patched coat. Let coming and going be the ashes you apply to your body O Yogi; then you shall conquer the universe. ||1|| Play that horn O Yogi. By that the unlimited divine music plays and remains attached to God's love. ||1||Pause|| Make truth and contentment your begging bag O yogi; and beg awns of God's sacred name. Make meditation your walking stick O Yogi, and make thinking as the horn you blow. ||2|| Be stable in your meditation posture then your worry will go. Go begging in the village of the body; then you receive the awns of God's name. ||3|| Simply blowing the horn the mind does not concentrate and does not obtain the truth O yogi. Blowing horn like this does not attain peace; self-pride does no leave. ||4|| Respect both, fear and love of God and make your body the weigh scale. The guru-willed plays this instrument; this way the greed goes away. ||5|| One who obeys God's command is the yogi. He attunes to God with love. His worry goes away; he becomes pure and realizes the way of yoga. ||6|| Whatever you see will vanish; therefore put your mind to God. Attuning to God lovingly attains this divine wisdom. ||7|| Page 909 Leave your family and wander around is not yoga. Visualize God in your mind through guru's grace and recite His name. ||8|| This world is a puppet of clay O Yogi; it is sick with greed. Making all ritualistic efforts, it cannot be cured. ||9|| God's name is the medicine O yogi; enshrine in the mind. The guru-willed realizes it and finds the way of yoga. ||10|| The path of Yoga is very difficult O Yogi; it is realized by God's grace. See God inside out and eliminate doubt from the mind. ||11|| Then the horn blows without blowing. God blows it. Says Nanak, thus the yogi shall be liberated, and he attunes to God with love. ||12||1||10|| Raamkalee, Third Master: The guru-willed realizes the treasure of worship learning from the guru. ||1|| O saints, God honours the guru-willed; ||1||Pause|| Being truthful; peace and contentment well up; lust and anger go away. ||2|| Eradicate ego, remain lovingly focused on God's name; guru's teachings burn away the worldly attachment. ||3|| God creates and destroys us; in the end His name comes to help. ||4|| He who created the creation is ever-present; don't think Him far. ||5|| Always follow guru's lesson in the mind lovingly attuned to God. ||6|| God's priceless name is realized in devotee's company; the fortunate realize it. ||7|| Do not be deluded by doubt; serve the guru and keep your mind in one place. ||8|| Without God's name, everyone wanders around in confusion. They waste away their lifes in vain. ||9|| O Yogi, you lost the way; you wander around confused. Hypocrisy does not realize Yoga. ||10|| Sitting in Shiva's yogic postures, yoga is realized through guru's teachings. ||11|| Guru's teaching eliminates cheating and God's name dwells in the mind. ||12|| This body is a sacred pool, O saints; bathe in it with love. ||13|| Bathing in God's name makes pure; guru's teachings eliminate the filth. ||14|| Trapped by the three qualities, he does not miss God's name. He will parish without God's name. ||15|| Brahma, Vishnu and Shiva the three images are lost in doubt in the world. ||16|| By guru's grace, three worldly qualities are eradicated, and one attains the fourth state. ||17|| The scholar reads and explains but the ignorant does not understand? ||18|| They are intoxicated by ill will and deluded by doubt; who are they teaching this o brother? ||19|| The sacred sermon of God's devotees prevails forever. ||20|| One who follows the sermon obtains honour and merges in truth through guru's teachings. ||21|| Page 910 Search your soul through guru's teachings and realize priceless treasure reciting God's name. ||22|| Conquering desire, the mind merges in peace, and praises God in the mind. ||23|| Seeing God's amazing show the mind is attuned to the unseen God. ||24|| The unseen Lord is forever unique; one's light merges in His Light. ||25|| I praise my guru forever, who taught me the true understanding. ||26|| Nanak offers one prayer; salvation attains through God's name. ||27||2||11|| Raamkalee, Third Master: Worshipping God is difficult O saints; it cannot be described. ||1|| O saints, the guru-willed find the perfect God. Reciting God's name is his worship. ||1||Pause|| Other than God everything is dirty; what can I offer to worship Him. ||2|| Whatever pleases God is the worship; enshrine His will in the mind. ||3|| Everyone worships Him, O saints, the self-willed goes nowhere. ||4|| If someone dies by guru's teachings O saints; this worship is accepted. ||5|| Those attuned to guru's teachings with love are sacred and truthful. ||6|| There is no worship other than God's name; the world is lost in doubt. ||7|| Lovingly attuning to God the guru-willed realizes himself. ||8|| The true Lord inspires us to worship Him; guru's teachings realize God. ||9|| He worships but does not know the way; he gets dirty deluded by duality. ||10|| The guru-willed knows how to worship enshrining God's will in the mind. ||11|| Obeying God's will attains happiness O saints; God's name helps in the end. ||12|| He does not realize himself; he praises the falsehood. ||13|| The devil of death does not spare the hypocrites; they depart in disgrace. ||14|| With guru's teachings in the mind, he realizes himself and attains salvation. ||15|| His mind enters in intuitive trance; his soul merges with supreme soul. ||16|| The guru-willed listens and says God's name in devotee's company. ||17|| The guru-willed sings God's praises and eliminates ego; he is honoured in God's court. ||18|| They truly speak true sermon truly attuning to the true name. ||19|| My God is the destroyer of fear and sins; he helps in the end. ||20|| He pervades in everything. O Nanak, sing His praises.

||21||3||12|| Raamkalee, Third Master: I am filthy polluted proud and egotistic. My filth is eliminated following guru's teachings. ||1|| O Saints, God's name liberates the guru-willed. Enshrining God's name in the mind, God takes care of you. ||1||Pause|| Page 911 Touching philosopher's stone turns into gold by God's grace. ||2|| Some egotistic make false pretences. They lose their lives in the gamble. ||3|| Some worship God day and night enshrining God's name in the heart. ||4|| Intuitively attuned to God enjoy contentment and eliminate ego. ||5|| Cannot worship without love; worship flourishes through love. ||6|| Guru's teaching eliminates worldly attachment and realizes divine wisdom. ||7|| The Creator inspires us to act. He blesses us with His treasure. ||8|| No one can find the limit of His virtues. I praise Him through guru's teachings. ||9|| I recite God, I praise God. It eliminated my ego. ||10|| I received God's sacred name from the guru; it shall never fall short. ||11|| He blesses His devotees and inspires them by His grace. ||12|| They are hungry for His name; they praise him through guru's teachings. ||13|| Soul, body and everything is His; to say or think anything else is bad. ||14|| Those who follow guru's teachings swim across the terrifying world-ocean. ||15|| No one swims across without God's name, think and see it. ||16|| We obtain what is written from destiny. God is realized through guru's teachings. ||17|| Dye your priceless body with God's love through guru's teachings. ||18|| The body is filled with nectar; it is realized through guru's teachings. ||19|| Those who seek God find Him; other egotistic die in vain. ||20|| Debating is a wastage; the devotees worship Him lovingly through guru's teachings. ||21|| He who realizes divine wisdom and eliminates ego and greed is a yogi. ||22|| They realize the bestowal guru by God's grace. ||23|| Those who do not serve the guru, and are attached to worldly wealth; they are egotistic and die drowning. ||24|| Serve the guru as long as you live; you will merge with God in the end. ||25|| Remain awake all the time in love of the beloved? ||26|| I offer my body and mind in praise of my guru; I admire Him. ||27|| Attachment to worldly wealth will go away; you attain salvation through guru's teachings. ||28|| Whom God awakens; remain awake and contemplate guru's teachings. ||29|| O Nanak, those who do not miss God die! The devotees live by contemplating Him. ||30||4||13||

Raamkalee, Third Master: I obtained the treasure of God's name from the guru. I am satisfied and fulfilled reciting God; ||1|| O saints; the guru-willed attain salvation. Page 912 God's name is enshrined in my mind by guru's grace. ||1||Pause|| He is the Creator and the enjoyer. He gives food to all. ||2|| Whatever He wants He does; no one else can do anything. ||3|| He creates the creation; He puts everyone to task. ||4|| Serve Him and attain peace; he is realized through the guru. ||5|| The Lord created Himself; the unexplainable cannot be explained. ||6|| He kills and revives; He does not have any greed. ||7|| He made some the giver, the others beggars. He makes us worship Him. ||8|| Those who know One Lord are fortunate and they merge with Him. ||9|| He is beautiful and wise; His worth cannot be expressed. ||10|| He gives pain and pleasure. He makes us wander in doubt. ||11|| The great giver is revealed to the guru-willed. Without the guru, the world wanders in darkness. ||12|| Those who taste enjoy it. He is realized through the guru. ||13|| He causes some to forget Him and reveals to the guru-willed. ||14|| O saints; praise Him forever; His greatness is great. ||15|| There is no other King except Him; He became so by worshipping. ||16|| His justice is always true; only a few follow His command. ||17|| O mortal, recite His name forever; who created the creation. ||18|| One, who surrenders to the guru gets his desire fulfilled enshrining God's name in the mind. ||19|| The true Lord is true; He reads His sermon through guru's teachings. ||20|| Nanak is amazed, hearing and seeing His Lord; my God is all pervading. ||21||5||14|| Raamkalee, Fifth Master, Ashtapadees: God is one. He is realized by guru's grace. Someone created the creation. Some started worship. Some practice self-cleansing through yoga. I the humble recite God. ||1|| I place my faith in You O beloved Lord. I do not know any other way. ||1||Pause|| Some abandon their homes, and live in the forest. Some become silent and call themselves hermits. Some claim that they do only one worship. I the humble seek God's refuge. ||2|| Some say that they live at sacred shrines. Some do not eat and are called renunciates. Some wander all over the world. I the humble have fallen at God's door. ||3|| Some say that they belong to noble families. Page 913 Some offer great admirations O brother. Some say that they are wealthy. I the humble; take God's support. ||4|| Some dance, wearing ankle bells. Some fast and take vows, and wear rosary. Some apply ceremonial marks to their forehead like Gopichand. I the humble recite God. ||5|| Some play mystic's drama. They make many imitations in many ways. Some put up show by saying loud words. I the humble serve God. ||6|| One calls himself a wise scholar. One performs rituals to appease the deity. One maintains pure lifestyle and does good deeds. I the humble seek God's refuge. ||7|| I studied the religions and rituals of all ages. Without God's name, this mind does not enlighten. Says Nanak, when I found the company of devotees. My greed ended and I became peaceful. ||8||1|| Raamkalee, Fifth Master: He created you out of this water. From mud He fashioned your body. He intuitively blessed you with mind to understand. In mother's womb, He preserved you. ||1|| Recite the name of the saviour Lord. Give up all others thoughts, O mind. ||1||Pause|| He gave you mother and father; He gave you jewel children and siblings; He gave you spouse and friends. Enshrine that Lord in your mind; ||2|| He gave you the invaluable air. He gave you the priceless water. He gave you fire to burn. Keep your mind in the sanctuary of that Lord; ||3|| He gave you the thirty-six varieties of tasty food. He gave you a place to live. He gave you the earth, and things to use. Enshrine that Lord's feet in your mind. ||4|| He gave you eyes to see, ears to hear. He gave you hands to work, and a nose and a tongue. He gave you feet to walk, and head to think. O mind, worship the feet of that Lord the master. ||5|| He made you pure from impure; He made you the head of all creatures; Now, it is up to you to succeed or not. Reciting God your affairs shall be resolved, O mind. ||6|| Here and there, only one God exists. Wherever I look, there You are. Even then the mind is reluctant to serve Him; Forgetting Him, I cannot survive even for an instant. ||7|| I am a sinner without any virtue. I do not serve You, or do any good deeds. By good fortune, I found the boat the guru. Slave Nanak the stone, has crossed over, with Him. ||8||2|| Raamkalee, Fifth Master: Some spend their lives enjoying pleasures and beauty. Page 914 Some pass their lives with their mother, father and children. Some pass their lives in power, estates and trade. The saints pass their lives with the support of Lord's name. ||1|| The world is created truthfully. He alone is the master of all. ||1||Pause|| Some pass their lives debating scriptures. Some pass their lives tasting flavours. Some pass their lives attached to women. The saints are absorbed in the name of God. ||2|| Some pass their lives gambling. Some pass their lives getting high on drug. Some pass their lives stealing the property of others. The humble servants of the Lord pass their lives reciting God. ||3|| Some pass their lives in Yoga, self-discipline and worship. Some are sick with sorrow and doubt. Some pass their lives practicing breath control. The saints pass their lives singing the praises of the Lord. ||4|| Some pass their lives walking day and night. Some pass their lives on battle field. Some pass their lives teaching children. The saints pass their lives singing Lord's praise. ||5|| Some pass their lives playing drama and dancing. Some pass their lives taking the lifes of others. Some pass their lives ruling by force. The saints pass their lives singing Lord's praises. ||6|| Some pass their lives counselling and giving advice. Some pass their lives forcibly serving others. Some pass their lives exploring life's mysteries. The saints pass their lives drinking the sublime essence of the Lord. ||7|| As God attaches us, so we do. No one is an ignorant, and no one is wise. Nanak praises those whom God blesses with His grace. ||8||3|| Raamkalee, Fifth Master: Even in a forest fire, some trees remain green. The infant is free of pain in mother's womb. Reciting His name the other concerns go away. Same way the sovereign Lord protects the saints. ||1|| Such is the kind Lord, my protector. Wherever I look, I see You O caretaker Lord. ||1||Pause|| As thirst is quenched by drinking water; As the bride becomes happy when her husband comes home; As wealth is the resolve of the greedy person. Same way God's devotees love God. ||2|| As the farmer protects his crop. As mother and father are kind to the children. As friend meets the friend. Same way God embraces His devotees. ||3|| As the blind is happy seeing. As the mute, sings in joy eating sweets. As the cripple crosses over the mountain. Same way God's name bestows salvation to all. ||4|| As cold is eliminated by fire. Same way the sins are destroyed in saints' company. As clothes are cleaned by soap. Same way reciting God eliminates fear and doubt. ||5|| As the chakvi (duck) bird longs for the sun. As the rain bird thirsts for raindrop. As the deer's ears are attuned to the sound. Same way God's name please His devotees. ||6|| Page 915 By Your grace, we love You. When You are kind, we start missing You. When the Creator is kind; I am released from my bonds. ||7|| I have seen all places with my eyes wide open. There is no other than God. Doubt and fear are dispelled by guru's grace. Nanak sees the amazing Lord's play. ||8||4|| Raamkalee, Fifth Master: All beings that I see are Your creation; ||1|| This mind is saved through the name of God. ||1||Pause|| In an instant, He creates and destroys the creation. It is all God's doing. ||2|| Lust, anger, greed, falsehood and slander are destroyed in devotee's company. ||3|| Reciting God the mind becomes pure and attains eternal peace. ||4|| One who comes to devotee's refuge, does not lose here or the next world. ||5|| Pleasure and pain are the state of my mind; I put it in front of You O God. |6|| You are the bestowal of all beings. You look after your creation. ||7|| Millions of times again and again Nanak praises You. ||8||5|| Raamkalee, Fifth Master, Ashtapadee: God is one. He is realized by guru's grace. Seeing the guru all sins go away and he unites you with God. ||1|| My guru is the transcendent Lord, the giver of peace. He teaches the name of the supreme Lord that helps in the end. ||1||Pause|| I applied the dust of guru's feet to my forehead; my pain is destroyed. ||2|| In an instant, He purifies the sinners and eliminates the ignorance. ||3|| God is the doer and cause of causes; Nanak seeks His refuge. ||4|| Eliminating all bonds I worship God humbly through guru's word. ||5|| He took me out of the dark well and attuned my mind to guru's teachings. ||6|| The fear of birth and death is eliminated. I shall never wander again. ||7|| This mind is imbued to reciting God's name. I am full by drinking nectar. ||8|| I sing God's praises in devotee's company and became content. ||9|| Perfect guru taught the perfect lesson. Other than God no one helps; ||10|| The fortunate obtained the treasure of God's name O Nanak, he will not go to hell. ||11|| I have no effort or intellect; it is all guru's blessing. ||12|| Reciting God; is meditation, penance and self-control; it is all God's grace. ||13|| In the midst of children, spouse and sins; the guru carries his devotees across. ||14|| Page 916 You take care of Your beings. You attach them to your lap. ||15|| He built the boat of true faith to cross over the terrifying world-ocean. ||16|| The Lord is unlimited and endless. Nanak praises Him forever. ||17|| He is immortal, does not take birth, came into existence on his own and enlightens in today's Dark Age. ||18|| He is the Inner-knower, bestowal of life; I am satisfied and fulfilled seeing him. ||19|| God is one; formless, unconcerned pervades water land and all. ||20|| He blesses His devotees with the gift of worship; Nanak longs for God O mother. ||21||1||6|| Raamkalee, Fifth Master, Hymn: Learn from guru's teaching O beloved, the support of life and death. You will be happy and peaceful forever reciting God O Nanak. ||1|| My mind and body are imbued with my beloved Lord. I worship God intuitively O saints. ||1|| The guru fulfilled his promise O saints; He gave the profit of God's name to his servant and threw greed into the air O saints. ||1||Pause|| I found jewel the God by searching; I cannot express its price. ||2|| My mind is focused to His lotus feet; I am absorbed in Him O saints. ||3|| Singing His praises I am content; reciting God I am satisfied and full. ||4|| God pervades all; neither he comes nor goes O saint. ||5|| He exists from the beginning for a long time. It is true that there is God; He blesses all beings O saints. ||6|| He is endless; His end cannot be found. He is omnipresent O saints. ||7|| God is my friend, companion, wealth, youth, son, father and mother, O Saints. ||8||2||7|| Raamkalee, Fifth Master: I recite God's name from my mind without fail. The horrible world-ocean is a whirlpool O Nanak, the guru-willed goes across. ||1||Pause|| Reciting God attains peace inside out; the evil are crushed; ||1|| God got rid of my sins I was committing, by His grace. ||2|| The saints who sought God's refuge are saved; the proud died rotting in the filth. ||3|| In devotee's company I realized this; only God's name helps in the end. ||4|| No one is strong, or weak; all are lit by Your light O Lord. ||5|| You are all-powerful, indescribable, permanent and omnipresent God. ||6|| O Creator; who can describe You; there is no limit. ||7|| O God; bless Nanak with Your name and the dust of saint's feet. ||8||3||8||22|| Page 917 Raamkalee, Third Master, Anand ~ The Song Of Bliss: God is one. He is realized by guru's grace. I am happy O my mother that I found my guru. Finding guru I attained peace and contentment and my mind sings songs of joy. The family and celestial beauties came to sing God's priceless praises through guru's teachings. All those who enshrine God in the mind sing God's praises through guru's teaching. Says Nanak, I am happy that I found my guru. ||1|| O my mind; remain absorbed in God forever. Remain absorbed in God O my mind; all sufferings will be eliminated. He will help you and fulfill your deeds. Our Lord is capable of doing everything; why forget Him from your mind? Says Nanak, O my mind, remain absorbed in God forever. ||2|| O true Lord; what do not you have in your home? Everything is in Your home; they receive whom You give. They say Your praises forever enshrining You in the mind. Those who have your name enshrined in the mind; infinite divine music plays in their mind through guru's teachings. Says Nanak, O true Lord; what do not You have in your home? ||3|| The true Name is my resolve. The true name is my resolve; it satisfies all hunger. It has brought peace and contentment to my mind and fulfilled my desires. I admire the guru forever, who possesses such greatness. Says Nanak, listen, O saints; enshrine guru's teachings in your mind with love. The true name is my resolve. ||4|| The homes where the divine music plays with five types of musical instruments through guru's teachings are fortunate. Blessed are those in whose home the divine music plays by God's grace. You controlled the five demons and destroyed the thorn of death; those who have such pre-ordained destiny recite God's name. Says Nanak, they are at peace, and the unlimited music plays in their home. ||5|| Without true love, the body is humble. The body is humble without God's name; what can it do? No one except You is powerful; please be kind O Lord of the universe. There is no place for me; please guide me through guru's teachings. Says Nanak, without Your love, what can the poor do? ||6|| Everyone talks of happiness but the happiness is realized through the guru. Eternal happiness is realized through the guru by God's grace. The sins are eliminated by His grace through the medicine of divine wisdom. Those who eradicate worldly attachment from their mind are saved through guru's teachings. Says Nanak; this is happiness that comes from the guru. ||7|| Page 918 O elder; whom You give obtains it. Whoever You give receives it; others cannot do anything. Some deluded by doubt wander in ten directions. Some recite God and are saved. By guru's grace, the mind becomes pure of those who believe in God's will. Says Nanak, whom God blesses receives it O beloved; ||8|| Come, beloved saints, let us speak the unspoken speech of the Lord. Let us talk the unspoken that tells how to find God. Surrender body, mind and wealth to the guru; obey his command and realize God. Obey guru's command, and sing the true word of His sermon. Says Nanak, listen, O saints, let us speak the unspoken speech of the Lord. ||9|| O fickle mind, through cleverness, no one has realized God. Through cleverness, no one has found Him; listen, O my mind. This worldly wealth is enticing, that deludes the mind. He who created the creation created the enticing worldly wealth. I admire Him who created the enticing emotional attachment; Says Nanak, O fickle mind, no one has found Him through smart ideas. ||10|| O beloved mind, recite God forever. This family, which you see, shall not go with you. If it does not go with you, why are you attached to it? Don't do anything that you will regret in the end. Listen to the teachings of the guru; these shall go with you. Says Nanak, O beloved mind, recite God forever. ||11|| O inaccessible and unfathomable Lord, Your limits cannot be found. No one can find Your limits; only You know You. All living beings are Your play; what can anyone say? You speak and look after everything; You created the universe. Says Nanak, You are inaccessible. Your limits cannot be found. ||12|| The demy-gods, beings and sages search for nectar which is obtained from the guru. Obtain the nectar by guru's grace and enshrine God in the mind. You created all beings. Some think and search for You. Their greed and ego are dispelled by guru's grace. Says Nanak, those with whom God is pleased, obtain the nectar through the guru. ||13|| The way of devotees is unique. The devotee's way is unique; it is a difficult way to follow. They renounce greed, ego and desire and do not talk too much. This way is sharper than a sword and finer than a hair. You have to follow that. Page 919 Those who self surrender by guru's grace, they start thinking of God. Says Nanak, the way of devotee's is unique in all ages and forever. ||14|| As You ask me, so I do O my Lord; I do not know any of Your virtues. As You cause them, so they do; whomever You guide they serve You. Those whom You inspire by Your grace; recite Your name. Those whom You speak Your sermon; find peace in guru's refuge. Says Nanak, O my Lord keep me as You please. ||15|| This song of praise looks adorable through guru's teachings. The guru told this adorable praise through his teachings. It enshrines in the mind of those with pre-ordained destiny. Some wander around talking a lot, but no one realizes God by talking. Says Nanak, guru revealed the beautiful God's praise through his teachings. ||16|| Those humble beings who recite God become sacred. The guru-willed who recite God become sacred. Their mother, father, family and their whole congregation becomes sacred. Those who say, those who listen to God's name, become sacred by enshrining His name in the mind. Says Nanak, the guru-willed who recite God become sacred; ||17|| By good deeds peace does not well up, without peace the doubt does not go away. The doubt does not depart by self-control; many have tried it. Wash your mind through guru's teachings and enshrine God in the mind. Says Nanak, peace comes by guru's grace; this is how the doubt departs. ||18|| Inwardly polluted but outwardly pure. Those who are pure outside but dirty inside lose their life in a gamble. They are sick with greed; they have forgotten God from the mind. The scriptures describe that God's name is pure but he does not hear this and wanders like a demon. Says Nanak, those who forsake truth and cling to falsehood, lose their lives in a gamble; ||19|| Those who are pure inside are pure outside as well. They are pure inside out; they obtained it by serving the guru. When truth wells in the mind, the affect of falsehood does not touch them. Those who earn the jewel God's name in this human life are good merchants. Says Nanak, those whose minds are pure, live with the guru forever. ||20|| If a disciple obeys and serves the guru devotionally; If a disciple obeys the guru sincerely and enshrines guru in the mind; He humbly worships the guru by enshrining him in the mind. Renouncing ego he remains attached to the guru; he does not know anyone else except the guru. Page 920 Says Nanak, listen, O saints: such a disciple follows the guru with love is a beloved of the guru. ||21|| One who turns away from the guru; no one attains salvation without the guru. No one attains salvation any other way; go ask the wise people. He may wander through many lifes still cannot attain salvation without the guru. Liberation is attained, when one is attached to guru's feet and the guru reads him the teachings. Says Nanak, think this; no one attains salvation without the guru. ||22|| Come, O beloved guru's disciples; listen to the true sermon. Sing guru's sermon, the supreme sermon of sermons. Those who are blessed by God enshrine it in the mind. Drink the nectar and fall in love with God and recite His name. Says Nanak, sing this true discourse forever. ||23|| Without the guru, other sermons are false. The sermon other than guru's lesson is false. The speakers are false; listeners are false; those who speak and recite are false. They may say God God forever but never think of it. Those enticed by the worldly wealth just make noise. Says Nanak, without the guru, other speeches are false. ||24|| Guru's teaching is a jewel studded by diamonds. If guru's teaching touches your mind then you enshrine it in the mind. When guru's teaching enshrines in your mind, you start loving God. He is the diamond; He is the jewel whom God reveals it. Says Nanak, guru's teaching is a jewel studded with diamonds. ||25|| He created the worldly power and yet God issues His command. He issues and enforces His command; only a few guru-willed realize it. They break bonds and attain liberation enshrining guru's teachings in the mind. Those whom God blesses become guru-willed and focus their mind on God. Says Nanak, God the Creator reveals His command. ||26|| The scriptures contemplate sin and sacred, but do not know the reality. The ignorant do not know the reality without the guru. The world is asleep in the three worldly qualities in doubt; it passes the night sleeping. Those who enshrine God in the mind wake up by guru's grace and speak sacred words. Says Nanak, those; who love God, know the reality and spend the nightlife awake. ||27|| He nourished us in the mother's womb; why forget Him from the mind? Why forget such a great giver, who gave us food in the fire of the womb? Nothing can harm one, whom the Lord inspires to love Him. Page 921 He inspires us to love Him and the guru-willed recite God forever. Says Nanak, why forget such a great giver from the mind? ||28|| As is the fire in the womb, so is worldly wealth outside. The fire and worldly wealth is the same. God sets this play. According to His will, the child is born, and the family is pleased. God's love wears off; the child becomes greedy. The worldly wealth runs its course. This is the worldly wealth that makes the child forget God, worldly attachment and the love of duality wells up. Says Nanak, those attuned to God by guru's grace, realize God even surrounded by worldly wealth. ||29|| The Lord is priceless. His worth cannot be estimated. His worth cannot be estimated, people get tired of trying. If you meet such a guru, surrender to him, then the ego will depart. You meet whom you belong; God comes to dwell in the mind. God is priceless; those attached to God are fortunate O Nanak. ||30|| The Lord is my capital; my mind is the merchant. The Lord is my capital, and my mind is the merchant. I realized this through the guru. Recite God all the time o my mind and reap the reward of your effort. This wealth is obtained by those who are pleasing to God's will. Says Nanak, the Lord is my capital, and my mind is the merchant. ||31|| O my tongue, you are enticed by other tastes. Your thirst will not go. Your thirst shall not be quenched by any means, until you enjoy the subtle essence of the Lord. If you obtain God's essence and drink it, you will not be thirsty again. Those who meet the guru acquire God's taste fortunately. Says Nanak, when God enshrines in the mind, all other tastes are forgotten; ||32|| O my body, God infused soul in you that is how you came into the world. God infused soul in you then you came into the world. God is the mother and the father who brought you in the world to see it. By guru's grace, some understand and start moving and see the world move. Says Nanak, He laid the foundation of the universe, and infused His light, then you came into the world; ||33|| My mind became happy, hearing of God's coming. Sing the songs of joy, O friends; my house has become a temple. Sing songs of joy every day; sorrow and pain will not bother you. When I touch guru's feet is an auspicious time, and then I realize my beloved. Divine sermon is realized through guru's teaching and I enjoy the love of God's name. Page 922 Says Nanak, I realized God the doer and cause of causes. ||34|| O my body, what did you do after taking birth in this world? Since you came in the world; what did you do O my body? God who created you, you did not enshrine him in the mind. By pre-ordained destiny God abides in the mind by guru's grace. Says Nanak; this body is accepted when one's mind attaches to the guru. ||35|| O my eyes, God infused His light in you; do not see anyone else but God. Do not see anyone other than God; you will be content by His grace. This poisonous world you see is God's image; you see God in it. By guru's grace, I understand and see One God; there is no one but God. Says Nanak, these eyes were blind; meeting the guru, I see everything now. ||36|| O my ears, you were created to hear the true

Lord. You were attached to the body really to hear God's sermon. Hearing it, the mind and body are rejuvenated, and the tongue is absorbed in sublime Godly taste. The true Lord is unseen and amazing; His divine state cannot be described. Says Nanak, listen to God's sacred name and become sacred. God sent you to listen to Godly truth. ||37|| God placed the soul in the cave and played the music of air. Playing the music of air he opened nine doors and kept the tenth secret. Lovingly attached to guru's refuge, then tenth door is revealed. There are many priceless forms of the Lord, his limits cannot be found. Says Nanak, God placed the soul in the body and started breathing air. ||38|| Sing this true song of praise in true Lord's home. Sing the song of praise in your true home, where God is recited forever. The guru-willed whom you reveal, recite Your name by Your grace. This truth is the Lord the master of all; whoever He blesses obtains it. Says Nanak, sing the true song of praise in true Lord's home (mind). ||39|| Listen with love O fortunate; your wishes are fulfilled. I realized God the supreme Lord and all sorrows are forgotten. Pain, illness and worry have departed listening to the true sermon. The saints and friends realized God through guru's teachings. Pure are the listeners and the speakers; true guru is omnipresent. Prays Nanak; touching guru's feet, the infinite divine music plays. ||40||1|| Page 923 Raamkalee, Sadd ~ The divine lesson: God is one. He is realized by guru's grace. God the bestowal the love of devotees abides in the whole universe. He is realized through love of guru's teachings not thinking of anyone else. Do not think of anyone else; recite God through guru's teachings. By the grace of guru Nanak, Lehna obtained the highest status (became guru). When the call came for Him to depart, He was merged in the name of God. God is immortal, eternal, and unweighed in the world. Amar Daas realized God through worship. ||1|| God's will pleases the guru and the guru goes to God. The guru prays to God, "Please, save my honour. This is my prayer". Save the honour of Your servant, O Lord; please bless him with Your name. In the end His name goes with you and destroys death and devil of death. God heard the prayer of the guru and granted His request. God united him with the guru; He blessed and praised him by His grace. !"||2|| Listen O my disciples, children and brothers, come with me by God's will. The guru accepted God's will, and my Lord applauded Him. He, who obeys God's will, is a devotee the guru. The joyous infinite divine music plays and God embraces him. O my children, siblings and family, look carefully in your minds and see. The pre-ordained destiny does not change; the guru goes to God. ||3|| The guru called his family by his will. Let no one weep for me after I am gone. That would not please me at all. One who preserves friends honour obtains friend's divine wisdom after he is gone. Consider this and see, O my children and siblings. God bestows guruship. The guru is transformed and established his divine rule by God's will. All disciples, relatives, children and siblings have fallen at the feet of guru Ram Daas. ||4|| Finally, the guru said, "When I am gone, sing God's praises for attaining salvation. By God's grace the messenger invited the scholarly Pandit to read the sermon of the Lord. Read God's sermon, hear God's name in the wild. Guru loves God's love. Offer a platter of worship offering, a lamp and a garland of flowers to God. The guru said by God's will that I have realized all-knowing God. The guru blessed sodhi Ram Daas with the ceremonial mark, the symbol of the guru's teachings. ||5|| Page 924 Whatever the primal Lord guru said; the disciples obeyed his will. His son Mohri got up and humbly touched Ram Daas's feet. Everyone touches guru's feet the way guru is worshipped. If someone did not bow because of envy, came later and touched guru's feet. God blessed the guru by His grace. The pre-ordained fate realized. Says Sundar, listen, O saints: the whole world fell at His feet. ||6||1|| Raamkalee, Fifth Master, Chhant: God is one. He is realized by guru's grace. Friend, my friend – standing near me is my friend! I see my beloved Lord with my eyes. I see God with my eyes, he lives in everybody. His nectar tastes sweet. He is with all but cannot be found; the ignorant does not know His taste. Intoxicated with worldly wealth; talks silly, he cannot realize God due to doubt. Says Nanak, without the guru, God cannot be realized though he stands close to all. ||1|| God, my God – the support of my life is my God. My merciful Lord – the giver of gifts is my merciful Lord. The giver of gifts is infinite and unlimited; He abides in all. He created His slave so powerful that she enticed all beings. One, whom the Lord saves, speaks the truth through guru's teachings.

Says Nanak, one who is pleasing to God; God is dear to him. ||2|| God is my honour, I honour my God. Realize God; my Lord is all wise and all knowing. All wise, all-knowing God is forever supreme; recite His sacred name. Tasting God fulfills those who have pre-ordained destiny. They worship and find Him. They place their faith in Him. Says Nanak, He sits on eternal throne. True is His royal court. ||3|| The song of joy, Lord's song of joy; listen to the song of joy of my God. The song, God's song; plays the infinite divine music. The infinite music plays through guru's teaching. It is praised forever. Reciting God attains everything He does not die or go away. The guru-willed realizes the absolute God; his deeds are fulfilled and greed ends. Says Nanak, songs of joy are heard in my God's home; ||4||1|| Page 925 Raamkalee Fifth Master: Recite God o my mind; do not forget Him even for a moment. Enshrine God in the mind and say God God God. Enshrine God in the mind the primal being, bestowal of salvation and formless. He destroys fear, sins and other sufferings. Contemplate the virtues of God, the cherisher and the virtuous Lord of the universe. Prays Nanak; recite God day and night joining devotee's company. ||1|| His lotus feet are the support and anchor of His humble servants. God's name is the treasure of property and wealth of many worlds. Those who enjoy reciting mighty God's name obtain his treasure. Recite God with every breath and enjoy the taste and beauty of the infinite God. Reciting God's name devotionally destroys sins and fear of death. Prays Nanak, the support of His lotus feet is His devotee's wealth. ||2|| O Master, Your virtues are endless, no one can describe; Seeing and hearing of You O merciful Lord, Your devotees narrate them. All beings recite You, O primal transcendent Lord the master. All are beggars. You are the giver, O kind Lord of the universe. He is a devotee a saint whom God accepts. Prays Nanak; they realize You by Your grace. ||3|| I the unworthy orphan came to your refuge. I praise the guru who teaches God's name to me. The guru blessed me with Your name. I became peaceful and my desires fulfilled. The fire extinguished, I became happy uniting with God after a long separation. I found joy, happiness and contentment by singing God's songs of joy. Prays Nanak, I obtained God's name from the perfect guru. ||4||2|| Raamkalee, Fifth Master:

Get up early morning and sing infinite God's praises in saint's company every day. Recite God through guru's teachings; all sins and sufferings will be erased. Recite God's name day and night and drink nectar with love. Falling at guru's feet and reciting God attains yoga and other worship. Worshipping the beloved God with love eliminates all sufferings. Prays Nanak; reciting God the Lord, one cross over the world-ocean. ||1|| O God the ocean of peace, Lord of the universe; Your devotees sing and recite your praises. Touching guru's feet enjoys happiness and many comforts. I obtained the treasure of peace, the pains destroyed and God saved me by His grace. Falling at God's feet the fear and doubt disappeared and I recite God's name. Miss One God, sing one God and visualize one God. Page 926 Prays Nanak, God became kind and I found the perfect guru. ||2|| Meet with God's devotees and sing God's praises in their company. God is the merciful master, Lord of wealth. There is no end to His virtues. The kind God the destroyer of pains eliminates sufferings in His refuge. Emotional attachment, sorrow and bad deeds are eliminated reciting God. All beings are Yours, O my God; be kind that I become the dust of all. Prays Nanak, O God, be kind that I live by reciting Your name. ||3|| God saves His humble devotees, attaching them to His feet. Twenty-four hours a day recite and worship One God. Those who recite God swim across the world ocean, their coming and going ends. Singing God's praises attains eternal peace and God's will pleases them. All my desires are fulfilled, meeting with the perfect guru. Prays Nanak, God united me with Him and pains will not bother again. ||4||3|| Raamkalee, Fifth Master, Chhant. Hymn: In the sanctuary of His lotus feet, I sing His praises with joy and peace. O Nanak, worship God the eradicator of misfortune. ||1|| Chhant: God is the eliminator of misfortune; there is none other than Him. Worship Him forever. he abides in water and land as well. He pervades water land and in between. Do not forget Him even for a moment. Blessed was the day, when I touched guru's feet the Lord of all virtues. So serve Him day and night, O servant, whatever pleases Him happens. Nanak praises the giver of peace; his mind and body are enlightened. ||1|| Hymn: Reciting God my mind and body became happy and thinking of duality ended. Nanak takes the support of the Lord of the world, the Lord of the universe, the destroyer of pains. ||1|| Chhant: The merciful Lord eradicated my fears and troubles. I sing God's praises in love. He is the master, cherisher of the poor. The caretaker immortal God is one. I am in love with Him. When I placed my hands and forehead on His feet, He united me with him and I am awake forever. My soul, body, household home youth wealth and property belong to Him. Nanak is indebted to the caretaker of all beings forever. ||2|| Hymn: My tongue says God God and virtues of the Lord of the universe. Nanak has taken support of one God. He protects the innocent. ||1|| Chhant: God, our Lord and master; protects us attaching to his lap. Recite kind God the Lord in devotee's company and forget own ideas. Page 927 Seek the support of one God, surrender your soul to Him; place your hopes in the sustainer of the world. In devotee's company dyed by God's name one swims across the world ocean. The birth death and other useless deeds ended. No stain should stick to you. Nanak praises the perfect primal Lord. His marriage is eternal. ||3|| Hymn: He is the bestowal of faith, wealth and other needs of salvation. One with pre-ordained destiny gets his deeds fulfilled O Nanak. ||1|| Chhant: All my desires are fulfilled, meeting with my sovereign Lord. I am happy O fortunate. God has revealed in my mind. My beloved came into my mind due to previous earning. I cannot say much about His virtues. God is perfect, infinite bestowal of peace and contentment. How can I say His praises? He unites us with him and embraces. I have no one other than Him. Nanak admires the Creator forever. He abides in all. ||4||4|| Tune Raamkalee, Fifth Master: Sing the song of joy O friends and recite One God. Serve your guru, O my companions, and obtain the fruits of your choice. Raamkalee, Fifth Master, Ruti ~ the seasons. hymn: God is one. He is realized by guru`s grace. Pray to the supreme Lord and seek the dust of the feet of devotees. Eliminate ego and recite God O Nanak, God is omnipresent. ||1|| He is the destroyer of sins and fear; the sovereign Lord is the ocean of peace. Kind to the poor, the destroyer of pain: O Nanak, recite Him forever. ||2|| Chhant: Sing His praises, O fortunate and God will bless you with His grace. Season, month, hours and every moment say the praises of the praiseworthy. Those who recite God whole heartedly are dyed by His virtues are admirable.

Those who realized God. Their life became fruitful. Doing good deeds, giving awns and other deeds do not match God the destroyer of sins. Prays Nanak, he lives by reciting God and his birth and death ends; ||1|| Hymn: Work for the inaccessible and unfathomable Lord, and bow humbly to His lotus feet. What pleases You is the true sermon. God`s name is Nanak`s resolve. ||1|| O friends seek saint's refuge and recite the infinite Lord. O Nanak, reciting God the dead branches become green; ||2|| Chhant: The spring season is joyful; first and second months are pleasant. My mind body and breath blossomed meeting my husband Lord. With my Husband Lord at home, I became stable and happy O friend and my mind blossomed taking support of His lotus feet. Page 928 God is beautiful, wise and all knowing and His virtues are priceless. I found Him fortunately; it eliminated my sufferings and my hope is fulfilled. Prays Nanak, I am in your refuge. My fear of death is eliminated. ||2|| Hymn: Without devotee's company I am tired of wandering doing all kind of deeds. O Nanak, all is bound by passive relations; it is written in the fate. ||1|| He unites and separates us by His will. Nanak has entered God's refuge. His greatness is great! ||2|| Chhant: Summer season is harsh; in the month of Jaith it is very hot. The divorcee without love is not looked upon by God at all. Lord does not look at her. Engrossed by ego she dies of separation. She is attached to worldly wealth and hurts like a fish in the net. God does not like her. She commits sins in life and is scared that devil of death will punish her. Prays Nanak, I take your support; please protect me and do the needful. ||3|| Hymn: I am lovingly attached to my beloved; I cannot live without him even for a moment. He abides in my mind and body intuitively O Nanak. ||1|| My friend of many lifes took me by the hand. He has made me His humble slave; O Nanak, God is in my mind. ||2|| Chhant: The rainy season is comfortable, the months of Saawan and Bhaadon and brings joy. It rains heavily, the land gets drenched and flowers bloom all over. God is all-pervading and all homes are filled with His name. Recite the inner knower God. All dynasties will be saved. Lovingly attached to God is not harmed by anything. God is always kind. Prays Nanak, I found my Husband Lord. He always pleases my mind. ||4|| Hymn: Thirsty with desire, I wander around; when will I see my

Lord of the world? Is there any friendly saint O Nanak, who will unite me with God? ||1|| I am restless without meeting Him. I cannot survive for a moment without Him. By God's grace my hope is fulfilled in devotee's refuge O Nanak. ||2|| Chhant: In cool, autumn season, the months of Assu and Katik, I am thirsty for God. I wander around searching for you. When will I see the virtuous Lord? There is no peace without the beloved Husband. Wearing ornaments is useless. She is beautiful, wise, clever and knowledgeable; but she is like a dead body. I look here and there, in ten directions; my mind is thirsty to meet God! Prays Nanak, be kind and unite me with You O God. ||5|| Hymn: The fire is extinguished, I am soothed and peaceful. O Nanak, I met my perfect God. The illusion of duality is erased. ||1|| Page 929 The Lord sent His devotees, to tell us that He is not far away. O Nanak, doubt and fear are dispelled, reciting the omnipresent God. ||2|| Chhant: In the winter season of Maghar and Poh, the Lord reveals Himself. My burning desire is quenched by visualizing Him, the enmity and worldly wealth departed. All my desires are fulfilled meeting the Lord. I am His servant, I serve His feet. The joy of wearing necklace and make up are obtained by singing the praises of the unseen mysterious God. I long for loving devotion to the Lord of the universe; the devil of death cannot rob me. Prays Nanak, God united me with Him. I shall not separate again. ||6|| Hymn: The happy soul bride found Godly wealth. Now my mind does not waver. Due to pre-ordained destiny I visualized the saint in my mind. ||1|| With my beloved Husband Lord, I enjoy millions of melodies, pleasures and joy. The fruits of mind's desires are obtained, O Nanak, reciting God's name. ||2|| Chhant: The snowy winter season, the months of Maagh and Phagun, are pleasing to the virtuous bride. O my friends and companions sing songs of joy; my Husband Lord has come home. Missing Him in my mind, my beloved came home and my bed looks adorable. My woods, meadows, the whole universe is lush green by visualizing Him. I met my Lord; reciting the pure word fulfills my desires. Prays Nanak, I enjoy that I met my Husband Lord the Lord of excellence. ||7|| Hymn: The saints are my help to take across the terrifying world ocean. O Nanak, those who love God's name are the highest of all. ||1|| Those who realize God swim across; they are brave

warriors. Nanak praises those who swam across reciting God. ||2||
Chhant: By His grace all sufferings are eradicated. Fear of coming and
going eliminated and God's worship entered in my mind. Imbued
with God's love attains peace. May I not forget him from my mind at
all? Renouncing ego I sought refuge of God the Lord of the universe.
Worship God the Lord of the universe, the treasure of virtue, the
Lord of excellence, our primal Lord and master. Prays Nanak, may
You live forever by Your grace. ||8||1||6||8|| Raamkalee, First Master,
southern language, Onkaar: God is one. He is realized by guru's grace.
First, God came into being by reciting God. From one the eternal
ages were created. From one created the Vedas. Page 930 Reciting
one God through guru's teachings attains salvation. Reciting God the
guru-willed are saved. Pay regard and listen to God's praises with
love. Praise God the cherisher of the universe. ||1|| Listen, O scholar,
what worldly entanglements you write about. O guru-willed, write
about God the Lord of the world. ||1||Pause|| Letter Sassa: He created
the universe with ease. His one light pervades the universe. The
guru-willed obtains the treasure. He picks gems and pearls. He
understands, reads and contemplates but finally there is only one
God. The guru-willed realizes and recites God. Without God the
world is false. ||2|| Letter Dhadha: In God's realm abides faith; the
virtuous attains peace there. Dhadha: If the dust of their feet touches
one's face, he is transformed from iron into gold. The Lord of the
earth is without birth, weighs perfect and speaks eternal truth. God
and guru know His divine power. ||3|| In love of duality, divine wisdom
is lost; he eats poison and rots in filth. Singing guru's praises do not
appeal to him, nor does he likes the profound, unfathomable Lord.
Listening to guru's true sermon obtains nectar, mind and body
become peaceful. He is the devotee. He is the bestowal and drinks
the nectar. ||4|| Everyone says that God is one, but they are troubled
by ego and pride. Realize God inside out; destiny attains this way.
God is near; do not think Him far. He abides the whole world. God
is one, not two. Nanak has merged with Him. ||5|| How can you
control Him. He is too powerful. Intoxicated with worldly wealth
they are cheated by falsehood. They are enslaved by greed; they will
repent forever. Serving One God attains salvation and coming and

going ends. ||6|| God's actions, colours and forms are one. He manifests in many shapes through wind, water and fire. One soul wanders through the universe. One who realizes one understands and attains honour. Obtaining divine wisdom and contemplation; he becomes stable. Only a few guru-willed realize God. Whoever he blesses with His grace attains peace. He speaks of God in guru's refuge. ||7|| Water and land are lit by His light. In the whole universe is the guru, the Lord of the world. The Lord reveals His various forms. By His grace, He enters the heart. It pours when it rains. It happens through sacred guru's teachings. One who knows the mystery of one God? He is the Creator the divine Lord. ||8|| When the sun rises, the demons are killed. Realize the mighty God through guru's teachings. God is above the origin the end of the universe. He acts, speaks and listens; Page 931 He is the architect of destiny. He blesses us with mind and body. That architect of destiny is in my mind and mouth. God is the life of the world; there is no other at all. O Nanak, imbued with God's name obtains honour. ||9|| One who lovingly recites the name of the sovereign Lord? Fights the battle and conquers his mind; Day and night, he remains imbued with Lord's love. He is famous throughout the universe and the four ages. One, who realizes the Lord, becomes like Him. He becomes absolutely pure and his body is sanctified. His is happy, in love with one Lord. With guru's teachings in the mind he lovingly attunes to God. ||10|| Don't be angry – drink the nectar; you will not live forever. The kings and paupers shall not live; they come and go in all four ages. By saying, no one lives forever; whom do I offer my prayer to? Only through guru's teachings reciting God's name attains honour. ||11|| Worried about honour she wore a veil; she died and veil is lifted in the end. I am freed of insane ignorant mother-in law. My beloved called me and I joined with him through guru's teachings. Imbued with love I the guru-willed became carefree and beloved of my beloved. ||12|| Recite God's name and obtain the real profit. Greed and ego are bad. Ladies who like gossip and slander are not trustworthy. The self-willed is blind, foolish and ignorant. You came into the world to get some benefit. You did hard labour; got cheated and departed. Take benefit of reciting God's name and earn faith. O Nanak, you will be truly honoured by the true emperor. ||13||

The world is ruined on the path of death. No one has the power to erase death. If wealth is in lowly person's home, seeing wealth, all pay respect to him. Even an idiot is smart, if he is rich. Without God's worship, the world is insane. One Lord abides among all. Whoever God blesses realizes Him; ||14|| The enemy less God exists in all ages. He is not subject to birth and death or worldly affairs. Whatever is seen is God Himself; Creating Him, He lives in the heart. He is unfathomable; He puts people to their deeds. He is the way of Yoga, the life of the world. Truthful living brings true peace. Without God's name, how can anyone find liberation? ||15|| Without God's name the body is useless. Why not realize God so that the pain of your mind is eliminated? The traveller comes and goes forever. What did he bring and what he has? Without God's name there is shortage everywhere. The profit is earned, when the Lord grants understanding. The merchant deals in trading. Without God's name there is no honour. ||16|| One who contemplates Lord's virtues is spiritually wise. Through His virtues, one obtains divine wisdom. There are only a few virtuous people in the world. The true way of life comes through guru's teachings. The Lord is inaccessible and unfathomable. His worth cannot be estimated. Page 932 You unite with Him if he unites you. The virtuous soul bride continuously contemplates His virtues. O Nanak, the friendly God is realized through guru's teaching. ||17|| Lust and anger destroy the body. As gold is dissolved by borax. The gold passes the test. When it is appraised by the goldsmith. The world is an animal and death is the butcher. God creates and the mortal gets the fruit of his doing. He, who created the world, knows its worth. What else can we say? There is nothing to say. ||18|| By searching I drink the nectar. By guru's blessing he became humble. Everyone calls him true and genuine. The true jewel is genuine in all four ages. Eating and drinking, one dies, but still does not know why? He dies in an instant, when he realizes guru's teachings. His mind became stable and the mind accepted death. By guru's grace, he realizes God's name. ||19|| The profound Lord dwells in the sky. Singing His praises, one dwells in peace. He, who goes, does not return and who comes does not go. By guru's grace, he remains lovingly focused on the Lord. The Lord is inaccessible, independent and beyond birth. He is stable in trance. Reciting God eliminates birth. Guru's teachings are the reality, anything else is useless. ||20|| I am tired of wandering in many houses. I do not know how many times I was born. I had so many mothers and fathers, sons and daughters. I had so many gurus and disciples. Through a false guru, liberation is not found. There are so many brides of one Husband Lord; know this. The guru-willed dies and lives with God. Searching in the ten directions, I found Him in my own home. I am united with God; the guru united me. ||21|| The guru-willed sings and speaks. The guru-willed checks the weight and weighs. The guru-willed comes and goes without any concern. His filth is taken away, and his stains are burnt off. The guru-willed hears, reads and contemplates. The guru-willed performs good deeds with good behaviour. The guru-willed realizes the nectar and reality through guru's teachings. O Nanak, the guru-willed crosses over. ||22|| The fickle mind does not remain stable. It is like a deer secretly nibbling at the green sprouts. One who enshrines Lord's lotus feet in the mind? Remembers God as long as he lives. Everyone seems to be worried. Reciting one God attains peace. When the Lord dwells in the mind; then he is absorbed in God's name. One attains liberation and goes home with honour. ||23|| The body falls apart and one knot is untied. People see others die every day. One who looks alike upon sunshine and shade? His bonds are cut and attains salvation. The world is lost in the false shade. Everything happens by pre-ordained destiny. Youth is wasting away, getting old, death hovers overhead. Page 933 The body is destroyed like algae on water. ||24|| God appears throughout the three worlds. Throughout the ages, He is the great giver none else. As it pleases You, keep me. I praise you that you bless me for fulfillment with branches and leaves. I keep praising if it please You. When You unite me with You, I merge with You. I recite and praise God the life of the world. All desires are fulfilled through guru's teachings. ||25|| Why bother talking nonsense and argue with the world? You see the reality and die repenting. He is born to die; he has no hope of living. He comes hopeful, and goes hopeless. He regrets talking ill and mixes with dirt. Death does not chew up, singing God's praises. I obtained the priceless treasure by reciting God's name; The Lord bestows intuitively. ||26|| He speaks spiritual wisdom innocently, and understands it. He understands it and realizes it. He accepts guru's word with love. The purity truly appeals to the true Lord. Guru is the ocean full of jewels. The treasure of jewels is truly inexhaustible. Do what the guru says. Why do you want to go after guru's actions? O Nanak, through guru's teachings; merge in true Lord. ||27|| What can you do when the love breaks? The arm is broken, when it is pulled from both sides. Love breaks, when one speaks bad words. The Husband Lord abandons and leaves behind the evil-minded bride. The broken knot is tied again through contemplation. Through guru's teachings your deeds will be completed. The profit of truth never falls short. The Lord of the universe is my best friend. ||28|| Control your mind, and keep it in place. The world is destroyed by obstructing and regrets doing sinful mistakes. There is one Husband Lord, all are His brides. The false bride makes many disguises. He stops her from going into the homes of others; He calls her home and nothing stops her. She is adorned by guru's teachings and Lord's love. She is the happy soul bride supported by her Husband Lord. ||29|| Wandering all over O my companion, my clothes are torn and makeup faded. Jealousy takes away the peace of mind, without fear the congregation is destroyed. One who is afraid of her knowledgeable Husband Lord? She is fearful of her guru and recites carefree God's name. He lives on a hill. I am very thirsty for him; when I realize then he is not far. Obeying guru's teachings the thirst is quenched and I drink the nectar. Everyone says, give give, but as He pleases, He gives. He gives at guru's refuge and eliminates the thirst. ||30|| Searching around I see the edges of the river falling and disappearing. The heavy fall and disappear, the light swim across. I admire those who realize unimaginable immortal God. I am intoxicated by the dust of their feet and united with God in their company. I surrendered my mind to my guru and obtained God's pure name from him. Page 934 I serve one who gave me God's name; I admire Him. He, who builds, also demolishes; there is no other than Him. By guru's grace, I recite Him; then my body does not suffer in pain. ||31|| No one is mine – whom should I hold on to? No one was and no one will be. One is ruined in coming and going afflicted with the disease of duality. Those without God's name are like mud wall which falls quick. Without the name, how can they find freedom? They go to hell in the end. We describe God through limited letters of alphabet, but God is beyond limit. The ignorant has no wisdom; without the guru, there is no divine wisdom. With a broken string the guitar does not play due to separation. God unites the separated with Him due to previous deeds O Nanak. ||32|| The body is a tree, the mind is a bird; the birds peck on the tree. They peck the fruit, and merge with one Lord. They are not trapped again. They fly around fast and look for more food. They are caught in the net and their wings are clipped. This happened due to doing bad deeds. How can they be saved without the true Lord? Reciting God is the supreme deed. When He frees them, only then they are freed. He is the great master. By guru's kindness, they are released by God's grace. Greatness is in His Hand. He blesses those with whom He pleases. ||33|| The soul shivers when it is without a place to rest. There is only one honourable place; nothing goes wrong there. God and guru are eternal and so is the true thinking. O Lord, You are the support of gods, men mystics and hopeless. O bestowal Lord; You abide everywhere, all high low places. Wherever I look, I see You; You have no end or limit. You abide everywhere, all high low places. You are realized through guru's teachings. You are great, permanent and beyond comprehension and bestow gifts that are not even asked for. ||34|| O Lord, You are kind and bestowal of gifts. You create and look after the creation. Please be kind and unite me with You. You destroy and rebuild in a moment. You are all wise and all seeing. You are the greatest giver of all. You destroy the poverty and sufferings. The guru-willed realize You contemplating divine wisdom. ||35|| Losing wealth, he worries a lot. The ignorant mind is in the wealth. Only a few collect the true wealth through God's sacred name. What if you lose wealth; dye yourself with God's love. Surrender your mind and head for God's support. Worldly affairs ended and enjoy guru's teachings in the mind. Enemies become friends, meeting the guru, the Lord of the universe. Wandering from forest to forest searching, but the treasure is at home. United by the guru, I remain united, the pain of birth and death ends. ||36|| One does not find freedom through rituals. Without virtues one goes to the village of death. He is neither here nor the next world. He regrets doing bad deeds. Page 935 He neither has divine wisdom nor meditation; neither faith in religion. Without God's name and with ego, the carefree God cannot be realized. I am tired – how can I get there? This ocean has no bottom or end. I have no beloved companions, who I can ask for help? O Nanak, cry, "beloved, beloved", God will unite you with him. He, who separated me, will unite again through the love of the guru. ||37|| Sin is bad, but it is dear to the sinner. He loads sins, and spreads all over. Giving up sins, one realizes him. He is not afflicted by sorrow or separation. How can one avoid going to hell? How can he cheat death? How can, coming and going be forgotten? Falsehood is bad, death is cruel. The mind is enveloped by entanglements and leads to more entanglements. Without God's name, how can anyone be saved? The sinners rot in sins. ||38|| Again and again, the crow falls in the trap. Then he regrets, what can he do now? Even in a trap, he pecks at food; he does not understand! Meeting the guru, his eyes open; like a fish, he is caught in the noose of death. Without the kind guru, there is no salvation. He keeps on coming and going again and again. If he is attuned to God with love. He will be freed and never caught in a trap again. ||39|| She keeps saying, O brother, O brother. The brother is far away. Her brother goes home and the sister feels separation. When the daughter is in father's home; the children love each other. If you long for your Husband Lord, O soul bride, serve the guru: Only a few wise people realize that the guru unites them with God. The honour is in God's hand; he gives whomever He wants. Only a few guru-willed contemplate guru's sermon. This is God's sermon; through which one realizes one. ||40|| Break and make, then break again; destroy the built and rebuild. He dries up the pools and fills the dried pools again. The all-powerful God is carefree. Deluded by doubt, they go insane; without destiny they get nothing? O guru-willed, God has the string of wisdom in His hand; the way he pulls so we go. Those who sing God's praises are dyed by His love; they do not repent later. Bhabha: the guru-willed searches and finds; he attains destiny that way. Bhabha: The path of the terrifying world-ocean is hard. He who gives up desire swims across. One who searches his soul by guru's grace becomes dead while alive. ||41|| Everyone yearns for wealth, but wealth does not go with them. The soul-swan departs; he forgets to take wealth with him. The false mind is robbed by the devil of death; the bad deeds go with him. The mind turns upside down at the time of death if the virtues are with him. Page 936 Crying mine, mine, they died; without God's name, they only find pain. Where are the forts, mansions, palaces and courts? It is like a juggler's show. O Nanak, without the true name, coming and going is false. He is clever and beautiful; He is wise and all knowing. ||42|| Those who come must go in the end; they repent when they come and go. They keep coming and going. It never ends. Those who love God are saved. They die engaged in worldly entanglements robbed by the worldly wealth. Whoever is seen shall depart; whom should I make friends with? Self-surrender yourself including mind and body. You are permanent O Creator; I lean on Your support. I died due to virtues hit by the love of guru's teachings in the heart. ||43|| The kings, the nobles, the rich or the poor will not remain forever. They go turn by turn, no one can stay here. The path is difficult and treacherous; the ocean and mountains are impassable. I am filled with faults; I am wondering; how can I go home without virtues? The virtuous realize God through virtues; how can I meet them with love? May I become like them by reciting God in my mind. He is filled with faults but virtues also dwell with it. Virtues cannot be acquired without the guru and his teachings. ||44|| He keeps army at home, it is written from destiny. They serve the supreme Lord and obtain profit. They renounce greed and evil deeds and forget them from their mind. Crying at God's door, no one loses at all. He who answers the call immediately is God's servant. He loses his wages and does not sit on the throne. Honour is in beloved's hand. He gives whom He wants. He does everything; whom else should we say? No one else does anything. ||45|| I cannot think of any other, who could be seated on the royal cushions. God the Lord of beings saves from hell; he exists and it is true. I wandered all over searching for Him; now I think in my mind. The treasure of diamonds, pearls, jewels and emeralds is in guru's hand. If I recite God single mindedly with love; I become pure and realize God. O Nanak, one who loves the beloved intently gets the benefit in the next world. He, who created the creation and the universe; O guru-willed worship the unlimited God; there is no end to His creation. ||46|| Rharha: The dear Lord is beautiful; there is no other emperor except Him. Rharha: Listen to His sermon; God lives in your mind. God is realized by guru's grace; do not doubt it. He is the true banker, who has the Godly wealth with him. He is a true guru-willed – applaud him! Through the beautiful sermon I realized God contemplating guru's teachings. Page 937 Eliminating ego the pain is gone and the soul bride found her Husband Lord. ||47|| Collect gold and silver. It is false wealth like dirty ashes. He hoards wealth and calls him a banker, he is deluded by duality. The truthful gather truth; the true name is priceless. God is pure and clean, speak the truth and you will be truly honoured. You are my friend and companion, all-knowing Lord. You are the lake and You are the swan. I admire those who enshrine God in the mind. God created worldly wealth and attachment and He knows it. Sin and sacred are alike; only the divine person realizes it. ||48|| Without kindness, countless hundreds of thousands have perished. Do not know how many died like this; it is beyond imagination. One who realizes his master is set free and not bound again. One realizes true God through guru's teachings and attains forgiveness, truth and peace. Enjoy Godly wealth as much as you want; He abides in your body. Recite Him with your mind body and mouth; virtuous peace giving God is in your mind. Those who sow useless seeds, die ruined by ego. God created the beings and seeded ego inside, the Creator is beyond it. ||49|| No one knows the mystery of the Creator of the world. Whatever the Creator of the world does, happens. For wealth, we recite God. By pre-ordained destiny, wealth is obtained. For the sake of wealth, some become servants or thieves. Wealth does not go with them; it goes to someone else. Without reciting God no one attains honour in His court. Drinking the subtle essence of the Lord attains freedom O ignorant. ||50|| Seeing and seeing, O my companions, I am surprised. My ego is dead by reciting guru's teaching and obtained divine wisdom. I am tired of wearing necklaces, hair-ties, bracelets and decorating myself. I found peace meeting the beloved the supreme necklace of all. O Nanak, the guru-willed realize God through love. No one attains peace without God; think in your mind; Read God, think God and love God; Recite

and contemplate God; make God's name your destiny. ||51|| O friend,
the writing in the fate by God, does not erase. He, who created the
universe, will be your turban exchange brother. Honour is in God's
hand; only a few realize it through guru's teachings. The writing
cannot be changed; it happens as he wishes. Nanak found peace by
your grace through guru's teachings. The self-willed are lost, they rot
and die. They rise again contemplating guru's teachings. The Lord
cannot be seen; what can we say about Him? I praise my guru who
revealed God in the mind! ||52|| He who speaks divine wisdom
intuitively is the real scholar. Page 938 He acquires knowledge and
realizes reality by lovingly attuning to God's name. The self-willed
sells knowledge; he earns poison and eats poison. The ignorant does
not contemplate guru's teachings. He has no intellect. ||53|| The
guru-willed who teaches wisdom to his disciples is a scholar. Praise
and gather God's name and reap the benefit in the world. Write truth
in your mind truthfully, read the reality through guru's teachings. O
Nanak, he who wears God's name's necklace is a learned scholar.
||54||1|| Raamkalee, First Master ~ Conversations With The mystics:
God is one. He is realized by guru's grace. The mystics sit in
congregation and applaud; I offer my prayer to the infinite
incomparable and beautiful Lord; I cut my head and offer to Him; I
offer my mind and body as well. O Nanak, meeting the saints obtains
truth, you praise them, and they praise you back. ||1|| What is the use
of wandering around? Truth comes through truth. Salvation is not
obtained without guru's true teachings. ||1||Pause|| Who are you?
What is your name? What is your faith? What is your goal? I say
truthfully that I praise the saints. Where is your seat? Where do you
live, O boy? Where did you come from and where you are going? Tell
us the truth O Nanak, what is your path, asks the mystic?"||2|| God
fully abides in all. He is realized following guru's will. I came peacefully
by God's command O Nanak by His will. I sit in the posture and
recite the immortal Lord. I learned this from the guru. The guru-willed
understands and realizes him and merges with true Lord. ||3|| The
world is a terrifying ocean; how can I cross it? Says Charpat O Nanak
yogi; give us your true reply; You say that you know it; what can I
reply to you says Nanak? I say the truth; if you have already attained

salvation, how can I argue with you? ||4|| The lotus flower floats untouched in the water and the duck swims in the stream; O Nanak, attuning to guru's teachings reciting God's name with love swims across the world ocean; One who truly enshrines God in the mind and detached in the midst of desire. Nanak is the servant of the one who realizes and reveals others the inaccessible, unfathomable Lord? ||5|| "Listen O master to my request; I honestly ask you? Don't be angry; please tell us: How can we find guru's refuge?" Stabilize the fickle mind and truth will well up through God's name O Nanak. If you truly love Him; he will unite you with Him; ||6|| Remain detached while shopping, walking in the forest and desert; Eat roots and fruits O yogi and speak divine wisdom. Page 939 We bathe at shrines to attain happiness and think that filth will not attach again. Gorakh's disciple says; this is yoga; |7|| He does not sleep while shopping, walking and the mind does not look at other's houses. O Nanak, the mind does not stabilize without God's name and greed does not go away. The guru revealed the shop and the city in the mind; where I trade for peace and truth. Sleep little, eat little; O Nanak, and contemplate the reality. ||8|| O yogi; you pretend by wearing earrings, begging bag and patched coat. Serve one God inside out and obtain the highest treasure of divine wisdom. Guide your mind this way and you will not be hurt again. Nanak speaks: the guru-willed understands. This is the yoga way. ||9|| Wear guru's teaching as earring; eliminate ego and worldly attachment. Eliminating lust, anger and ego; attains realization through guru's teachings. Your patched coat and begging bag will be filled says Nanak; God bestows salvation. There is one God; it is true. Realize Him through guru's teachings. ||10|| This head the hat made of five elements will be turned upside down. Let the body be your worship mat, and the mind your loincloth. Let truth, contentment and self-discipline be your companions. O Nanak, the guru-willed recite God's name. ||11|| "Who is hidden? Who is liberated? Who is united inside out? Who comes, who goes? Who is permeating and pervading the universe?"||12|| He is hidden in each and every heart. The guru-willed is liberated. He is realized inside as well outside through guru's teachings. The self-willed perishes and comes and goes. O Nanak, the guru-willed merges in truth. ||13|| "How is one bound and consumed by worldly wealth? How does one lose, how does one gain? How one becomes pure? How is one in the dark? One who understands this reality is my guru."||14|| Engrossed by ill deeds is consumed by worldly wealth. The self-willed loses the guru-willed gains. Meeting the guru, darkness is eliminated. O Nanak, eradicating ego one merges in the Lord. ||15|| Focus your mind continuously on one God. The soul-swan does not fly away and the body wall does not collapse. Then, one realizes God in his peaceful cave. O Nanak, truth pleases the true Lord. ||16|| "Why did you leave your home O renunciates? Why did you become like this? What merchandise do you trade? How will you go across?||17|| I became renunciate searching for God. I adopted these robes to visualize God. I trade the merchandise of truth. O Nanak, the guru-willed goes across; ||18|| Why have you changed the course of your life? What have you linked your mind to? Page 940 How have you subdued your hopes and desires? How have you found the Light in you? Without teeth, how can you eat? Give us your true answer O Nanak."||19|| The guru eliminates birth in his refuge. My mind is attached and attuned to the infinite God. Through guru's teachings the hope and desire are eliminated. The guru-willed found the real enlightenment. Eradicating the three qualities, one realizes the reality. O Nanak, the bestowal bestows salvation. ||20|| What can you tell us about origin? Where did God live then? Who was contemplating divine wisdom and who lived in everyone? Why to avoid the beating of death and how to go to destiny? How to obtain peace and contentment and how to drive away the ill will? Eliminating the evil ego through guru's teachings one reaches the destiny? One who created the creation through guru's teachings; Nanak is his slave. ||21|| Where we come from? Where we go? Where we will be absorbed? One who realizes guru's teachings; does not have to worry at all; the guru-willed realizes the essence of immortality through love. He knows all, He is the Creator; says Nanak by contemplating. We come by His command, go by His command and we merge with Him by His command. Practice truth through the guru and attain divinity through the guru. ||22|| This is how the amazing God is contemplated and truly merge with absolute God. Unthinkingly contemplate guru's wisdom and realize God in all.

Through guru's teachings we merge with God realizing God intuitively. O Nanak, there is no other way; the disciple who serves finds God. One who realizes God's command through His command realizes the way to realize Him. One who eradicates ego becomes desire free. He is called the Yogi. ||23|| Realizing the unknown God makes pure; the creation is created from absolute. Pleasing the guru attains salvation through guru's teachings. One realizes God by eliminating ego and duality. He who is enlightened through guru's teachings is the real yogi. If one dies while alive understands everything. He realizes the kind God in him. O Nanak, he is blessed with greatness; who sees God in all. ||24|| We emerge from truth, merge in truth again. The truthful merges in true Lord. The false come and find no place to rest; in duality, they come and go. Coming and going end through guru's teaching. God finds and forgives. One, who suffers from the disease of duality, does not recite God. Page 941 Whom God inspires realizes God through guru's teachings and attains salvation. O Nanak, the bestowal bestows salvation by eliminating pride and duality. ||25|| The self-willed are deluded, under the fear of death. They look into the homes of others and lose. The self-willed confused by doubt, wander in the wilderness. Having lost their way, they are robbed by the mantra of the fake and dead. They do not contemplate guru's teachings instead they talk silly. O Nanak, imbued with truth obtains happiness. ||26|| The guru-willed (guru's follower) loves the true Lord. The guru-willed speaks the unspoken sermon. The guru-willed becomes pure by singing God's praises. The guru-willed becomes sacred and attains salvation. The guru-willed recites God through every pour of the body. O Nanak, the guru-willed merges in truth. ||27|| The guru-willed contemplates the scriptures. The guru-willed contemplates and crosses over the world ocean. The guru-willed who realizes guru's teachings becomes divine. The guru-willed realizes his inner-self. The guru-willed attains the unseen the infinite Lord. O Nanak, the guru-willed attains salvation. ||28|| The guru-willed speaks the unspoken wisdom. In the midst of his family, the guru-willed lives a spiritual life. The guru-willed recites God with love. The guru-willed acquires good behaviour through guru's teachings. Contemplating guru's teachings He realizes the reality. O Nanak, He merges with God eliminating ego. ||29|| True Lord created the earth for the sake of the guru-willed. There, he set the play of creation and destruction. One who is imbued with God's love through guru's teachings? Attuned to the truth, he goes home with honour. Without guru's teachings no one obtains honour. O Nanak, without God's name, how can one be absorbed in truth? ||30|| The guru-willed attains all mystic powers and divine knowledge. The guru-willed swims across the world ocean through truth. The guru-willed knows the ways of true and false. The guru-willed knows worldliness and renunciation. The guru-willed crosses over, and carries others across as well. O Nanak, the guru-willed attains salvation through guru's teachings. ||31|| Attuned to God's name eliminates ego. Attuned to God's name merge in truth. Attuned to God's name, contemplate the way to salvation. Attuned to God's name attain salvation. Attuned to God's name, understand the universe. O Nanak, attuned to God's name attains eternal peace. ||32|| Attuned to God's name he converses with mystics. Attuned to God's name is eternal and self-discipline. Attuned to God's name are truthful and true deeds. Attuned to God's name they contemplate the divine wisdom. Without God's name, people talk useless. O Nanak, those attuned to God's name are praiseworthy. ||33|| Through the perfect guru, one obtains God's name. This is the way of Yoga; and remains absorbed in truth. The Yogis wander in the twelve schools of Yoga; renunciate in sixty-four. He, who remains dead while alive through guru's teachings, attains salvation. Page 942 Without guru's teachings all are enticed by duality; check it out. O Nanak, those who enshrine God's name in the mind are fortunate. ||34|| The guru-willed obtains the jewel lovingly focusing on God. The guru-willed appraises the jewel intuitively. The guru-willed practices truthful action. The mind of the guru-willed is pleased with the true Lord. The guru-willed sees the unseen by God's grace. O Nanak, the guru-willed does not have to endure punishment. ||35|| The guru-willed bathes in God's name. The guru-willed intuitively enters in trance. The guru-willed obtains honour in God's court. The guru-willed realizes the supreme Lord, the destroyer of fear. The guru-willed does good deeds and inspires others to do so. O Nanak, the guru-willed unites with God. ||36|| The guru-willed contemplates the scriptures. The guru-willed knows the secrets of each and every heart. The guru-willed eliminates hate and opposition. The guru-willed erases all accounts. The guru-willed is imbued with the love of the name of God. O Nanak, the guru-willed realizes his master. ||37|| Without the guru, one wanders in coming and going. Without the guru, one's work is not completed. Without the guru, the mind is totally unsteady. Without the guru, one is unsatisfied, and eats poison. Without the guru, one is stung by the poisonous snake and dies on the way. O Nanak without the guru, all is a loss. ||38|| One who meets the guru is carried across. His sins are erased, and obtains salvation through virtues. The eternal peace and liberation is attained, contemplating guru's teachings. The guru-willed never loses. The body is the shop and the mind is the shopkeeper. O Nanak, it deals intuitively in truth. ||39|| The guru-willed is the bridge, built by the architect of destiny. He robbed Lanka and the miserable demon. Ram Chander – killed Raawan. The guru-willed bhabhekhan gave the secret. The guru-willed floats the rock in the ocean. The guru-willed saves millions of gods. ||40|| The comings and goings of guru-willed ends; The guru-willed is honoured in the court of the Lord. The guru-willed distinguishes the true from false. The guru-willed focuses his mind intuitively. In the court of the Lord, the guru-willed is absorbed in His praises. O Nanak, the guru-willed is not bound by bonds. ||41|| The guru-willed realizes the name of the formless Lord. Through guru's teachings the guru-willed eliminates ego. The guru-willed sings the praises of the true Lord. The guru-willed merges with true Lord. Through the true name, the guru-willed attains honour. O Nanak, the guru-willed understands the universe. ||42|| "What is the root, the source of all? What is the time for guru's teaching? Who is your guru? Whose disciple are you? What is that speech, by which you remain unattached? Listen to what we say, O Nanak, you boy. Give us your answer to what we said. How guru's teaching carries us across the terrifying world-ocean?"||43|| Page 943 From the air came the beginning. Guru's teaching is the time to learn. Lovingly attuning to guru's teachings the disciple realizes God. Speak the unspoken speech and remain unattached. O Nanak, throughout the ages, the guru is the Lord of the world. I contemplate the sermon through guru's teachings. The guru-willed puts out the fire of ego. ||44|| How can you eat with teeth made of wax? What is that, which takes away pride? How can the house of snow wear a robe of fire? Where is that cave, the mind goes after death? Where does the soul live here and the next world? What is the process by which God enters the mind? ||45|| How one eradicates ego and possessiveness from the mind? Eliminates duality and becomes one with one. The world is difficult for the foolish, self-willed. Practicing guru's teachings you eat everything. Know that God is inside out. O Nanak, the fire is extinguished by guru's will. ||46|| Imbued with love, eliminates self-pride. Realize God contemplating guru's teachings. Through guru's teachings, God enshrines in the mind. The body and mind are soothed dyed by God's love. Extinguish the fire of lust, anger and corruption. O Nanak, by the grace of the beloved God. ||47|| How does moon give soothing like snow? How does the sun give heat? How death robs every day? How the guru-willed obtains honour? Who is the brave who conquers Death? Give us your thoughtful reply, O Nanak."||48|| Through guru's teachings the moon illuminates; the sun gives light to moon. Feel pleasure and pain alike through the help God's name. He carries us across the world ocean. Following guru's sermon, truth dwells in the mind. Nanak says humbly, and then death does not kill him. ||49|| God's name is essence of everything. Without God's name, one suffers the pain of death. When realty merges with reality, then the mind agrees. Duality is gone and one merges with God. Then the wind blows and the cloud thunders. O Nanak, one obtains peace intuitively. ||50|| The absolute Lord dwells inside, outside and the whole universe. One, who knows the fourth state, is not subject to virtue or vice. He knows the secret of everyone. He is primal being formless God. Whoever is dyed by the name of the formless God? O Nanak, he is the primal being the architect of destiny. ||51|| "Everyone speaks of the absolute Lord. Where did the infinite God come from? How do those dyed by the infinite God look like? They are like the Lord, from whom they originated. They are not born, they do not die; they do not come or go. O Nanak, the guru-willed teach their minds. ||52|| Nine pools are half empty, the tenth is full. There the infinite God plays the divine music. Those who love God, realize Him in the mind. God pervades all. Page 944 The secret sermon wells up. O Nanak, the true Lord is revealed to them. ||53|| They realize God intuitively and attain peace. The guru-willed stays awake never sleeps. He enshrines the infinite unimaginable God in the mind through guru's teachings. Reciting God through guru's teaching attains salvation. Through guru's blessing they are dyed with God's love. O Nanak, eliminating ego they realize God now not tomorrow. ||54|| One, who follows evil will, finds no place to rest; Why he cannot understand the reality and suffers in pain? No one can save him when tied up at death's door. Without guru's teaching he does not obtain honour. "How can one obtain understanding and cross over?" O Nanak, the ignorant self-willed does not understand? ||55|| Evil thoughts are erased, contemplating guru's teachings. Following the true guru obtains liberation. The self-willed does not understand the reality and is burnt to ashes. His evil-mindedness separates him from the Lord and suffers. Obeying God's command obtains virtues and divine wisdom. O Nanak, he is honoured in the court of the Lord. ||56|| He obtains the wealth of true God. He crosses over the world ocean by God's grace. Imbued with contentment, he realizes God and obtains honour. No one can estimate his worth. Wherever I look, I see the Lord pervading. O Nanak, through the love of the true Lord, one crosses over. ||57|| "Where guru's teaching comes from, which takes us across the world ocean? The life, which is said to be beyond ten fingers, who supports it? He speaks plays and becomes stable, How can the unseen be seen?" Listen, O master; Nanak prays truly, by guiding his mind. The guru-willed attunes to guru's teachings with love and unites with God by his grace. He is all-knowing and all-seeing. By perfect destiny, we merge in Him. ||58|| Enshrining guru's teachings in the mind he sees God wherever he looks. The air comes from place of the Lord. He has the power of bestowing wisdom. Guru's teachings enshrine in the mind by God's grace and eliminate doubt. The body and mind become pure through the sermon enshrining God's name in the mind. Swim across the world ocean through guru's teachings and see God everywhere. He has no form or colour, shadow or illusion; O Nanak, He is realized through guru's teachings. ||59|| O hermit, the life beyond ten fingers, comes from the true Lord. The guru-willed speaks and churns the reality, and realizes the unseen infinite Lord. Eradicating the three qualities, he enshrines guru's teachings in the mind and eliminates self-pride. If one realizes God inside out, falls in love with God. When God inspires, even the leper understands the two important divine veins. O Nanak, God is above these veins. He is realized by guru's teachings. ||60|| "The air is said to be the soul of the mind. But what does the breath live on? What is the way of divine wisdom O hermit? What the mystic attains. Page 945 O hermit; without guru's teachings the thirst of ego does no vanish. Imbued with guru's teachings obtains sacred taste and gets fulfilled. "What is the wisdom to remain stable? What food brings satisfaction?" O Nanak, when one sees pain and pleasure alike and death does not consume by guru's grace. ||61|| One who is dyed by God's love does not enjoy sublime taste. Without guru's teachings he is burnt by fire. He controls sexual urge and does not recite guru's teachings. He does not control breathing; he does not worship the true Lord. One who speaks the unspoken speech, and remains stable. O Nanak, then he realizes God the Lord of soul. ||62|| By guru's grace, he is attuned to Lord's love. He drinks nectar and gets intoxicated with truth. Contemplating guru's teachings eliminates the fire. Drinks the nectar and attains eternal peace. Reciting true Lord the guru-willed swims across. O Nanak, a few realize it by contemplating. ||63|| "Where does this intoxicated mind live? Where does the air live? O hermit where guru's teachings abide that eliminated mental wandering? By God's grace one meets the guru and attains destiny. When he eliminates ego, he becomes pure and wandering mind stabilizes. How to realize the origin of soul and how sun gives light to moon? The guru-willed eliminates ego, then O Nanak he merges in peace. ||64|| When the pure mind abides in the heart, the guru-willed realizes the origin. When the breathing is controlled from the naval, then the guru-willed realizes the reality. When one enshrines guru's teachings in the mind, he can see the universe. He eliminates hunger and pain through true Lord and gets satisfied. The guru-willed realize the divine sermon, but only a few understand it. Nanak speaks the truth; one dyed by God's tint does not fade away. ||65|| If there was nobody and the heart, where will the mind live? If there was no naval then where would breathing come from? When there was no form or shape, then how could anyone lovingly focus on guru's teachings? When there was nobody, how will anyone realize God? When there is no colour, dress and form; how could the true Lord be known?" O Nanak, those attuned to God's name lovingly are true everywhere. ||66|| When the heart and the body did not exist, O hermit, then the mind resided in God; If there was no naval, where would the beloved breath live? If there was no form shape or social class, then how would the lowly realize guru's lesson. When the world and the sky did not exist, where God the light of the universe live? Page 946 Colour, dress and form are one God; He is realized through guru's teachings. O Nanak, no one becomes pure without truth, this is the unspoken story. ||67|| How the world is created and how the pain is eliminated? In ego the world was created, O man; forgetting God's name suffers pain. The guru-willed contemplates divine wisdom and the ego eliminates. His body and mind become pure through sermon and merge with true Lord. Through God's name they remain detached enshrining God in the mind. O Nanak, without God's Name, Yoga is never attained; think and see it; ||68|| Only a few guru-willed contemplate true guru's teachings. The True discourse is revealed to the guru-willed. The mind, of only a few guru-willed accepts and realizes it. The guru-willed attains the destiny. The guru-willed realizes the way of Yoga. O Nanak, the guru-willed knows only one God. ||69|| Without serving the true guru, Yoga is not attained; without meeting the guru, the salvation is not obtained. Without meeting the guru, God's name cannot be obtained. Without meeting the guru, one suffers in terrible pain. Without meeting the guru, there is only the deep darkness of egotistic pride. O Nanak, without the guru, one dies losing the benefit of this life. ||70|| The guru-willed conquers his mind by eliminating ego. The guru-willed enshrines truth in his heart. The guru-willed conquers the world and drives away the devil of death. The guru-willed does not lose in the court of the Lord. The guru-willed who unites with God knows it; O Nanak, the guru-willed realizes God through guru's teachings. ||71|| O hermit; listen to the result of guru's teachings. Without guru's teachings, yoga is not realized. Those attuned to

God's name are intoxicated forever. Reciting God's name attains peace. Everything originates through God's name and attains understanding. People pretend a lot without God's name. They are deluded by God. The guru bestows God's name; that is the yoga way. Think in the mind O Nanak, salvation does not attain without God's name. ||72|| Only You know your divine power; no one can say anything about it. You are hidden, You are revealed. You enjoy all pleasures. The seekers, the mystics, the gurus and disciples keep searching by your grace. They beg for Your name and obtain awns. They praise visualizing You. The immortal God plays this game; the guru-willed understand it. O Nanak, God is omnipresent, none else; ||73||1|| Page 947 God is one. He is realized by guru's grace. Vaar of Raamkalee, Third Master, To be sung to the tune of 'Jodha and Veere Poorbaanee': Hymn, Third Master: The guru is the field of contentment; who intuitively inspires to love Him? Sow God's name, God's name grows and then merges with God's name. This seed eliminates ego and worry. If you sow nothing, nothing grows; then you eat what God gives you. When water mixes with water, it cannot be separated again. O Nanak, this happens to the guru-willed; come and see O people. What can the poor people see? They do not understand. Whom God reveals see it, but only those who enshrine God in the mind. ||1|| Third Master: The self-willed is the field of suffering. He sows pain and suffers pain. He is born in pain, dies in pain and spends life in ego. He does not understand the coming and going; the blind acts blindly. He does not realize the giver, but he is attached to what is given. O Nanak, he acts according to his pre-ordained destiny. He cannot do anything else. ||2|| Third Master: He who God inspires meets the guru and attains everlasting peace. This is the true meaning of peace, and one becomes pure. The doubt of ignorance is eradicated and divine wisdom is obtained. O Nanak, I see one God wherever I look. ||3|| Ladder: The true Lord created His throne, He sits on it. He is everything. This is what guru's teachings reveal. He created the universe and places to rest. He made sun and moon two lamps and completed the system. He sees, He hears; realized through guru's teachings reciting His name. ||1|| Hail to the Lord; truly You are there. ||1||Pause|| Hymn: O Kabeer, I grounded myself into henna paste. O my Husband Lord, You do not notice me. You never allow me to touch Your feet; ||1|| Third Master: O Nanak, my Husband Lord keeps me like henna paste by His grace. He grinds and grinds and He applies it also. This is the cup of love of my Lord. He gives it as He chooses. ||2|| Ladder: He created the world in variety of ways. Everyone comes and goes by his command and merges with Him by His command. You look after and enjoy none else. Keep me as You please. You are realized through guru's teachings. Everyone is under your power. You lead us as You wish. I do not know anyone as great as You; who do I tell this? ||2|| Hymn, Third Master: Deluded by doubt, I wandered all over the world. I am ashamed of it. Page 948 My Husband Lord has not blessed me with peace; what will work with Him? By guru's grace, I recite God enshrining Him in the mind. O Nanak, you find God sitting at home if God blesses. ||1|| Third Master: He spent the day working and the night sleeping. Telling lies, he eats poison; the self-willed departs crying. The devil of death beats over his head; the moral departs in disgrace. He never recited God. He keeps coming and going. By guru's grace, the Lord enshrines in the mind; then the devil of death does not beat over the head. O Nanak, he merges intuitively with God; he obtains the fruit of his doing. ||2|| Ladder: Some are linked to His praises through guru's teachings. Some are blessed with the name of the eternal, unchanging true Lord. Water, air and fire, worship Him by His command. They are worried about the next world by His will. God's one command pervades all; accepting it attains peace. ||3|| Hymn: O Kabeer, the false do not pass God's test. He who dies while living passes the test of the Lord. ||1|| Third Master: How can this mind be conquered? How can it die? It does not listen to guru's teachings and does not eliminate ego. By guru's grace, ego is eradicated, then one attains salvation. O Nanak, whom he blesses, obtains it No obstacles block his way. ||2|| Third Master: Everyone talks about dieing while living, but how one can attain salvation? If he is content through love and applies medicine of love. One attains peace and contentment; sings God's praises and swims across the terrifying world ocean reciting God's name. O Nanak, the guru-willed realizes this by God's grace. ||3|| Ladder: God created the love of duality, and three qualities prevail the universe. He created Brahma, Vishnu and Shiva, who act according to His will. The scholars and the astrologers study but they do not understand by thinking. Everything is Your play, O true Creator Lord. You bless whom You wish; You are realized through guru's teachings. ||4|| Hymn, Third Master: The false minded practices falsehood. He runs after worldly wealth, yet calls himself the self-disciplined. Deluded by doubt, he visits all shrines of pilgrimage. How can such a self-disciplined man attain the supreme status? By guru's grace, one earns truth. O Nanak, such a man of self-discipline attains liberation. ||1|| Third Master: He is a self-disciplined, who practices this discipline. Meeting with the guru, he contemplates guru's teachings. Serving the guru – this self-discipline is accepted. O Nanak, such a disciplined man is honoured in the court of the Lord. ||2|| Ladder: He created night and day, for the activities of the world. Page 949 Following guru's teachings, one's heart illuminates, and the darkness dispelled. Everything is created by His command and he abides in everything. He is everything; O guru-willed recite His name forever. He is realized through guru's teachings by His grace. ||5|| Hymn, Third Master: Those who have doubt in the mind cannot be called devotees of God. They teach others what they know O Nanak. He is hungry for the supreme status of the fearless Lord; O Nanak, only a few obtain this food. ||1|| Third Master: Those who eat at other's house are not God's devotees. For the sake of their bellies, they make disguises. Those who search their soul are God's devotees. They find their Lord and live with Him. ||2|| Ladder: He separates the sky and earth with His support in the middle. Where truth dwells is a truthful house. God's command prevails all and the guru-willed merge in truth. He is true, and true is His throne. Sitting on it, He administers true justice. Truth prevails everywhere and the guru-willed speaks the unspoken. ||6|| Hymn, Third Master: God is infinite and abides in everything; the false come and go. One, who follows own will, suffers severe punishment. God bestows everything. It is realized by pre-ordained destiny. O Nanak, following His will obtains the priceless treasure. ||1|| Third Master: One, who does not intuitively serve the guru, loses his life in ego. His tongue does not taste the sublime essence of the Lord, and his heart-lotus does not blossom. The self-willed eats poison and dies. He is ruined by love of worldly attachment. Without the name of one Lord, his life and living is cursed. When God bestows His grace, then one becomes the slave of His slaves. Night and day, he serves the guru, and never leaves His side. As the lotus flower floats unaffected in the water, so he remains detached in his own household? O Nanak, the Lord acts, and makes everyone to act as it pleases Him. ||2|| Ladder: For thirty-six ages, there was utter dark. Then, the Lord revealed Himself. He created the entire universe. He blessed it with understanding. He created the scriptures; He calculates the accounts of virtue and vice. Whom He inspires, realizes Him through guru's teachings. He is all-pervading. He unites us with Him by His grace. ||7|| Hymn, Third Master: This body is all blood; without blood, the body cannot exist. Those who are attuned to their Lord; they do not have bloody greed in them. In fear of God, the body becomes week, and the blood of greed leaves the body. Page 950 As heat purifies metal, so does God's love eradicates the filth of evil-deeds? O Nanak, beautiful are those, who are imbued with God's love. ||1|| Third Master: By God's grace I have enshrined God in my mind; thus I have been adorned. I have blossomed through guru's teachings and he offered me the treasure of worship. My doubt is erased and I woke up. The darkness of ignorance is erased. She, who is in love with God, is beautiful forever. Such an admirable happy soul-bride enjoys her Husband Lord forever. The self-willed does not know how to decorate her; she wastes her life away. Those who worship others than God; keep taking birth and are ruined. They do not obtain respect in this world; only God knows what happens next. O Nanak, God is one. The world is in duality. He makes them do good or bad by His will. ||2|| Third Master: Without serving the guru, peace does not well up. There is no other such place. No matter how much one wants; cannot obtain anything without luck? Those filled with greed and other useless ideas in the mind are ruined by duality. The cycle of birth and death does not end. They suffer in ego. Those who focus their mind to the guru do not go empty. They have no worry of the devil of death. They do not suffer. O Nanak, the guru-willed rise and merge with true guru's teachings. ||3|| Ladder: God remains detached forever; all others engage in worldly affairs. He is unchanging and unmoving;

the others continue coming and going. Reciting His name all the time, the guru-willed attains happiness. He attains his destiny and merges in true God by praising Him. God is profound and unfathomable. He is realized through guru's teachings. ||8|| Hymn, Third Master: Recite God's name; He pervades all. O Nanak, who realizes His command; obtains the true reward; He keeps telling tell tales but does not realize the real command. O Nanak, one who obeys God's will is His devotee. Without obeying he is really false. ||1|| Third Master: The self-willed cannot say this; they are filled with lust, anger and pride. They do not know right or wrong. They are filled with useless greed. They talk their self-interest. They are killed by the devil of death. The account is asked for in God's court; the false are beaten and disgraced. How can the filth of falsehood be washed off? Can anyone think about it? Meet the guru and recite God's name the destroyer of sins. Those who recite and worship God's name; bow in respect to them O people. Page 951 God's name washes away the filth of falsehood; reciting name makes truthful. O servant Nanak, one who has this virtue; the bestowal lives forever. ||2|| Ladder: No one is as great a giver as You are. Who can I tell this? He is realized by guru's grace and the ego departs. You are beyond sweet and sour tastes; true is Your greatness. Whoever He blesses obtains it and unites with God. The nectar is in the body; only a few drink it by His grace. ||9|| Hymn, Third Master: the children tell the stories of ancestors. They accept what is pleasing to the guru and act accordingly. Go and consult the Simritees, the Shaastras, the writings of Vyaas, Sukhdey, Naarad, and all those who preach to the world. Those, whom God attaches, are attached to the truth. They contemplate the true name forever. O Nanak, their coming into the world is approved. They redeem all their ancestors. ||1|| Third Master: The disciples of an ignorant guru are also ignorant. They follow their will and talk false all the time. They practice falsehood and deception and endlessly slander others. Slandering others, they drown and drown their entire dynasty as well. O Nanak, they do what they are made to do; what can they do? ||2|| Ladder: He keeps everything under His control, the entire universe. He puts some to do ill deeds. The self-willed are robbed. The guru-willed recite God all the time with love. Those bestowed with the treasure of virtues sing God's praises. O Nanak, recite God's name worthy of praising. ||10|| Hymn, First Master: After committing sins if one does a truthful deed. The guru goes to his home to offer wisdom. The woman and men earn the benefit. Whether they come or go. No one obeys the Shaastras or the Vedas. Everyone worships himself. Becoming judges, they sit and administer justice. They count beeds of rosary and say God. They accept bribes, and block justice. If someone asks, they read from their books and tell. The Muslim scriptures are in their ears and in their hearts. They take bribe and rob people. They paint the kitchen and say that it has become sacred. That is what the Hindus do. A house holder calls him a yogi by matting his hair and applying ashes on his body. He walks back and forth. He does not attain Yoga – he has lost his way. Why does he apply ashes to his body? O Nanak, this is the order of today's age (Kalyug). Everyone says that he knows it. ||1|| First Master: The Hindu comes to Hindu's house. He puts the sacred thread around his neck and reads the scriptures. He wears the sacred thread and does bad deeds. His cleansings and washings go waste. The Muslim glorifies his own faith. Page 952 Without the guru or a spiritual teacher, no one attains anything. They may be shown the way, but only a few go there. Without doing good deeds, no one goes to heaven. The way of Yoga is preached in Yogi's monastery. Because of that they wear earrings. Wearing earrings, they wander around the world. The Creator is everywhere. There are as many wanderers as there are beings. When one's death warrant is issued, there is no delay. They are identified here as well in the next world. They are poor ignorant, whether Hindus or Muslims. Everyone's account is read in the court of the Lord; without good deeds no one attains salvation. Only a few know the truth. O Nanak, they are not questioned in God's court. ||2|| Ladder: The fortress of the body is the place of worship of God. The rubies and gems are inside O guru-willed recite God's name. The body, God's temple is beautiful. Recite God's name O mortal. The self-willed ruin them; they boil in worldly wealth forever. One God is the master of all; with good luck, He is realized. ||11|| Hymn, First Master: Truth is not found by pleasure or pain or swimming in water like animals. Shaving head or reading or wandering all over does not find truth. Truth is not found on trees or stones. They suffer pain by being scraped. Chaining the elephants or grazing the cows does not find truth. He, who has the power, bestows it; whom He bestows gets it. O Nanak, he who enshrines guru's teachings in the mind obtains honour. God says, all hearts are mine, and I am in all hearts. Who can tell the confused? Who can confuse him; who has been shown the way? One who lost the way, who can guide him? ||1|| First Master: He is a real householder, who controls his passions He begs for meditation, austerity and self-discipline. He gives donations. Such a householder is as pure as the water of the Ganges. He recites God the embodiment of truth. The supreme Lord has no shape or form. ||2|| First Master; He is a detached hermit, who burns away his ego. He begs for eliminating the worries. In his heart, he begs for awns. Such a devotee climbs to the city of God. Says Gorakh Naath; God is the embodiment of truth. The supreme Lord has no shape or form. ||3|| First Master: He is a renounce who practices renunciation. He sees the formless God here and the next world. He makes a connection between the sun and the moon. Nothing obstructs such a renounce. Says Gopi chand; God is the embodiment of truth. The supreme Lord has no shape or form. ||4|| First Master: He who pretends to cleanse his body is a pretender. He burns his inner fire on God. He does not waste his celibacy even in a dream. Page 953 Such a pretender does not grow old or die. Says Charpat, God is the embodiment of truth. The supreme Lord has no shape or form. ||5|| First Master: He is a renounce, who turns to God. He supports the universe through his mind. He always contemplates in the mind. Such a renounce is just like the true Lord. Says Bharthari, God is the embodiment of truth. The supreme Lord has no shape or form. ||6|| First Master: How is evil eradicated? How can the true way of life be found? What is the use of piercing the ears, or begging for food? Existence or non-existing is the same. What is that Word, which controls the mind? When you look alike upon sunshine and shade, says Nanak, what the guru said. The students follow the six systems. They are neither worldly people, nor renunciates. One who remains absorbed in the formless Lord why should he go begging? ||7|| Ladder: Where we realize God is the real place of worship. Attained human life through guru`s teachings by God`s grace. Don't look outside; the architect of destiny is inside. The self-willed does not know where God lives; he wastes away his life. God pervades all; he is realized through guru`s teaching. ||12|| Hymn, Third Master: The ignorant listens to the ignorant. What are the signs of an ignorant? What does the ignorant do? He who is engrossed in ego is an ignorant. His actions always bring pain. He lives in pain. Doing so; such a person goes to hell; the guru-willed contemplates and remains detached. Reciting God he attains salvation. Even the drowned swims across following him; O Nanak, he acts in accordance with God`s will; he accepts what he gets. ||1|| First Master: Says Nanak, listen to the truth O mind; God will ask for your account. He has opened the account book. Those rebels who have unpaid accounts shall be singled out. The devil of death will come and arrest you. You cannot run. He puts the tight chain in your neck. Falsehood will end; O Nanak, and truth will prevail in the end. ||2|| Ladder: Everyone belongs to God. He is omnipresent. Lord's value cannot be estimated; nothing can be said about it. Praise Him by guru`s grace and worship him with love. The mind and body are rejuvenated, and ego eradicated. Everything is God`s play; only a few guru-willed realize Him. ||13|| Hymn, First Master: Giving millions of awns Indra still cried. Paras Raam returned home crying. Ajai cried when he had to beg. Such punishment is received in the court of the Lord. Raam Chander wept when he was sent into exile. Page 954 He separated from Sita and Lakhshman. The ten-headed Raawan wept when he lost Lanka. He brought Sita with the beating of drums. The Paandavas became labourers and wept. They had the prophet living close by. Janmeja wept, that he had lost his way. One mistake; he became a sinner. The scholars, seekers and spiritual teachers weep. At the last moment, may they suffer in pain? The kings weep piercing their ears. They go begging from house to house. The miser cries when he loses his collected wealth. The scholars cry without divine knowledge. The young woman weeps because she has no husband. O Nanak, the whole world is suffering. He who believes in Lord's name is the winner. No other action attains anything. ||1|| Second Master: Meditation, austerity and everything come through belief in Lord's name. All other actions are useless. O Nanak, the mind realizes God through guru`s teachings. ||2|| Ladder: The union of the body and the soul is pre-ordained by the Creator. He is hidden, yet pervading all. He is revealed to the guru-willed. He sings God`s praises and speaks virtues and merges in virtues. True is the true sermon; it unites one with God. He is everything. He bestows honour. ||14|| Hymn, Second Master: O Nanak, the blind goes to appraise jewels. He does not know what jewels are; it is written in his destiny. ||1|| Second Master: The jeweller opens the secret pouch of jewels. The merchandise and the merchant are merged together. O Nanak, only the knowledgeable deal in jewels. One without light the blind cannot appraise jewel; ||2|| Ladder: The fortress of body has nine gates; the tenth gate is kept hidden. The rigid door of mind does not open; it opens with guru`s teachings. The infinite divine music plays listening to guru`s teachings. Reciting God enlightens the devotees. He, who created the creation, abides in all. ||15|| Hymn, Second Master: The blind follows the blind. O Nanak, why should he get lost if he can see? Those without eyes are not the only blind? O Nanak, those who forget God are the real blind; ||1|| Second Master: Whom Lord made blind – Lord can make him see again. He only gets what he earns; you may say anything. Where the real thing is not seen, he who creates it knows it. O Nanak, if customer does not know the merchandise, why should he buy it? ||2|| Second Master: He who is blind by God's command; why do we call him blind? O Nanak, one who does not understand God's command is the real blind. ||3|| Page 955 Ladder: There is a fort in the body everywhere. God sits in trance there in everyone. He created the creation and hides in all. Serving the guru, the Lord is revealed. Everything is true; it is realized through the guru. ||16|| Hymn, First Master: Like the night in the month of Saawan and day in the month of Ahaadh, are lust and anger the two fields. Greed prepares the soil, sows seeds of falsehood; attachment and love are the farmer and hired hand. He sows and contemplates falsehood. He earns and eats it by God's command. O Nanak, when his account is opened; the widower goes without children. ||1|| First Master: Make God's love the farm, purity the water, truth and contentment the oxen. Humility the plough, mind the ploughman, missing God the preparation of land and union with God the time to seed; Seed God's name and obtain His blessing; the world is false. O Nanak, if God bestows his blessing, all sorrows go away. ||2|| Ladder: The self-willed is filled with worldly attachments and dwells in duality. Deluded in duality is ever painful; he churns water instead of milk. The guru-willed recite God and find the essence of reality. He is enlightened inside and finds God. God leads them to doubt; what can they do? ||17|| Hymn, Second Master: O Nanak, don't worry. God worries about you. He created the creatures in water and He gives them food. There are no shops and no one farms there. Nothing transacted there, and no one buys or sells. Animals eat animals; this is what God made their food? He created them in the oceans and provides for them as well. O Nanak, don't worry; God worries for you. ||1|| First Master: O Nanak, this soul is the fish, and death is the hungry fisherman. The blind mind does not think of this. Suddenly he is caught in the net. O Nanak, mind is ignorant; it departs caught in worry. But if God bestows His grace. He unites us with Him. ||2|| Ladder: Those who drink God's sublime essence become true forever. God abides in their mind; they bought the truth. Everything is in the mind; the fortunate realize it. Singing God's praises the greed is eliminated. He unites with Him by His grace. ||18|| Hymn, First Master: The cotton is ginned, woven and spun; the cloth is spun washed and bleached. The tailor cuts it with scissors and sews with needle and thread. Same way the disgraced attains honour praising God O Nanak and lives this way. Becoming old the clothes get torn and stitched with needle and thread. It does not last for a month or a week. It barely lasts for moment. Page 956 Truth does not get old is not sewn or torn; O Nanak, God is ever true. He is realized reciting His name; ||1|| First Master: Truth is the teeth and truth is the food. Its workmanship is incomparable and beyond comprehension. It is sharpened on the grindstone of guru's teachings. It merges in guru's scabbard. If the scholar is killed with that; then the blood of greed will spill out. One, who dies this way, obtains justice. O Nanak, he visualizes God and merges with Him. ||2|| First Master: A beautiful dagger hangs by the waist and beautiful is the rider. O Nanak, do not be proud; you may fall with head down. ||3|| Ladder: The guru-willed follows devotee's company. They recite God and become truthful and carry Godliness to spend. The devotees look beautiful, singing God's praises through guru's teaching. The priceless jewel enshrines in the mind through guru's teaching. He unites in His Union and grants honour by His grace. ||19|| Hymn, Third Master: Everyone is filled with hope; hardly anyone is free of hope. O Nanak, he who dies while living; his coming here is worthwhile. ||1|| Third Master: Nothing is in the hands of hope. How can one become free of hope? What can the poor do? When God leads him to it? ||2|| Ladder: Cursed is the life in this world, without the true name. God is the great giver. His wealth is permanent forever. He who recites God with every breath becomes pure. The inner-knower Lord is infinite; this tongue is one to recite Him. He is all pervading. Nanak praises Him. ||20|| Hymn, First Master: The union between the lake and swan is pre-ordained; it is God's will. The pearls are in this lake; they are the food of the swans. The cranes and crow will not stay at the lake if they are smart. They do not have food there. Their food is different. Practicing truth obtain truth, practice false obtain false. O Nanak, those with pre-ordained destiny meet the guru. ||1|| First Master: My Lord makes you pure if you miss Him devotionally. O Nanak, serve Him, who gives forever. O Nanak, serve Him. By serving Him, sorrow is dispelled. Demerits vanish, merits take their place; peace comes to dwell in the mind. ||2|| Ladder: He is all pervading. He sits in a trance. He guides the guru-willed and they believe him. He causes some to wander in the wild, while he makes others to worship Him. Whom He inspires realizes and recites His name. O Nanak, recite God's name; it is a great honour. ||21||1|| declaration|| Page 957 Vaar of Raamkalee, Fifth Master: God is one. He is realized by guru's grace. Hymn, Fifth Master: As I heard about the true guru, so I see Him. He re-unites the separated with God. He is the lawyer at God's court. He implants the lesson of Lord's name and eradicates the sickness of ego. O Nanak, those with a pre-ordained destiny meet the guru. ||1|| Fifth Master: If one is friendly, all are friends; if one is enemy then all are his enemies. The perfect guru has shown me that without the name, everything is useless. The faithless evil people; attached to other tastes wander around. Servant Nanak realized God, by the grace of the guru. ||2|| Ladder: The Creator created the creation. He is the perfect banker and earns His profit. He created the universe and imbued them with His love. The value of God's creative power cannot be estimated. He is inaccessible, unfathomable, endless and the farthest. He is the great emperor. He is the minister. No one knows His worth, or the greatness of His resting place. He is our true Lord. He reveals Himself to the guru-willed. ||1|| Hymn, Fifth Master: Listen, O my beloved friend: please take me to the true guru. I offer my mind to him and enshrine him in the mind. Those without the guru; their living in the world is useless. O servant Nanak; those who live with the guru forever are united with him. ||1|| Fifth Master: I have yearning to meet with you; how can I find You O God? I will search for a friend, who will unite me with my beloved. The perfect guru has united me with Him. Wherever I look, there He is. Servant Nanak serves that God. There is no other as great as He. ||2|| Ladder: He is the great giver. With what mouth can I praise Him? By His grace He protects, preserves and sustains us. No one is under anyone else's control. He is the support of all. He takes care all like a child and supports by giving His hand. He stages His happy plays, which no one understands at all. The all-powerful Lord gives His support to all. I admire Him. Night and day, sing the praises of the one worthy of praise. Those who fall at guru's feet, enjoy the sublime essence of the Lord. ||2|| Hymn, Fifth Master: He widened the narrow path and preserves the honour of my family. He resolved all my affairs. I dwell upon God forever. God is my mother and father. He embraces and cherishes me like a child. O Nanak, all beings are kind to me by God's grace. ||1|| Page 958 Fifth Master: To ask from anyone other than You, brings pain and more pain. Please bless me with Your name that I become content and eliminate hunger. The guru made woods, meadows green again O Nanak, what to say of man? ||2|| Ladder: Such is that great giver; may I never forget Him from my mind. I cannot survive without Him, for an instant, for a moment, or a second. He is with me inside out; how can I hide! Whoever he blesses, swims across the world ocean. Whom God blesses, is a devotee, divine, and disciplined. Whom He blesses is perfect and above all. He endures the unendurable; that the Lord inspires. He who enshrines God in the mind obtains the true lesson. ||3|| Hymn, Fifth Master: Blessed are those beautiful tunes, which quench thirst by singing. Blessed are those beautiful guru-willed who recite God's name? I admire those who single-mindedly worship God. I yearn for the dust of their feet. It is obtained by luck. I admire those who are imbued with love of the Lord of the universe. I tell them the state of my mind and pray that I unite with my beloved. The perfect guru united me with Him and the pain of birth and death ended. Servant Nanak found the inaccessible, infinite beautiful Lord, now he does not have to go anywhere else. ||1|| Fifth Master: Blessed is the time, hour, second and the moment. Blessed is the day, the opportunity, when I saw the guru in person. My mind's desires are fulfilled, I found the inaccessible, unfathomable Lord. Ego and worldly attachment is eradicated, only God's name is my resolve. O servant Nanak; serving God the whole world is saved. ||2|| Ladder: Those who praise God are rare in the world. Whoever God blesses the treasure, does not question again. Those who are imbued with His love are absorbed in love. They take the support of one name; One name is their food. Following them those who eat that food are also fulfilled. They love God; that is their yoga. Those who meet the guru; they realize God. I admire those who are pleasing to their Lord the master. ||4|| Hymn, Fifth Master: O God; I am friends with one and I love one Lord. The Lord is my only friend and companion O God. O God I consult with one. He never makes me worry. He knows the state of my mind. He never ignores my love. He is my only counsellor, all-powerful to destroy and create. The Lord is my only giver. He places His hand on everyone's head. I take the support of one Lord. He is powerful of all. He united me with the saint guru by placing His hand on my forehead. Page 959 The guru united me with the great master; who saved the world. The desires of the mind are fulfilled. I attained Him by pre-ordained destiny. Nanak has obtained the true name. He enjoys it forever. ||1|| Fifth Master: Friendship with self-willed is for worldly wealth. They leave you in front of your eyes. They never stand firm. As long as they get food and clothing, they stick around. The day they receive nothing, they start cursing. The self-willed ignorant do not know the essence of mind! They are blind. The false bonds do not last. It is like stones thrown in the mud. The blind do not understand; they are engrossed in false worldly entanglements. Entangled in false attachments, they pass their lives in ego and self-conceit. Whoever God blesses; does good deeds from destiny. O Nanak, those seek guru's refuge are saved. ||2|| Ladder: Those who are imbued with realizing God, speak the truth. They realize God why should they go after dirt. The mind, stained by corruption, becomes pure by associating with them. One finds the destiny and the lock of doubt opens. Whom God bestows salvation; they are not pushed around. The mind and body become content by His glance of grace. The priceless treasure is realized following guru's teachings. The fortunate apply the dust of the saints to their forehead. ||5|| Hymn, Fifth Master: O deer-eyed bride, I speak the truth, which shall save you. Listen to the beautiful words O beautiful bride; your beloved Lord is in your mind. You have fallen in love with an evil person. Tell me why? I lack nothing and I am not sad or depressed. I have no deficiency at all. I lost my beloved Husband lord due to bad deeds. I am not mistaken or confused. I have no ego and commit no sin and I have no blame. As You have linked me, so I do; listen to my true message. She, who is blessed by God, is blessed and happy soul-bride. Her Husband Lord eliminates her demerits. He embellishes and embraces her. The unfortunate soul-bride prays: O Nanak, when will my turn come? All the blessed soul-brides enjoy; bless me for one night O Lord. ||1|| Fifth Master: Why do you waver, O my mind? The Lord is the fulfiller of desires. Recite the true Lord. He eliminates all sufferings. Recite God's name in the mind, all sins will be eliminated. Those with pre-ordained destiny fall in love with formless God. They gave up the interest of worldly wealth and gather Godly wealth. Twenty-four hours a day, they are lovingly absorbed in one Lord. They obey the will of the infinite Lord. Page 960 Servant Nanak begs for one gift: O beloved may I visualize You. ||2|| Ladder: One who misses You is at peace forever. One who misses You is not troubled by the devil of death. One who misses You has no worry. One who has the Creator his friend – all his affairs are resolved. One who misses You is accepted by You. One who misses You is rich. One who misses You has a large family. One who misses You is saved along with his family. ||6|| Hymn, Fifth Master: Blind inside, is blind outside, the false sings false. He washes his body, and draws ritual marks on it, he is after wealth. The inner filth of ego does not wash away; they keep taking birth again and again. Bothered by sleep and worried about sex yet he says God God from the mouth. He is called a devotee, he does egotistic deeds; how can he obtain fruit by beating the shell. The crane sitting with swans does not become a swan. It is just looking for fish. When the swans sit and contemplate; the crane never joins them. The swans peck at the diamonds and pearls, the crane chases after frogs. The poor crane flies away, so that his secret is not exposed. They do what they are asked to; who can they blame when this pleases God. The guru is full of pearls. He who meets the guru obtains it. The devotee swans gather at the lake by guru's command. The lake is filled with the wealth of these jewels and pearls. They spend and consume, but they never run out. The swan never leaves the lake. It is by God's will. O Nanak, one with pre-ordained destiny meets the guru. He saves himself, all his family and the whole world. ||1|| Fifth Master: He is called a scholar, yet he wanders along many paths. He is as hard as uncooked beans. He is filled with attachment, and troubled by doubt; his body falls apart. Looking for worldly wealth the false comes and goes. If someone speaks the truth, he is troubled and gets angry. The ignorant bothered by evil will and ill intellect is attached to worldly wealth. The cheat meets the cheat and enjoys similar company. When the jeweller appraises, the iron shows up. Mixed with genuine many times, but the secret opens immediately. Coming to guru's refuge whole-heartedly changes the iron to gold. The guru treats everyone equally. He eliminates demerits and cleanses the body. O Nanak one with pre-ordained destiny falls in love with God. Page 961 Guru's sermon is sacred; whom He is kind enshrines in the mind. His coming and going ends and attains eternal peace. ||2|| Ladder: He who obeys your will realizes You. He who obeys your will is honoured in Your court. Whoever you bless eliminates ego. Whoever you are satisfied with eliminates his filth. One, who has the Lord on his side, becomes carefree. One, who is blessed with Your grace, becomes truthful. One, who is blessed with Your Kindness, is not touched by fire. You are forever kind to those who learn from the guru. ||7|| Hymn, Fifth Master: O kind Lord be kind and bless me. That I recite your name forever and touch guru's feet. Please, dwell in my mind and body and end my sufferings. Please give me Your hand that I am not bothered by concerns. May I sing Your praises day and night; please commit me to this task? Associating with the humble saints, the disease of ego is eradicated. One Lord is pervading and permeating everywhere. By guru's grace, I have truly found the truest of the true. O kind Lord, please be kind and bless me to praise You. Nanak has this longing to visualize You and attain contentment. ||1|| Fifth Master: Recite one God in the mind and seek his refuge. Be in love with one Lord; there is no other such place. Beg from one Lord the great giver. He will bestow you with everything. In your mind and body, with each breath and morsel of food, recite one God. Truly the guru-willed realize the treasure of sacred name. The saints who enshrine God in the mind are fortunate. He is pervading in water and land; there is no other at all. I recite God's name, speak God's name O Nanak by God's grace. ||2|| Ladder: One You protect; who can kill him? One You protect is a winner O sister. One who has You on his side, he is a happy face. One who has You on his side is the purest of pure. One who is blessed by You is not called to give his account. One with whom You are pleased obtains the nine treasures. One who has You on his side O God? Why should he rely on others? One who is blessed with Your Kindness worships You. ||8|| Hymn, Fifth Master: Be kind, O my Lord that I spend my life in the society of saints. Those who forget You are born and die again and again; their sufferings never end. ||1|| Fifth Master: Recite your true guru all the time everywhere all the time. Reciting God's name, no one will block your path. ||2|| Ladder: Page 962 Where no one helps; You are there. You protect in the heat of the womb. Hearing Your name, the devil of death leaves one alone. The terrifying, treacherous, impassable world-ocean is crossed over, through guru's teachings. Those who feel thirst for you, drink the nectar. In today's age singing God's praises is the greatest deed. God protects and cares for all forever. Those who come to You with love do not go empty. ||9|| Hymn, Fifth Master: O supreme Lord; whom You bless with Your name; do not know any other. Inaccessible, unfathomable Lord is all-powerful the true great giver. You are eternal without enemy. Your court bestows true justice. Your worth cannot be described. You have no end or limit. Forsake God and beg from others; all are useless and taste like dirt. They find peace. Those who deal in truth are the true kings. Those who love God's name, attain contentment and happiness. O Nanak, recite one God and be the dust of the feet of saints. ||1|| Fifth Master: Singing God's praises all the time, attains joy, peace and comfort. Give up all other intelligent ideas and attain salvation reciting God. ||2|| Ladder: No one can control you, by hating the world. No one can control You by reading scriptures. No one can control you by bathing at shrines. No one can control You by wandering all over the world. No one can control You by clever tricks. No one can control You by giving large donations. Everyone is under Your control O inaccessible, unfathomable Lord. You are under the control of devotees. You are devotee's strength. ||10|| Hymn, Fifth Master: You are a doctor and God. These physicians of the world increase the pain of mind. They drink nectar through guru's teachings. O Nanak, those who enshrine God in the mind; their sufferings are eradicated. ||1|| Fifth Master: He overflows by God's command and lives by God's command. By His command he thinks of pain and pleasure alike. By His command, he recites God day and night. O Nanak, only he does so, who is blessed. He lives and dies by His command. By His command the tiny become large. By His command, he enjoys happiness and sorrow. By His command, he recites absolute guru's teachings. By His command, coming and going ends. O Nanak, whom God links to worship God. ||2|| Ladder: I admire the minstrel who serves You. I praise the minstrel, who sings the praise of infinite Lord. Blessed is the minstrel, who longs for the formless God. That minstrel is fortunate who reaches the court of the Lord. That minstrel recites You and sings your praises day and night. He begs for the sacred name and never loses. His clothes and his food are true, and lives loving You. Praiseworthy is that minstrel, who loves God. ||11|| Page 963 Hymn, Fifth Master: The sacred sermon tastes sacred and God's name is sacred. Recite God in the mind, body and heart twenty-four hours a day. Listen to these teachings, O guru's followers. This is the true purpose of life. This priceless human life will be fruitful; embrace love of Lord in your mind. Reciting God obtains peace, contentment and joy. The sufferings depart. O Nanak, reciting God's name peace wells up and attains honour in God's court. ||1|| Fifth

Master: O Nanak, recite God`s name through perfect guru`s teachings. By Lord's will, they practice meditation, austerity and self-discipline. By Lord's will and they are saved. By Lord's will, they wander in reincarnation. By Lord's will, they are blessed. By Lord's will, pain and pleasure are experienced. By Lord's will, we do deeds. By Lord's will, He creates the being. By Lord's will, He infuses the light in it. By Lord's will, enjoyments are enjoyed; by Lord's will, they are denied; By Lord's will, they go to heaven and hell; by Lord's will, they fall to the ground. By Lord's will, those committed to His worship O Nanak, are rare. ||2|| Ladder: I live by listening to the praises of God`s name. The ignorant animals and ghosts are saved in a moment. Day and night, recite God`s name forever. Greed, hunger and other useless desires depart reciting Your name. Disease, sorrow and pain run away enshrining God`s name in the mind. He, who recites God through guru`s teachings; obtains the treasure. O saviour of the worlds, solar systems and unlimited others. You are your glory, O my beloved Lord. ||12|| Hymn, Fifth Master: O Nanak, I abandoned my beloved friend and fooled by the transitory colour of safflower, which fades away. I did not know Your value, O my friend; without You, I am worth nothing. ||1|| Fifth Master: My mother-in-law is my enemy, O Nanak, my father-in-law is argumentive and my brother-in-law burns me at every step. They are all like dust, when You are my friend, O Lord. ||2|| Ladder: Those, who enshrine You in the mind, eliminate their pain. Those, who enshrine You in the mind, do not ever lose. One who meets the perfect guru will surely be saved. One, who is attached to truth, contemplates truth. One, who finds the treasure, stops searching. He, who is dyed by God`s love is God`s devotee. He is the dust of the feet of all; yearns for love of Lord's feet. Everything is Your amazing play; the whole creation is Yours. ||13|| Hymn, Fifth Master: I have discarded praise and slander, O Nanak, I have abandoned everything. When I found that all relation are false. I held on to Your lap. ||1|| Fifth Master: O Nanak, I felt ashamed of wandering all over. Since I found my beloved through the guru, I sleep in peace. ||2|| Page 964 Ladder: When I forget You, I endure all pains and worries. Making thousands of efforts, they are still not eliminated. One, who forgets God`s name becomes poor. One, who forgets God`s

Name, wanders in life's. One who does not remember God, is punished by the devil of death. One, who does not remember God, is a sick person. One who does not remember God is an ignorant proud. One who forgets God's name is miserable in this world. ||14|| Hymn, Fifth Master: I have not seen anyone like You. You are pleasing to Nanak's mind. I admire that friend the middleman who led me to recognize my Husband Lord. ||1|| Fifth Master: Beautiful are those feet, which walk towards You; beautiful is that head which falls at Your feet. Beautiful is that mouth which sings Your praises; beautiful is that soul which seeks Your sanctuary. ||2|| Ladder: Meeting the ladies in true Congregation, I sing the songs of joy. I became stable and I do not wander anymore. Bad learning and thinking bad of others is dispelled, so is falsehood. I am known as being calm and truthful. Inside out I follow one Lord. My mind is thirsty to visualize Him and become the servant of His feet. I am glorified wearing jewellery, when my Lord enjoys with me. I met Him through my destiny by pleasing Him. ||15|| Hymn, Fifth Master: O Nanak, You bestowed all virtues on me; what can I the virtueless do? There is no other giver as great as You. I the beggar beg of You forever. ||1|| Fifth Master: My body is wasting away and depressed. The guru, my friend consoled me. My whole world sleeps in peace and joy. Ladder: Your court is eternal and Your throne is true. You are the emperor of emperors with an eternal canopy flying over Your head. Whatever pleases God is the true justice. If it pleases God, the homeless finds a home. Whatever the Creator does, is a good thing. Those who realize God the master find a place in God's court. True is Your Command; no one can challenge it. O merciful Lord, cause of causes, You are the Creator of the universe. ||16|| Hymn, Fifth Master: Listening to His praises my mind and body blossom. Reciting God it gets dyed deep red. Walking on that path, I am soothed. Seeing the guru I am content. ||1|| Fifth Master: I have found the jewel in my heart. I did not buy it; my guru gave it to me. My search has ended and I have become stable. O Nanak, I have conquered this priceless human life. ||2|| Ladder: One, with pre-ordained destiny starts to serve God. One, who blossoms, meeting the guru, remains awake forever. All doubt and fear runs away from the one who is in love with Lord's lotus feet. Page 965 He conquers his soul; following guru's teachings and becomes immortal. He who recites the supreme Lord attains salvation in today's age. In devotee's company he became as pure as bathing at sixty-eight shrines. He who realizes God is fortunate person. Nanak admires such a person whose destiny is so great! ||17|| Hymn, Fifth Master: When the Husband Lord is in the heart, the worldly wealth goes out. When one's Husband Lord is out, then the worldly wealth rules. Without God's name, one wanders all over. The true guru reveals God in the mind. Servant Nanak truly merges in the truest of the true. ||1|| Fifth Master: Making all sorts of efforts, they do not accomplish anything. O Nanak, only a few know the effort, which bestows salvation. ||2|| Ladder: The greatest of the great, infinite is Your status. Your colours and tints are numerous; no one can know Your actions. Everything is in the mind; know that! Everything is under Your control. Your home is gracious. Your home is filled with bliss and honour. Your honour, importance and glory are Yours alone. You are omnipresent. I see You wherever I look. Nanak, the slave of Your slaves, prays to You. ||18|| Hymn, Fifth Master: In the covered bazaar, the traders look beautiful. O Nanak, there is one priceless merchandise; whoever earns it is lucky. ||1|| Fifth Master: O Kabeer, no one is mine, I belong to no one. I am absorbed in the one, who created this creation. ||2|| Ladder: The Lord is the beautiful fruit tree, bearing fruits of nectar. My mind longs to meet Him; how can I ever find Him? He has no colour or form; He is inaccessible and unconquerable. He who opens the secret of life is my beloved. I shall serve you forever, if you tell me of my friend. I praise, dedicated, devoted to Him. The beloved saints explain; listen carefully? One who has such pre-ordained destiny, O slave Nanak, is blessed with God's name by the guru. ||19|| Hymn, Fifth Master: O Kabeer, the land of devotee's is occupied by thieves. The earth is not affected if the thieves come and sit on it. ||1|| Fifth Master: O Kabeer, for the sake of rice, the husk is beaten. When one sits in evil company, the justice of destiny asks questions. ||2|| Ladder: He has the large family. He is alone also. He alone knows His own worth. He is everything, he created Himself. Only He can describe His creation. Blessed is the place, where You live. Page 966 Blessed are Your devotees, who see You, O true Lord. He, who is blessed by You; praises You. One, who meets the guru O Nanak, becomes pure; ||20|| Hymn, Fifth Master: O Fareed; this world is beautiful, but there is a poisonous garden in it. Those who are blessed by their spiritual teacher are not touched by it. ||1|| Fifth Master: O Fareed; blessed is the life with such a beautiful body. There are only a few who love the beloved God. ||2|| Ladder: He obtains meditation, austerities, self-discipline, compassion and faith, whom the Lord blesses. He recites God's name; whose burning fire is extinguished by God's grace. The inner-knower, immortal God sees everything with one eye. One gets imbued with God's love in devotee's company. One's faults are eradicated, happiness bestowed and attains salvation. The concern of birth and death is eliminated. One does not take birth again. God pulls him out of the deep, dark pit by attaching him to the hem of His robe. O Nanak, God unites him with Him and embraces him. ||21|| Hymn, Fifth Master: One who loves God is imbued with the deep crimson colour of love. O Nanak, such a person is rare; his value cannot be estimated. ||1|| Fifth Master: He is pierced by true name inside out. O Nanak, God pervades all places, forest; grass the hair and the universe. ||2|| Ladder: He created the universe; He imbued it in His love. He is one and He is all. He is in all, and He is beyond all. He is known to be far away, and He is seen close. He is hidden and He is revealed. No one can estimate the value of Your creation O Lord. You are deep profound, unfathomable, infinite and invaluable. O Nanak, One Lord is all pervading. You are one and only one. ||22||1||2|| declaration|| Vaar Of Raamkalee, Uttered By Satta And Balwand The Drummer: God is one. He is realized by guru's grace. One who recites the name of the almighty Creator? How can his words be weighed? His divine virtues are the true sisters and brothers. Through them, the gift of salvation is obtained. Nanak established the kingdom; He built the fortress of truth on a very strong foundation. He installed the royal canopy over Lehna's head. Singing God's praises he drank the nectar. By the grace of guru's teachings, he was united with God reciting God. The guru bowed down to His disciple, while Nanak was still alive. He put the mark of guruship on his forehead while living. ||1|| Nanak proclaimed Lehna's succession. He earned it. The soul and the process became one; his body changed immediately. Formless Lord's canopy waves over him; He sits on the throne in guru's shop. He does as the guru commands; He licked the rock of salt of yoga. Page 967 The common kitchen runs. There is no limit of benefits from guru's teachings. He spent His master's gift and distributes it to all. The praises of the master were sung, and divine Light descended from the heavens to the earth. Seeing You O my Lord; the filth of many a life is eliminated. The guru taught the truth; then why should we stop telling truth? His sons did not obey His word. They are pulled from the ear and suffer. The evil-minded became rebellious. They carry loads of sin on their backs. Whatever the guru says; do it. You get what you earn. Who lost, and who won? ||2|| You get what you earn; earn shell you get shell, earn rice you get rice? The justice of destiny is the judge. He takes a cut to take your case. If you do what the guru says that is accepted in God's court. Guru Angad was proclaimed, and the true Creator confirmed it. Nanak merely changed his body. He still sits on the throne, with hundreds of branches reaching out. Standing at His door, His followers serve Him; by this service, their filth is removed. The saintly recites God's name with love and accepted at God's court. Balwand says that Khivi, guru's wife, is a noble woman, who gives soothing, leafy shade to all. She distributes rice pudding added with sugar and butter the wealth of guru's kitchen. The faces of the guru-willed are happy and the self-willed bad like straw. The master gave His approval, when Angad proclaimed him the guru. Such is the Husband of mother Khivi; He sustains the world. ||3|| Guru Nanak touched Angad's feet; the process is reversed? Nanak the Lord, the Lord of the world, spoke the words out loud. He churned the mountain with the fragrance of guru's teachings. From it, He extracted the fourteen jewels and illuminated the world. He appraised guru Angad by his mighty power. He raised the royal canopy to wave over the head of Lehna, and raised His glory to the skies. His light merged into the light and He blended him into Himself. Guru Nanak tested His followers and His sons, and everyone saw what happened. When Lehna was found to be pure, then He was put on the throne. ||4|| Then, the guru, the son of Pheru, came to live at Khadoor. Meditation, austerities and self-discipline rest with You; the egotistic will fall. Greed ruins mankind, like the algae in the water. In guru's court, the divine light shines by God's grace. You are the mountain where the hand does not reach. You are filled with treasure of God's name. Whoever slanders You will be destroyed in pieces. The world is seen close by but You can see far beyond. Then the true guru, the son of Pheru, came to live at Khadoor. ||5|| Page 968 The same mark on the forehead, the same throne, and the same Royal court. Just like the father and grandfather, the son is approved. He churned the essence with a string of love. He churned the world ocean with mountain as churning machine. He extracted the fourteen jewels, and enlightened the world. He made contentment his horse, and renunciation his saddle. He placed the arrow of Lord's praise in the bow of truth. It is dark in today's age. Then, He rose like the sun after night. He grew the field of truth and spread the canopy of truth. Your kitchen always has butter and flour to eat. Enshrining guru's teachings in the mind, one can see the whole world. Coming and going ends by God's grace. You are the prophet, the incarnation of the all-knowing primal Lord. You are not pushed or shaken by the windstorm; you are a mountain. You know the state of the soul. You are all knower. How can I praise You, O true Lord; You are divine and all knowing? The blessings that please the guru are the blessing for Satta. Seeing Nanak's canopy waving over Your head, everyone was surprised. The same mark on the forehead, the same throne, and the same Royal court. Just like the father and grandfather, the son is approved. ||6|| Blessed is guru Raam Daas; He who created You also dignified You. Perfect is Your miracle; the Creator Lord installed You on the throne. The followers and the Congregation recognize You as the supreme Lord and bow down to You. You are unchanging, unfathomable and immeasurable. You have no end or limit. Those who serve You with love – You bestow salvation to them. Greed, envy, lust, anger and emotional attachment – You have beaten and driven them out. Blessed is Your place, and true is Your magnificent glory. You are Nanak, You are Angad, and You are Amar Daas, so I see! When I saw the guru, my mind was consoled. ||7|| The four gurus enlightened the four ages. God assumed the fifth form. He created Himself, and He is the supporting pillar of the universe. He is the paper, the pen, and the writer. His entire congregation comes and goes. He is ever fresh and new. Guru Arjun sits on the throne; the royal canopy waves over the guru. From east to west, He illuminates the four directions. Those self-willed who do not serve the guru die in shame. Your miracle power increase two to four-fold; truth wells truth. The four gurus enlightened the four ages. God assumed the fifth form. ||8||1|| Raamkalee, The Word Of The Devotees. Kabeer Jee: God is one. He is realized by guru's grace. Make your body the pot and the mix. Put guru's teachings as jagry in it. Page 969 Cut up desire, lust, anger, pride and envy, and let them be the fermenting bark. ||1|| Is there any saint, with peace and contentment; I will pay commission to him if he offers me meditation and self-discipline. If he gives me a drop of that intoxication, I will offer my mind and body. ||1||Pause|| I made the fourteen worlds the furnace and burnt my body with godly fire. My yogic stick as an intoxicant and intoxicated with contentment and paint it with divine words. ||2|| I mortgage pilgrimage, fast, principle, cleansing, self-discipline even the sun and moon for it. I make my mind the cup and pour nectar as the pure juice and drink it. ||3|| The pure stream constantly flows down and my mind is intoxicated by the sublime essence. Says Kabeer, all other intoxicant is tasteless. This is the only true taste. ||4||1|| Make knowledge the molasses, meditation the mix and the fear of God the fire enshrined in your mind. The spinal vein merges in peace by drinking it. ||1|| O hermit, my mind is intoxicated. When the liquor intoxicates; I can see the whole universe. ||1||Pause|| Joining the two channels of the breath, I have lit the furnace and I drink the sublime essence. I burnt both lust and anger and I am saved from the world. ||2|| I learnt this from the guru and attained divine wisdom enlightenment and joy. Slave Kabeer is intoxicated with that wine, which never wears off. ||3||2|| You are my mountain O my Lord; I have grasped Your support. You do not shake, I do not fall. You have preserved my honour. ||1|| Now and then, here and there, You, only You! By Your grace, I am forever in peace. ||1||Pause|| Believing in You I settled at Magahar and my burning fire is extinguished. First, I visualized You at Magahar and then came and settled at Kashi. ||2|| As is Magahar, so is Kashi; I see them one and the same. I the poor attained this wealth; the proud die breaking in pieces. ||3|| The proud feels the pinch of thorns; no one will take them out. They are crying of pinching and go to hell crying. ||4|| What is hell, what is heaven? The saints reject both. I do not say any fault of anyone by guru's grace. ||5|| Now, I reached the throne of the Lord and met the sustainer of the world. God and Kabeer became one, no one can differentiate anymore. ||6||3|| I obey the saints, and punish the wicked; this is my duty; Day and night, I massage Your feet. I wave my hair as a fan. ||1|| I am a dog at Your Court O Lord; I lie down and bark in front of You. ||1||Pause|| Page 970 I am Your servant from the previous life. I cannot leave you now. The divine music plays on my forehead at Your door. ||2|| Those who were wounded before, will fight the battle, those who were not wounded will run away. The devotee will recognize the devotee and treasure the godliness. ||3|| In the fortress is the chamber; that sacred chamber is realized by contemplating. The guru blessed Kabeer with the merchandise to keep it safe. ||4|| Kabeer gave it to the world. The fortunate obtain it. Those who obtain the taste of nectar; their marriage is eternal. ||5||4|| The mouth which spoke prayer and the Vedas; why should a scholar forget that! The whole world falls at His feet Why not those scholars say God from their mouth? ||1|| Why, O my scholar; you do not say God from your mouth? If you don't recite God O scholar, you will go to hell. ||1||Pause|| You think you are high but you eat at the lowly houses; you fill your belly by practicing rituals. On the fourteenth day of new moon, you beg all over; even you hold the lamp in your hand; still you fall into the pit. ||2|| You are a scholar; I am only a weaver from Banaras. How can I compare with you? I attained salvation saying God's name; you will drown believing in Vedas; ||3||5|| There is one tree, with countless branches full of leaves and flowers. This world is a garden of nectar. The perfect Lord created it. ||1|| I have come to know the story of my sovereign Lord. The soul has realized God in it. Only a few guru-willed know it. ||1||Pause|| The bumblebee, addicted to the nectar enshrining twelve yogic sects in the mind. It drenched the sixteen sects when flies in the sky. ||2|| In the profound void of contentment one tree grew up and soaked the water of the earth. Says Kabeer, I am the servant of those who have seen this tree. ||3||6|| Make silence your earrings and compassion the begging bag and reciting the begging bowl. Sew this body as your patched coat, and take God's name as your support. ||1|| Practice such Yoga, O Yogi. The guru-willed, enjoy meditation, austerities and self-discipline. ||1||Pause|| Apply the ashes of wisdom to your body and your mind the horn. Be detached, and wander through the city of your body and blow the horn of your mind. ||2|| Enshrine the five elements in your mind and be in real trance. Says Kabeer, listen, O Saints: make faith of kindness your garden. ||3||7|| For what purpose you came into the world and what did you attain? You never missed God the bestowal of salvation even for a moment. ||1|| Page 971 O Lord of the universe, I am such a sinner! God gave me body and soul, but I did not practice His worship lovingly. ||1||Pause|| I do not give up other's wealth, other's bodies, other's slander and bad mouthing others. I keep coming and going; it never stops. ||2|| That house, where God's saints speak God's sermon; I never went there; Drunkards, thieves and evil-doers; I constantly live with them. ||3|| I am attached to lust, anger, worldly wealth and false attachments. I do not even dream about kindness, faith or serving the guru. ||4|| He is merciful to the meek, kind and benevolent, the love of His devotees and the destroyer of fear. Says Kabeer, please protect Your servant from disaster; O Lord, I serve only You. ||5||8|| Reciting His name attains salvation. You shall go to heaven and not return to this earth. In the home of the carefree Lord, the divine music plays. The infinite divine music plays there all the time. ||1|| Practice such recitation o my mind. Salvation is not obtained without reciting God. ||1||Pause|| There is no stopping reciting God. You will be liberated and the great load will be taken away. Bow in humility in your heart; Your coming and going will end. ||2|| Reciting Him gives you happiness. God has lit the lamp without oil. That lamp makes the world immortal. It conquers and drives out the poisons of lust and anger. ||3|| Reciting Him saves you. Recite that recitation in your heart forever. Practice that recitation and never let it go. By guru's grace, you shall cross over. ||4|| Reciting God; you will not suffer any shortage. You shall sleep in your mansion, in covers of silk. Your soul shall be peaceful and mind joyous. Drink that recitation all the time. ||5|| Reciting Him, your troubles will depart. Reciting Him the worldly wealth will not rob you. Recite and sing God God in your mind. This recitation is obtained from the guru. ||6|| Recite God forever day and night. While standing sitting with every breath and morsel of food. While awake and asleep, enjoy the essence of recitation. Reciting God is pre-ordained. ||7|| Recitation that will not load you down. Make that recitation of God's name your resolve. Says Kabeer, He has no limits. No ritual works in front of it. ||8||9|| Raamkalee, Second House, the word Of Kabeer Jee: God is one. He is realized by guru's grace. I am trapped by worldly deeds. The liberated guru extinguished my fire. Page 972 When I searched my mind thoroughly through guru's teachings; I cleansed my mind. ||1|| God the preserver of honour abides in the mind. He does not die or go through life. ||1||Pause|| Turn away from worldly powers. And fly in the universe. Get pierced by the yogic mysticism. And merge with the Lord intuitively. ||2|| My attachment to worldly wealth and attachment is gone. The moon engulfed the sun. When the pool got filled to the brim. The infinite divine music starts to play. ||3|| The guru read his teachings. The listener listened and enshrined in the mind. Reciting God attains salvation. Says Kabeer to the world. ||4||1||10|| The moon and the sun are both the embodiment of light. Within their light, is the incomparable God; ||1|| O wise man, contemplate God. God's light pervades the universe. ||1||Pause|| One diamond enlightens the next diamond. Says Kabeer, the Lord is indescribable. ||2||2||11|| You are being robbed while awake. You are being robbed O brother. While the Vedas stand guard watching, the devil of death takes you away. ||1||Pause|| He thinks that the bitter neem fruit is a mango, and the mango is a bitter neem. He imagines the thorny bush bears the ripe banana fruit. He thinks that the ripe coconut hangs on the simbal tree. What a stupid ignorant he is! ||1|| The Lord is like sugar spilled in the sand; it cannot be picked by hand. Says Kabeer, give up your ancestry, social status and honour. Be tiny like an ant; then pick and eat it. ||2||3||12|| The Word of Naam Dev Jee, Raamkalee, First House: God is one. He is realized by guru's grace. Cut a paper, make a kite and fly in the sky. Talking with the friends, he still keeps his attention on the kite string. ||1|| My mind has been pierced by the name of the Lord; like the goldsmith, whose attention is held by his work. ||1||Pause|| The princess goes to the well and fills the pitcher with water. She laughs, plays and talks with her friends, but she keeps her mind on the pitcher. ||2|| There is one divine abode with ten doors and cows graze there. The cow grazes five miles away but she focuses her mind on the calf. ||3|| Says Naam Dev, listen, O Trilochan: the herder's child sleeps on the ground. The mother works all over but she keeps her mind on the child. ||4||1|| There are countless scriptures; I do not sing their songs and hymns. Page 973 In the imperishable realm of the formless Lord, I play divine music. ||1|| Becoming detached, I sing Lord's praises. Imbued with divine music from the past goes to immortal God's home. ||1||Pause|| Then the yogi who breathes through two veins will live by breathing air. Those who look sun and the moon the same way merge with God. ||2|| Seeing the sacred shrine, do not bathe in it. You disturb the beings there. The guru showed me sixty-eight shrines in the body; bathe in it; ||3|| Entangled in five passion and attain worldly admiration. I do not care about it. Says Naam Dev; my mind is imbued with God. I am absorbed in absolute state. ||4||2|| When there was no mother and father, no deeds and no human body. Then I was not and you were not there, then who came from where? ||1|| O Lord, no one belongs to anyone else. We are like birds perched on a tree. ||1||Pause|| When there was no moon and no sun, then water was merged in air. When there were no scriptures; where did the fate come from? ||2|| Living in the sky or earth, sacred shrubs and rosary are obtained by guru's grace. Naam Dev prays; this is the reality, realized through guru's teachings. ||3||3|| Raamkalee, Second House: Some practice austerities at Banaras, or hang upside-down, die at a sacred shrine, sit in the middle of fire; do such practices. Perform the horse-sacrificial ceremony, or donate lot of gold; nothing equals reciting God's name. ||1|| O hypocrite, abandon your hypocrisy. Do not practice deception. Recite God's name all the time. ||1||Pause|| Some go to Ganges, others to Godawary, some to Kumbh, some go to Kaidar Nath, some to Gomti river to bathe. Some donate hundreds of cows. He may make millions of pilgrimages, or destroy his body in the Himalayas; still, nothing equals reciting God's name. ||2|| Some donate horses and elephants, or women of their beds, or land; they may donate such things day and night. He may purify his soul by donating gold equal to his weight. Nothing equals to reciting God's name. ||3|| Do not be angry Do not blame the devil of death; then find the pure state of salvation. My Sovereign Lord King is Raam Chander, the son of the King Dasrath; prays Naam Dev, I drink the divine nectar. ||4||4|| Raamkalee, the word of Ravi Daas Jee: God is one. He is realized by guru's grace. By reading, thinking and hearing God's name, still God is not visualized. How can iron be transformed into gold, unless it touches philosopher's stone? ||1|| Page 974 O Lord, the knot of skepticism does not open. Lust, anger, worldly wealth, intoxication and jealousy. These five have joined to plunder the world. ||1||Pause|| I am a great poet, noble heritage; a scholar, a yogi and a renunciate; I am a preacher, a warrior and a bestowal; such thinking never ends. ||2|| Says Ravi Daas, no one understands; they are all lost like an insane. Lord's name is my support. He is my life and wealth. ||3||1|| Raamkalee, the word of Baynee Jee: God is one. He is realized by guru's grace. Three energy veins abide in one place. Says Baynee, three veins, bathing at Sangam and bathing at Piraag, is in the mind. ||1|| O saints, the Lord dwells there. Only a few search the mind. That is where God dwells. ||1||Pause|| What is the sign of divine Lord's dwelling? The infinite divine music plays there. There is no moon or sun, no air or water there. The guru-willed become aware and realize God through guru's teachings. ||2|| Divine wisdom wells up, and evil-mindedness departs. The universe gets drenched with sublime nectar. One who knows the secret of this process? Surrenders to You o sacred guru. ||3|| The tenth gate is the home of the inaccessible, infinite supreme Lord. There is a shop and niche on top of it and in it is the wealth. ||4|| One, who remains awake, never sleeps. He realizes the universe. He enshrines the seed of teachings in the mind. His mind changes and attains the absolute state. ||5|| He remains awake, and he does not lie. He keeps the five sensory organs under his control. He enshrines guru's teachings in the mind. He offers his mind and body for God's love. ||6|| Even if for a moment he contemplates guru's teachings. He does not lose his life in a gamble. He plugs up the source of the river of evil tendencies. He makes the sunrise from the west. He bears the unbearable and the nectar trickle down within. He speaks with the Lord of the world. ||7|| The four-sided lamp burns in God's abode.

The primal Lord is at the centre of the countless leaves. He abides there with all His powers. He mixes the jewels into the pearl of the mind. ||8|| The lotus is at the forehead, and the jewels surround it. There, lives God the rich Lord of the universe. Five divine tunes of purity play there. The religious fan waves and the conch shell sounds like thunder. The guru-willed tramples and destroys the demons through divine knowledge. Baynee longs for Your name O Lord. ||9||1||

Page 975 Tune Nat Naaraayan, Fourth Master:

God is one. It is true. He is the Creator. He is carefree. He has no enemy. He is immortal. He does not take birth. He came into existence own His own. He is realized by guru's grace.

O my mind, recite God's name forever. I committed millions of sins. All are with me. Please eliminate them. ||1||Pause|| The devotees sing God's praises and recite His name with love. All sins are erased, just as water washes off the dirt. ||1|| O mortal; sing praises of God from your mouth. In a moment God will get rid of the five incurable diseases of the body. ||2|| The fortunate God's devotees recite God's name. I beg for their company O God so that I the ignorant fool attain salvation. ||3|| O life of the world, I am at your refuge. Be kind and save me. Servant Nanak is at your refuge O God; preserve my honour; ||4||1|| Nat, Fourth Master: Reciting God the devotees merge with God. I recite God's name through guru's teachings and God became kind to me. ||1||Pause|| The devotee merges with inaccessible and unfathomable God with ease reciting His name intuitively. Devotees of God enjoy God's love in the congregation. I admire them. ||1|| God's devotees sing supreme God's name. Their poverty and pain is erased. There are five thieves in the body. God drove them away quickly. ||2|| God's saint loves God in his mind, like the lotus flower seeing the moon. Hearing the thunder of a dark cloud the peacock dances in love. ||3|| My Lord made me think and I live by realizing and visualizing God. Servant Nanak is addicted to God. I am peaceful visualizing God. ||4||2|| Nat, Fourth Master: O my mind my friend; recite God's name. Page 976 By guru's grace, I recite God's name and wash my guru's feet. ||1||Pause|| The sacred Lord the master of the universe keeps me a sinner in His refuge. You are the great Lord, destroyer of the pain of the poor; You made me recite Your name. ||1|| I the lowly sing God's praises in the company of my guru. Like the bitter neem tree, growing near the sandalwood tree and acquires the smell of sandalwood. ||2|| I commit sins and acts of corruption countless times. I am virtueless, heavy like a rock. God took me across along with others. ||3|| Those whom You save O Lord; their sins are destroyed. O Nanak's kind Lord and master. You saved many sinner demons. ||4||3|| Nat, Fourth Master: O my mind, recite God with love. The Lord of the universe became kind to me. I recite God and touch the feet of His devotees. ||1||Pause|| Making mistakes for many a life; now I came to God's refuge. O Lord; You save those who come to Your refuge. Please save me the sinner. ||1|| Who would not be saved in Your Company? God saves the sinners. The seamster Naam Dev was driven out by the evil. You preserved the honour of Your humble servant. ||2|| Those who sing Your praises, O Lord; I admire them. You sanctified the homes, where the dust of your devotee's fell. ||3|| I cannot describe Your virtues O God. You are the greatest primal Lord. Please be kind to Your servant Nanak that I serve the feet of Your devotees. ||4||4|| Nat, Fourth Master: O my mind, recite God's name with love. The master of the universe became kind, I recite God's name through guru's teachings. ||1||Pause|| Listening to guru's teachings, God's devotees sing God's praises. God's name cut the sins like a farmer cuts the crop. ||1|| Only You know Your greatness. I cannot describe God's virtues. You are what You are O God; You alone know Your Virtues. ||2|| The mortals are bound by worldly wealth. Reciting God removes the bonds. Like the elephant, which was caught in the water by an octopus. He was freed reciting God. ||3|| O my master and transcendent Lord, throughout the ages, mortals search for You. Your extent cannot be known, O great God of servant Nanak. ||4||5|| Nat, Fourth Master: O my mind, sing and pray to God in today's age. Kind God became kind and I recite God in guru's refuge. ||1||Pause|| Page 977 O my Lord, You are great, inaccessible and unfathomable. All recite Your name o beautiful Lord. Those whom You see with grace the guru-willed recite God. ||1|| You created the universe O Lord, may you live forever O life of the world. As the waves rise little by little and merge again with water. ||2|| You know whatever You do. O Lord, I do not know. I am Your child; please enshrine Your praises in my heart so that I recite Your name O God; ||3|| O God, You are deep Like lake Mansarovar. Whoever worships reaps the reward. Servant Nanak longs for God; please bestow Your name on Him. ||4||6|| Nat Naaraayan, Fourth Master, Partaal: God is one. He is realized by guru's grace. O my mind, serve the Lord, and receive the fruits of your effort. Receive the dust of guru's feet. All poverty will be eliminated and your pains will disappear. O God, be kind and bestow peace on me by your grace. ||1||Pause|| God embellishes His house. It looks beautiful and entices me. God came to my house by His grace. My guru represented me and I am content visualizing Him. ||1|| The guru told me of God's coming and I became happy O my friend. Servant Nanak became intoxicated and content meeting God; ||2||1||7|| Nat, Fourth Master: O mind, join the society of saints, and become adorable. Listen to the unspoken speech of the peace-giving Lord. All sins will be washed away. Meet the Lord, according to pre-ordained destiny. ||1||Pause|| Praising God in today's age is the highest. Recite Him through guru's teachings. I am a sacrifice to the person who listens and believes. ||1|| Those who enjoy the untold story of God; their hunger disappears. O Nanak; they became content and became God by listening to God's discourse. ||2||2||8|| Nat, Fourth Master: If someone would come and tell me Lord's sermon. I admire Him forever. That humble servant of the Lord is gentle of all. Page 978 Meeting the Lord, you become content. ||1||Pause|| The guru showed me the way to divinity and way to walk on it. O my guru-brothers, eliminate inner corruption and worship God with pure mind and be content. ||1|| Those guru's followers please God; who realize God with them. God guided servant Nanak; Seeing God close by he is contented. ||2||3||9|| Tune Nat Naaraayan, Fifth Master: God is one. He is realized by guru's grace. O Lord, What do I know what pleases You? I have a great yearning to visualize you in the mind. ||1||Pause|| He, who you are kind to; becomes your devotee and divine; Whoever You are kind to; sings Your praises forever. ||1|| What sort of Yoga, spiritual wisdom or meditation, and what virtues please you? Whom You inspire to love you becomes your devotee. ||2|| That is intelligence, wisdom and cleverness, which inspires one not to forget God, even for an instant. I obtained this benefit in saint's company and recite God's praises forever. ||3|| I see the amazing beautiful scene. I see nothing else at all. Says Nanak, the guru eliminated my filth; that eliminates rebirth. ||4||1|| Tune Nat Naaraayan, Fifth Master, Du-Padas: God is one. He is realized by guru's grace. I don't blame anyone else. Whatever You do is sweet to my mind. ||1||Pause|| Obeying Your word I find peace and I live by listening to Your name. Here and hereafter, O Lord, only You are there. The guru taught me this lesson. ||1|| Since I came to realize this, I became happy and content. Nanak is enlightened in devotee's company, not anyone else. ||2||1||2|| Nat, Fifth Master: Whoever has You for support; Their fear of death removed; peace found and the pain of ego eliminated. ||1||Pause|| The fire extinguished through sacred sermon, I am content like a child with milk. The saints are my mother, father and friends brothers and my support. ||1|| Page 979 The doors of doubt opened. I met God and enlightened like a diamond touching diamonds. Nanak is amazed reciting God's praises the treasure of virtues. ||2||2||3|| Nat, Fifth Master: He saved His humble servant. Twenty-four hours a day, He dwells with His humble servant. He never forgets him from His mind. ||1||Pause|| He does not look at his colour form or considers the ancestry of His slave. By His grace, God blesses him with His name and takes care intuitively. ||1|| The ocean of fire is treacherous and difficult, but he is carried across. Witnessing this Nanak is joyous and admires Him forever. ||2||3||4|| Nat, Fifth Master: I say God God God in my mind. Millions of sins are erased in an instant and pain is relieved. ||1||Pause|| By searching, I became detached. I recite God in devotee's company. Renouncing everything, I am lovingly focused on God. I seek God's refuge. ||1|| Those who recite or listen or seek God's refuge attain salvation. Says Nanak; reciting God he is very happy. ||2||4||5|| Nat, Fifth Master: I am in love with Your lotus feet. O Lord, ocean of peace, please, bless me with the supreme status. ||1||Pause|| He attaches His devotee with Him and pierces His mind with love. Singing His praises, love wells up in the devotee, and the trap of worldly pleasure is broken. ||1|| The Lord, the ocean of mercy, is all-pervading. I do not see anyone else. He has united slave Nanak with Him. His love never diminishes. ||2||5||6|| Nat, Fifth Master: O my mind, recite the word God. I shall never forget Him from my mind. Twenty-four hours a day, I sing His praises. ||1||Pause|| I bathe in devotee's dust daily. All my sins and sufferings eliminated. The Lord, the ocean of mercy, is all-pervading and abides in all. ||1|| All kind of meditations, austerities and worships do not equal to reciting God. With his palms pressed together, Nanak begs for this blessing, that he may become the slave of Your slaves. ||2||6||7|| Nat, Fifth Master: The treasure of God's name is everything for me. By God's grace I met God's devotees and the guru blessed me. ||1||Pause|| Singing the praises of God the bestowal of happiness and destroyer of sins attains divine wisdom. Lust, anger and greed are destroyed. Ignorance and self – pride eliminated. ||1|| What virtues of Yours should I say? O God, You know all. I seek the refuge of Your lotus feet, O Lord, ocean of peace; Nanak admires You forever. ||2||8|| Page 980 Nat, Fifth Master: I praise the guru, the Lord of the world. ||1||Pause|| I am unworthy. You are the perfect giver. You are kind Lord of the meek. ||1|| While standing sitting sleeping and awake, You are my life wealth and property. ||2|| I am thirsty of visualizing You. Nanak will be content visualizing You. ||3||9|| Nat Partaal, Fifth Master: God is one. He is realized by guru's grace. Is there any friend or companion of mine? Who will read God's name to me daily? And get rid of my pains and evil tendencies? I will surrender my mind, body and everything. ||1||Pause|| There are only a few who will make me their own. In his refuge my mind will soothe. By his grace he bestows God's praises on me. ||1|| Reciting God the priceless life is conquered. Millions of sinners are sanctified. Slave Nanak admires Him. ||2||1||10||19|| Nat Ashtapadees, Fourth Master: God is one. He is realized by guru's grace. O Lord, Your name is the support of my mind and body. I cannot survive for a moment without serving You. I recite Your name through guru's teachings. ||1||Pause|| I recite God God in the mind. I love God's name. God became kind to the poor and took my care through guru's teachings. ||1|| Almighty Lord is the slayer of demons, life of the world, my Lord and master, inaccessible and infinite: I pray to my guru that I may wash the feet of devotees. ||2|| Unique God is one but he has millions of eyes. God is one but seen in many forms. Guru's teachings bestow salvation. ||3|| Obeying guru's teachings, I realized God, reciting and enshrining His name in the mind. God's sermon tastes sweet to me like a mute enjoys sweets. ||4|| Deluded by duality the tongue enjoys other tastes that are bland and useless. The guru-willed enjoys the taste of God's name forgets other tastes. ||5|| I realized the wealth of God's name through guru's teachings. Listening or saying God eliminates the sins. The devil of death or justice of destiny do not come close to my Lord's beloved devotees. ||6|| I recite God with every breath through guru's teachings. Any breath without reciting God goes waste. ||7|| O God, bless me in your refuge by your grace and unite me with Your devotees. Page 981 Nanak, the slave of Your slaves, says, I am the water-carrier of Your slaves. ||8||1|| Nat, Fourth Master: O Lord, I am a virtueless stone. O God, unite me with the guru by your grace that I the stone attain salvation through guru's teachings. ||1||Pause|| The guru reads God's sweet name and spreads fragrance like sandalwood. Through God's name, my awareness extends in ten directions. The fragrance of the fragrant Lord permeates the air. ||1|| Your virtuous sermon is sweet. I recite God through guru's sacred word. I always sing God's praises. The guru bestows salvation singing praises. ||2|| The guru has discerning thinking and knows all; meeting him eliminates doubt. Meeting the guru attains salvation. I admire my guru. ||3|| Practicing hypocrisy and deception, people are confused. Greed and hypocrisy are evils in this world. Here and hereafter it is painful. The devil of death hits them over the head. ||4|| At the day break they engage in evil deeds the expanse of evil worldly wealth. When night falls, they see dreams and see pain in dreams also. ||5|| They grow false in the salty land and harvest false. The faithless people are always hungry. The mighty devil of death is waiting at the door. ||6|| The self-willed gathered lots of loan. It is paid by contemplating guru's teachings. All debtors and creditors, obtain salvation touching God's devotee's feet. ||7|| The whole creation is under the control of the Lord of the universe. O Nanak, as God pulls, so we go; the way it please my beloved God; ||8||2|| Nat, Fourth Master: O Lord; may I bathe in divine pool. Bathing in guru's divine wisdom is pure. It washes the filth of sins. ||1||Pause|| The virtues of devotee's company are great! A prostitute attained salvation listening to a parrot saying God. The hunch back attained salvation by touching by Lord Krishna. ||1|| Ajaamal loved his son and called him God. By God's grace and intuitive love, the pain of devil of death was driven away. ||2|| The mortal reads and explains others but does not follow what he says. Meeting devotee's company the faith wells up and attains salvation reciting God. ||3|| As long as his soul and body are healthy, he does not think of God. But when his home catches fire, then he wants to dig a well and extinguish fire by drawing and pouring water from the well. ||4|| O mind, do not accompany the faithless who forgot God's name. The faithless word stings like a scorpion; leave and stay away from him. ||5|| Page 982 I fell in love and embellished in devotee's company. I believe in guru's teachings and love my master the Lord. ||6|| I earned it in previous life bit by bit reciting God's name with love. By guru's grace, I obtain sacred taste. I sing and think God's name. ||7|| O Lord, all forms and colours are Yours O my beloved, my deep crimson ruby. The love You bestow is obtained; what can the poor Nanak do? ||8||3|| Nat, Fourth Master: O God; God saves us in guru's refuge. He protected the elephant, when caught by octopus. He pulled him out of water. ||1||Pause|| God's servants are sublime and exalted. They enshrine God in the mind. Faith and devotion please my God. He saves the honour of His devotees. ||1|| God's servant serves God and visualizes God's expanse. He sees one and only one God, Who sees all with one eye. ||2|| God pervades all and looks after His devotees. The kind Lord kindly gives His kindness as gifts even to worms in stones. ||3|| The fragrance of musk is in the deer, he wanders all over deluded by doubt. He is tired of wandering in the forest; the perfect guru bestows salvation at home. ||4|| Guru's word is guru's lesson. Guru's teaching has nectar in it. The devotee follows what guru says. Guru definitely bestows salvation. ||5|| All is God, God is the creation. Man eats what he plants. When Chandarhaans was tormented by bad intellect; he burnt his house. ||6|| When a devotee misses God in the mind; God saves him. By God's grace the devotee worships God. He and his followers are saved. ||7|| God is all in all and looks after the universe. O servant Nanak, everything happens by God's grace. Salvation obtains by God's grace. ||8||4|| Nat Master Fourth Grant Your Grace O Lord and save me. You saved Dropadi from shame when she was brought before the evil court. ||1||Pause|| Be kind to Your beggar. I beg for one gift O Lord. I long for my guru; please unite me with the guru. ||1|| The actions of the faithless are like churning water. He churns water and gets water. Joining the true congregation, the supreme status is obtained; the butter is produced churning milk and eaten with delight. ||2|| He constantly washes his body and rubs and cleans it. Page 983 If the word of my guru is not pleasing to his mind, then all his preparations and beautiful decorations are useless. ||3|| Walk playfully and carefree, O my friends and enjoy the virtues of God. God is pleased with guru-willed's service; I realize God through the guru. ||4|| Women and men all belong to God the primal Lord; The dust of God's devotee's pleases me. God bestows salvation in devotee's company. ||5|| I wandered all over but God's servant find God in the mind. With love, God unites us with the guru and the guru bestows salvation. ||6|| Contemplating guru's teachings my breath has been purified. I drink nectar in my home and see the world without eyes. ||7|| I cannot describe Your Virtues O Lord; You are great and I am a tiny worm. Be kind to Nanak and unite with the guru. My mind is at peace reciting God. ||8||5|| Nat, Fourth Master: O my mind, recite the inaccessible and infinite Lord the master. I am a sinner and unworthy. O guru, be kind and save me. ||1||Pause|| I pray to my guru that I meet holy devotees. Please, bless me with the wealth of God`s name and eliminate my greed and hunger. ||1|| The moth, the deer, the bumblebee, the elephant and the fish are ruined, each by the one passion that controls them. Five demons control the body. The guru eliminates the sins. ||2|| I searched the Shaastras and the Vedas. Naarad also says the same words. Recite God`s name and attain salvation in guru`s company. ||3|| I am in love with my beloved Lord like the lotus blooms seeing the sun. The peacock dances on the mountain, when dark clouds thunder; ||4|| Water the faithless with nectar; even then the branches and flowers are bitter. As one bows down to the faithless, the faithless spits poison. ||5|| When saints and devotees get together they talk divine wisdom. The saints enjoy meeting the saints, like the lotus enjoys meeting water. ||6||

The waves of greed are like mad dogs with rabies. Their madness ruins everything. When the news reached the court of my Lord, the guru took up the sword of divine wisdom and killed them. ||7|| Save me O my God; shower me with Your kindness and save me! O Nanak, I have no other support; the guru has saved me. ||8||6|| First Set of Six Hymns||

Page 984 Tune Maalee Gauraa, Fourth Master:

God is one. It is true. He is the Creator. He is carefree. He has no enemy. He is immortal. He does not take birth. He came into existence on His own. He is realized by guru's grace.

Many have tried, but none have found Lord's limit. The Lord is inaccessible, unapproachable and unfathomable. I humbly bow to God the Lord. ||1||Pause|| Lust, anger, greed and emotional attachment bring continuous conflict and strife. Save me I am your humble creature, O Lord; I came to Your refuge O God; ||1|| You protect those who come to Your refuge O God; You look after your devotees. Your humble servant Prahlaad was caught by Harnaakhash; You saved Him and carried him across. ||2|| Recite God O my mind the bestowal of destiny and destroyer of pain. O Lord; eliminate the fear of birth and death. God is realized through guru's teachings. ||3|| I recite the name of saviour of sinners and destroyer of fear with love. I wear God's necklace in my mind and servant Nanak is merged with God's name. ||4||1|| Maalee Gauraa, Fourth Master: O my mind, recite the name of God the bestowal of happiness. The guru-willed enjoys reciting God in devotee's company and realizes God. ||1||Pause|| The fortunate visualized the guru; meeting the guru realizes God. The filth of evil is washed away and I bathe in God's sacred pool. ||1|| Blessed are the devotees who realized God. I ask them God's stories. I fall at their feet and pray to unite me with God the architect of destiny. ||2|| Through pre-destined fate I met the devotee guru. My mind is imbued by guru's teachings. Meeting God I attained peace and all sins are destroyed. ||3|| Those who recite God through guru's teachings; their words are sacred. The fortunate obtains the dust of their feet; servant Nanak touches their feet. ||4||2|| Page 985 Maalee Gauraa, Fourth Master: All mystics, seekers and sages recite God with love. The supreme Lord is limitless. The guru knows the unknown Lord. ||1||Pause|| I am low and I do evil deeds. I do not recite God the Lord. The Lord united me with the guru. He liberated me from bonds in a minute. ||1|| God wrote in my fate and I recite God with love through guru's teachings. The five instruments play in God's court. I sing songs of joy realizing God. ||2|| The name of the Lord is the purifier of sinners. It does not appeal to the unlucky. They rot in the womb for birth like salt dissolves in water. ||3|| O inaccessible Lord, please guide me that I put my mind to guru's feet. Servant Nanak remains attached to God's name and merges with it. ||4||3|| Maalee Gauraa, Fourth Master: My mind is addicted to the taste of Lord's name. Meeting the guru, my mind enlightened. The doubt and fear departed. ||1||Pause|| I worship God with love. My sleeping mind woke up through guru's teachings. My sins are erased and I found peace by enshrining God in the mind by good fortune; ||1|| The self-willed is like the false colour of the safflower. The flowers last only for a few days. He perishes in an instant by God's power. He is punished by the justice of destiny. ||2|| The love of devotee's company is deep. It is like dying with deep red colour. The cloth of the body may be torn to shreds, but still this beautiful colour of Lord's love does not fade; ||3|| Dyed by God's love obtains guru's glory, God dyes one with deep crimson colour. Servant Nanak washes the feet of those who fall at God's feet. ||4||4|| Maalee Gauraa, Fourth Master: O my mind, recite God's name the Lord of the world. My mind and body are merged in Lord's joyous name through guru's teaching. ||1||Pause|| Recite God's name through guru's teachings. Recite God in the rosary of mind. Those with pre-ordained destiny realize God wearing a garland of flowers. ||1|| Those who recite God's name; their entanglements end. The devil of death does not come close to them; the guru, the saviour Lord, saves them. ||2|| I am a child. I know nothing. The Lord cherishes me as my mother and father. I continuously put my hands in worldly fire. Kind to the poor guru saved me. ||3|| I the filthy became pure. Singing God's praises eliminated my sins. My mind became happy meeting the guru. Servant Nanak became content through guru's teachings. ||4||5|| Maalee Gauraa, Fourth Master: Page 986 O my mind, recite God and all sins will be eliminated. I enshrined God in my mind through the guru. May I walk on guru`s path; ||1||Pause|| Whoever tells me the stories of my Lord; I will cut my mind and offer to him. The perfect guru united me with my friend. I am sold on guru`s word. ||1|| I offered awns in the month of Maagh. I cut and offered half of my body as well. No one attains salvation without God`s name. He may donate huge amount of gold. ||2|| I sing God`s praises through guru`s teaching and my mind opened. The three qualities are shattered, doubt and fear ran away, the rope broke and the pitcher broke. ||3|| In today`s age, those with a pre-ordained destiny meet the perfect guru. Servant Nanak drinks the nectar. His hunger and thirst are quenched. ||4||6|| Set of Six Hymns || Maalee Gauraa, Fifth Master: God is one. He is realized by guru`s grace. O mind, true peace comes from serving the Lord. Other services are false, the devil of death beats over the head all the time. ||1||Pause|| Those with pre-ordained destiny meet devotee's company. God the infinite saint carried the world across the terrifying world-ocean. ||1|| Serve devotee's feet forever eliminating greed and useless attachment. Abandon all other hopes, and rest your hopes in one formless Lord. ||2|| Some faithless are deluded by doubt. Without the guru, there is pitch dark. Whatever is pre-ordained; comes to pass. No one can erase it. ||3|| The beauty of the Lord of the universe is profound and unfathomable. The names of the infinite Lord are unlimited. Blessed are those O Nanak, who enshrine God`s name in the mind. ||4||1|| Maalee Gauraa, Fifth Master: I humbly bow to the name of the Lord. Reciting it, one is saved. ||1||Pause|| Reciting Him, conflicts end. Reciting Him, one's bonds are cut. Reciting Him, the ignorant becomes wise. Reciting Him, one's dynasty is saved. ||1|| Reciting Him, fear and pain are taken away. Reciting Him, misfortune is avoided. Reciting Him, sins are erased. Reciting Him, pain ends. ||2|| Reciting Him, the mind becomes happy. Reciting Him, the worldly wealth becomes servant. Reciting Him, one obtains the priceless treasure. Reciting Him, the ignorant attains salvation. ||3|| The name of the Lord is the purifier of sinners. It saves millions of devotees. I the meek seek the refuge of God`s servants. Nanak puts his forehead on the feet of the saints. ||4||2|| Maalee Gauraa, Fifth Master: Such a help is God`s name. Reciting God in devotee's company fulfills deeds. ||1||Pause|| It is like a boat to a drowning man.

Page 987 It is like oil to the lamp whose flame is dying out. It is like water poured on the burning fire. It is like milk poured into baby's mouth. ||1|| As one's brother comes to help on the battlefield. As one's hunger is satisfied by food. As rain saves the crops. As one is protected in tiger's den. ||2|| As Guruda bird is not satisfied eating snakes. As the cat cannot eat the parrot in a cage. As a bird cherishes egg in the heart. As the grains are spared, by sticking to the central post of the mill. ||3|| Your glory is so great. I can describe only a tiny bit of it. O Lord, You are inaccessible, unapproachable and unfathomable. You are lofty and high, utterly great and infinite. O Nanak, reciting God one swims across the world ocean. ||4||3|| Maalee Gauraa, Fifth Master: Please let my deeds be fulfilled. Please honour Your servant. ||1||Pause|| I put my forehead on the feet of the saints. May I see his face day and night? With my hands, I serve the saints. I dedicate my life, mind and wealth to the saints. ||1|| My mind loves the society of the saints. The virtues of the saints abide in my mind. The will of the saints is sweet to my mind. Seeing the saints, my heart-lotus blossoms. ||2|| I dwell in the society of the saints. I have a great thirst for the saints. Words of the saints are the lesson of my mind. By the grace of the saints, my corruption is eliminated. ||3|| This way of liberation is my treasure. O merciful God, please bless me with this gift. O God, shower Your mercy on Nanak. I have enshrined the feet of the saints in my heart. ||4||4|| Maalee Gauraa, Fifth Master: He is with all. He is not far. He is the cause of causes, ever-present. ||1||Pause|| Hearing His name, one sings God`s name. Pain is dispelled; peace dwells in the mind. The Lord is a priceless treasure. The silent sages and mortals serve Him. ||1|| Everything is in His home. No one is without Him. He takes care of all beings. Serve the merciful Lord forever. ||2|| True justice is dispensed in His court forever. He is carefree and owes allegiance to no one. He does everything. O my mind, recite His name. ||3|| I admire the company of devotees. Meeting him attains salvation. My mind and body are attuned to God`s name. God has blessed Nanak with this gift. ||4||5|| Maalee Gauraa, Fifth Master, Du-Padas: God is one. He is realized by guru`s grace. I seek the refuge of all-powerful Lord. My soul, body and wealth belong to God, the cause of causes. ||1||Pause|| Reciting Him attains eternal peace. He is the source of life. He is all-pervading from smallest to the largest. ||1|| Page 988 Abandon all your entanglements and corruption; sing God's praises daily. With palms pressed together, Nanak begs for this blessing. Please bless me with Your name. ||2||1||6|| Maalee Gauraa, Fifth Master: God is all-powerful, divine and infinite. Who knows Your amazing plays? You have no end or limit. ||1||Pause|| In an instant, You establish and disestablish; You create and destroy O Lord. As many beings as You created O God, You bless them all. ||1|| I have come to Your sanctuary. I am Your slave, O inaccessible Lord! Pull me out of the terrifying world-ocean. Servant Nanak admires You forever. ||2||2||7|| Maalee Gauraa, Fifth Master: The Lord of the world abides in my mind and body. Friend of the poor, love of His devotees is kind forever. ||1||Pause|| You are from the beginning, in the end and the middle, no one is without You. He the master is pervading in the whole world; ||1|| With my ears I hear God's praises. I visualize Him with my eyes and sing His praises with my tongue. Nanak admires You forever; please, bless me with Your Name. ||2||3||8||6||14|| Maalee Gauraa, the word of devotee Naam Dev Jee: God is one. He is realized by guru's grace. Blessed is that flute which the Lord plays. The sweet, infinite divine music plays. ||1||Pause|| Blessed is the rain from the cloud that rejuvenates everything. Blessed is the blanket worn by Krishna. ||1|| Blessed are you, O mother Devakee: In your home the Lord was born. ||2|| Blessed are the forests of Brindaaban. The supreme Lord plays there. ||3|| He plays the flute and herds the cows. Naam Dev's Lord the master plays happily. ||4||1|| O my father, Lord of wealth; how handsome you are? ||1||Pause|| You hold the steel ring in Your hand. You came down from Heaven, and saved the life of the elephant. In the court of Duhsaasan, You saved the honour of Dropati, when her clothes were being removed. ||1|| You saved Ahliyaa, the wife of Gautam; how many have You purified and carried across? Such a lowly outcaste Naam Dev has come to Your sanctuary. ||2||2|| Everybody says God God. What else they say; other than God? ||1||Pause|| Out of the same clay, the elephant the ant; many species are formed. In stationary life forms, moving beings, worms, moths and in each and every heart, God abides. ||1|| Remember the one, infinite Lord; abandon all other hopes. Naam Dev prays humbly, I am the servant of that Lord. ||2||3||

Page 989 Tune Maaroo, First Master, First House, Chau-Padas:

God is one. It is true. He is the Creator. He is carefree. He has no enemy. He is immortal. He does not take birth. He came into existence on His own. He is realized by guru's g race.

Hymn: O my Friend, I shall forever be the dust of Your feet. Nanak seeks Your refuge and sees You ever-present. ||1|| Lesson: Recite God's name in the last phase of the night. Tents, canopies, pavilions and carriages are prepared and made ready for them. Those who recite Your name. You invite and meet them. ||1|| O elder, I am unfortunate and a fraud. I did not find Your name. My mind is blind and deluded by doubt. ||1||Pause|| I taste the blooming pains. They are pre-ordained O mother. Less happiness, more pains and I suffer in pain. ||2|| What to say of the separated and what to say of the united? Praise the Lord, who created this play. ||3|| By good destiny, they are united because of their past deeds. The unfortunate separate after union O Nanak, this is also by luck. ||4||1|| Maaroo, First Master: The union of the mother and father brings the body into being. The Creator inscribes the fate in him. You get the enlightenment and honour according to your fate. You lost your intellect seeing the worldly wealth. ||1|| O ignorant mind, why are you so proud? You will depart according to God's will. ||1||Pause|| Abandon the tastes of the world and find intuitive peace. All must leave their home; no one remains here forever. Eat some, and save the rest for future. If you are coming back into the world. ||2|| He adorns his body and dresses in silk robes. He issues all sorts of recommendations. He sleeps in a comfortable bed. He does everything, why to cry then? ||3|| Household affairs are whirlpools of entanglements, O brother; Page 990 Sin and stone do not float. So let the love of God be the boat to carry you across. Says Nanak, only a few attain it; ||4||2|| Maaroo, First Master, First House: Actions are the paper, mind is the ink; good and bad are written on it. Past deeds govern our present; there is no end to Your virtues O God. ||1|| Why do not keep this in mind O ignorant? Forgetting God, your virtues are finished and rot. ||1||Pause|| The night and the day is a net. There are as many traps as there are moments. You peck on the bait with love and get caught; how will you escape? ||2|| The body is a furnace, and the mind is the iron in it. The five fires are heating it. Sin is the charcoal put on it; which burns the mind and the pliers to hold is the worry. ||3|| The burnt mind becomes gold again if he meets the guru; He blesses with sacred God's name and the body's thirst quenches. ||4||3|| Maaroo, First Master: In the middle of filth there is pure water and lotus grows there. The lotus flower lives in water and is not bothered by pollution. ||1|| You frog, you will never understand; You eat dirt, while you live in pure waters. You do not know about nectar. ||1||Pause|| You live in water; the bumblebee does not live there, that is worth talking. Intuitively sensing the moon in the distance, the lotus bows its head. ||2|| You think you are smart and enjoy nectar milk and honey. You never give up your habits like a slanderer. ||3|| The ignorant lives with a scholar and listens to the scriptures. You do not leave your habits like the tale of a dog. ||4|| Some hypocrites do not recite God's name; others are absorbed in God's feet. You get what you earn. O Nanak recite God's name. ||5||4|| Maaroo, First Master, Hymn: Attaching to God's feet many sinners become sacred. Reciting God's name is as good as bathing at sixty eighty shrines by pre-ordained destiny. ||1||Lesson: O friends and companions, filled with pride. Listen to this one joyous story of your Husband Lord. ||1|| Who can I tell about my pain, O my mother? My mind cannot live without God. What can I do O mother? ||1||Pause|| I am a discarded bride, I am miserable. I have lost my youth. I regret and repent. ||2|| You are my wise Lord and master over my head. I serve You as Your humble slave. ||3|| Nanak humbly prays this is my only concern: Without seeing you, how can I recite You with love? ||4||5|| Page 991 Maaroo, First Master: You bought me, I am Your dedicated servant and I am called a fortunate. I was sold through guru's word; I do what he said. ||1|| What cleverness Your servant can have? I do not follow Lord's command. ||1||Pause|| My mother and father are Your slaves and I am their child. She dances and he sings and I worship You O Lord; ||2|| If You wish to drink, I get water for You O Lord; if You wish to eat, I shall grind grain for You. I wave fan and wash Your feet and continue reciting Your name. ||3|| Your slave Nanak is thankless. It is your greatness if You forgive him. From the beginning for a long time O kind bestowal, salvation is not attained without You. ||4||6|| Maaroo, First Master: Some call him a ghost; some say he is a demon. Some call him a man; it is only poor Nanak! ||1|| Nanak has gone insane after his Lord the King. I know of none other than the Lord. ||1||Pause|| He is known to be insane, when he goes insane with love of God. He recognizes none other than one Lord. ||2|| Call him real insane if he works for only one Lord. He realizes Lord's command; what other cleverness is there? ||3|| Call him insane, if he falls in love with his master. He sees himself bad and rest of the world good; ||4||7|| Maaroo, First Master: This wealth is all pervading and permeating all. The self-willed wanders around thinking that it is far away. ||1|| That merchandise the wealth of God's name is in my mind. Whoever You bless with it, is liberated. ||1||Pause|| This wealth does not burn. A thief cannot steal it. This wealth does not drown; its owner is never punished. ||2|| See; greatness of this wealth. You spend your life imbued in peace. ||3|| Listen to this incomparably beautiful story, O my brothers. Tell me, without this wealth, who has ever obtained salvation? ||4|| Says Nanak humbly the unspoken speech of the Lord. This wealth is obtained meeting with the guru. ||5||8|| Maaroo, First Master: Dry the sun and drink the ego and control your breath through yoga practice. Stabilize your fishy mind that the swan neither flies nor jumps the wall. ||1|| You ignorant, why are you deluded by doubt? You do not remember the detached Lord of supreme bliss. ||1||Pause|| Give up wandering and drink the nectar. Stabilize your fishy mind, then you will never waver. ||2|| Page 992 Nanak humbly prays, if a mortal recites God from the mind; the mind drinks nectar with every breath. Stabilize your fishy mind; then you will never waver. ||3||9|| Maaroo, First Master: Worldly wealth or the mind; do not die neither do the waves in the ocean; The boat crosses over the water, carrying the true merchandise. The jewel mind conquers the mind. Nothing affects the truth. The king sits on the throne imbued with the fear of God and the five qualities. ||1|| O elder; do not see God far; He is the light, the life of the world; He writes the fate of everyone. ||1||Pause|| Brahma and Vishnu, saints, sages, Shiva and Indra, penitents and beggars Those who obey His command are honoured in His court. The rebels die in disgrace. The wandering beggars, warriors, celibates and hermits – contemplate through the perfect guru: Without service, no one receives the reward. Service is the essence. ||2|| You are wealth of the poor, guru of the guru-less, the honour of the humble. The guru gave the jewel to the blind. You are the strength of the weak. He is not known through burnt offerings and ritual chanting. The true Lord is realized through guru's teachings. Without God's name, no one finds shelter in God's court. The false keep coming and going. ||3|| So praise the true name, through the true name you will find satisfaction. When the mind is cleaned with the jewel of spiritual wisdom, it does not become dirty again. As long as the Lord dwells in the mind, nothing obstructs you. O Nanak, by self-surrendering one is freed; the mind and body become true. ||4||10|| Maaroo, First Master: The way of yoga is to recite pure name and then the filth does not attach. See the beloved Lord always with you and the cycle of birth death ends. ||1|| O Lord of the universe what is Your name and how it is realized? If You call me in. I will ask one unique question? ||1||Pause|| He who bathes in divine wisdom and worships God is a scholar. One name, one Lord, and His one light pervade the universe. ||2|| My tongue is the weigh scale and this heart is the pan of the scale. I weigh the immeasurable God's name. There is one shop and one banker above all; the merchants deal in one merchandise. ||3|| The true guru saves us at both ends. He who is lovingly focused on God realizes it. his soul becomes peaceful. Enshrining guru's teachings in the mind eliminates the doubt and the devotee worships God day and night. ||4|| Above is the sky and beyond that is the Lord; that is where immortal guru lives. Through guru's word Nanak became detached and sees God inside out. ||5||11|| Page 993 Tune Maaroo, First Master, Fifth House: God is one. He is realized by guru's grace. Day and night, he remains awake. He never sleeps. He who has the pain knows it. My body is pierced through with the arrow of love. The doctor does not know the cure? ||1|| Whom the true Lord links to His praise; He guides only a few guru-willed to realize it. He who deals in nectar; knows its value; ||1||Pause|| The soul-bride is in love with her Husband Lord. Then focuses her mind to guru's teachings.

The soul-bride is joyous intuitively; her hunger and thirst are eliminated. ||2|| Tear down skepticism and dispel your doubt. With intuition, draw the bow of the praise of the Lord. One who conquers the mind through guru's teachings is the real yogi. ||3|| Burnt by ego, one forgets God from his mind. In the city of death, he is attacked with massive swords. Then, even if he asks for it, he will not receive Lord's name. O soul, you shall suffer terrible punishment. ||4|| You are distracted by the worldly attachments. In the city of death, the noose of the devil of death will catch you. You cannot break the bonds of worldly attachment; the devil of death will torture you. ||5|| I did nothing; I do nothing. The guru blessed me with God's sacred name. Whoever You give, he has no say in it. Nanak seeks Your refuge. ||6||1||12|| Maaroo, Third Master, First House: God is one. He is realized by guru's grace. Wherever You seat me, there I sit, O Lord; wherever You send me, I go. In the whole world, there is only One King. All places are sacred. ||1|| O elder, you dwell in my body and I sing the true praises. By that I may intuitively merge with You. ||1||Pause|| Good or bad deeds; come from within; this is the source of all evil. All happens by God's command in the whole world ||2||. Senses are said to be powerful. Where did the senses come from? The Creator stages all the plays. Only a few realize this. ||3|| By guru's grace, the mind focuses on one Lord and the duality ends. Obey and accept God's will; your noose of devil of death will be cut. ||4|| Prays Nanak, who can call him to account, when the egotistic pride of his mind has been eliminated? Even the justice of destiny recites God and seeks God's refuge. ||5||1|| Maaroo, Third Master: Coming and going ends and one becomes immortal. He bestowed the treasure of truth. He only knows it. ||1|| Page 994 O my mind, miss God and eliminate useless things. Recite God through guru's teachings with love. ||1||Pause|| He, who forgets the name in this world, shall not find a place to rest anywhere. He shall wander in many lifes and rot in filth. ||2|| The fortunate met the guru due to pre-ordained destiny, O mother; Night and day, I practice true worship. I am united with the true Lord. ||3|| He created the entire universe. He looks after as well. O Nanak, God bestows the greatness of His name if He wishes. ||4||2|| Maaroo, Third Master: Please forgive my past sins, O Lord; put me on right path now. I remain attached to Lord's feet and eradicate self-conceit from within. ||1|| O my guru-willed mind, recite God's name. May I be attached to God's feet whole-heartedly with love? ||1||Pause|| I have no social status or honour. I have no place or home. Contemplating guru's teachings eliminated the doubt; the guru taught me God's name. ||2|| This mind wanders around driven by greed attached to greed. He is engrossed in false deeds. He shall endure pain in the city of death. ||3|| O Nanak, God is all in all. There is no other. He bestows the treasure of worship and the guru-willed attains peace. ||4||3|| Maaroo, Third Master: Seek and find those imbued with truth; they are rare in this world. Meeting with them, one becomes happy reciting the name of the Lord. ||1|| O elder; enshrine God's name in the mind. Ask your guru and find the priceless treasure. ||1||Pause|| All serve one Lord. Through pre-ordained destiny, they meet Him. The guru-willed merge with Him and never separate again and realize true Lord. ||2|| Some do not know the value of worship. The self-willed are deluded by doubt. God guides them. They cannot do anything by themselves. ||3|| Where power does not help; one should humbly stand and pray. O Nanak, when God's name dwells in guru-willed's mind; then God applauds him. ||4||4|| Maaroo, Third Master: He transforms the burning desert into a cool oasis; and iron into gold. So praise the true Lord. There is none other as great as He. ||1|| O my mind, night and day, recite God's name. Recite God through guru's teachings and sing His praises forever. ||1||Pause|| The guru-willed realizes one God through guru's teachings. Praise the true guru, who has this wisdom. ||2|| Those who forsake the guru and attach to duality – what will they do when they go to the world hereafter? Tied in the city of death, they are beaten and punished severely. ||3|| Page 995 My God is carefree. He has no greed at all. O Nanak, seek His refuge. He will unite you with Him by His grace. ||4||5|| Maaroo, Fourth Master, Second House: God is one. He is realized by guru's grace. Sukhdev and Janak recited God's name through guru's teachings and sought God's refuge. God met Sudama and removed his poverty. He attained salvation through worship. God is the love of His devotees and his name is fulfilling by His grace. ||1|| O my mind, reciting God attains salvation. The guru-willed Dhroo, Prahlaad and Bidar the servant girl's son attained salvation reciting God's name. ||1||Pause|| In today's age God's name is the essence. God's devotees attain salvation. Naam Dev, Jai Dev, Kabeer, Trilochan and Ravi Daas the leather-worker. Their sins were eliminated. Those guru-willed who recite God's name attain salvation and their sins are eliminated. ||2|| Even the sinners who recite God's name; their sins are forgiven. Ajaamal, who loved a prostitute, was saved, by reciting God from the mouth. Reciting God's name, Ugar Sain obtained salvation. His bonds were broken and he was liberated. ||3|| God became kind to His devotees and made them His own. My Lord of the universe saves the honour of His servants; those who seek His sanctuary are saved. The Lord blessed servant Nanak; he enshrined God's name in the mind. ||4||1|| Maaroo, Fourth Master: The mystics recite God in trance; the seekers and sages also recite God. The celibates, the truthful, content, Indra and his followers recited God. Those who seek Him, recite God in love and the guru-willed attain salvation. ||1|| O my mind, reciting God's name attains salvation. Dhanna the farmer and Balmik the highway robber, the guru-willed crossed over. ||1||Pause|| Demy gods, men, heavenly heralds and celestial singers and the poor saints sing God's praises. Shiva, Brahma and the goddesses recite God's name from their mouth. Those whose minds are drenched with God's name the guru-willed attain salvation. ||2|| Millions of gods recited God; they still did not find God's limits. The scholars recite God reading from the scriptures. Those whose minds are filled with God's name the guru-willed cross over. ||3|| Those who recite God's name with love. I still cannot count their number. He who pleases God attains salvation by the grace of the Lord of the world. By guru's grace and teachings, servant Nanak recites God's name. ||4||2|| Page 996 Maaroo, Fourth Master, Third House: God is one. He is realized by guru's grace. Reciting God's name through guru's teachings attains honour. Here and hereafter, it goes with you; in the end, He shall free you. In difficult path and narrow streets, reciting God frees you there. ||1|| O my true guru; I say God God. The Lord is my mother, father, child and relative. I have no other than the Lord, O my mother. ||1||Pause|| I have yearning for God's name. May someone come and unite me with God. I pray to him if he unites me with my beloved. The almighty kind guru united me with God immediately. ||2|| Those who do not recite God's name are unlucky and die. They wander in life again and again. They die, and are re-born, and continue coming and going. They are tied and beaten at death's door, and punished in God's court. ||3|| O God, I seek Your refuge. Please unite me with You O Lord. O Lord, life of the world; be kind and grant me the refuge of the guru. The dear Lord became kind and united servant Nanak with Him. ||4||1||3|| Maaroo, Fourth Master: I inquire about the wealth of God's name; will someone tell me about Godly wealth? I will praise him from the bottom of my heart if he unites me with God. I am filled with love of my beloved; how can I meet my friend. ||1|| O my beloved friend my mind, I obtained the wealth of God's name. The perfect guru implanted God's name in me; the Lord is my support. I celebrate the Lord. ||1||Pause|| O my guru, please unite me with God and show me Godly wealth. Without the guru, love does not well up; check it out; The Lord dwells in the guru; realize God through guru's praises. ||2|| The ocean of the treasure of worship rests with the perfect guru. When it pleases the guru, He opens the treasure and the guru-willed are enlightened. The unfortunate self-willed die of thirst on the bank of a river. ||3|| The guru is the great giver. I beg for this gift from the guru. I am separated from God for a long time. My mind and body long for God. If it pleases You, O my guru, please listen to servant Nanak's prayer. ||4||2||4|| Maaroo, Fourth Master: Listening to God's sermon through guru's teaching. God is enshrined in my mind. Recite God's sermon O fortunate; God is sacred and bestowal of salvation. Page 997 The minds of the guru-willed are respectful. Through the perfect guru, they absorb in the name of the Lord. ||1|| O my mind, the sermon of the Lord is pleasing to my mind. O guru-willed; speak the unspoken discourse of God continuously forever. ||1||Pause|| I searched my mind and body; how can I know the unspoken speech? Meeting the saints, I heard the unspoken speech and enjoy it. God's name is the support of my mind and body. I am united with all knowing primal Lord. ||2|| The guru, the primal being, united me with the primal Lord. My mind has merged in the supreme mind. The fortunate worshipped God and realized wise and all-knowing God. The self-willed are unfortunate, their night passes in pain. ||3|| I am Your meek beggar; please bestow the sacred sermon to my mouth. The guru is my friend. He unites me with my wise, all-knowing Lord. Servant Nanak seeks Your refuge. Be kind that I merge in your name. ||4||3||5|| Maaroo, Fourth Master: I the detached am in love with God. O fortunate keep God in the mind. Joining the devotees, love wells up. Then enjoy God's taste through guru's teachings. Reciting God's praises through guru's teachings the mind and body rejuvenate; ||1|| O my beloved mind; enjoy the taste of God's name. I realized God through the guru. He preserves my honour everywhere. ||1||Pause|| O guru-willed; recite God's name and enjoy the taste of God's name. Plant Godly seed in the body field. God abides in devotee's company. God's name is sacred; enjoy it through the perfect guru. ||2|| The self-willed filled with greed wander in ten directions and all over. Living without God's name is a curse; the self-willed rot in filth. They come and go and keep wandering many lifes eating filth. ||3|| I humbly seek Your refuge O God; be kind and save me. Unite me with devotee's company that I enjoy God's name from tip to toe. Servant Nanak obtained the wealth of God's name through guru's teachings. ||4||4||6|| Maaroo, Fourth Master, Fifth House: God is one. He is realized by guru's grace. Reciting God fills the store. The guru-willed obtains salvation reciting God's name. Whoever God is kind to; sings God's praises. ||1|| O Lord, be kind to me. I recite You in my mind forever. O my mind recite God's name. Reciting God frees you. ||1||Pause|| Page 998 God's name is sacred ocean of peace. The beggar begs for it. O Lord, please bless him with Your kindness. True is the Lord; he appeals to my mind forever. ||2|| New nails get filled with filth. Reciting God's name all deeds become sacred. If my God is pleased listening to reciting His name, the filth is washed away reciting His name. ||3|| Attachment to worldly wealth is terribly treacherous. How can one cross over the difficult world-ocean? The Lord bestows the boat of the true guru; reciting God he takes us across. ||4|| You are everywhere; all are Yours. Whatever You do O God that happens. Poor servant Nanak sings

Your praises. If it pleases God then He accepts it. ||5||1||7|| Maaroo, Fourth Master: O my mind recite God's name. The Lord shall eradicate all your sins. Gather and hoard God's wealth. God's name goes with you on departure. ||1|| Whoever God blesses, recites God's name. He recites God's recitation and attains happiness. By guru's grace, God's sublime taste is acquired. Reciting God he takes us across. ||1||Pause|| The carefree, formless Lord exists. It is true. To recite God is a sacred deed. Enemy devil of death kicks people, but they do not come close to God's servant. ||2|| Whoever God is pleased with. That servant is known in all four corners. If some sinner speaks evil of him, the devil of death eats him up. ||3|| One Creator Lord abides in all. He creates tests and looks after. Whom God protects and frees; who can kill him? ||4|| I recite God all the time. He saves all His servants and devotees. Consult, eighteen Puraanas and four Vedas O servant Nanak, only God's name saves us. ||5||2||8|| Maaroo, Fifth Master, Second House: God is one. He is realized by guru's grace. The earth, the sky and the stars are scared. Tough God hovers over their head. Wind, water fire and poor Indra, all are scared of God. ||1|| I have heard one thing that one Lord alone is carefree. He who sings God's praises in guru's company is happy and content. ||1||Pause|| The mortals, gods, mystics and seekers die of God's fear. The whole creation dies to be reborn and keep taking birth forever. ||2|| Page 999 The kings, faithless and greedy along with many others are afraid of God. The enticing worldly wealth and the justice of destiny are afraid of God. ||3|| The entire universe is bothered and scared; only the Creator is free of fear. Says Nanak, God is the companion of His devotees. His devotees look beautiful in His court. ||4||1|| Maaroo, Fifth Master: The five year old orphan boy Dhroo, became immortal reciting God. In love of his son, he recited God; the thorn of devil of death was driven away. ||1|| My Lord has saved many, countless beings. I the poor with low intellect and virtue less has come to Your refuge. ||1||Pause|| Baalmeek the outcaste was saved, and the poor hunter was saved as well. The elephant was saved saying God in the mind for a moment. ||2|| He saved devotee Prahlaad, and tore Harnaakhash with his nails. Bidar, the son of a slave, was purified, and his entire dynasty was redeemed. ||3|| What sins of mine should I speak of? I am intoxicated with false emotional attachment. Nanak has come to God's refuge; please accept me with open arms. ||4||2|| Maaroo, Fifth Master: For the sake of riches, I wander around in so many ways. I make all sorts of efforts. The deeds I did in ego and pride; have all gone waste. ||1|| Other days are of no use to me. Please bless me with the day, when I sing God's praises. ||1||Pause|| Seeing the children, spouse, household possessions, I am entangled in these. Tasting the worldly wine, one is intoxicated and never sings God's praises. ||2|| I tried all sort of methods; God is not realized without saint's company. You are the great giver, O almighty God; I came to beg a gift from You. ||3|| Abandoning all pride and self-importance; the servant humbly came to Your refuge. Says Nanak, realizing God, I became one with one and found eternal peace. ||4||3|| Maaroo, Fifth Master: Where does God's name abide and where dwells the ego? What high status did you attain listening to abuses? ||1|| Listen: who are you, and where did you come from? You don't know how long you will stay here. You do not know when you shall depart. ||1||Pause|| Wind water and the earth have patience and tolerance; are all forgiving without saying. You are made up of five elements; where are you running around? ||2|| The primal Lord, the architect of destiny created you. He also gave you ego. That causes you to take birth and death and keep coming and going. ||3|| There is no colour or symbol of the creation. It is all imaginary; Prays Nanak; when He finishes the play; then there is only one God. ||4||4|| Page 1000 Maaroo, Fifth Master: Do not sow the useless pride, emotional attachment, greed and corruption in your mind. I bought a jewel of God's name. I am going loaded with priceless treasure. ||1|| Finally devotee's love is realized. I serve God while living and enshrine in the mind on departure. ||1||Pause|| I have not turned away from my Lord and master's command. My house is filled with joy and contentment and searching for more. ||2|| Obeying His command even hungry is happy. I do not differentiate between sorrow and happiness. Whatever is the command of my Lord; I take it on my forehead and accept it. ||3|| The Lord became kind to His servant. He saved me here and the next world. Blessed and fruitful is his birth O Nanak, who realizes his master. ||4||5|| Maaroo, Fifth Master: By

God's grace my luck blossomed and I sing God's praises. My struggle is gone, I became peaceful and my wandering ended. ||1|| Now, I have obtained the eternal state. I miss God the architect of destiny in saint's refuge. ||1||Pause|| Lust, anger, greed emotional attachment and enemies are eliminated. God is always with me; he never goes far. ||2|| I attained peace, soothing, and devotion by saint's help. He purified the sinners in an instant. I cannot express His glory. ||3|| I became carefree eliminating all concerns and took shelter of the feet of the Lord of the universe. Nanak sings God's praises day and night with love. ||4||6|| Maaroo, Fifth Master: He is all-powerful, master of all virtues, but you never sing His praises! What leaves you in a moment; you keep going after that forever; ||1|| Why do you not contemplate your God? You are entangled in association with enemies and the enjoyment of pleasures. Your soul is burning with them! ||1||Pause|| Hearing His name, the devil of death will free you, and yet, you do not enter His sanctuary! He, who drives away the jackal; seek the shelter of that God; ||2|| Praising Him, you shall cross over the terrifying world-ocean, why do not you fall in love with Him? You are stuck to listen and watch the short-lived dream. ||3|| When our Lord the ocean of mercy grants His grace, one finds honour in the society of saints. Says Nanak, I am free of the doubt of three qualities by God's grace. ||4||7|| Maaroo, Fifth Master: The inner-knower, knows everything; what can anyone hide from Him? Your hands and feet will fall off in a moment when burnt in the fire. ||1|| Page 1001 You ignorant; you have forgotten Lord from your mind! You eat His salt, and you are not faithful to Him. Before your very eyes, you shall be destroyed. ||1||Pause|| The incurable disease has arisen in your body; it cannot be cured. Forgetting God, one endures utter pain; Nanak found that by contemplating. ||2||8|| Maaroo, Fifth Master: I have enshrined the lotus feet of God in my mind. I sing the praises of the Lord continuously. There is none other than Him. He alone exists, in the beginning, in the middle, and in the end. ||1|| He is the support of the saints. ||1||Pause|| The entire universe is under His control. He is the formless Lord, He is He. Nanak holds tight to the true Lord. He has found peace and shall never suffer pain again. ||2||9|| Maaroo, Fifth Master, Third House:

God is one. He is realized by guru's grace. He is the bestowal of peace and life, why did you forget him O ignorant? You are intoxicated with bland alcohol. You waste this precious human life. ||1|| O man, you practice such a useless deed. Forgetting God you are lost in doubt. You are in love with the slave not the master. ||1||Pause|| Forgetting the cherisher of earth you serve the lowly and spend your life in ego. O ignorant self-willed; you do useless deeds and you are called blind. ||2|| You think the true is untrue; you think the perishable is immortal. You hold on to what belongs to others; you are completely lost; ||3|| The Khshatriya, Brahmins, Soodras and Vaishyas all cross over, through the name of one Lord. Nanak speaks guru's teachings; whoever listens to it is carried across. ||4||1||10|| Maaroo, Fifth Master: You act in secrecy, but God is still with you. You can deceive other people. Forgetting God you enjoy evil deeds; you are embracing the red-hot pillars. ||1|| O man, why do you go to other's houses? You filthy, heartless, lustful donkey! Haven't you heard of the justice of destiny? ||1||Pause|| The useless stone tied around your neck and the load of slander on your head. You cannot go across the mighty world ocean. ||2|| You are engrossed in lust, anger, greed and emotional attachment. You have turned your eyes away from truth. You cannot even raise your head above water of the vast, impassable sea of worldly wealth. ||3|| The sun and the moon are liberated; the all – knowing God is a mystery. His inner nature is like that of fire, untouched and forever pure. ||4|| The veil of the fortunate is lifted of those who lovingly obey guru's will. Page 1002 Guru gave a word of medicine of God's name; servant Nanak does not have to go through pain of birth. ||5||2|| O man, this way, you shall cross over to the other side. Recite God and be humble and eradicate the affect of duality. ||Second Pause||2||11|| Maaroo, Fifth Master: I quit searching outside; the guru showed me God in me. I witnessed the carefree, amazing beautiful face and my mind does not want to go anywhere leaving him behind. ||1|| I found the jewel. I have found the perfect Lord. It is priceless, cannot be bought. The kind guru gave it to me. ||1||Pause|| The supreme Lord is imperceptible and unfathomable. Meeting the devotees, I speak the unspoken speech. The infinite divine music plays in tenth Gate. God's sacred name trickles down there. ||2|| I lack nothing; the greed is eliminated. I obtained the unending treasure. I serve the feet of the guru and manage the unmanageable. I have found the juice, the sublime essence. ||3|| Intuitively I come and go; my mind intuitively plays. Says Nanak, the guru eliminated the doubt and I realized God in me. ||4||3||12|| Maaroo, Fifth Master: You feel no love for the one who created you and looks after. When you sow the seed out of season; it does not bear flower or fruit. ||1|| O mind, this is the time to plant the seed of God's name. Focus your mind and sow the crop. It is the right time; ||1||Pause|| Eradicate the doubt of your mind and go to the sanctuary of the guru. One with a pre-ordained destiny performs this deed. ||2|| He fell in love with the Lord of the universe and his efforts are rewarded. My crop has grown and it shall never fall short; ||3|| I obtained the priceless merchandise which shall never leave me and go anywhere. Says Nanak, I found peace. I am satisfied and fulfilled. ||4||4||13|| Maaroo, Fifth Master: The egg of doubt has burst. My mind has been enlightened. The guru has shattered the shackles from my feet and set me free. ||1|| My coming and going in life ended. The boiling cauldron has cooled down; the guru blessed me with God's soothing name. ||1||Pause|| Since I joined devotee's company, those who were eyeing me have left. One, who tied me, has freed me; what can the watchman do? ||2|| The load of my deeds has been removed and I am carefree now. I crossed the world-ocean and reached the shore. The guru blessed me with faith. ||3|| True is my place and true is my seat. I have made truth my life's destiny. True is my capital and the merchandise, Nanak found it in the mind. ||4||5||14|| Maaroo, Fifth Master: Page 1003 The scholar reads the Vedas but he is slow to act on them. Another person sits silently, but his heart is tied to desire. He becomes detached, leaves home but attachment does not vanish. ||1|| Who can I tell about the state of my mind? Where can I find such a person who is liberated and liberates me? ||1||Pause|| He practices self-discipline and cures body but the mind runs around. The celibate practices celibacy, but he is filled with pride. He becomes detached and goes to pilgrimage but filled with anger. ||2|| The followers of Bhairov tie bells around their ankles to earn their living. Others go on fasts, take vows and perform the six rituals. It is all show business. Some sing melodious songs and hymns, but their minds do not sing God. ||3|| Only pure God's saints are without joy, sorrow and greed. My mind obtains the dust of their feet when God shows mercy. Says Nanak, I met the perfect guru and the anxiety of my mind is removed. ||4|| My sovereign Lord is the inner-knower. The beloved of my soul knows everything. All trivial talk is forgotten. ||1||Second Pause||6||15|| Maaroo, Fifth Master: One who has Your name in his mind is the king of millions. Those whom my guru did not bless with God's Name; the ignorant die to be reborn; ||1|| My true guru preserves my honour. When I miss You I obtain honour. When I forget You I am like dirt. ||1||Pause|| The mind's pleasures of love and beauty bring useless blames. God's name is the treasure of salvation. It brings peace and contentment. ||2|| The worldly pleasures fade away in an instant, like the shade of a cloud. They are dyed in God's deep red colour, those who say God God meeting the guru. ||3|| My Lord is lofty exalted, beyond imagination and infinite. His court is permanent. Glory and greatness obtains reciting the name of my beloved God. ||4||7||16|| Maaroo, Fifth Master, Fourth House: God is one. He is realized by guru's grace. One Creator created the creation. He made all the days and nights. The forests, meadows, three worlds and water; The four Vedas and the four sources of creation. The countries, the continents and the whole world. Everything was created with one command. ||1|| Hey – understand the Creator Lord. If you meet the true guru, then you'll understand; ||1||Pause|| He created the creation in three worldly qualities. And heaven and hell. In ego, they come and go. The mind cannot stabilize even for an instant. Page 1004 Without the guru, there is pitch dark. Meeting with the true guru, one attains salvation. ||2|| They do deeds in ego. The chains are tied around their neck? Harbouring self-conceit and self-interest Is just like placing chains around one's ankles. He meets with the guru and realizes the Lord; who has such destiny written on his forehead? ||3|| He, who is pleasing to God, realizes Him. He is deluded, who is deluded by God. No one is ignorant or wise. He recites God's name if God inspires him. You have no end or limits. Servant Nanak praises Him forever. ||4||1||17|| The enticer entices through three worldly qualities.

The false world is engrossed in greed. Crying mine, mine! they collect. In the end they are all cheated. ||1|| Lord is carefree, formless and merciful. He looks after all beings. ||1||Pause|| Some collect wealth, and bury it in the ground. Some cannot abandon wealth, even in dreams. The king exercises his power, and fills his moneybags, but this fickle companion does not go with him. ||2|| Some love wealth even more than their body and life. Some collect it even forsaking their fathers and mothers. Some hide it from their children, friends and siblings, but it does not remain with them. ||3|| Some become hermits and sit in trance. Some are Yogis, celibates, religious scholars and thinkers. Some dwell in homes, graveyards, cremation grounds and forests; it sticks to their lap. ||4|| When the Lord cuts their bonds; God's name dwells in their mind. They attain salvation in devotee's company O Nanak, they are honoured by God's grace. ||5||2||18|| Maaroo, Fifth Master: Recite one formless God. No one is turned away from Him empty-handed. He cherished and preserved you in your mother's womb. He blessed you with body and soul and embellished you. Each and every moment, recite the architect of destiny. Reciting Him all evil deeds are covered up. Enshrine God's lotus feet in your mind. Save your soul from the sins. Your cries and shrieks shall be ended. Reciting Lord of the universe, your doubts and fears shall be dispelled. Only a few realize God in devotee's company. Nanak admires them. ||1|| Lord's name is the support of my mind and body. Whoever recites Him is liberated. ||1||Pause|| He believes that the imaginary things are true. The foolish ignorant falls in love with it. He is intoxicated with the wine of lust, anger and greed. He loses this human life in exchange for a shell. He abandons his own and loves others. His mind and body are permeated with the intoxication of worldly wealth. His desires are not eliminated, he indulges in pleasures. His hopes are empty and all his words are false. He comes alone, and goes alone. Page 1005 What we talk among us is false. The Lord deluded us to forget Him. O Nanak, the deeds you do, cannot be erased. ||2|| Beasts, birds, demons and ghosts. They wander in many other lifes. Wherever they go, they cannot remain there. They have no place of their own; they have to get up and go. Their minds and bodies are filled with different smell.

The poor are robbed by ego. They suffer lot of pain and punishment. God's worth cannot be estimated. Forgetting God, they go to hell. There are no mothers, no siblings, no friends and no spouses there. Those whom God is kind; O Nanak, they cross over. ||3|| Wandering around, I came to God's refuge. He is the master of the meek, the father and mother of the world. The merciful God is the destroyer of sorrow and suffering. He emancipates whoever He pleases. He pulls some out of the deep dark pit. Emancipation comes through loving worship. He is the embodiment of devotees. He saves us from the great fire. Practice meditation, austerities, penance and self-discipline obtain no reward. In the beginning and in the end, the inaccessible and unfathomable God exists. Please bless me with Your name. Your slave begs for this. O Nanak, my Lord is the giver of life. ||4||3||19|| Maaroo, Fifth Master: Why do you deceive people O beloved God kind to the poor? ||1|| This is what I understood. The brave guru, preserves the honour of those who seek his refuge. ||1||Pause|| He listens to his devotees and bestows peace forever. ||2|| Please be kind to me that I recite Your name. ||3|| Poor Nanak begs for the gift of Your name to eliminate the doubt and duality. ||4||4||20|| Maaroo, Fifth Master: My Lord is very powerful. I am just His poor servant. ||1|| My enticing beloved is dear to my mind and life. He blesses me with His gift. ||1||Pause|| I have seen and tested all. I do not depend on anyone else. ||2|| He sustains and nurtures all beings. He was, He is and He will be. ||3|| O Lord; be kind to me. Nanak worships You. ||4||5||21|| Maaroo, Fifth Master: He is the saviour of sinners to carry them across. I admire Him forever. May I meet some saint and recite the name of God. ||1|| No one knows me. I am called Your slave. This is my support and food. ||1||Pause|| You support and cherish all. Listen to the prayer of the poor. You know Your way; You are water, I am the fish. ||2|| O all pervading Lord I follow You around. O God, You are pervading all the worlds, solar systems and galaxies. ||3|| Page 1006 You are eternal and unchanging, imperishable, invisible and infinite, O fascinating Lord. May I receive a gift of the dust of the feet of saint's in their company? ||4||6||22|| Maaroo, Fifth Master: The saints are fulfilled and satisfied. Those who know guru's word of teachings. They cannot even be described. They are blessed with the greatness of God's name. ||1|| My beloved is a priceless jewel. He is called the unattainable and immeasurable. ||1||Pause|| My mind accepts the unexplainable God. The guru-willed realizes the reality of divine wisdom. He sees all and looks after all. He abandons self-pride. ||2|| Permanent is the place of those; who realize the destiny through the guru? Meeting the guru, they remain awake night and day. They are committed to Lord's service. ||3|| They are perfectly fulfilled and satisfied. Intuitively they get in trance. Lord's treasure comes into their hands. O Nanak, through the guru, they attain it. ||4||7||23|| Maaroo, Fifth Master, Sixth House, Du-Padas: God is one. He is realized by guru's grace. Abandon clever ideas and eliminate self-pride meeting the devotees. Everything else is imaginary. Recite God God with your tongue. ||1|| O my mind, with your ears; listen to the name of God. The sins of your many lifetimes shall be erased. Forget about the poor devil of death? ||1||Pause|| Pain, poverty and fear shall not afflict you, you find peace and contentment. By guru's grace, Nanak speaks the essence of knowledge and God's worship. ||2||1||24|| Maaroo, Fifth Master: Those who forgot God's name; I saw them turned to dust. The love of children friends and spouse ends. ||1|| O my mind, recite God's name all the time. You shall not burn in the ocean of fire and attain peace of mind and body. ||1||Pause|| Like the shade of a tree, blowing wind and clouds all vanish. O Nanak, recite God in devotee's company. It will help you. ||2||2||25|| Maaroo, Fifth Master: The perfect, primal Lord giver of peace is always with you. He does not die, does not come or go, does not perish, not affected by heat or cold. ||1|| O my mind; fall in love with God's name. Miss the treasure of God's name in your mind; this is the right way. ||1||Pause|| Whoever recites the merciful compassionate Lord of the universe, finds the way. He is always new, fresh and young, clever and beautiful. O Nanak, pierce your mind with his love. ||2||3||26|| Maaroo, Fifth Master: While walking sitting sleeping and awake; recite guru's word in your mind. Recite God humbly in devotee's company and go across the world ocean. ||1|| Page 1007 O my mind, enshrine God's name in your heart. Love the Lord in your mind and body whole-heartedly and forget everything else. ||1||Pause|| Soul, mind, body and life, belong to God.

Eliminate your self-conceit. All deeds are fulfilled reciting God O Nanak, you will never lose. ||2||4||27|| Maaroo, Fifth Master: Renounce your ego, and the fever shall depart; become the dust of the feet of devotees. Whoever You bless with Your kindness obtains Your name. ||1|| O my mind; drink the nectar of God's name. Abandon other bland tastes. Become immortal and live forever. ||1||Pause|| Savor the essence of God's name and fall in love with God's name. Nanak has made God his only friend, companion and relative. ||2||5||28|| Maaroo, Fifth Master: He nourishes and preserves mortals in the womb of the mother. The heat does not hurt him. Same Lord protects you in the world; think and realize this in your mind. ||1|| O my mind; take the support of God's name. Understand the one who created you. God is the cause of causes. ||1||Pause|| Remember God in the mind; give up smart ideas and disguises. O Nanak, recite God all the time; many have gone across doing so. ||2||6||29|| Maaroo, Fifth Master: His name is the purifier of sinners. He is the master of orphans. In the vast terrifying world-ocean, he is the raft for those with pre-ordained destiny. ||1|| Many gatherings have drowned without God's name. They do not miss God, the cause of causes and who supports them. ||1||Pause|| Praise God's name in devotee's company; that is the sacred path. Be kind O Lord of the world; Nanak lives by listening to Your sermon; ||2||7||30|| Maaroo, Anjulee ~ With Hands Cupped In Prayer, Fifth Master, Seventh House: God is one. He is realized by guru's grace. Union and separation are pre-ordained from destiny. The puppet is made from the five elements. By pre-ordained command of the Lord, the soul enters the body. ||1|| There the fire rages like an oven. In that darkness, where the body lies face down. He recites God with every breath and God saves him there. ||2|| Then, one comes out of the womb. He forgets God and attaches his mind to the world. He comes and goes, wanders in life. He cannot stay anywhere. ||3|| The merciful Lord saves him. He created and established all beings. Those who worship God in the priceless human life O Nanak, their coming into the world is approved. ||4||1||31||Page 1008 Only God helps where there is no doctor friend brother or sister. ||1|| He does everything, washes the filth of sins; recite that supreme Lord. ||2|| He abides in each and every heart, dwells in all; His seat is eternal. ||3|| He does not come or go, He is always with us. His actions are perfect. ||4|| He is the protector of His devotees. The saints live by reciting God the support of life. The almighty Lord is the cause of causes. Nanak praises Him. ||5||2||32|| God is one. He is realized by guru's grace. Maaroo, Ninth Master: God's name bestows happiness forever. Reciting Him, Ajaamal and a prostitute attained salvation. ||1||Pause|| Dropadi the princess of Panchaal remembered God's name in the royal court. The Lord, the embodiment of mercy, removed her suffering. Thus His own glory was increased. ||1|| Whoever sings praises of the kind God; God comes to help them. Says Nanak; believing that I have come to the refuge of the Lord. ||2||1|| Maaroo, Ninth Master: What should I do now, O mother? I wasted my life in sin and corruption. I never recited God. ||1||Pause|| When the devil of death puts the chain around the neck. I lose my senses. In this disaster, other than God's name; who else will help me? ||1|| That wealth, which he believes is his, in a moment it became some else's. Says Nanak, I kept thinking this in my mind and never praised God in the mind. ||2||2|| Maaroo, Ninth Master: O mother, I have not renounced the pride of my mind. I wasted my life intoxicated with worldly wealth. I did not worship God. ||1||Pause|| When devil of death hits on the head, then the sleeping mind wakes up. What can you do now; you cannot be freed or run away? ||1|| When this anxiety rose in the heart, then one loves guru's feet. Life becomes fruitful, O Nanak, when I am absorbed in God's praises. ||2||3|| Maaroo, Ashtapadees, First Master, First House: God is one. He is realized by guru's grace. Reciting and listening to scriptures, countless wise men have grown weary. They wandered at sixty-eight shrines, got tired of making imaginary faces. Enshrining and worshipping in the mind realize the pure true Lord. ||1|| You are eternal; You are immortal. All others pass away. Recite God's name with love; will eliminate all sufferings. ||1||Pause|| Page 1009 Study God and understand God. God's name saves through guru's teachings. Perfect guru teaches perfect lesson; contemplate through his teachings. God's name is as good as bathing at sixty-eight shrines and eliminates sins. ||2|| The ignorant churns water and gets water, but the blind wants butter. Through guru's teachings churn milk and get butter the God's name. The self-willed does not know the reality. He is like an animal. ||3|| Dyed in ego and possessiveness, one dies to be born again and again. One who dies through guru's teachings; does not die again. When the life of the world enshrines in the mind through guru's teachings; his dynasty is saved. ||4|| God's name is the true priceless merchandise; its trade is also true. Take advantage of God's name in the world through guru's teachings. To work in love of duality, brings loss in the world. ||5|| True is one's association, one's place, and one's home. When one has the support of God's name, his food and faith become true as well. One attains contentment through guru's teachings and true sermon. ||6|| Enjoying princely pleasures, one shall suffer in pain and pleasure. Being called great, one strings heavy sins around his neck. Man cannot give gifts. You alone are the giver of everything. ||7|| You are inaccessible and unfathomable; O Lord, You are immortal and infinite. Through guru's teachings one seeks God's door the treasure of salvation. O Nanak, this union is not broken when trading with true Lord. ||8||1|| Maaroo, First Master: The boat is loaded with sin and corruption and launched into the sea. The shore cannot be found on this side or the other side. There are no oars, no boatmen, to cross over the terrifying world-ocean. ||1|| O elder, the world is caught in the great net. Reciting the true name one is saved by guru's grace. ||1||Pause|| The guru is the boat and his teaching carries across. There is neither wind nor fire, neither water nor the atmosphere. God dwells there; reciting His name takes across the terrifying world ocean. ||2|| The guru-willed cross over and attain salvation attuning to God with love. Their coming and going ends, and their light merges in supreme Light. Contentment originates from guru's teachings and merges with God. ||3|| The snake may be locked in a basket, but it is still poisonous and angry in the mind. One obtains what he earns and is pre-ordained. Why does he blame others? If the guru-willed hears and believes in saying God's name, he finds peace. ||4|| The crocodile is caught by the hook and net. Caught in the net due to evil-deeds, he regrets and repents, again and again. He does not understand birth and death. The inscription of one's past actions cannot be erased. ||5|| Page 1010 Injecting the poison of ego the world was created. The poison eliminates enshrining guru's teachings in the mind. Old age cannot bother one who remains lovingly absorbed in the true Lord. He, who eliminates ego, is liberated from life. ||6|| The world is after the worldly affairs; they do not think or understand at all. The foolish, ignorant, self-willed has forgotten birth and death. Those protected by the guru are saved through guru's teachings. ||7|| Like a parrot dyed by love, keeps saying God God. It pecks at the truth and drinks the nectar. It flies once for all. Meeting the guru one finds his Lord. Says Nanak, he attains liberation. ||8||2|| Maaroo, First Master: One who dies by guru's teachings; where can he run and go? Who we are afraid of and run away from; his name is sacred. You kill and protect; other than You, there is no place at all. ||1|| O elder, I am filthy, shallow and totally without understanding. Without God's name one is nothing. The perfect guru teaches perfect lesson. ||1||Pause|| I am full of faults, with no virtue. Without virtues, how can I go home? Through guru's teachings peace wells up, the unlucky do not get this wealth. Those who do not enshrine God's name in the mind are tied and suffer. ||2|| Those who forgot God's name; why did they come in the world? Here and hereafter, they do not find peace. Their carts are loaded with ashes. The separated, do not reunite with God; they suffer pain at death's door. ||3|| I do not know what is ahead; I am confused. Please teach me O God! I am lost; I will fall at the feet of the one who shows me the way. Without the guru, there is no bestowal. His value cannot be described. ||4|| If I see my friend, I will embrace Him. I truly sent Him a letter. The guru-willed soul-bride stands at the door of liberation. I see with my eyes. You live in the mind if it pleases You by Your grace. ||5|| One who is hungry and thirsty – what can anyone ask and get from him? I cannot think of anyone else; who can bestow complete mind and body. One who created me takes care. He blesses me with honour. ||6|| The controller of the body is ever new. His child like play is beautiful. He is not a woman, or a man, or a bird. The true Lord is wise and beautiful. Whatever pleases You happens. You are the lamp and the incense. ||7|| He hears the songs and tastes the flavours, but these flavours are useless and bring sickness to the body. One who loves truth and speaks the truth, escapes from the pain of separation.

O Nanak, do not forget God's name; whatever happens let it be. ||8||3|| Maaroo, First Master: Practice truth – other greed and attachments are useless. True Lord has enticed my mind; my tongue enjoys the taste of truth. Without God's name, there is no taste. Others depart loaded with poison. ||1|| I am such a slave of Yours, O my beloved master; I walk as You order O my true beloved. ||1||Pause|| Night and day, the slave works for the Lord of lords. I sold my mind through guru's word. My mind is content through guru's teachings. Page 1011 I praise the perfect guru who erases the pain of my mind. ||2|| I am the servant and slave of my Lord; what greatness of His can I say? The master forgives by His grace if you do truthful deeds. I praise the guru who unites the separated. ||3|| The slave servant became intelligent through guru's pure teachings. The truthful thinking looks beautiful. Thinking of the self-willed is bland. My mind and body belong to You O God; truth is my resolve from destiny. ||4|| In truth I sit and stand; I eat and speak the truth. My mind is truthful, my wages are truth and I enjoy the taste of truth. The true Lord keeps the truthful in His home through guru's teachings. ||5|| The self-willed is very lazy; he is trapped in the wilderness. He is trapped and pecks on the bait; he is ruined by doing so. By guru's grace, one is liberated worshipping God in trance. ||6|| His slave is pierced by the love of the Lord. Without the true Lord, the soul of the false, corrupt burns to ashes. Abandoning all evil actions he crosses over swimming in truth. ||7|| Those who forget God's name have no home, no place to rest. Lord's slave renounces greed and obtains Lord's name. If You bless him, then You unite him with You; Nanak admires You. ||8||4|| Maaroo, First Master: Lord's slave renounces his ego through guru's love intuitively. The slave realizes his master; that is his greatness! Meeting with Lord he finds peace. His value cannot be described. ||1|| I am the slave and servant of my Lord; all glory is His. By guru's grace, I am saved in the sanctuary of the Lord. ||1||Pause|| The slave has been given the task, by the Lord from destiny. The slave realizes God's command and lives by God's will. The Lord of the lords, grants his grace. His greatness is great. ||2|| He is true, everything is true. He is revealed through guru's teachings. Whom You cause; serves you. Without serving no one finds Him. In duality and doubt, they are ruined. ||3|| Why do you forget him who gives you more and more every day? Soul and body, all belong to Him. He infused the breath in us. We serve Him by His grace and merge with Him. ||4|| He is the real slave who dies while alive and eliminates ego. His bonds are broken, the fire of desire extinguished and he is liberated. The treasure of God's name dwells in all. Only a few guru-willed realize it. ||5|| The slave has no virtues; he is virtueless. There is no giver as great as You; You are the bestowal. Your slave obeys Your order; that is the essence. ||6|| The guru is the ocean of nectar; whatever one desires gets it. By enshrining immortal God's priceless name in the mind. Page 1012 Those whom God inspires; obtain eternal peace serving the guru; ||7|| Gold and silver are elements; it will merge with dirt. Without God's name nothing goes with you; the guru teaches this. O Nanak, those imbued with God's name are pure and merge with God. ||8||5|| Maaroo, First Master: Order is issued, he cannot stay here. He ran out of luck. This mind is tied to ill deeds. It suffers terrible pain in the body. The perfect guru forgives all the mistakes of the beggar at His door. ||1|| How can he stay here? He must get up and depart. Contemplate guru's teachings and understand this. Whom You unite through Your infinite command, unites with You. ||1||Pause|| As You keep me, so I remain; whatever You give I eat. As You lead me, I follow and recite Your sacred name from my mouth. All glories rest with my Lord. My mind yearns to unite with Him. ||2|| Why should anyone praise the deeds of others. God does it and checks it? The one who created me abides in my mind; there is no other. So praise that true Lord and you shall be honoured. ||3|| The scholar, reads, but does not reach the Lord. He is totally entangled in worldly affairs. He follows both virtue and vice, the devil of death is hungry for him. He, who is protected by the perfect Lord forgets the fear of separation. ||4|| Those who are honoured in God's court are perfect O brother. Pure is the intellect of the pure Lord. True is His greatness His gifts never run short. Those who receive it get tired of receiving. ||5|| Searching the salty sea, one finds the pearl. It looks beautiful for a few days; then the dirt eats it. If one serves the guru the ocean of truth, his gifts never run short. ||6|| Those who please my God are pure; others filled with filth. The filthy becomes pure, when it touches philosopher's stone. Who can estimate the value and colour of the true jewel? ||7|| It cannot be found by imitation or going to pilgrimage or giving awns. Ask those who read scriptures. Without faith, the world is robbed. O Nanak, he who learns wisdom from the guru knows the value. ||8||6|| Maaroo, Fifth Master: The self-willed abandons his home in greed and is ruined; then he spies on the homes of others. Without surrendering to the guru, he loses home and faith and falls prey to the whirlpool of evil deeds. He wanders all over and tired of reading scriptures, but his greed increases. His perishable body does not search guru's teachings. He fills his belly like an animal. ||1|| O elder, this is the life of the detached from the world. Those attuned to God through guru's teachings dyed by God's name are content. ||1||Pause|| He dyes his clothes with saffron dye; he wears and goes begging like a beggar. Tearing his robes, he makes a patched coat, and makes the begging bag of worldly wealth. He begs house to house and preaches the world. He is spiritually blind and loses his honour. He is deluded by doubt. He does not contemplate guru's teachings and loses his life in a gamble. ||2|| Page 1013 The inner fire does no extinguish without the guru; the fire still burns outside. Without serving the guru, worship is not possible. How can one search his soul any other way. Slandering others, one goes to hell. God abides inside. He goes on pilgrimage to sixty-eight shrines. He is ruined by doubt. How can he wash the filth of sins? ||3|| He sifts the ashes and applies to the body; but the worldly wealth robs him. He does not see God inside or out. If I say the truth, he gets angry. He reads the scriptures, but tells lies; that is the thinking of a guru less. How can he find peace without reciting God; how will he look good without God's name? ||4|| Some shave their heads; some keep their hair braided, while some keep silent, but all filled with egotistic pride. Their minds waver and wander in ten directions without being dyed with divine wisdom. Intoxicated by worldly wealth. He drinks poison instead of nectar. Past actions do not leave; without obeying God's command, he is like an animal. ||5|| With bowl in hand, wearing his patched coat, great desires well up in his mind. Abandoning his wife, he is troubled by sex and puts his mind to other's wives. He preaches, but does not follow guru's teachings. He is lost in useless deeds. Filled with poison, he is quiet outside. The devil of death will humiliate him. ||6|| He, who serves the guru is a renounce and eliminates ego. He does not ask for clothes or food; whatever he gets accepts it happily. He does not speak empty words; he gathers the wealth of tolerance, and burns away his anger with God's name. He is a blessed householder, a renounce and a Yogi, who focuses his mind on Lord's feet. ||7|| Amidst hope, the renounce remains unmoved by hope; he remains lovingly focused on one Lord. He drinks the sublime essence of the Lord and finds peace and remains absorbed in trance. His mind does not waver; the guru-willed understands. He restrains his mind from wandering. He searches his body through guru's teachings and obtains the treasure of God's name. ||8|| Brahma, Vishnu and Shiva are sacred, imbued with and reciting God's name. The sources of creation, speech, the heavens and the underworld, all beings are infused with Your light. Enshrining in the mind and singing God's name with love attains eternal peace and salvation. Without God's name no one is saved O Nanak, swim across the world ocean through truth. ||9||7|| Maaroo, First Master: Through the union of mother and father, the fetus is formed. The egg and sperm join together to make the body. Inside the womb, he worships God with love and God bestows the gift. ||1|| How can he cross over the terrifying world-ocean? The guru-willed obtains the name of formless God and the unbearable load of sins is removed. ||1||Pause|| I have forgotten Your virtues. I am insane and a sinner – what can I do now? You are the kind giver to all. You give gifts and take care of all. ||2|| One is born with four treasures of life. But he lives in worldly wealth. Page 1014 He is hungry for worldly wealth and robbed of the treasure of liberation. ||3|| He does not look hard. He looks here and there then gets tired. Bothered by lust, anger and ego, he falls in love with false relations. ||4|| He eats and enjoys, listens and watches, and dresses up to show off in this house of death. Without guru's teachings, he cannot recognize him. Death does not spare without God's name. ||5|| The more attachment and ego delude and confuse him, the more he cries, mine, mine; and more he loses. His body and wealth are lost and he is torn by worry and doubt. In the end, he regrets when the dust falls in his mouth. ||6|| He grows old, his body and youth waste away and his throat is plugged with mucous. Water flows from his eyes. His feet fail him, his hands shake; the faithless does not enshrine God in his heart. ||7|| His intellect fails him, hair turns white, and no one wants to keep him at home. Forgetting God's name gives such pains and the devil of death kills him and takes to hell. ||8|| The record of previous life does not erase; who do you blame for your birth and death? Without the guru, birth and death is useless. Without guru's teachings one will keep taking birth and death. The pleasures enjoyed in happiness bring pain. Acting in corruption is useless. Forgetting God's name, one loses the origin in greed. The stick of the justice of destiny strikes over the head. ||10|| The guru-willed whom God blesses, sings God's praises. Those beings are pure, perfect and infinite. In this world, they are the embodiment of the guru, the Lord of the universe. ||11|| Recite God through guru's teachings O God – willed; enjoy devotee's company. God's servant is in charge at guru's abode. Nanak begs for the dust of his feet. ||12||8|| God is one. He is realized by guru's grace. Maaroo, Kaafee, First Master, Second House: Come on O double minded; who are you friends with? The soul-bride separated from her Lord; how can she feel comfortable? ||1|| My mind is imbued to the love of my Husband Lord. I am devoted and praise You. Be kind for a moment! ||1||Pause|| I am a rejected bride in my parents' home; how can I go to my in-laws? I am full of faults; I will die worrying without my beloved Lord. ||2|| If I care for my beloved in parents home; I will live happily with my in-laws. The happy soul-brides sleep in peace. They found the virtuous Husband Lord. ||3|| Their blankets and mattresses are made of silk, so are the clothes they wear. The impure soul-brides rejected by the Lord; spend their lives in pain. ||4|| Page 1015 I have tasted many flavours and made many disguises. Without my Husband Lord, my youth is slipping away uselessly. I am separated from Him and cry in pain. ||5|| I have heard the true Lord's message through guru's teachings. Truthful sit in true company lovingly by God's grace. ||6|| The divine person wears the eye lashes of truth and the Lord sees it. The guru-willed realize God eliminating ego and pride. ||7|| Those who please You are like You.

There are many like me also. O Nanak, those imbued with true Lord's love do not separate. ||8||1||9|| Maaroo, First Master: Neither the sisters, nor the sisters-in-law, nor the mother-in-law, shall remain. The true relation does not break when the guru unites with the beloved. ||1|| I praise my guru forever. I wandered all over without the guru. The guru united me with my beloved Lord. ||1||Pause|| Aunts, uncles, grandparents and sisters-in-law. They come and go. No one stays forever; all go like boat loads. ||2|| Uncles, aunts, brothers, mother or father, do not remain. Friend who used to sit and enjoy ran away when the trouble arose. ||3|| O sister-friends, my Husband Lord is dyed in the colour of truth. One who is truly dyed with love; never separates. ||4|| All seasons are good, when you are in love with the true Lord. That soul-bride, who knows her Husband Lord, sleeps in peace forever. ||5|| At the dock the ferryman announces, "O travelers, hurry and cross over." I have seen them crossing over on the boat of the true guru. ||6|| Some are getting on board and some are already there; some are weighed down with their loads. Those who deal in truth, remain with their true Lord. ||7|| I am not good; I see no one bad. O Nanak, he who eliminates ego becomes like the true Lord. ||8||2||10|| Maaroo, First Master: I do not know if anyone is stupid or intelligent. Imbued with God's love, I recite God's name forever. ||1|| O elder, I am a ignorant but I praise God's name. You are the Creator wise and all-knowing. I will go across reciting Your name. ||1||Pause|| Ignorant and wise are same; they have the same soul but two different names. Those who do not believe in God's name are the real ignorant. ||2|| God's name is talked about at guru's refuge but it does not sink in without the guru. It enshrines in the mind by guru's grace; then devotees enjoy forever. ||3|| Power, pleasure, beauty, wealth, youth and the gamblers. They play under God's command. The play is same all the time. ||4|| The wise and clever world is deluded by doubt; they read scriptures and called scholars. They recite scriptures not God's name. They are lost. Those who call them scholars are also lost. ||5|| Page 1016 He is like the crop in baron land, tree on the river bank, or the white clothes sprinkled with dirt. This world is the house of desire; whoever enters is burnt by self – pride. ||6|| Where are the kings and their subjects?

Those deluded by doubt perished? Says Nanak, the ladder of the guru will take to divinity forever. ||7||3||11|| Maaroo, Third Master, Fifth House, eight stanzas: God is one. He is realized by guru's grace. One, who enshrines love in the mind through guru's teachings intuitively; He only knows the pain. What does anyone else know about the cure? ||1|| He unites in His Union. He inspires us with His love. Whoever You bless; he only knows the essence of love. ||1||Pause|| Far sightedness wells up and doubt disappears. By guru's grace, he obtains the supreme status. He who contemplates guru's teachings and finds the way is a Yogi. ||2|| By good destiny, the soul-bride is united with her Husband Lord. Following guru's teachings, she eradicates her evil-will. She is the beloved of her husband Lord and enjoys with him forever. ||3|| Other than the guru, there is no other doctor. He is the formless God. Meeting with the guru, evil is conquered, and divine wisdom wells up. ||4|| Whoever God inspires to the reality through guru's teachings. The guru-willed eliminates the greed of hunger. Nothing happens by own effort; all happens by God's grace. ||5|| The true guru has revealed the essence of scriptures. By his grace, he came to his home. Whoever You bless realizes God in the midst of worldly wealth; ||6|| The guru-willed realizes the reality. He eradicates ego. Without the guru, everything you do is useless; check it out? ||7|| Some are deluded by doubt. They are filled with ego. Some guru-willed eliminate ego. Attuned to God's love through guru's teachings one become detached. Others ignorant are deluded by doubt. ||8|| The individuals who do not obtain God's name; are self-willed wasting away their life. No one is your friend in the next world; realize it through guru's teachings. ||9|| God's sacred name is the bestowal of happiness. He is realized through guru's teachings in all four ages. Whoever You give receives it; Nanak says by contemplating the truth. ||10||1|| Page 1017 Maaroo, Fifth Master, Third House, Ashtapadees: God is one. He is realized by guru's grace. Wandering through many different lives, I took birth as a human now. ||1|| O ignorant, you are enticed by the bland taste. The nectar abides with you, but you are entangled in ill deeds. ||1||Pause|| You come to trade in gems and jewels but you have loaded the salty soil. ||2|| The home where you have to live; you do not remember that house. ||3|| You do not sing praises of Him, who is immovable, indestructible, the giver of peace. ||4|| You forgot the place where you have to go; never thought of it even for a moment. ||5|| Seeing children, spouse and household, you are entangled in them. ||6|| As God guides so are they linked and so are the deeds they do. ||7|| When He becomes kind then one joins the company of devotees O Nanak, then he recites God. ||8||1|| Maaroo, Fifth Master: By His grace He protects me in devotee's company. My tongue says God's name with sweet deep love. ||1|| He is the place of rest for my mind. He the inner-knower is my beloved, friend, companion and relative. ||1||Pause|| He created the world-ocean. I seek the sanctuary of that God. By guru's grace, I worship God; the devil of death does not say anything. ||2|| Salvation obtains at His door. He is the treasure in the hearts of the saints. The all-knowing God shows the true way of life. He is our saviour forever. ||3|| Pain, suffering and troubles are eradicated, when the Lord abides in the mind. Death, hell and the horrible place of sins and pain do not bother him. ||4|| Wealth, mysticism and priceless treasures are His. He bestows the nectar. He is from the beginning, middle and end. He is sacred permanent and unfathomable. ||5|| The mystics, seekers, gods, sages and the Vedas speak of Him. Reciting the Lord obtains happiness and contentment. He is endless. ||6|| Reciting God lovingly in the mind eliminates all sins in a moment. Reciting Him makes one purest of the pure and is blessed with the merits of millions of donations and cleansing baths. ||7|| God is power, intellect, life, wealth, and everything for the saints. May I never forget Him from my mind, this is Nanak's prayer. ||8||2|| Maaroo, Fifth Master: The sharp tool cuts down the tree, but it does not feel anger in the mind. It serves the purpose of the cutter and does not blame him at all. ||1|| O my mind, recite God continuously. The saints listen to the name of kind Lord of the universe intuitively. ||1||Pause|| Page 1018 He puts the witness down and sits. He does not have strength anymore. The great ocean does not bother him; he went across instantly. ||2|| He does not love sandalwood, fragrance, and camphor-paste etc. He digs out filth bit by bit. He does not like the bad deeds. ||3|| High and low, bad and good and all other comforts available to him. He does not differentiate between friend and foe; all are same to him. ||4|| He is enlightened with beaming light and the darkness eliminated. He became sacred touched by sacred ray. He does not hate anyone. ||5|| The cool and fragrant wind gently blows at all places alike. He touches everywhere. He does not have any doubt or pride. ||6|| Good or bad, whoever comes close to fire; his cold is eliminated. He does not differentiate between him and others intuitively forever. ||7|| His mind is imbued with the love of the lotus feet of the Lord. O Nanak, sing praises of the kind and merciful God forever. ||8||3|| Maaroo, Fifth Master, Fourth House, Ashtapadees: God is one. He is realized by guru's grace. Moonlight lights up the yard. God's name enlightens the inside. ||1|| Recite God's name; reciting God is sacred. ||2|| Renounce lust, anger and greed. Renouncing them is good. ||3|| Beg for God's praises from the guru. Begging God's praises is sacred. ||4|| Stay awake singing God's praises. Singing God's praises is sacred. ||5|| Touch, guru's feet. Touching guru's feet attaches the mind to guru's feet. ||6|| Those with good luck obtain the above mentioned. ||7|| Says Nanak, he who obtains God's refuge; everything is good for him. ||8||1||4|| Maaroo, Fifth Master: Please come to my home and speak God's praises. ||1||Pause|| Your coming rejuvenates my mind and body. I sing God's praises with you. ||1|| By saint's grace, God abides in my mind and eliminates the love of duality. ||2|| By devotee's kindness the intellect is enlightened and pain and evil-mindedness are eradicated. ||3|| Seeing them, makes sacred and getting in the womb for birth eliminates. ||4|| By Your grace I obtain priceless treasures, wealth and mystic power. ||5|| I have no other place but the saints. I do not feel like going anywhere else. ||6|| I am unworthy; no one gives me refuge. But I am merged with the saints||7||. Says Nanak, the guru showed me the way reciting God in the mind. ||8||2||5|| Page 1019 Maaroo, Fifth Master: Fruitful is the life of one who hears and recites God's name. ||1||Pause| Drink that which satisfies the mind; that is God's sacred name. ||1|| Eat that which eliminates hunger, makes content and fulfills. ||2|| Wear Godly clothes which protect honour and never be naked again. ||3|| Enjoy God's love in your mind in devotee's company lovingly. ||4|| Sew your mind without thread and needle but with God's worship. ||5|| Imbued and intoxicated with God's love never suffers pain. ||6|| One is blessed with all treasures, when God blesses him. ||7|| O Nanak, serving the saints brings peace. I wash saint's feet and drink the water. ||8||3||6|| Maaroo, Fifth Master, Eighth House, Anjulees ~ With Hands Cupped In Prayer: God is one. He is realized by guru's grace. He, who has lot of wealth, has lot of worry. He, who has less, wanders for more. He, who is free of both; is content; ||1|| Householders, kings, renounce and angry; all go to hell. Those who study and recite the Vedas in so many ways; but one, who is merged within himself; his efforts are fulfilling. ||2|| He sleeps even when he is awake; he is robbed by doubt. Without the guru, liberation is not obtained O friend. In devotee's company the bonds and ego depart and one becomes content reciting God. ||3|| Doing deeds, one is tied in bonds; but if he does not, he is slandered. Intoxicated with emotional attachment, the mind is afflicted with anxiety. One who sees pleasure and pain alike by guru's grace; sees God in all. ||4|| The world is bothered by doubt. He does not know the imperceptible unspoken speech of the Lord. Whom He guides, understands it; He looks after him like a child. ||5|| He may try to abandon but cannot; If he collects then he is worried in the mind. Among all this if God bestows honour; devotees wave fan over his head. ||6|| Only the brave can die. One who runs away will wander in different lifes. Whatever happens, accept it good. Obeying God's command burns ill will. ||7|| Whatever He makes us, that we do. He creates and watches over His creation. O Nanak's perfect bestowal of happiness; I recite Your name by your grace. ||8||1||7|| Maaroo, Fifth Master: Under the tree, all beings have gathered. Some are hot-headed and some speak sweet. Like the sun rise and sunset, they get up and go as the life passes away. ||1|| Those who committed sins are sure to be ruined. The devil of death catches and tortures them. Page 1020 The Creator sends them to hell and the shopkeeper wants the account paid. ||2|| No brothers or sisters can go with them. Leaving behind their property, youth and wealth, they go; They do not know the kind and compassionate Lord; they shall be crushed like sesame seeds in the oil-press. ||3|| You happily, cheerfully steal the possessions of others. God is with you, watching and listening to everything. Driven by worldly greed he falls in the pit and cannot know the future. ||4|| He is born to die; dies and reborn again. He suffers heavy punishment in faraway land. The blind does not realize the Creator and suffers pain. ||5|| Forgetting the Lord, he is ruined. The worldly play is bad; it brings sadness and happiness. He does not meet the saint, does not have faith or contentment; he wanders on his own. ||6|| The Lord plays the play. He pulls some out and throws some into the waves. We dance to His tune; everyone gets what he sows. ||7|| When God blesses, we recite His name. In the society of saints, one does not go to hell. Please bless Nanak with the gift of sacred name; that he always sings the songs of Your glory. ||8||2||8||12||20|| Maaroo, Sohlays, First Master: God is one. He is realized by guru's grace. It is true that there is God; there is no other. He, who creates, shall destroy in the end. Keep me as You please; what can I say? ||1|| You create and destroy. You put them to their work. You make us worthy by your will and put us on the right path. ||2|| You are all-wise and all-knowing. You faithfully created the creation. You are air, water and fire; You unite in Your union. ||3|| You are the moon, the sun, the perfect of the perfect. You are divine, You meditate, and You are the brave guru. The net of death cannot catch those who are lovingly attuned to true Lord. ||4|| You are the male and female. You are the chess-game and the player. You staged the play of worldly arena and You evaluate the players. ||5|| You are the bumblebee, the flower, the fruit and the tree. You are water, the desert, the ocean and the pool. You are the big fish, the tortoise, the cause of causes. Your form cannot be known. ||6|| You are the day and the night. You are pleased by guru's discourse. You are from the beginning for a long time beyond limits and forever. You are realized in the mind through guru's teachings. ||7|| You are the beautiful priceless jewel. You are the assessor and the perfect weighing person. Page 1021 You test and bless some. You give and take, O brother; ||8|| He is the bow He is the archer. He is all-wise beautiful and all-knowing. He is the speaker, the orator and the listener. He made everything. ||9|| Using air as a culture the life has been created by the reaction of water and earth. As the day and night begin and end, same way everyone in the world takes birth and dies. ||10|| You are the fish and the net. You are the cows and You are the keeper. Your

Light burns in all beings of the world according to God's order. ||11|| You are the Yogi and You are the enjoyer. You are the enjoyer; You are the supreme unitor. You are speechless, formless and fearless, absorbed in trance; ||12|| The sources of creation and speech are contained in You O Lord. All that is seen; keeps coming and going. They are true bankers and traders, who realize God through the guru. ||13|| The perfect guru teaches through his teachings. The true Lord is filled with all powers. You are fulfilled and carefree forever. You do not have any greed. ||14|| Birth and death are meaningless, for those, Who enjoy the contentment through guru's teachings? He is bestowal of liberation, satisfaction and blessings to the devotees who love Him in their minds. ||15|| He is unique; He is realized through guru's divine wisdom. Whatever is seen shall merge in You. Poor Nanak begs for awns at your door. Bless him with Your name; ||16||1|| Maaroo, First Master: He is the earth and the sky and their support. He reveals His virtues on His own. He is celibate, truthful and content. He is the doer of deeds. ||1|| He, who created the creation, creates and tests the quality and looks after. No one can erase the writing of the true Lord. He is the doer, the cause of causes. He bestows honour as well. ||2|| The five thieves cause the fickle mind to waver. It robs other's homes, but does not search own. The body crumbles into dust; he loses honour without guru's teaching. ||3|| Learning from the guru, realizes the universe. He eliminates his desires and struggles with his mind. Those who serve You, become like You. The carefree God looks after them like his children. ||4|| You are in the heaven and the fish in the deep underworld. You are the embodiment of light and forever young. With matted hair, horrible or dreadful form. You have no form or feature. ||5|| The Vedas and the western scriptures do not know the mystery of God. He has no mother, father, child or brother. You create and destroy the mountains; Your virtues cannot be explained. ||6|| I have grown weary of making friends. No one can eliminate my sins. God is the Lord of angels, mortals, yogis and all. Lovingly attuning to Him eliminates the fear. ||7|| He puts them back on the path who have wandered stray. You misguide and guide them again. I see nothing without God's name; I obtain salvation through God's name. ||8||

Page 1022 You are said to be living at Ganges, the Jamunaa, Kaydar Naat'h, Banaras, Kanchivaram, Puri, Dwaarkaa; The Ganges empties into the ocean. Trivaynee where the three rivers meet and the sixty-eight sacred shrines; are all merged in the Lord. ||9|| He is the mystic the seeker contemplates everything. He is the king and the council. God sits on the throne and delivers justice. He eliminates doubt, duality and fear. ||10|| He is the Qazi; He is the Mullah. He is infallible; He never makes mistakes. He is the bestowal of kindness and honour. He is no one's enemy. ||11|| Whoever He blesses, bestows honour. He is the giver of all. He does not have any greed. He is pure and hidden yet abides everywhere. ||12|| How can I praise the inaccessible, infinite Lord? The true Creator Lord is the enemy of ego. He unites those whom He blesses and unites them in His union. ||13|| Brahma, Vishnu and Shiva stand at His door. They stand and serve the unseen, infinite Lord. Millions of others are seen crying there. I cannot count them. ||14|| His sermon and praises are true. I can see no other in the Vedas and the Puraanas. Truth is my capital. I sing His praises. I have no other place to go. ||15|| God exists from beginning, from ages, now and will be. Who has not died? Who shall not die? Poor Nanak offers this prayer; see Him in your mind focusing lovingly. ||16||2|| Maaroo, First Master: In duality and evil-mindedness, the soul-bride is blind and deaf. She wears the false dress of lust and anger. She does not know that her Husband Lord is inside; but she cannot sleep without him. ||1|| The flames of fire burn inside. The self-willed looks around in four directions. Without serving the guru, happiness does not well up; honour is Lord's hand. ||2|| She eradicates lust, anger and ego. She destroys the five thieves through guru's teachings. She fights with her mind with a sword of divine wisdom and controls the desires of mind. ||3|| From the union of the mother's egg and the father's sperm. The face and beauty has been created by the grace of infinite Lord. All beings are Your blessing O Lord; You are omnipresent. ||4|| You created birth and death. Why should anyone fear, if they understand You through the guru? You are kind and bestow your blessing; the pain and suffering depart. ||5|| He, who sits at home, eats and digests love. He controls the wandering mind and keeps in place. His heart-lotus blossoms in the overflowing greenery and over flowing pools and the Lord of his soul supports him. ||6|| Death is written before birth. How can they remain here? They have to go to the world beyond. God is immortal, His abode is true. He bestows honour to those who go there. ||7|| He created the whole world. He, who created them; puts them to work. Page 1023 I cannot see any other above God. God cannot be priced. ||8|| In this green pasture the mortal stays only a few days. He plays around like mad. The jugglers staged their show and left, like people mumbling in a dream. ||9|| They are blessed with greatness at God's court. Who enshrine the carefree God in the mind with love? In the galaxies and solar systems, underworld, celestial realms and the universe, God sits in trance. ||10|| True is the village, and true is the throne. The guru-willed meet Him and attain peace. Honour is obtained in true Lord's court eliminating ego and calculations. ||11|| Calculating and counting, the soul becomes anxious. How can one find peace, through duality and three qualities? The bestowal formless Lord is pure. He is realized through the guru. ||12|| In all ages only a few guru-willed realize Him. He abides in the mind and realized dyeing the mind with His love. Seeking His shelter, they find peace; filth does not attach to the mind and body. ||13|| Their tongues recite Him imbued with His love. Those attuned to God have no concern or relation with anyone else. Hearing guru's sermon the ears get fulfilled and the soul merges with soul. ||14|| One by one I place my feet on the ground. Wherever I go, I see Your refuge. In pain and pleasure You appeal to me and I am in harmony with You. ||15|| No one is a friend in the end. The guru-willed realize You by praising. O Nanak, imbued with God's name become detached and sit in trance within themselves. ||16||3|| Maaroo, First Master: From the beginning and throughout the ages, you are infinite and incomparable. You are my primal, formless Lord and master. I contemplate Him through Yoga way and see Him in trance. ||1|| For many ages, there was pitch dark. The Creator sat in trance. Reciting God's name attains true greatness and honour in God's court. ||2|| In the first Age of truth, truth and contentment filled the bodies. Profound and unfathomable truth prevailed everywhere. The true Lord appraises the truth and issues the true command. ||3|| The perfect guru is truthful and content. He, who enshrines guru's teaching in the mind, is brave. Truthful abide in His court. God's command prevails there. ||4|| In the age of truth, everyone spoke the truth. Truth prevailed. Everyone was truthful. God destroyed the self-willed's, doubt, fear, and became a friend with guru-willed. ||5|| In the second Age of Traytaa, one power of faith was lost. Three feet remained; one dried through doubt. The guru-willed realized the truth; the self-willed lost in useless deeds. ||6|| The self-willed never wins in God's court. Without guru's teachings, how can he be happy inside? They come and go tied up; they do not understand anything. ||7|| In the third Age of Dwaapur, kindness was cut in half. Page 1024 Only a very few guru-willed search. The faith puts two feet on the ground and the guru-willed live there. ||8|| The kings do justice there. Enticed by desire they give awns. Salvation is not obtained without God's name; many got tired of doing deeds. ||9|| Practicing religious rituals they seek liberation. The treasure of liberation comes from praising God through guru's teaching. Without guru's teaching, salvation is not obtained; practicing hypocrisy, they wander around confused. ||10|| Love and attachment to worldly wealth cannot be abandoned. Those who practice truth are freed. Dyed by God's worship day and night they realize and follow God's will. ||11|| Some recite and practice self discipline then bathe at shrines. Whatever pleases You; they do. Stubborn rituals without belief do not please God. Without guru the God, no one obtains honour. ||12|| In today's age, there is only one leg left. Without the perfect guru, no one has described it. The self-willed deals in falsehood! Doubt does not vanish without guru. ||13|| The carefree guru plays the music. There is no fear of devil of death or anyone to sing. Whoever pleases God becomes immortal; death does not bother him. ||14|| God abides in the guru. Million of guru-willed attain salvation through him. God the life of the world is the giver of all beings. The carefree is not touched by filth. ||15|| Everyone begs from the guru the storekeeper. He is the formless, unknowable, infinite Lord. Nanak speaks the truth and begs from God to bless him with truth by Your will. ||16||4|| Maaroo, First Master: Devotees are united with true Lord through guru's teachings. When it pleases Him, we intuitively merge with Him. The light of the transcendent Lord pervades the universe; there is no other O brother. ||1|| I am His servant; I serve Him. He the unknowable and mysterious is realized through guru's teaching. The Creator is the supporter of His devotees. He blesses them with His greatness. ||2|| There is no shortage to His giving. The false receive and then deny having received. They do not know their origin, they are not pleased with truth and they wander in duality and doubt. ||3|| The guru-willed remain awake day and night. Love of the true Lord is realized through guru's teaching. The self-willed remain asleep and are robbed. The guru-willed are saved O brother. ||4|| The false come, the false go. Imbued with falsehood the false practice falsehood. Those imbued with guru's teachings go to God's court. The guru-willed focus their mind on God. ||5|| The false are cheated and robbed by the robbers. Like the garden in the wild is destroyed. Without God's name, nothing tastes good; forgetting God they suffer pain. ||6|| Receiving the food of truth, one is satisfied. True is the greatness of the jewel of God's name. One who searches his soul realizes God. His soul merges with God. ||7|| Page 1025 Forgetting God's name she wanders hurt. Even great smartness does not dispel doubt. Unconsciously he does not remember God. He dies in filth and carries a heavy load on the head. ||8|| No one is free of conflict and rivalry. If someone can show me, I will admire him. Surrendering mind and body to God the life of the world, he becomes friendly with God. ||9|| No one knows the divine wisdom of God. Whoever calls himself great, will be eaten by his greatness. There is no lack of gifts from God. He created all. ||10|| Great is the greatness of the carefree Lord. He created all, and gives to all. The bestowal God is not far away; he is realized intuitively by His grace. ||11|| Some are sad and some are sick with disease. It is all by God's grace. Love of worship comes from guru's teachings and the divine music plays. ||12|| Some wander and roam around hungry and naked. Some die acting stubborn, but do not know the value of God. They do not know the difference between good and bad; it is realized through guru's teachings. ||13|| Some bathe at sacred shrines and do not eat. Some torment their bodies in burning fire. Salvation cannot be achieved without God's name. There is no other way. ||14||

Abandoning guru's teaching; some wander in the wild. The self-willed wander uselessly; they do not recite God's name. They earn filth and drown in filth; death is the enemy of false. ||15|| We come and go by His command. One, who realizes His command; merges in the true Lord. O Nanak, he merges in God by his will; the guru-willed has earned it. ||16||5|| Maaroo, First Master: He is the Creator Lord, the architect of destiny. He came into existence on his own and knows it. He is the guru and the devotee. He created the universe. ||1|| He is near not far away. The guru-willed understand Him; they are perfect beings. Their company is beneficial; that is the greatness of guru's congregation. ||2|| O God; Your saints are sacred in all ages. They sing God's praises with their tongue and enjoy it. They praise God. It eliminates pain poverty and worries. ||3|| They remain awake and do not appear sleepy. They serve the true Lord and attain salvation along with their congregation and dynasty. They are not stained by filth of sins; they are pure, and remain absorbed in devotional worship. ||4|| O humble servants of the Lord; understand guru's teachings. This youth, breath and body shall pass away. O mortal, you will die today or tomorrow; recite God in your mind. ||5|| O mortal, abandon falsehood and worthless deeds. Death viciously kills the false. The faithless and false die in filth of ego. They die deluded by duality. ||6|| Page 1026 Give up slander and envy of others. Reading and studying, they burn, they do not find peace. Join true company and praise God's name. God will help you. ||7|| Abandon lust, anger and wickedness. Abandon egotistic deeds and looking at other's spouses. Join and be saved in guru's refuge. This way the world ocean is crossed. ||8|| In the hereafter, you have to cross the filthy river and burning fire. No one else will be there. Your soul shall be all alone. The self-willed are destroyed in the rising waves in the ocean. ||9|| Liberation comes from the guru by his will. He, who obtains knows it. Ask one who has obtained it O brother. Serve the guru and earn it. ||10|| Without the guru, he dies entangled in useless deeds. The devil of death beats over the head and humiliates. The slanderers are tied and they drown slandering others. They cannot be saved. ||11|| Speak the truth and realize the Lord inside. He is not far away; look and see. No obstacle comes your way. The guru-willed swim across terrifying world Ocean. ||12|| God's name dwells in the body. The Creator is immortal. The soul does not die, or killed; God watches over. He is realized through guru's teachings by His grace. ||13|| He is pure, not blind. True Lord sits on His throne. The faithless false engaged in deeds keep wandering. They are born and dead again and again. ||14|| Guru's servants are the love of the guru. The guru sits on the throne and they contemplate His teachings. They realize the reality and know the state of their mind; it is realized through devotee's company. ||15|| He saves himself and his ancestors as well. His companions are liberated and carry others across. Nanak is the servant of the guru-willed attuned to God with love. ||16||6|| Maaroo, First Master: For many ages, only darkness prevailed; The infinite God sat in trance. He sat unaffected in absolute darkness; the conflicting world did not exist. ||1|| Thirty-six ages passed like this. He causes all to happen by His will. He has no rival. He is infinite and endless. ||2|| God is hidden throughout the four ages – know this well. He pervades each and every heart and every belly. He prevails in all ages; he is realized through guru's teachings. ||3|| From the union of the sperm and egg, the body was formed. From the union of air, water and fire, the living being is created. He enjoys in His abode. Rest is the entanglement of attachment to worldly wealth. ||4|| Within mother's womb, upside-down, the mortal recites God. The inner-knower knows everything. With every breath, he recites God's name when in the womb. ||5|| Page 1027 He came into the world with four priceless treasures. The worldly power entered in his mind. He lost out by forgetting God; the blind forgot God's name. ||6|| The child engages in his childish games. The loving child keeps talking and crying. The Lord who owns him took him back. They forgot to weep for God. ||7|| What can they do, if he dies in his youth? They cry saying him mine, mine! They cry for the sake of wealth and are ruined; their living in world is useless. ||8|| Their black hair, turned grey. Without God's name, they lose their wealth and leave. The evil-minded are blind – they are ruined and robbed and cry in pain. ||9|| One, who understands himself, does not cry. When he meets the true guru, he understands. Without the guru, the heavy door of the mind does not open. Realization comes through guru's teaching. ||10|| The body grows old and falls apart. Still, he does not recite God, which will help in the end. Forgetting God's name he goes with a black face; the false is humiliated in God's court. ||11|| Forgetting God's name the false departs. While coming and going, dust falls on their heads. She finds no place in in-law's home. She ponders at her father's home. ||12|| She eats, dresses and plays. But without devotional worship of the Lord, she dies uselessly. She does not distinguish between good and bad. When the devil of death kills her; she cannot do anything; ||13|| He, who realizes and honours the customs of others! He reaches the destiny through guru's teaching. He never talks bad of others; truth is always truth. ||14|| Without truth, no one wins in the court of the Lord. Through guru's true teachings, one obtains honour. He blesses those who eliminate ego and self-pride by His will; ||15|| One realizes His command through guru's grace. He realizes the process required in all ages. O Nanak, recite God and swim across. God will carry you across. ||16||1||7|| Maaroo, First Master: I have no other friend like God. He gave me body and mind, and infused consciousness in me. He cherishes and cares for all beings. He is wise, all-knowing Lord. ||1|| Guru is the ocean and I am His beloved swan. In the ocean, there are many jewels and rubies. Singing and dyeing your mind with God's praises attains all pearls and gems. ||2|| The Lord is inaccessible, inscrutable, unfathomable and unattached. The limits of God the guru the lord of the world cannot be found. The bestowal bestows salvation through guru's teaching and unites those dyed with His love. ||3|| Without the true guru, salvation cannot be achieved? He is eternal, for ages and a friend of God. By His grace, He grants salvation in His court and forgives their sins. ||4|| Page 1028 The true guru, the giver, grants liberation; Eradicates all diseases and blesses the taste of nectar. Their fire eliminates and become soothed; death tax does not apply to them. ||5|| The body has developed a great love for the soul. He is a Yogi, and she is a beautiful woman. Day and night, he loves her but does not tell her on departure. ||6|| God created the universe and decorated it. He created air, water and fire. The mind wavers in the company of evil. He gets what he earns. ||7|| Forgetting God's name one suffers the pain of evil deeds. When the order to depart is issued, he has to go, cannot stay back? He falls in the pit of hell and suffers like a fish out of water. ||8|| The faithless goes through hell millions of times. He gets what he earns. Without the guru, there is no liberation; he follows his deeds. ||9|| This path is very narrow, like the sharp edge of a sword. He is crushed like sesame seed in oil mill to check his account. Mother, father, spouse and child – none is anyone's friend in the end. No one is freed without God's love. ||10|| You may have many friends and companions in the world. But without the guru the transcendent Lord no one is yours? Serving the guru is the way to salvation by praising God forever. ||11|| Abandon falsehood, and pursue the truth; You obtain the fruit of your choice. There are only a few traders of true wealth; they make a deal and reap the reward. ||12|| They depart with priceless merchandise of God's name. Visualize Him and attain contentment. O guru-willed the perfect being, search yourself; this is how the all-knowing God is realized. ||13|| God is endless; following guru's teachings, some find Him. Through guru's teaching he guides his mind. Believe in guru's sermon; this way you realize God. ||14|| Naarad and Saraswati are Your servants. Servants of the universe and the elders. The universe is Yours; You are the Lord of all. You created all. ||15|| Some serve at Your door and their sufferings are dispelled. They are honoured in God's court; the guru frees them. The guru breaks the bonds of ego and does not let the mind to be fickle. ||16|| Meet the guru and follow his way. By which you find God and not have to answer for your account. Eliminate ego and serve the guru; servant Nanak is drenched with God's love. ||17||2||8|| Maaroo, First Master: My God is the destroyer of demons. My beloved Lord is pervading each and every heart. The unseen Lord is totally unexplainable; the guru-willed write and say so. ||1|| The guru-willed devotees seek Your sanctuary. Page 1029 O God; be kind and carry me across. The ocean is very deep, filled with fiery water; the guru carries us across. ||2|| The blind, self-willed does not understand. He comes and goes in life, dieing, and dieing again. Previously written fate does not erase; they are humiliated at the time of death. ||3|| Some come and go, and do not find a home to stay. Bound by their past deeds they commit sins. The blind have no understanding and wisdom; they are trapped and ruined by greed and ego. ||4|| Without her Husband Lord, what good are the soul-bride's decorations? She forgot her husband Lord and is in love with another's husband. As the son of a prostitute has no family name; so are his useless deeds. ||5|| The ghost in the cage suffers all sorts of pain. Those who are spiritually blind die in hell. Those, who forgot God's name; will have to pay the remaining loan to the justice of destiny; ||6|| The scorching sun blazes with flames of poison. The self-willed animal demon is disgraced. Trapped by hope and desire, he practices falsehood. The sickness of doing bad deeds is also bad. ||7|| He carries the heavy load of sins on his forehead and head. How can he cross the terrifying world-ocean? Boarding guru's boat from the beginning and for ages reciting God's name attains salvation. ||8|| The love of children and spouse is sweet in this world. The universe is attached to worldly wealth. The guru breaks the chains of death; the guru-willed realizes the reality. ||9|| Cheated by falsehood, they walk on many paths. The heat of fire destroys the self-willed. The guru is the great giver of sacred name. Reciting God's name attains eternal peace. ||10|| The amazing true guru teaches the truth. Eliminates all sufferings and puts on the right path. No thorn pinches the foot of one who has the guru as his protector. ||11|| Dust to dust when the body disintegrates. The self-willed does not get wet like a stone. He cries a lot; but keeps going to heaven and hell. ||12|| They live with the poisonous snake of worldly wealth. This duality has ruined many homes. Without guru, love does not well up. Imbued with devotional worship, the soul is satisfied. ||13|| The faithless chase after wealth. Forgetting God's name, how can they find peace? They sink in three worldly qualities; cannot swim across this way; ||14|| The false are called pigs and dogs. They bark to death; they bark and bark and howl in fear. False in mind and body practice falsehood; the evil-minded lose in God's court. ||15|| Meeting the true guru, the mind is stabilized. In his refuge they obtain God's name. He bestows God's priceless name. Singing God's praise in God's court is accepted with love. ||16|| Page 1030 Recite God's name in devotee's refuge. Salvation attains through guru's teachings. O Nanak, recite God in the mind; God will unite you with Him. ||17||3||9|| Maaroo, First Master: O childish ignorant mind; stay at home. Recite God in the mind with love. Renounce greed and create the infinite love. Obtain salvation this way; ||1|| Forgetting God; the devil of death starts robbing. All peace will be gone and you will suffer in pain in the world after. O guru-willed recite God's name in the mind; this is the essence of all. ||2|| Recite God's name and enjoy the sweet taste. The guru-willed find Godly taste inside. Get imbued with God's love forever; this is the essence of meditation and self-discipline. ||3|| Recite God's name through guru's teachings. This essence is found in devotee's congregation. Search your soul through guru's teachings. You will never go through womb again. ||4|| Bathe at the sacred shrine of truth and sing God's praises. Contemplating God with love realizes the reality. In the end the devil of death cannot rob those who say God with love. ||5|| The guru the bestowal is very wise. Those with truth inside merge with truth. One, whom the guru unites with him, gets rid of the fear of death. ||6|| The body is formed combining five elements. God the jewel abides in it. The soul is God, God is soul; God is realized through guru's teachings. ||7|| O brother; be truthful and content. Be kind and stay at guru's refuge. Search your soul and find God; it is realized through guru's company. ||8|| The faithless are stuck in falsehood and deceit. Day and night, they slander others. Without reciting God they come and go through the hell of mother's womb. ||9|| The faithless cannot get rid of fear of death. The punishment of devil of death never ends. They pay the dues of justice of destiny; they are loaded heavily. ||10|| Tell me: without the guru, who the faithless has been saved? Acting in ego he falls into the terrifying world-ocean. Without the guru, no one is saved; one crosses over reciting God. ||11|| No one can erase guru's blessings. The Lord carries across those whom He blesses. The pains of birth and death do not touch those who have the unlimited infinite God in the mind. ||12|| Those who forget the guru come and go in reincarnation. They are born, only to die and continue committing sins. The ignorant faithless does not miss God innocently; he says God when hurt. ||13|| Pleasure and pain are the earning of previous life. The giver, who blesses us with these, knows it. Who can you blame O man; you reap the reward of your doing? ||14|| Page 1031 Practicing ego and false attachment, you came into the world. You are driven and bound by hope and desire. You keep saying mine mine; you cannot take anything with you. You are going loaded with sins and dirt. ||15|| O brother; worship God. Speak the unspoken speech in the mind. Control your wandering mind; God will eliminate your suffering. ||16|| I seek the support of the perfect guru the God. The guru-willed attuning to God with love realizes God. O Nanak, through God's name the intellect improves. God blesses and bestows salvation. ||17||4||10|| Maaroo, First Master: O my guru, I came to your refuge. You are the almighty kind Lord. No one knows Your amazing plays. You are the perfect architect of destiny. ||1|| From the beginning of time, throughout the ages, You take care of all. You the kind and beautiful Lord abide in each and every heart. As You wish, You cause all to follow; everyone acts according to Your command. ||2|| O life of the world, your kind light shines in all. Everyone enjoys you and drinks your essence with love. He gives and He takes in the whole universe. He is the mother and father of the world. ||3|| He created the world and set the play in motion. He placed the soul in the body of air, water and fire. The body has nine gates; the tenth gate remains hidden. ||4|| There are four terrible rivers of fire. Only a few guru-willed realize Him through guru's unique teachings. The faithless are drowned and burnt through evil-mindedness. The guru saves those who are imbued with God's love. ||5|| You created water, fire, air, earth and the sky. You created life combining the five elements. They remain imbued with guru's teaching eliminating worldly wealth and ego O brother. ||6|| The mind drenched with guru's teaching gets satisfaction. Without God's name there is no place to rest. They are being robbed inside; the faithless do not know the devil of death. ||7|| The scary messengers and ghosts make lot of noise. These demons create lot of trouble. Without realizing guru's teaching he keeps coming and going and loses his honour in the process. ||8|| The body of the false person is like a pile of salty dirt. Without God's name what honour you have? Tied this way they do not attain salvation even in all four ages; the thorn of devil of death hurts them. ||9|| Tied at death's door, they are punished. Such a sinner does not obtain salvation. He cries in pain, like the fish caught in the hook. ||10|| The faithless alone is hanged.

The miserable blind person is controlled by the devil of death. Without God's name; salvation is not obtained; today or tomorrow he is going to fall in the hands of death. ||11|| There is no friend without the guru. Here and hereafter, God is the saviour. He bestows God's name by His grace and unites with him like water in water. ||12|| Page 1032 Guru guides the misguided followers. He puts them on the right path when they are going stray. Serve the guru forever day and night; He is the destroyer of pain and he is your friend. ||13|| O mortal; how can you worship the guru? Even Brahma, Indra and Shiva did not know and could not do it. Tell me, how can the virtues of the guru be known? Whoever God blesses; realizes it. ||14|| One, with love in the mind visualizes God. By being in love with guru's sermon intuitively; God's pure soul abides everywhere; the guru-willed get enlightened. ||15|| The food of spiritual wisdom is very sweet. Whoever tastes it visualizes God. Visualizing God the renounce meets and merges with God eliminating desires. ||16|| Those who serve the true guru are supreme. They realize God in everybody. O Nanak, those who realize guru the God, sing God's praises in devotee's company. ||17||5||11|| Maaroo, First Master: The true Lord is the Creator of the universe. He created the earth and other planets systematically in the universe. He created the creation and looks after; true Lord is carefree. ||1|| He created many species creeds and races. There are two travelers and both walk on different paths. Without the perfect guru salvation is not obtained. Recite God's name and reap the benefit. ||2|| The self-willed reads but does not know the way to follow. They do not realize God's name and are lost in doubt. They take bribes and testify; doing evil deeds a chain of death ties in their neck. ||3|| They read the scriptures; They explain and debate, but do not know the reality. Without the perfect guru, reality is not obtained. The pure and truthful walk on the path of truth; ||4|| They hear and tell others to praise God. He is the bestowal and appraises the truth. The guru-willed, whom God blesses, praise Him through guru's teaching. ||5|| They listen to guru's sermon and tell others. They listen and then tell others, but they do not know His limits. Whoever God guides; they only know the unexplainable story. ||6|| At birth, the congratulations pour in. The ignorant sing

songs of joy. Whoever is born has to die. They get what they earn.
||7|| Union and separation are created by my God. Creating the
universe, He put pain and pleasure inside. The guru-willed wear the
amour of peace; they are not affected by pain or pleasure. ||8|| The
good people trade in truth. They purchase the true merchandise
contemplating guru's teaching. One, who has the true priceless
merchandise; he enjoys it through guru's true teaching. ||9|| Making
false deal brings loss. The guru-willed does a business, which pleases
God. His merchandise and wealth are safe and sound. The noose of
death is cut from his neck. ||10|| Page 1033 Everyone speaks as they
please. The self-willed do not know any other way. The blind thinks
blind and speaks blind; he suffers pain in coming and going. ||11|| In
pain he is born and in pain he dies. His pain is not relieved without
seeking the refuge of the guru. Born in pain die in pain, what did he
bring and what did he take? ||12|| True deeds are done in guru's
guidance. They do not come and go and they are not subject to the
laws of death. Leaving the branches he holds on to the trunk and is
truly happy in the mind. ||13|| Death cannot kill God's people. They
do not see pain or a difficult path. They recite and worship God's
name in the mind nothing else. ||14|| There is no limit to the ways of
preaching and praising. As it pleases You, I live by Your will. This
way going to Your court becomes easy by Your order O Lord. ||15||
What can I say; your virtues are many to express? Even the elders
cannot find it. Please bless Nanak with truth, and preserve his honour
O emperor of emperors. ||16||6||12|| Maaroo, First Master, written in
southern language: Inside the body-village, is the fortress. The true
Lord dwells in it. This place is permanent and pure forever. He
created it. ||1|| Within the fortress are balconies and bazaars. He
takes care of His merchandise. The door of the tenth gate is closed
shut. It opens through guru's teaching. ||2|| There is a cave in the
mind fortress. He created nine doors by His will. In the tenth gate,
the unknowable and infinite Lord dwells; the unseen Lord reveals
there. ||3|| Within the body of air, water and fire, lives one Lord. He
stages this drama. By His grace the burning fire extinguished, He
pours water on it. ||4|| Creating the earth, He created the faithful
place to rest. Creating and destroying, He remains unattached. He

stages the play of the breath everywhere. He destroys it by His power. ||5|| Your garden is the vast vegetation of nature. The wind blowing like a fan around You. You created sun and moon two lamps; sun gives the light to moon. ||6|| The five birds do not fly wild. The tree of life is fruitful, it bears the sacred fruit. The guru-willed intuitively sings God's praises and pecks on sublime essence. ||7|| The dazzling light glitters without the moon or the stars; There is no sunray or lightening strike. I describe the indescribable of the formless. Lord pleasing to my mind lives there. ||8|| The ray of divine light illuminates the soul. Having created the creation, the kind Lord watches it. Divine music plays in carefree God's home. ||9|| Page 1034 The divine music plays and the affect of doubt goes away. The adorable Lord pervades all. All belong to You; the guru-willed realize You by singing praises at Your door. ||10|| The formless pure God exists from the beginning. I do not know anyone else. God dwells in the mind and pleases me. He eliminates ego and pride. ||11|| I drink nectar given by the guru. I do not know any other, second or third. He is one, unique, infinite and endless Lord; He evaluates and puts in the treasury. ||12|| True Lord is full of divine wisdom, meditation and is unfathomable. No one knows Your vastness. The whole creation begs from You. Those with pre-ordained destiny realize You. ||13|| Doing good deeds and faith are under your control. You are carefree and Your stores are never empty. O God; You are kind and compassionate; You unite us with You. ||14|| You see and cause others to see. You create and destroy. You unite and separate; You kill and give life. ||15|| The whole creation is in You. You see everything sitting in Your royal palace. Nanak prays and speaks the truth; visualizing God obtains peace. ||16||1||13|| Maaroo, First Master: I can only visualize You if I please You. In devotional worship, O true Lord, I sing Your praises. By Your will O Lord. You become pleasing to me and make me recite You. ||1|| The devotees look beautiful in Your court. Your slaves are liberated O Lord. Eliminating ego they dye in Your love and recite Your name forever. ||2|| Shiva, Brahma, gods and goddesses; Indra, ascetics and sages serve You. Celibates, truthful and many renounce as well. No one knows Your limits. ||3|| No one knows You, unless You make them know. Whatever happens;

happens by Your will. You created millions of species; they breathe by Your will. ||4|| Whatever pleases You happens. The self-willed plays his drum and cries. Forgetting God's name, he finds no place to rest; he suffers in coming and going. ||5|| Pure is the body and the soul is sacred. Inside that, dwells the child of God's name. He drinks all pains like nectar and never suffers again. ||6|| Tasting many flavours gives pain. He suffers with sickness and is ruined in the end. Pleasure can never erase his pain; he wanders around without obeying God's will. ||7|| The whole world wanders without divine wisdom. The true Lord is pervading everywhere with love. The carefree God is realized through guru's teachings and the souls merge. ||8|| He is the eternal, unchanging, immeasurable Lord. He destroys and rebuilds in a moment. He has no form or shape, no limit or value. He is honoured through guru's teachings. ||9|| Page 1035 I am the slave of Your slaves, O my beloved. The seekers of truth are good and think of You. Whoever believes in Your name, realizes You; You teach the truth. ||10|| Truly the truthful carries truth in his lap. True Lord is pleased with those who love guru's teaching. Lord created the universe with His true power; He is pleased by truth. ||11|| Everyone calls Him the greatest of the great. No one understands anything without the guru. The truthful please the true Lord; they merge with Him and never separate again. ||12|| Separated from destiny cry and are ruined. They die only to be reborn, when their time comes. He honours those whom he blesses; they do not regret after union. ||13 || He is the Creator and He is the enjoyer. He is satisfied and He is liberated. The Lord of liberation grants liberation and eradicates greed and attachment. ||14|| Your gift is the best gift of all. You are the cause of causes, almighty infinite Lord. You create and test for quality; You cause all to do their deeds. ||15|| Those who please God, sing His praises. They originate from You and merge with You. Nanak offers this true prayer; meeting with the true Lord obtains peace. ||16||2||14|| Maaroo, First Master: For billions of years, there was utter darkness. There was no earth or sky; there was infinite God; His rule prevailed. There was no day or night, no moon or sun; God sat in absolute trance. ||1|| There were no sources of creation or sermon and no air or water. There was no creation or destruction, no coming or going.

There were no continents, underworld, seven seas, rivers or flowing water. ||2|| There was no heavenly being, no prophet or the underworld. There was no heaven or hell, no fear of death. There was no hell or heaven, no birth or death, no coming or going. ||3|| There was no Brahma, Vishnu or Shiva. There was no one but One God. There was no female or male, no social class or caste of birth; no one experienced pain or pleasure. ||4|| There were no celibates, truthful or renounce. There were no mystics, seekers or peaceful people. There were no Yogis, beggars with ringing bells or a spiritual master. ||5|| There was no meditation, body purification, self-discipline, fasting or worship. No one spoke or talked in duality. He created Himself and rejoiced; He evaluated Himself. ||6|| There was no purification, no self-restraint and no garland of basil leaves. There were no beloved ones, no cows or cow herder. There were no false teachers with false lessons, no one played the flute. ||7|| There was no good deed, faith, wealth or worldly flies. Social class and birth were not seen. There was no enticement of greed, no pre-determined death; no one worshipped anyone as well. ||8|| There was no slander, no seed, no soul and no life. There was no Gorakh and no Maachhindra (mystics). There was no spiritual wisdom or meditation, no dynasty or creation, no checking of accounts. ||9|| Page 1036 There were no castes or social classes or caste. There were no demy-gods or temples, no cows or goddesses prayer. There were no burnt offerings, no ceremonial feasts, no cleansing rituals at shrines and no one worshipped. ||10|| There was no Mullah, or Qazi. There was no scholar or pilgrims to Mecca. There was no king or subjects, and no worldly ego; no one spoke of him. ||11|| There was no love or devotion, no worldly power as well. There were no friends or companions, no semen or blood. He was the banker, the merchant. Only that appealed to the true Lord. ||12|| There were no Vedas, Qurans or Bibles, no Simritees or Shaastras. There was no recitation of the Puraanas, no sunrise or sunset. The unfathomable Lord was the speaker and the preacher; the unseen Lord knew everything. ||13|| When He wanted, He created the world. Without any support, He sustained the universe. He created Brahma, Vishnu and Shiva and created the worldly attachment. ||14|| Guru's teaching was spoken to a rare one. He created the creation and controlled by His command. He created the planets, solar systems and underworld and hid in it. ||15|| No one knows His limits. He is realized through the perfect guru. O Nanak, those attuned to truth are amazed; They enjoy singing His praises. ||16||3||15|| Maaroo, First Master: He created the creation and remains unattached. The kind Lord established His true home. Combining air and water he created the being. ||1|| The Creator established nine gates. In the tenth gate, the unseen unexplainable infinite God lives. The seven seas are filled with pure water. The filth does not attach to Him. ||2|| The lamps of the sun and the moon give light to all. Creating them, He watches His greatness. Embodiment of beauty, light and bestowal of happiness is honoured through truth. ||3|| Within the fortress are the stores and markets; the business is transacted there. The supreme merchant weighs with the perfect weights. He buys and sells jewel and He determines the price as well. ||4|| The appraiser appraises its value. The carefree is full of treasures. He has all powers, He pervades all; only a rare guru-willed understand Him. ||5|| By His grace one meets the guru. The devil of death cannot strike him. He blossoms like the lotus in water; he recites God with joy. ||6|| He rains the stream of nectar, jewels, diamonds, and priceless rubies. Meeting the guru realizes the perfect God through priceless love. ||7|| Whoever receives the priceless treasure of love? It never decreases in weight. It is weighed correctly. The trader of truth buys the true merchandise. ||8|| Very few buy the true merchandise. Meeting the perfect guru, one meets God. Page 1037 The guru-willed understand God's command. Obeying His command they merge with Him. ||9|| By His command we come, and by His command we merge with Him. By His command the world we see was formed. By His command, people go to heaven, fish lives deep in the underworld. His command supports everything. ||10|| He holds the earth in its place by His command. By His command, air, water and fire came into being. By His command the worldly power came into existence. Everything plays by His command. ||11|| By His command the birds fly in the sky. By His command the creatures dwell in the water and the whole world. By His command we eat breathe and see. ||12|| By His command He created ten prophets. And the uncounted and infinite gods and demons. Whoever obeys His command honourably goes to His court and merges with Him. ||13|| By his command, the thirty-six ages passed. By His command the mystics and seekers contemplate Him. He is the master and controls all; he bestows salvation by His grace. ||14|| The emperor sits in the body fort with a beautiful door along with His courtiers. Those gripped by falsehood and greed do not live there. Greedy and sinners regret. ||15|| Truth and contentment govern this body-village. Celibacy, truth and self-control are in the sanctuary of the Lord. O Nanak, intuitively one meets the Lord, life of the world; he obtains honour through guru's teaching. ||16||4||16|| Maaroo, First Master: In absolute, the infinite God created Him. He is unique, infinite and incomparable. He creates by His power and watches. The absolute God creates in trance. ||1|| From the absolute, He created air and water. He created the universe and the king in the fortress of the body. Your light pervades fire, water and souls; Your power pervades all. ||2|| From the void, Brahma, Vishnu and Shiva were created. This primal Lord pervades in all the ages. The mortal who contemplates this way is perfect; meeting with him, doubt is dispelled. ||3|| From the absolute the seven oceans were created. He, who created them, knows about it. The guru-willed who swims in those seven oceans lovingly, does not take birth again. ||4|| From this primal void, came the moon, the sun and the earth. His light shines in the whole universe. The absolute God is unseen, infinite and unique and sits in trance. ||5|| From this primal void, the earth and the sky were created. They are supported without pillars by His power. Creating the universe He tied it with the worldly wealth. He creates and destroys. ||6|| From the absolute came the four divides of creation and the Godly sermon. They originate from absolute and merge with absolute. The Creator started the play. Amazing show is seen through guru's teaching. ||7|| From this primal void, He made both night and day. He creates and destroys and gives pleasure and pain. He is beyond pain and pleasure; the guru-willed finds his destiny. ||8|| Page 1038 The Saam Veda, the Rig Veda, the Jujar Veda and the Atharvan Veda From the mouth of Brahma; they speak the three worldly qualities. They cannot describe

God; they say as He makes them say; ||9|| From the primal void, He created the seven underworlds. From the primal void, He created the world; all remain attuned to Him with love. The infinite Lord created the creation. Everyone does what You ask them to do? ||10|| Power, greed and truth are created by You; They take birth and die in ego and suffer pain. Whoever God blesses with virtues; the guru-willed attains salvation in the fourth state. ||11|| From the primal void, came the ten prophets. Creating the universe, He made the expanse. He created demy-gods demons, the heavenly heralds and celestial musicians; they act according to their past deeds. ||12|| The guru-willed understands and does not suffer the disease. Very few guru-willed realize guru's ladder to climb. They attain salvation in all ages and attain honour. ||13|| From the primal void, the five elements were created. Then joined to form the body, which engages in actions. Both bad and good are written in fate, the seeds of vice and virtue. ||14|| The guru is unique and sacred. He is imbued with divine teaching and is intoxicated with it. Riches, intellect, mysticism are realized from the guru; one meets him with good luck. ||15|| This mind is in love with the worldly wealth. O divine people; tell me something and close the case; In hope, desire, ego and skepticism, the greedy man acts falsely. ||16|| From the true guru, one understands the reality. He sits in trance in the house of the true Lord. O Nanak, the pure sound of guru's teaching wells up and he absorbs in God's name. ||17||5||17|| Maaroo, First Master: Wherever I look, I see God merciful to the meek. The kind God does not come or go. He carefully abides in the beings and yet remains unattached. ||1|| The world is His image. He has no father or mother. He does not have sister or brother. He does not take birth or death, has no family or caste. He is free of aging and death and appeals to my mind. ||2|| You are immortal; death does not hover over Your head. You are the unexplainable inaccessible and unique. You are true, content and very cool through guru's teachings and intuitively filled with love. ||3|| The three qualities are pervasive; God dwells in the fourth state. He has made death and birth like a morsel of food. God the life of the world is a pure soul; the guru reveals Him through divine teachings. ||4|| The saints are sacred, good and beloved of God.

Intoxicated with God's sublime taste, they go across the world ocean. Nanak is the dust of saint's congregation; God is realized by guru's grace. ||5|| You are the inner-knower. All beings belong to You. Page 1039 You are the bestowal; I am Your servant. Be kind and bestow me with sacred name and enlighten me with guru's divine wisdom. ||6|| You created this body uniting five elements. Realizing God the supreme soul, peace is obtained. By good deeds sacred fruit rewarded, obtaining the jewel of God's name. ||7|| The mind is fulfilled and feels no hunger or thirst. The formless God pervades in everybody. Only the detached is imbued with God's essence through guru's teachings intuitively. ||8|| He does spiritually wise deeds day and night. Sees the immaculate divine light inside. Reciting the tasteful guru's teachings he plays the tasteful flute. ||9|| He plays the sweet music of this flute. He, who knows the universe; O Nanak, realize this through guru's teaching and attune to God's name with love. ||10|| Such people are rare in the world. Who contemplate guru's teaching and remain detached. They save themselves, their congregation and dynasty; their coming in the world is fruitful. ||11|| He knows the home of his heart, and the door to the temple; who obtains realization from the perfect guru. In the body-fortress, lives God establishing His true kingdom inside. ||12|| Inside fourteen shops, there are two lamps as witnesses. Lord's servants, do not taste the poison of corruption of five thieves. The beautiful, priceless merchandise lives inside. It is realized by meeting the guru. ||13|| The worthy sits on the throne. He controls five passions through guru's teachings. Let there be no doubt? God exists from the beginning, for ages. He is and will be; ||14|| May God's rule prevail forever? This true honour is realized through loving guru's teachings. O Nanak, recite God and swim across; God helps in the end; ||15||1||18|| Maaroo, First Master: O brother; collect Godly wealth; Serve the guru and remain in His refuge. Thieves do not steal from him. He remains awake through guru's teaching. ||1|| You are the one universal Creator the unique emperor. You resolve the affairs of Your humble servants. You are immortal, immovable, infinite and priceless. O Lord, Your place is beautiful and eternal. ||2|| In the body-village is the most sacred place. The five passions control everything there. Above them is detached

God. He sits in trance there. ||3|| There are nine gates to the body-village; The Creator Lord fashioned them for every person. In the tenth gate lives the unique God; Only He knows Himself. ||4|| The primal Lord cannot be explained; true is His court. Truth prevails in His court by His command. O Nanak, search your soul; God the Lord is realized by reciting His name. ||5|| Page 1040 The primal, formless and all-knowing God is everywhere. He administers justice. He is absorbed in guru's teachings. He chokes the lust and anger to death, and eliminates ego and greed. ||6|| In that true place, the formless Lord lives. He is realized contemplating guru's teaching. He reaches and lives in God's home and coming and going ends. ||7|| His mind does not waver and he is not blown away by wind. Such a Yogi plays the infinite music through guru's teaching. God plays and sings the five divine tunes there intuitively. ||8|| In love of detachment, he intuitively merges in peace. Renouncing ego he is imbued with the infinite divine music. He realizes the essence of the medicine to realize the Lord of the universe. ||9|| Immortal God is the destroyer of pain and fear. He cures the disease and cuts away the noose of death. O Nanak, God the destroyer of concerns is realized meeting the guru. ||10|| He realizes the lotus the formless God destroyer of death. He, who understands the reality, realizes God through guru's teaching. He knows and realizes Himself. This whole world is His play. ||11|| He is the banker and the merchant. He is the appraiser and appraises. He tests with a touchstone and He estimates the value. ||12|| God is kind by His grace. The gardener of the universe pervades all. The Lord beyond the universe is happy within Himself. The primal guru unites with primal God. ||13|| God is wise and all knowing; He eliminates ego. Eradicating duality, One Lord reveals Himself. In hope and uniqueness life; one sings praises of formless and ancestor less God. ||14|| Eradicating ego he obtains peace through guru's teaching. He, who searches his soul, is a divine person. O Nanak, singing God's praises in devotee's company is beneficial. ||15||2||19|| Maaroo, First Master: Speak the truth and live in the home of truth. Die while living; one swims across the terrifying world ocean. The guru is the boat, the ship, the raft; reciting God in the mind one goes across. ||1|| Ego, possessiveness and greed are eliminated. He is liberated from the nine gates, and obtains a place in the tenth gate. He is high beyond imagination and unlimited; He came into existence on his own. ||2|| Through guru's teachings, lovingly attuned to God, one crosses over. Sing the praises of the absolute Lord, why should you be afraid of the devil of death? Wherever I look, I see You; I do not sing praises of any other. ||3|| True is Lord's name, and true is His sanctuary. True is guru's teaching; following it one swims across the world ocean. He speaks the unspoken; infinite Lord watches and he never goes through womb again. ||4|| Without truthfulness, no one finds truth or contentment. No one is liberated without the guru; they keep coming and going. Reciting God, the primal word, says Nanak; he realizes the primal God. ||5|| Page 1041 Without the truth, the terrifying world-ocean cannot be crossed. This ocean is vast and unfathomable; it is full of worst poison. He goes beyond everything through guru's teaching and realizes the carefree God within. ||6|| False is the cleverness of loving attachment of the world. In no time, it comes and goes. The proud lives forgetting God's name; he keeps coming and going. ||7|| Bound by bonds they are born and dead. The noose of ego and worldly wealth is around their necks. Whoever does not recite God's name through guru's teaching is tied and taken to the city of death. ||8|| How can anyone be liberated without the guru. Without the guru, how can anyone recite God's name? Swim across the terrifying world ocean through guru's teaching; be happy being saved; ||9|| Through guru's teachings, Krishna protected the cows on mount Govardhan. Through guru's teachings, floats the stones in the ocean. Following guru's teaching obtains highest status O Nanak, guru eliminates the doubt. ||10|| Follow guru's teaching and swim the swimming of truth. Search God the destroyer of sins in your mind. Reciting God cuts the noose of death and realizes the family less Lord. ||11|| Through guru's teachings, the five passions become friend and brothers of same faith. Through guru's teachings, the inner fire is extinguished. O self-willed; recite God's name the life of the world in your mind and know the unknown. ||12|| The guru-willed understands and obtains honour through guru's teaching. Why do you praise or slander anyone? Search your soul and recite God; God the Lord of the universe is pleasing. ||13|| Know the one who pervades all the realms of the universe. O guru-willed, understand and realize Him through guru's teaching. The enjoyer enjoys each and every soul, yet remains detached from all. ||14|| Through guru's teachings, praise the true Lord; Through guru's teachings, visualize the highest Lord. Whoever listens to God's sermon O Nanak, dyes with God's love. ||15||3||20|| Maaroo, First Master: Give up lust, anger and the slander of others. Renounce greed and possessiveness and become carefree. Break the chains of doubt and remain unattached and enjoy the sublime taste of God inside. ||1|| As one sees the flash of lightning in the night. See the divine light merged inside forever same way. The Lord, the embodiment of bliss, incomparably beautiful is revealed by the perfect guru so meet with the guru and God will save you. He placed the lamp of sun and moon in the sky. See the invisible Lord and whole universe by lovingly attuning to Him. Obtaining the sublime sacred taste, desire and fear are dispelled. He attains the supreme status and eliminates ego. The highest status is obtained through guru's pure teaching. ||4|| The name of the invisible and unfathomable Lord is infinite. The name of the invisible and unfathomable Lord is infinite. Page 1042 The sublime taste of God's name is very sweet; O Lord, bless Nanak with Your praise and may I recite God forever. ||5|| Enshrining God's name inside obtains a jewel. Reciting God stabilizes the mind and body. It eliminates duality of mind and rebirth as well. ||6|| Through the love of guru's teaching one gets inspired. And begs for singing the priceless God's name. By God's will the guru unites us with God; God saves the whole world. ||7|| One who recites God; the guru teaches him. The painful messenger of death becomes a servant at his feet. Noble congregation makes one noble and crosses over the terrifying world ocean. ||8|| Swim across the terrifying world ocean through guru's teaching. Burn the inner doubt from inside. Take five arrows; draw on the celestial bow and kill the devil of death. ||9|| How can the faithless attain the knowledge through guru's teaching? Without awareness of guru's teaching, one keeps coming and going. O Nanak, the guru-willed obtains salvation and unites with God through good fortune. ||10|| The carefree God is the protector. Devotional worship is obtained through the guru, the Lord of the world. The joyful limitless music plays. God is realized through guru's teaching. ||11|| He, who has no account to pay; is carefree. God is unseen. He is revealed through the creation. He is beyond birth, He is self existent O Nanak, He is realized through guru's teaching. ||12|| The guru knows the state of one's inner being. He the carefree is realized through guru's teaching. Seeing inside he sees the eternal Lord, his mind does not waver anymore. ||13|| He the carefree dwells deep in the mind. He is realized by reciting His name with love day and night; O Nanak, join devotee's company and sing God's praises and merge with God with ease. ||14|| See God inside out. Remain detached and bring the wandering mind back to its home. He is the Lord of the universe; the taste of nectar is obtained through truth O Nanak. ||15||4||21|| Maaroo, First Master: The Creator Lord is infinite. His creative power is wondrous. The created beings have no power over Him. He creates and feeds all beings and His command rules all. ||1|| The all-pervading God administers His command. Who is near, and who is far? He secretly abides in all. The unique Lord is permeating all. ||2|| Whoever He unites with Him enshrines in His soul. Through guru's teaching he recites God's name. God is the embodiment of bliss, beautiful and unfathomable; meeting with the guru eliminates the doubt. ||3|| God's name is dearer than mind body and wealth to me. In the end at the time of departure, He is my companion; Page 1043 Enticement of worldly wealth does not accompany you. Who found happiness without guru the God? ||4|| He, whom the perfect guru grants His grace; the brave guru unites with God through his teaching. O Nanak, serve guru's feet, who showed you the way when you were lost. ||5|| The wealth of Lord's praise is very dear to the humble saints. Through guru's teachings, I have obtained Your name. The beggar serves at Lord's door and sings His praises in His court. ||6|| When one meets the guru, he is invited to God's palace. In the true court, he is blessed with salvation and honour. The faithless has no place in God's palace. He suffers the pain of birth and death. ||7|| So serve the guru, the unfathomable ocean, and obtain the jewel of God's name and reap the reward. Bathing in sacred pool of nectar eliminates filth of evil and makes content in guru's pool. ||8|| So serve the guru without hesitation. And in the midst of hope, remain unaffected. Serve the eradicator of worry and suffering; you shall never be sick again. ||9|| Praising God pleases Him. Who else can teach him anything? The Lord and the guru is same O Nanak, God the guru pleases him. ||10|| Some read scriptures, the Vedas and the Puraanas. Some sit and listen, and read to others. Tell me, how the heavy door of mind opens? Without the guru the reality is not realized. ||11|| Some smear their bodies with ashes; they are angry wicked and egotistic. Practicing hypocrisy, Yoga is not obtained; without the guru, the unseen Lord is not found. ||12|| Some make vows, visit sacred shrines, keep fast and live in the forest. Some practice chastity, charity and self-discipline, and speak of spiritual wisdom. Peace does not well up without God's name; the doubt does not dispel without the guru. ||13|| Body cleansing through yoga exercises and sitting in the middle of fire; Inhaling, exhaling and holding the breath forcibly. By empty hypocrite religious ritual practices, God's love does not well up. The supreme taste is obtained through guru's teachings. ||14|| Seeing Lord's creative power, my mind is satisfied. Through guru's teaching, I have realized God. O Nanak, the Lord of the world is revealed through guru's teaching. ||15||5||22|| Maaroo, Sohlay, Third Master: God is one. He is realized by guru's grace. God created the universe by His command intuitively. Creating the creation, He watches His greatness. He acts and inspires all to act; by His will; He pervades all. ||1|| The world is blinded by the worldly attachment. Only a few guru-willed realize it. He realizes God by His grace and unites with Him by His grace. ||2|| Page 1044 Uniting with Him, He bestows honour. By guru's grace, one realizes God's value. The self-willed wanders crying, he is ruined by the love of duality. ||3|| Ego is instilled in the worldly wealth. The self-willed is deluded, and loses his honour. The guru-willed gets absorbed in God's name and merges with Him. ||4|| The jewel of God's name is realized through the guru. Controlling the desires, he enshrines it in the mind. The Creator sets His plays; He himself reveals to them. ||5|| One who serves the guru eradicates ego. Meeting with his beloved, he finds peace through guru's teaching. He is imbued with God's worship and becomes content. ||6|| The destroyer of pain is realized through the guru. God the life of the world unites them with Him. Whom He guides, realizes Him. The love of doubt disappears from the body. ||7|| He blesses the guru-willed by His grace. They worship the guru through guru's teaching. Old age and death cannot rob them. They are in harmony with true Lord. ||8|| The world is burning in the fire of greed. It burns and is destroyed badly. The self-willed finds no place to rest; the guru imparts this understanding. ||9|| Those who serve the guru are fortunate. They are attuned to God with love. God's name abides in the mind; guru's teaching eliminates greed. ||10|| Guru's teaching is true and his sermon is true. Only a few realize this. Those imbued with guru's teaching become detached and their coming and going ends. ||11|| Eliminating evil mindedness eliminates the filth. The pure God's name enshrines in the mind. He serves his guru forever and ego is eradicated from within. ||12|| If one understands through the guru, finds the destiny. Without God's name they explain and argue. The greatness of serving the guru eliminates greed and hunger. ||13|| When the Lord unites them with Him, then they come to realize. Without spiritual wisdom, they understand nothing at all. Enshrining the gift of guru's teaching in the mind, he speaks the sermon. ||14|| He acts according to pre-ordained destiny. No one can erase the order from destiny. Those with pre-ordained destiny, live in devotee's company. ||15|| Those blessed by guru meet devotee's company. They sit in trance with God's love through guru's teaching. Servant Nanak says humbly that awns of God's name are obtained at His door. ||16||1|| Maaroo, Third Master: One Lord is pervading and permeating everywhere. Only a few guru-willed realize this. One God abides in all; no one is without Him. ||1|| He created millions of species. Page 1045 The spiritual teachers and the meditators proclaim this. He feeds all; no one else can estimate His value. ||2|| Love and attachment of the worldly wealth is dark. Ego and possessiveness are spread throughout the universe. They burn day and night and find no peace without the guru. ||3|| He unites and separates. He establishes and disestablishes. True is His command and creation. No one else can issue that command. ||4|| Whoever He guides follows Him; by guru's grace, the fear of death runs away. Enshrining guru's teaching in the mind attains peace; very few guru-willed realize it. ||5|| God unites them in His union. The pre-ordained destiny cannot be erased. Night and day the guru-willed devotees worship and serve the guru. ||6|| Serving the guru lasting peace is obtained. He, the bestowal of all comes to meet them. Subduing ego eliminates the fire of greed; peace attains through guru's teaching. ||7|| One who is attached to his body and family, does not understand. But the guru-willed see everything. Night and day they recite God's name forever and find happiness meeting the beloved. ||8|| The self-willed wanders distracted, attached to duality. Why the unfortunate did not die at birth? He wastes away his life in coming and going. Without the guru, liberation is not obtained. ||9|| The body is stained with the filth of ego and falsehood. The filth does not wash away even by washing hundred times. It cleanses through guru's teaching and filth does not attach again. ||10|| The five demons destroy the body. He dies and reborn again and again but he does not follow guru's teaching. The darkness of emotional attachment to the worldly wealth is like a dream which does not come true; ||11|| Some conquer the five demons and follow guru's teaching. The fortunate meet the guru with ease. Filled with truth and dyed with love, they merge in peace. ||12|| Guru's way is known through the guru. His perfect servant realizes it through guru's teaching. He recites guru's teaching in the mind and the tongue tastes God's love. ||13|| Ego is conquered and subdued by guru's teaching. By enshrining God's name in the heart; they know no other than one God; then let that happen what happens; ||14|| Without the guru, no one obtains intuitive happiness. The guru-willed understands and merges with truth. He serves the Lord attuned to guru's teaching. Guru's teaching eliminates ego. ||15|| He contemplates the virtues of the bestowal. The guru-willed throws the final dice. O Nanak, he merges with God reciting His name and obtains honour. ||16||2|| Maaroo, Third Master: Only true Lord the life of the world is the bestowal. He is realized by serving the guru through his teaching. Page 1046 There is one rule and one supreme Lord. It stays the same in all ages. ||1|| Those who realize themselves are pure. The Lord, the giver of peace comes and meets him. His tongue is imbued with guru's teaching; he sings God's praises and honoured at His door. ||2|| The guru-willed obtains honour reciting God's name. The self-willed slanderer loses his honour. Attuned to God's name, the supreme soul-swan remains detached within him. ||3|| That humble being who dies by guru's teaching is a perfect man. The brave guru explains that; the true pool of nectar is in the body; he drinks it intuitively. ||4|| The scholar reads and explains to others. But he does not realize that his own home is burning. Without serving the guru, God's name is not realized; they are tired of reading but do not find peace. ||5|| Some smear their bodies with ashes and wander in disguise. Without guru's teaching, who has killed the ego? Night and day, they continue burning forever; they wander in doubt and disguise. ||6|| Some, in the midst of household and family, remain always unattached. They die by guru's teaching and dwell in the Lord's name. Night and day, they remain forever attuned to His love; they focus their mind to God with love. ||7|| The self-willed slanders others and is ruined. He is full of greed and barks like a dog. The messenger of death never spares him, and regrets in the end. ||8|| Through guru's true teaching one obtains honour. Without the name, no one attains liberation. Without the guru, no one obtains God's name; God has set such a play; ||9|| Some mystics and seekers think a lot. Some remain imbued with God's name forever. Whoever God unites with Him, understands it. ||10|| Some take cleansing baths and give awns but do not understand; Some conquer their mind and fight with their mind. They are imbued with God's love through guru's teaching; they unite with God through guru's teaching. ||11|| He creates and bestows honour. He unites them with Him by His will. He lives in the mind by His grace; my God's command prevails this way. ||12|| Those who serve the guru are truthful. The false, self-willed do not know to serve him. The Creator creates and watches over; He puts them to work by His will. ||13|| Throughout the ages, there is only one true bestowal. He is realized through guru's teaching by good fortune. Those united through guru's teaching never separate again; they merge in peace by God's grace. ||14|| Acting in ego they are stained with worldly filth. They die and die again, only to be reborn in love of duality. Without serving the guru, liberation is not obtained; check it out! ||15|| He does what He pleases. Page 1047 No one has done, or can do anything by himself. O Nanak, through God's name, one obtains greatness and honour in God's court. ||16||3|| Maaroo, Third Master: Whoever has come has to go. In love of duality, the noose of the devil of death catches them. Those protected by the guru are saved and truly merge with true Lord. ||1|| The Creator creates the creation and watches over it. He accepts those whom God blesses. The guru-willed attains divine wisdom and understands everything. The ignorant act blindly. ||2|| The self-willed is doubtful; he doesn't understand. He dies and reborn again and again and loses his life uselessly. The guru-willed dyed by God's name obtain peace and merge with true Lord intuitively. ||3|| Chasing after worldly affairs, their mind has been burnt. But meeting with the perfect guru, he is transformed into gold once again. God forgives him and blesses with happiness through guru's teaching. ||4|| The false and evil-minded are the most wicked of the wicked. They are the most sinful of the sinful. With false intellect they talk false words. God's name is not obtained through ill will. ||5|| The unworthy soul-bride is not pleasing to her Husband Lord. False-minded acts in falsehood. The ignorant does not know essence of her husband Lord; He is not realized without the guru. ||6|| The evil-minded, does evil deeds. She decorates herself, but her Husband Lord is not pleased. The virtuous soul-bride enjoys her Husband Lord forever the true guru unites her with Him. ||7|| God issues the order and watches over. He blesses some according to the pre-ordained destiny. Night and day, they are imbued with God's name and obtain peace. God unites them with Him by His grace. ||8|| God created the enticement of ego. The guru-willed merges in peace through true love. He unites and watches over; He is not realized without the guru. ||9|| Some contemplate guru's teaching and remain awake forever. Some unfortunate remain asleep attached to the worldly wealth. He acts and inspires all to act; no one else can do anything. ||10|| Through gurus teaching the death is conquered and killed. Enshrining God's name in the mind, serving the guru attains peace and one absorbs in God's name. ||11|| In love of duality, the world wanders around insane. Immersed in love and attachment of worldly wealth it suffers in pain. Wearing all kind of disguises. Without the guru, peace is not obtained. ||12|| Who to blame, when God makes us do everything? As He wishes He makes us to follow the path. He the bestowal is kind; as He pleases so we follow; ||13|| He is the Creator and the enjoyer. He is content and knows the way. He is pure, compassionate, the lover of nectar; His order cannot be erased. ||14|| Those who know one Lord are fortunate. Page 1048 God the life of the world abides in everyone. He hides and reveals the same time. He eliminates the fear of doubt of the guru-willed. ||15|| The guru-willed knows only one Lord. Enshrining God's name, he realizes God through guru's teaching. Whom You give, receives it. O Nanak, reciting God attains honour. ||16||4|| Maaroo, Third Master: I praise the true, profound and unfathomable Lord. The whole world is in His power. He enjoys all hearts forever day and night. He dwells in peace. ||1|| It is true that there is God. By guru's grace, I enshrine Him in my mind. He has come to dwell in my heart; the noose of death has been cut. ||2|| Who should I serve and who should I praise? I serve the guru and praise God through guru's teaching. The intellect becomes sacred through guru's teaching and the lotus mind blossoms. ||3|| The body is frail and perishable, like paper. With a drop of water on it, it crumbles and dissolves instantaneously. The guru-willed understands the priceless body enshrining God's name in the mind. ||4|| Pure is that kitchen, which is enclosed by spiritual awareness. Lord's Name is my food and truth is my support. He who has God's name enshrined in the mind becomes sacred and content forever. ||5|| I admire those who are attached to truth. They sing God's praises and remain awake forever. True peace fills them forever and their tongues savor God's sublime essence. ||6|| I miss God's name and no other. I serve one Lord, and no other. The perfect guru revealed me the truth; God's name dwells in me. ||7|| Wandering in different lifes I came in this life. I was lost by God's will. When God unites him, then the guru-willed realizes and searches God through guru's teachings. ||8|| I am a sinner filled with lust and anger. With what mouth should I say? I have no virtue or service to my credit. O immortal true God; please unite me the sinking stone with You through guru's teaching. ||9|| No one does anything; no one is able to do anything. What the Lord does and causes to be done happens. We attain happiness by His grace; He is realized by reciting His name. ||10|| This body is the land; the infinite lesson is the seed. Deal and trade with the true God; When the true wealth grows; it never falls short enshrining God's name in the mind. ||11|| O dear Lord, please bless me the worthless sinner, with virtues. Forgive me and bless me with Your Name. Enshrining God's name in the mind the guru-willed obtains honour. ||12|| Godly wealth is inside but the mortal does not realize it. By guru's grace, some understand it; The guru-willed acquires this wealth and abides by God's name forever. ||13|| The never ending greed leads one to doubt. Page 1049 In love of worldly attachment, he does not understand anything. The blind, self-willed knows nothing; God's name enshrines in the mind through guru's teaching. ||14|| The self-willed are asleep in ego and worldly wealth. They do not watch over their homes, and are ruined in the end. They slander others and burn in anxiety; they live in pain and suffering. ||15|| The Creator leads us to do our deeds. He blesses the guru-willed with understanding. O Nanak, those imbued with God's name become pure; God's name dwells in the mind by reciting. ||16||5|| Maaroo, Third Master: I serve only the eternal God. Attached to duality, the whole world is false. I praise God through guru's teaching; God pleases with truth only; ||1|| Your virtues are many but I do not know any. The life of the world the great giver attaches us to him by His grace. He blesses and bestows honour and the mind gets drenched through guru's teaching. ||2|| Guru's teaching eliminates greed of the worldly wealth. The mind becomes pure eliminating ego. Imbued with God's love I sing God's praises intuitively and my tongue recites God. ||3|| He spends life saying mine mine. The childish self-willed does not understand; The devil of death has decided the time; life decreases every moment. ||4|| He is full of greed and does not realize anything. Death hovers over the head but he does not know it. Whatever one earns here gets the reward in the next world; nothing can be done in the end. ||5|| Those attached to truth become true. The self-willed attached to duality weep and wail. God is the master at both ends; He enjoys His virtues. ||6|| The mortal looks adorable following guru's teaching. His mind is enticed by reciting God's name. The filth of false attachment and worldly wealth does not touch him who recites God's name through guru's teaching. ||7|| One Lord abides in all. He is revealed by guru's grace. Eliminating ego attains happiness and drink nectar reciting God's name. ||8|| God is the destroyer of sin and pain. The guru-willed serves Him contemplating guru's teaching. Everything happens by God's grace. The mind and body of the guru-willed get drenched. ||9|| The world is burning in the fire of worldly pleasure. The guru-willed eliminates it through guru's teaching. Reciting God's name through guru's teaching attains peace and joy. ||10|| Even Indra, seated on his throne is subject to devil of death. The devil of death does not spare him, though he tries hard. Surrendering to the guru, attains salvation reciting God's name from the tongue. ||11|| There is no devotion in the mind of the self-willed. The guru-willed attains peace and happiness through God's worship. God's sermon is sacred and saviour, and drenches the mind with guru's teaching. ||12|| Brahma, Vishnu and Shiva also contemplate. They are bound by the three qualities. But the salvation is different. Page 1050 The guru-willed knows God through divine wisdom and recite His name. ||13|| He reads scriptures but does not understand God's name. For the sake of wealth he reads again and again and argues. The ignorant is filled with ignorance; how can he be saved through duality? ||14|| He reads preaches and discusses the scriptures. His mind does not believe it and he does not follow guru's teaching. The Vedas tell about virtue and vice, but the guru-willed drinks nectar. ||15|| God is one. It is true. There is no one except Him. O Nanak, imbued with God's name the mind becomes truthful and dwells in truth. ||16||6|| Maaroo, Third Master: True Lord established the throne of truth. He dwells there; no false or worldly attachment exists there. True Lord dwells in the mind; that is the essence of the guru-willed. ||1|| True is his merchandise, and true is his trade. There is no doubt or duality there. Earned true wealth does not fall short; only a few think and realize it. ||2|| Those guided by God are attached to Him. They are fortunate enshrining God's name in the mind. They praise God through guru's teaching; they contemplate God imbued with guru's teaching. ||3|| It is true that there is God and I truly praise Him. I see one Lord and no other. Guru's teaching is the top step of the ladder; the jewel of divine wisdom eliminates ego. ||4|| Emotional attachment to the worldly wealth is eliminated through guru's teaching. The truth dwells in the mind by Your grace. True are the actions of the truthful and the thirst of ego is subdued. ||5|| God created the false and worldly attachment. Only a few guru-willed realize it. Only the guru-willed earns the truth; truth is the reality of his deeds. ||6|| He does those deeds which are pleasing to God; Ego and greed are eliminated through guru's teaching. Following the guru's teachings, the mind becomes soothed forever and the ego is driven away. ||7|| Those who are attuned to truth are pleased with everything. They look adorable following guru's teaching. Truthful here are truthful in God's court. God bestows His blessing on them. ||8|| Those who are attached to duality not the truth; attached to worldly pleasure they suffer forever. Without the guru, they do not understand pain and pleasure; attached to the worldly wealth they suffer terrible pain. ||9|| Those who are pleased with true guru's teaching! They act according to pre-ordained destiny. They serve and recite the true Lord and contemplate truth imbued with truth. ||10|| Service to the guru seems sweet to them. Night and day, they are intuitively immersed in peace and trance. Saying God the mind becomes pure and they love guru's service. ||11|| Those beings are at peace that the true guru attaches to the truth. He unites them with Him by His grace. Those protected by the guru are saved; others are ruined by the love of worldly pleasure. ||12|| Page 1051 The guru-willed realizes the true Lord through guru's teaching. He has no family or mother. One God abides in all and He is the support of all. ||13|| Ego, possessiveness are the love of duality. They can do nothing. It is all pre-ordained from destiny. Through the true guru, they practice truth. God eliminates their pain. ||14|| I obtain peace through Your blessing. Through true guru's teaching they earn the truth. Enshrining truth in the mind, the mind and body become true and are filled with the treasure of worship. ||15|| He issues orders and watches over. He makes us obey His will. O Nanak, the detached are imbued with God's name; their mind and body look adorable dyed by God's name. ||16||7|| Maaroo, Third Master: He came into existence on his own. He pervades all but hidden. God the life of the world takes care of all those who realize themselves. ||1|| He who created Brahma, Vishnu and Shiva, He put them to pre-ordained deeds. The guru-willed who realize one God, merge with Him by His grace. ||2|| The world keeps coming and going in reincarnation. Attached to worldly wealth; he thinks of many useless deeds. One who realizes guru's teaching becomes eternal and truthful forever. ||3|| Some are attached to the root, they find peace. Those attached to the branches, waste their lives away. Those, who speak the sacred words; bear the sacred fruit; ||4|| I have no virtue; what can I say? You see all, and weigh them on Your scale. The guru-willed knows only one God; he lives by God's will. ||5|| According to Your will, You link me to the true task. Renouncing vice, I am immersed in virtue. The virtuous God dwells in virtues. He is realized through guru's teaching. ||6|| Wherever I look, I see Him there. Duality and evil-mindedness are destroyed by guru's teaching. God is one and only one; He is happy within Himself. ||7|| The body is withering away. The ignorant self-willed does not realize guru's teaching. He who searches himself by guru's grace realizes God the Lord of the universe. ||8|| The Lord frees him from the entanglement of sins. By enshrining God's name in the mind. Reap the reward of your choice by dying with unfading divine love. ||9|| The self-willed discusses wisdom but it does not sink in. Again and again, he comes into the world but finds no place to rest. The guru-willed praises divine wisdom and realizes God in all ages. ||10|| The self-willed does deeds that bring pain all the time. He does not believe in guru's teaching; how can he go to God's court? The guru-willed enshrines God in the mind through guru's teaching and serves the bestowal of happiness forever. ||11|| Page 1052 Wherever I look, I see You everywhere. I realized this through the perfect guru. I recite God's name forever and my mind is dyed by it. ||12|| Imbued with God's name the body is sanctified. Those without God's name drown without water and die. They come and go but do not realize God's name. The guru-willed realize Him through guru's teaching. ||13|| The perfect guru has imparted this understanding. Without God's name, no one attains liberation. Reciting God's name attains honour and intuitively remain dyed with love. ||14|| The body-village crumbles and collapses into a pile of dust. Without guru's teaching the cycle does not end. The guru-willed who praise God, merge in God and know only one God. ||15|| Whoever God blesses, realize Him. God dwells in the mind through guru's teaching. O Nanak, those imbued by God's name become formless. Truth is recognized in God's court. ||16||8|| Maaroo, Sohlay, Third Master: O Creator, You do everything. All beings are under Your refuge. You abide in all yet hidden. You are realized through guru's teaching. ||1|| The treasure of worship of devotees of God is full. He blesses them through guru's teaching. They do what pleases You and their minds are imbued with Your love. ||2|| You are the priceless diamond and jewel. You weigh them with Your blessing. All beings are in Your refuge. They realize You by Your blessing. ||3|| Those who are blessed by you from destiny; they do not die or take birth. Their cycle of reincarnation ends. They praise God day and night. One God prevails through all ages. ||4|| Emotional attachment to worldly wealth exists in the whole world. Including Brahma, Vishnu and all the demy-gods; those who please you recite Your name. You are realized through divine lesson. ||5|| The world is engrossed in vice and virtue. Happiness and sorrow are loaded with pain. The guru-willed realize You by reciting Your name and attain happiness. ||6|| No one can erase the record of one's actions. Salvation attains through guru's teaching. He, who eliminates ego, realizes God. He only gets what he earns. ||7|| Enticed by the worldly wealth, he does not enjoy God's name. In love of duality, he suffers serious pain. The hypocrite, self-willed and imitators are lost and repent in the end. ||8|| Praise God through God's will. All sins and sufferings will be eliminated. God is pure, so is His sermon. Dye your mind with God's love. ||9|| Whoever He blesses, obtains the treasure of virtues. Ego and possessiveness are brought to an end. God is the bestowal of virtue and vice. Only a few guru-willed realize Him. ||10|| My God is pure and infinite. God unites us with Him contemplating guru's teaching. Page 1053 He blesses and implants the truth. My mind and body are attuned to God. ||11|| The supreme soul lives in filthy mind and body. He is realized contemplating guru's teaching. Conquering ego, the mind becomes pure forever. Recite the name of the bestowal of peace with your tongue. ||12|| In the fortress of the body there are many shops and bazaars. Infinite God lives there. Adored by guru's teaching; one looks adorable. God is realized by killing ego. ||13|| The jewel is priceless, inaccessible and infinite. How can the poor estimate its worth? It is weighed through guru's teaching and realized reciting guru's lesson. ||14|| The volumes of the Simritees and the Shaastras only extend the extension of attachment to the worldly wealth. The ignorant read and do not understand guru's word; only a few guru-willed realize it. ||15|| The Creator acts and causes all to act. Through true sermon he teaches the truth. O Nanak, honour is obtained through God's name. One God prevails through all ages. ||16||9|| Maaroo, Third Master: Serve the true Creator. He eliminates sufferings through guru's teaching. He is inaccessible and unfathomable. He cannot be evaluated. He is inaccessible and immeasurable. ||1|| The true Lord bestows truth. He attaches some humble beings to the truth. They serve the true Lord and practice truth and merge with truth through God's name. ||2|| The primal Lord unites His devotees with Him. He attaches them to devotional worship. They sing God's praises through true sermon and get the benefit of life. ||3|| The guru-willed trades and realizes himself and others. He knows no other than one Lord. The true banker trades with true traders and they trade true merchandise. ||4|| He came into existence on His own; then created the universe. He guides a few to realize guru's teaching. Those who serve the guru are truthful. Their noose of death is cut. ||5|| He destroys, creates, embellishes and fashions all beings. And attaches them to duality and worldly attachment; the self-willed wander acting blindly forever. Chain of death hangs around their neck; ||6|| He blesses and puts them to serve the guru. Through guru's teachings, they enshrine God's name in the mind. Night and day, they recite God's name. They make profit reciting God's name in the world. ||7|| He is true and true is His name. He bestows to the guru-willed and they enshrine Him in their mind. Those who enshrine Him in the mind look adorable; no one attacks them. ||8|| He is inaccessible and unfathomable; His value cannot be appraised. By guru's grace, He lives in the mind. Praise the bestowal of virtues through guru's teaching and no one will ask for your account; ||9|| Brahma, Vishnu and Shiva serve Him. They cannot find the limits of the unseen, unknowable Lord. The guru-willed whom You bless know the unknown. ||10|| Page 1054 The perfect guru has imparted this understanding. I have enshrined God's name in my mind. Reciting God's name is worship, praising God one attains divinity. ||11|| The servant serves and obeys the command of the infinite Lord. The self-willed does not know the essence of God's command. Obeying His command attains honour and one becomes carefree through God's command. ||12|| By guru's grace, one recognizes God's command. The wandering mind is controlled and brought back to stability. Imbued with God's name becomes detached; God's name is a jewel. ||13|| One Lord pervades the world. He is revealed by guru's grace; Those who praise guru's teaching become pure and reach God's home. ||14|| The devotees are forever in Your sanctuary. You are inaccessible and unfathomable; Your value cannot be estimated. As it pleases Your will, You keep me; the guru-willed recites your name. ||15|| I sing Your praises forever. O true Lord, may I become pleasing to Your mind. Nanak offers this true prayer: O Lord, please bless me with truth that I merge in truth. ||16||1||10|| Maaroo, Third Master: Those who serve the guru are very fortunate. Night and day, they remain lovingly attuned to the true name. Lord, the giver of peace, abides in their hearts forever; they enjoy guru's teaching. ||1|| When Lord grants His grace, one meets with the guru. He enshrines God's name in the mind. Enshrining God in the mind attains eternal peace; they enjoy guru's teaching. ||2|| By His grace, God unites us with Him. Ego and attachment are burned away by guru's teaching. Imbued with God's love he is liberated forever. He has no conflict with anyone. ||3|| Without serving the guru, there is pitch dark. Without guru's teaching, no one goes across. Those imbued with guru's teaching become totally detached and enjoy benefit of guru's teaching. ||4|| Pain and pleasure are pre-ordained by the Creator. He created the duality. The guru-willed remain absorbed in God. The self-willed do not believe in it. ||5|| Those who do not understand guru's teaching are called self-willed. They do not know the essence of the love of the guru. How can anyone find the carefree Lord without love? The devil of death will take their breath away. ||6|| The overfed devil of death cannot be killed. But he does not come close to those who follow guru's teaching. Hearing to guru's teaching he runs away from far; may the Lord beat him ||7||. The dear Lord is the ruler of all. What can this poor devil of death do? The obedient servant obeys God's order. God takes away the breath by His command. ||8|| God created the universe following guru's teaching. Then God created the creation. The guru-willed realizes it and obtains honour reciting guru's teaching. ||9|| The guru-willed realizes the architect of destiny. Page 1055 In all four ages, God is realized through guru's teaching. The guru-willed does not die or take birth; he is absorbed in guru's teaching. ||10|| The guru-willed praises God through guru's teaching. God is inaccessible, unfathomable and carefree. God's name bestows salvation in all four ages believing in guru's teaching. ||11|| The guru-willed obtains eternal peace and happiness. The guru-willed enshrines God's name in the mind. Becoming a guru-willed, he realizes God's name and forgets the ill will. ||12|| When one becomes guru-willed, he merges in truth. He does not die and take birth, and not consigned to rebirth. The guru-willed remains forever imbued with God's love and takes advantage forever. ||13|| The guru-willed devotees look beautiful in God's court. They are cared for through true sermon and guru's teachings. Night and day, they sing God's praises and reach the destiny with ease. ||14|| The perfect guru speaks his teaching. He preaches to worship God night and day with love. One who sings God's praises forever becomes pure; purity is God's virtue; ||15|| True Lord is the giver of virtues. Rare are the guru-willed who realize Him. Servant Nanak enjoys praising the name of carefree God! ||16||2||11|| Maaroo, Third Master: Serve the inaccessible and infinite God; He has no end or limit. Recite Him in the mind through guru's teaching. The mind has the divine wisdom. ||1|| One Lord is pervading all. By guru's grace, He is revealed. The life of the world nurtures and gives food to all. ||2|| The perfect guru has imparted this understanding. The universe is created by His command. He who obeys God's order finds peace. His command is the highest of all. ||3|| The teaching of the true guru is infinite. Through His teaching, the world is saved. The Creator creates and checks the quality. He bestows life and food. ||4|| Out of millions, only a few understand; They are imbued with God's love through guru's teaching. They praise God the giver of peace forever; God blesses those who worship Him. ||5|| Those who serve the guru are truthful. Those who die to be reborn again are the false of the false. The inaccessible, invisible, carefree and unfathomable Lord is the love of His devotees. ||6|| The perfect guru implants truth. Praise God forever through true guru's teaching. The bestowal of virtues abides in all. Everybody's fate and death is pre written. ||7|| The guru-willed knows that God is ever-present. He who serves him through guru's teachings obtains satisfaction. Night and day, he serves the true sermon. He enjoys guru's teaching. ||8|| The ignorant and blind performs all sorts of rituals. The stubborn-minded performs these rituals and takes birth again and again. Page 1056 For committing sins, they act in greed and evil-minded duality. ||9|| The perfect guru teaches God's worship. Enshrine God's name in the mind through guru's teaching. God abides in mind and body. The mind enjoys praising and worshipping God. ||10|| My true God is the destroyer of demons. Worshipping Him through guru's teaching bestows salvation. My true Lord is forever true. He is the emperor of emperors. ||11|| True are those devotees, who are pleasing to Your Mind. They sing Your praises at Your door through guru's teaching and look beautiful. Night and day, they sing the true sermon. God's name is the support of the poor. ||12|| Those whom You unite, are never separated again. They praise You through guru's teaching forever. You are the master of all. They praise Your name through guru's teaching. ||13|| No one can realize You without guru's teaching. You speak the unspoken speech. Everyone; recite God's name through guru the bestowal. ||14|| You are the Creator of the universe. No one can erase what You have written. You bless the guru-willed with Your name; his doubt and account is erased. ||15|| Your true devotees stand at the door of Your court. They serve You through guru's teaching with love. O Nanak, those imbued with God's name become detached. Their deeds are fulfilled reciting Your name. ||16||3||12|| Maaroo, Third Master: My True Lord staged a play. He created no one like anyone else. He made them different, and is happy seeing it. All tastes are in the body. ||1|| You made them breathe air. You put worldly power in the body. By guru's grace, one turns away from it, and attains the jewel of spiritual wisdom through guru's teaching. ||2|| He created darkness and light. He pervades all, no one else is; One who realizes himself by guru's grace, the lotus of his mind blossoms by Your grace. ||3|| You know your depth and extent. Other people hear say. The divine person realizes God and truly praises God. ||4|| The priceless merchandise is in the body. He opens the mental doors. The guru-willed intuitively drinks nectar and extinguishes fire of greed. ||5|| All sublime tastes are in the body. Only a few obtain guru's teaching. Search God inside through guru's teaching, why do you search outside? ||6|| No one enjoys the taste without tasting. He drinks nectar through guru's teaching. Drinking nectar he becomes immortal; Your taste is enjoyed through guru's teaching. ||7|| One, who realizes himself, knows all virtues. Page 1057 He recites God's name through guru's teaching. Imbued with God's name forever, eliminates the attachment of worldly wealth. ||8|| Serving the guru, everything is obtained. Ego, possessiveness and self-conceit are taken away. God the giver of peace grants His grace; he looks beautiful through guru's teaching. ||9|| Guru's teaching is a sacred sermon. Night and day, recite God's name. When true God dwells in the mind, the body becomes pure. ||10|| The servant serves You by praising guru's teaching. Imbued forever with God's love, he sings God's praises. By His grace He unites us with Him and imparts sandalwood scent in us. ||11|| He praises God and speaks the unspoken through guru's teaching. My true God is carefree. The giver of virtue imparts guru's lesson. Lesson's taste is Your taste. ||12|| The confused, self-willed finds no place of rest. They do the pre-ordained deeds. Imbued with poison, they search for poison, and suffer the pain of death and birth. ||13|| He is He and praises Himself. Your virtues are in You O God; You are true, Your sermon is true. Only You are unknown and unfathomable. ||14|| Without the guru, the giver, no one finds the Lord. He may do millions of good deeds. God dwells in the mind by guru's grace. Praise Him through guru's teaching. ||15|| Those with pre-ordained destiny, unit with You. They are adorned by true sermon and guru's teaching. Servant

Nanak sings God's praises all the time. Singing His praises one merges with Him. ||16||4||13|| Maaroo, Third Master: Only God is eternal forever. He is realized through the guru. Those imbued with God's taste; recite Him forever. They become peaceful through guru's teaching. ||1|| Enshrine true love of the true Lord in the mind. Through guru's teaching; recite beloved God's name. Enshrine treasure of God's name in the mind and forget the worldly wealth. ||2|| Both the king and his subjects are involved in evil-deals and duality. Without serving the guru, they do not unite with God. They recite one God and attain peace forever. Their rule becomes eternal. ||3|| No one can save them from coming and going. Birth and death come from Him. O guru-willed; recite the true Lord forever. He bestows salvation. ||4|| Truth and self-control are found at the door of the guru. Ego and anger are eliminated through guru's teaching. Serving the guru, obtains lasting peace; humility and contentment come from Him. ||5|| Ego and false attachment well up in the world. Forgetting God's name, the whole world parishes. God's name is not obtained without serving the guru. God's name is beneficial in the world. ||6|| True immortal God is adored through guru's teaching. Five divine tunes are played with musical instruments. Page 1058 All deeds are fulfilled through God's name. What kind of work anyone does without guru's teaching? ||7||He laughs and cries in a moment. Through ill will and duality the deed is not fulfilled. Union and separation are pre-ordained by the Creator. Actions taken cannot be reversed. ||8|| Salvation is obtained through guru's teaching. He remains forever submerged in the Lord. By guru's grace, one obtains greatness and the sickness of ego does not affect him. ||9|| Eating tasty delicacies, he increases his body weight. He wears disguises but does not follow guru's teaching. The disease inside is painful and one sinks in the filth. ||10|| He studies the scriptures and preaches others. God is in the body. He does not recognize Him through guru's teaching. The guru-willed churns the essence and enjoys singing God's name. ||11|| He forsakes the essence at home and wanders outside. The blind, self-willed do not taste the flavour. Imbued with other tastes she speaks bland and does not enjoy God's taste. ||12|| The self-willed doubts the husband Lord. She is deluded by ill will and suffers forever. Through lust and anger her mind is attached to duality. She does not find peace even in a dream. ||13|| The body becomes adorable through guru the Lord's teaching. Night and day, she enjoys the husband Lord with love. The stranger finds a place in her mind. God is realized by obeying His will. ||14|| The great giver gives by His grace. No one has any say in front of Him. She unites with Him by His grace through guru's teaching. Guru's teaching is unfathomed. ||15|| Body and soul, all belong to Him. True Lord is my Lord and master. Nanak realized God through guru's sermon. Reciting God's recitation he merged with God. ||16||5||14|| Maaroo, Third Master: The guru-willed realizes God by reciting, listening to scriptures and thinking. The guru-willed attains infinite spiritual wisdom and meditation. The guru-willed does deeds pleasing to God. The guru-willed realizes God through perfect deeds. ||1|| The mind of the guru-willed turns away from the world. The guru-willed plays the sermon through speaking. The guru-willed attuned to the truth becomes detached and dwells in His home. ||2|| The guru speaks the sacred words. Guru's teaching is easily understood. My mind remains imbued with God's love and merges with Him. ||3|| Guru-willed's mind becomes pure and he bathes in the pool of truth. No filth attaches to him; he merges in the true Lord. He truly practices truth forever and performs true worship. ||4|| The guru-willed speaks truth and sees truth. The guru-willed practices and lives the truth. He speaks truth forever and inspires others to speak truth. ||5|| The guru-willed speaks the true and sacred sermon. Truly the guru-willed preaches truth. The guru-willed serves the true Lord and imparts guru's teaching. ||6|| Page 1059 One who becomes a guru-willed understands. He gets rid of ego, worldly wealth and doubt. He climbs the sacred high guru's ladder and sings God's praises at His door. ||7|| The guru-willed practices truth self-control, and does good deeds. The guru-willed obtains salvation. Through loving devotion, he remains forever imbued with Lord's love. Eradicating self-conceit, he merges in the Lord. ||8|| One who becomes a guru-willed, searches and tells others. He is lovingly attuned to the true name forever. They do whatever appeals to the true Lord. ||9|| When it pleases God, he unites them with the guru.

As it pleases Him, He comes to dwell in the mind. He is happy by His will and enshrines in the mind by His will. ||10|| Those who act stubborn-mindedly are destroyed. Wearing all sorts of religious rituals, they do not please the Lord. They commit sins and suffer and sink in pain. ||11|| The guru-willed earns happiness. He understands death and birth. One, who sees birth and death alike, pleases God. ||12|| When the guru-willed dies, he is accepted by God. He realizes the coming and going through guru-s teaching. He does not die or reborn, and does not suffer in pain; his mind merges with God. ||13|| Those who meet the guru are fortunate. They eradicate ego and attachment from inside. Their mind becomes pure and filth does not attach again. They are honoured in God's court. ||14|| He acts and inspires all to act. He establishes and disestablishes and watches over. The service of the guru-willed is pleasing to God. He puts in his account when He hears the truth. ||15|| The guru-willed practices truth and only truth. The guru-willed is immaculate; no filth attaches to him. O Nanak, those who contemplate God's name are imbued with it. Reciting God's name they merge with God. ||16||1||15|| Maaroo, Third Master: He created the universe by His command. He establishes and disestablishes, and embellishes with grace. God administers justice; through truth, we merge in the truth. ||1|| The body is a fortress of creation. Emotional attachment to worldly wealth prevails everywhere. Without guru's teaching one becomes dust and merges with dust. ||2|| The body is the infinite fortress of gold. Guru's infinite teaching abides in it. The guru-willed sings praises of God and finds peace meeting the beloved. ||3|| The body is the temple of God. God Himself embellishes it. The dear Lord dwells in it. The businessmen trade in guru's teachings and unite with God by His grace. ||4|| He who eradicates anger is pure. He realizes this through guru's teaching and reforms. The Creator acts, and inspires all to act. He abides in the mind. ||5|| Pure and unique is devotional worship. The mind and body are washed clean, contemplating guru's teaching. Page 1060 One who remains forever imbued with His love? God attaches him to worship by His grace. ||6|| The mind in the body wanders around. Forgetting the bundle of happiness, he suffers in terrible pain. Without meeting the true guru, he finds no place to rest. God sets this play. ||7|| He is infinite. He contemplates Himself. He unites us with Him. That is the essence. What can the poor creatures do? God unites them by His grace. ||8|| God unites us with the perfect guru. Through guru's teaching he becomes very powerful and brave. Uniting them with Him He bestows honour. He inspires them to focus their mind to the true Lord. ||9|| True Lord dwells in the mind. Only a few guru-willed understand this. God's priceless name dwells in the mind and realized by reciting His name. ||10|| He wanders in foreign lands, but does not look inside. Attached to the worldly wealth, he is arrested by the devil of death. Those who dwell in duality, the noose of devil of death around their neck never breaks; ||11|| There is no meditation, penance or self-control, Till one practices guru's teaching. Truth is obtained through guru's teaching and truly merges with truth. ||12|| Lust and anger are very powerful in the world. They lead to all sorts of actions, but only add to pain. Those who serve the guru find peace; they unite with God through guru's teaching. ||13|| There are Air, water and fire. Emotional and worldly attachments abide in all. If you realize the Creator, the worldly attachment eliminates. ||14|| Some are bothered by pride of worldly wealth. They are proud and egotistic. They never think of the devil of death and depart repenting. ||15|| He, who created it, knows the way. He guides the guru-willed to know God through guru's teaching. Slave Nanak offers this prayer; O mortal, enshrine God's name in the mind. ||16||2||16|| Maaroo, Third Master: The kind and bestowal of honour God; exists from the beginning for ages. He is realized through perfect guru's teaching. Those who serve You merge with You by Your grace. ||1|| You are inaccessible and hidden. Your price cannot be found. All beings seek Your sanctuary. You guide them as You please. You put them on the correct path. ||2|| There is God and He always will be. He creates and no one else can. The bestowal of peace takes care of all and feeds them. ||3|| You are inaccessible, hidden, unexplainable and infinite. No one knows Your extent. You know You. Through guru's teachings, You reveal You. ||4|| Your almighty command prevails throughout the underworlds, realms and the universe. Page 1061 God creates and destroys by His order and unites with Him by His order. ||5|| One, who realizes Your command, praises Your command. You are inaccessible, hidden and carefree. What You teach, they learn. You are realized through guru's teaching. ||6|| Night and day, the life decreases. Both night and day are the witness. The blind self-willed does not know that the death hovers over the head. ||7|| The mind and body become soothed by entering guru's refuge. Doubt is eliminated from within and fear runs away. He is happy forever and sings God's praises and speaks the true sermon. ||8|| O architect of destiny; whoever realizes You; the fortunate realizes you through guru's teaching. God bestows self-control, honour and truthfulness. He is realized by eliminating ego. ||9|| The stubborn mind is attached to duality. Deluded by doubt the unfortunate wander around in confusion. With good luck he serves the guru and attains peace with ease. ||10|| He created millions of species. Worship God in this human life. Without worship they live in filth and get absorbed in filth again. ||11|| Doing good deeds the guru teaches the way to worship. Without good luck, how can anyone find Him? The Creator acts and inspires all to act; as He wills, he guides us. ||12|| The Simritees and the Shaastras do not know His limits. The blind ignorant does not recognize the essence of reality. The Creator acts and inspires all to act; He deludes some in doubt. ||13|| He causes everything to be done. He puts everyone to task. He establishes and disestablishes, and watches over; He reveals Himself to the guru-willed. ||14|| True Lord is profoundly deep and unfathomable. Praising Him forever, the mind is consoled. He is inaccessible and unfathomable. His value cannot be estimated. The guru-willed enshrines Him in the mind. ||15|| He remains unaffected; rest of the world is entangled in their affairs. By guru's grace, one realizes Him. O Nanak, enshrine God's name in the mind. He is realized through guru's teaching. ||16||3||17|| Maaroo, Third Master: For thirty-six ages, utter darkness prevailed. Only You know this, O Creator Lord; What can anyone else say or preach? You only know Your value. ||1|| Saying once, you created the universe. All the plays and dramas are by Your greatness. The True Lord makes distinctions; He makes and breaks as well. ||2|| The Juggler has staged His juggling show. One watches it through the perfect guru; One who remains forever detached through guru's teaching and focuses his mind to the true Lord. ||3|| The divine musical tunes play in the universe. God the player plays them. Everyone breathes in the same air and all live by breathing. ||4|| Page 1062 Whatever the Creator does, happens definitely. Through guru's teaching, he eliminates ego. He bestows honour on some by guru's grace and they recite Gods name. ||5|| There is no other benefit as great as service to the guru. They enshrine God's name in the mind and praise God through his name. Reciting His name attains peace by His grace and reaps the reward. ||6|| Without reciting God's name the world suffers. The more actions one does, more the corruption increases. How can one find peace without reciting God's name? He suffers pain without God's name. ||7|| He acts and inspires all to act. By guru's grace, He reveals Himself to a few. The guru-willed breaks the bonds and reaches the destiny. ||8|| One who calculates and counts, burns in the world. His skepticism and corruption are never dispelled. The guru-willed forgets counting and merges with true Lord. ||9|| If God bestows truth, then we attain it. By guru's grace, it is revealed. Attune to God with love, praise God's name and attain peace by guru's grace. ||10|| Through God's love one obtains meditation, penance and self-control. God, the destroyer, destroys sins. Through God's name the body and mind are soothed and merge in peace intuitively. ||11|| With greed inside, the filth attaches to filthy mind. They do filthy deeds and suffer in pain. The false deal in false and suffer pain by telling lies. ||12|| Only a few enshrine the pure sermon in the mind. By guru's grace, his skepticism is removed. He follows guru's will day and night and finds peace missing God's name. ||13|| The true Lord is the Creator. He creates and destroys. The guru-willed praises Him forever and finds peace uniting with Him. ||14|| Making countless efforts, the senses do not come under control. Everyone is burning in the fire of lust and anger. Serving the guru, the mind is controlled. Controlling the mind merges with supreme mind. ||15|| You created the sense of 'mine' and 'yours.' All beings are Yours; O Nanak, recite God's name all the time and enshrine in the mind through guru's lesson. ||16||4||18|| Maaroo, Third Master: The bestowal Lord is inaccessible and unfathomable. He does not have any greed; He is carefree. No one

can reach Him; He unites us with Him by His grace. ||1|| Whatever
He does surely happens. There is no other giver, except Him.
Whoever He blesses with His name, obtains it. He is realized through
guru's teaching. ||2|| The fourteen worlds are Your markets. The true
guru reveals them in the mind. One, who deals in God's name, finds
Him through guru's teaching. ||3|| Page 1063 Serving the guru, one
obtains peace and joy. Lord of the universe comes to dwell in the
heart. He intuitively practices worship day and night. God guides
him to worship. ||4|| Those who are separated from the guru, suffer
in pain Night and day, they are punished and they suffer more pain.
Their faces are blackened and they do not reach the destiny and
suffer pain and more pain. ||5|| Those who serve the guru are very
fortunate. They intuitively attune to God with love. They practice
truth all the time and unite with true Lord. ||6|| He obtains the truth,
which the true Lord blesses. Filled with truth eliminates doubt.
Truly, God is the bestowal of truth; whomever He bestows receives
it. ||7|| He is the Creator of all. Whoever He guides, realizes Him. He
blesses and bestows honour and unites with Him. ||8|| Acting in ego,
one wastes his life. Even in the world hereafter, attachment to
worldly wealth does not leave him. In the next world, the devil of
death checks his account and crushes him like sesame seeds in the
oil-press. ||9|| By perfect destiny, one serves the guru. If God blesses,
then one serves. The devil of death does not come close to him. He
reaches the destiny and attains peace. ||10|| Those who please you
find happiness. By good fortune they serve the guru. Honour is in
Your hand. Whoever You bestow receives it. ||11|| The enlightenment
comes from the guru. By enshrining the priceless God's name in the
mind, the jewel of divine wisdom enlightens the mind forever and
eliminates the darkness of ignorance. ||12|| The blind ignorant are
attached to duality. The unfortunate drown without water. When
they depart from the world, they do not find God's door or home;
they are tied at the door of devil of death and suffer pain. ||13||
Without serving the guru, no one finds liberation. Go ask any spiritual
teacher or those who meditate. Whoever serve the guru obtain
honour and are honoured in God's court. ||14|| He who serves the
guru, God unites him with Him. Eliminating worldly attachment, he

lovingly attunes to God. The merchants deal in truth forever and profit from God's name. ||15|| The Creator acts and inspires all to act. He who dies through guru's teaching attains salvation. O Nanak, enshrine God's name in the mind and recite God's name. ||16||5||19|| Maaroo, Third Master: Whatever You want to do is done. Only a rare one obeys Your will. One, who obeys Your will, finds peace. Peace dwells in God's will; ||1|| The guru-willed obeys Your will. He intuitively practices truth and finds peace. Many long to follow Your will. You inspire them to follow your will. ||2|| One, who surrenders to Your will, meets with You. Page 1064 One who believes in Your will merges with You. Greatness rests in God's will; rare are those who accept it. ||3|| When it pleases Him, He leads us to meet the guru. The guru-willed finds the treasure of God's name. You created the universe through Your will. Whoever You bestow Your will enjoys it. ||4|| The blind, self-willed practice cleverness. They do not surrender to Lord's will and suffer terrible pain. Deluded by doubt, they come and go in life; they never find destiny. ||5|| The guru unites them with God and bestows honour to them. Guru's service is pre-ordained. Serving the guru, one obtains God's name and obtains peace through God's name. ||6|| Everything originates from God's name and merges in God's name. By guru's grace, the mind and body are pleased. Reciting God's name obtains enjoyment and joy increases through taste. ||7|| Within the body, only a few reach the destiny. They enshrine truth in the mind through guru's teaching. Whoever He blesses with truth obtains the truth and merges with truth. ||8|| Forgetting God's name the mind and body suffer pain. Attachment to the worldly wealth brings sickness. Without God's name, his mind and body are sick with leprosy, and he goes to hell. ||9|| Those imbued with God's name; their body becomes pure. Their soul-swan becomes pure and enjoys eternal happiness. Praising God's name attains eternal peace and attains destiny. ||10|| Everyone deals in business. Without God's name they fall short in the world. Naked they come and naked they go; without God's name they suffer. ||11|| Whoever God blesses obtains God's name. Through guru's teaching he enshrines God in the mind. God's name dwells in the mind by guru's grace and he recites God's name. ||12|| All those who are born, long for God's name; those who obtain God's name are fortunate. They unite with God through guru's teaching. ||13|| The fortress of the body is infinite. God sits in it and contemplates. He administers true justice and trades in truth; through Him one finds the eternal place. ||14|| Inside the body is a beautiful place. Only a few guru-willed find it. If one stays there and praises God's name. God comes to dwell in the mind. ||15|| My Creator has created a system. He placed every priceless merchandise in the body. O Nanak, those imbued with God's name deal in God's name. Only a rare guru-willed obtains God's name. ||16||6||20|| Maaroo, Third Master: Contemplating guru's teaching the body becomes priceless. God abides there; He has no end or limit. Night and day, he serves God through true sermon. God is realized through guru's teaching. ||1|| Page 1065 I admire those who recite God. They unit with God through guru's teaching. I apply the dust of their feet to my face and forehead and sing God's praises in devotee's company. ||2|| I sing God's praises if it pleases Him. Enshrining God's name in the mind through guru's teaching pleases me. Guru's sermon is heard in all four corners. Listening to it one merges with God's name. ||3|| He who searches God inside is truthful. He attains God's grace through guru's teaching. He takes the medicine of divine wisdom through guru's teaching and unites with God by His grace. ||4|| By good fortune, I obtained this body; in this human life, I have focused my mind to guru's teaching. It is all dark without guru's teaching; only the guru willed realizes it. ||5|| Why are some here to waste away their life? The self-willed are attached to the love of duality. This opportunity does not come again. He regrets when the steps start slipping. ||6|| The body becomes sacred through guru's teaching. True Lord, the ocean of virtue, dwells in it. He sees truth everywhere and enshrines truth in the mind by hearing; ||7|| Ego and mental calculations are eliminated through guru's teaching. By enshrining God in the mind; He praises God through guru's teaching and attains peace uniting with God. ||8|| He, whom the Lord inspires to remember Him, recites His name. Through gurus teaching, He dwells in the mind. He sees, He understands and He merges in Him. ||9|| In whose mind He puts the priceless merchandise, knows it; He realizes Himself through guru's teaching. He, who realizes himself becomes pure and speaks the sermon through guru's lesson. ||10|| This body is sacred. He misses the virtuous God through guru's teaching. He sings God's praises imbued with love and merges in virtuous God singing His praises. ||11|| This body is the source of all worldly pleasure. In love of duality, it is deluded by doubt. He does not miss God and suffers. He suffers for not missing God; ||12|| One who serves the guru is approved. His body and soul-swan are pure; it is known in God's court. He serves God and enshrines Him in the mind. He looks adorable singing God's praises. ||13|| One cannot serve the guru without luck. The self-willed are deluded, and die crying. Those, who are blessed by the guru; God unites them with Him. ||14|| In the body fortress, are the solid built markets? The guru-willed buys the merchandise and keeps it safe. Reciting God's name day and night, he attains high status. ||15|| True Lord is the giver of peace. He is realized through perfect guru's teaching. O Nanak, those who praise God's name obtain this by good luck. ||16||7||21|| Page 1066 Maaroo, Third Master: The formless Lord created the universe. By His command, He created the worldly attachment. The Creator stages all the plays. Listen and enshrine Him in the mind. ||1|| He gave birth to worldly wealth with three qualities. Proclaimed the four Vedas to Brahma; Creating the years, months, days and dates, He gave thinking to the world. ||2|| Service to the guru is the essence of all. Enshrine Lord's name in your heart. Guru's sermon wells up in the world. God's name is obtained through it. ||3|| He reads Vedas and argues night and day. He does not remember Gods name. He will be arrested by the devil of death. In love of duality, he suffers in pain forever; through three worldly qualities he is deluded by doubt. ||4|| The guru-willed loves God only. He controls the three qualities in the mind. He gets liberated through guru's teaching and eliminates the worldly attachment. ||5|| Those who are attuned to God from destiny are attuned now. By guru's grace, they are intuitively intoxicated by it. Serving the guru they find God. He unites them with Him. ||6|| They are not affected by worldly attachment and doubt. Attached to the love of duality, one suffers in pain. This deep colour does not last long; it takes a moment to fade. ||7|| They get their mind dyed with love. Dyed in this colour, they merge in the true Lord. By perfect destiny, some obtain this colour. Through guru's teachings, this colour is applied. ||8|| The self-willed are proud. They are never honoured in the court of the Lord. Attached to duality, they waste their lives in vain; they suffer without understanding. ||9|| God is hidden in me. By guru's grace, one unites with God. God is true; true is His trade, through which God's priceless name is bought. ||10|| No one found this body's value. My Lord has made it this way. The guru-willed purifies the body and unites with God by His grace. ||11|| Gain and loss are in the body. The guru-willed search for the carefree God. The guru-willed trades and finds peace forever; he intuitively merges in God. ||12|| True is God's mansion, and His treasure. The great giver Himself blesses it. The guru-willed praises the giver of peace in the mind and unites with God, and knows His worth. ||13|| The merchandise is in the body but he does not realize it. God bestows honour to the guru-willed. The shopkeeper knows the priceless merchandise. He gives it to the guru-willed without hesitation. ||14|| God abides in all. He is found by guru's grace. He unites us with Him by His grace. One merges with Him through guru's teaching intuitively. ||15|| Page 1067 True Lord is realized through guru's teaching. Guru's teachings eliminated the doubt from inside. O Nanak, Reciting God's name obtains honour and happiness. ||16||8||22|| Maaroo, Third Master: He is inaccessible, unfathomable and carefree. The kind Lord is inaccessible and unlimited. No one can reach Him. He is realized through guru's teaching. ||1|| He, who pleases You serves You. He merges in truth through guru's teaching. Night and day, he praises God and enjoys Godly taste. ||2|| Those who die through guru's lesson take care of their life. They enshrine Lord's glories in their hearts. Falling at God's feet the life becomes fruitful and affect of duality eliminates. ||3|| God unites us with Him by His grace. One eliminates ego through guru's teaching. He worships God with love day and night and takes advantage in the world. ||4|| I praise Your virtues but I cannot praise enough. You have no limit. Your value cannot be estimated. God bestows His kindness and one merges in His virtues through virtues. ||5|| In this world, emotional attachment is spread all over. The ignorant, self-willed is immersed in utter darkness. Chasing after worldly affairs, he wastes away his life; without God's name, he suffers in pain. ||6|| If it is written in his fate; he meets the guru. The filth of ego is eliminated through guru's teaching. The mind becomes pure and enlightened through divine wisdom and the darkness of ignorance is eliminated. ||7|| Your names are countless; Your value cannot be estimated. I enshrine Lord's true name in my heart. Who can estimate Your value O God? You are merged in peace. ||8|| God's name is priceless, inaccessible and infinite. No one can weigh it. Only He can weigh himself. He is weighed through guru's teaching. ||9|| Your servant serves and offers this prayer. You unite us with you and make us sit near you. Bestowal of peace to all is recited by perfect destiny. ||10|| Chastity, truth and self-control come by practicing truth. This mind becomes pure, singing the praises of the Lord. In this worldly poison, the nectar is obtained, if it pleases my Lord. ||11|| He understands whom God inspires to understand. Singing the praises of the Lord, one's inner being is awakened. Ego and possessiveness are subdued, and one intuitively finds the truth. ||12|| Without good fortune, countless others wander around. They die only to be reborn; they cannot escape the cycle of birth and death. Imbued with sins, they commit sins and never find peace. ||13|| Many disguise themselves in many ways. Without guru's teaching, no one has conquered ego. One who dies while alive is liberated, and merges in the true name. ||14|| Spiritual ignorance and desire burn this human body. Page 1068 Those who follow guru's teachings, their fire is extinguished. Their body and mind are soothed, anger and ego eliminated and they merge with God. ||15|| True is the Lord and true is His greatness. By guru's grace, a rare few realize this. Nanak offers this prayer: one merges with God reciting His name. ||16||1||23|| Maaroo, Third Master: You unite Your devotees with You by Your grace. Your devotees praise You with love forever. Those in your refuge are saved O Creator; You unite them with You. ||1|| Worship looks adorable through perfect guru's teaching. Peace prevails inside. They are pleasing to Your Mind. His mind and body are imbued with devotion and focuses his mind to God. ||2|| The body burns in ego forever.

With good fortune, one meets the perfect guru. The inner ignorance goes away through guru's teaching and attains peace. ||3|| The blind, self-willed acts blindly. He is in terrible pain and wanders in many a life. He can never snap the noose of death; in the end, he suffers in horrible pain. ||4|| Guru's teaching eliminates the coming and going. He enshrines God's name in the mind. He dies through guru's teaching and eliminates ego from the mind and merges with God. ||5|| They lose their honour in coming and going. Without the guru, no one can become immortal. His soul becomes peaceful through guru's teaching and merges with supreme soul. ||6|| The five demons think of evil and corruption. This is caused by emotional attachment and worldly wealth. Serving the guru, one is liberated, and the five demons are brought under control. ||7|| Without the guru, there is darkness of worldly attachment. They drown again and again turn by turn. Meeting the guru, one speaks the truth and the true name pleases his mind. ||8|| True is His door and true is His divine court. They serve the true Lord through guru's teaching with love. Singing the praises of God through true tune they merge with true Lord. ||9|| Some realize God in their mind. Through guru's teaching intuitively. They are not troubled by sorrow or separation, they merge with God intuitively. ||10|| The evil people live in love of duality. They wander around; they are thirsty of false attachment. They sit in evil company and suffer pain forever; they earn pain through pain. ||11|| Without the guru, there is no congregation. No one goes across the world ocean without guru's teaching. One who intuitively praises God day and night merges with supreme soul. ||12|| The body is the tree; the bird of soul dwells in it. It pecks nectar through guru's teaching. It never flies away, does not come or go; it dwells there permanently. ||13|| They purify themselves contemplating guru's teaching. They eliminated false attachment and doubt. God the bestowal unites them with Him by His grace. ||14|| Page 1069 He is always nearby. He is never far away. Find Him close by through guru's teaching. The lotus blossoms by dawn of sun ray and illuminates with it. ||15|| True Lord is the Creator. He kills and gives life; there is no other at all. O Nanak, honour obtains through God's name and peace obtains by eliminating ego. ||16||2||24|| Maaroo,

Sohlay, Fourth Master: God is one. He is realized by guru's grace. True Lord looks after all. I cannot think of anyone else. Truth abides in the mind of a guru-willed. He merges with truth intuitively. ||1|| True Lord dwells in the minds of all. By guru's grace, they intuitively merge with Him. Saying, "guru, guru", I found eternal peace by focusing my mind to guru's feet. ||2|| The guru is divine wisdom and worship. I serve the true guru, no other. I obtained the jewel of God's name from the guru and guru's service appeals to me. ||3|| Without the guru, those who are attached to duality They come and go and the unfortunate die in doubt. O Nanak, even they are liberated if they become guru-willed and remain in guru's sanctuary. ||4|| The love of the guru-willed is true forever. I beg for the invaluable God's name from the guru. O dear Lord, be kind and protect me in guru's refuge. ||5|| True guru trickles the nectar into my mouth. My tenth gate has been opened. The infinite divine music plays there through guru's sermon and one merges in it intuitively. ||6|| Those who have it pre written by the Creator; They pass their night and day saying guru, guru, guru. Without the guru, no one understands anything. Focus your mind to guru's feet; ||7|| Lord blesses those with whom He is pleased. The guru-willed obtain the priceless name. God blesses them with His name by His grace O Nanak, they merge in His name. ||8|| The jewel of spiritual wisdom is revealed in the mind. The wealth of God's name obtained with ease. This greatness is obtained from the guru; I admire my guru forever. ||9|| With the sunrise the darkness disappeared. The ignorance disappeared through guru's priceless jewel; Guru's jewel of divine wisdom is priceless. It is obtained by good luck. ||10|| The guru-willed is enlightened through divine wisdom. In all four ages he is considered to be pure in the world. Imbued with God's name obtain peace by lovingly attuned to God's name. ||11|| The guru-willed obtains God's name. He sleeps and wakes up in peace. Page 1070 The guru-willed merges with God and Nanak recites God's name||12|| The devotees recite the sacred sermon. The guru-willed recite and speak God's name. Saying God, the mind becomes happy focusing the mind to God's feet. ||13|| I am an ignorant and fool. I have no wisdom at all. From the true guru, I understood in the mind. O God, be kind and bless me with guru's service. ||14|| Those who know the guru know God. The giver of peace is all-pervading everywhere. Searching the soul attains eternal peace and the mind merges in service. ||15|| Those who are blessed with honour from destiny; the guru dwells in their mind with love. The bestowal of life of the world unites by His grace O Nanak, the devotee merges with Him. ||16||1|| Maaroo, Fourth Master: The Lord is inaccessible unfathomable eternal and imperishable. He dwells in the body of everyone. There is no other giver except Him; worship the Lord, O mortal. ||1|| Whoever God protects; no one can kill him. Serve such Lord, O saints, His sermon is sacred. ||2|| When it seems that there is nothing anywhere. God abides there fully. He causes the dried branch to turn green. Recite God who does this; ||3|| The one who knows the pain of all beings I admire that Lord. Offer your prayer to Him, who bestows all happiness. ||4|| One who does not know the state of the soul? Do not say anything to such an ignorant person. Do not argue with ignorant, O mortal. Recite God the bestowal of salvation. ||5|| Don't worry! The Creator worries for you; The Lord gives to all creatures in the water and on land. My God bestows His blessings without worry, even to worms in soil and stones. ||6|| Do not place your hopes in friends, children and siblings. Do not place your hopes in banker or the business of others. Without God there is no friend, recite God the Lord of the world. ||7|| Night and day, recite the name of the Lord. He will fulfill your hope and desire. O servant Nanak, recite the name of the destroyer of fear and spend the night in peace and contentment. ||8|| Those who serve the Lord find peace. They are intuitively absorbed in Lord's name. The Lord preserves the honour of those who seek His sanctuary, go and check the Vedas and the Puraanas. ||9|| Whoever God inspires, serves Him. Through guru's teaching the fear of doubt goes away. In his own home, he remains unattached, like the lotus in water. ||10|| Page 1071 One who serves in ego, his service is not approved. He keeps taking birth and death again and again. Perfect is the penance and service, which pleases my Lord; ||11|| What virtues of Yours should I say O my Lord? You are the inner-knower of all souls. I beg for Your blessing O Creator; that I recite Your name forever. ||12|| Some are proud of talking with ego. Some are proud of authority and wealth. I have no support other than God. Protect the humble O Creator! ||13|| You bless the humble with honour by Your grace. Many others argue in conflict and keep coming and going in reincarnation. Whoever You side with O Lord; you bestow them with honour. ||14|| Those who recite God's name forever. They obtain the highest status by guru's grace. Those who serve God find peace; without serving Him, they repent; ||15|| You are pervading all, O Lord of the world. He recites God upon whose forehead the guru places his hand. Entering God's refuge, Nanak the servant of servants recites God. ||16||2|| Maaroo, Sohlay, Fifth Master: God is one. He is realized by guru's grace. He created the earth by His power. He holds the sky at His feet by His command. He created fire locked it in the wood. That God protects all, O brother. ||1|| He gives food to all beings. He is all-powerful Creator, the cause of causes. He establishes and disestablishes in a moment. He is your support; ||2|| He took care of you in your mother's womb. With every breath and morsel of food, recite Him. He is with you and takes care of you. Recite the beloved forever; His greatness is the greatest. ||3|| The kings and scholars are reduced to dust in an instant. God looks after the poor and makes them into rulers. He is the destroyer of ego and Support of all. His value cannot be estimated. ||4|| He is honourable and wealthy. He, who has God enshrined in his mind; He who created the universe is my mother, father, child, relative and sibling. ||5|| I came to God's refuge without any concern. In the company of devotees one definitely attains salvation. One who recites God wholeheartedly is never punished. ||6|| God the treasure of virtue abides in the mind and body. He does not wander through birth and death cycle. Pain vanishes and peace prevails, when one is satisfied and fulfilled. ||7|| My master is my best friend. Page 1072 The inner-knower is in all high and low places of concern. Reciting the perfect transcendent Lord my worry and counting ended. ||8|| God's name is as good as millions of other efforts. Singing God's praises is your wealth. By His grace, God drove away the demons with a sword of divine wisdom. ||9|| Recite God's name with a rosary. Be a winner and abide in your home. You shall not go through the hell of millions of births, by singing God's praises with love. ||10|| He is the saviour of worlds and galaxies. He is lofty, unfathomable, inaccessible and infinite. Whoever God blesses, recites God's name. ||11|| God has broken my bonds, and bought me. By His grace He made me His servant. The infinite divine music plays with love through peace giving tune; that is the true deed and earning. ||12|| O God, I respect You in my mind. My egotistic intellect has been driven away. God made me His and now I am honoured and known in the world. ||13|| Proclaim His glory and recite the name of the Lord of the universe. I praise my God. I do not see anyone else but Him. One Lord pervades the world. ||14|| True, true, true is God. By guru's grace, my mind is attuned to Him forever. O Lord, Your devotees live by reciting Your name and merge with You. ||15|| The dear Lord is the beloved of His humble devotees. My Lord is the saviour of all. Reciting His name my desire is fulfilled. God preserved servant Nanak's honour. ||16||1|| Maaroo, Sohlay, Fifth Master: God is one. He is realized by guru's grace. The body-bride is attached to the Yogi, the husband-soul. She is entangled with him, enjoying pleasure and delights. They met due to past actions. They play and enjoy each other. ||1|| Whatever the husband does, the bride willingly accepts. The husband adorns his bride, and keeps her with him. They live together day and night; the beloved Lord comforts his wife. ||2|| Whatever the bride asks for, the husband tries his best to get it. Whatever he finds, he brings and shows to his bride. But he cannot get one thing that she is hungry and thirsty of. ||3|| With her palms pressed together, the bride offers her prayer; O my beloved, do not leave me and go to foreign lands; please stay here with me. Do such business at home that relieves my hunger and thirst. ||4|| All sorts of religious rituals are performed for ages; without the sublime essence of the Lord, there is no peace; By God's grace they joined devotees congregation O Nanak, both husband wife became happy. ||5|| Page 1073 The body-bride is blind, and the groom is childish. The creation was created mixing the five elements. The priceless merchandise you came for; is obtained from the guru. ||6|| The body-bride says, Please live with me. O my beloved, peaceful, young lord. Without you, I am worth nothing; promise that You will not leave me; ||7|| The soul-husband says, I am the slave of my commander.

He is my great master, who is fearless and very strong. Till He wants, I will stay with you; when He calls back, I have to go; ||8|| The husband speaks truth to the bride; But the bride is restless and inexperienced and she does not understand anything. Again and again, she begs her husband's company; she thinks that he is just joking. ||9|| The order comes, and the husband-soul is called. He does not consult with his bride, and does not ask her opinion. He gets up and goes, and the body crumbles to dust O Nanak, this attachment is imaginary. ||10|| O greedy mind – listen! Serve the guru day and night forever. Without the guru, the faithless rot and die. The noose of death is around the necks of those who have no guru. ||11|| The self-willed comes, and goes. The self-willed suffers beating again and again. The self-willed endures as many hells as there are; the guru-willed is not even touched by them. ||12|| He who pleases God is a guru-willed. Who can destroy him who is robed in honour by the Lord? The blissful one is forever in bliss; he is dressed in robe of honour. ||13|| I appraise the perfect guru. He offers refuge and fulfills his word. I met such Lord the bestowal of peace. He does not separate or goes anywhere. ||14|| He is the treasure of virtue. His value cannot be estimated. He abides in everyone and everywhere. Nanak seeks the sanctuary of the destroyer of pain of the poor. I am the dust of the feet of Your slaves. ||15||1||2|| Maaroo, Sohlay, Fifth Master: God is one. He is realized by guru`s grace. My blissful Lord is forever in bliss. He fills each and every heart, and judges each and everyone. He is the emperor of emperors; there is none else. ||1|| He is joyful, blissful and merciful. God's light gives light everywhere. He creates checks and enjoys it. He worships Himself. ||2|| He contemplates His own creative power. He truly created the universe. He stages the play, day and night. He listens, hears and rejoices. ||3|| True is His throne, and His kingdom. True is the treasure of the true banker. Page 1074 He is true, and created everything true. Truth prevails everywhere. ||4|| True is the justice of the true Lord. Your place is true forever, O God. True is Your creative power, and true is Your sermon. True is the peace, which You give, O my Lord. ||5|| You are the greatest emperor. By Your command, our deeds are fulfilled. You know everything in and out and You believe Yourself.

||6|| You are the great taster and enjoyer. You are liberated, You are the Yogi. All peace and contentment in Your house and Your blessing trickles down. ||7|| You alone give Your gifts. You give gifts to all beings of the world. Your treasures are full, never run short. Those who receive it are fulfilled. ||8|| The mystics, seekers and forest-dwellers beg from You. The celibates and truthful and peaceful beg from You. You alone are the bestowal; all others are beggars. You bless the whole world with Your gifts. ||9|| Your devotees worship You with infinite love. In an instant, You establish and disestablish. Your command is very heavy. Obeying it is Your worship. ||10|| They alone know You, whom You bless with Your visualization. Through guru's teaching they enjoy Your love. Those who please Your mind are clever, handsome and wise. ||11|| One who misses You becomes carefree. One who misses You is the true banker. One who misses You, has no concern. Others can do nothing to him. ||12|| His thirst quenches and inside becomes soothed. The true guru has mended the broken knot. The mind woke up through guru's teaching and drinks nectar with love. ||13|| He does not die, he lives forever. He became immortal and imperishable. Nothing comes and nothing goes. The guru eliminated the doubt. ||14|| Perfect is the sermon of the perfect guru. He, who is attached to the perfect Lord, merges with Him. His love increases day by day, and it does not decrease when weighed. ||15|| The gold is purified twelve times and became absolutely pure. It is appraised by the appraiser. Assaying it, it is placed in the treasury by the jeweller and do not need to melt it again. ||16|| O Master; Your name is sacred. Servant Nanak admires You forever. In the society of the saints, I found great peace; seeing them my mind got drenched. ||17||1||3|| Maaroo, Fifth Master, Sohlay: God is one. He is realized by guru's grace. Guru is the Lord of the world, the master of the universe. Guru is merciful, and always forgiving. Guru is the Shaastras, the Simritees and the six rituals. Guru is the holy shrine. ||1|| Page 1075 Reciting the guru, all sins are erased. Reciting the guru the devil of death does not arrest. Reciting the guru the mind becomes pure and eliminates ego. ||2|| Guru's servant does not go to hell. Guru's servant recites the supreme Lord. Guru's servant joins the company of devotees and the guru bestows

blessings to them. ||3|| At guru's shrine the praises of God are sung and heard. Meeting with the guru, one sings God's praises. The guru eradicates sorrow and suffering, and bestows honour in God's court. ||4|| The guru has revealed the inaccessible and unfathomable Lord. The guru shows the way to the lost. Nothing stops guru's servant from worship. He taught him the perfect divine wisdom. ||5|| The guru reveals the Lord everywhere. The Lord of the universe is permeating and pervading water and land. High and low are the same to Him. His mind is focused intuitively. ||6|| Meeting with the guru, his thirst is quenched. Meeting with the guru, the worldly wealth does not rob him. The perfect guru bestows truth and contentment; he drinks the nectar of God's name. ||7|| Guru's sermon is contained in all. He hears and He preaches it. Those who recite it are emancipated; they attain eternal place. ||8|| Glory of the guru is known only to the guru. Whatever He does; does according to his will. Your humble servants beg for the dust of the feet of devotee's. Nanak praises You forever. ||9||1||4|| Maaroo, Sohlay, Fifth Master: God is one. He is realized by guru's grace. The primal God is formless. The detached Lord is prevailing in all. He has no race or social class, no identifying mark. He created the universe by His command. ||1|| All the millions of species of beings; God blessed mankind with honour. A person, who misses the ladder, suffers and repents in coming and going. ||2|| What I can tell him, who created everything? The guru-willed contemplates and recites God's name. Whoever He misguides forgets Him, whoever He wants; He guides them. ||3|| This body has been made the village of joy and sorrow. Those who seek guru's refuge are saved. The guru-willed who stays away from three worldly qualities obtains honour. ||4|| He does many deeds; whatever he does is a chain in the feet. The seed sowed at the wrong time does not grow and loses the benefit. ||5|| In today's age, singing God's praises is the essence. The guru-willed recite God with intent. Page 1076 He along with his ancestors attains salvation and goes to God's court with honour. ||6|| All continents, underworld, islands and worlds God made them all subject to death. God is immortal. He who recites Him becomes immortal. ||7|| God's servant becomes like God. Do not think that he is different, because of his human body. Like the waves rise from water many ways and merge again intuitively. ||8|| A beggar begs for awns at His door. When God pleases, He blesses him. Please bless me with Your visualization to satisfy my mind. Singing God's praises the mind stabilizes. ||9|| The handsome Lord is not controlled in any way. The Lord does whatever pleases His saints. They ask Him whatever they want. They do not have to come second time. ||10|| Wherever the mortal faces a difficulty. There he should recite the Lord of the universe. Where there are no children, spouse or friends, God saves them; ||11|| The great master is inaccessible and unfathomable. How can anyone meet with the carefree God? Those, whom He puts on the right path by cutting the noose, join devotee's company. ||12|| One who realizes God's command is His devotee. He bears bad and good equally. The guru-willed who realizes God merges in peace. ||13|| The devotees of the Lord dwell forever in peace. Innocent like a child he remains detached and aloof. They enjoy pleasures in many ways like the love of father and son. ||14|| He is inaccessible and unfathomable. His value cannot be estimated. We meet Him, only when He causes us to meet. The Lord reveals to those guru-willed who have pre-ordained destiny. ||15|| You are the Creator, the cause of causes. You created the universe, and You support the whole world. Servant Nanak seeks the sanctuary of Your door, O Lord; if You wish, preserve his honour. ||16||1||5|| Maaroo, Sohlay, Fifth Master: God is one. He is realized by guru`s grace. Whatever is seen is You, O Lord; We hear Your discourse with our ears. There is nothing else to be seen. It is all Your blessing. ||1|| You know Your creation. You came into being on Your own O God. Creating Yourself, You created the universe and look after all. ||2|| You created some to hold royal courts. Some become renounce and some house holders. Page 1077 Some are hungry and some are satisfied and satiated, but You support all. ||3|| The true Lord is true forever. He is with His devotees, through and through. He is hidden and He is revealed. He creates everything. ||4|| God exists and will always be. He is lofty, inaccessible, unfathomable and infinite. He fills the empty, and empties the filled; this is all His doing; ||5|| With my mouth, I praise my true Lord king. With my eyes, I see the inaccessible and unfathomable Lord. Listening with my ears, my mind and body are rejuvenated; my Lord saves all. ||6|| He created the creation and checks for quality; All beings and creatures recite Him. He knows His creative power. He blesses with His grace. ||7|| Where the saints gather and sit, God is with them. They abide in bliss and joy and watch Lord's wondrous play. They sing the divine sermon with love; servant Nanak recites God there. ||8|| Coming and going is all Your play. Creating the creation, the infinite Lord watches over; The Creator creates and looks after. ||9|| I live by listening to Your praises. I praise You forever. With my palms pressed together, I recite You day and night O my inaccessible, infinite Lord. ||10|| Other than You, who else can I praise? I recite one and only Lord in my mind. Realizing God's command the mortal become content; that is their effort. ||11|| Recite the true Lord in the mind through guru's teaching. Fall in love with God through guru's teaching. All bonds break through guru's teaching; doubt and false attachment are burnt. ||12|| Wherever He keeps me, is a peaceful place. Whatever naturally happens, I accept that as good. Hatred is gone. I have no enemy and I see God in all. ||13|| Fear has been removed, and darkness has been dispelled. The primal, detached Lord has been revealed. Leaving ego, I have entered His refuge and work for Him. ||14|| Rare are those few blessed people; who recite the master twenty-four hours a day? Everyone in their company as well their family is saved. ||15|| This blessing is obtained from the Lord. Twenty-four hours a day, with my palms pressed together, I recite His name. I recite God's name and merge in peace; O Nanak, I always recite You. ||16||1||6|| Maaroo, Fifth Master: Do not be fooled by appearance, you ignorant; all that you see is imaginary and false. No one stays in the world forever; only God is forever. ||1|| Seek the sanctuary of the perfect guru. He shall eradicate all emotional attachment, sorrow and doubt. He only teaches one lesson, sing the true God's name in the mind. ||2|| Page 1078 Many gods yearn for God's name. All devotees serve Him. He is the master of orphans, the destroyer of the pain of the poor. His is realized through the perfect guru. ||3|| I cannot think of any other door. Wandering through universe, one still does not realize anything. The guru is the banker, and has the treasure of

God's name; this jewel is obtained from him. ||4|| The dust of His feet purifies. Even the gods and heroes cannot realize Him O friend; the guru is the transcendent Lord; surrendering to him attains salvation. ||5|| O my beloved mind, if you wish for an ever fruit bearing tree. If you wish forever milk giving cow at your home; Serve the perfect guru with intent and be content and practice God's name! ||6|| Through guru's teaching the five passions are killed. You become pure through God's love. When the perfect guru touches with touchstone, the iron becomes gold. ||7|| Many heavens do not come close to it. The divine person gives up the liberation as well. One universal Creator is found through the guru. I admire seeing my guru. ||8|| No one knows how to serve the guru. Guru is the unfathomable, supreme Lord. Whoever he guides, those with pre-ordained destiny start serving him. ||9|| Even the Vedas do not know guru's glory. They narrate only a tiny bit by hearing. The guru the supreme Lord is beyond comprehension, reciting him the mind is soothed. ||10|| My mind lives by listening to God's virtues. When He dwells in the heart, one becomes peaceful. Saying guru from the mouth obtains glory and he does not follow the path of death. ||11|| I have entered the sanctuary of the saints. I put my soul life and wealth in front of him. I know nothing about service and awareness; please take pity on this worm. ||12|| I am unworthy; please unite me with You. Please bless me that I serve You. I wave fan, and grind grain for the saints and find peace washing their feet. ||13|| After wandering around at many doors, I have come to Your door, O Lord. By Your grace, I have entered Your sanctuary. Keep me in saint's company and bless me with the gift of your name. ||14|| My Lord has become kind. I have visualized the perfect guru. I have found eternal peace, poise and bliss; Nanak is the slave of Your slaves. ||15||2||7|| Maaroo, Sohlay, Fifth Master: God is one. He is realized by guru's grace. The earth and the sky recite Your name. The moon and the sun sing Your praises. Air, water fire and the whole creation recites Your name. ||1|| Page 1079 All the continents, islands and worlds recite Your name. Those in the underworld praise the true Lord. The sources of creation, the sermon and all God's devotees recite God. ||2|| Brahma, Vishnu and Shiva recite Your name. The three hundred thirty million gods recite Your name. The gentle people and demons recite Your name. I do not know how many more recite Your name. ||3|| The animals, birds and ghosts recite Your name. The forests, mountains and hermits recite Your name. The vines and branches recite You. The Lord abides in every mind. ||4|| All beings, small or large recite Your name. The mystics and seekers recite God's lesson. All visible and the invisible recite God's name. God is Lord of the universe. ||5|| Men and women recite Your name in their places of worship. All social classes and souls of all races recite Your name. All the virtuous, clever and wise people, and day and night recite You. ||6|| Hours, minutes and seconds recite Your name. Death and life, and thoughts of purification, recite Your name. The sleeping and those who command others also recite Your name. No one can explain even a bit of You. ||7|| The Lord is the doer, the cause of causes. He is the inner-knower of all hearts. Whoever You bless with Your worship, obtains the priceless treasure in life. ||8|| Those, in whose mind God dwells; they recite guru's word by good fortune. He realizes the all-pervading Lord and does not go through life again. ||9|| He who has guru's teaching dwelling in the mind, his pain suffering and doubt go away. Reciting God's name he obtains peace contentment and joy and divine music plays intuitively. ||10|| He, who recites God, is rich. He, who attains devotee's company, is honourable; He, who has the bestowal of liberation in the mind, his deeds are fulfilled without fail. ||11|| The Lord is pervading water and land. There is no other said to be so. The ointment of guru's spiritual wisdom has eradicated all doubts! Other than one Lord, I do not see any other. ||12|| Lord's court is the highest of the high. His limit and extent cannot be described. The Lord is profoundly deep, unfathomable and unweighable; how can He be measured? ||13|| You are the Creator; all is created by You. Without You, there is no other at all. You are in the beginning, the middle and the end. You are the origin of the creation. ||14|| The devil of death does not come close to him; who sings God's praises in devotee's company. All his desires are fulfilled, who listens to God's praises through ears; ||15|| You belong to all; all belong to You, O my true, deep and profound Lord! Page 1080 Says Nanak, those beings that please You are sacred.

||16||1||8|| Maaroo, Fifth Master: God is the almighty giver of all peace and joy. Be kind to me, that I recite Your name. God is the giver and all beings are beggars. Your servant begs for awns. ||1|| I beg for the dust of the feet of the humble, that I may be librated. The filth of countless lifetimes will be erased. The chronic diseases are cured by the medicine of Lord's name; I beg to be imbued with the pure Lord. ||2|| With my ears, I listen to the pure praises of my Lord. Take God's support and give up sins and lust. I humbly bow and fall at the feet of Your slaves. I do not hesitate to do good deeds. ||3|| O Lord, I sing Your praises with my tongue. The sins which I have committed are erased. I live by reciting my Lord's name and got rid of five passions. ||4|| Reciting on Your lotus feet, I have come aboard Your boat. Joining the society of saints, I cross over the world-ocean. I offer flowers and scent to realize God who dwells in all; and I shall never be naked again. ||5|| Please make me the slave of Your slaves, O Lord of the world. O treasure of blessing and kind to the poor O Lord; the perfect transcendent Lord is my friend and a companion; once united with you shall never be separated again. ||6|| I dedicate my mind and body, and place before the Lord. Asleep for countless lifetimes, I have awakened. He, whom I belong, is my cherisher and nurturer. I have killed and discarded my murderous self-conceit. ||7|| The inner-knower is pervading the water and the land. The undeceivable Lord abides in each and every heart. The perfect guru eliminated the wall of doubt. He is omnipresent. ||8|| Wherever I look, I see God, the ocean of peace. Lord's treasure is never exhausted. He is the store of jewels. He is beyond comprehension and His limits cannot be measured; whoever He blesses realize Him. ||9|| My heart is cooled, and my mind and body are calmed and soothed. The craving for birth and death is eliminated. By His grace he pulled me out by trickling His kindness on me. ||10|| One and only Lord is permeating and pervading everywhere. There is none other than Him at all. God exists from the beginning, the middle and the end; my greed and doubt ended. ||11|| The guru is the transcendent Lord; the guru is the Lord of the universe. The guru is the Creator, the guru is forever kind. I obtained the fruit of reciting guru's lesson and the lamp of wisdom is lit in saint's company. ||12|| Whatever I see, is

my master. Whatever I hear is God's sermon. I do what You make me do; You are the help of saints in Your refuge; ||13|| The beggar begs, and worships You. Reciting the perfect God the sinners are purified. Please bless me with one gift, O treasure of all bliss and virtue; I do not ask for anything else. ||14|| Page 1081 God is the Creator of the body-vessel. In the society of the saints, the dye is produced. Through God's sermon my thinking became pure and mind dyed with deep permanent love of God's name. ||15|| I obtained the reward of God's sixteen powers. Becoming humble I realized God. Lord's Name is Nanak's bliss, play and peace; he drinks and is fulfilled with God's nectar. ||16||2||9|| Maaroo, Sohlay, Fifth Master: God is one. He is realized by guru's grace. You are my master. You have made me Your servant. My soul and body are all gifts from You. You are the Creator, the cause of causes; nothing belongs to me. ||1|| When You sent me, I came into the world. Whatever pleases You, I do. Without You, nothing is done, so I have no worry. ||2|| In the world hereafter, I hear Your command. In this world, I sing Your praises. You write and erase the account; no one can argue with You. ||3|| You are our father; we are all Your children. We play as You make us play. You made the path in the forest; no one goes on the opposite side. ||4|| Some sit in their home. Some wander across the country and foreign lands. Some are grass-cutters and some are kings. Who among them is false? ||5|| Who is liberated, and who goes to hell? Who is worldly, and who is a devotee? Who is giver, and who is shallow? Who is wise and who is ignorant? ||6|| By His command one is liberated, and by His command one goes to hell. By His command, one is worldly, and by His command one is a devotee. By His order, one is shallow, and by His order, one is a bestowal. There is no other side except His. ||7|| You made the ocean vast and huge. Some ignorant foolss live in the deep underworld. Some are carried across in the ship of truth of the true guru. ||8|| You issue Your command for the amazing death. You create all beings and absorb them back in You. You see and enjoy everything in the worldly arena You created. ||9|| Great is master and His name is greater. He is the great giver; great is His place. He is inaccessible and unfathomable, infinite and unweighable. He cannot be measured. ||10|| No one else knows His value. You O formless God, do Your own worship; You are divine, You meditate and You are very truthful. ||11|| For many days, You remained invisible. For many days, You remained in absolute state. For many days, there was pitch dark and then the Creator revealed Himself. ||12|| You are the most powerful. Page 1082 You are the hero exerting Your regal power. You created the worldly power and You are cool and calm; ||13|| One whom You bless, make him a guru-willed. They enshrine Your name in the mind and divine music plays. He is peaceful, he is the master; the devil of death does not go close to him. ||14|| His value cannot be described on paper. Says Nanak, the Lord of the world is infinite. God exists from the beginning, in the middle and in the end. Judgment is in His hands alone. ||15|| No one equals Him. No one can stand up against Him by any means. Nanak's God is all-in-all. He creates and watches His amazing play. ||16||1||10|| Maaroo, Fifth Master: The sacred supreme transcendent Lord is the inner-knower of hearts. He is the slayer of demons, our supreme Lord the master. The supreme saint, the master of the sensory organs, the lifter of mountains, the joyful Lord playing His enticing flute; ||1|| The enticer of hearts, the Lord of wealth, Krishna, the enemy of ego. The Lord of the universe, the dear Lord, the destroyer of demons; Life of the world, immortal master abides and accompanies all. ||2|| The support of the earth, the man-lion, the supreme God; The protector who tears apart demons with His teeth and supports the earth; O Creator, You came as Baavan prophet; You are good to everyone. ||3|| You are the great Lord, who has no form or feature. Adorned with flowers, holding the circular weapon in Your hand, Your form is beautiful. You have thousands of eyes, and thousands of forms. You alone are the giver, and all are beggars of You. ||4|| You are the love of Your devotees, the master of the orphans. The Lord of the milk-maids, You are the companion of all. O bestowal formless Lord. I cannot describe Your virtues. ||5|| Liberator, enticing Lord, Lord of Lakshmi (Vishnu) the supreme Lord; Saviour of Dropadi's honour; O amazing Vishnu, You enjoy everything and yet detached. ||6|| Visualizing You is rewarding. You do not take birth, You are self-existent; You are immortal, cannot be destroyed. O imperishable, eternal, unfathomable Lord, everything is attached to You. ||7|| The honourable God lives in heaven. By the pleasure of His will, He came as a prophet of fish and the tortoise. Your do unique deeds; whatever You wish happens. ||8|| He does not eat and has no enemy. He staged His play. He is called the four-armed Lord. He came in beautiful brown body and enticed everyone playing the flute. ||9|| He is adorned with garlands of flowers, with lotus eyes. His earrings, crown and flute are beautiful. He carries the conch, the circular armament and the war club; He is the great charioteer, who stays with His saints. ||10|| The Lord of yellow robes, the master of the universe. The Lord of the universe, the Lord of the world. I recite His name from my mouth. He is the archer, the beloved Lord; I cannot count all His limbs. ||11|| He is said to be free of anguish, and absolutely immaculate. The Lord of prosperity, pervading the water and the land; Page 1083 In the living world including the underworld, Your abode is imperishable. ||12|| You are the purifier of sinners, the destroyer of pain and fear. You are the eliminator of ego and eliminator of birth and death. He the merciful to the meek is pleased with devotional worship. He is not happy any other way. ||13|| The formless Lord is undeceivable and unchanging. The whole world blossoms through His light. He unites with Him those whom He Himself unites. No one can find Him on his own. ||14|| He is the milkmaid, and Lord Krishna. He grazes the cows in the forest. You create, and destroy. No filth attaches to You. ||15|| O my beloved Lord; which of Your virtues can I say? Even the thousand-headed serpent does not know Your limit. One may recite You with new names day and night, but no one can describe any of Your virtues. ||16|| I take Your support; O mother and father of the world; the fear of devil of death, duality and evil worldly wealth is dangerous. Be kind and keep me in the company of saints by Your grace. ||17|| All that is seen is an illusion. I beg for one gift, the dust of the feet of the saints, O Lord of the universe. Applying it to my forehead, I obtain liberation; whom he gives receives it; ||18|| those, unto whom the Lord, the giver of peace, grants His grace; He enshrines devotee's feet in the mind. They obtain the priceless treasure through God's name and the infinite divine music plays. ||19|| I recite You with many imaginary names with my tongue. It is true that You exist from the beginning. Says Nanak; Your devotees have entered Your sanctuary. Please visualize to me; my mind is dyed with Your love. ||20|| You alone know Your divine wisdom. You speak, and describe it. Make Nanak the slave of Your slaves, O Lord; please keep me with You if it pleases You. ||21||2||11|| Maaroo, Fifth Master: O Godly person; God is inaccessible; Forsake thoughts of worldly entanglements. Become the dust of the feet of the humble saint. This is how the gentle devotee is accepted at His door: ||1|| Let truth be your prayer and faith your prayer mat. Subdue your desires, and overcome your hopes. Let your body be the mosque, and your mind the priest and God's sermon will purify you. ||2|| Make first code (Shariat) as your daily work. Make second code (Tareekat) to complete the search for God. Make third code (maarfat) to kill the ego. When you obtain fourth code (Hakeekat); you shall not die again. ||3|| Practice in your heart the teachings of the Quran and the Bible; Let the ten sensory organs not misguide you. Control five passions faithfully; the awns of contentment will be rewarded. ||4|| Let kindness be your Mecca and the dust of devotee's feet be the fast. Let paradise be your practice of the Prophet's word. Make God the beauty, the light and the fragrance and pray God at the place of worship. ||5|| Page 1084 He, who practices truth, is the real Qazi; He is a pilgrim to Mecca, who purifies his heart. He is a Mullah, who banishes evil; he is a gentle saint, who praises God. ||6|| Always, at every moment, remember God, the Creator in your heart. Missing God with ten senses is your rosary and the contentment your circumcision. ||7|| You should know everything in your heart by now. Family, household and siblings are all entanglements. Kings, rulers and nobles will all die; only one place of God's place is eternal. ||8|| First, is the Lord's praise; second the contentment; Third the humility and fourth, giving awns; Fifth is to keep five passions in check. This is the essence of your five times of prayer. ||9|| Save yourself from bad deeds. Giving up the evil actions and make your hands the water-jug you carry. Eat what you earn. Wash your filthy mind in the river; One who realizes the prophet attains heaven. The devil of death cannot take him to hell. ||11|| Let good deeds be your body, and faith your bride. Control your senses and enjoy. Purify the impure by following prophet's words and you will wear the turban of honour. ||12|| To be Muslim is to be kind-hearted, and wash away the filth from the heart. The worldly love should not bother you, as the flower, silk and butter are not affected by anything. ||13|| One who is blessed with the mercy and by kind Lord? He is the real man; He is a scholar, preacher, a pilgrim and God's slave, whom God blesses. ||14|| God, the Creator of the universe and cause of everything is merciful. The praises and love of the merciful Lord are unfathomable. His justice and command is true; realizing Him O Nanak attains salvation. ||15||3||12|| Maaroo, Fifth Master: The seat of the supreme Lord is the highest of all. He creates, destroys and recreates. Going to God's refuge attains peace and no concern bothers the child. ||1|| He saved you from the fire of the womb; He did not destroy you, when you were an egg in your mother's ovary; He preserved you by blessing you by reciting Him. He owns everybody. ||2|| I have come to the sanctuary of His lotus feet. I sing God's praises in the company of devotees. It eliminated the fear of birth death and pain. Reciting God eliminates the fear of death. ||3|| God is all-powerful, indescribable, unfathomable and divine. All beings and creatures serve Him. He creates the creation in the way of egg, womb, sweat and earth. ||4|| He obtains the priceless treasure. Who savors and enjoys Godly taste in the mind. He pulls His few followers out of the deep dark well. ||5|| Page 1085 God exists from the beginning, in the middle and in the end. Whatever the Creator does; comes to pass. Doubt and fear are erased in devotee's company and pain does not bother. ||6|| I sing the sacred sermon of the Lord of the universe. I beg for the dust of the feet of devotees. Eradicating desire, I became free of desire and burnt away all my sins. ||7|| This is the unique way of the saints; they see God with them. They recite God with every breath; why delay reciting? ||8|| Wherever I look, I see the inner-knower; I never forget God, my Lord even for a moment. Your slaves live by reciting You in the forest, water and land. ||9|| The hot wind does not touch them; They remain awake, reciting God's name day and night. They enjoy reciting God's name; they have no concern of worldly wealth. ||10|| Disease, sorrow and pain do not affect him; they sing God's praise in devotee's company. O Lord; listen to my prayer and bless me with Your name. ||11|| Your name is a jewel, O my beloved Lord. Your slaves are imbued with Your infinite love. Those imbued with Your love, become like You; but they are rare. ||12|| My mind longs for the dust of their feet. They never forget the Lord. Associating with them, I obtain the supreme status; the Lord is always with me. ||13|| He is my beloved friend and companion. Reciting His name the evil thinking disappears. He speaks pure words and it eliminates lust anger and pride. ||14|| Other than You, O Lord, no one is mine. The guru has led me to grasp the feet of God. I praise the perfect guru, who has destroyed the illusion of duality. ||15|| With each and every breath, I never forget God. Twenty-four hours a day, I say God God God. O Nanak, the saints are imbued with Your Love; You are all powerful. ||16||4||13|| Maaroo, Fifth Master: God is one. He is realized by guru's grace. I enshrine Lord's lotus feet continuously in my heart. Each and every moment, I humbly pay regards to my guru. I offer my body, mind and everything to God. His name is adorable in the whole world. ||1|| Why forget the Lord from your mind? He created your body and soul and takes care as well. With every breath and morsel of food, the Creator takes care of His beings but you get what you earn. ||2|| No one returns empty-handed from Him. Keep the Lord in your mind twenty-four hours a day. Page 1086 Recite the sacred Lord in devotee's company and obtain honour in His court. ||3|| The four great blessings, and the eighteen miraculous spiritual powers; The priceless treasure peace and contentment is obtained reciting God's name. If you want happiness then recite God in the company of devotees. ||4|| The Shaastras, the Simritees and the Vedas proclaim O mortal; conquer your priceless life. Forsaking lust, anger and slander and sing God's praises O Nanak, ||5|| He has no form or shape, no ancestry or social class. The perfect Lord is perfectly pervading everywhere day and night. Whoever recites His name is fortunate and will not take birth again. ||6|| One who forgets the primal Lord, the architect of destiny? Wanders around burning, and remains tormented. No one helps the thankless; they go to the most horrible hell. ||7|| He blessed you with your soul, life, your body and wealth; He preserved and nurtured you in your mother's womb. Forsaking His love, you are imbued with another; no one will take you across like this. ||8|| O my master; be kind to me. You live in everyone and are near everyone. Nothing is in my hands; he alone knows, whom You inspire to know. ||9|| One who has such pre-ordained destiny inscribed on his forehead? The worldly wealth does not bother him. Slave Nanak seeks Your sanctuary forever; there is no other to go to; ||10|| He made pain and pleasure by His grace. Very few search for the sacred name. His value cannot be described. He is prevailing everywhere. ||11|| He is the devotee; He is the great giver. He is the perfect primal Lord, the architect of destiny. He is your help since childhood; He fulfills your desires. ||12|| Death, pain and pleasure are pre-ordained. They do not increase or decrease by any means. Only that happens what God wants; why waste your life claiming. ||13|| He pulls us out of the deep dark pit. He unites those with Him, who were separated for many life's. Recite God in devotee's company and he will protect you by His grace. ||14|| Your worth cannot be described. Wondrous is Your form, and Your glory is great. Your servant begs for the gift of worship. Nanak praises You forever. ||15||1||14||22||24||2||14||62|| Vaar of Maaroo, Third Master: God is one. He is realized by guru's grace. If you sell the virtue without a real buyer; it sells cheap. But if one meets a buyer of virtue, then it sells for hundreds of thousands. Page 1087 One obtains virtues meeting with a virtuous guru and merges with him. Priceless virtues are not obtained for any price; they are not bought in a shop. O Nanak, their weight is full and perfect; it never decreases. ||1|| Fourth Master: Without the name of God, they wander around and keep coming and going all the time. Some are bound, some are free; some are happy in love of God. O Nanak, believe in the true Lord and practice truth. This is the true way. ||2|| Ladder : From the guru, I have obtained the powerful sword of spiritual wisdom. I cut the fortress of duality and doubt, attachment, greed and ego. God's name dwells in my mind contemplating guru's teaching. Through truth, self-discipline and sublime understanding, the Lord has become very dear to me. Truly, the true Creator Lord is all pervading. ||1|| Hymn, Third Master: You find the way to destiny through singing tunes falling in love with guru's teaching. If one remains in the true congregation and loves the true Lord. He eliminates filth from within and attains salvation along with His generations. He gathers the wealth of virtue, and drives away the sins. O Nanak, he who meets the guru knows it. He does not leave him and falls in love with anyone else. ||1|| Fourth Master: I get scared seeing the ocean, but I do not get scared seeing you. Through guru's teaching I become content and happy reciting God's name. ||2|| Fourth Master: I get on board the boat and set out, but the ocean pushes around with waves. The boat of truth encounters no obstruction, if the guru supports. He takes us across to the other side, as the guru watches over. O Nanak, by God's grace one obtains honour in God's court. ||3|| Ladder: Enjoy the kingdom without obstruction O guru-willed; this is the true earning. God administers justice sitting on the throne. He is realized through devotee's company. Recite God through true lesson and become friends with God. If God the bestowal of happiness abides in the mind; he helps in the end. Love for the Lord wells up, when the guru imparts understanding. ||2|| Hymn, First Master: Confused and deluded, I wander around, but no one shows me the way. I go and ask the elders, if anyone can eliminate my pain. If the true guru abides in my mind; I see my beloved there. O Nanak, my mind is satisfied praising the true name. ||1|| Third Master: He does everything by His will. He blesses some and He does the needful. O Nanak, meeting the guru obtains enlightenment. The pains and sins are burnt away through God's name. ||2|| Ladder: O ignorant self-willed, do not forget God seeing the worldly wealth. It does not go with you on departure. Collecting wealth is false. The blind ignorant do not understand that the sword of death is hanging over their head. Those who enjoy God's taste are saved by guru's grace. Page 1088 He is the doer, the cause of causes and saves by His grace. ||3|| Hymn, Third Master: Those who do not meet the guru do not know about the amazing fear. They suffer seriously while coming and going and their worry never goes away. Like beating the clothes while washing and beating the bell. O Nanak, without the true name, the entanglements hanging over their head do not go away. ||1|| Third Master: I have searched the universe O my friend; ego is bad for the world. Don't worry, O my soul; speak the truth, O Nanak, truth and only truth. ||2|| Ladder:

God blesses the guru-willed and they absorb in reciting His name. He puts them to worship through guru's teaching as their goal. Those who serve and enshrine the guru in the mind look beautiful and honoured in God's court. Those who realize God are free here and the next world. Blessed are those devotees who serve God and I admire them. ||4|| Hymn, First Master: The rude, ill-mannered, living in graveyard, with black heart and impure; the virtuous enjoys her husband Lord and the virtueless is blind O Nanak. ||1|| First Master: She is truthful, peaceful, self discipline and she has a perfect family. O Nanak, day and night, she is always good; she loves her beloved Husband Lord. ||2|| Ladder: One, who obtains the treasure of God's name; realizes himself; By God's grace he obtains guru's teaching. Guru's sermon is pure; one drinks nectar through it. Those who taste the sublime essence of the Lord, forsake other taste. Drinking the sublime essence of the Lord, they are satisfied forever; their hunger and thirst are quenched. ||5|| Hymn, Third Master: Her Husband Lord is pleased, and He enjoys His bride; the soul-bride adorns her heart with God's name. O Nanak, that bride standing before Him is a noble and respected woman. ||1|| First Master: In her father-in-law's home and in her parents' home, she belongs to her Husband Lord. Her Husband is inaccessible and unfathomable. O Nanak, she is a happy soul-bride, who is pleasing to her carefree Lord. ||2|| Ladder: The king worthy of the throne sits on the throne; those who realize the true Lord are the true kings. These mortal rulers are not called kings; they suffer in pain of duality. Why should we praise those who are created? They depart in no time. Only God is eternal. The guru-willed who realize Him become eternal. ||6|| Hymn, Third Master: One Lord is the Husband of all. No one is without the Husband Lord. O Nanak, those who merge with the guru are happily married forever. ||1|| Third Master: With unstable mind like waves; how can one be saved? Those dyed with permanent love of the infinite Lord; O Nanak, those lovingly attached to true Lord are saved by guru's grace; Ladder: The name of the Lord is priceless. How can anyone estimate its value? Page 1089 He created the entire universe, and He is pervading all. The guru-willed praise Him forever and realize its true value. The lotus blossoms through guru's teaching and drinks God's sublime essence. Coming and going in life ends and one sleeps in peace and contentment. ||7|| Hymn, First Master: Neither dirty, nor dull, nor saffron, nor any colour that fades; O Nanak, truly dyed by truth is permanent deep red; ||1|| Third Master: The fearless bumblebee intuitively lives in flowers and fruits. O Nanak, there is only one tree, one flower, and one bumblebee. ||2|| Ladder: Those humble beings that struggle with their minds are brave and well known; those who realize themselves merge with God forever. This is the honour of the divine people that they remain absorbed in their mind. They reach God's palace truly focusing their mind on Him. Those who conquer their mind, by guru's grace, conquer the world. ||8|| Hymn, Third Master If I was a Yogi, I wander around the world, begging from door to door; But when the account is asked for in God's court; who do I answer to? Beg for God's name in the temple; He is always with you; nothing is obtained by imitating; all are subject to death. O Nanak, do not talk false; contemplate the true name. ||1|| Third Master: The court where the account is asked for; no one serves that court. Seek and find such a guru, who has no equal. You are freed in his refuge and no one will ask for your account. He practices and teaches the truth and bestows true teaching. One who has truth in his heart – his body and mind also become true. O Nanak, if one obeys God's order obtains true honour. Whoever He bestows His grace to, merges in truth. ||2|| Ladder: They are not brave, who die of ego and suffer in pain. The blind do not realize themselves; they rot in love of duality. They struggle with great anger; here and hereafter they suffer in pain. Self-pride does not please God; the Vedas proclaim this clearly. Those who die in ego do not find salvation. They die and reborn again. ||9|| Hymn, Third Master: The crow does not become white, and an iron boat does not go across. The caretaker blesses one who obeys the priceless name of the beloved. One who realizes God's command becomes happy and goes across like the iron attached to wood. Forsake greed and live in fear of God; this is the essence O Nanak, Third Master: Those who want to conquer their mind, the ignorant cannot do it; O Nanak, if this mind is to be conquered, contemplate guru's teaching. This mind is not conquered by trying, even though everyone thinks so. O

Nanak, the mind conquers the mind, if one meets with the guru. ||2||
Page 1090 Ladder: He created both sides, worldly power and Godly
power. No one becomes divine through worldly power; they keep
taking birth and death. Serving the guru, peace is found, reciting
God with every breath and morsel of food. Search through Simritees
and Shaastras; God`s servant is the highest. O Nanak, no one lives
forever without God`s name; I praise God`s name. ||10|| Hymn, Third
Master: If I was a scholar or an astrologer. I read four Vedas with my
mouth. I will be worshipped in the world for my wisdom and
thinking. Let me not forget the word of truth, that no one touches
my cooking square! Such cooking squares are false, O Nanak, only
one Lord is true. ||1|| Third Master: He creates and does everything
by His grace. He the true Lord bestows greatness O Nanak. ||2||
Ladder: Only death is painful; I cannot see anything else as painful.
It is overpowering and stalks the world, and fights the sinners. Search
God through guru`s teaching and realize God by reciting Him. He,
who fights with his mind is saved in God`s refuge. One who
contemplates and recites God is honoured in God`s court. ||11||
Hymn, First Master: Submit to the will of the Lord the commander;
Truth prevails in His court. God will ask for your account; do not
forget this seeing the world. One, who watches his heart, is a saint
and his heart is pure. Love and affection, O Nanak, in the account
are placed before the Creator. ||1|| First Master: He, who is unique
like the bumblebee, sees the Lord of the world everywhere. The
diamond pierces the diamond with light by touch intuitively O
Nanak. ||2|| Ladder: The self-willed attached to worldly wealth is
afflicted by death. Those in love with duality are thrown to the
ground and killed in a moment. This opportunity does not come
back; the devil of death hits over the head. Those who love God are
not hit with a stick by the devil of death. All are Yours, they are
attached to You and You save them. ||12|| Hymn, First Master: The
immortal God abides everywhere; worldly wealth brings serious
pain. Loaded with dust, you have to cross over the world-ocean; you
have no profit or wealth with You; ||1|| First Master: Carry the wealth
of true name, which is inexhaustible and infinite. O Nanak, this
merchandise is pure; blessed is the banker who trades in it. ||2|| First

Master: O mortal love with great Lord of previous life goes with you. O Nanak those blessed with God's name push the devil of death to ground face down. ||3|| Ladder: He looks after the body and places the treasure of His name inside. Those with fruitless deeds; He confuses them in doubt; some guru-willed realize the Lord of the soul. Some listen and obey Him; reciting God is the sacred deed. God's love wells up in the mind and sings the name of virtuous God. ||13|| Hymn, First Master: Page 1091 The fear of God abides in the mind of the innocent; this is the straight path to one Lord. Jealousy and envy bring terrible pain, and one is cursed in the whole universe. ||1|| First Master: Play the drum of Vedas! It makes lot of noise. O Nanak, recite God's name; there is no one like Him. ||2|| First Master: The world-ocean of the three qualities is unfathomable; who has seen the bottom? If I meet with the great, carefree guru, then I go across. This ocean is filled with pain and suffering. O Nanak, without the true name, no one's hunger is appeased. ||3|| Ladder: Those who search inside through guru's teaching look adorable. Reciting God's name they get what they want. Whoever God blesses, meets the guru and sings God's praises. The justice of destiny is their friend. He does not have to walk on the path of death. He recites God's name day and night and merges with Him. ||14|| Hymn, First Master: Listen to and speak the Name of one God, who permeates the heavens, this world and the underworld. His command cannot be erased; whatever is written goes with you. Who died, and who kills? Who comes and who goes? Who is happy O Nanak, and who merges in God? ||1|| First Master: In ego, he dies; possessiveness kills him, and the breath flows out like a river. Desire vanishes O Nanak, when the mind is imbued with God's name. His eyes are imbued with God's eyes and his ears hear divine wisdom. His tongue recites and enjoys the taste dyed with God's deep love. His inner being is drenched with Lord's fragrance; it cannot be described. ||2|| Ladder: In this age, God's name is the priceless treasure and it goes with you. It is inexhaustible; it is never empty, no matter how much one may eat, consume or takes with him. The devil of death does not come close to God's devotee. They are the true bankers and traders, who have Godly wealth in their lap. God is realized by God's grace when

God sends for him. ||15|| Hymn, Third Master: The self-willed does not know the essence of business. He trades poison, collects poison and loves poison. Outwardly, they are called scholars but they are ignorant in the mind. They do not focus their mind to God; they love arguing. They speak the stories of fights; they make their living by telling lies. In this world, Lord's name is pure; rest of the world is filthy. O Nanak, those who do not recite God's name become filthy and die in ignorance. ||1|| Third Master: Without serving the Lord, he suffers in pain; the pain goes away by obeying His order. He is the giver of peace; He gives punishment also. O Nanak, know this well; that everything happens by His will. ||2|| Ladder: The world is poor without God's name; no one is satisfied without God's name. Deluded by duality and doubt, in ego, he suffers in pain. Page 1092 Nothing is obtained without good fortune, no matter how much he wants. They come and go, take birth and die. They are freed through guru's teaching. He does everything. Who can we complain to? When there is no one else? ||16|| Hymn, Third Master: In this world, the saints earn the wealth; they meet guru the God. The guru teaches the truth; the value of this wealth cannot be described. Obtaining this wealth, hunger is relieved, and peace comes to dwell in the mind. Only those who have pre-ordained destiny, obtain it. The world of the self-willed is poor, they cry for worldly wealth. Night and day, he wanders around, his hunger never vanishes. He is never content; peace does not dwell in the mind. He is always worried and his doubt never vanishes. O Nanak, without the guru, his intellect is perverted; if he meets the guru, then he practices guru's teaching. He dwells in peace forever and merges in true Lord. ||1|| Third Master: He, who created the world, takes care of it. Recite one God O brother; no one is without Him. Eat the food of guru's lesson; eating it gives satisfaction forever. Dress yourself in the praise of the Lord. He is pure forever, never gets dirty. Earning the wealth of contentment and truth never fall short. The body adorned with guru's teaching is at peace forever. O Nanak, the guru-willed realizes God, whom He reveals Himself. ||2|| Ladder: Reciting guru's teaching attains meditation, self-discipline and restraint. Reciting God's name eliminates ego and ignorance. The mind is full of nectar. Enjoy the taste only by tasting. Those who taste it become carefree; they are satisfied with God's sublime taste. Those who drink it by God's grace are not troubled by death. ||17|| Hymn, Third Master: People tie bundles of demerits; no one trades in virtue. The buyers of virtues are rare O Nanak, Virtues are obtained by guru's grace, whoever God blesses. ||1|| Third Master: Merits and demerits are the same; the Creator creates them both. O Nanak, obeying God's order obtains peace contemplating guru's teaching. ||2|| Ladder: The King sits on the throne inside the body; He administers justice. God's court is realized through guru's teaching. His support is also inside. The genuine are appraised and put in the treasure; there is no place for counterfeit. Truth prevails everywhere and truth administered forever. Enshrining God's name in the mind enjoys the taste of nectar. ||18|| Hymn, First Master: When I act in ego, You are not there. When You are there then there is no ego. Page 1093 O spiritual man, understand this; the unspoken speech in the mind. Without the guru, the reality is not found. The invisible Lord dwells in all. He is realized by meeting the guru when his teaching enshrines in the mind. When ego departs, doubt and fear also depart, and the pain of birth and death is removed. Following guru's teachings, the unseen Lord is seen; the intellect is exalted, and one is carried across. O Nanak, recite the word Sohang (He is me, I am He). The universe is absorbed in Him. ||1|| Third Master: Those who appraise the jewel mind through guru's teaching. They are rare in the world in today's age. One, who realizes himself, his ego and duality disappear; O Nanak, those imbued with God's name swim across the difficult poisonous world ocean. ||2|| Ladder: The self-willed do not search inside; they are deluded by egotistic pride. They are tired of wandering in four corners; they are burning with greed. They do not follow the scriptures; the self-willed are ruined. No one attains divinity without the guru and God's true name. Reciting God obtains salvation contemplating the essence of divine wisdom. ||19|| Hymn, Second Master: He knows, He acts, and He does it right. So stand before Him, O Nanak, and offer your prayer. ||1|| First Master: He, who created the creation, watches over it and knows it. Who do I speak to O Nanak, when it happens in every house? ||2|| Ladder: Forget everything, and be friends with one Lord; Your mind and body shall be content, and sins destroyed. Your coming and going ends; you will not take birth and die again. Take support of God's true name; sorrow and old age will not bother. O Nanak, enshrine the treasure of God's name in the mind. ||20|| Hymn, Fifth Master: You do not forget the worldly wealth from your mind; you beg for it with each and every breath. You do not miss God O Nanak; it is not in your fate. ||1|| Fifth Master: Worldly wealth does not go with you; why do you cling to it? Recite guru's feet, the bonds of worldly wealth will break. ||2|| Ladder: By His will, the Lord inspires us to obey His order and bestows happiness. By His will, He unites us with the guru and inspires to recite the true God. There is no other gift as great as His will; I speak the truth. Those with pre-ordained destiny practice truth. Nanak has entered His sanctuary who created the world. ||21|| Hymn, Third Master: Those who do not have spiritual wisdom and fear of God; O Nanak, why kill those who are already dead? The Lord of the universe killed them. ||1|| Third Master: Read the horoscope of the mind; it is the essence of peace. He, who contemplates the divine wisdom, is a good scholar. He praises God, reads God contemplating guru's teaching. Page 1094 He, who obtains salvation for his entire dynasty; his coming in the world is approved. Your caste is not questioned in the next world; practicing guru's teaching is the reality. Other studies and actions are false; love of bad deeds is false as well. The self-willed does not find peace inside and ruins his life. O Nanak, those imbued with God's name are saved through guru's love. ||2|| Ladder: He creates and checks it out; He is complete truth. One who does not understand God's command is false. The way the true Lord pleases; He puts the guru-willed to work; He is the Lord of all; we merge with Him through guru's teaching. O guru-willed; praise Him forever; everyone looks to Him. O Nanak, as He makes us dance, so we dance. ||22||1|| declaration|| Vaar of Maaroo, Fifth Master, in southern language, Fifth Master: God is one. He is realized by guru's grace. If You tell me O my friend, I will cut my head and offer it to You. My eyes long for You; when will I see You; ||1|| Fifth Master: I am in love with You; I have seen that other love is false. Even clothes and food scare me, if I do not see my beloved. ||2|| Fifth Master: I rise up like a wave O my Husband Lord, to visualize you. Eye makeup, garlands of flowers, and the flavour of betel leaf, are like dust, without seeing You. ||3|| Ladder: You are true, O my true Lord. You created everything true. You created the world, making a place for the guru-willed. By the will of God, the Vedas came into being; they contemplate sin and virtue. You created Brahma, Vishnu and Shiva, the worldly virtues. Creating the world of the nine regions, O Lord, You adore it with Your love. Creating the beings of various kinds, You infused Your power in them. No one knows Your limit, O true Creator. You know all ways and means; You save the guru-willed. ||1|| Dakhanay, Fifth Master: If You are my friend, don't separate me from You even for a moment. You enticed my mind; when will I see You, O my beloved? ||1|| Fifth Master: O evil minded; may you burn in fire and die in separation. Sleeping with my Husband Lord, my all sufferings disappeared. ||2|| Fifth Master: Love of duality is evil and the separation is the sickness of ego. The true Lord King is my friend; meeting with Him, I enjoy; ||3|| Ladder: You are inaccessible, kind and infinite; who can estimate Your value? You created the entire universe; You are the master of the whole world. No one knows Your creative power, O my all-pervading Lord; No one can equal You; You are immortal and the saviour of the world. Page 1095 You established the four ages; You are the Creator of the world. You created the coming and going in life; no filth touches You. Whoever You are kind to; You attach him to guru's feet. You cannot be found by any other means; You are immortal Creator of the universe. ||2|| Dakhanay (southern language), Fifth Master: If You come into my yard, the whole earth becomes beautiful. Without my Husband Lord, no one cares for me; ||1|| Fifth Master: All my adornments look beautiful, when my Husband sits in my yard. Whoever comes to my house, does not go empty hand. ||2|| Fifth Master: I made my bed for my Husband Lord, and applied all my decorations. I cannot contain myself by wearing the necklace. ||3|| Ladder: O supreme Lord, O transcendent Lord, You do not take birth. You created the universe by Your command and dwell in it. I cannot see Your face; then how can I worship You? You pervade all; You reveal Your creative power. Your treasures of worship are full; they never fall short. These are gems, jewels and diamonds – their value cannot be estimated. Whoever You are kind to; You put them to serve the guru. He, who sings God's praises does not fall short of anything. ||3|| Dakhanay (southern language), Fifth Master: When I look in me, I see my beloved with me. All pains are gone by God's grace O Nanak, ||1|| Fifth Master: Nanak sits and waits for the news and serves for a long time at His door. O my beloved, You know my purpose; I stand, waiting to see Your face. ||2|| Fifth Master: What should I say to you, o ignorant? Don't look at other's wives – be a true husband; O Nanak, the entire world is blooming, like a garden of flowers. ||3|| Ladder: You are very intelligent and beautiful; You are pervading and permeating all. You are the master and the servant; You worship You. You are all caring bestowal and truthful. O my Lord, You are celibate, truthful and pure. You created the universe and set the play in motion. You created the coming and going and watch Your amazing play. One, whom You bestow with guru's lesson, does not go through the womb again. All do as You make them do; nothing is in the hands of the beings. ||4|| Dakhanay, Fifth Master: You are walking along the riverbank, but the ground under you is sinking. You are a sinner; the devil of death is pulling your feet. ||1|| Fifth Master: You believe that the false and temporary are true, and you go after them. O Nanak, like butter in the fire, it will melt; it shall fade away like the water lily. ||2|| Fifth Master: O my ignorant soul, why are you so lazy to serve? The time is going by. When will this opportunity come again? ||3|| Page 1096 Ladder: You have no form or shape, social class or race. These humans believe that You are far away; but You are very close. You enjoy every heart, and no filth sticks to You. You are the blissful and infinite primal Lord; Your light is all pervading. You are the greatest God of all gods O architect of destiny O Lord of all men. How can my one tongue worship You? You are immortal and beyond imagination; One, whom You unite with the guru; his dynasty is saved. All Your servants serve You; servant Nanak is at Your door. ||5|| Dakhanay, Fifth Master: He builds a hut of straw and the ignorant burns it with fire. Those with pre-ordained destiny are saved in guru's refuge. ||1|| Fifth Master: O

Nanak, he grinds the grain, cooks it and places it before him. But without his guru, he sits and waits for his food to be blessed. ||2|| Fifth Master: O Nanak, cook chapattis and put in the plate. Those who consoled with the guru, eat to the full. ||3|| Ladder: You staged this play in the world, and put ego in it. Five thieves live in the body, they do bad deeds daily. There are ten senses in one body; they all entice with their taste. This worldly wealth entices all and they wander in doubt daily. You created both sides Godly and worldly powers. Worldly power loses to the Godly power; that pleases God. You saved one from within and united him with devotee's company. Bubble originates from water and merges in water. ||6|| Dakhanay, Fifth Master: Go forward; don't turn your face back; O Nanak, deal with it this time and you will not be born again. ||1|| Fifth Master: My beloved is a happy soul. Everyone calls him friend. All think Him their own. He never breaks anyone's heart. ||2|| Fifth Master I found the hidden jewel; it appeared on the forehead. O Nanak, that place is beautiful where my beloved lives. ||3|| Ladder: When You are on my side O Lord, why do I look to others? You entrusted everything to me, when I became Yours. My wealth does not fall short, I keep spending and consuming. All of the millions of species serve You. All enemies have become my friends, and no one wishes me ill. No one asks for my account, since God blessed me. I have become happy and peaceful, meeting the guru, the Lord of the universe. All my affairs have been resolved, since You are pleased with me. ||7|| Dakhanay, Fifth Master: I am eager to see You, O Lord; how does Your face look like? I wandered in a miserable state, but when I saw You, my mind is satisfied. ||1|| Page 1097 Fifth Master: The painful suffer in pain. You alone know their pain O Lord. I may know millions, but I live by seeing my beloved. ||2|| Fifth Master: I have seen the riverbank washed away and rivers changing course. Those who meet the guru become humble. ||3|| Ladder: No pain afflicts that humble being who is hungry for You. Those, guru-willed who realize You are known in all four corners. The mortal who seeks his refuge, the sins run away from him. The filth of many a life is washed away bathing in the dust of guru's feet. Whoever obeys God's will does not suffer in sorrow and pain. O Dear Lord, You are the friend of all; You know all. The glory of God's humble servant is as great as God. God pervades all. He is realized through His devotees. ||8|| Dakhanay, Fifth Master: Those, whom I followed, now follow me. Those, whom I hoped for, they hope for me. ||1|| Fifth Master: The wet pieces of gooey gluey jagry, is thrown all over. Whoever sits on it, is caught; those with good fortune are saved; ||2|| Fifth Master: I see Him in all. No one is without Him. Those, my friends are lucky who enjoy my beloved Lord. ||3|| Ladder: I the minstrel sing His praises at His door, it pleases my God; My God is permanent forever; others continue coming and going. I beg for that gift from the Lord of the world, which will satisfy my hunger. O dear God, please visualize to the minstrel so that he is satisfied. God, the bestowal hears the prayer and invites the minstrel to His palace. Seeing God my pain and hunger disappeared. The minstrel forgot to beg. All desires are fulfilled, touching the feet of God. The primal Lord freed me the minstrel without filing charges. ||9|| Dakhanay, Fifth Master: When the soul leaves, the body, it becomes dust; the lonely soul does not realize the husband Lord. You are in love with evil people; by what virtues will you enjoy God's love? ||1|| Fifth Master: O Nanak, without Him, you cannot survive, even for an instant; you cannot survive for a moment forgetting Him; Why do you get angry with him who worries about you? ||2|| Fifth Master: Imbued with the love of the supreme Lord, their minds and bodies are dyed deep red. O Nanak, without the name, all other thoughts are filthy. ||3|| Ladder: O dear God, when You are my friend, why do I worry? You have beaten and destroyed the cheats that cheat the world. The guru carried me across the terrifying world-ocean and won the battle. I enjoy every pleasure in the mighty world arena through guru's lesson. The true Lord has brought all my senses under my control and my lust is gone. Page 1098 Wherever He attaches them, they stay there; they do not create any problem. I obtain the fruits of my desires; the guru has a garden inside. Says Nanak, when the guru is pleased O brother; God dwells close by. ||10|| Dakhanay, Fifth Master: When I miss You; I enjoy all comforts. O Nanak: my mind is imbued with Your love O beloved; ||1|| Fifth Master: Enjoyment of clothes and corrupt pleasures are all like dust. I long for the dust of the feet of those who are imbued to visualizing God. ||2|| Fifth Master: Why do you look in other directions? O my heart; take support of one Lord. Become the dust of the feet of saints, and find God the giver of peace. ||3|| Ladder: Without good luck God is not found; without the guru, the mind does not concentrate; Faith and contentment are in the body and this evil mind does not realize. He reaps what he sows; he gets it instantly. I checked all four ages; self-pride does not go away without congregation. Ego is never eradicated without the company of devotees. As long as the mind does not like the Lord, it does not find a place to rest. Whoever serves God; he is supported by God forever. He obtains peace by God's grace by attaching to guru's feet. ||11|| Dakhanay, Fifth Master: I have searched everywhere for the emperor of emperors. That master is in my heart; I recite His name from my mouth. ||1|| Fifth Master: O my mother, the master has blessed me with the jewel. Reciting God from my mouth soothes my heart. ||2|| Fifth Master: I have laid the bed of my beloved on my eyes. If You look at me, even once, I shall find peace beyond imagination. ||3|| Ladder: My mind longs to meet the Lord; how can I visualize Him? I turned and twisted in my bed millions of time if he would call me once. I have searched in four corners; there is none as great as You. Show me the path, O saints. How can I meet God? I offer my mind and renounce my ego. This is the path I will take. I serve my master in devotee's company. The guru invited me to his palace and my hopes are fulfilled. I cannot think of any other as great as You, O my friend Lord of the world. ||12|| Dakhanay, Fifth Master: I found Your throne O my beloved Lord. He calls me close to his feet; I am happy like a lotus in water. ||1|| Fifth Master: I am hungry to meet my beloved and see His amazing expanse. I know that sugar is in sugarcane. It does not yield without crushing. ||2|| Fifth Master: Break off your love with the cheaters; know that it is an enticing scent. Your pleasure lasts for only two moments; this traveler wanders through many homes. ||3|| Ladder: God is not found by intelligent ideas; He is unknowable and unseen. Page 1099 The followers of the six orders wander around in disguises. Disguises do not realize God. They keep the lunar fasts, but they are of no use. They read Vedas completely, but still they do not know the reality. They apply ceremonial marks on the forehead, and take cleansing baths, but they are black inside. God cannot be realized by disguises and without true learning. He, who has pre-ordained destiny, finds the way. One, who sees the guru with his eyes, liberates his life. ||13|| Dakhanay, Fifth Master: Focus on that which will not pass away. Abandon your false actions, and recite the true master. ||1|| Fifth Master: God' is seen in the soul like the reflection of moon in water. He reveals to those O Nanak, who have pre-ordained destiny. ||2|| Fifth Master: Praising God twenty – four hours a day one looks beautiful. O Nanak, he is accepted in God's court and the homeless finds a home. ||3|| Ladder: Imitating outside does not realize God. God abides inside and knows all. Without One dear God, all wander around aimlessly. Their minds are imbued with attachment to family and they are full of pride. The arrogant wander in the world; what is the pride of wealth? Pride and wealth do not go with you. They leave you in a moment. They wander around in the world, according to God's command. I am lucky that I found the guru the God the master. He, who is God's devotee; God works for him; ||14|| Dakhanay, Fifth Master: All talk about death, but rare are those who realize death. Nanak is the dust of the feet of those who have faith in one God. ||1|| Fifth Master: Know that He lives inside; rare are those who realize Him. There is no veil between God and him who surrenders to the guru. ||2|| Fifth Master: Those who find the way by contemplating I wash their feet and drink the water; My body is filled with infinite love to see my true master. ||3|| Ladder: He forgot the name of concern free God and is attached to worldly wealth. He comes and goes, and wanders, dancing in many lives. He gives his word, and then backs out. He speaks all false. The false person is hollow inside; he is totally sunk in falsehood. He creates enmity with enemyless for the sake of false greed. The true Lord kills him, looking into his deeds from the beginning. He is chased by the devil of death and rots in pain. O Nanak, true justice is administered in true Lord's court. ||15|| Dakhanay, Fifth Master: Recite God in the morning and worship guru's feet. Singing the praises of True Lord erases the filth of birth and death. ||1|| Fifth Master: The body is in the dark, blind and lonely without God's name. O Nanak, fruitful is the birth of the one, in whose heart God lives. ||2|| Fifth Master: With my eyes, I have seen the light and my thirst quenched. Page 1100 O Nanak, those eyes are different that see my beloved Husband Lord. ||3|| Ladder: The humble being, who worship God, obtain all happiness. He is saved, along with his family and the whole world as well. He collects the wealth of Lord's name, and his thirst is quenched. He renounces worldly greed, and lovingly attunes to God. Peace dwells in his home forever; God is his friend and support. He looks alike upon enemy and friend intuitively. He is worshipped in the world and inspires to recite guru's wisdom. He obtains what is pre-ordained for him and he consoles with God. ||16|| Dakhanay, Fifth Master: The truthful is said to be beautiful; false thinks false. O Nanak, rare are those who have truth in their laps. ||1|| Fifth Master: The face of my friend is beautiful; I watch Him, twenty-four hours a day. In sleep, I saw my Husband Lord; I admire the dream. ||2|| Fifth Master: O my friend; realize the true Lord. Just to talk about Him is useless. See Him in your mind; your beloved is not far away. ||3|| Ladder: The earth, sky, the underworld, moon and sun all will parish. Emperors, bankers, long life and princes will demolish their abode and depart. The happy, rich, poor and the intoxicated, all these people shall pass away. The Qazis, scholars and preachers shall all get up and go. The spiritual teachers, prophets and mighty, none of them remains forever. Those who keep fast, call to pray and read scriptures. All will go without understanding anything. The millions of species of beings shall all continue coming and going. One God and His devotee servant are eternal. ||17|| Dakhanay, Fifth Master: I have searched everything. Nothing is without God. Come, and show me Your face, O my friend, so that my body and mind are soothed. ||1|| Fifth Master: The lover is without hope, but in my mind, there is great hope. In the midst of hope and despair are You! O Lord; I admire You. ||2|| Fifth Master: Even if I hear of separation from You, I am in pain; I die without seeing You. Without her beloved, the separated lover takes no comfort. ||3|| Ladder: Riverbanks, sacred shrines, idols, temples, and places of pilgrimage like Kaydar Naath, Matura and Banaras; Three hundred thirty million gods, along with Indra, shall

all pass away. The Simritees, Shaastras, the four Vedas and the six systems of philosophy shall vanish. Granth sahib, religious scholars, songs, poems and poets shall also depart. The celibate, truthful and detached hermits are all subject to death. The sages, the Yogis and the nude saints, and the devil of death, all will die. Whatever is seen shall perish; all will die and disappear. Only the supreme Lord the transcendent Lord and His devotees are immortal. ||18|| Hymn Dakhanay, Fifth Master: The naked does not make the person naked; tens of thousands of hungry do not make him hungry; Millions of pains do not cause him pain. O Nanak, the Lord looks after them with His grace. ||1|| Page 1101 Fifth Master: Enjoy the eternal peace in the whole world. O Nanak, those without God's name, die of all kind of disease. ||2|| Fifth Master: Yearn for one God and realize one God. O Nanak, He fulfills your hopes; you should be ashamed of going to others. ||3|| Ladder: God is eternal, inaccessible and incomprehensible. The treasure of God's name is eternal; reciting it finds God. O guru-willed sing the praises of immortal God; truthfully and faithfully worship the immortal God day and night. Those who have pre-ordained destiny worship God and become kind and faithful. The writing in the fate is eternal; it does not change by any means. Devotee's company makes immortal, guru's and devotee's word is eternal. Those with pre-ordained destiny recite God forever. ||19|| Hymn, Dakhanay, Fifth Master: How can the drowning man carry others across? O Nanak, one imbued with God's love swims across and takes others with him. ||1|| Fifth Master: Wherever someone speaks and hears the name of my beloved Lord; I will go there O Nanak, I will rejuvenate seeing Him. ||2|| Fifth Master: Why are you calling your children and spouse as mine and love them? O Nanak, without God's name it means nothing. ||3|| Ladder: I See the guru with my eyes and put my forehead on his feet. When the guru walks I wave fan over his head. I recite the immortal God in my mind day and night. Believing in God, by guru's grace I gave up possessiveness. The guru bestowed the treasure of God's name and my pain went away. O brother eat digest and carry in the lap the unimaginable God's name. Bathe in God's name and speak guru's sermon wholeheartedly forever. I realized God intuitively and fear of devil of death eliminated. ||20|| Hymn, Dakhanay, Fifth Master: The eyes focused on the beloved are never satisfied. God abides in all; I do not see any other. ||1|| Fifth Master: The sayings of the saints are the paths of peace. O Nanak, those with good fortune find it. ||2|| Fifth Master: The mountains, water, land, forest, fruits and the deep gullies; the underworld and the sky. God abides in all. O Nanak see that everything is strung on one thread. ||3|| Ladder: The dear Lord is my mother and father. He looks after everyone. God cares for me, I am His child. Slowly and steadily, He feeds me. He never delays. He does not remind me of my faults; He embraces me. Whatever I ask for, He gives me. God is my peace-giving father. Page 1102 He considered me worthy and blessed with knowledge and wealth of God's name. He seated me alongside the guru and I obtained all happiness. He never leaves me; God the father does everything. ||21|| Hymn, Dakhanay, Fifth Master: O Nanak, break away from the false, and find true saint friend. The false leave you while alive; the saints do not leave even after death. ||1|| Fifth Master: O Nanak, the lightning flashes, and dark cloud thunders. It rains heavy O Nanak, the bride looks adorable in her husband's company. ||2|| Fifth Master: The ponds and land are full of water and cool breeze blows. Her bed is adorned with gold, diamonds and rubies; She wears beautiful clothes O Nanak, but without her Husband Lord she is miserable. ||3|| Ladder : He does whatever the Creator asks him to do. No matter where you run; you only get what is written in your fate from above. Cannot find anything without luck; you may wander the whole earth. Meet the guru and realize God's love and the fear will depart. He, who misses God through love, wanders around searching Him. The contentment wells up by searching. Birth and death ends. Recite God intently from the mind and find Him in devotee's company. Whoever the Lord puts on the boat of Guru Nanak, is carried across the terrifying world-ocean. ||22|| Hymn, Dakhanay Fifth Master: First, accept death, and give up hope of living. Become the dust of the feet of all, then come to me; ||1|| Fifth Master: He, who dies while living, lives forever; seeing him, the living should die while living. Those who are in love with one God are the supreme people. ||2|| Fifth Master: Pain does not come close to those, who have God dwelling in the mind; Hunger and thirst do not affect him; the devil of death does not approach him. ||3|| Ladder; Your worth cannot be estimated, O true, unmoving Lord. The mystics, seekers, spiritual people and meditators; who among them can measure You? You are all-powerful, to make and break; You create and destroy all. You are all-powerful to act; You abide in everyone. You give food to all; why should mankind waver? You are deep, profound unfathomable virtuous divine and priceless. They do the deeds, which they are pre-ordained to do by God. There is nothing beyond You; Nanak praises You. ||23||1||2|| Tune Maaroo, the word of Kabeer Jee: God is one. He is realized by guru's grace. O religious scholar, what ignorant deeds are you engaged in? You will drown along with your family; O unfortunate you do not recite God's name. ||1||Pause|| What is the use of reading Vedas and Puraanas? It is like loading a donkey with sandalwood. Page 1103 You do not know the way of God's name; how will you go across? ||1|| You kill and call it a good act. Tell me O brother, what is a bad act? You call yourself a sage; then who will you call a butcher? ||2|| O mentally blind, you do not know you, how can you teach others? You sell knowledge for the sake of money; you waste your life away. ||3|| Naarad and Vyaas say these words; go and ask Sukhdev as well. Says Kabeer, you will be saved reciting God; otherwise you will drown. ||4||1|| How can you find God living in the forest, till you do not eliminate useless feelings from the mind? Those who see home and forest alike are perfect in the world. ||1|| You shall find real peace reciting God. Recite God in your mind with love. ||1||Pause|| What is the use of having matted hair, apply ashes to the body and live in a cave? Conquering the mind, one conquers the world, and the sins go away. ||2|| Wearing eye lashes and look through corner of the eye does not entice the lover. The eyes that wear the eye lashes of wisdom are approved; ||3|| Says Kabeer, now I know my Lord; the guru has blessed me with spiritual wisdom. I surrendered myself to God; now my mind does not go anywhere else. ||4||2|| He, who realizes the power of mysticism; why should he worry about anyone else? What can I say about divine wisdom; I feel ashamed if I say; ||1|| One who has found the Lord? He does not wander from door to door. ||1||Pause|| The false world wanders all over for wealth;

it is useful only for two days. The mortal, who drinks Lord's water, never feels thirsty again. ||2|| Whoever realizes God by guru's grace becomes free of hope in the midst of hope. One sees the Lord everywhere when the soul becomes detached. ||3|| I tasted the sublime essence of God's name; God's name carries all across. Says Kabeer, I have become like gold; the doubt has gone to the other side of the ocean. ||4||3|| Like a drop of water in the ocean and like waves in the river, merge again. Merging with absolute God, I have become like wind. ||1|| Why should I come into the world again? Coming and going is by His command; realizing His command I shall merge in Him. ||1||Pause|| When the body of five elements perishes, then any such doubts shall end. Giving up the process of seeing I became all seeing reciting one name. ||2|| I do what He asks me to do and keep doing the same deeds. When God grants His grace, then I am absorbed in guru's teaching. ||3|| Die while yet alive, and live by dieing; thus you shall not be reborn Page 1104 Says Kabeer, whoever is absorbed in God's name is absorbed in God. ||4||4|| If You keep me away from You, then tell me, what is liberation? I have become one and all. How can I wander all over now? ||1|| O Lord, where will You take me after liberating? Tell me; what kind of liberation You will give me by Your grace; ||1||Pause|| You talk about liberation only till you know it? Now I become pure in my heart, says Kabeer, and my mind is pleased; ||2||5|| Raawan, who had golden castles; he is gone leaving it behind. ||1|| Why do you act your own way? When devil of death came and caught you from the hair. Only God's name can free you then. ||1||Pause|| The Lord created death and immortality and created the body of five elements. Says Kabeer, those who enshrine God's name in the mind attain salvation. ||2||6|| The body is a village, and the soul is the owner and farmer; the five farm hands live there. The eyes, nose, ears, tongue and senses do not listen to me. ||1|| O elder, now I will not live in this village. They ask for my account every moment. When will I recite God's name? ||1||Pause|| When the justice of destiny asks for my account, I will owe a lot; the five farm hands will run away, and the bailiff will arrest my soul. ||2|| Says Kabeer, listen, O saints: forget about the farm; O Lord, bless the mortal this time so that he does not come back.

||3||7|| Tune Maaroo, the word of Kabeer Jee: God is one. He is realized by guru's grace. No one has seen the carefree God, O renunciate; without the fear of God, how can the carefree God be realized? ||1|| If you see the beloved face to face then only love wells up O renunciate; If he realizes God's command then he becomes carefree O forest dweller; ||2|| God does not believe in hypocrisy, O renunciate! The whole world is filled with hypocrisy O forest dweller. ||3|| Greed does not leave you O renunciate. The false attachment burns away the body village. ||4|| Burn the worry that burns the body, O renunciate, If one lets his mind become dead. ||5|| Without the guru, there can be no renunciation; Even if all the people may wish for it O forest dweller; ||6|| With good fortune, one meets the guru O renunciate, intuitively finds God O forest dweller. ||7|| Says Kabeer, I offer this one prayer, O renunciate. Carry me across the terrifying world-ocean O forest dweller; ||8||1||8|| Page 1105 O king who will come to your home? I have seen such love from Bidar, that poor man pleases me. ||1||Pause|| Seeing his power, he was lost in doubt; he did not know that He was God; He accepted water from Bidar as a nectar and as good as your milk; ||1|| He ate grass like your milk pudding and spent the night singing God's praises; Kabeer's Lord is joyous and blissful; He does not care about anyone's caste; ||2||9|| Hymn, Kabeer: The battle of life has been declared by beating the drum. O braves; those with pre-ordained destiny come in the field and show your fighting skills. ||1|| He, who fights within the code of conduct; is a real brave; Then if he dies by cutting into pieces but never leaves the battle field. ||2||2|| Word of Kabeer, Tune Maaroo, the word of Naam Dev Jee: God is one. He is realized by guru's grace. Following four systems of mystics the bridegroom went to God's refuge; He is liberated and is known in four ages and has a canopy over his head and sings God's praises. ||1|| Tell me, who did not attain salvation reciting God? Those who follow guru's teaching and join devotee's company are called God's devotees; ||1||Pause|| He blows a conch, wears a circular weapon and has mark on the forehead. Seeing his glory the devil of death is scared. He becomes fearless, and the power of the Lord thunders through him; the pains of birth and death are taken away. ||2|| The Lord blessed Ambreek

with honour of fearlessness and made Bhabhikhan a king. God blessed Sudama, Dhroo and Prahlaad with a priceless treasure; He has not stopped there; ||3|| For the sake of His devotee Prahlaad, God assumed the form of a man-lion and killed Harnaakhash. Says Naam Dev, the beautiful-haired Lord is under the control of His devotees; He is standing at Bal king's door, even now! ||4||1|| Maaroo, Kabeer Jee: O ignorant man you have forgotten the faith. You fill your belly, and sleep like an animal; you have wasted the human life. ||1||Pause|| You never joined devotee's company; always engaged in false deed. You wander like a dog, a pig, a crow; soon, you will get up and go; ||1|| You believe that you are great, and others are nothing compared to you. Those who follow their desire, word and deed, I saw them going to hell. ||2|| The lustful, the angry, clever and jugglers are all useless. You spend your life slandering and do not recite God; ||3|| Says Kabeer, the fools, the idiots and the ignorant do not miss God. They do not even know Lord's name; how can they be carried across? ||4||1|| Page 1106 Tune Maaroo, the word of Jai Dev Jee: God is one. He is realized by guru's grace. I wandered through seven moons playing seven drums, and worshipped the seven suns in sixteen ways. I eliminated ego, stabilized the flickering mind, controlled the uncontrollable mind, and then I drank the nectar. ||1|| I sing praises of the primal virtuous God in my mind. My doubt disappeared by Your grace. ||1||Pause|| I worship God worthy of worship, worthy of merging intuitively and became one with one. Says Jai Dev, I recite God lovingly and attained salvation. ||2||1|| Kabeer, Maaroo: Recite God O my mind otherwise you will regret. My sinful mind is greedy. Today or tomorrow I will get up and go. ||1||Pause|| Attached to greed and deluded by doubt I wasted my life away. Do not take pride in wealth and youth; it will rot like a paper. ||1|| When the devil of death catches and throw you to the ground, you will be powerless. You do not recite God and you are not kind; You will be slapped in the face and suffer. ||2|| When the justice of destiny calls your account, how will you show your face? Says Kabeer, listen, O saints: salvation is obtained in devotee's company. ||3||1|| Tune Maaroo, the word of Ravi Daas Jee: God is one. He is realized by guru's grace. O beloved; who else but You can do such a thing? O supporter of the poor, Lord of the world, You have put the canopy of Your grace over my head. ||1||Pause|| Only You can be kind to that person whose touch pollutes the world. You elevate the lowly, O Lord of the universe; You are not afraid of anyone. ||1|| Naam Dev, Kabeer, Trilochan, Sadhana and Sain attained salvation. Says Ravi Daas, listen, O saints, everyone obtains salvation reciting God. ||2||1|| Maaroo: Ocean of peace; the miracle tree of life, fulfiller of deeds and the ever milk giving cow; all are under His power. The four great blessings, the eight miraculous powers of mystics and nine treasures are in the palm of His hand. ||1|| Why don't you recite God's name? Abandon all other written sermons. ||1||Pause|| Many epics, the Puraanas and the Vedas are all composed with thirty-four letters of the alphabet. Vyaas thinks and says sacred words that nothing equals God's name. ||2|| In intuitive trance, without any status I am attuned to God fortunately. Says, detached humble servant Ravi Daas that his fear of birth and death ran away. ||3||2||15|| Page 1107 Tukhaari Chhant, First Master, Baarah Maahaa ~ The Twelve Months:

God is one. He is realized by guru's grace.

Listen O man: You act according to your previous earning. Everyone gets happiness or sorrow of what he earns. Whatever You give is good. O Lord, what is my state in your creation; I cannot live without God for a moment. Without my beloved, I am miserable; I have no friend. The guru-willed drink nectar. The formless Lord created the creation. Enshrining God in the mind is a good deed. O Nanak, the soul-bride is content listening to Your praise O Lord; ||1|| The rain bird cries for rain and the song-bird sings God's sermon. The soul-bride enjoys all the pleasures, and merges in her beloved. She merges with God if she pleases Him and she is a happily married woman. God established nine houses and then made the tenth high one for Himself. All are Yours, You are my beloved; I am in love with You night and day. O Nanak, the rain bird cries for rain and the songbird looks beautiful while singing; ||2|| You are drenched with God's love listening to Your beloved. Recite Him from your mind and body and never forget Him. How could I forget You even for a moment? I praise You and live by singing Your praises. No one is mine; whom do I belong to? I cannot survive without God. I took shelter at His feet and became sacred. O Nanak, visualizing Him I find eternal happiness and my mind is at peace through guru's teaching. ||3|| The nectar rains down heavily! Its drops look beautiful! I met my beloved intuitively and I fell in love with God. If it pleases God. He comes into my body and the bride sings His praises. In each and every home, the Husband Lord enjoys the happy soul-brides; why has He forgotten me? The dark cloud clouds over and rains intuitively and my mind and body enjoy the love. O Nanak, the sacred sermon rains down. He comes home by His grace. ||4|| In first month (Chayt) the month of spring, the bumblebees hum with joy. Page 1108 The forest blossoms in front of my door, if my beloved would come home! If her Husband Lord does not return home, how can the soul-bride find peace? Her body is wasting away with the sorrow of separation. The beautiful songbird sings, perched on the mango tree; why I endure so much pain? The bumblebee is buzzing around the flowering branches; but how can I became humble while I am alive, O my mother! O Nanak, in first month (Chayt), the bride obtains peace and contentment if her Husband Lord is at home; ||5|| Baisakh the second month is pleasant; the branches blossom with new leaves. The soul-bride yearns to see the Lord at her door. Please be kind and come to my home O Lord. O beloved, come home and take me across the world ocean; I am worth nothing without You. Who can estimate the joy I get if I am pleasing to You? If I see You by Your grace O beloved. I know that You are not far; You are in me and I realize Your palace. O Nanak, I find God in the month of Baisakh by consoling my mind and intellect through guru's teaching. ||6|| The month of Jaith is good. How can I forget my beloved? The earth is hot; with a load on her head the soul-bride offers her prayer. The bride offers her prayer, and sings His praises. Singing His praises, she becomes pleasing to God. The unattached Lord dwells in His true mansion. If He allows me, then I will come to Him. The bride is humble and powerless; how will she find peace without her Lord? O Nanak, in Jaith, the virtuous fortunate bride meets her husband Lord. ||7|| The month of Aasaarh is such that the sun blazes in the sky. The earth suffers in pain, parched and roasted by heat. She absorbs the heat and is dieing in worry; still she does not quit her work. Time passes by, the soul-bride seeks shade. The crickets chirp in the forest. She carries the faults with her and suffers pain ahead. She finds peace if she recites God. O Nanak, whom I surrendered my mind; I will live and die with him. ||8|| In Saawan, be happy, O my mind. The rainy season has come, it rains heavy. My mind and body long for my Husband Lord but he is gone abroad. My beloved does not come home, I am worried and the lightning flashes. I alone suffer in the bed and I am suffering in pain. How can I sleep without God? Wearing clothes do not give peace to me. O Nanak, she, who merges with her beloved Lord, is a happy soul-bride. ||9|| In Bhaadon, the youthful woman confused by doubt, repents. The lakes and fields are filled with water in rainy season. It is time to enjoy. It rains in the dark night, frogs and peacock make noise but the girl is restless. The rain bird chirps in happiness, stinging snakes are out. The mosquitoes bite, the ponds are overflowing; how can she find peace without God? O Nanak, I go and ask my guru; take me where God is? ||10|| In Assu, come my beloved; the soul-bride is worried. She can meet Him only when God inspires her to meet. She is ruined by duality. Robbed by falsehood rejected by husband, her hair turned grey. Page 1109 Summer is behind and the winter is ahead. My mind wanders seeing this. In all ten directions, the branches are green and alive. That which ripens slowly, is sweet. O Nanak, in Assu, I meet my beloved when the guru is my lawyer. ||11|| In Katak, I do whatever pleases God. The lamp burns in peace and burns the sins. The lamp enjoys the oil, bride and husband unite and the bride is filled with joy. Filled with demerits, neither she dies nor her deeds fulfill. She will die (humble) through virtues. If the devotee recites God's name at home, still there is hope! O Nanak: may I realize God and open the door of my mind even for a moment! ||12|| The month of Maghar is good; I praise God's virtues and merge with Him. The virtuous sings His praises. I am pleased with eternal Lord. The primal Lord is unmoving, clever and wise; the entire world is fickle. If it pleases God, then one absorbs in wisdom, meditation and virtues. I heard the songs, sounds and the poems of the poets; but the pain goes away only by listening to God's name. O Nanak, the soul bride who worships her Lord lovingly, is loved by the Lord; ||13|| In Poh, the snow falls, and the sap of the trees and the fields dry up. He dwells in my mind, body and mouth. Why He does not come? God the life of the world dwells in my mind and body and I enjoy His love through guru's teaching. His light shines in all those born of eggs, womb, sweat or earth. O bestowal of honour visualize and teach me so that I attain salvation. O Nanak, the enjoyer of taste enjoys God through love. ||14|| In Maagh, I became pure; I realized God's shrine inside me. I met my beloved intuitively and merged with Him praising His virtues. O my virtuous beloved Lord, please listen: I bathe in your sacred pool if it pleases You. I merge with Ganges, Jamunaa and Saraswati, at the junction; then flow and merge in seven oceans. Good deed, donations and God's worship, are the same in all ages. O Nanak, in Maagh, reciting God is the most sublime essence. It is as good as bathing at sixty-eight shrines. ||15|| In Phalgun, her mind enjoys her husband's love intuitively. She eliminated ego and became peaceful forever. Emotional attachment is eradicated from her mind, when it pleases him and he came home by his grace. I tried many ways, but without the Lord there is no place to rest. I wore stringed necklaces scented oils and silk robes for the sake of my beloved. O Nanak, the guru has united me with Him. The soul-bride has found her Husband Lord in her heart. ||16|| The twelve months, the seasons, the weeks, the days are all good; So are the hours, the minutes and the seconds, when one intuitively meets the true Lord. When one realizes the beloved Lord, her deeds are fulfilled. The Creator knows every way. He, who loves her, also adores her. They are united and enjoy. The bed looks beautiful when she enjoys with her Lord; the guru-willed is lucky. Page 1110 O Nanak, she enjoys with her Lord forever and her marriage is eternal. ||17||1|| Tukhaari, First Master: In the first watch of the night, O bride with beautiful eyes; save the priceless treasure; your turn will come. When your turn comes, who will wake you up? The devil of death will suck your blood while asleep. In the darkness of night the thieves break in and steal everything. What happens to your honour then? O saviour, inaccessible and infinite Lord, please hear my prayer. O Nanak, the ignorant never misses God; what can he see in the dark of night? ||1|| In the second watch, she wakes up subconsciously! Protect your wealth, O mortal; your farm is being eaten. Protect your crop through guru the God's love and remain awake; then the thief will not break in. Then you do not follow the path of death and suffer. The fear and concern of devil of death will go away. The lamps of sun and moon are lit at guru's refuge through his teachings and the mind recites the true Lord. O Nanak, the ignorant still does not miss Him; how can he find peace in duality? ||2|| The third watch has begun, and he is fast asleep. The mortal suffers in pain, from worldly attachment, children and spouse. Worldly wealth, children, wife and the whole world are dear to him; he bites the bait, and is caught. When he recites God's name, he attains peace through guru's teaching and the death does not seize him. He cannot escape from birth and death; without the name, he suffers. O Nanak, in the third watch of the three-phased worldly wealth, the world is engrossed in worldly attachment. ||3|| The fourth watch has begun, and the day is about to dawn. Those who remain awake night and day, protect their homes. Those who recite God's name and remain awake, following guru's teaching, their night passes peacefully; those who follow guru's teaching do not take birth and God becomes their friend. His hands feet and body shake, he goes blind and finally body turns to dust. O Nanak, people suffer throughout the four ages, without enshrining God's name in the mind. ||4|| The letter is opened; get up; the order has come! Pleasures and comforts are gone. He is tied and taken away O God; You will be tied and taken away by God's will. You cannot see or hear. Everyone will have their turn; the crop ripens, and then it is harvested. The record of every moment is accounted for. All good or bad deeds you did. O Nanak, the gods and heroes, all unite with God through guru's teaching; this is how God sets it up! ||5||2|| Tukhaari, First Master: The morning star has risen. How can it be seen with eyes O God? The devotee with good fortune sees it through guru's teaching O God! Guru's teaching reveals it by reciting God and then watches it forever; by self-realization the five passions go away. Lust anger and sins erased. His inner soul is illuminated, by guru's teachings and the fortunate finds God; Page 1111 O Nanak, killing his ego, he is satisfied; the morning star has risen; ||1|| The guru-willed remain awake; their egotistic pride is eradicated. The day has dawned forever and he merges in true Lord O God; the guru-willed are merged in the true Lord and they are happy. They are fully awake. The guru blesses them with God's sacred name. They are lovingly attached to guru's feet. Their soul is enlightened and realized God in the soul. The self-willed are lost in doubt. O Nanak, The day has dawned the mind is satisfied and spends the night awake. ||2|| The demerits are forgotten and merits have entered the mind O God. One Lord pervades everywhere; there is no other at all. He is all pervading; there is no other. The mind has conquered the mind. He, who created water, land, universe and all beings, the guru-willed realized that God. The infinite, all-powerful Lord is the Creator, the cause of causes; erasing the three-phased worldly pleasure we merge with Him. O Nanak, the demerits are dissolved in merits; such is guru's teaching. ||3|| My coming and going has ended and the ignorance eliminated O God; Conquering my ego, I wear the gown of truth O God. The guru eliminated my ego sorrow and suffering. I am enlightened. My soul merged with supreme soul and I realized me. Following guru's teaching in parents home, I am pleasing to my husband in in-laws home. O Nanak, the guru has united me in His union; my public weakness ended. ||4||3|| Tukhaari, First Master: Deluded by doubt, misled and confused, the soul-bride regrets and repents. Abandoning her Husband Lord, she sleeps and does not appreciate his virtues. Leaving her Husband Lord, she sleeps. She is robbed by her faults. The night is painful for this bride. Lust, anger and ego destroy her. She burns in ego. When the soul-swan flies away by God's order; she became dust and merged with dust. O Nanak, without the true name, she is lost and regrets. ||1|| Please listen, O my beloved Husband Lord, to my one prayer. You live in your home and I became a pile of ashes. Without my Husband Lord, no one likes me; what can I say or do? Recite and enjoy God's sacred name and drink nectar through guru's teaching. Without God's name, you have no friend or a companion. You will keep coming and going forever. O Nanak: make profit and go home. Your teaching is truly true. ||2|| My beloved has gone abroad and I send a message. I miss my beloved and my eyes are filled. My eyes are filled and I sing your praises; how will I meet my beloved God? The path is treacherous and I do not know the way. How will I meet my beloved husband Lord? The separated bride meets the Lord through guru's teaching and offers her mind and body to him. O Nanak, the sacred tree bears the sweet fruits; meeting with my beloved, I taste the sweet juice. ||3|| The Lord is calling you, do not delay! Page 1112 Imbued with love forever attains peace. Eliminating self-pride she merged with God; she became peaceful and content and her sorrows eliminated. Imbued with truth, she unites with God. The self-willed keeps coming and going. When you dance, what is the idea of veil? Take off the veil and be carefree; O Nanak, the guru-willed realizes himself contemplating the reality. ||4||4|| Tukhaari, First Master: O my dear beloved, I am the slave of Your slaves. The guru has shown me the invisible Lord, now I do not seek any other. The guru showed me the invisible Lord, when it pleased Him by God's grace. The life of the world, the architect of destiny, the Lord of woods I met Him with ease. Bestow Your grace and carry me across. Please bless me with truth O Lord, kind to the poor. Prays Nanak, I am the slave of Your slaves. You take care of all beings. ||1|| My dear beloved is pervading throughout the universe. The guru the embodiment God is realized through guru's teaching. The guru, the embodiment of God, abides in the whole universe; His limits cannot be found. He created the beings of various colours and creeds. His blessings increase day by day. The infinite Lord creates and destroys; whatever pleases Him happens; O Nanak, the diamond enlightens the diamond and the garland of virtues is strung. ||2|| The virtuous merges in virtuous Lord; God's name is the resolve of the fortunate. The true person merges in the true Lord, his coming and going ended. The true person realizes the true Lord, and is imbued with truth. Merging with the true Lord pleases him. No one else is above the true Lord. The true person merges in the true Lord. The enticer enticed my mind and freed me from bonds. O Nanak, my light merged in the divine light when I met my beloved. ||3|| By searching, the true home, the place of the true guru is found. The self-willed does not realize God; the guru-willed does, through divine wisdom. Whoever God approves bestows them with true gift; God is a great giver forever. He is immortal, unborn and permanent; His true palace is everlasting. When God's light wells up in the mind the daily account keeping ends. O Nanak, the true person is absorbed in true Lord; the guru-willed crosses over to the other side. ||4||5|| Tukhaari, First Master: O my ignorant, unconscious mind; realize yourself O God. O my mind, abandon demerits and gather merits O God. Those who do deeds enticed by many tastes get separated from God and never reunite. How can the difficult world-ocean be crossed? The fear of the devil of death scares. The path of death is very painful. The mortal does not recite God's name in the morning and evening; what can he do on a difficult journey? Bound in bonds is freed if the guru-willed serves God. ||1|| O my mind; abandon your useless deeds. O my mind; serve the unique primal Lord. Page 1113 Recite one God, who created the whole world. He controls air, water and fire; the guru staged the drama of the world. Recite God's name, you will improve character, dealing, restraint, meditation and self-discipline. Reciting God's name will make friends; companions and the beloved will love you. ||2|| O my mind, remain stable, and you will not be hurt O God. O my mind, sing God's praises and merge in peace intuitively O God. Sing God's praises with love through guru's teaching; that is the essence. Guru's teaching enlightens the universe and five demons are destroyed. Eliminate fear and become carefree and swim across the horrible world-ocean. Meeting the guru all deeds are fulfilled. You will find joy beauty and love of God by God's grace. ||3|| O my mind, what did you bring and what will you take with you O God? O my mind, you will only be saved if you eliminate doubt. Collect the treasure of God's name. You will realize it through guru's teaching. The filth will be removed through guru's pure teaching and you will find the destiny. You will obtain honour through God's name and go straight home, and drink nectar with love. Recite God's name and enjoy through guru's teaching; the fortunate sing God's praises. ||4|| O my mind, without a ladder, how will you climb God's temple O God? O my mind, you cannot not reach the other shore without a boat. Your beloved infinite Lord is on the other side. Attuning to guru's teaching you will go across. You enjoy in devotee's company and never repent. O merciful God, be kind and bless me with Your name in devotee's company. Please hear Nanak's prayer O my beloved; guide my mind through guru's teaching. ||5||6|| Tukhaari Chhant, Fourth Master: God is one. He is realized by guru's grace. I am in love with my beloved; how will I live without my beloved O God? How can I drink nectar if I do not see him? How can I drink nectar and live without God? I cannot survive without Him. Night and day, I keep calling my beloved! My thirst does not quench without my beloved. O My beloved God; bless me so that I recite Your name forever. I realized my beloved through guru's teaching; I admire my guru; ||1|| When I see my beloved Lord, I sing God's praises with love. Page 1114 I call my beloved with love and become enlightened. I call my beloved with love through guru's teaching and attain salvation. I do not get satisfaction without seeing him. Adorned by guru's teaching the soul bride recites God's name all the time. Your servant begs for a gift, please be kind and unite him with his beloved. Night and day, I recite guru the Lord of the world and I praise my guru; ||2|| I am a stone in guru's boat. Please carry me across the terrifying ocean. O guru, please, bless me with your lesson intuitively so that I the ignorant am saved. I am an ignorant fool; I know nothing about Your divine wisdom. You are known as inaccessible and great. You are kind. You united me the virtueless with you by Your grace. I committed sins and wandered through many lifes. Now I came to your refuge. Be kind and save me O God; I touch guru's feet. ||3|| The guru is philosopher's stone; I the iron became gold by his touch O God. My light merged into supreme light, and my body-fortress looks beautiful. My body-fortress looks beautiful. My God fascinates me. How can I forget Him, even for a breath, or a morsel of food? I have caught the unseen and unfathomable Lord through guru's teaching. I praise my guru. I offer my head to the guru if it pleases him. Be kind O kind God so that Nanak merges with You. ||4||1|| Tukhaari, Fourth Master: God is inaccessible, unfathomable, infinite and beyond comprehension. Those who recite You O Lord of the universe; they swim across the terrifying world ocean. Those who recite God's name swim across the terrifying world-ocean and become content. Those who listen to guru's word and follow it; God unites them with Him. By God's grace their soul merges with God's soul. God is inaccessible, unfathomable, infinite and beyond comprehension. ||1|| O my Lord, You are inaccessible and unfathomable. You abide in everyone. You are unseen unfathomable; You are realized through guru's word. Blessed are those perfect people, who sing God's praises in devotee's company. Through supreme intellect and contemplating, the guru-willed recite God all the time through guru's teaching. Wherever the guru-willed sits or stands; says God God God. O my Lord; You are inaccessible and unfathomable. You abide in all. ||2|| People worship God but those who worship through guru's teaching are accepted. God eliminates their millions of sins in a moment. Those who recite God with love, their sins and sufferings are erased. Page 1115 The Creator fulfills their life who recite God through guru's teaching. Those who recite God through guru's teaching swim across the terrifying world-ocean and are blessed with greatness and perfection. Those who recite and serve God through guru's teaching are accepted. ||3|| O God; You know all; I walk the way you want me to; Nothing is in my hand; when You unite me, I come and unite with You. Those whom You unite with You O my Lord! Their accounts are settled. Those, who realize God through guru's teaching, no one can go through their account O brother! O Nanak, the Lord becomes kind to those who obey guru's will. O God; You know all; I walk the way You want me to; ||4||2|| Tukhaari, Fourth Master: You are the life of the world, the Lord of the universe, our master, the Creator of the universe. Those, with pre-ordained destiny recite You O my Lord. Those, with pre-ordained destiny say God God O Lord. Those, who recite God through guru's teaching their sins are eliminated in a moment. Blessed are those humble beings who recite God's name. Seeing them I became guru-willed. You are the life of the world, the Lord of the universe, our master, the Creator of the universe. ||1|| You pervade in water and land. You are the master of all. Those who recite God whole-heartedly! They attain salvation by reciting. Those who recite God attain salvation and are happy in God's court. They are happy here and hereafter. God the protector protects them. Listen to Lord's name in saint's company O brother. The service of the guru-willed is rewarded. You pervade in water land and sky. You are the master of all. ||2|| O Lord; You pervade all high and low places of interest. The forests, the straw, the universe and the creation; all recite Your name. All recite God`s name O Creator. Unlimited numbers recite God. The saints and devotees, who please God are admirable. Those who recite God`s name in the mind all the time; You reward them with visualizing. O Lord, You pervade all high and low places of interest. ||3|| Unlimited numbers of treasures are filled with Your worship; whoever You give, only they get it O my God. Those, on whose forehead the guru places his hand. God`s praises enshrine in their mind. God`s praises enshrine in the mind of those who have love and devotion in the mind; Page 1116 No one falls in love or carries across the world ocean without God`s fear. O Nanak, whom You bless, falls in love devotionally; There are unlimited number of treasures of Your worship; Whoever You bless obtains it O master. ||4||3|| Tukhaari, Fourth Master: To meet the guru is above bathing at all shrines. The filth of evil thinking washed away, and the darkness of ignorance erased. Ignorance eliminated by visualizing the guru and the soul got illuminated. The pains of birth and death vanished in an instant, and realized the immortal God. The Creator celebrated the festival and the guru came to bathe at Kurukshayter. At the festival I visualized the unconquerable guru. ||1|| The guru and the devotees walked the path together. Night and day, devotional worship services were held and we saw the guru at every step. God was worshipped and everyone came to see. Whoever saw the guru saw God? The guru made the pilgrimage to the sacred shrine, for the sake of saving all the people. The guru and the devotees walked the path together. ||2|| First the guru came to Kurukshayter and celebrated the festival. The news spread throughout the world, and the entire universe came to see. The gods, sages, heroes and others from the three worlds came to see. Those whom the perfect guru touched; their sins were erased. The Yogis, the nude saints, the renunciates and those from six schools of philosophy came and contemplated divine wisdom. First the guru came to Kurukshater and celebrated the festival. ||3|| Second, the guru went to the river Jamunaa and worshipped God. The tax collectors met the guru and gave Him offerings and let him go. All those, who recited God`s name with the guru attained salvation. Whoever follow guru`s teaching, the devil of death does not come close to them. The whole world says guru guru. Saying guru everyone is freed. Second, the guru went to the river Jamunaa and worshipped God. ||4|| Third, He went to the river Ganges, something amazing happened there. All were fascinated, seeing the guru; nobody charged any money from him. No tax was collected, and the mouths of the tax collectors were sealed. They said, O brother, what could we do? Who should we ask? Everyone is running after the true guru. Page 1117 The tax collectors were smart; they thought about it and saw. They broke their cash-boxes and left. Third, He went to the Ganges, and an amazing thing happened there. ||5|| The important people of the city came and sought guru's protection. They asked the guru the Lord of the universe and read simritees. They read Simritees and the Shaastras. Pressing their palms together they recited God the guru the Lord of the universe like Sukhdev and Prahlaad. They destroyed the five thieves from their bodies. They praised the Puraanas and offered awns daily and worshipped God through guru's word. The important people of the city came and sought guru's protection. ||6||4||10|| Tukhaari Chhant, Fifth Master: God is one. He is realized by guru's grace. O my beloved, I praise you and I have surrendered my mind to the guru. Listening to your teaching, my mind is happy. This mind is happy like the fish in water. I am lovingly attached to the Lord. I cannot say anymore. you are beyond comprehension. O Lord the bestowal of all virtues; listen to the prayer of the humble; Please bless Nanak with your visualization; my mind praises you lovingly. ||1|| This body and mind and all virtues are Yours. I love and praise to visualize You. Listen O my God; I live by seeing You all the time. I have heard that Your name is the nectar; be kind so that I drink it. I am thirsty of You O Lord, like the rain bird for a drop of rain. Says Nanak, please visualize O God; I praise You; ||2|| You are my true Lord O infinite King. You are my life soul and heart O my dear beloved. The guru-willed realized God the bestowal of life and I am in love. O God, whatever You say the mortal does. He, whom the Lord of the universe blessed, conquered his mind in devotee's company. Says Nanak, my soul praises You. You gave me my soul and body. ||3|| I the unworthy have been saved by saint's grace. The guru has covered the faults of a

sinner like me. O God, You cover the faults and bestow life and soul.
O My Lord; You are immortal incomprehensible perfect and architect
of destiny. Your praise cannot be described; how can anyone
understand you? Slave Nanak admires Him who blesses him with
Lord's name, even for a moment. ||4||1||11||
Page 1118 Kaydaaraa, Fourth Master, First House:
God is one. He is realized by guru's grace.
O my mind, sing continuously the name of God. The inaccessible,
unfathomable Lord cannot be realized. He is realized by meeting the
perfect guru. ||Pause|| Whoever my Lord is kind to; attunes to God
with love. Everyone worships God; but those who please Him are
accepted. ||1|| God has the priceless name with Him; whom God
bestows obtains it. Whoever God blesses with His name; his account
is erased. ||2|| Those with pre-ordained destiny recite God's name,
they are blessed. My mind is happy seeing them, like the child is
happy embracing mother. ||3|| I am a child, God is my father. He
teaches me the way to realize God. As a cow is happy seeing her calf,
same way God embraces Nanak. ||4||1|| Kaydaaraa, Fourth Master,
First House: God is one. He is realized by guru's grace. O my mind,
say the praises of God. Worship God by washing his feet and realize
God this way. ||Pause|| Stay away from lust, anger, greed, attachment
and pride. Discus God in devotee's congregation. Discus with
devotees and recite God's name with love. Page 1119 You know that
you enjoy the self-pride; throw it away from you; O Lord; be kind to
servant Nanak and bless him with the dust of the saints. ||2||1||2||
Kaydaaraa, Fifth Master, Second House: God is one. He is realized
by guru's grace. O mother, I have awakened in the society of the
saints. I recite the priceless name of my beloved devotionally. ||Pause||
I have the yearning to visualize my beloved. My eyes are focused on
Him. I have given up pretending. ||1|| Now, I have found my
peace-giving guru with ease. I am very happy to see him. Seeing my
Lord, joy has welled up in my mind. O Nanak, my beloved's sermon
is sweet. ||2||1|| Kaydaaraa, Fifth Master, Third House: God is one.
He is realized by guru's grace. O kind Lord; listen to the prayer of the
humble. There are five thieves and the three sinners and I have one
mind O Lord Pause|| O God; be kind and protect me. I make all sorts

of efforts and go on pilgrimages; I perform the six rituals, and meditate the right way. I got tired of doing all this but the useless deeds do not leave me. ||1|| I pray for Your refuge O master of kindness. You are the destroyer of fear, O Lord; You alone are kind to the meek. Nanak takes the support of God's Feet. I have been rescued from the ocean of doubt and false attachment, by humbly touching saint's feet. ||2||1||2|| Kaydaaraa, Fifth Master, Fourth House: God is one. He is realized by guru`s grace. I have come to Your sanctuary, O Lord the priceless treasure. I am in love with Your name and I beg for You. ||1||Pause|| O perfect transcendent Lord, giver of peace, be kind and preserve my honour. O Lord; bless me with devotees love and to praise God with my tongue. ||1|| O Lord of the world, merciful Lord of the universe, Your sermon and spiritual wisdom are pure. Please dye Nanak with God's love and focus his mind on Your Lotus feet. ||2||1||3|| Kaydaaraa, Fifth Master: My mind yearns to visualize God. Be kind and unite me with devotee's company and bestow Your name. ||Pause|| I serve my true beloved Lord. When I hear His praise, my mind becomes happy. Page 1120 I praise You again and again; how you look like and where You live? ||1|| You cherish and nurture all and take care of all and protect all. O primal Creator Nanak's God; I see You in everyone. ||2||2||4|| Kaydaaraa, Fifth Master: I love my beloved. My mind is intoxicated and filled with hope; my eyes are focused on you; ||Pause|| What day, hour, minute and second and moment will be? When the door of my mind opens and greed ends by seeing you; ||1|| What is the method, the effort, the service and contemplation? When Nanak gives up pride, arrogance and worldly attachment and obtains salvation in saint's company. ||2||3||5|| Kaydaaraa, Fifth Master: Sing the praises of God; be kind O life of the world, Lord of the universe, that I recite Your name. ||Pause|| Please lift me out of other bad deeds and guide my mind to devotee's company. Eliminate my doubt, concern, and worldly attachment that I visualize You following guru's teaching. ||1|| May my mind become the dust of all; may I abandon my egotistic intellect. O kind God, bless fortunate Nanak with your worship and realization. ||2||4||6|| Kaydaaraa, Fifth Master: Without the Lord, life is going waste. Forgetting the Lord you are attached to other love; you wear and eat imaginary and temporary things. ||Pause|| You enjoy wealth, youth, property and comforts. They do not go with you at all. O ignorant, you are enticed by the mirage and in love with the shade of clouds. ||1|| You are enticed by, pride, attachment and liquor. You fell in the ditch of lust and anger. O God, give Your hand to servant Nanak and help him. ||2||5||7|| Kaydaaraa, Fifth Master: Other than God, nothing goes with you. He is the master of the meek, the Lord of kindness and master of orphans. ||Pause|| Children, wealth and the enjoyment of corrupt pleasures do not go with you on the path of death. Singing the praises of priceless God's name, the Lord of the universe and go across the deep ocean. ||1|| Reciting God in the sanctuary of the all-powerful, indescribable, unfathomable Lord eliminates the sufferings. Humble Nanak longs for the dust of the feet of Lord's humble servant. He will get what is written in his fate. ||2||6||8|| Kaydaaraa, Fifth Master, Fifth House: God is one. He is realized by guru's grace. I do not forget God from my mind. Now this love has become very strong and other bad deeds are eliminated. ||Pause|| How can the rain bird without rain – drop or fish survive without water? Page 1121 To sing God's praises has become my habit. ||1|| It is like a deer fascinated by the sound got pierced by an arrow; Nanak enjoys the joy of God's Lotus feet and tied them in a knot. ||2||1||9|| Kaydaaraa, Fifth Master: My beloved dwells in the cave of my heart. O God; eliminate my doubt and fear and take me towards you. ||1||Pause|| The world-ocean is unfathomable, pleas be kind and take me across. In the company of the saints, aboard the boat of God's feet I crossed over. ||1|| He, who placed you in the womb of your mother; the poison of the forest will not harm you; the power of Lord's sanctuary is all-powerful; Nanak does not seek any other. ||2||2||10|| Kaydaaraa, Fifth Master: Recite the name of God with your tongue. Sing God's praises day and night; your sins will be eradicated. ||Pause|| Know that death hovers over the head; you will leave wealth behind on departure. Believe that the imaginary attachments and evil hopes are false. ||1|| Enshrine the true immortal God in your mind. O NANAK, God accepts the profit of treasure of God's name. ||2||3||11|| Kaydaaraa, Fifth Master: God's name is my support. Dealing with saints the suffering and conflict do not bother; ||Pause|| God saved me by His kindness and evil ideas do not arise. Whoever receives His grace, recites Him; worldly fire does not burn him. ||1|| Peace, joy and bliss come from reciting God. God's feet are the essence. Slave Nanak seeks Your refuge; he is the dust of the feet of Your saints. ||2||4||12|| Kaydaaraa, Fifth Master: Hearing anything other than God's name is useless. Those who forget the embodiment of life; what is the use of their living? ||Pause|| One who eats and drinks countless delicacies is no more than a donkey, a beast of burden. He is absorbed in hard work twenty-four hours a day like the soul in a body tree. ||1|| Those who forget God and attach to others, cry in many ways. With his palms pressed together, Nanak begs for this gift; O Lord, please keep me strung around Your Neck. ||2||5||13|| Kaydaaraa, Fifth Master: I take the dust of the feet of the saints and apply to my face. He is sacred virtuous and perfect forever. No pain bothers him in today's age. ||Pause|| His deeds are fulfilled through guru's word and he does not waver here or there. One God in many forms is completely perfect; fire or sin cannot burn Him. ||1|| God took His servant by the arm and the souls merged. Nanak, the orphan, has come to the refuge of God's feet and walks along God's side. ||2||6||14|| Kaydaaraa, Fifth Master: Page 1122 My mind has yearning for God's name. So that my burning chest cools with eternal peace; ||Pause|| Walking on saint's path the lowly and sinners attain salvation. Applying the dust of devotees to the forehead equals bathing at many sacred shrines. ||1|| Recite God every moment enshrining His lotus feet in the mind. O Nanak, in infinite God's refuge the devil of death does not bother. ||2||7||15|| Kaydaaraa Chhant, Fifth Master: God is one. He is realized by guru's grace. Please meet me, O my dear beloved. ||Pause|| He is all-pervading, architect of destiny. The path created by God is realized in saint's company. God the architect of destiny is realized in saint's company. He abides in all. One, who comes to His sanctuary, finds all peace; his work does not go waste. Sing God's praises the treasure of virtues intuitively and get intoxicated with love. Slave Nanak seeks Your sanctuary O perfect Creator Lord, the architect of destiny. ||1|| The devotee pierced by God's worship does not go anywhere else. The fish cannot bear the separation of water. She dies without water. Why to live without God and suffer pain like the rain bird suffers of raindrop. When will the night end and sun rise so that chakvi (duck) finds peace? When my mind visualizes God, will be my lucky day and I sing God's praises forever. Slave Nanak says this prayer; how will I breathe without God? ||2|| What good is the body without breathing? Without seeing the guru, the devotee is restless. When the mind is pierce by God's lotus feet; living without God is living in hell. Attuned to God's name the detached enjoys God and the humble does not go anywhere else. Living in devotee's company realizes God and he merges in peace. O Nanak's master, be kind so that he merges with Your feet. ||3|| By God's grace I found God by searching. I am unworthy, a lowly orphan, but He does not consider my faults. He does not consider my faults; He blessed me with perfect peace. The bestowal of salvation did his deed the natural way. Hearing that He is the love of His devotees, I grasped the hem of His robe. He is totally permeating each and every heart. I found God the ocean of peace intuitively. The pains of birth and death are gone. He took Nanak his servant by the hand and enshrined God's name in his soul. ||4||1|| Page 1123 Tune Kaydaaraa, the word of Kabeer Jee: God is one. He is realized by guru's grace. Eliminate praise slander pride and ego. He, who looks at iron and gold alike; is the image of God. ||1|| Hardly anyone is a humble servant of Yours, O Lord. He who eradicates lust, anger, greed and attachment follows Godly path. ||1||Pause|| Kings, greed and truthfulness are worldly qualities that You created. He, who realizes for the fourth state attains the highest state. ||2|| Amidst pilgrimages, fasting, rituals, purification and self-discipline, he remains humble. Greed and doubt of worldly wealth eradicates and he recites God. ||3|| The being, who is enlightened; his ignorance departs. Says Kabeer the servant of servants; he realizes the carefree God and his doubt departs. ||4||1|| Some deal in bronze and copper, some in cloves and betel nuts. The saints deal in the name of the Lord of the universe. I buy such merchandise. ||1|| I am a trader of the name of God. The priceless diamond has come in my hands and the worldly dealing ended. ||1||Pause|| The merchant of truth become such traders by God's grace. I loaded the merchandise of truth and went to God the treasurer. ||2|| He is the pearl, the jewel, the ruby; He is the jeweller as well. He goes out in ten directions. He is the eternal trader. ||3|| Make mind the ox, thinking the distance and load it with divine wisdom. Says Kabeer, listen, O saints: my merchandise has reached its destination! ||4||2|| O liquor dealer, fool and ignorant; you blow the wind to the wrong side. Let your mind be intoxicated with nectar, which trickles down from the pool high above. ||1|| O brother, I swear by God. O saints; drink and get intoxicated by difficult to obtain intoxicant and quench your thirst. ||1||Pause|| If someone fears God and falls in love with Him and enjoys God's taste O brother; the nectar abides in everybody. Whoever pleases God, drinks it. ||2|| There are nine gates to one city of the body; restrain your mind from escaping through them. When the desire of three qualities is erased, then the mind becomes intoxicated O brother. ||3|| He reaches the state of no coming back; says Kabeer after deliberation. I found this intoxicant walking on a difficult path and got intoxicated with it; ||4||3|| Engrossed with lust, anger and greed, you did not think of God. Your are blind, you cannot see. You will drown and die without water. ||1|| Page 1124 Why do you walk in that crooked, zigzag way? You are a bundle of bones, wrapped in skin and stinking. ||1||Pause|| You do not recite God. What doubts are you lost in; death is not far from you? You look after your body making lots of efforts and live a full life. ||2|| Nothing can be done by own efforts. What can the mortal do? When it pleases God, the mortal meets the guru and recites God's name. ||3|| You live in a house of sand, you are proud of yourself O ignorant. Says Kabeer, those who do not miss God; many clever like that drown; ||4||4|| Your turban is crooked, you walk crooked; and you chew the betel leaves. You have no concern with love of God or His worship but you call yourself in charge in God's court. ||1|| O egotistic, you have forgotten God Seeing Gold and beautiful spouse, you think it is permanent. ||1||Pause|| You are happy engrossed in greed, falsehood and corruption. This is how you go through your life. Says Kabeer, in the end the death will catch you O ignorant; ||2||5|| You depart when your turn comes after blowing your horn for four days. You collect and hoard wealth but nothing goes with you. ||1||Pause|| The wife mourns sitting at doorstep and mother goes up to the door. Other people and relatives go till the cremation ground and then the swan goes alone. ||1|| The children, wealth and the town; he will never come and see again. Says Kabeer, why do you not recite God? The life is going waste. ||2||6|| Tune Kaydaaraa, the word of Ravi Daas Jee: God is one. He is realized by guru's grace. He performs six religious rituals and comes from a good family, but does not worship God in the mind. He does not like God's lotus feet or sermon. He is a lowly person. ||1|| O ignorant, recite God in your mind subconsciously. Why do you not look at Baalmeek? From a low caste, what an immortal status he obtained by worshipping God. ||1||Pause|| The enemy of dogs, the lowest of all, was lovingly embraced by Krishna. How much can the people praise; he was known in the entire universe. ||2|| Ajaamal leper and lustful elephant went to the Lord. Such evil beings were saved! Why will you not be saved, O Ravi Daas? ||3||1|| Page 1125 Tune Bhairao, First Master, First House, Chau-Padas: *God is one. It is true. He is the Creator. He is carefree. He has no enemy. He is immortal. He does not take birth. He came into existence on His own. He is realized by guru's grace.* Nothing happens without You. You create, check and know; ||1|| What can I say? I cannot say anything. Whatever exists is by Your will. ||Pause|| Whatever is to be done, rests with You. To whom should I offer my prayer? ||2|| I speak and hear Your discourse. You know all Your amazing play. ||3|| You act, inspire all to act; only You know You. Says Nanak, You look after, establish and disestablish. ||4||1|| God is one. He is realized by guru's grace. Tune Bhairao, First Master, Second House: Through guru's teaching many sages including Indra and Brahma attained salvation. Sanak, Sanandan and many renunciates went across by guru's grace. ||1|| How can anyone cross over the terrifying world ocean without guru's teaching? Without God's name the world is troubled and dies drowned in duality. ||1||Pause|| The guru is divine; the guru is unfathomable and mysterious. Serving the guru realizes the universe. The bestowal guru blessed me with a gift and I realized the inscrutable, mysterious Lord. ||2|| The mind is king; the mind conquered the mind and the desire absorbed in the mind. The mind is the Yogi sorrowful after separation. Singing God's praises controls the mind. ||3|| Those who conquer their mind through guru's teaching are rare in the world. O Nanak, the Lord pervades all;

liberation is obtained through guru's teaching. ||4||1||2|| Bhairao, First Master: He cannot see, the body is weak, old age is upon him and the death hovers over the head. Beauty, loving attachment and the pleasures of life are not permanent. Why should the net of devil of death free him? ||1|| O mortal; recite God, life is going by; Page 1126 Without guru's teaching, freedom is not possible and the life goes waste. ||1||Pause|| Lust, anger, ego and attachment are in the body and give serious pain. O guru-willed recite God with love. You will be able to swim across the world ocean this way. ||2|| Your ears are deaf, your intellect is worthless, and still, you do not realize peace through guru's teaching. The self-willed loses the priceless life. The blind does not understand without guru. ||3|| Whoever remains detached and free of desire in the midst of desire, and intuitively contemplates God and remains unattached. Prays Nanak, the guru-willed is freed lovingly attuning to God. ||4||||2||3|| Bhairao, First Master: He walks clumsy, his feet and hands shake, speaks with difficulty and his body is weakened. His cannot see or hear properly; still the self-willed does not know God's name. ||1|| O blind man, what did you gain by coming into the world? Never missed God or served the guru; you are going after losing the principle. ||1||Pause|| Your tongue is not imbued with God's love. Whatever you say is tasteless. Slandering the saints troubles you; you are an animal; you will never be good. ||2|| Only a few obtain the taste of nectar meeting the guru. Till you find the secret of guru's teaching, the death will bother you. ||3|| You do not know any other door because there is only one true door. Humble Nanak says; salvation is obtained by guru's grace. ||4||3||4|| Bhairao, First Master: He spends the entire night sleeping with a chain tied around his neck. His day is wasted in worldly entanglements. He does not think of God even for a moment; that created this world. ||1|| O mind, how will you escape this terrible disaster? There is nothing to bring or take with you; reciting God is worth it. ||1||Pause|| The heart-lotus of the self-willed is upside-down; his intellect is shallow; his mind is blind, and he is entangled in worldly affairs. Death and re-birth constantly hang over your head; without God's name, your neck shall be caught in the noose. ||2|| Your steps are unsteady, cannot see properly and you have no understanding of guru's teaching O brother. The Shaastras and the Vedas tie the mortal to three worldly qualities and he performs blind deeds. ||3|| He loses his principle; how can he make profit; he is evil minded without divine wisdom. Contemplating guru's teaching he enjoys Godly taste O Nanak and finds true God. ||4||4||5|| Bhairao, First Master: He remains with the guru, day and night, and his tongue savors the savoury taste of Lord's Love. He does not know any other; he realizes God inside through guru's teaching. ||1|| Such a humble person is pleasing to my mind. He conquers ego and is imbued with the infinite Lord and serves the guru. ||1||Pause|| The primal formless God is inside and out. That is the lesson of primal Lord. God completely pervades all. He is omnipresent. ||2|| Page 1127 Those imbued with truth, speak the truth and become sacred and the imaginary dirt does not attach to them. They taste pure nectar of God's name. They obtain honour dyed with guru's teaching. ||3|| The virtuous meet the virtuous and earn the profit; the guru-willed obtain greatness through God's name. Serving the guru erases all sufferings; O Nanak, God's name is a friend. ||4||5||6|| Bhairao, First Master: Enshrining God's name in the mind is the essence. It is obtained by guru's grace. Everlasting priceless merchandise is obtained by intuitively focusing the mind. ||1|| O my mind; focus your mind to God's worship. O guru-willed recite God's name in the mind and go home in peace. ||1||Pause|| Doubt, separation and concern never end and one keeps coming and going without knowing God. No one attains salvation without God's name; they drown without water. ||2|| They lose honour engaged in deeds and the doubt does not end O ignorant. Without guru's teaching, salvation is not obtained; the blind is entangled in worldly deeds. ||3|| When the mind consoles with formless God then the mind conquers the mind. See one God inside out O Nanak not any other. ||4||6||7|| Bhairao, First Master: You may give feasts, make burnt offerings, donate to charity, perform austere penance and worship; you punish your body and suffer pain doing so. Salvation is not obtained without God's name. The guru-willed obtains salvation through God's name. ||1|| Without God's name, birth in the world is useless. Without God's name, the mortal eats poison and speaks poisonous words; he dies fruitlessly, and wanders in reincarnation. ||1||Pause|| He reads scriptures, studies grammar and says prayers three times a day. O mortal, salvation is not possible without guru's teaching. It is all entanglements without God's name. ||2|| He has a walking stick, begging bowl, tuft hair, sacred thread, loin cloth, goes to shrines and wanders all around. Peace is not obtained without God's name. He, who recites God, goes across. ||3|| He has matted hair, ash applied to the body and wanders naked removing the closes. Satisfaction is no obtained without God's name. He makes disguises just to do something. ||4|| You live in all beings in water and land and sky; O guru; save your servant by your grace. Nanak mixes and drinks Godly juice. ||5||7||8|| Tune Bhairao, Third Master, Chaupadas, First House: God is one. He is realized by guru's grace. No one should be proud of his caste. He, who realizes God, is a scholar. ||1|| Do not be proud of your caste O ignorant fools! Page 1128 His pride creates many useless deeds. ||1||Pause|| Everyone says that there are four castes; they all emanate from the drop of God's seed. ||2|| The entire universe is made of the same clay. The potter shapes the pots in many ways. ||3|| The body is made of five elements. Who knows the difference? ||4|| Says Nanak, this soul is bound by its actions. Without surrendering to the guru, salvation is not obtained; ||5||1|| Bhairao, Third Master: The Yogis, the householders, scholars and imitators. They are all asleep in ego. ||1|| They are asleep, intoxicated with worldly wealth. No one can rob them if they are awake; ||1||Pause|| He, who meets the guru, remains awake. He controls the five demons. ||2|| One, who contemplates the reality, remains awake. He kills his ego and does not kill anyone else. ||3|| One, who realizes God, remains awake. He abandons the service of others, and realizes the essence of reality. ||4|| Among all four castes, if someone remains awake? He is freed from birth and death. ||5|| Says Nanak, he remains awake; Who applies the ointment of divine wisdom to his eyes; ||6||2|| Bhairao, Third Master: Whomever the Lord keeps in His sanctuary; attaches to truth, and obtains true fruit. ||1|| O mortal, who do you complain to? Everything happens and runs by His command. ||1||Pause|| This creation is created by You. It is destroyed in a moment; does not take long; ||2|| By His grace, He staged this play. The supreme status is obtained by guru's grace. ||3||

Says Nanak, He kills and revives. Understand this, do not doubt it? ||4||3|| Bhairao, Third Master: I am the bride; the Creator is my Husband Lord. As He inspires me, I adorn myself. ||1|| When it pleases Him, He enjoys with me. My mind and body is for the true Lord. ||1||Pause|| Why people praise or slander? When one God abides in all; ||2|| By guru's grace, I am attracted by His love. When I meet my kind Lord; divine music will play in five tunes. ||3|| Prays Nanak, what can anyone do? Whom He unites, unites with Him; ||4||4|| Bhairao, Third Master: He, who kills the duality of mind, is a sage. ||1|| Page 1129 Eliminating duality, he contemplates God. Search your mind O brother; Searching the mind obtains the treasure of God's name. ||1||Pause|| The Creator created the world, through worldly attachment. Attaching to worldly wealth, he led the world into doubt. ||2|| From this Mind come all bodies and life. Thinking with the mind, one merges with God by realizing His command. ||3|| When one earns then the guru grants his grace. This mind is awakened, and duality died. ||4|| It is the nature of mind to remain detached. The detached Lord dwells hidden in all. ||5|| Says Nanak, one who understands the mystery; becomes the embodiment of the primal, formless Lord; ||6||5|| Bhairao, Third Master: The world is saved through God's name. It carries the mortal across the terrifying world-ocean. ||1|| Recite God's name by guru's grace. It shall stand by you forever. ||1||Pause|| The ignorant self-willed does not recite God's name. How will he cross over without God's name? ||2|| God the great giver gives the gifts. Celebrate and praise the great giver! ||3|| He unites us with the guru by His grace. O Nanak, enshrine God's name in the mind; ||4||6|| Bhairao, Third Master: Those who recite God's name attain salvation. The guru-willed obtain God's name. ||1|| When dear God becomes kind; He blesses the guru-willed with the honour of God's name; ||1||Pause|| Those who love God's name; They obtain salvation along with their dynasty. ||2|| Without God's name self-willed go to the city of death. They suffer in pain and endure beating. ||3|| When the Creator gives; O Nanak, the mortals receive God's name. ||4||7|| Bhairao, Third Master: Loving the Lord of the universe saved Sanak and his brother; they recited God's name through guru's teaching. ||1|| O dear God; be kind to me. That the guru-willed loves

God's name; ||1||Pause|| Love of God in the mind is the true worship. It wells up meeting the perfect guru. ||2|| He intuitively dwells in his home; Then God's name enshrines in the mind. ||3|| God watches everything. O Nanak, enshrine God's name in the mind. ||4||8|| Bhairao, Third Master: In today's age, enshrine Lord's name in your heart. Without God's name, ashes will fall in your face. ||1|| God's name is difficult to obtain, O brother; by guru's grace, it comes to dwell in the mind. ||1||Pause|| That humble being who seeks Lord's name; receives it from the perfect guru. ||2|| Those who obey God's will are accepted. They make God's name their resolve through guru's teaching. ||3|| So serve the one, who supports the universe. O Nanak, the guru-willed loves God's name. ||4||9|| Bhairao, Third Master: He does many deeds in today's age. Without proper time the deeds do not produce result. ||1|| In today's age, God's name is the essence. The guru-willed falls in love with true Lord; ||1||Pause|| Searching my body and mind, I found Him in me. The guru-willed focuses his mind to God's name. ||2|| Page 1130 The guru applies the ointment of divine wisdom. God's name is pervading the three worlds. ||3|| In today's age there is one God. There is nothing else. O Nanak, the guru-willed enshrines God's name in the mind. ||4||10|| Bhairao, Third Master, Second House: God is one. He is realized by guru's grace. Duality and burning in greed trouble the self-willed. He dies to be reborn again and again and finds no place to rest. He wastes away his life. ||1|| O my beloved, be kind and make me understand; the world was created in the disease of ego; this sickness is not cured without guru's teaching. ||1||Pause|| Many sages read the scriptures, but without guru's teaching they do not understand anything. All are sick with three worldly qualities; they are lost in false attachment. ||2|| God pulls some out and puts them to serve Him. They obtain the treasure of God's name and peace wells up in the mind. ||3|| The guru-willed dwell in the fourth state; they reach their destiny. They eliminate ego by the grace of a perfect guru. ||4|| He, who created Brahma, Vishnu and Shiva; rules the universe. O Nanak, God is forever. He does not die or take birth. ||5||1||11|| Bhairao, Third Master: The self-willed is sick with duality, so is the whole world. The guru-willed realizes it through guru's teaching. ||1|| O dear God, please unite me with true congregation. O Nanak, God bestows honour to those, who focus on God's name; ||1||Pause|| Death kills all those sick with false attachment. The devil of death rules them. The devil of death does not come close to the guru-willed, who enshrine God in the mind; ||2|| O guru-willed; those who do not realize God's name; why did they come in the world? They never serve the guru; they waste their life away. ||3|| O Nanak, those whom guru enjoins to His service are fortunate. They obtain what they want and obtain peace through guru's sermon. ||4||2||12|| Bhairao, Third Master: He is born in pain, dies in pain and works in pain; He is never free from the womb of reincarnation; he rots in filth. ||1|| The self-willed wastes his life away. He does not serve the perfect guru; he does not love God's name. ||1||Pause|| Whoever God inspires eliminates all sickness through guru's teaching. Page 1131 Those who enshrine God's name in the mind obtain honour. ||2|| Surrendering to the guru obtains the reward. True deeds are the essence. Those who attach to God's name with love become pure. ||3|| If I get the dust of the feet of those who worship the perfect guru; I will apply it to my forehead; O Nanak, those who focus their mind to God's name; to obtain their dust is lucky. ||4||3||13|| Bhairao, Third Master: Those who enshrine God in the mind and contemplate guru's teaching become truthful. If one performs true worship day and night, then his body will not feel pain. ||1|| Everyone calls him, God's devotee. Without serving the guru, worship is not obtained. Only through perfect destiny, one realizes God. ||1||Pause|| The self-willed loses the principle and wants profit; where will he get the profit? The devil of death always hovers over their head. In love of duality, they lose their honour. ||2|| Trying all sorts of rituals day and night, the sickness of ego does not cure. They read argue and debate; attached to worldly pleasure they lose their awareness. ||3|| Those who serve the guru obtain supreme status and honour through God's name. O Nanak, those who enshrine God's name in the mind obtain honour in God's court. ||4||4||14|| Bhairao, Third Master: The self-willed cannot escape false hope. He is ruined in love of duality. His river like belly never fills up. He rots in the fire of greed. ||1|| Those imbued with God's love are happy forever. With God's name in the mind the duality departs and drinking nectar fulfills him.

||1||Pause|| God the bestowal of salvation, who created the universe, puts everyone to work; He created the enticement of worldly wealth and attaches us to duality. ||2|| What can we say if there was anyone else; all merge in You. The guru-willed contemplates divine wisdom and his soul merges with supreme soul. ||3|| God is true, will remain true and the universe is true as well. O Nanak, the guru teaches the reality and salvation obtains through God's true name. ||4||5||15|| Bhairao, Third Master: In today's age those who do not realize God are ghosts. In first age (Satyug) they contemplated God. In second and third age the human prevailed; only a few killed ego. ||1|| In today's age, God's name brings honour. In all ages the guru-willed realize God. Salvation is not possible without God's name. ||1||Pause|| The truthful realizes and enshrines God's name in the mind; Those who are lovingly focused on God's name attain salvation along with their dynasty. ||2|| My God is the giver of merits. Guru's teaching burn away the demerits. Page 1132 Those who enshrine God's name in the mind are adorable. ||3|| The guru reveals God's home His court and palace; I enjoy His love. Whatever He says, I accept as good; Nanak recites God's name. ||4||6||16|| Bhairao, Third Master: Conquer you mental desires by contemplating guru's teaching. You get understanding through the perfect guru and do not die again. O my mind, take the support of God's name. By guru's grace, I obtained the supreme status; my desires fulfilled. ||1||Pause|| God abides in all but cannot be realized without the guru. God reveals to the guru-willed by singing His praises day and night. ||2|| One God is the giver of peace; peace is not found anywhere else. Those who do not serve the bestowal guru, depart regretting in the end. ||3|| Serving the guru obtains lasting peace and the pain does not bother anymore. Nanak realized God's worship; his soul merged with supreme soul. ||4||7||17|| Bhairao, Third Master: Without the guru, the world is insane; it suffers in delusion. It dies and reborn time and again and suffers forever. He is unaware of God's door. ||1|| O my mind; always remain in guru's refuge. God's name is always pleasing to the mind. Terrifying world-ocean is crossed over following guru's teaching. ||1||Pause|| The mortal wears disguises but he is filled with lust, anger and ego. He is very hungry and thirsty inside. He barks door to door. ||2|| He,

who dies through guru's teaching, obtains salvation and lives forever. He is peaceful and content inside because he enshrined God in the mind. ||3|| As it pleases Him, He inspires us to act. We cannot do anything. O Nanak, the guru-willed recites guru's teaching and obtains honour reciting God's name. ||4||8||18|| Bhairao, Third Master: He is troubled by ego, worldly pleasure and attachment. He earns and eats pain. He is filled with greed, gone insane and suffers; he runs around mad. ||1|| The life of the self-willed is not worth living. He does not remember God's name even in a dream; he cannot fall in love with God. ||1||Pause|| He acts like an animal, does not understand anything. He earns false and reaps false. Thinking reverses by meeting the guru. Only a few search and find God. ||2|| God's name dwells in the mind permanently and attains the treasure of virtues. By guru's grace, he finds the perfect Lord; his self-pride eradicates. ||3|| The Creator acts, and causes all to act. He puts us on the right path. Page 1133 God blesses the guru-willed and he absorbs in God's name. ||4||9||19|| Bhairao, Third Master: I write the name of God the Lord of the universe on my writing plank. Those in duality are caught in the net of devil of death. The guru nurtures and sustains me. God the giver of peace is always with me. ||1|| Following guru's teachings, Prahlaad says God God God. The child does not obey teacher's order. ||1||Pause|| Prahlaad's mother gave her beloved son some advice: "My son, you must abandon Lord's Name, and save your life!" Prahlaad said: Listen, O my mother; The guru told me not to abandon God's name. ||2|| Sandaa Markaa, his teachers, went to his father and complained: Prahlaad has gone astray, and he leads all the other pupils astray. In the court of the wicked king, a plan was hatched. Let us see if God can save Prahlaad; ||3|| With sword drawn, Prahlaad's proud father ran up to him. Where is your Lord, who will save you? In an instant, God appeared in a scary form from the pillar. He tore Harnaakhash apart with his nails and saved Prahlaad. ||4|| God took care of the task of the saint. He saved twenty-one generations of Prahlaad's descendents. Guru's teaching eliminated the poisonous ego. O Nanak, God's name liberates the saints. ||5||10||20|| Bhairao, Third Master: God makes demons pursue the saints; then He saves them. Those who remain forever in Your refuge, they do not suffer in the mind. ||1|| In each and every age, Lord saves the honour of His devotees. Prahlaad, the demon's son, knew nothing of Brahmin's self-fulfilling prayer. He realized God through guru's teaching. ||1||Pause|| He worshipped God all the time through guru's teaching and eliminated doubt. Those imbued with truth become pure forever, enshrining God in the mind. ||2|| The ignorant read duality, they do not understand reality; they waste their lives away. The demon slandered and got mad at the saint. ||3|| Prahlaad did not fall in duality, he did not abandon God's name and he was not afraid of anyone. God protected the saint and killed the demon. ||4|| God saved His honour and blessed His devotee with greatness. O Nanak, Harnaakhash was torn apart by God with His claws; the blind demon knew nothing of Lord's court. ||5||11||21|| Tune Bhairao, Fourth Master, Chaupadas, First House: God is one. He is realized by guru's grace. By God's grace the devotees attach to saint's feet. Page 1134 Recite God through guru's teaching wholeheartedly. ||1|| O my mind, recite the name of God. When God the bestowal of peace bestows his blessing; the guru-willed recite God's name and go across the terrifying world ocean. ||1||Pause|| They sing God's praises in devotee's company. They enjoy reciting God's name through guru's teaching. ||2|| The devotees bathe in guru's pool filled with nectar and divine wisdom. All of their sins are eliminated. ||3|| You are the Creator of the universe. Please unite Nanak the servant of servants with You. ||4||1|| Bhairao, Fourth Master: Fruitful is the moment when one says God's name. Guru's lesson eliminates all sufferings. ||1|| O my mind, recite the name of God the Lord of humans. O Lord, be kind and unite me with the guru so that I go across the terrifying world ocean. ||1||Pause|| O my mind, recite God the life of the world. It will eliminate millions of your sins. ||2|| May the dust of devotees fall in your face? It is equal to taking bath at sixty-eight rivers. ||3|| God became kind to me the ignorant. The saviour Lord has saved servant Nanak. ||4||2|| Bhairao, Fourth Master: To do good deeds is the best rosary. Reciting God in the mind goes with you. Recite the name of God O jungle dweller. Be kind and unite me with devotee's company, so that net of the devil of death breaks. ||1||Pause|| The guru-willed who work hard attain above. They mint the true coins through guru's teaching. ||2|| The guru has revealed to me the inaccessible and unfathomable Lord. I found God in the body by searching. ||3|| I am a child; God my father looks after me. Please liberate servant Nanak, by Your grace. ||4||3|| Bhairao, Fourth Master: All beings are Yours O Lord; You are in all. No one is beyond You. ||1|| O my mind, recite the name of peace giving God. I praise You O God; You are my father. ||1||Pause|| Wherever I look, I see God; All are under Your control; there is no other; ||2|| You save whoever You please O God; No one harms him. ||3|| You fully pervade in water land and the sky. Servant Nanak recites the ever-present Lord. ||4||4|| Page 1135 Bhairao, Fourth Master, Second House: God is one. He is realized by guru's grace. God's saint who enshrines God in the mind is God's image. One with pre-ordained destiny recites God's name through guru's teaching. ||1|| Enshrine God in your heart and recite His name. The five thieves rob the body; God drives them away through guru's teaching. ||1||Pause|| Whose minds are satisfied with God; God resolves their affairs. They do not beg from others; God helps them. ||2|| You should consult others only if they are beyond God. Whatever God does is good. Recite God's name night and day. ||3|| God does everything on His own. He does not ask for advice. O Nanak, recite God forever; who unites you with the guru. ||4||1||5|| Bhairao, Fourth Master: O master; unite me with devotees that I recite God in their company and attain salvation. And I enjoy seeing their faces and I praise them forever; ||1|| I recite God's name in the mind. O father the master of the world, be kind that I the servant of servants carry water for them. ||1||Pause|| He who enshrines God in the mind, his thinking and honour becomes high. O master; put me to their service; reciting them I obtain salvation. ||2|| Those who do not find such a holy guru are beaten, and driven out of the court of the Lord. These slanderers have no honour; the Creator cuts their noses. ||3|| The Lord speaks, inspires all to speak; He is immaculate and formless, and does not eat. Whoever You unite; unite with You O Nanak, what the poor beings can do? ||4||2||6|| Bhairao, Fourth Master: The company where singing of Your praises is heard is the true congregation. The minds of those who listen to God's name are drenched with bliss; I worship their feet forever. ||1|| Recite God the life of the world and attain salvation. You have unlimited number of names; so many that I cannot count them. ||1||Pause|| O guru-willed; say God, sing God, and recite God through guru's teaching. Whoever listens to guru's teachings attains eternal happiness. ||2|| Blessed are the ancestry, the father, and the mother who gave birth to this humble servant. Those who recite God with every breath and morsel of food; they are called God's servants in His court. ||3|| O God, Your names are infinite; Your devotees cherish them. Servant Nanak realized God through guru's teaching and obtained salvation reciting God. ||4||3||7|| Page 1136 Bhairao, Fifth Master, First House: God is one. He is realized by guru's grace. He searched every date and kept record. God was born on eighth day of lunar calendar. ||1|| Deluded and confused by doubt, the mortal practices falsehood. The Lord is beyond birth and death. ||1||Pause|| You prepare sweet treats and feed the thieves. God is not born, and does not die, you are faithless animals! ||2|| You commit all sins. May that mouth burn that says God and takes birth again; ||3|| God does not take birth or dies. He neither comes nor goes. Nanak's God is pervading and permeating everywhere. ||4||1|| Bhairao, Fifth Master: I am at peace sitting or standing. I have no fear, because this is what I understand; ||1|| God my master is my protector. He is the inner-knower of everyone. ||1||Pause|| I sleep without worry, and wake up without worry. O God, You are pervading everywhere. ||2|| I live in peace in my home and I am at peace outside. Says Nanak, the guru taught me the lesson. ||3||2|| Bhairao, Fifth Master: I do not keep fasts or observe the month of Ramadaan. I serve the one, who protects in the end. ||1|| One Lord, the Lord of the world, is my God Allah. He administers justice to both Hindus and Muslims. ||1||Pause|| I do not make pilgrimages to Mecca, nor I worship at Hindu shrines. I serve one Lord, not any other. ||2|| I do not perform Hindu worship service, nor I offer Muslim prayers. I enshrine the formless God in my mind and worship Him. ||3|| I am not a Hindu, or a Muslim. My body and life belong to Allah – to Raam – the God of both. ||4|| Says Kabeer, this is what I say: Meeting the guru, my spiritual teacher, I realized God my Lord. ||5||3|| Bhairao, Fifth Master: I easily tied up the deer – the ten senses. I pierced five deer through God's sermon. ||1|| I go hunting in devotee's company. And we capture the deer without horses or weapons.

||1||Pause|| I came home after hunting. I brought the hunted animals at home in the village. ||2|| I caught the deer and brought them home. Dividing them up, I shared them, bit by bit. ||3|| I donated all the animals. Nanak is left with God's name at home. ||4||4|| Bhairao, Fifth Master: If he is burdened with hundreds of thoughts; still the faithless does not remember God. ||1|| Learn from the humble saints and obtain salvation in devotee's company. ||1||Pause|| You may keep the stone in water; It never absorbs water and remains completely dry. ||2|| Page 1137 The six Shaastras may be read to a ignorant; It is like wind blowing from ten directions. ||3|| How can you thresh without the crop? In the same way, no benefit comes from the faithless. ||4|| As the Lord attaches them, so are they attached? Says Nanak, God has set such a play. ||5||5|| Bhairao, Fifth Master: He created the soul, life and the body; He created all beings and feels the pain. ||1|| The guru, the Lord of the universe, is the helper of the soul. Here and hereafter, He always provides shade. ||1||Pause|| Reciting God is a sacred deed. In devotee's company the enmity vanishes. ||2|| Friends, well-wishers and wealth will not support you. Blessed is my Lord. ||3|| Nanak speaks the sacred sermon. Do not realize any other than one God. ||4||6|| Bhairao, Fifth Master: God is in front and behind me. In the middle is the taste of God's love. ||1|| God is my scriptures and good omen. In His Home I find peace, contentment and bliss. ||1||Pause|| I live by reciting and listening to God's name. Reciting God, one becomes immortal. ||2|| The pains of countless lifetimes have been erased. The infinite divine music plays at His court. ||3|| God united me with Him by His grace. Nanak has entered God's refuge. ||4||7|| Bhairao, Fifth Master: It fulfills millions of desires. On the path of death, it will go with you. ||1|| God's name is sacred like the water of Ganges. Whoever recites and drinks God's nectar; attains salvation and does not wander in different lives. ||1||Pause|| It is my worship, meditation, austerity and cleansing bath. Reciting God's name I became free of desire. ||2|| The kingdom, wealth, riding horses and the court; Reciting God fulfills all desires; ||3|| Slave Nanak thought and came to this conclusion: Without God's name the world is temporary and shall vanish. ||4||8|| Bhairao, Fifth Master: It had absolutely no harmful effect. But the wicked Brahmin died in pain.

||1|| The supreme Lord saved His humble servant. The sinner died by the power of the guru. ||1||Pause|| The humble servant recites his master. He destroyed the ignorant sinner. ||2|| God is the mother, the father and the protector of His slave. The face of the slanderer is blackened here and hereafter. ||3|| The transcendent Lord has heard the prayer of servant Nanak. The filthy sinner lost hope and died. ||4||9|| Bhairao, Fifth Master: Excellent, excellent, excellent, excellent, excellent is Your name. False, false, false, false is pride of the world. ||1||Pause|| You devotees are priceless and visualizing them is also priceless. Page 1138 Without God's name the world is just like ashes. ||1|| Your creative power is amazing and Your lotus feet are admirable. Your praise is priceless, O true King. ||2|| God is the support of the unsupported. Recite the name of God, kind to the poor. ||3|| God has been kind to Nanak. May I never forget God; He is my heart, soul and life. ||4||10|| Bhairao, Fifth Master: O guru-willed, obtain the true wealth. Accept the will of God as true. ||1|| And live forever. Get up in the morning and drink the nectar of the Lord. Say God God God with your tongue. ||1||Pause|| In today's age God's name is the essence. Nanak speaks, the wisdom bestowed by God. ||2||11|| Bhairao, Fifth Master: Serving the guru, all fruits are obtained. The filth of many lifetimes is washed away. ||1|| Your name O God is the purifier of sinners. Because of the past deeds written in the fate I sing God's praises. ||1||Pause|| Devotee's company attains salvation. And honour in God's court. ||2|| Serving at God's feet, all comforts are obtained. All demy-gods, angels and heroes long for the dust of their feet. ||3|| Nanak has obtained the treasure of God's name. Reciting God the whole world has been saved. ||4||12|| Bhairao, Fifth Master: God embraces His servant. He throws the slanderer in the fire. ||1|| The Lord saves His servants from the sinners. No one can save the sinner. The sinner rots in his actions. ||1||Pause|| God's slave is in love with dear God. The slanderer's fate is reversed. ||2|| The supreme Lord has revealed His instinctive nature. The evil-doer obtains the fruits of his actions. ||3|| God does not come or go; He is all-pervading. Slave Nanak seeks the sanctuary of the Lord. ||4||13|| Tune Bhairao, Fifth Master, Chaupadas, Second House: God is one. He is realized by guru's grace. The fascinating Lord, the Creator of all, the formless

Lord, is the giver of peace. You abandoned such God, and serve others. Why are you intoxicated with such evil pleasures? ||1|| O my mind, recite the Lord of the universe. I have seen all other deeds; whatever you think, spoils your work. ||1||Pause|| The blind, ignorant, self-willed forget God and worship the servant. They slander those who worship God; without guru they are like animals. ||2|| Soul, life, body and wealth all belong to God; the faithless says it is his; Page 1139 They are arrogant, ill minded and dirty. Without the guru they keep coming and going in the world. ||3|| Through burnt offerings, charitable feasts, ritualistic chants, penance, all sorts of austere self-discipline and pilgrimages to shrines and rivers, do not find God. He, who eliminates ego in guru's refuge; the guru-willed attains salvation and takes the world with him O Nanak. ||4||1||14|| Bhairao, Fifth Master: I saw God in the woods, in the fields, in the household and in renunciates. I saw Him as a Yogi carrying a stick, with matted hair, fasting, making vows, and visiting shrines. ||1|| I saw Him in the mind in the society of the saints. He is pervading in the sky, in the underworld and in everything. I sing His praises with love and happiness. ||1||Pause|| I saw Him in Yogis, the renunciates, the celibates, the wandering hermits and the wearers of patched coats. I saw Him in men of self-discipline, the sages, the drama actors and dancers. ||2|| I saw Him in the four Vedas, six Shaastras, eighteen Puraanas and Simritees; All say that there is only One God. So tell me, from whom is He hidden? ||3|| The infinite God is beyond comprehension. He is beyond pricing. Servant Nanak admires those, in whose heart He is revealed. ||4||2||15|| Bhairao, Fifth Master: How can anyone do evil, if he realizes that the Lord is near? One, who gathers poison, constantly feels fear. He is near, but this mystery is not understood. Without the guru, all are enticed by worldly wealth. ||1|| Everyone says that He is near at hand. Only some guru-willed find the secret. ||1||Pause|| He does not see nearby but goes to the homes of others. He steals their wealth and lives in falsehood. Drugging cheats him, and he cannot see God nearby. Without the guru, he is lost in doubt. ||2|| He does not realize God, who is very near and talks false. The ignorant is robbed by attachment to worldly wealth. God is inside but he searches in foreign lands. Without the guru, he is deluded by doubt. ||3|| One, who has destiny written on the forehead; He serves the guru and his mind opens up. God is inside out and very close. O servant Nanak, he does not come or go. ||4||3||16|| Bhairao, Fifth Master: Who can kill the person whom You protect, O Lord? All beings, and the entire universe, are in You. The mortal makes millions of plans; That alone happens, which the amazing Lord does. ||1|| Save me O Lord by your kindness. I seek Your sanctuary, and Your court. ||1||Pause|| Whoever serves the carefree God the bestowal of peace? He gets rid of fear and attaches to one God. Whatever You do that happens. No one else can kill or save. ||2|| What do you think, with your humanly habits? The all-knowing Lord is sacred. One and only Lord is my support and protection. The Creator knows everything. ||3|| Whoever God blesses by His grace; Page 1140 All his affairs are resolved. The one Lord is his protector. O servant Nanak, no one can equal him. ||4||4||17|| Bhairao, Fifth Master: We should feel sad, if God is outside. We should feel sad, if we forget God. We should feel sad, if we are in love with duality. Why should we feel sad when God is in us? ||1|| Those attached to worldly wealth feel sad. They are consumed by sadness. Without God's name, they get tired of wandering. ||1||Pause|| We should feel sad, if there was another Creator; We should feel sad, if someone dies by injustice. We should feel sad, if God does not know anything. Why should we feel sad when God pervades all? ||2|| We should feel sad, if God was a tyrant. We should feel sad, if He made us suffer by mistake. The guru says; whatever happens is all by God's will. So I abandon sadness and I sleep without anxiety. ||3|| O God, You are the master; all belong to You. According to Your will, You pass judgment. There is no other; One Lord is pervading everywhere. Please save Nanak's honour; I have come to Your sanctuary. ||4||5||18|| Bhairao, Fifth Master: How can one dance without music? Without a voice, how can one sing? Without strings, how can a guitar be played? Without God's name, all affairs are useless. ||1|| Tell me, who attains salvation without God's name? Without the guru, how can anyone cross over to the other side? ||1||Pause|| Without tongue, how can anyone speak? Without ears, how can anyone hear? Without eyes, how can anyone see? Without God's name the mortal is of no use;

||2|| Without learning, how can one become a scholar? Without power, how can anyone rule? Without understanding, how can the mind become stable? Without God's name the whole world is insane. ||3|| Without detachment, how can one be a detached hermit? Without renouncing ego, how can anyone be a renunciate? Without overcoming the five thieves, how can the mind be subdued? Without God's name the mortal repents forever. ||4|| Without guru's teachings, how can anyone obtain divine wisdom? Without seeing – tell me: how can anyone focus? Without fear of God, all preaching is useless; Says Nanak, this is what happens in God's court. ||5||6||19|| Bhairao, Fifth Master: Mankind is afflicted with the disease of ego. The disease of lust overwhelms the elephant. Because of the disease of vision, the moth is burnt to death. Because of the disease of the sound, the deer is lured to death. ||1|| Whoever I see is sick; only my guru the Yogi is free of disease. ||1||Pause|| Because of the disease of taste, the fish is caught. Because of the disease of smell, the bumblebee is destroyed. The whole world is sick with the disease of attachment. In the disease of the three qualities, corruption increases. ||2|| In sickness they die, in sickness they are born. In disease they wander in different life again and again. Page 1141 Entangled in disease, they cannot stay free of disease. Without the guru, the disease is never cured. ||3|| When the supreme Lord grants His grace; He takes by the arm and pulls them out of sickness. Joining the company of devotees, the bonds are broken. Says Nanak, the guru cures him of the disease; ||4||7||20|| Bhairao, Fifth Master: When He comes to mind, then I am very happy. When He comes to mind, then all my pain is destroyed. When He comes to mind, my hopes are fulfilled. When He comes to mind, I never feel sad. ||1|| God has revealed Himself to me in me. The perfect guru has inspired me to love Him. ||1||Pause|| When He comes to mind, I am the king of all. When He comes to mind, all my affairs are completed. When He comes to mind, I am dyed in His deep love. When He comes to mind, I am content forever. ||2|| When He comes to mind, I am wealthy forever. When He comes to mind, I am free of doubt forever. When He comes to mind, I enjoy all pleasures. When He comes to mind, I am not short of anything. ||3|| When He comes to mind; I am at peace in my home. When He comes to mind, I am

absorbed in the absolute; when He comes to mind, I sing God's praises. Nanak's mind is pleased and satisfied with the Lord. ||4||8||21|| Bhairo Fifth Master; my father is immortal. My brothers live forever. My friends are imperishable. My family abides in the eternal home. ||1|| If I am at peace, then all are at peace. The perfect guru has united me with my father. ||1||Pause|| My mansions are the highest of all. My countries are infinite and countless. My kingdom is eternal and stable. My wealth is inexhaustible and permanent. ||2|| My reputation resounds throughout the ages. My fame has spread in all places of importance. My praises echo in every house. My worship is known in the universe. ||3|| My father has revealed Himself in me. The father and son have joined together in partnership. Says Nanak, when my father is pleased; then the father and son have become one in love. ||4||9||22|| Bhairao, Fifth Master: O enemyless primal guru the bestowal God; I am a sinner; You are the forgiver. The sinner, who finds no place to rest; If he seeks Your sanctuary, he becomes pure. ||1|| Consoling with the guru, I have found peace. Reciting the guru, I have obtained all rewards. ||1||Pause|| The guru reveals the supreme Lord. My mind and body are Yours; the whole world is Yours. When the veil was removed, I saw Him. You are my master; You are the King of all. ||2|| When it pleases Him, even the dry wood becomes green. When it pleases Him, rivers flow across the desert sands. When it pleases Him, all fruits and rewards are obtained. Grasping hold of the guru's feet, my anxiety is dispelled. ||3|| Page 1142 I am ungrateful, but He has been kind to me. My mind and body are soothed; the nectar rains down in my mind. The supreme Lord the guru has become kind to me. Slave Nanak is content seeing Him. ||4||10||23|| Bhairao, Fifth Master: My true guru does not need any help. My true guru is adorned with truth. My true guru is the giver of all. My true guru is the architect of destiny. ||1|| There is no deity equal to the guru. Those with good fortune serve him. ||1||Pause|| My true guru is the sustainer of all. My true guru kills and revives. The greatness of my guru, has become manifest everywhere. ||2|| My guru is the power of the powerless. My true guru is my home and court. I praise my true guru forever He has shown me the known path of liberation. ||3|| One, who serves the guru, has no concern. One who serves the guru does not suffer in pain. Nanak has studied the Simritees and the Vedas. There is no difference between the guru and God; ||4||11||24|| Bhairao, Fifth Master: Reciting God's name, I realized Him in the mind. Reciting God's name sin is banished from the body. Reciting God's name, all festivals are celebrated. Reciting God's name is equal to bathing at sixty-eight shrines. ||1|| God's name is my sacred shrine of pilgrimage. My guru taught me the essence of divine wisdom. ||1||Pause|| Reciting God's name the pain goes away. Reciting God's name the ignorant becomes divine. Reciting God's name the divine light is lit. Reciting God's name, worldly entanglements are eradicated. ||2|| Reciting God's name the devil of death does not come near. Reciting God's name, one finds peace in God's court. Reciting God's name. God admires you. God's name is my true wealth. ||3|| The guru taught me this reality. Singing God's praises is the support of the mind. Nanak is saved by instinctively reciting God's name. Other actions are just to please the people. ||4||12||25|| Bhairao, Fifth Master: I bow humbly to Him millions of times. I offer this mind to Him. Reciting God eliminates the sufferings. Joy wells up, and no disease is contracted. ||1|| God's name is such a pure diamond; Reciting His name all deeds are fulfilled. ||1||Pause|| Seeing Him the house of pain is demolished. The mind is soothed reciting God's sacred name. Millions of devotees worship His feet. He is the fulfiller of all deeds. ||2|| In an instant, He fills the empty to over-flowing. In an instant, He transforms the dry into green. In an instant, He gives the homeless a home. In an instant, He bestows honour to the humble. ||3|| Page 1143 One God pervades all. He, whose guru is perfect; recites God; Praising God is his resolve. Says Nanak, whom God is kind; ||4||13||26|| Bhairao, Fifth Master: I was discarded but He has adorned me. He has blessed me with beauty and love through His name. All my pains and sorrows have been eradicated. The guru has become my mother and father. ||1|| O my friends and companions, my family life is joyous. By His grace I met my husband Lord. ||1||Pause|| The fire of desire is extinguished, and all my desires are fulfilled. The darkness has been dispelled, and the divine light is lit. The infinite divine music plays and I am overwhelmed seeing the amazing play. Perfect is the grace of the perfect guru. ||2|| He, who has realized God; seeing him makes others content. He obtains all virtues and priceless treasures. Whoever guru blesses with God's name; ||3|| He who meets his master. Saying God God, their mind and body are soothed. Says Nanak, those who please God. Only a few are blessed with the dust of their feet. ||4||14||27|| Bhairao, Fifth Master: The mortal does not hesitate to think about sin. He is not ashamed to spend time with prostitutes. He works all day long; but when it is time to recite God; then a heavy stone falls on his head. ||1|| Attached to worldly pleasure the world is lost; God made him that way and now he is engrossed in worthless worldly affairs. ||1||Pause|| He is happy seeing the worldly wealth. He loves the shell, and ruins his life. His mind is attached to blind worldly affairs. He does not miss the Creator in his mind. ||2|| He keeps doing this and suffers. His affairs of worldly pleasure are never completed. His mind is saturated with lust, anger and greed. He dies hurting like fish out of water. ||3|| One who has God as his protector. He recites God's name all the time. He sings God's praises in devotee's company. O Nanak, he has found the perfect guru. ||4||15||28|| Bhairao, Fifth Master: He, who God is kind to, obtains it; He enshrines God's name in his mind. He enshrines guru's true teaching in his mind and heart. The sins of countless lifes vanish. ||1|| God's name is the support of the soul. O brother recite God by guru's grace; you will swim across the world-ocean. ||1||Pause|| Those who have this treasure of God's Name written in their destiny; they are honoured in God's court. Singing His praises with peace, poise and bliss; the homeless obtains a home hereafter. ||2|| This is the essence and reality in all ages. Reciting God is the true thinking. Page 1144 Whoever He attaches to Him, attaches; Asleep for countless births, he wakes up. ||3|| Your devotees belong to You, and You belong to Your devotees. You inspire them to sing Your praises. All beings are in Your hands. Nanak's God is always with him. ||4||16||29|| Bhairao, Fifth Master: The name of God is the inner-knower of my heart. God's name is useful to me. Lord's name permeates each and every hair of mine. The perfect guru has given me this gift. ||1|| The Jewel of God's name is my treasure. It is inaccessible, priceless, infinite and incomparable. ||1||Pause|| God's name is unmoving and wealthy. The glory of God's name pervades all. God is my perfect banker through His name. God's name makes me independent. ||2|| God's name is my food and love. God's name is the objective of my mind. By the grace of the saints, I do not forget God's name. Reciting God's name the infinite divine music plays. ||3|| By God's grace, I have obtained the treasures of God's name. By guru's grace, I am attuned to God's name. Those who have the treasure of God's name are wealthy and supreme. ||4||17||30|| Bhairao, Fifth Master: You are my father, You are my mother. You are my soul, my life and the giver of peace. You are my master; I am Your slave. Without You, I have no one else. ||1|| O God, please be kind and bless me with the gift, that I sing Your praises, day and night. ||1||Pause|| I am Your musical instrument and You are the musician. I am Your beggar; please bless me with awns, O great giver. By Your grace, I enjoy love and pleasures. You are merged in each and every heart. ||2|| By Your grace, I recite Your name. In devotee's company I sing Your praises. By Your kindness, You take away our pains. By Your kindness the heart-lotus blossoms; ||3|| I admire my guru. Visualizing him is fulfilling and serving is sacred. O my God and master, be kind to me, that Nanak sings Your praises all the time. ||4||18||31|| Bhairao, Fifth Master: His court is the highest of all. I humbly bow to Him, forever. His place is the highest of the high. Reciting God's name erases millions of sins. ||1|| In His sanctuary, we find eternal peace. Whoever he unites with Him by His grace; ||1||Pause|| His amazing actions cannot be described. Everybody has faith in Him. He is revealed in devotee's company. The devotees recite Him with love. ||2|| He keeps giving and His stores never empty. In an instant, He establishes and disestablishes. No one can erase His command. He is the emperor of emperors. ||3|| He is my anchor and support; I place my hopes in Him. Page 1145 My pain and pleasure is in His hand. He covers the faults of His humble servant. Nanak sings His praises. ||4||19||32|| Bhairao, Fifth Master: The whiner whines every day. He thinks of God just to obtain the household requirements. If someone realizes and becomes detached; He will not suffer the pain of birth and death again. ||1|| All deeds are filled with sins. Rare are those who make God's name their resolve; ||1||Pause|| The three-phased worldly wealth infects all. Those who cling to it suffer in pain. There is no peace without reciting God's name. The fortunate obtain the treasure of God's name. ||2|| One who loves the juggler. He regrets when the juggler is finished with his tricks. The shade of a cloud is transitory; same is the worldly attachment and other useless things; ||3|| If someone obtains one merchandise; His deeds are fulfilled. One, who obtains God's name by guru's grace; O Nanak, his coming into the world is worthwhile. ||4||20||33|| Bhairao, Fifth Master: Slandering the saints, the mortal wanders in reincarnation. Slandering the saints, he gets sick. Slandering the saints, he suffers in pain. The slanderer is punished by the devil of death. ||1|| Those who argue and fight with the saints; those slanderers find no happiness. ||1||Pause|| Slandering the devotees, the wall of the mortal's body falls; Slandering the devotees, he goes to hell. Slandering the devotees, he rots in the womb. Slandering the devotees, he loses his kingdom. ||2|| The slanderer finds no salvation at all. He eats what he sows. He is worse than a thief, a cheat or a gambler. The slanderer places an unbearable burden on his head. ||3|| The devotees of the supreme Lord are enemyless. Whoever worships their feet is emancipated. The slanderer forgot the primal Lord. O Nanak, your deeds cannot be erased. Bhairao, Fifth Master: God's name is my listening and singing of Vedas. Through God's name, my work is completed. God's name is my worship of gods. God's name is my service to the guru. ||1|| The perfect guru has implanted God's name in me. God's name is the highest work of all. ||1||Pause|| God's name is my cleansing bath. God's name is my perfect donation. Those who recite God's name are sacred of all. Those who recite God's name are my friends and brothers. ||2|| God's name is my good omen and good fortune. God's name satisfies me intuitively. God's name is my good conduct. God's name is my good dealing. ||3|| Thos who have God enshrined in the mind; they have God's support. O Nanak, they sing God's praises with mind and body. Whom God blesses with His name in devotee's company; ||4||22||35|| Page 1146 Bhairao, Fifth Master: O God; bless the poor with wealth; So that their sins are eliminated and mind becomes pure. May all their desires and deeds be fulfilled? Please bless Your devotees with Your name. ||1|| Service to the Lord, our sovereign King, is fruitful. God does and makes us do; no one goes empty handed from His door. ||1||Pause|| O God; cure the sickness of the sick; O God; eliminate the sorrows of the sufferer. Please give home to the homeless. Please link Your slave to Your worship. ||2|| O God bestow honour on the dishonoured. You make the fools ignorant intelligent and divine. The fear of all fears disappears. God's name dwells in the mind of His humble servant; ||3|| The supreme Lord is the treasure of peace. God's sacred name is the essence of divine wisdom. He guides them to serve the saints by His grace. O Nanak, the devotees merge with God; ||4||23||36|| Bhairao, Fifth Master: In the realm of the saints, the Lord dwells in the mind. In the realm of the saints, all sins run away. In the realm of the saints, one's thinking becomes pure. In the society of the saints, one loves God. ||1|| That place is called the realm of the saints; Where only God's praises are sung; ||1||Pause|| In the realm of the saints, birth and death are ended. In the realm of the saints, the devil of death does not bother. In the society of the saints, one speaks sacred words. In the realm of the saints, God's name is recited. ||2|| The realm of the saints is eternal. In the realm of the saints, sins are destroyed. In the realm of the saints, the sacred sermon is spoken. In the society of saints, the pain of ego runs away. ||3|| The realm of saints cannot be destroyed. In the realm of saints, abides the virtuous God. The realm of saints is the resting place of God. O Nanak, He is completely merged there. ||4||24||37|| Bhairao, Fifth Master: When God protects there is no sickness. That person, whom the Lord protects, does not suffer pain and sorrow. That person, upon whom God showers His mercy, death turns away from him. ||1|| God's name is his help forever. He, who misses God, obtains eternal peace and the devil of death does not come close to him. ||1||Pause|| When this being did not exist, who created him? What has been produced from what source? He kills and He gives life. He cherishes His devotees forever. ||2|| Know that everything is in His hand. My God is the master of orphans. His name is the destroyer of pain. Singing His praises you shall find peace. ||3|| O Lord, please listen to the prayer of saints. My soul, life and wealth are yours. This world is Yours; all worship You. Page 1147 Please be kind that Nanak obtains happiness. ||4||25||38|| Bhairao, Fifth Master: I survive in today's age by Your support. With Your support, I sing Your praises. With Your support, death cannot touch me. With Your support, my entanglements vanish. ||1|| You support the whole world. One God abides in all. ||1||Pause|| With Your support, I enjoy; With Your support, I recite guru's word. With Your support, I cross over the terrifying world-ocean. The protector God is an ocean of peace. ||2|| With Your support, I have no fear. The true Lord is the inner-knower. With Your support, my mind enjoys your support. Here and there, You are my court. ||3|| I believe in Your support. Everyone recites You O virtuous God. Your servants recite and enjoy. O Nanak, recite the virtuous God; ||4||26||39|| Bhairao, Fifth Master: First, I gave up slandering others. All anxiety of my mind is dispelled. Greed and attachment are eliminated. God's devotee sees the supreme Lord close. ||1|| Such a renunciate is rare. Who recites God's name; ||1||Pause|| I have forsaken my egotistic thinking. Love of lust and anger has vanished. I recite God saying God God God. In the company of devotees I am emancipated. ||2|| Enemy and friend are same to me. The perfect Lord is permeating all. Obeying God's will I obtain peace. The perfect guru taught me to recite God's name. ||3|| Whoever He protects by His grace; that devotee recites the recitation of God's name. His mind enlightens through guru's lesson; Says Nanak, he is totally fulfilled. ||4||27||40|| Bhairao, Fifth Master: There is no peace in earning lot of money. There is no peace in watching dances and plays. There is no peace in working in many countries. All peace comes from singing God's praises. ||1|| You shall obtain peace, poise and bliss, The fortunate joins devotee's company and recites God's name. ||1||Pause|| Mother, father, children and spouse are bonds. Religious rituals and actions done in ego are bonds. If God the destroyer of bonds dwells in the mind; then he obtains peace and dwells in his house. ||2|| Everyone is a beggar; God is the giver. The treasure of virtues is the infinite, endless Lord. He, whom God grants His grace; He recites God's name. ||3|| I offer my prayer to my guru. O primal Lord, treasure of virtue, please bless me with Your grace. Says Nanak; I have come to Your sanctuary. Keep me as You please O Lord of the world. ||4||28||41|| Bhairao, Fifth Master: Meeting with the guru, I have forsaken the love of duality. Page 1148 The guru-willed recites God's name. My anxiety is gone, and I am in love with God's name. I was asleep for many lifetimes, but I have awakened now. ||1||

By His grace he put me to His service. I obtained eternal peace in devotee's company. ||1||Pause|| Guru's teaching eliminated all diseases and suffering. Medicine of God's name has entered my mind. Meeting with the guru, my mind is happy. All treasures are in the name of God. ||2|| My fear of birth and death and devil of death has been dispelled. In devotee's company the inverted lotus of my heart has blossomed. Singing God's praises I have found eternal and lasting peace. All my deeds are fulfilled. ||3|| This hard to get human body is approved by the Lord. It became fruitful by reciting God's name. Says Nanak, God blessed me with His kindness. With every breath and morsel of food, I say God God God. ||4||29||42|| Bhairao, Fifth Master: His name is the highest of all. I sing His praises, forever. Reciting His name eliminates all suffering. All peace entered in the mind. ||1|| O my mind, recite the true Lord; In this world and the next, you shall be saved. ||1||Pause|| The primal formless God is the Creator of all. He gives sustenance to all beings. He forgives millions of sins in an instant. Through devotional worship, one is emancipated forever. ||2|| True is His wealth and greatness; I obtained the complete wisdom from the guru. Whom He protects by His grace; their ignorance is eliminated. ||3|| I focus my mind on the supreme Lord. The bestowal of salvation abides in all. Eradicating doubt and fear, I have realized the Lord of the world. The guru has become kind to Nanak. ||4||30||43|| Bhairao, Fifth Master: Reciting His name the mind is illuminated. Suffering is eradicated, and one dwells in peace. They alone receive it, to whom God gives it. They serve the perfect guru. ||1|| All peace and comfort are in Your name O God. O my mind, sing His praises twenty-four hours a day. ||1||Pause|| You shall receive the fruit of your desire; Enshrining God's name in the mind; Reciting God's name the coming and going ends. Through devotional worship, lovingly focus your mind to God. ||2|| Lust, anger and ego are dispelled. Love and attachment to worldly wealth is eliminated. Through God's support day and night, whomever the supreme Lord gives this gift. ||3|| Our Lord is the Creator, the cause of causes. He is the inner-knower of all hearts. By His grace, he inspires us to sever Him; Slave Nanak has come to Your sanctuary. ||4||31||44|| Bhairao, Fifth Master: One who does not recite God's name shall die of shame. How can he be happy without God's name? He forsakes reciting God and yet wants to obtain salvation; Page 1149 How can the branches flourish without the roots? ||1|| O my mind, recite guru the Lord of the universe. It eliminates the filth of many a life and unites with God; ||1||Pause|| How can a stone be purified by bathing at a sacred shrine? The filth of ego clings to the mind. Millions of rituals are the roots of entanglements. Without worshipping God he is useless like a bundle of straw. ||2|| Without eating, hunger is not eliminated. When the disease is cured, the pain goes away. The mortal is bothered by lust, anger, greed and attachment. He does not recite God, who created him; ||3|| Blessed is the devotee who recites the admirable God's name. Twenty-four hours a day, he sings God's praises. Blessed is God's devotee and blessed is the Creator. Nanak seeks the sanctuary of the primal, infinite God; ||4||32||45|| Bhairao, Fifth Master: When the guru is pleased, my fear is taken away. I enshrine the name of the formless God in the mind. He is kind to the meek and compassionate forever. All my entanglements have ended. ||1|| I have found peace, poise, and many pleasures. My fear and doubt erased in devotee's company and I recite God's sacred name. ||1||Pause|| I have fallen in love with Lord's lotus feet. In an instant, the terrible demons are destroyed. Twenty-four hours a day, I recite God; the guru is the saviour the Lord of the universe. ||2|| He looks after His devotees forever. He looks after His devotees at every breath. What can you say about the human beings? God saves them from the devil of death by His grace. ||3|| His glory and nature are admirable. Who remember the supreme Lord in their minds? The guru granted this gift by his grace. Nanak has obtained the treasure of God's name. ||4||33||46|| Bhairao, Fifth Master: My guru is the all-powerful the Creator, the cause of causes. He is the bestowal of soul life and happiness. The sovereign Lord is the destroyer of fear; He is immortal. Visualizing Him all pains go away. ||1|| Wherever I look, I see Your refuge. I praise the feet of the guru. ||1||Pause|| My tasks are accomplished, meeting the guru. He is the giver of all rewards. Serving Him is sacred. He reaches out to His slaves. And enshrines God's name in their mind; ||2|| They are happy forever, and do not feel sorrow. No pain, sorrow or disease afflicts them. Everything is Yours, You are the Creator. The guru is the supreme Lord, the inaccessible and infinite God; ||3|| His admiration is sacred and His sermon is wonderful; the perfect supreme Lord is pleasing to my mind. He is pervading in water and land. O Nanak, everything comes from God. ||4||34||47|| Bhairao, Fifth Master: My mind and body are imbued with the love of Lord's feet. Page 1150 All my deeds have been fulfilled. Twenty-four hours a day, I sing God God God. The guru taught me the perfect lesson. ||1|| He, who loves God's name, is fortunate. The world attains salvation with him. ||1||Pause|| He, who recites one God, is divine. He, who has discriminating intellect, is rich. He, who recites God the master, belongs to a good family. He, who realizes himself, is honourable. ||2|| By guru's grace, I have obtained the supreme status. Day and night I sing God's praises. My bonds are broken and my hopes are fulfilled. The feet of the Lord abide in my heart. ||3|| Says Nanak, he has the perfect luck. He who comes to God's refuge; He is pure and he sanctifies all. He recites God and searches his soul. ||4||35||48|| Bhairao, Fifth Master: Reciting God's name, no obstacles block his way. Listening to God's name the devil of death runs away from far. Reciting God's name, all pains vanish. Reciting God's name, he dwells at God's feet. ||1|| Recite and worship God without any obstruction. Sing God's praises with joy. ||1||Pause|| Reciting God, the other tastes do not bother. Reciting God, the demons do not touch you. Reciting God, the attachment and self-pride do not entice. Reciting God, one does not go through the process of birth. ||2|| Any time is a good time to recite God. Among many, only a few recite God. Social class or no class, only a few recite God. Whoever recites God obtains liberation. ||3|| Recite God's name in devotee's company. God's name dyes with true love. O God, be kind to Nanak, that he recites God with every breath. ||4||36||49|| Bhairao, Fifth Master: He is the Shaastras, He is the Vedas. He knows the secrets of everyone. He is the embodiment of light; all beings belong to Him. He is the all-powerful Creator, the cause of causes. ||1|| O my mind; take God's support. O guru-willed recite God's lotus feet. The enemy or pain, do not come close. ||1||Pause|| He is the essence of the forests and fields, and the entire universe. The universe is strung on His thread. He is the worldly power. He bestows salvation and enjoys it. ||2|| Wherever I look, I see

Him. Without Him, there is no one else. In love of God's name, the world-ocean is crossed. Nanak sings His praises in devotee's company. ||3|| The way of liberation and enjoyment are under His control. His humble servant lacks nothing. Whoever he is pleased with; O slave Nanak that humble servant is admirable. ||4||37||50|| Bhairao, Fifth Master: The minds of God's devotees are filled with bliss. They become immortal and all their anxiety goes away. Page 1151 Their fears and doubts are dispelled in an instant. The supreme Lord dwells in their minds. ||1|| God's name is the support of the saints. Inside out God is with them. God abides in all places. ||1||Pause|| The Lord of the world is my wealth, property, youth and ways and means. He continuously cherishes and brings peace to my soul and life. He reaches out with His hand and saves His slave. He does not abandon us at all; He is always with us. ||2|| There is no other beloved like the Lord. The true Lord takes care of all. The Lord is our mother, father, son and a relative. Since the beginning of time, and throughout the ages, His devotees sing His praises. ||3|| I belong to Him and my mind is united with God. Without one God, there is no other. Nanak has this goodness in his mind. God fulfills our desires. ||4||38||51|| Bhairao, Fifth Master: Reciting God the fear changed in love. All diseases of worldly three qualities erased and devotee's desires got fulfilled. ||1||Pause|| God's devotees sing His praises forever; they find the perfect place. Even the justice of destiny and devil of death long to visualize Him day and night so that they become sacred; ||1|| In devotee's company, lust, anger, greed, intoxication slender and pride are eliminated. The fortunate meet such saints; Nanak admires them forever. ||2||39||52|| Bhairao, Fifth Master: He, who harbours five thieves, is one of them. He gets up each day and tells lies. He acts as astrologer and practices hypocrisy. He feels sad like divorced woman. ||1|| Everything without God's name is false. Without the perfect guru, liberation is not obtained. In true court the faithless are robbed. ||1||Pause|| One who does not know Lord's creative power is filthy. Painting the kitchen does not make it pure in the eyes of the Lord. He is dirty inside and washes the outside every day. He loses honour in the true court. ||2|| He works for the sake of wealth. He never walks on the right path. He never remembers the one who created him. He speaks false with his mouth. ||3|| Whoever God grants His grace; He deals with God's devotees. He recites God's name with love. Says Nanak – no obstacles block his way. ||4||40||53|| Bhairao, Fifth Master: The entire universe curses the slanderer. False are the dealings of the slanderer. The slanderer is characterless. God protects His servant. ||1|| The slanderer dies with the rest of the slanderers. The supreme lord, the transcendent Lord, protects and saves His humble servant. Death roars over the head of the slanderer. ||1||Pause|| Page 1152 No one believes what the slanderer says. The slanderer tells lies, and regrets. He wrings his hands and hits his head against the ground. God does not forgive the slanderer. ||2|| God's slave does not wish anyone bad. The slanderer suffers, as if stabbed by a spear. Like a crane, he spreads his feathers, to look like a swan. When he speaks with his mouth, he is exposed. ||3|| The Creator is the inner-knower. Whatever God's devotee does happen? Lord's slave is true in the court of the Lord. Servant Nanak speaks, after contemplating the reality. ||4||41||54|| Bhairao, Fifth Master: With my palms pressed together, I offer this prayer. My soul, body and wealth are His property. He is the Creator, my Lord and master. I admire Him million times. ||1|| The dust of the feet of devotees brings purity. Reciting God the evil thinking disappears from the mind and the filth of many life's washes away. ||1||Pause|| All treasures are in His house. Serving Him, the mortal attains honour. He is the fulfiller of all desires. He is the support of the soul and life of His devotees. ||2|| His Light shines in each and every heart. The devotees live by reciting His name. Service to Him does not go in vain. By reciting one God in the mind and body; ||3|| Following guru's teachings, kindness and contentment are obtained. Reciting the treasure of God's name obtains these in abundance. Please attach me to the hem of Your robe by Your grace. Nanak continuously recites Lord's lotus feet. ||4||42||55|| Bhairao, Fifth Master: The guru has listened to my prayer. All my affairs have been resolved. I recite God in my mind and body. The perfect guru dispelled all my fears. ||1|| The guru is the most powerful of all. Serving Him, I obtain all comforts. ||Pause|| Everything is done by Him. No one can erase His eternal verdict. The supreme Lord the transcendent Lord, is very beautiful. Guru is His true image. ||2|| The name of the Lord abides in him. Wherever he sees, he sees the Wisdom of God. His mind is totally enlightened. The supreme Lord abides in him. ||3|| I humbly bow to that guru forever. I praise the guru forever. I wash the feet of the guru, and drink this water. Nanak lives by reciting the guru. ||4||43||56|| Page 1153 Tune Bhairao, Fifth Master, Partaal, Third House: God is one. He is realized by guru's grace. God is compassionate cherisher. Who can count His virtues? He is imbued with many colours and waves of joy. He is the master of all. ||1||Pause|| There are many spiritual ways, contemplations, meditation and self-discipline. Countless virtues, musical notes and playful sports. Countless sages enshrine Him in their hearts. ||1|| Countless melodies, countless instruments, countless tastes, and each and every instant; countless mistakes and diseases are removed by hearing His praise. O Nanak, serving the infinite Lord, one earns all rewards and merits of performing the six rituals, fasts, worship services, pilgrimages to sacred rivers, and journeys to sacred shrines. ||2||1||57||8||21||7||57||93|| Bhairao, Ashtapadees, First Master, Second House: God is one. He is realized by guru's grace. God is the soul, soul is God. He is realized through guru's teaching. The sacred sermon is realized through guru's teaching. It eliminates pain and ego. ||1|| O Nanak, the disease of ego is bad; wherever I look, I see the same pain. God blesses all through guru's teaching. ||1||Pause|| God the appraiser appraises the mortal then he is not tested again. Those, whom God blesses, meet the guru; it happens by God's will. ||2|| Air, water and fire and the whole world is sick; Mother, father, the worldly body and the whole family is sick. ||3|| Brahma, Vishnu and Shiva are sick; the whole world is sick. Those who search God through guru's teaching obtain salvation. ||4|| The seven seas, the rivers; the continents and the underworld are all sick. Only God's devotees are truly happy. God's grace pervades all places. ||5|| Those who follow six Shaastras, the imitators and many stubborn are sick. The ignorant read scriptures but do not follow what is in them; ||6|| Eating sweets makes them sick and there is no happiness eating roots. Those who forget God's name and follow others, repent in the end. ||7|| Going to sacred shrines does not cure sickness. They read scriptures and waste their time arguing. The disease of duality is a serious sickness; it makes them dependant on worldly wealth. ||8||

The guru-willed praises guru's teaching. His mind becomes pure and the sickness is cured. O Nanak, the fortunate God's devotees are pure forever. ||9||1|| Page 1154 Bhairao, Third Master, Second House: God is one. He is realized by guru's grace. The Creator has staged the wondrous Play. He plays the divine music through guru's teaching. The self-willed are confused, while the guru-willed understand. The Creator creates the cause. ||1|| I enshrine guru's teaching in my mind intently. I never abandon God's name. ||1||Pause|| Prahlaad's father sent him to school, to learn. He took his writing wooden plank and went to the teacher. He said, I will not learn anything other than God's name. Write Lord's name on my wooden plank; ||2|| Prahlaad's mother said to her son. I advise you not to read what your mind says. He answered! The carefree God is with me. If I forget God then my family will be cursed and disgraced. ||3|| Prahlaad has corrupted all other students. He does not listen to what I say, he does his own thing. He tells everyone to worship God in the whole town. The gathering of the wicked people could not do anything to him. ||4|| Sanda Marka, his teacher, complained; All demons tried in vain. The Lord protects and preserves the honour Of His devotees. What can be done by the created beings? ||5|| Because of his past deeds, the demon ruled over his kingdom. He did not think of God; God confused him. He created enmity with his son Prahlaad. The blind did not understand that his death was approaching. ||6|| He put Prahlaad in a room and locked the door. The fearless child was not afraid at all. He said that God is in him. If he can do anything then he can rival God! It cannot be done. Whatever was written in his fate, happened; he created enmity with God's devotee. ||7|| The father raised the club to hit Prahlaad. Where is your God, the Lord of the universe? Finally God the life of the world came to help. Wherever I look, I see Him. ||8|| Tearing apart the pillar, the Lord appeared. He killed the proud demon. The devotees became happy and admirations started to come. He blessed His servant with greatness. ||9|| He created birth, death and attachment. The Creator wrote coming and going in reincarnation. For the sake of Prahlaad, the Lord appeared. The word of the devotee came true. ||10|| The gods proclaimed victory of Lakshmi. O mother, make this form of the man-lion disappear! Lakshmi said, it cannot be done; Page 1155 The humble servant Prahlaad came and fell at the Lord's feet. ||11|| The guru taught him to recite the priceless God's name. Power, property and all worldly pleasure are false. But still, the greedy people continue clinging to them. Without God's name they are punished in God's court. ||12|| Says Nanak, everyone acts as the Lord makes them act. Those who focus their mind to God are accepted. He helps His devotees all the time. The Creator showed His natural way. ||13||1||2|| Bhairao, Third Master: Serving the guru obtains sacred fruit and eliminates ego and greed. Enshrining God's name in the mind and controlling the desire. ||1|| O dear Lord, be kind to me; the humble begs to praise God forever. Guru's teaching bestows salvation. ||1||Pause|| The devil of death cannot rob the saints. He cannot cause any pain to them. Those who enter Your refuge attain salvation along with their dynasty. ||2|| You preserve the honour of your devotees. This is your greatness. You eliminate the sins and doubt of many a life. ||3|| I am foolish and ignorant, I understand nothing. You bless me with realization. You do whatever pleases You; others cannot do anything. ||4|| Creating the world, You put them to work; even the evil deeds; they lose this precious human life in a gamble. They do not realize guru's teaching. ||5|| The self-willed die not knowing anything; they are filled with the darkness of evil-mindedness and ignorance. They do not cross over the terrible world-ocean; without the guru, they drown and die. ||6|| True are those humble beings that are imbued with true guru's teaching; God unites them with Him. They realize guru's sermon through his teaching and lovingly attach to it. ||7|| You are pure. Your devotees become pure contemplating guru's teaching. Nanak admires them forever, who enshrine God's name in the mind. ||8||2||3|| Bhairao, Fifth Master, Ashtapadees, Second House: God is one. He is realized by guru's grace. He, who enshrines God's name in the mind, is an emperor. One who enshrines God's name in the mind, his deeds are fulfilled. One, who enshrines God's name in the mind, obtains wealth in millions. Without God's name the life goes waste. ||1|| I praise him, who has Godly wealth. He, who has guru's blessing, is fortunate. ||1||Pause|| One, who enshrines God's name in the mind, keeps army of millions. One, who enshrines

God's name in the mind, obtains eternal peace and contentment. Page 1156 One, who enshrines God's name in the mind, becomes cool and calm. Without God's name, his life is worthless. ||2|| One, who enshrines God's name in the mind, obtains salvation. One, who enshrines God's name in the mind, understands everything. One, who enshrines God's name in the mind, obtains the priceless treasure. Without God's name, the mortal keeps coming and going. ||3|| One, who enshrines God's name in the mind, becomes carefree. One, who enshrines God's name in the mind, reaps the profit forever. One, who enshrines God's name in the mind, has a large family. Without God's name the self-willed is ignorant. ||4|| One, who enshrines God's name in the mind, becomes immortal. One, who enshrines God's name in the mind, sits on the throne. One, who enshrines God's name in the mind, is a true banker. Without God's name, no one obtains honour or faith. ||5|| One, who enshrines God's name in the mind, is famous among all. One, who enshrines God's name in the mind, is the architect of destiny. One, who enshrines God's name in the mind, is the highest of all. Without God's name the ignorant wanders in different lifes. ||6|| One, who enshrines God's name in the mind, knows all calculations. One, who enshrines God's name in the mind, becomes enlightened. God accepts one, who enshrines God's name in the mind. Without God's name, coming and going continues. ||7|| He, whom God becomes kind, obtains God's name. God is realized in devotee's company. Their coming and going ends and become peaceful. Says Nanak; the soul merges with supreme soul. ||8||1||4|| Bhairao, Fifth Master: He created millions of incarnations of Vishnu. He created millions of places to worship in the universe. He created and destroyed millions of Shivas. He employed millions of Brahmas to create the worlds. ||1|| Such is my Lord, the Lord of the universe. I cannot describe His virtues. ||1||Pause|| Millions of worldly pleasures are His maidservants. Millions of souls realize divine wisdom and attain peace; Millions adorn You with love. Millions of devotees abide with the Lord. ||2|| Millions of kings bow before Him. Millions of Indras stand at His door. Millions of heavens are in His realm. I do not know how many names He has. ||3|| Millions blow horn to worship Him. Millions of arenas stage His play and enjoy. Millions of worldly powers are obedient to Him. He gives food to millions of beings. ||4|| In His feet are millions of sacred shrines of pilgrimage. Millions recite His sacred name with love. Millions of worshippers worship Him. His creation extends in millions; there is no other at all. ||5|| Millions of swan-souls sing His praises. Millions of Brahma's children sing His praises. He creates and destroys millions, in an instant. Millions are Your virtues, they cannot be counted. ||6|| Millions of spiritual teachers teach His spiritual wisdom. Millions of meditators focus on meditation. Millions of austere penitents practice austerities. Page 1157 Millions of sages remain silent. ||7|| God is eternal, imperishable, and incomprehensible. The inner-knower pervades all. Wherever I look, I see You there. The guru has blessed Nanak with enlightenment. ||8||2||5|| Bhairao, Fifth Master: The guru has blessed me with this gift. He has given me the priceless jewel of Lord's name. Now, I intuitively enjoy endless pleasures and amazing play. God has met with Nanak care freely. ||1|| Says Nanak; true is Lord's praise. Again and again, my mind remains immersed in it. ||1||Pause|| Care freely, I feed on the love of God. Care freely, I recite God's name. Care freely; guru's teaching saves me. Care freely; my treasures are filled to overflowing. ||2|| Care freely, my works are completed. Care freely, I got rid of sorrow. Care freely, my enemies have become friends. Care freely, I have controlled my mind. ||3|| Care freely, God has comforted me. Care freely, my hopes have been fulfilled. Care freely, I have realized the reality. Care freely; I have been blessed with guru's word. ||4|| Care freely, I have no enemy. Care freely, my darkness has been dispelled. Care freely, God's praises appeal to me. Care freely, I see God in everyone. ||5|| Care freely; all my doubts have been dispelled. Care freely; peace and harmony fill my mind. Care freely, the infinite divine music plays. Care freely, the Lord of the universe has revealed to me. ||6|| Care freely, my mind believes. I have care freely realized the eternal, unchanging Lord. Care freely; the discriminating wisdom has welled up in me. Care freely; I have the support of God. ||7|| Care freely, God has recorded my destiny. Care freely, I realized God my master. Care freely; all my worries have been taken away. Nanak has merged in God. ||8||3||6|| Bhairao, The Word Of The Devotees, Kabeer Jee, First House: God is one. He is realized by guru's grace. God's name is my wealth. I do not tie in a knot, or sell it to make my living. ||1||Pause|| God's name is my crop and field. Your humble servant worships You in Your refuge; ||1|| The Name is my wealth and property. Forgetting You I do not know anyone else. ||2|| God's name is my relative and my brother. God's name will help me in the end. ||3|| One, whom God keeps detached in the middle of the worldly wealth. Says Kabeer, I am his slave. ||4||1|| Naked we come, naked we go. No king or queen shall remain. ||1|| Page 1158 The sovereign Lord is my priceless treasure. You are in love with possessions and spouse. ||1||Pause|| They do not come or go with you. What happened to the elephants tied up at his door? ||2|| The fortress of Lanka was made of gold; What did the ignorant Raawan take with him? ||3|| Says Kabeer, think of doing some good deeds. In the end, the gambler shall depart empty-handed. ||4||2|| Brahma is filthy, Indra is filthy. The sun is polluted, the moon is polluted. ||1|| This world is polluted with pollution. Only God is pure; there is no limit or end to His creation. ||1||Pause|| The rulers of the world are polluted. Nights and days, and the days of the month are polluted. ||2|| The pearl is polluted, the diamond is polluted. Wind, fire and water are polluted. ||3|| Shiva and other gods are polluted. The mystics, seekers and strivers, and imitators are polluted. ||4|| The Yogis and wandering hermits with their matted hair are polluted. The body, along with the soul, is polluted. ||5|| Says Kabeer, those beings are approved and pure, who realize God; ||6||3|| Let your mind be Mecca, and your body the temple of worship. Let the supreme guru be the one who speaks. ||1|| O Mullah, say the call to prayer. The one mosque has ten doors. ||1||Pause|| Kill your evil nature, doubt and cruelty; Consume the five demons and you will be content. ||2|| Hindus and Muslims have the same God. What can the Mullah or the elder do? ||3|| Says Kabeer, I have gone insane. Stealing and robbing I have merged in celestial peace. ||4||4|| River Saraswati merged with Ganges and became Ganges. ||1|| Same way Kabeer has changed. He has merged in truth and he does not go anywhere else. ||1||Pause|| Associating with the sandalwood tree, the tree nearby is changed; That tree begins to smell like the sandalwood tree. ||2|| Coming in contact with the philosophers' stone, copper is transformed;

That copper is transformed into gold. ||3|| In the society of the saints, Kabeer is transformed; That Kabeer is transformed into God. ||4||5|| Some apply ceremonial marks to their forehead, hold rosary in the hand and wear religious robes. People think that God is a toy; ||1|| If I am insane, then I am Yours, O Lord. How can people know my secret? ||1||Pause|| I do not pick leaves to worship idols. Without God's worship, all other worship is useless. ||2|| I worship the guru; and console with him all the time. By such service, I find peace in the court of the Lord. ||3|| People say that Kabeer has gone insane. Only God knows the secret of Kabeer. ||4||6|| I gave up on caste and family. Now I weave in trance and contentment. ||1|| I have no quarrel with anyone. Page 1159 I have abandoned both Pandits and mullahs. ||1||Pause|| I weave and wear what I weave. Where there is no ego, there I sing God's praises. ||2|| Whatever the Pandits and mullahs have written; I left it behind and do not take anything. ||3|| My heart is pure, You can check it O Lord. Searching his soul, Kabeer has found God. ||4||7|| No one respects the poor man. He may make thousands of efforts, but no one pays any attention to him. ||1||Pause|| When the poor man goes to the rich man; He sits in front of him, but the rich man turns away from him. ||1|| But when the rich man goes to the poor man; The poor man welcomes him with respect. ||2|| The poor man and the rich man are both brothers. God's doing cannot be erased. ||3|| Says Kabeer, he who does not have God's name in the heart is really poor? ||4||8|| Serving the guru, devotional worship is practiced. Then, this human body is obtained. Even the gods long for this human body. So worship God with that body. ||1|| Do not forget to worship the Lord of the universe. This is the benefit of a human body; ||1||Pause|| As long as the disease of old age has not taken over. As long as death has not seized the body. As long as you have not lost your speech; O mortal, recite God in your mind; ||2|| If you do not recite God now; when will you O brother? When the end comes, you will not be able to recite God. Whatever you have to do – now is the best time. You will regret later and will not go across. ||3|| He, whom God puts to serve Him, is His servant. He realizes God. Meeting with the guru, his mind has opened up. He does not come back in the world again. ||4|| This is your chance, and this is your time. Look deep in your heart, and reflect on it. Says Kabeer, you win to lose. I say this loud in many ways. ||5||1||9|| In the city of God, essence of understanding prevails. You should congregate there and discus; Thus, you shall understand this world and the next. What is the use of possessions, if you have to die in the end? ||1|| I focus my mind on myself. God's name is my divine wisdom. ||1||Pause|| I am sitting at God's door. I see moon above the sun. The sun blazes in the west. Those who claim possessions get beaten on the head with a stick. ||2|| The western gate is closed with a rock. There is a window above the rock. Above that window is the tenth gate. Says Kabeer; it has no end or limit. ||3||2||10|| He, who fights with his mind, is a real mullah; He unites with God through guru's teaching. He serves God with love. I offer my greetings to that mullah. ||1|| Page 1160 God is near, why you say that He is far. Stop making noise and realize the beautiful God. He, who searches his soul, is a Qazi. Burn your energy on reciting God. He does not let his mind flicker even in a dream. Such a Qazi does not get old or dies. ||2|| He is a real king, who wins both worlds. He searches his soul instead of searching outside. He assembles his army in the realm of God. That king wears a royal crown. ||3|| The Yogi says "Gorakh, Gorakh (God)". The Hindu says Raam Raam. The Muslim has one God. Kabeer's master abides in all. ||4||3||11|| Fifth Master: Those who call a stone their god; their service goes waste. Those who fall at the feet of a stone god; their work goes in vain. ||1|| My Lord speaks forever. God gives gifts to all beings. ||1||Pause|| God is inside but the blind does not know it; Deluded by doubt, he gets entangled. The stone does not speak; it does not give anything to anyone. Such rituals are useless; such service is fruitless. ||2|| If someone puts sandalwood on the dead; what good does it do? If the dead is thrown in the filth. What does the dead lose? ||3|| Says Kabeer, I proclaim this; O faithless ignorant; look and understand? The love of duality has ruined many homes. The Lord's devotees are forever in bliss. ||4||4||12|| The fish in the water is attached to the worldly pleasure. The moth fluttering around the lamp is pierced by the worldly pleasure. The lust bothers the elephant. The snakes and wasps are stuck in the worldly pleasure. ||1|| O brother; the worldly pleasure is such an enticer; as many beings there are; all are deluded by it. ||1||Pause|| The birds and the deer are imbued with worldly pleasure. Jagry is a deadly trap for the flies. Horses and camels are absorbed in worldly pleasure. The eighty-four mystics play in the worldly pleasure. ||2|| The six celibates are slaves of worldly pleasure. So are the nine masters of Yoga, and the sun and the moon. The austere disciplinarians and saints are asleep in worldly pleasure; Death and the five demons are in worldly pleasure. ||3|| Dogs and jackals are imbued with worldly pleasure. Monkeys, leopards and lions; Cats, sheep and fox. The roots of the trees are planted in the worldly pleasure. ||4|| Even the gods are drenched with worldly wealth. As are the oceans, the sky and earth. Says Kabeer, whoever has the stomach, is controlled by the worldly wealth; they are freed by meeting with God's devotees. ||5||5||13|| As long as he says, mine! mine! Till then nothing is accomplished. When such possessiveness is erased; Page 1161 Then God comes and resolves his affairs. ||1|| Contemplate such spiritual wisdom, O my mind. Why do not you recite God the destroyer of pain? ||1||Pause|| As long as the tiger lives in the forest; the forest does not bloom. But when the jackal eats the tiger. The entire forest blooms. ||2|| The victorious are drowned, the defeated swim across. By guru's grace, one crosses over the world ocean. Slave Kabeer speaks and teaches: Remain lovingly absorbed in God; ||3||6||14|| He has 700 courtiers; and hundreds of thousands of prophets; He is said to have millions of elders. And millions of guards; ||1|| Who listens to a poor like me? The distance is long; only a few reach there. ||1||Pause|| He plays millions of games. Millions wander insane. When Adam found out something; He went to heaven. ||2|| He, who is disturbed and gone pale by listening to sermon; He forsakes Quran and practices evil. O Loie (His wife); he is just blaming the world; He reaps what he sows. ||3|| You are the giver, O Lord; I am a beggar forever. Please deny me if I commit any sin. Slave Kabeer has entered Your shelter. O kind Lord; keep me close; it is heaven for me. ||4||7||15|| Everyone speaks of going there; I do not know where the heaven is. ||1||Pause|| One, who does not know his own cure? He talks about heaven; ||1|| As long as the mortal hopes for heaven; Till then he cannot live at God's feet. ||2|| There is no moat, no plastered walls with mud; I do not know what heaven's gate is like; ||3|| Says

Kabeer, now what more can I say? The company of devotee's is the heaven. ||4||8||16|| How can the beautiful fortress be conquered, O brother? It has double walls and triple moats. ||1||Pause|| It is defended by the five elements, the twenty-five types of attachments, pride, jealousy and powerful worldly wealth. The poor mortal does not have the strength to conquer it; what should I do O Lord? ||1|| Lust is the window; pain and pleasure are the gatekeepers. Virtue and sin are the gates. Anger is the noisy commander and the mind is the rebel king there. ||2|| Their armour is the pleasure of tastes and flavours, their helmets are worldly attachments; they take aim with their bows of corrupt intellect. The greed that fills their hearts is the arrow; this way the fort cannot be conquered. ||3|| Intoxicate with love and fire the shell of divine wisdom through breathing into the mind. The fire of God is lit by intuition and with one shot, the fortress is conquered. ||4|| He fights with truth and contentment and broke through the door of duality. By guru's grace in devotee's company I arrested the king of my body; ||5|| Page 1162 The devotees are lining up to recite God and their chain of death is cut. Slave Kabeer has climbed to the top of the fortress and realized the immortal kingdom. ||6||9||17|| The mother Ganges is deep and profound. Tied up in chains, they took Kabeer there. ||1|| My mind was not shaken; why should my body be afraid? My mind is absorbed in God's lotus feet. ||1||Pause|| The waves of the Ganges broke the chains; Kabeer was seated on a deerskin. ||2|| Says Kabeer, I have no friend or companion. In water or land, the Lord is my protector. ||3||10||18|| Bhairao, Kabeer Jee, Ashtapadees, Second House: God is one. He is realized by guru's grace. God constructed a fortress, inaccessible and unreachable, He lives there. There, His divine Light shines. Lightning flashes and joy prevails, the ladder where the child God climbs; ||1|| This mind is attuned to God with love. He is saved from old age and death, his doubt ran away. ||1||Pause|| Those who believe in high and low social classes; they only sing songs of ego. The infinite divine music plays. The ladder which my supreme Lord climbs; ||2|| He dwells in all lands surroundings and divisions; He pervades in three places and three divisions. The inaccessible and unfathomable Lord dwells in the heart. No one can find the limits or the secrets of the Lord of the world. ||3|| His light shines in trees and flowers. He dwells in the pollen of the lotus flower. Lord's secret is within the twelve petals of the heart-lotus. The supreme Lord, the Lord of Lakshmi dwells there. ||4|| Who else do I see in this world and the next world? He lives in a lonely place. There is no sun or the moon. The primal Lord enjoys there. ||5|| He pervades the universe. Take your cleansing bath in Mansarovar Lake. Recite the recitation of Sohang (you are me I am You). He is not affected by either virtue or vice. ||6|| He is not affected by either high or low social class, sunshine or shade. You do not find Him anywhere else except the refuge of the guru. He cannot be changed. He does not come or go. He is absorbed in trance and obtains peace. ||7|| If one realizes in the mind. Whatever He says happens. He stabilizes the soul and mind through guru's lesson. Says Kabeer, that person obtains salvation. ||8||1|| His light gives as much light as millions of suns. Millions of Shivas and Kailash mountains; Millions of Durga goddesses massage His feet. Millions of Brahmas speak the Vedas to Him. ||1|| When I beg, I beg only from God. I have nothing to do with any other deities. ||1||Pause|| Millions of moons shine in the sky. Page 1163 Millions of gods perform offering to God. The nine astrology stars stand at His door million times. Millions of religious people stand guard at His court. ||2|| Millions of winds blow around Him from four directions. Millions of serpents churn and spread His bed. Millions of oceans are His water-carriers. The eighteen million loads of vegetation are His hair. ||3|| Millions of treasurers fill His treasury. Millions of Lakshmis adorn themselves for Him. Millions commit sins and good deeds. Millions of Indras serve Him. ||4|| Fifty-six million are His guards. He is praised in every town and village. Many wander with their hair hanging all over. God plays countless games. ||5|| Millions of charitable feasts are held in His court; Millions of celestial singers celebrate Him. Millions of learned one's sing His praises. Even then, they cannot find God's limits. ||6|| Rama, with millions of monkeys, conquered Raawan's army. Billions of Puraanas praise Him; He humbled the pride of Duryodhan. ||7|| Millions of beauties cannot compare with him. He steals the hearts of all beings. Says Kabeer, please hear me, O Lord of the world. I beg for the blessing of state of immortality. ||8||2||18||20|| Bhairao, The Word

Of Naam Dev Jee, First House: God is one. He is realized by guru's grace. O my tongue, I will cut you into seven pieces; If you do not recite the name of the Lord; ||1|| Dye your tongue with God's name. Recite God with utmost love. ||1||Pause|| O my tongue, other deeds are imaginary. Only God's name is the eternal state of liberation. ||2|| I performed unlimited number of other worships. Naamaa did not worship God at all. Prays Naam Dev, this is my occupation. O Lord, Your forms are endless. ||4||1|| One who stays away from other's wealth and other's spouses? God abides near that person. ||1|| Those who do not recite God; I do not want to see their faces. ||1||Pause|| Those who have difference in the mind; they are just like animals. ||2|| Prays Naam Dev; without being humble; Thirty-two good signs do not look good. ||3||2|| Naam Dev milked the ever milk giving cow in one bowl and brought water in another bowl. ||1|| Please drink this milk, O my sovereign Lord; Drink this milk and my mind will be happy. Otherwise, my father will be angry with me. ||1||Pause|| Taking the golden cup, Naam Dev filled it with the nectar; and placed it before the Lord; ||2|| The Lord looked at Naam Dev and smiled. This devotee pleases me. The Lord drank the milk, and the devotee returned home. Page 1164 Naam Dev visualized God; ||4||3|| I am insane – the Lord is my Husband. I decorate and adorn myself for Him. ||1|| Slander me, slander me, slander me, O people. My body and mind are united with my beloved Lord. ||1||Pause|| I do not engage in any argument or debate with anyone. I recite God's name with my tongue. ||2|| Now, my mind and life have become such; that I realized God and I play His tune. ||3|| Anyone can praise or slander me. Naam Dev has met God. ||4||4|| Sometimes, people do not appreciate milk, sugar and butter. Sometimes, they have to beg for bread from door to door. Sometimes, they have to pick out the grain from the chaff. ||1|| As God keeps us, so we live, O brother? God's glory cannot be described. ||1||Pause|| Sometimes, people parade the horses. Sometimes, they do not even have shoes on their feet. ||2|| Sometimes, people sleep on cozy beds with white sheets. Sometimes, they do not even have straw under them; ||3|| Says Naam Dev; only God's name bestows salvation. One, who meets the guru, is carried across to the other side. ||4||5|| Laughing and playing, I came to Your temple, O Lord. While Naam Dev was worshipping, he was grabbed and driven out. ||1|| I am of a low caste, O Lord; Why was I born into a family of a seamster? ||1||Pause|| I picked up my blanket and went to the back side and sat behind the temple; ||2|| As Naam Dev uttered praises of the Lord; Devotee's temple started to move; ||3||6|| Bhairao, Naam Dev Jee, Second House: God is one. He is realized by guru's grace. As the hungry loves food; as the thirsty wants water; as the ignorant is attached to his family; same way Naam Dev loves God. ||1|| Naam Dev is in love with the Lord. He became detached intuitively. ||1||Pause|| Like the woman who falls in love with another man. As the greedy loves wealth. As the sexually promiscuous man who loves women. Same way; Naam Dev loves God; ||2|| Only that is real love, which the Lord bestows. By guru's grace, duality is eradicated. Such love never breaks. Through it, the mortal merges with God. Naam Dev has focused his mind to the true name. ||3|| Like the love between the child and mother; so is my mind imbued with God? Prays Naam Dev; I am in love with God. The Lord of the universe abides in my mind. ||4||1||7|| The blind ignorant abandons his wife. Page 1165 He has an affair with another woman. As the parrot is pleased seeing the simbal tree. But in the end, he dies, stuck to it. ||1|| The home of the sinner is on fire. It keeps burning, the fire cannot be extinguished. ||1||Pause|| He does not go to see where the Lord is worshipped. He abandons Lord's path, and takes the wrong path. He forgets the reality and keeps coming and going. He abandons nectar, and gathers poison and eats. ||2|| He is like the dancer who comes to dance. She wears beautiful clothes, and jewellery. She dances to the beat and captivates the audience. But the noose of the devil of death is around her neck. ||3|| One who has good fortune written on his forehead? He goes to guru's sanctuary. Says Naam Dev, consider this: O saints, this is the way to cross over to the other side. ||4||2||8|| Sanda Marka went and complained to Harnaakhash; Your son does not learn. We are tired of trying to teach him. He recites God and dances. He spoils all other students also. ||1|| He recites God's name. He has enshrined God's recitation in the mind. ||1||Pause|| Your father the king has conquered the world, said his mother the queen. My son Prahlaad does not listen, he is stuck to something else. ||2|| The demon council passed a resolution to kill Prahlaad. Prahlaad was thrown off a mountain, into the water, and into a fire, but the sovereign Lord saved him, by changing the laws of nature. ||3|| Harnaakhash thundered with rage and threatened to kill Prahlaad. Tell me, who can save you? Prahlaad answered. The Lord of the universe, is even in this pillar to which I am tied; ||4|| The Lord, who tore Harnaakhash apart with His nails proclaimed Himself the Lord of gods and men. Says Naam Dev; I recite God the bestowal of salvation. ||5||3||9|| The king said, listen, Naam Dev: Let me see the actions of your Lord."||1|| The king arrested Naam Dev. And said, "Let me see your beloved Lord."||1||Pause|| Bring this dead cow back to life. Otherwise, I shall cut your head right now; ||2|| Naam Dev answered, "O king, how can this happen? No one can bring the dead back to life by saying. ||3|| I cannot do anything. Whatever the Lord does happens; ||4|| The king was proud. He incited an elephant to attack. ||5|| Naam Dev's mother began to cry. Why don't you abandon your Lord Raam, and worship Allah? ||6|| Naam Dev answered, I am not your son, and you are not my mother. When the trouble arises, then you sing God's praises. ||7|| The elephant attacked him with his trunk. God protects Naam Dev. ||8|| The Qazi and the Mullah bow down and say. These Hindus has destroyed our honour. ||9|| The people pleaded with the king, Hear our prayer, O king. Page 1166 We offer gold equal to Naam Dev's weight. ||10|| The king replied. If I take the gold, then I will go to hell. By forsaking my faith I will suffer in the world. ||11|| With his feet in chains, with his hands pressed together Naam dev sings the praises of the Lord. ||12|| Even if the Ganges and the Jamunaa rivers flow backwards; I will still continue singing the praises of the Lord. ||13|| Seven moments have passed. Still the Lord of the universe did not come. ||14|| Playing on the instrument of the feathers. The Lord of the universe came, riding the eagle guruda. ||15|| He looked after His devotee. The Lord came, riding the eagle guruda. ||16|| The Lord said to him, If you wish, I shall turn the earth sideways. If you wish, I shall turn it upside down. ||17|| If you wish, I shall bring the dead cow back to life. Everyone will see and believe; ||18|| Naam Dev prayed; let us tie the back legs of the cow. He brought the calf to the cow, and milked her. ||19|| When the pitcher was filled with milk; Naam Dev took it and placed it before the king. ||20|| The king went into his palace; His heart was troubled. ||21|| He prays and tells Qazis and Mullahs; Forgive me, please, O Hindu; I am your cow. ||22|| Naam Dev said, Listen, O king: This was my test? ||23|| The purpose of this test is; O king, you should walk on the path of truth and humility."||24|| Naam Dev became famous everywhere. The Hindus got together and went to Naam Dev. ||25|| If the cow had not been revived; Naam dev would fail the test. ||26|| The fame of Naam Dev spread throughout the world. The humble devotees were saved and carried across with him. ||27|| All sorts of troubles and pains troubled the slanderers. There is no difference between Naam Dev and God. ||28||1||10|| Second House: By the grace of guru, one meets the Lord. By the grace of guru, one is carried across to the other side. By the grace of guru, one swims across to heaven. By the grace of guru, one remains dead while yet alive. ||1|| True is the guru. False are all other worship services. ||1||Pause|| By the grace of the guru, the devotee recites God's name. By the grace of the guru, one does not wander in ten directions. By the grace of the guru, the five demons are kept far away. By the grace of the guru, one does not die regretting. ||2|| By the grace of the guru, one speaks the sacred sermon. By the grace of the guru, one speaks the unspoken speech. By the grace of the guru, one's body becomes sacred. By the grace of guru, one recites God's name. ||3|| By the grace of the guru, the devotee realizes the universe. By the grace of the guru, the devotee obtains high status. By the grace of the guru, the devotee obtains honour. By the grace of the guru, the devotee is admired forever. ||4|| By the grace of the guru, one remains detached forever. By the grace of the guru, he gives up slandering others. Page 1167 By the grace of the guru, good or bad is the same. By the grace of the guru, the fate written on the forehead improves. ||5|| By the grace of the guru, the wall of the body does not erode. By guru's grace, the door of the temple moves. By the grace of the guru, one builds his house. By the grace of the guru, the discarded gifts are revived. ||6|| By the grace of the guru, one bathes at sixty-eight shrines. By the grace of the guru, one makes the body a worship offering. By guru's grace, one worships on twelfth day of moon; by guru's grace, all poisons become fruits.

||7|| By guru's grace the doubt is erased. By guru`s grace, one is freed from the devil of death. By guru`s grace, one swims across the terrifying world ocean. By guru`s grace the birth and death end. ||8|| By guru`s grace, one studies eighteen scriptures. By guru`s grace, one makes the offering of eighteen loads of vegetation. Other than the guru, one should not go anywhere else. Naam Dev has entered the sanctuary of the guru. ||9||1||2||11|| Bhairao, the word of Ravi Daas Jee, Second House: God is one. He is realized by guru`s grace. Without seeing, the desire does not arise. Whatever is seen shall pass away. Whoever; from any caste recites God`s name; that is the true Yogi, who is free of desire. ||1|| When someone utters the name of the Lord with love; It is like touching philosopher's stone; his duality is eradicated. ||1||Pause|| He, who eliminates the duality from mind, is a saint. He merges in the universe with no door. Everyone acts according to the inclinations of the mind. Attuned to the Creator, one remains free of fear. ||2|| Plants blossom to produce fruit. When the fruit is produced, the flowers wither away. For the sake of divine wisdom, people act and practice good deeds. When divine wisdom wells up, then fate is eliminated. ||3|| For the sake of butter, the ladies churn milk. They are freed from life and attain salvation. Says Ravi Daas, O supreme renunciate; why do not you recite God in your mind! ||4||1|| Naam Dev: Come O Lord; with beautiful hair; Wearing the robes of a Sufi saint; ||Pause|| You wear sky the crown and the seven underworlds your throne; Your body is covered with skin; this is how you live O Lord; ||1|| Your gown is made of millions of yards of cloth and your waste is very large. The eighteen loads of vegetation is Your food and the entire world is Your plate. ||2|| The body is the mosque, and the mind is the priest, who prays intuitively. O Lord; Lakshmi (wealth) is Your maidservant. ||3|| I lost my cymbals while dancing in Your love; who do I complain to! Naam Dev's Lord, the inner-knower lives everywhere. ||4||1|| Page 1168 Tune Basant, First Master, First House, Chau-Padas, Du-Tukas:

God is one. It is true. He is the Creator. He is carefree. He has no enemy. He is immortal. He does not take birth. He came into existence on His own. He is realized by guru's grace.

Among the months, blessed is this month when the spring arrives. O my mind, blossom and recite God the Lord of the universe forever. ||1|| O ignorant; forget your egotistic thinking. Kill ego and contemplate virtues and find the essence in the virtues. ||1||Pause|| Deed is the tree with green branches. The faith is flower and fruit of wisdom. Realize God and enjoy the shade of leaves that eliminates pride of mind. ||2|| See nature with eyes, listen sermon with ears and say God's name with tongue. Attain the perfect wealth of honour, intuitively focusing to reciting God. ||3|| The months and the seasons come; you keep doing your deeds. O Nanak, the guru-willed who merge with God do not wither away. They remain green forever. ||4||1|| First Master, Basant: The spring has arrived and everything is green. I recite Your name with love. Who else should I worship? At whose feet should I bow? ||1|| I am the slave of Your slaves, O my sovereign Lord; O life of the universe, there is no other way to meet You. ||1||Pause|| You are one, yet You have countless forms. Which one should I worship? In front of which one should I burn incense? Your limits cannot be found. How can anyone find them? I am the slave of Your slaves, O my sovereign Lord; ||2|| The cycles of years and the places of pilgrimage are Yours, O Lord. Your name is true, O transcendent Lord. Your divine wisdom cannot be understood? I recite Your name unknowingly. ||3|| What can poor Nanak say? All people praise one God. Nanak places his head on the feet of such people. I praise every one of Your names. ||4||2| Basant, First Master: The kitchen is golden, and the cooking pots are golden. Silver line marks the cooking square. The water is from the Ganges, and the firewood is sandalwood. The food is rice pudding, cooked in milk. ||1|| O my mind, these things do not obtain salvation. Page 1169 If you are not drenched with the true name. ||1||Pause|| One may have the eighteen Puraanas written in his own hand; He may recite the four Vedas by heart. Takes ritual baths at holy festivals and gives donations. He observes fast, recites one word and performs religious ceremonies day and night. ||2|| He may be a Qazi, a Mullah or an elder, or a Yogi or a wandering hermit wearing saffron robe. He may be a householder, working at his job; without realizing God, they will tie and take him away. ||3|| All beings have their fate written on the forehead. According to their deeds, they are judged. Only the ignorant and the ignorant issue commands. O Nanak, the treasure of praise belongs to God alone. ||4||3|| Basant, Third Master: He removes his clothes and becomes naked. What Yoga does the matted hair perform? If the mind is not pure, you cannot reach the tenth door. The ignorant wanders in life again and again. ||1|| O ignorant mind; recite one God. You will be liberated in a moment. ||1||Pause|| Some recite the scriptures. Some sing the Vedas and read the Puraanas; they practice hypocrisy and do bad deeds. God does not come near them. ||2|| If someone practices self-discipline. Performs worship in a special way. If he is filled with greed, and his mind is engrossed in corruption; how can he realize the formless God? ||3|| What can the created being do? The Lord makes him do. If God blesses, the doubt is erased. If the mortal realizes God's command, he realizes God. ||4|| If someone is filthy inside. If he bathes at sacred shrines all over the world O Nanak, when one meets the guru. Then the bonds of the terrifying world-ocean are broken. ||5||4|| Basant, First Master: The whole world is enticed by the worldly wealth. I do not see any other but You; You are everywhere. You are the master of Yogis, God of gods. Serving guru's feet, the name of the Lord is received. ||1|| O my beautiful, deep and profound beloved Lord. The guru-willed sings Your praise O infinite caretaker of the world; ||1||Pause|| Without devotee's company God's love is not obtained. Without the guru, one's body is dirty with filth. Without God's name, one cannot become pure. Praise the true Lord through guru's teaching. ||2|| O saviour Lord, whoever You save by your grace; You unite him with the guru and he takes care of him. Eliminate poisonous ego and attachment. Reciting God all pains are eliminated. ||3|| Singing God's praises he becomes spiritually wise. Through guru's teaching the jewel God's name is realized. He is lovingly attuned to God's name and the love of duality is erased. O Lord, unite the servant Nanak with the guru; ||4||5|| Basant, First Master: O my friends and companions, listen with intent; My handsome Husband Lord is always with me. He is hidden. He cannot be seen. How can I describe Him? Page 1170 The guru has shown me that my sovereign Lord is in me. ||1|| Joining my friends and companions, I am adorned by God's praises. My husband Lord plays with me; the guru-willed realizes it.

||1||Pause|| The self-willed divorcee does not understand this mystery. The beloved God of all abides in all. The guru-willed searches God inside. The guru has implanted God's name and I recite it. ||2|| Without the guru, devotional love does not well up. Without the guru, one is not blessed with the society of the saints. Without the guru, the blind cry entangled in worldly affairs. The mind of the guru-willed becomes pure through guru's teaching. ||3|| The guru brought my mind under control with ease. Day and night, he savors the Yoga of devotional worship. In saint guru's company, suffering and sickness are erased. Servant Nanak merges with her Husband Lord, in contented Yoga. ||4||6|| Basant, First Master: He created the universe and the beings. The King of kings administers true justice. The sacred lesson is obtained in guru's company. Reciting God's name obtains contentment. ||1|| Say God God; do not forget it; God is infinite, inaccessible and incomprehensible; O guru-willed. God guides to weigh the unweighed. ||1||Pause|| The devotee serves guru's feet to the end. Serving the guru, I have forgotten claiming mine, your etc. The slanderous and greedy people are stone hearted. Those who do not love to serve the guru are the thieves of thieves. ||2|| When the guru is pleased, He blesses with devotional worship of God. When the guru is pleased, the devotee finds God's place. Renounce slandering and wake up in devotional worship of the Lord. Those with pre-ordained destiny look adorable worshipping God. ||3|| The guru unites with the Lord by his grace. The guru loves His followers day and night. They obtain the fruit of God's name, when the guru bestows it. Says Nanak, only a few obtain it. ||4||7|| Basant, Third Master, Ik-Tukas: When it pleases God, then the devotee serves Him. He dies while yet alive and redeems his entire dynasty as well. ||1|| I will not give up Your worship, even if people laugh at me. The true name abides in my heart. ||1||Pause|| As the mortal remains enticed by the worldly attachment; same way the saint keeps saying God God God. ||2|| I am an ignorant fool O Lord; please be kind to me. May I remain in Your sanctuary? ||3|| Says Nanak, worldly affairs are fruitless. By guru's grace, only a few realize the sacred God's name. ||4||8|| First Master, Basant Hindol, Second House: God is one. He is realized by guru's grace. O Brahmin, you worship and believe in your stone-god, and wear a ceremonial

rosary beads. Recite God's name and build a boat! O kind God, be kind to me. ||1|| Page 1171 Why do you water the salty soil? You are wasting your life away! This wall of mud is crumbling. Why bother to patch it with plaster? ||1||Pause|| Let your hands be the buckets, strung on the chain, and yoke the mind as the ox to pull it and draw water from the well. Irrigate your fields with nectar then you belong to God the gardener. ||2|| Let lust and anger be your two shovels, to dig your farm, O brother; More you dig more peace you find; past actions cannot be erased. ||3|| The crane is transformed into a swan, if You so will, O merciful Lord. Prays Nanak, the slave of Your slaves. Be kind O God; ||4||1||9|| Basant, First Master, Hindol: In the Husband's home, the treasure is commonly owned by everyone but in parents home everyone has separate treasure. She is ill mannered and does not know how to care for things; then how can she blame others? ||1|| O my Lord, I am deluded by doubt. I sing the written words but I do not know any other sermon. ||1||Pause|| If she knits and wears those clothes; then she is a real woman. If she maintains the house and does not do bad things; then she is loved by her husband; ||2|| If you are a learned and wise religious scholar, then make a boat of the letters of God's name. Prays Nanak, One Lord shall carry you across, if you merge in true Lord. ||3||2||10|| Basant Hindol, First Master: The boy is a king, his city is vulnerable. He is in love with his enemies. He learns from two mothers and two fathers; O scholar reflect on this. ||1|| O Master the scholar, teach me about this; How can I obtain the Lord of life? ||1||Pause|| There is fire inside the plants which bloom; the ocean is tied into a bundle. The sun and the moon both are in the mind. You did not know this; ||2|| One, who recites God and enjoys one Godmother; He intuitively gathers the wealth of forgiveness. ||3|| He is friends with those who do not listen and do not admit what they eat. O Nanak, the slave of Lord's slaves pray little by little. ||4||3||11|| Basant Hindol First Master The guru the bestowal is the true banker; he unites me with God and eliminates my hunger. He guides to worship God and sings God's praises forever. ||1|| O my mind, do not forget; recite God. Without the guru, no one is liberated in the universe. The guru-willed obtains God's name. ||1||Pause|| Without worship, the guru is not found. God is not worshipped without luck. Devotee's company is not found without luck; those with pre-ordained destiny recite God's name. ||2|| He creates and watches by hiding. He is revealed to the guru-willed saints. Those who say God God are dyed with God's sacred name with love. ||3|| Page 1172 The guru-willed are honoured in God's court and are known in the world. Touching philosopher's stone, they become philosopher's stone; they become the same in God's the guru's company. ||4||4||12|| Basant, Third Master, First House, Du-Tukas: God is one. He is realized by guru's grace. Throughout the months and the seasons, there is always spring; it rejuvenates all beings. What can I say? I am just a worm. No one has found Your beginning or end, O Lord. ||1|| Those who serve You O Lord; they find eternal peace O God; ||1||Pause|| They serve the guru if it is in their fate. By guru's grace, he remains dead while yet alive. Night and day, he recites God's name. In this way, he crosses over the treacherous world-ocean. ||2|| The Creator created both poison and nectar. He attached both fruits to the worldly tree. The Creator is the doer, the cause of all. He feeds all as He pleases. ||3|| O Nanak, when He casts His glance of grace. He bestows the sacred name. Thus, He eliminates the desire for sin. The Lord carries out His will. ||4||1|| Basant, Third Master: Those who are imbued with God's name are content. O God kind to the poor; be kind to me. Without Him, I have no one. As it pleases Him, He keeps me. ||1|| The guru, the Lord, is pleasing to my mind. I cannot survive, without seeing him. I meet Him when the guru unites me. ||1||Pause|| The greedy mind is enticed to greed. Forgetting the Lord, he regrets in the end. The separated are reunited, when imbued with guru's service. He bestows God's name to the fortunate. ||2|| This body is made of air and water. The body is afflicted with illness of ego and gives terrible pain. The guru-willed takes the medicine of singing God's praises. The guru cures the sickness by his grace. ||3|| The four evil rivers of fire flow through the body. It is burning in greed and pride. The guru saved and liberated the fortunate. Servant Nanak enshrines the sacred God in the mind. ||4||2|| Basant, Third Master: One who serves the Lord is the Godly person. He dwells in intuitive peace, and never suffers in sorrow. The self-willed died not enshrining God in the mind. They die and take birth again and again.

||1|| Those who have God in the mind, live forever. They contemplate the truth and merge in truth. ||1||Pause|| Those who do not serve the Lord are far from the Lord. They wander in foreign lands, with dust thrown on their face. The Lord enjoins His humble servants to serve Him. They live in peace forever, and have no greed. ||2|| Page 1173 By God's grace the ego eliminates. The mortal is honoured in the court of the true Lord. He sees the dear Lord always close; He realizes God through guru's teaching. ||3|| The Lord cherishes all beings. By guru's grace, recite Him forever. You shall go to your true home in Lord's court with honour. O Nanak, he obtains honour through God's name. ||4||3|| Basant, Third Master: One who worships God in his mind? Sees only one God, and no other. People in duality suffer terrible pain. The guru has revealed one God to me. ||1|| My God is in bloom, and there is spring forever. This mind blossoms, singing the praises of the Lord of the universe; ||1||Pause|| Ask the guru, and think; Then, you shall fall in love with God. Abandon your ego and be His servant lovingly. Then God the life of the world shall come to dwell in your mind. ||2|| Worship Him and see Him always close; My God pervades all. If one knows the secret of this worship. My God is the Lord of the soul. ||3|| The guru unites us with God. He links our mind to the Lord, the life of the world. Thus, our minds and bodies are rejuvenated with ease. O Nanak, he attunes to God's name with love. ||4||4|| Basant, Third Master: The Lord the love of His devotees dwells in their minds. By guru's grace intuitively he worships God and eliminates ego. Thus, he meets the true Lord. ||1|| His devotees look adorable in God's court. They fall in love with God through guru's love. ||1||Pause|| He, who worships God, becomes pure. He eliminates ego through guru's teaching. Dear God comes to dwell in the mind; the mortal merges in peace and contentment. ||2|| Those who are imbued with truth are forever in bloom. Their minds and bodies are rejuvenated by singing praises of the Lord of the universe. Without Lord's name, the world is dry. It burns in the fire of greed over and over. He does what pleases God. Obeying God's will, he finds peace. He serves His God with ease. O Nanak, God's name dwells in his mind. ||4||5|| Basant, Third Master: He burns the enticement of worldly wealth through guru's teaching. The mind and body are rejuvenated by the love of

the guru. The tree bears fruit at God's door; In love with God's name through true sermon, ||1|| This mind is rejuvenated, with ease; And bears the fruit of truth by guru's grace; ||1||Pause|| He is close, he is far. He sees God close through guru's teaching. The plants have blossomed and give dense shade. The guru-willed blossoms intuitively; ||2|| Night and day, he sings God's praises. The guru drives out the stink of falsehood and impurity from inside. Page 1174 Seeing God's amazing play he is amazed. The guru-willed realize God reciting God's name. ||3|| The Creator enjoys all delights. Whatever He does surely happens. The great bestowal has no greed. O Nanak, he is realized by practicing gurus teaching. ||4||6|| Basant, Third Master: By perfect destiny, one acts in truth. He remembers one God and does not take birth again. Fruitful is his coming in the world. He becomes content through God's true name. ||1|| O guru-willed, do deeds with love. Recite God's name and ego will depart. ||1||Pause|| True is the sermon of that humble being. It spreads in the world through guru's teaching. His glory is realized in all four ages. Imbued with God's name, the devotee is enlightened. ||2|| Some are attuned to guru's teaching with love. They become true through true God's love. They recite the true God and see Him close. They become dust of the lotus feet of the humble saints. ||3|| There is only one Creator, none else. He is realized through guru's teaching. Whoever serves the true Lord finds the taste. O Nanak, he is intuitively absorbs in God's name. ||4||7|| Basant, Third Master: He worships God and sees Him close. He becomes the dust of the lotus feet of the humble saints. Those who are attuned to God with love; they realize God through perfect guru's teaching. ||1|| There are only a few servants of servants. He obtains the supreme status. ||pause|| So serve one Lord, no other. Serving Him, eternal peace is obtained. He does not die; He does not come and go. Why should I serve any other than Him, O my mother? ||2|| True are those humble beings who realize true God. Conquering their ego, they merge intuitively in God's name. The guru-willed obtain God's name. Their mind and thinking become pure. ||3|| Know the Lord, who gave you spiritual wisdom; and realize one God, through guru's teaching. Enjoying God's love, one becomes pure. O Nanak those imbued with God's name become truthful. ||4||8|| Basant, Third

Master: Those imbued with God's name save their dynasty reciting God's name with love through true sermon; Why have the wandering self-willed come in the world? Forgetting God's name they waste their life away. ||1|| One, who dies while yet alive, obtains salvation after death. He enshrines God in the mind through guru's teaching. ||1||Pause|| The body of the guru-willed becomes sacred enjoying truth. His mind becomes pure and treasure of virtues. He does not take birth or dies. Nor does he come or go. By guru's grace, he merges in the true Lord. ||2|| Serving the true Lord, one realizes the truth. Through guru's teaching he goes to God's court with honour. Page 1175 In the court of the true Lord, he obtains true glory. He attains his destiny. ||3|| True God does not forget. All others forget and lose honour deluded in duality. So serve the true Lord, through true sermon. O Nanak, they merge in truth through God's name. ||4||9|| Basant, Third Master: Without good fortune, all are lost in doubt. They suffer in pain in love of worldly wealth. The blind, self-willed find no place of rest. The worms of filth rot in filth. ||1|| He, who obeys God's command, is accepted by God. Through guru's teaching he makes God's name his resolve. ||1||Pause|| Those who have such pre-ordained destiny are imbued with God. The name of the Lord is forever pleasing to their minds. Through guru's sermon, one obtains eternal peace. And the souls merge. ||2|| God's name saves the world. By guru's grace, through the love of God's name; without God's name no one obtains liberation. Through the perfect guru, one obtains God's name. ||3|| Whoever He guides, understands it. Serving the guru, he recites God's name. God accepts those who realize God. O Nanak, imbued with God's name they go to God's court with honour. ||4||10|| Basant, Third Master: By his grace, God unites us with the guru. The Lord comes to abide in the mind. His intellect becomes stable, and his mind becomes content. He sings the praises of the Lord, the ocean of virtues. ||1|| Those who forget God's name die eating poison. Their lives are wasted uselessly, they continue coming and going. ||1||Pause|| They make many disguises, but their minds are not at peace. They are proud and they lose their honour. Those who obtain guru's teaching are fortunate. The one they thought was outside found Him in the mind. ||2|| The inaccessible and infinite God abides in the mind. The devotees find Him contemplating guru's teaching. They found the treasure of God's name in their home; they are dyed with God's love and merge with God. ||3|| God does everything; no one can do anything by himself. When it pleases God, he unites us with Him. All are near Him; no one is far. O Nanak, God is realized reciting His name. ||4||11|| Basant, Third Master: Recite God through guru's teaching intuitively. You will be fulfilled lovingly reciting God's name. The sins of millions of lifes shall be burnt away. Reciting God's name one dies in the mind while yet alive. ||1|| God knows His blessing. This mind blossoms through guru's teaching and recites the virtuous God. ||1||Pause|| Wearing saffron clothes does not obtain salvation if he is doubtful. Even with self-discipline and happiness, he does not realize God. God's name obtains through guru's teaching. The fortunate realizes God. ||2|| In today's age God's name is an honour. Page 1176 Through the perfect guru, it is obtained. Those imbued with God's name obtain everlasting peace. But without God's name, he burns in ego. ||3|| The fortunate contemplates God's name. Through Lord's name, all sorrows are eradicated. He abides in the mind and outside as well. O Nanak, the Creator knows all. ||4||12|| Basant, Third Master, Ik-Tukas: You created all worldly beings. If you bless me, then I will recite Your name forever. ||1|| I recite and contemplate God's virtues O mother. Reciting His name I fall at Lord's feet. ||1||Pause|| By guru's grace, God's name becomes enjoyable. Why waste your life in hatred and conflict? ||2|| When the guru granted His grace, my ego was eradicated. I became peaceful by obtaining God's name. ||3|| To practice guru's teaching is the highest deed. Nanak recites the true name. ||4||1||13|| Basant, Third Master: The spring has arrived and all vegetation has bloomed. This mind blossoms in guru's company. ||1|| O ignorant mind, recite the true Lord. Only then, you will find peace, O my mind. ||1||Pause|| This mind blossoms and I am happy. I obtained the sacred fruit of the name of the Lord of the universe. ||2|| Everyone says, there is one God; Obeying His command, one realizes Him. ||3|| Says Nanak, no one can describe God by speaking with ego. All saying and seeing happens by God's grace. ||4||2||14|| Basant, Third Master: You created all ages, O Lord. Surrendering to the guru the intellect becomes divine; ||1|| God unites us with Him by His will. One merges in true Lord through guru's teaching. ||1||Pause|| When the mind blossoms the whole world blossoms; Blossoming and flowering through God's name obtains peace. ||2|| Contemplating guru's teaching is always a spring season. Enshrining God's name in the mind; ||3|| When the mind blossoms, the body and mind are rejuvenated; O Nanak, this body is the tree which bears the fruit of God's name. ||4||3||15|| Basant, Third Master: Those who sing God's praises enjoy the spring season. God inspires us to worship Him through good luck. ||1|| This mind is not touched by spring. This mind is burnt by duality and double-mindedness. ||1||Pause|| This mind does deeds entangled in worldly affairs. Robbed by worldly wealth, he cries in pain forever. ||2|| This mind is freed by meeting the guru. Then, he is not pushed around by the devil of death. ||3|| This mind is freed, when the guru frees it. O Nanak, guru's teaching eliminates the love of worldly wealth. ||4||4||16|| Basant, Third Master: Spring has arrived and the whole forest is flowering. These beings bloom by attuning the mind to God. ||1|| Page 1177 In this way, this mind is rejuvenated. He recites God's name day and night and washes away the filth of the guru-willed. ||1||Pause|| The guru speaks the sermon through His teaching. This world blossoms by guru's grace. ||2|| They bear flower and fruit, when God so wills. He, who attaches to the roots, meets the guru. ||3|| God is the spring and the world is His garden. O Nanak, God's unique worship is obtained with luck. ||4||5||17|| Basant Hindol, Third Master, Second House: God is one. He is realized by guru's grace. O brother, I admire guru's sermon and teaching O brother. I praise my guru forever, O brother. I focus my mind to guru's feet. ||1|| O my mind; focus on God's name. Your mind and body will bloom and bear the fruit of God's name. ||1||Pause|| Those protected by guru drink the nectar of God's name O brother. The pain of ego is eradicated O brother; and peace welled up in the mind. ||2|| Those, whom He blesses O brother; unite with Him through guru's teaching. Join devotee's company O brother and obtain the dust of their feet. ||3|| He does and causes all to do O brother; He makes everything green. O Nanak, peace fills their minds and bodies forever and unites with God O brother. ||4||1||18||12||18||30|| Tune Basant, Fourth Master,

First House, Ik-Tuka: God is one. He is realized by guru's grace. Just as the light of the sunrays spread out; same way, God is merged in everybody completely. ||1|| One God pervades all places. He is realized through guru's teaching O my mother; ||1||Pause|| One God abides in every heart. God is realized meeting the guru. ||2|| One Lord is pervading everywhere. The greedy, faithless thinks that God is far away; ||3|| One and Only one Lord pervades the world. O Nanak, whatever God does happens. ||4||1|| Basant, Fourth Master: Day and night, the two calls are sent out. O my mind, recite God; He will save you in the end. ||1|| O my mind, recite God forever. I realized God the destroyer of laziness and pain by singing His praises through guru's teaching. ||1||Pause|| The self-willed are deluded by doubt forever. Page 1178 The death destroyed the demons, and they went to the city of death; ||2|| The guru-willed are lovingly attuned to God. Their pains of both birth and death are taken away. ||3|| God showers His kindness on His humble devotees. Nanak has united with honourable God. ||4||2|| Basant Hindol, Fourth Master, Second House: God is one. He is realized by guru's grace. God's name is a jewel, hidden in a chamber of the body-fortress. Meeting the guru He is found and the soul merges with supreme soul. ||1|| O Lord, lead me to meet the devotees. Seeing them all sins go away and obtains the supreme status. ||1||Pause|| The five thieves got together and plundered the body-village and stole the wealth of God's name. I arrested them through guru's teaching and recovered the wealth. ||2|| They got tired of practicing hypocrisy and doubt, but they are filled with greed of worldly wealth. The devotees realized the Lord of humans and darkness of ignorance eliminated. ||3|| The Lord of earth, and the universe, united me with His devotees by His grace. O Nanak, singing God's praises in the mind obtains peace. ||4||1||3|| Basant, Fourth Master, Hindol: You are the great Supreme Being, the vast and inaccessible Lord of the world; I am an insect, a worm created by You. O kind Lord be kind to me. I long to touch guru's feet. ||1|| O Lord of the universe, be kind and unite me with devotee's company. I was filled with filth of sins for many lifes. Please unite me with devotee's company and purify me. ||1||Pause|| Your humble servant, whether high or low class; becomes pure by reciting God. God made him the highest of all in the universe and bestowed honour. ||2|| Anyone, from high or low class, who recites God, becomes the perfect person. Those, who enshrine God in the mind, are admirable and perfect. ||3|| I am very low a big pile of mud, O God, be kind and unite me with You. Servant Nanak met the honourable guru; he made me sacred from sinner. ||||4||2||4|| Basant Hindol, Fourth Master: My mind cannot survive, even for a moment, without God; I am imbued with God's name. As the baby enjoys mother's breast, he sucks her breasts with joy. ||1|| O Lord of the universe, my mind and body are pierced by the name of God. Fortunately I found God right in the body; ||1||Pause|| Page 1179 As many times I breathe, I recite God with every breath. As the lotus loves water, it dries up without it. ||2|| The devotee recites God's name with love through guru's teaching. Bathing in God's sacred name the filth of many lifes is washed away. ||3|| Please, do not count my deeds; preserve the honour of Your own. If it pleases God, then the servant Nanak will fall at His feet. ||4||3||5|| Basant Hindol, Fourth Master: My mind wanders in doubt every moment. It does not stay at home at all. When the guru hits with the medicine of his teaching over the head, then it stays at home. ||1|| O dear Lord of the universe; unite me with devotee's company that I recite God. The sickness of ego is cured and I became peaceful and content. ||1||Pause|| This house is loaded with countless gems, jewels, rubies and emeralds, but the wandering mind cannot find them. As the diver finds things lost in the well, likewise the guru finds the lost jewels. ||2|| Those who do not find such a devotee guru, live a worthless life. They sell their treasure of priceless life for a shell. ||3|| O Lord, be kind and unite me with the guru. Servant Nanak sings God's praises in devotee's company and attains salvation. ||4||4||6|| Basant Hindol, Fourth Master: The self-willed are left alone and suffer the pain of coming and going. He does not recite God's name at all; the devil of death will catch and take him away. ||1|| O dear Lord of the universe; please eliminate my ego and false attachment. God loves devotee's company; enjoy God's love joining devotee's company. ||1||Pause|| Please be kind and unite me with Your devotees. I seek their refuge. O kind God, take me the sinking stone out of water and eliminate my pain. ||2|| I enshrine Your praise in my mind, so that I am enlightened.

I have fallen in love with God's name; I praise God. ||3|| O Lord, bestow me with Your name and fulfill my deeds. The guru gave me the sermon of God's name and Nanak's mind and body are happy. ||4||5||7||12||18||7||37|| Page 1180 Basant, Fifth Master, First House, Du-Tuka: God is one. He is realized by guru's grace. I serve the guru and humbly bow to Him. Today is a day of celebration for me. Today I am very happy. Surrendering to the Lord of the universe dispels my anxiety. ||1|| Today, it is springtime in my house. I sing Your praises, O infinite Lord. ||1||Pause|| Today, I am celebrating the festival of Holi. Joining God's companions, I have begun to play. I celebrate the festival of Holi by serving the saints. I am imbued with deep crimson colour of God's love. ||2|| My mind and body have blossomed beautifully. They do not dry up in sunshine or shade; They flourish in all seasons. It is always springtime, when I meet the guru. ||3|| The wish-fulfilling Elysian tree has grown. It bears flowers and fruits of jewels of all sorts. I am satisfied and fulfilled, singing the praises of the Lord. Servant Nanak says God God God. ||4||1|| Basant, Fifth Master: The shopkeeper deals in merchandise for profit. The gambler's mind is focused on gambling. The addict lives by taking drug. Same way God's devotee lives by reciting God. ||1|| Everyone plays his game. He is attached to whatever God attaches him to. ||1||Pause|| When the clouds thunder, the peacocks dance. Seeing the moon, the Greek partridge enjoys. The mother enjoys seeing the child. Same way God's devotee lives by reciting God the Lord of the universe. ||2|| The tiger always wants to eat meat. The warriors are happy going to the battle. The miser loves wealth. God's name is the resolve of God's devotees. ||3|| All love is contained in the love of the Lord. All comforts are obtained reciting God's name. He alone receives this treasure O Nanak, whom the guru gives His gift. ||4||2|| Basant, Fifth Master: He enjoys the spring season, to whom God is kind. He experiences the springtime, to whom the guru is kind. He is happy, who does only one work. He who has God's name in the mind; it is always spring for him. ||1|| This spring comes to those homes; those who sing God's praises with love. ||1||Pause|| O my mind, bloom with God's love. Follow God's devotee's and practice divine wisdom. He, who enjoys devotee's company, is an abstinent. He, who is dyed by guru's love, meditates forever. ||2|| He, who loves God, becomes carefree. He is peaceful, whose doubts are dispelled. He is a hermit, whose heart is steady and stable. He is immortal, who has found the true place. ||3|| He seeks God, and loves one God. He loves to visualize God with love. He intuitively enjoys the love of the Lord. Slave Nanak admires that humble being. ||4||3|| Page 1181 Basant, Fifth Master: You gave us soul, life and body. I am an ignorant, but You have made me beautiful with Your light in me. We are all beggars, O God; You are kind to us. Reciting Your name I am content. ||1|| O my beloved, you do everything. I receive everything from you in abundance. ||1||Pause|| Reciting God's name the mortal attains salvation. Reciting God's name, the mortal obtains peace and contentment. Reciting God's name the mortal obtains honour and glory. Reciting God's name, no obstruction comes his way. ||2|| The reason, you obtained this hard to obtain body! Tell me that reason O my God; this peace is found in devotee's company. May I always recite Your name in the mind O God; ||3|| Other than You, there is no one at all. Everything is Your play; it all merges again in You. As it pleases You, keep me O Lord. O Nanak, peace is obtained by meeting the perfect guru. ||4||4|| Basant, Fifth Master: My beloved God, my King is with me. Realizing Him, I live O my mother. Reciting Him, there is no pain or suffering. Please, be kind and unite me with him. ||1|| My beloved is the support of my life and mind. This soul, the life and wealth are all Yours, O Lord. ||1||Pause|| He is sought by angels, mortals and gods. The sages, the humble, and the elders do not understand His mystery. His divine wisdom cannot be described. God pervades all beings. ||2|| His devotees are happy. His devotees cannot be destroyed. His devotees are not afraid. His devotees are victorious forever. ||3|| What praises of Yours can I say? God, the giver of peace, is pervading and permeating everywhere. Nanak begs for one gift. Be kind and bless me with Your name. ||4||5|| Basant, Fifth Master: As the plant turns green by watering; Same way the ego goes away in devotee's company. Just as the servant believes in his ruler; same way the guru the divine teacher bestows salvation. ||1|| You are the bestowal, O kind Lord. I humbly bow to You forever. ||1||Pause|| Whoever enjoys devotee's company? He is dyed with God's love. He is liberated from bonds. His devotees worship Him in yoga's way. ||2|| My eyes are content, visualizing Him. My tongue sings infinite praises of God. My thirst is quenched, by guru's grace. My mind is satisfied, with the sublime taste of Lord's essence. ||3|| Your servant is committed to the service of Your feet; O primal infinite divine Lord; Your name is the saving grace of all. Nanak has received this treasure. ||4||6|| Basant, Fifth Master: You the great giver keep giving. You live in my soul and body. You have given me all sorts of foods to eat. I am unworthy; I have no virtue. ||1|| I do not understand anything of Your reality. Page 1182 Save me, O my kind God. ||1||Pause|| I have not practiced meditation, austerities or good actions. I do not know the way to meet You. I have one hope in my mind. To obtain salvation with the support of your name. ||2|| You are all powerful O God. The fish cannot find the limits of water. You are inaccessible and unfathomable, the highest of high. I am small, You are great. ||3|| Those who recite You are well known. Those who realize You are rich. Those who serve You are peaceful. Nanak seeks the sanctuary of the saints. ||4||7|| Basant, Fifth Master: Serve the one who created You. Worship the one who gave you life. Become His servant, and you shall never be punished. Become His trustee and you shall never suffer pain. ||1|| Those who are that lucky; Attain salvation. ||1||Pause|| Life is wasted uselessly in the service of duality. No work is completed. It is painful to serve the mortals. Serving God's devotee brings contentment. ||2|| If you long for eternal peace, O brother; Then join devotee's company; guru said this. Only God's name is recited there. Salvation is obtained in devotee's company. ||3|| Among all, divine wisdom is the essence. Focusing on God's name is the best focus. Best tune to sing God's praises is; O Nanak, sing God's praises in devotee's company. ||4||8|| Basant, Fifth Master: Saying His name, one's mouth becomes pure. Reciting Him the thinking becomes pure. Worshipping Him the devil of death does not bother; Serving Him, everything is obtained. ||1|| Say God God God. Abandon all desires of your mind. ||1||Pause|| He keeps the sky and the earth in its place. His light illuminates each and every heart. Reciting His name the sinners become sacred. They will not cry in the end. ||2|| Among all religions, this is the ultimate religion. Among all rituals and codes of conduct, this is above all. The angels, mortals and gods long for

Him. Serve the congregation of devotees; ||3|| One whom the primal Lord blesses with His gift; Obtains the treasure of the Lord; His state of divine wisdom cannot be described. Servant Nanak says God God God. ||4||9|| Basant, Fifth Master: My mind and body are thirsty. The kind guru has fulfilled my hopes. In devotee's company my sins are erased. I recite God's name with love. ||1|| By guru's grace, this spring has arrived. I have enshrined God's lotus feet in my mind and I listen to God's praises forever. ||1||Pause|| Page 1183 All-powerful Lord is the doer, the cause of all causes. I am an orphan – I seek Your sanctuary O God. All beings and creatures take Your support. Be kind and save me O God. ||2|| God takes us across the world ocean and destroys the suffering. The angels, beings and sages serve Him. The earth and the sky are in His power. All beings eat what You give. ||3|| The inner-knower God is kind. He blesses His devotees with His grace. Please be kind and bless me with this gift; That Nanak may live by reciting Your name. ||4||10|| Basant, Fifth Master: Dyed with God's love all sins are eradicated. Reciting God, all worries have departed. Reciting the name of God of the universe, all ignorance is dispelled. Reciting God, the cycle of birth and death ends. ||1|| Love of God is springtime for me. Company of saints is always enjoyable. ||1||Pause|| The saints have taught me. Blessed is that country where the devotees of the Lord of the universe live; Without God's worship the gardens become deserted. See God in everyone through guru's teaching. ||2|| Sing God's praises and enjoy the taste. O mortal, the sins you commit remain with you forever. See God the Creator close by. Here and hereafter, God shall resolve your affairs. ||3|| I focus my mind to Lord's lotus feet. God has blessed me with this gift by His grace. I yearn for the dust of the feet of Your saints. O Nanak, recite God, he is always with you. ||4||11|| Basant, Fifth Master: True transcendent Lord is ever new. By guru's grace, I enjoy Him daily. God is my protector, my mother and father. Reciting His name there is no worry. ||1|| I recite God whole-heartedly with love. I seek guru's refuge and enshrine God in my mind. ||1||Pause|| God protects His humble servants. The demons and enemies have grown weary of wandering in doubt. Without the guru, there is no place to go. They wander all over and suffer pain. ||2|| The record of their past actions cannot be erased.

They harvest what they sow; The Lord is the protector of His humble servants. No one can rival the humble servant of the Lord. ||3|| By His grace, God protects His slave. God's glory is perfect and unbroken. Sing the praises of the Lord of the universe with your tongue forever. Nanak lives by reciting the feet of the Lord. ||4||12|| Basant, Fifth Master: Serving guru's feet my suffering departed. The supreme Lord is kind to me. All my desires and tasks are fulfilled. Nanak lives by reciting God's name. ||1|| When I miss God, that season is adorable. The self-willed are seen crying without the guru and they keep coming and going. ||1||Pause|| Page 1184 Those who have Godly wealth are rich. Through guru's teaching the lust and anger are destroyed. Their fear is dispelled, and they become fearless. Meeting with the guru, Nanak recites God the master. ||2|| God dwells in the company of devotees. Reciting God my desires are fulfilled. God pervades water land and in between. Meeting with the guru, Nanak says God God God. ||3|| The eight mystic powers and nine treasures are obtained by the fortunate, whom God blesses with His name. Your slaves, O God, live by reciting Your name. O Nanak, the heart-lotus blossoms meeting the guru. ||4||13|| Basant, Fifth Master, First House, Ik-Tukay: God is one. He is realized by guru's grace. Reciting God, my all desires are fulfilled. I found God after a long separation. ||1|| Recite God worthy of worship. Reciting Him obtains peace and contentment. ||1||Pause|| By His grace, He blessed me with contentment. God took care of His slave. ||2|| My bed has been beautified by His love. God, the giver of peace, has come to meet me. ||3|| He does not consider my merits and demerits. Nanak worships the feet of God. ||4||1||14|| Basant, Fifth Master: singing the glories of God erases the sins; Peace and joy have welled up forever. ||1|| My mind has blossomed in God's refuge. He united me with devotees and I am dyed by God's love. ||1||Pause|| The Lord of the world has revealed Him to me by His grace. The Lord, merciful to the meek, has attached me to Him and saved me. ||2|| This mind has become the dust of devotees; I see God close by all the time. ||3|| Lust, anger and desire have vanished. O Nanak, God has become kind to me. ||4||2||15|| Basant, Fifth Master: God has cured my disease. He creates and protects His children. ||1|| The spring has arrived and peace and contentment prevail in my home. I have sought guru's refuge and attained salvation reciting God through the lesson. ||1||Pause|| God has dispelled my sorrow and suffering. I worship my guru forever. ||2|| That humble being who recites Your name; Singing Your praises obtains all rewards and the devotee becomes stable. ||3|| O Nanak, the way of the devotees is good. They recite God the bestowal of peace all the time with love. ||4||3||16| Basant, Fifth Master: By His command He makes us happy. He shows mercy to His servant. ||1|| The perfect guru makes everything perfect. He implants God's sacred name in the mind. ||1||Pause|| He does not consider the deeds or faith. Page 1185 Taking me by the arm, He saved me and carried me across the terrifying world-ocean. ||2|| God has eliminated my filth and made me pure. I have sought the sanctuary of the perfect guru. ||3|| He does, and causes everything to be done. By His grace, O Nanak, He saves us. ||4||4||17|| Basant, Fifth Master: God is one. He is realized by guru's grace. I am blooming visualizing Him. Renounce and abandon your ego. Hold on to His lotus feet. Meet with God, O fortunate. O my mind; miss God; ||Pause|| The tender trees give tender smell. While others remain hard like dry wood; The spring season has arrived. May it blossom forever; ||1|| Now, today's dark age has arrived. Seed one name; it is not the season to plant other seeds. Do not wander lost in doubt. Those with pre-ordained destiny realize God through the guru. O my mind, it is the season to plant God's name. Nanak praises God saying God God God. ||2||18|| Basant, Fifth Master, Second House, Hindol: God is one. He is realized by guru's grace. O brothers, get together and eliminate duality enshrining God's love in the mind. O guru-willed, spread the prayer mat and put your mind to God. ||1|| O brother, throw the dice this way; O guru-willed, recite God's name day and night; you will not suffer in the end. ||1||Pause|| Make your deeds and faith the chess game and make truth the pawns. Conquer lust, anger, greed and worldly attachment through God's such love. ||2|| Recite God when you get up in the morning and continue till you sleep. My guru will help you to play the difficult moves and you go home in peace and content. ||3|| God plays and watches. He created the play. O servant Nanak, the guru-willed who plays this game wins and goes home. ||4||1||19||

Basant, Fifth Master, Hindol: You know Your creative power, O Lord; no one else knows it. Whoever You bless with Your grace, realizes You. ||1|| I praise Your devotees. Your place is ever beautiful O God; Your love is infinite. ||1||Pause|| Your worship comes from You; there is no other O Creator. He, who pleases You; You dye him by Your love; he is Your devotee. ||2|| Page 1186 You are the great giver. There is no other like You. You are my all-powerful master; I do not know how to worship You. ||3|| You are hidden O my beloved; Your will is amazing. Says Nanak; I have fallen at Your door. Please protect the ignorant fools; ||4||2||20|| Basant Hindol, Fifth Master: He does not know the origin and does not understand himself. The egotistic is engrossed in doubt. ||1|| My father the supreme Lord is rich. Please save the virtueless. ||1||Pause|| Creation and destruction come from God; this is the belief of God's devotees. ||2|| Those, imbued with God's name are judged peaceful in today's age. ||3|| O Nanak, I see no other way to obtain salvation but guru's teaching. ||4||3||21|| God is one. He is realized by guru's grace. Tune Basant Hindol, Ninth Master: O devotees know that this body is temporary. God, who lives in it, recognize Him; He is real. ||1||Pause|| The worldly wealth is a dream; why are you so proud of it? None of it shall go with you; why do you cling to it? ||1|| Give up praise and slander and sing God's praises in your mind. O servant Nanak, one primal Lord completely abides in all. ||2||1|| Basant Hindol Ninth Master The sinner is filled with lust in the mind. He cannot control his fickle mind. ||1||Pause|| The Yogis, wandering ascetics and renunciates; All are caught in this net. ||1|| Those who recite God's name; They cross over the terrifying world-ocean. ||2|| Servant Nanak seeks the sanctuary of God. Please bless me with Your name that I sing Your praises. ||3||2|| Basant, Ninth Master: O mother, I have gathered the wealth of Lord's name. My mind has stopped wandering, and now, it has come to rest. ||1||Pause|| Attachment to worldly wealth has disappeared and divine wisdom welled up. Greed and attachment cannot touch me; I worship God with love. ||1|| The worry of many lifes is erased when I obtained the jewel of God's name. The greed of my mind disappeared and merged in eternal peace. ||2|| Whoever the kind God is kind; sings praises of the Lord of the universe. Says Nanak, only a few guru-willed obtain this kind of wealth. ||3||3|| Basant, Ninth Master: O my mind, why did you forget God's name? When the body perishes, you will have to deal with the devil of death; ||1||Pause|| This world is a mountain of smoke. Page 1187 What makes you think that it is real? ||1|| Wealth, spouse, property and household; Understand that nothing goes with you; ||2|| Only God's worship goes with you. Says Nanak, recite God with love. ||3||4|| Basant, Ninth Master: Why are you lost in false greed? Nothing has been lost yet. Still time to wake up; ||1||Pause|| Know that this world is like a dream. In an instant, it shall perish; know that it is true; ||1|| The Lord lives with you forever. Night and day, recite Him O friend; ||2|| It helps you in the end. Says Nanak, sing His praises. ||3||5|| Basant, First Master, Ashtapadees, First House, Du-Tukas: God is one. He is realized by guru's grace. The world is like a crow; it does not remember God's name. See that you will fall on the ground forgetting God's name; The mind wavers doing bad deeds. False love with the world will break. ||1|| The burden of lust, anger and corruption is unbearable. Without God's name, how will you be good and virtuous? ||1||Pause|| The world is like a house of sand in a whirlwind. It is like a bubble formed by drops of rain. It forms in a small drop, when it falls on the ground and vanishes. The whole universe is the servant of God's name. ||2|| My guru does everything for me. I worship God and touch His feet. Imbued with Your name, I long for You. Those who do not recite God's name run away like thieves. ||3|| The mortal loses his honour, gathering sins. Those attuned to God's name go home with honour. whatever happens; happens by God's grace. He who is fearful of carefree God O my mother; ||4|| The woman desires beauty and pleasure. But betel leaves, garlands of flowers and sweet tastes lead only to disease. The more she plays and enjoys, the more she suffers. Whatever she wishes, happens seeking God's refuge. ||5|| She wears beautiful clothes with all sorts of decorations. But the flowers turn to dust, and her beauty becomes useless. Hope and desire are sitting tied at the door. Without God's name, one's home is deserted. ||6|| O princess my daughter, go away from here; Recite God truthfully, and enlighten yourself. Serve your beloved Lord, and lean on the support of His love. Eliminate the thirst of sins through guru's teaching. ||7|| My beloved has enticed my mind; I realize you through gurus teaching. Nanak stands lovingly at God's door. I am content with Your name O kind God; ||8||1|| Basant, First Master: The mind is deluded by doubt; it keeps coming and going in reincarnation. It is greedy and enticed by the evil worldly wealth. It does not remain stable in love of One Lord. Like the fish, the hook pierces its neck. ||1|| The deluded mind understands through the true name. He contemplates guru's teaching and attains peace through love. ||1||Pause|| Page 1188 The mind, deluded by doubt, buzzes around like a bumblebee. It is looking for useless unwanted things all the time. It is like an elephant that gets trapped intoxicated by lust. It is caught due to enticement and gets hit on the head. ||2|| The mind without worship is like an ignorant frog. It is cursed and condemned in God's court without reciting God's name. He has no class or honour, and no one even mentions his name. One without a virtue suffers all kind of pain. ||3|| His mind flickers and cannot stabilize. Without being imbued with God's love he goes nowhere. You know everything and protect everything. You the Creator create, know and look after everything. ||4|| When You make me wander, then who do I complain to? Meeting the guru, I will tell Him of my pain, O my mother. Abandoning my bad deeds I will do good deeds. Imbued with guru's teaching I will merge in true Lord. ||5|| Meeting the guru, the intellect becomes sacred. The mind becomes pure and ego is washed away. He is liberated forever, and no one can put him in bonds. He recites God's name all the time, nothing else. ||6|| The mind comes and goes according to the will of God. One God abides in all, I cannot say anymore. Everything happens by God's command and merges with Him by God's command. Pain and pleasure all come by His Will. ||7|| You are infallible; You never make mistakes. Those whom guru teaches his teaching, think ahead. O my great Lord, You are realized by guru's teaching. O Nanak, my mind is pleased praising the true Lord. ||8||2|| Basant, First Master: A person, who is thirsty for visualizing God; He is absorbed in one Lord, leaving duality behind. His pains are taken away, as he churns and drinks the nectar. The guru-willed realizes and merges with one God. ||1|| Many try and cry to visualize You. Only a few find Him following guru's teaching. ||1||Pause|| The Vedas say that we should recite one God. He is endless; who can find His limits? There is only one Creator, who created the world. Without any pillars, He supports the earth and the sky. ||2|| There only one way of wisdom, contemplation and singing God's sermon. God is unique and He cannot be explained. The true way to find Him is through guru's teaching. It is realized from the perfect guru. ||3|| There is only one faith; only a few follow that. He is realized through guru's teaching in all ages. Imbued with the infinite God with love intuitively; That guru-willed realizes the unexplainable and unlimited God; ||4|| There is one throne and one emperor. The carefree pervades all places. The universe is created by His will. God is unfathomable and incomprehensible. ||5|| God is one. It is true. True justice is administered there. Those who practice truth are honoured and accepted. They are honoured in the court of the true Lord. ||6|| There is only one-way of worship that is the love of the Lord. Without the fear and worship of God, they keep coming and going. He who realizes God through the guru is treated like a guest in God's court. Page 1189 Imbued with God's love the devotee is accepted. ||7|| I see Him here and there; I am content reciting Him. I do not love any other but You, O Master. O Nanak, my ego has been burnt away by guru's teaching. The true guru has visualized God to me. ||8||3|| Basant Hindol First Master The fickle mind cannot attain salvation. It is caught in coming and going without fail. I am suffering and dying, O my Creator. No one cares for me, except my beloved. ||1|| All are better than me, who I say is worse! Worshipping God by reciting His name I am honoured. ||1||Pause|| I am tired of taking all sorts of medicines; How can this disease be cured without my guru? Without worshipping God, there are many sufferings. My Lord and master is the giver of pain and pleasure. ||2|| The disease is serious; how can I find peace? He, who knows the sickness, will eliminate the pain. My mind and body are filled with faults; I searched and found the guru, O my brother! ||3|| Reciting God's name through guru's teaching is the medicine. As You keep me, so I live. The world is sick; where should I look? The Lord is pure; reciting His name makes one pure as well. ||4|| He, who sees and shows the home within the home; the guru lives in that palace and invites the devotee to his palace. When the mind conquers the mind, then he remembers God in the mind. This is what Godly people go through; ||5|| They remain free of any desire for happiness or sorrow; Tasting the nectar, they dwell in God`s name. They recognize themselves, and remain lovingly attuned to God; they win the battle of life through guru`s teaching; the pains go away. ||6|| The guru has given me the true nectar and I drink it; I die in peace and live in peace. Please, make me Your own, if it pleases You. Becoming yours, one merges in You. ||7|| Painful diseases afflict those who enjoy worldly pleasure. It appears that God dwells in all. One remains free of pain and pleasure through guru`s teaching. O Nanak, he, who recites God wholeheartedly. ||8||4|| Basant, First Master, Ik-Tukee: Do not be proud of rubbing ashes on your body. O naked Yogi, this is not the way of Yoga! ||1|| O ignorant; why do you forget God`s name; It will help you in the end; ||1||Pause|| Consult the guru and think it over. Wherever I look, I see the Lord of the world. ||2|| What can I say? I am nothing. All my status and honour are in Your name. ||3|| Why are you proud of property and wealth? You have nothing when you leave. ||4|| Control the five thieves, and stabilize your mind; this is the basis of the way of Yoga. ||5|| Your mind is tied with the rope of ego. You do not miss God O ignorant; you will not attain salvation! ||6|| If you forget God; you will be in the hands of devil of death; It will hurt you in the end O ignorant; ||7|| Page 1190 Search yourself through guru's teaching. True Yoga shall come to dwell in your mind. ||8|| He, who gave you the soul and body; you do not miss Him You ignorant; visiting graves and cremation grounds is not Yoga. ||9|| Nanak speaks the virtues and honourable words. If you can see, will recognize it; ||10||5|| Basant, First Master: Duality and evil will are blind deeds. The self-willed wanders, lost in whirlwind. ||1|| The blind man follows blind advice. The doubt does not dispel without guru's grace. ||1||Pause|| The self-willed does not appreciate guru's teaching. He is like an animal and his pride does not go away. ||2|| God created millions of species of beings. God creates and destroys them by His will. ||3|| All are confused, without guru's teaching and good conduct. He, whom the guru the God blesses understands it; ||4|| Guru's servants are pleasing to God. The Lord forgives them and they no longer fear the devil of death. ||5|| Those who enshrine God in the mind; He dispels their doubt and unites them with Him. ||6|| God does not need any favour; He is endless and infinite. The Creator is pleased with truth. ||7|| O Nanak, the guru instructs the lost soul. He implants the truth in him and shows him one Lord. ||8||6|| Basant, First Master: He is the bumblebee, the flower and the vine. He unites us with friendly devotee's congregation. ||1|| O bumble bee, suck that fragrance; which causes the trees to flower, and lush green forest; ||1||Pause|| He is Lakshmi, and He is her husband Vishnu. He creates guru's teaching and recites it. ||2|| He is the calf, the cow and the milk. He is the support of the body temple. ||3|| He is the deed, He is the doer. He is the guru-willed who contemplates Himself. ||4|| You create the creation and check for quality O Creator Lord. You give Your support to countless beings and creatures. ||5|| You are the unfathomable ocean of virtues. You are the unknowable, formless priceless jewel; ||6|| You are the Creator, capable of doing everything. You do not need any help O emperor and your subjects are happy. ||7|| Nanak is satisfied enjoying God's name with love; without the beloved guru the God; the life is meaningless. ||8||7|| Basant Hindol, First Master, Second House: God is one. He is realized by guru's grace. The nine regions, the seven continents, the fourteen worlds, the three qualities and the four ages – You created them from four sources; He placed the four lamps, one by one, into the hands of the four ages. ||1|| O kind Lord, destroyer of demons, Lord of Lakshmi, such is Your power; ||1||Pause|| Your fire burns in every heart and the religion rules over it. The earth is source of food and the fortunate is your storekeeper. ||2|| He, who is not content, will beg again; The devil will create trouble. Page 1191 Greed is the dark dungeon and demerits are the chains on his feet. ||3|| He is burdened by the weight of greed of wealth and commits millions of sins. Whatever good or bad they do is by Your grace. ||4|| O elder; it is time to miss the primal God, Sheikhs say Allah. He makes his living by worshipping gods, what a way? ||5|| The worship bowl, prayer mat and blue clothes are required to pray; Whom you worship, abides in every house and every one; but you say different words. ||6|| O my master, you are the king of the earth, what can I say? All four corners of the universe wish You well and everyone praises You. ||7|| Go to pilgrimage, read scriptures and give awns. Do something good every day. O Nanak, recite God's name every moment and obtain honour. ||8||1||8|| Basant Hindol, Second House, Fourth Master: God is one. He is realized by guru's grace. Within the body-village there lives a child who cannot stay still even for a moment; He is tired of making all efforts but still keeps wandering. ||1|| O my Lord, Your child has come home to be one with You. Meeting the guru, he finds the perfect Lord by reciting the symbol of God's name. ||1||Pause|| Those, who do not enshrine God's name in the mind, are like a dead body in the graveyard. The guru leads us to taste the water of God's name and we rejuvenate enjoying the taste; ||2|| I searched my body carefully and the guru-willed showed me the way. The faithless die searching outside; I realized God inside through guru's teaching. ||3|| God is kind to the humble, as Krishna was to Bidar and went to his home. Sudama came to see him with love; his poverty ended. ||4|| Great is the glory of God's name; God preserves it. Even if all faithless slander Him; it does not reduce a bit; ||5|| God's name is the honour of devotees; he is known in all ten directions. The slanderers and faithless cannot endure it; they burn their home. ||6|| The humble meeting the humble obtains honour. Virtues breed virtues. He, who becomes the servant of servants, is the beloved of my Lord. ||7|| The Creator is water; He unites us in water. O Nanak, the guru-willed merges in peace as water merges in water; ||8||1||9|| Page 1192 Basant, Fifth Master, First House, Du-Tukee: God is one. He is realized by guru's grace. Listen to the stories O my mind, and recite God with love. Ajaamal said God once and attained salvation. Baalmeek found the company of devotees. The Lord met Dhroo without doubt. ||1|| I beg for the dust of the feet of Your saints. Please be kind and bless me that I apply it to my forehead. ||1||Pause|| The prostitute was saved, saying God after her parrot said God. The elephant recited God and was saved. He eliminated Brahmin Sudaamaa's poverty. O my mind, you too recite the name of the Lord of the universe. ||2|| Even the hunter who shot an arrow at Krishna was saved. The hunchback was saved, when God placed His foot on her thumb. Being humble saved Bidar. O my mind, you too recite God; ||3|| God preserved the honour of Prahlaad. He preserved Dropadi's honour when her clothes were being removed; those who serve God in the end; O my mind, serve Him, and you shall be carried across to the other side. ||4|| Dhanna served the Lord, with the innocence of a child. Meeting with the guru, Trilochan attained salvation. The guru blessed Baynee with divine wisdom. O my mind, you too become God's slave. ||5|| Jai Dev gave up his ego. Sain the barber was saved through selfless service. Do not let your mind waver or wander; do not let it go anywhere. O my mind, you too shall cross over in God's refuge; ||6|| Whoever God blesses by His grace; You saved those devotees. You do not consider their merits and demerits. Seeing these ways, I started to serve You; ||7|| Kabeer recited God with love. Naam Dev lived with the dear Lord. Ravi Daas recited the beautiful God; Guru Nanak Dev is the embodiment of the Lord of the universe. ||8||1|| Basant, Fifth Master: The mortal wanders in reincarnation through countless lifes. Without reciting God they go to hell. Without God's worship, he is cut into pieces. Without realizing, the devil of death punishes them. ||1|| O my friend, recite the name of the Lord of the universe forever. Love guru's teaching forever. ||1||Pause|| Contentment does not come any other way. The worldly wealth thunders like the cloud. The mortal does not hesitate to commit sins. Intoxicated with poison, he comes and goes in reincarnation. ||2|| Acting in ego increases the useless deeds. The world is drowning in worldly attachment and greed. Lust and anger control the mind. He does not say God even in a dream. ||3|| Sometimes he is a king, sometimes he is a beggar. The world is bound by pleasure and pain. The mortal makes no arrangements to save himself. He keeps committing sins. ||4|| He has no friends or companions. He eats what he plants. Page 1193 The deeds that bring useless ideas; the ignorant leaves and goes away in a moment. ||5|| He wanders enticed by the worldly wealth. He does the deeds written in his fate. The Creator remains hidden. God is not affected by virtue or vice. ||6|| Please save me, O merciful Lord of the universe! I seek Your sanctuary, O perfect kind God; Without You, I have no other place of rest. Please be kind and bless me with your name. ||7|| You are the Creator, You do everything. You are the highest and infinite. Be kind and attach me to You. Slave Nanak has entered the sanctuary of God. ||8||2|| Basant Kee Vaar, Fifth Master: God is one. He is realized by guru's grace. Recite God's name and rejuvenate yourself. You get what you earn. This is the right season to earn. Every bit of the universe has bloomed and bears sacred fruit. Peace wells up meeting God's devotees and all desires end. O Nanak, recite one name and you will not wander anymore. ||1|| I have controlled the five thieves by God's support. God leads us to worship His feet by His grace. All sorrows and sicknesses are eradicated; I became ever new and strong. I recite His name day and night and I will not die again. O Nanak, where I came from I went back to the same place. ||2|| Where we come from? Where we live? Where we go? All creatures belong to God our master. Who realizes this? Those who say, recite and listen to God's name are called God's devotees. The Lord is inaccessible and unfathomable; there is no other equal to Him. The perfect guru has taught this truth. Nanak only tells it. ||3||1|| Basant, the word of devotees, Kabeer Jee, First House: God is one. He is realized by guru's grace. The earth is in bloom, the sky is in bloom. Each and every heart has blossomed and the soul is illuminated. ||1|| My sovereign Lord King blossoms in countless ways. Wherever I look, I see Him there. ||1||Pause|| Secondly the four Vedas blossomed in duality. The Simritees blossom along with the Quran and the Bible. ||2|| Shiva blossoms in Yoga and meditation. Kabeer's Lord equals all together. ||3||1|| The Hindu scholars are intoxicated by reading the Puraanas. The Yogis are intoxicated in Yoga and meditation. The renunciates are intoxicated in ego. The penitents are intoxicated with the mystery of penance. ||1|| All are intoxicated with the wine; no one is awake; the thieves are robbing their home. ||1||Pause|| Sukhdev and Akrur are also awake. Page 1194 Hanuman with his tail is awake. Shiva is awake and serves at God's feet. In today's age Naam Dev and Jai Dev are awake. ||2|| There are many ways of being awake, and sleeping. The guru-willed remain away, that is the essence of all. This body has many things to do. Says Kabeer, recite God's name; ||3||2|| Whoever God gave birth to; the son played with the father. Without breasts the mother nurses her baby. ||1|| See O people, this is the way in today's age. The son marries his mother. ||1||Pause|| Without feet, the mortal jumps. Without a mouth, he laughs loudly. Without feeling sleepy he lies down and sleeps. Without a rope he churns milk. ||2|| Without udders, the cow gives milk. Without travelling, a long journey is made. Without the guru, the path is not found. Says Kabeer, see this and understand. ||3||3|| Prahlaad was sent to school. He took many of his friends with him. He asked his teacher, why do you teach me about worldly affairs? Write the name of the dear Lord on my plank; ||1|| O elder, I will not give up the name of God. I will not bother with any other learning. ||1||Pause|| Sanda Marka went to the king and complained. He sent for Prahlaad to come at once. He said to him to give up the habit of saying God; I will free you immediately if you listen to me. ||2|| Prahlaad answered, why do you bother me again and again. God created water, land, hills and mountains. I will not forsake one Lord; if I did, I will be abusing my guru. You might as well throw me into the fire or kill me. ||3|| The king became angry and drew his sword. Show me your protector now! God emerged from the pillar, and assumed a mighty form. He killed Harnaakhash, tearing him apart with his nails. ||4|| The supreme Lord, God of gods; Through His worship with love, he came in the form of a lion. Says Kabeer, no one can know Lord's limits. He saves His devotees like Prahlaad over and over again. ||5||4|| Within the body and mind are thieves like lust; they stole my jewel of divine wisdom. I am an orphan, O God; whom should I complain? Who has not been ruined? What am I? ||1|| O Lord, I cannot endure this agonizing pain. What power does my fickle mind has against it? ||1||Pause|| Sanak, Sanandan, Shiva and Sukhdev Brahma was born out of lotus. The poets and the Yogis with their matted hair all lived their lives and went away. ||2|| You are unfathomable; I cannot know Your depth. O God, master of the meek; unto who should I tell my pains? Please, get rid of my pains of birth and death, and bless me with peace. Kabeer sings the praises of God the ocean of peace. ||3||5|| There is one leader and five traders. The twenty-five oxen carry glass. There are nine poles, which hold the ten bags. The seventy-two ropes tie the body. ||1|| I don't do such business. Page 1195 It decreases my principle and increases the interest. ||Pause|| Weaving the seven threads together, they carry on their trade. They take their mind and fate with them. The three tax collectors argue with them. The traders depart empty-handed. ||2|| Their capital is exhausted, and their trade is ruined. The caravan is scattered in the ten directions. Says Kabeer, O mortal, your tasks will be accomplished; if you want peace then forget the doubt. ||3||6|| Basant Hindol, Second House: God is one. He is realized by guru's grace. The mother is impure, father is impure. The fruit they produce is impure. Impure they come, impure they go. The unfortunate die impure. ||1|| Tell me, O religious scholar, which place is pure? Where I sit to eat my meal? ||1||Pause|| The tongue is impure, it speaks impure. The eyes and ears are impure. The impurity of senses does not depart; the fire burns the Brahmin. ||2|| The fire is impure, water is impure. The place where you sit and cook is impure. Impure is serving spoon. Impure is the one who eats it. ||3|| Impure is the cow dung, the kitchen square and the lines that mark it. Says Kabeer, those who think pure are pure, this is the truth. ||4||1||7|| Raamaanand Jee, First House: God is one. He is realized by guru's grace. Where should I go? My home is filled with bliss. My mind cannot do anything. It is flying like bumblebee. ||1||Pause|| One day, a desire welled up in my mind. I ground up sandalwood, along with several fragrant oils. I went to God's place to worship Him. The guru' showed me that God in the mind. ||1|| Wherever I go, I find water and stones. You are pervading and permeating in all equally. I have searched all the Vedas and the Puraanas. I will go there, if God is not here. ||2|| I admire You, O my guru. You have cut all my seen and unseen doubts. Raamaanand Master recites the all-pervading God. Guru's teaching eliminates millions of doubts. ||3||1|| Basant, the word of Naam Dev Jee: God is one. He is realized by guru's grace. When the master is in trouble and the servant runs away. He will not live long; he brings shame to both side of his family. ||1|| I will not abandon Your worship O Lord, even if the people laugh at me. God's lotus feet are enshrined in my heart. ||1||Pause|| The mortal will even die for the sake of his wealth; same way, Your saints do not give up God's name. ||2|| Pilgrimages to the Ganges, the Gaya and Godawari are worldly affairs. Page 1196 If the Lord is pleased, then Naam Dev is His servant. ||3||1|| The tidal waves of greed constantly assault me. My body is drowning, O Lord. ||1|| Please carry me across the world-ocean, O Lord of the universe. Carry me across, O my father. ||1||Pause|| I cannot steer my ship in this storm. I cannot find the other shore, O beloved Lord. ||2|| Please be kind and unite me with the guru; He will carry me across, O Lord. ||3|| Says Naam Dev, I do not know how to swim. Give me Your arm; give me Your Arm, O beloved Lord. ||4||2|| Slowly at first, the body-cart loaded with dust starts to move. It is driven from behind with a stick. ||1|| The body moves like the ball of dung, driven on by the dung beetle. The beloved soul goes to the pool to wash its hair. ||1||Pause|| The washer man washes, imbued with Lord's love. My mind is imbued with Lord's lotus feet. ||2|| Naam Dev recites God. Please be kind to Your devotee. ||3||3|| Basant, the word of Ravi Daas Jee: God is one. He is realized by guru's grace. Nothing comes to your mind; seeing your clothes, you are so proud. The proud bride does not find a place anywhere. The crow is sitting on your neck to cut it. ||1|| Why are you so proud? You ignorant; You are more eager than the mushroom in rainy season; ||1||Pause|| The deer does not know the secret; the musk is in its body, but it searches for it all over. Whoever reflects on his body? The devil of death does not abuse him. ||2|| The man is so proud of his sons and his wife; The Lord shall call his account. The soul suffers in pain for the actions it committed. Afterwards, whom shall you call, "dear, O dear."||3|| If you seek the support of the devotee. Millions of your sins will be erased. Says Ravi Daas, one who recites God's name; He has nothing to do with caste, birth or life. ||4||1|| Basant, Kabeer Jee: God is one. He is realized by guru's grace. You walk like a cow, the hair on your tail, are shiny. ||1|| You look around and eat anything you find in this house. But do not go out to any other house. ||1||Pause|| You lick the grinding stone and eat the flour. Where have you taken the kitchen rags? ||2|| Your eyes are fixed on the hanging basket. Watch out – a stick may strike you on the back from behind. ||3|| Says Kabeer, you have enjoyed enough; Watch out – someone may hit you with a brick or a rock. ||4||1||

Page 1197 Tune Saarag, Chau-Padas, First Master, First House:

God is one. It is true. He is the Creator. He is carefree. He has no enemy. He is immortal. He does not take birth. He came into existence on His own. He is realized by guru's grace.

I am the maidservant of my master. I have grasped God's feet, the life of the world. He killed my ego. ||1||Pause|| He is the perfect, supreme light; supreme Lord my beloved is my life. The beloved enticed my mind and I realized Him through guru's teaching. ||1|| The worthless self-willed with false and shallow intellect suffers pain in the mind and body. Since I am imbued with God's love, I recite God and attain peace. ||2|| Abandoning ego, I have become detached. And now, I am absorbed in true realization. My mind has consoled with formless God and gave up worrying about what the other people say. ||3|| There is no other like You, in the past or future, O my beloved the support of my life. The soul-bride is imbued with God's name O Nanak, God is my husband. ||4||1|| Saarag, First Master: How can I survive without God? I am troubled by pain; my tongue does not enjoy the taste; the death worries me without reciting God; ||1||Pause|| I am hungry and thirsty for him till I see my beloved. As I see him, my mind is happy like the lotus in water. ||1|| The cloud thunders and rains; the rain bird and the peacock are joyous. The snakes hang from the trees. The bride and husband enjoy at home. ||2|| She is filthy and ugly, unfeminine and ill mannered – she has no intuitive understanding of her Husband Lord. She is not satisfied by her Lord's love; she the evil-minded and suffers in pain. ||3|| She does not come or go, and does not suffer pain in the body. O Nanak, she is enticed by God; visualizing Him she finds peace. ||4||2|| Saarag, First Master: My beloved Lord is not far away. Guru's teaching pleases me. I found God the support of my life. ||1||Pause|| Page 1198 This is the way to meet your Husband Lord. Blessed is the soul-bride who is loved by her Husband Lord. Contemplating guru's teaching eliminates the doubt of caste, status and family. ||1|| One, whose mind accepts; he forgets self-pride, anger and greed. The soul-bride intuitively enjoys her Husband Lord; the guru-willed is adorned by love. ||2|| Burn away the love of family and relatives, which increases attachment to worldly wealth. He, who does not savor God's love, lives in duality and corruption. ||3|| The priceless jewel is inside; the beloved is not far away. O Nanak, The guru-willed enshrines the priceless God's name in the mind in all ages. ||4||3|| Saarang, Fourth Master, First House: God is one. He is realized by guru's grace. I am the dust of the feet of the humble saints of the Lord. Joining the true congregation, I have obtained the supreme status. God the lord of soul abides everywhere.

||1||Pause|| Meeting the saintly guru obtains peace and the sins are erased and taken away. The divine light burns inside and I realize God close by. ||1|| By good fortune, I found the true congregation and I am filled with God's name. ||2|| Bathing in the dust of true congregation equals bathing at sixty-eight shrines. She is evil-minded corrupt filthy and shallow minded with impure heart, she is enticed by false attachment. Without good luck, how can I find the congregation? Engrossed in ego, the mind regrets. ||3|| Be kind and bless me O dear Lord; I beg for the dust of the feet of the true congregation. O Nanak, meeting the saints, the Lord is realized. Lord's humble servant meets honourable God. ||4||1|| Saarang, Fourth Master: I praise the feet of the Lord of the universe. I cannot swim across the terrifying world ocean. I swim across by reciting God. ||1||Pause|| I am in love with God and I contemplate to serve Him. Night and day, I recite the name of all-powerful and virtuous God. ||1|| God is inaccessible and unfathomable. The infinite and invisible. God pervades everywhere in the mind and body. When the guru becomes kind, then the unseen Lord is seen in the heart. ||2|| God the Lord of the universe abides in my mind. He is far away from the proud faithless; His burning desire never quenches; he loses the game of life in a gamble. ||3|| When the guru becomes kind a little bit; the devotee sings God's praises while sitting or standing. O Nanak, whoever God is kind to; He preserves their honour: ||4||2|| Page 1199 Saarang, Fourth Master: O my beloved Lord, bless me with the sacred God's name. Those, who God is pleased with; he resolves their affairs. ||1||Pause|| Those, who became humble before the guru; their pains are eliminated. They worship God in front of the guru day and night; they are adorned by guru's teaching. ||1|| He enshrines and recites God's sacred name with tongue; he sings and contemplates God's love. They enjoy the sacred nectar by guru's grace and attain salvation. ||2|| The primal guru is unmoving and unchanging. He recites God's name devotionally and God is his support. I offer my soul to Him; I praise my guru. ||3|| The self-willed are attached to duality; they are filled with the darkness of ignorance. They do not see the guru, the giver; they are not on this shore, or the other. ||4|| The all-powerful God abides in all beings. Nanak, the slave of His slaves, says; please

be kind and save me! ||5||3|| Saarag, Fourth Master: Do such a service for God; Whatever He does, accept it true. O guru-willed enshrine God's name in the mind with love. ||1||Pause|| Love of the Lord of the universe tastes very sweet. I forgot everything else. Night and day, I am at peace; my soul has merged in supreme soul. ||1|| Singing God's praises my mind is satisfied and I am peaceful in my mind. When the guru becomes kind, the mortal finds God. He focuses his mind to God's lotus feet. ||2|| Reciting God the intellect is enlightened by lovingly attuning to the divine wisdom. The divine light shines inside and mind is pleased; he is in trance with God intuitively. ||3|| He is filled with corruption and does corrupt deeds daily; yet he says God from the mouth. He is filled with extreme false attachment; he thrashes the shell and eats it with pain. ||4|| When my God is pleased, the guru-willed obtains divine wisdom. Nanak has obtained the name of the Lord. He finds peace reciting His name. ||5||4|| Saarag, Fourth Master: My mind is pleased with God's name. The guru has implanted divine love in my heart. God's sermon gives peace to my mind. ||1||Pause|| O God kind to the humble; be kind to Your servant and bless him with your untold story. Meeting with the humble saints, I have found the sublime essence of the Lord. Lord tastes sweet to my mind and body. ||1|| Those, who realize God's name through guru's teaching are dyed with God's love and become unattached; The mortal meets the primal being and obtains peace; his coming and going ends. ||2|| I visualized the amazing God with my eyes and my tongue recites His name. Page 1200 I listen to God's praises with my ears and saying God appeals to my mind. ||3|| The guru controlled the five senses; then I became divine reciting God's name. God became kind to servant Nanak; he has merged in God's name. ||4||5|| Saarag, Fourth Master: O my mind, recite and study the essence of God's name. No one remains forever. Without God's name, everything else is a false show. ||1||Pause|| O ignorant; what to give and what to take. What you see is all dust. The poison which you think is your; it becomes a burden on the head, leave it behind. ||1|| The life decreases every moment; the ignorant cannot understand this. He does whatever does not go with him; this is the character of the faithless. ||2|| O ignorant, join the company of saints and obtain salvation. Without the true congregation, no one finds peace. Go and ask the scholars that contemplate Vedas. ||3|| All the kings and queens shall depart; they must leave this false expanse. O Nanak, the saints, who take support of God's name, are immortal. ||4||6|| Saarag, Fourth Master, Third House, Du-Padas: God is one. He is realized by guru's grace. O son, why do you argue with your father? It is a sin to argue with the one who fathered you and raised you. ||1||Pause|| That wealth, which you are proud of; does not belong to anyone; the evil wealth that you enjoy so much; you will leave behind in a moment and regret. ||1|| He, who is your master the God; recite the recitation of His name; Servant Nanak teaches you this; whoever listens to it, his worry departs. ||2||1||7|| Saarag, Fourth Master, Fifth House, Du-Padas, Partaal: God is one. He is realized by guru's grace. O my mind, recite the Lord of the world, master of the universe, life of the world, the enticer of the mind; fall in love with Him and take God's support day and night. ||1||Pause|| Many sing God's praises like Sukhdev, Naarad and Brahma. Your virtues O Lord cannot be counted. O God my master, You are infinite. Only You know the likes of You. ||1|| Those, who live, close to God; they are His devotees and worshippers. Those God's servants mix with God like water with water. ||2||1||8||Page 1201 Saarang, Fourth Master: O my mind, recite the Lord the master of humans, God of gods and my beloved God in the mind. ||1||Pause|| Where people sing God's praises, the divine music plays in the house of the fortunate in five tunes. All their sins, pains, sickness, lust, anger, false attachment and self-pride go away and the five thieves are driven out as well. ||1|| O God's devotees; recite God the Lord of the world and worship God with devotion. Say God God God. It will eliminate all sins. Recite the Lord of the world and remain awake and enjoy forever. Unite with God O servant Nanak; do good deeds and obtain salvation and receive the reward of your choice. ||2||2||9|| Saarang, Fourth Master: O my mind, recite the Lord of wealth, the source of nectar, the supreme Lord the transcendent Being, the inner-knower God; He is the destroyer of all suffering, giver of all peace; sing the praises of my beloved God. ||1||Pause|| God pervades everybody, the water, land all high low places of interest; I long to visualize God; May some my beloved God's saint come and show me the way. I will wash and massage the feet of that humble being. ||1|| God's servant realizes God with devotional worship. My mind and body are joyous visualizing God. God the Lord of the world became kind to servant Nanak. I recite God's name all the time and forever. ||2||3||10|| Saarang, Fourth Master: O my mind, recite the carefree God. He is true forever. He has no enemy. He is immortal. He is beyond birth and self-existent. O my mind, recite the formless God who does not eat. ||1||Pause|| Billions of gods, mystics, penitents, and yogis go to bathe at shrines and keep fast. Those upon whom God becomes kind; their service is accepted; ||1|| Those Godly saints who please God are gentle God's devotees. Those who have my master on their side – O Nanak, God preserves their honour. ||2||4||11|| Page 1202 Saarang, Fourth Master, Partaal: O my mind, worship God the Lord of the universe, treasure of virtues, God of the universe by saying God God the immortal Lord. ||1||Pause|| Those, thirsty for God recite and drink the nectar of God's name; Whoever God unites with the guru by His kindness; enjoys the taste of saying God's name. ||1|| Those who serve my Lord, forever, their pain, doubt and fear are eliminated. Servant Nanak lives by reciting God's name and gets satisfied like the rain bird by drinking water. ||2||5||12|| Saarang, Fourth Master: O my mind, recite the honourable God. Say God God God. It is true, there is God. O brother say God God God; He pervades everywhere. ||1||Pause|| God the Creator of all pervades everywhere. Whoever God the sovereign Lord blesses; he recites God's name with love. ||1|| O saints; see the greatness of God's name; He preserves the honour of His devotees in today's age and further. My sovereign Lord has taken servant Nanak's side; his enemies and pains have all run away. ||2||6||13|| Saarang, Fifth Master, Chau-Padas, First House: God is one. He is realized by guru's grace. I praise the image of the true guru. I am thirsty to visualize him like the rain bird for rain; when will I see him? ||1||Pause|| He is the master of orphans and care taker of all; He is called the love of devotees who recite His name. Whoever is not supported by anyone; You support him. ||1|| You are support of the unsupported, saviour of the unsaved and home of the homeless; I wander in ten directs and You are with me. Singing your praises is my job. ||2|| You created everyone and abide in all. I cannot describe Your divine wisdom. You are infinite; Your limit cannot be found; all that I see is Your play. ||3|| I join devotee's company and discuss with them and I am attuned to God's devotees with love. Servant Nanak has found God through guru's teaching; I am filled with joy visualizing You. ||4||1|| Saarang, Fifth Master: Know that God is the inner-knower; You do bad deeds hiding from people but God is present everywhere. ||1||Pause|| You call yourself a devotee of Vishnu and you practice the six rituals, but your inner being is polluted with greed. Those who slander the society of saints; the ignorant shall drown. ||1|| Page 1203 He eats specially prepared food for him, steals from others and filled with falsehood and ego; He knows nothing about Vedas or Shaastras; his mind is troubled by pride. ||2|| He says evening prayers, and observes all the fasts, but it is just a show. Forgetting God, he wanders in the wild and all his deeds are fruitless. ||3|| Whoever God blesses, is a divine teacher, and Vishnu's devotee. Serving the guru, he obtains the supreme status and saves the whole world. ||4|| What can I say? I don't know what to say. As God wills, so I speak; I beg for the dust of devotee's feet. Servant Nanak seeks their refuge. ||5||2|| Saarang, Fifth Master: Now, my dancing is over. I have intuitively realized my beloved through guru's teaching. ||1||Pause|| The way the maid laughs about a husband in friend's company. When the kindhearted God came in the mind; my veil of sins is lifted. ||1|| When gold is melted in the crucible, it flows freely everywhere. But when it is made into pure solid bars, then it remains that way. ||2|| As long as one lives, the clock ticks by hours, minutes and seconds. When the gong player gets up and leaves, the gong is not sounded again. ||3|| When the pitcher is filled with water; the water in it looks different; Says Nanak, when the pitcher is emptied, the water mixes with water. ||4||3|| Saarang, Fifth Master: Now if he asks, what can he say? Reciting God's name is sacred O ignorant; you are attached to poison. ||1||Pause|| I obtained this hard to obtain human life after a long time; I am exchanging it for a shell. He came to buy musk; instead he has loaded dust and thistle grass. ||1|| He came to earn profit; instead he is entangled and enticed in cheating. He loses the jewel in exchange for glass. When will this time come again? ||2|| He is full of sins, he has no virtue. He worships the servant instead of the master. When the silence prevails then the thieves break in. ||3|| I find no other way; I sought the refuge of God's devotees. Says Nanak; I will obtain salvation only when I eliminate all faults. ||4||4|| Saarang, Fifth Master: O mother, I am impatient. I miss my beloved a lot. There are many kinds of pleasures, but I am not interested in them. ||1||Pause|| Night and day, I utter my beloved from my mouth and cannot sleep at all. Necklaces, eye make-up, fancy clothes and decorations; without my Husband Lord, these are all poison to me. ||1|| Page 1204 I ask around humbly, if someone will tell me where my Husband Lord lives? I will offer my mind, soul and body and put my head on their feet; ||2|| I the servant will bow at their feet and pray for blessing of devotee's company. Be kind and unite me with God. I long to see him for a moment. ||3|| By His grace he came into my body; my mind and body became soothed. Says Nanak, I sing the songs of joy; and infinite divine music plays through guru's teaching. ||4||5|| Saarag, Fifth Master: O mother, God is true and His devotees are also true. The word which the perfect guru said; I have tied it in a knot. ||1||Pause|| Night day the stars the sun and the moon will vanish. The mountains, earth, water and the air shall vanish. Only devotee's word is eternal; ||1|| Those born of eggs, the womb, the earth and sweat shall pass away. The four Vedas and the six Shaastras shall vanish. Only devotee's word will remain. ||2|| Kings, the greedy and the faithless will vanish. All that is seen shall vanish. Only devotee's word is beyond destruction. ||3|| God is everything; all that we see is His play. He cannot be found by any means. O Nanak, He is found meeting the guru. ||4||6|| Saarag, Fifth Master: The guru, the Lord of the universe, dwells in my mind. Wherever my Lord is recited; that village is filled with peace and joy. ||1||Pause|| Wherever my beloved Lord is forgotten; all misery and misfortune is there. Where God's praises are sung in joy; peace and wealth are enjoyed there forever. ||1|| Wherever God's sermon is not spoken or heard; it is scary jungle there; Where God's praises are sung in devotee's company with love; lot of fragrance spreads around there. ||2|| Without reciting God, even if he lives for million years, the whole life goes waste. But if he recites God even for a moment, he lives forever. ||3|| O God, be kind and bless me with the refuge of the devotees by Your grace. O Nanak, the all-virtuous God abides in all. ||4||7|| Saarag, Fifth

Master: Now, I believe in God. Those who sought the refuge of God the ocean of mercy are carried across the world-ocean. ||1||Pause|| They sleep in peace, and become content; the guru eliminates their doubt. God does whatever they want; they obtain the reward of their choice. ||1|| Recite Him in the mind, see Him with eyes and listen to his sermon through ears. Page 1205 I walk on my master's path and sing God's praises. ||2|| May I see the amazing enjoyable beauty; the saint has changed my thinking. I have found the priceless name of the beloved Lord; it never leaves me or goes anywhere else. ||3|| What praise, what glory and what virtues should I say to please God? The kind God became kind to humble Nanak the servant of servants. ||4||8|| Saarang, Fifth Master: Whom can I tell and explain the peace I get? Visualizing God I am joyful and my mind sings God's praises with love. ||1||Pause|| I am wonderstruck, seeing the amazing God pervading everywhere. I drink nectar of God's name and smile like a mute. ||1|| God controls the wind such a way that we do not know where it comes from and where it goes. He, who realizes God; his story cannot be told; ||2|| Whatever other efforts anyone says, I studied them all. My beloved, carefree God has revealed Himself in my heart; thus I have realized the inaccessible God. ||3|| The absolute, formless, eternal, unchanging, immeasurable Lord cannot be measured. Says Nanak, whoever endures the unendurable, becomes like Him; ||4||9|| Saarag, Fifth Master: The evil person passes his days and nights uselessly. He does not recite God the Lord of the universe; he is intoxicated with egotistic intellect. He loses his life in a gamble. ||1||Pause|| He does not love God's priceless name instead he loves slandering others. He builds a hut out of straw and burns it. ||1|| He carries a load of baron earth on his head and forgets nectar from his mind; He falls in black pit and then he shakes his clothes again and again. ||2|| Standing on the branch he cuts the branch and smiles seeing what he does. He falls head down and shatters into bits and pieces. ||3|| He creates enmity with the enemyless, the ignorant goes nowhere. Says Nanak, the formless God the Lord of salvation protects the saints. ||4||10|| Saarag, Fifth Master: All others are lost; they cannot find the way wandering around. Who has God abiding in his mind; he realizes the essence of Vedas. ||1||Pause|| Whatever the sacred way, the people say; it is the way of pleasing themselves. Till there is enlightenment in the mind, it is dark all over. ||1|| They prepare field in every way, but nothing grows without seeding. No one obtains salvation without God's name, and the self-pride does not leave. ||2|| The mortal works hard to churn water; but how can he find butter in it? No one finds salvation and realizes the Lord of the world without the guru; ||3|| Page 1206 I came to this conclusion by contemplating that reciting God's name gives the greatest peace. Says Nanak, he, who has pre-ordained destiny obtains it. ||4||11|| Saarag, Fifth Master: Night and day, sing God's praises. You shall obtain all wealth, pleasure, success and the fruits of your choice. ||1||Pause|| Come, O peace giving saints of my life; let us recite immortal God. Master of the orphans and destroyer of pain of the humble pervades all. ||1|| Sing, listen and tell God's praises with devotion and enjoy God's love O fortunate! All their sufferings and struggles are eliminated and they recite God's name with love. ||2|| So abandon lust, anger, greed, falsehood and slander. Reciting God cuts all bonds; the intoxication of false attachment, ego and blind possessiveness are eradicated by guru's grace. ||3|| You are all-powerful, O supreme Lord and master; please be kind to Your humble servant. My Lord is pervading everywhere; O Nanak, God is very near. ||4||12|| Saarag, Fifth Master: I praise the feet of my guru. I recite God the bestowal of salvation in his company. His lesson bestows me the liberation. ||1||Pause|| Whoever seeks refuge of God's saints; his pain and sickness are destroyed. He recites and inspires others to recite God's name. He is all-powerful and bestowal of salvation. ||1|| His lesson drives away the doubt, and fills the empty to over flowing. Those who obey the order of Lord's slaves; do not enter into the womb of reincarnation again; ||2|| Whoever serves God's devotees and sings God's praises; his pain of birth and death is erased. Whoever the kind God is kind to; they burn in the fire of separation from God. ||3|| Those who are satisfied by God's sublime essence merge intuitively in peace; their caste or status cannot be described. By guru's grace, O Nanak, they are content and attain salvation reciting God; ||4||13|| Saarag, Fifth Master: I sing the songs of joy of my Lord, the treasure of virtues. Fortunate is the time, the day and the moment, when I become pleasing to the Lord of the world. ||1||Pause|| I touch my forehead to the feet of the saints. The saint has placed his hand on my forehead. ||1|| My mind is filled with God's devotee's teaching. And I have been saved from three qualities||2|| Seeing the devotees, my eyes are filled with love. Greed, worldly attachment and doubt are eliminated. ||3|| Says Nanak, I have found intuitive peace and joy. Eliminating the wall, I have met God the embodiment of supreme bliss. ||4||14|| Saarang, Fifth Master, Second House: God is one. He is realized by guru's grace. How can I express the pain of my soul? I am thirsty of visualizing my enticing beloved; my mind is out of control with joy. ||1||Pause|| Page 1207 I feel separation from my loving beloved in my mind; when will I visualize God? I try, but this mind does not stabilize! Is there any saint who will unite me with God? ||1|| I meditate; do penance, self-control, good deeds and give awns; so that my pain goes away. ||2|| I am in love and offer many prayers and serve Him day and night. I renounce pride and ego and listen to, whoever tells me about my beloved. ||3|| I am amazed seeing His amazing play that he united me with the guru. I have found the kind God in my heart O Nanak, it extinguished my burning fire. ||4||1||15|| Saarag, Fifth Master: You ignorant, why you do not recite God now? In the awful hell of the fire of the womb, you did sincere penance and sang God's praises every moment. ||1||Pause|| You wandered through countless births, until you attained this priceless human life. Leaving the womb when you came out, you became attached to other places. ||1|| You do evil deeds and cheat day and night, you do useless deeds. You thresh the straw, without grain; you wander around and suffer. ||2|| The false is attached to falsehood. He is entangled in enticing flavour of flowers. O ignorant, when the justice of destiny arrests you then you will go away with blackened face. ||3|| Whoever realized God is by God's grace; he has pre-ordained destiny written on his forehead. Says Nanak; I admire the being, who thinks in the mind a little bit. ||4||2||16|| Saarag, Fifth Master: How can I live without my beloved, O my mother? One dies separating from him and is not allowed to stay at home. ||1||Pause|| He, who has the beloved God the helper and bestowal of life on his side. O saints, be kind to me so that I sing God's praises with love; ||1|| I touch my forehead to the feet of the saints. My eyes long for their dust. O

Nanak, I admire them, by whose grace I realize God; ||2||3||17|| Saarag,
Fifth Master: I admire that occasion. Reciting God twenty-four hours
a day, the fortunate has realized God. ||1||Pause|| Good are Kabeer
the servant of servants and Sain the barber; Highest of the high is
Naam Dev, who looked upon all alike; Ravi Daas was in tune with
the Lord. ||1|| My soul, body and wealth belong to the saints; my
mind is dust of the saints. By saint's grace my doubt disappeared and
Nanak has united with God; ||2||4||18|| Saarag, Fifth Master: The true
guru fulfills the desires. Page 1208 O my mind; worship Him
twenty-four hours a day, who bestows all priceless treasures by
worshipping. ||1||Pause|| O Lord; Your name is the nectar; whoever
drinks it gets satisfied. The sins of many lifes are eliminated and
freedom obtained in God's court. ||1|| I have come to Your refuge O
Creator, O perfect supreme immortal God; Please be kind that I
worship Your lotus feet. Nanak is thirsty of visualizing you; ||2||5||19||
Saarang, Fifth Master, Third House: God is one. He is realized by
guru's grace. O my mind, why are you enticed by other things? Here
and hereafter, God is forever your support. He is with you for your
deeds. ||1||Pause|| The sacred name of my enticing beloved God fulfills
by drinking. The immortal God is the shelter and place of worship of
devotee saints. ||1|| They enshrine the sermon and lesson of divine
people in the mind and enjoy. Nanak found the place of peace by
searching God's name to enjoy. ||2||1||20|| Saarag, Fifth Master: O my
mind, sing forever the songs of joy of the Lord of the universe. Reciting
God's name a little in the mind, all your sickness and sorrow will go
away in a moment. ||1||Pause|| Abandon your smart ideas and clever
tricks and go to devotee's refuge. When God the destroyer of pain of
the humble becomes kind; then the devil of death becomes the justice
of destiny to administer justice. ||1|| Without one Lord, there is no
other at all. No one else can equal Him. God the bestowal of happiness
and life is Nanak's mother, father and brother; ||2||2||21|| Saarag, Fifth
Master: God's humble servant saves all those who accompany him.
Their minds are freed and purified; their pain of many a life is
eliminated. ||1||Pause|| Those who walk on that path find peace; those
with whom they talk about God are saved. Drowning in deep dark
well, they also go across in devotee's company. ||1|| Those with good

fortune O brother; are attached to devotee's company. Nanak longs for the dust of their feet; if my God blesses; ||2||3||22|| Saarag, Fifth Master: The humble servants of God, say God God God; Celebrating in devotee's congregation for one moment; they realize million heavens. ||1||Pause|| This hard to obtain human life becomes sacred and the thirst of devil of death is quenched. Even the sins of terrible sinners are washed away, by enshrining God's name in the mind. ||1|| Whoever listens to sacred God's praises; their pain of birth and death goes away. Says Nanak, the fortunate find God and their mind and body become happy. ||2||4||23|| Page 1209 Saarag, Fifth Master, Du-Padas, Fourth House: God is one. He is realized by guru's grace. O my beloved Lord, I pray to You: please come to my house; I am proud, I speak with pride that I am your servant even if I make mistakes. ||1||Pause|| I hear that You are near, but I cannot see You because I am deluded by doubt. The guru became kind and removed the veil and I found God in the mind. ||1|| If I forget my master even for a moment, it becomes like millions of years; When I joined devotee's company then Nanak met God. ||2||1||24|| Saarag, Fifth Master: Now what should I think? I have given up thinking. You do what You want to do; Please bless me with Your name by Your grace. ||1||Pause|| The poison of corruption is flowering in the four directions; I have taken guru's lesson as my antidote. God made me His own by giving His hand, like the lotus in water. ||1|| I have no ego, I am nothing. Whatever I am; it is by Your grace? Nanak runs after God; please save me by Your grace O saint. ||2||2||25|| Saarag, Fifth Master: Now I have abandoned all efforts. My Lord the all-powerful Creator the cause of causes is my saviour. ||1||Pause|| I have seen many beautiful faces and forms; none is like You; You give Your support to all O my Lord; You are the giver of peace, to soul and life. ||1|| Wandering all over, when I got tired, I fell at guru's feet. Says Nanak, I found eternal peace and spend my nights in peace. ||2||3||26|| Saarag, Fifth Master: Now I have found the support of my Lord. The peace-giving guru became kind; the blind found the jewel. ||1||Pause|| My ignorance is gone. I became pure and happy with discriminating intellect. As the waves rise out of water and again merge in water; so does the servant in master. ||1|| He came back where he went from; everything is one and one God; O Nanak, I see God the master of life everywhere. ||2||4||27|| Saarag, Fifth Master: My mind longs for one beloved Lord. I have looked everywhere in every country, nothing comes close to my beloved; ||1||Pause|| I served many delicate foods many ways; my mind does not like them anymore. I long for God's love and I call my beloved from my mouth; like the bumblebee longs for lotus flowers. ||1|| Page 1210 The treasure of virtue, the enticer of mind, my beloved is the giver of peace to all. Guru sent Nanak to God. I met my friend and embraced Him. ||2||5||28|| Saarag, Fifth Master: Now my mind is pleased with my Lord. The kind devotee became kind and drove away the stranger demon. ||1||Pause|| You are beautiful, and wise; You are elegant and all knowing. All Yogis, spiritual teachers and meditators do not know even a bit of Your value. ||1|| You are the master; You are the emperor ruling all O Lord; Please bless me with the gift of serving the saints; O Nanak, I am a sacrifice to the Lord. ||2||6||29|| Saarag, Fifth Master: I miss my beloved in my mind with love. I have forgotten the entanglement of worldly wealth and spend my nights fighting the evil. ||1||Pause|| I serve God enshrining Him in the mind and realize God in devotee's company. I have realized my enticing beautiful beloved; I obtained peace, which I asked for. ||1|| The guru has brought my beloved under my control, and I enjoy Him care freely. I became carefree and my concern eliminated O Nanak, I found God by reciting. ||2||7||30|| Saarag, Fifth Master: I praise visualizing God; I listened to guru's lesson intently and merged with my beloved. ||1||Pause|| I am happily married from a discarded one; I found handsome all-knowing God; The home, where I was not allowed to sit! Now I live there. ||1|| He the love of saints, who protects the honour of His saints; now he is under their control; Says Nanak, my mind is pleased with God, and worry of people tell tale is gone. ||2||8||31|| Saarag, Fifth Master: Now my association with five thieves has ended. Visualizing God my mind became happy. I am freed by guru's grace. ||1||Pause|| There are many sinful places on the earth and there are many holes to fire at the enemy. The sinners and egotistic cannot go there; I robbed it in saint's company. ||1|| I have found a great treasure, a priceless, inexhaustible supply of jewels. O servant Nanak, when God showered His grace, I started to enjoy God's love in my mind. ||2||9||32|| Saarag, Fifth Master:

Now my mind is absorbed in my Lord. The perfect guru has blessed me with the gift of life. I am entangled with the Lord, like the fish with water. ||1||Pause|| I have eradicated lust, anger, greed, ego and envy; I have given all this as a gift. The guru gave the medicine of his lesson; then I realized the all-knowing God; ||1|| My house is Your, You are my master. My guru eliminated the ego of the humble. Page 1211 Says Nanak, I have found at home the treasure of God's worship intuitively. ||2||10||33|| Saarag, Fifth Master: O my beloved Lord, all beings are Yours – You save them. By a little bit of Your kindness the destruction ends and then You bestow salvation to millions in the universe. ||1||Pause|| I offer countless prayers; I remember You at every moment. Please be kind O destroyer of pain of the poor; give me Your hand and save me. ||1|| What to say of the ignorant kings; tell me who kills whom? O Nanak, O bestowal of peace, the world is Yours and you look after it. ||2||11||34|| Saarag, Fifth Master: Now I have obtained the wealth of God's name. I became carefree, and all my thirst is quenched; this is written on my forehead. ||1||Pause|| I became detached searching for You and finally I came to my body village. The kind guru sold me this merchandise; I obtained the priceless jewel; ||1|| Any other business you do; gives you more pain. God's love is the wealth of the carefree traders of worship of the Lord of the universe. Nanak recites the name of God. ||2||12||35|| Saarag, Fifth Master: When I say my beloved God; it tastes sweet to my mind. The guru took me by the arm and put me to serve ever kind and beloved God. ||1||Pause|| O God, You are my Lord the cherisher of all. I and my wife are Your servants. You are my honour and power. Your name is my shelter. ||1|| If You seat me on the throne, then I am Your slave. If You make me a grass-cutter, then what can I say? Servant Nanak's God is the primal Lord, the architect of destiny, unfathomable and immeasurable. ||2||13||36|| Saarag, Fifth Master: The tongue looks adorable saying God. He creates and destroys in a moment. Seeing this wonder He entices my mind; ||1||Pause|| My mind becomes happy listening to His name and my pain and pride depart. I have found peace; my pains have been taken away, since I became Yours. ||1|| Sins departed, my mind became pure; the guru eliminated the enemy worldly pleasure. Says Nanak; I have found God, the all-powerful Creator, the cause of causes. ||2||14||37|| Saarag, Fifth Master: With my eyes, I have seen the amazing play. He is far from all, yet near all. He is inaccessible and unfathomable, and dwells in every heart. ||1||Pause|| The infallible Lord never makes a mistake. He does not suggest or consult anyone. He creates, cares for and destroys in a moment. He is the love of devotees. ||1|| The lamp is lit in the dark; the guru has enlightened my mind. Page 1212 Says Nanak, visualizing Him I found peace and my desire is fulfilled. ||2||15||38|| Saarag, Fifth Master: The most beautiful path to follow is the path of the Lord of the universe. The more you walk on any other path, the more pain and sorrow you suffer. ||1||Pause|| The eyes became sacred by seeing Him and the hands became sacred by serving him. With God dwelling in the mind, the mind became sacred and my forehead became sacred with the dust of the saints. ||1|| Reciting God obtains priceless treasure; those with pre-ordained destiny obtain it. Servant Nanak has met the perfect guru; he passes his life in peace and pleasure. ||2||16||39|| Saarag, Fifth Master: Recite God; He will be your friend in the end. Where your mother, father, children and siblings cannot help; You protect there. ||1||Pause|| He recites God in the dark house (body); who has it written in his fate; His bonds are untied, and the guru liberates him. He sees You everywhere. ||1|| Drinking sacred God's name, his mind is satisfied. Tasting it, his tongue is satiated. Says Nanak, I have obtained celestial peace and contentment; the guru has quenched all my thirst. ||2||17||40|| Saarag, Fifth Master: Meeting such a guru, I recite God; He has become kind and compassionate to me. He is the destroyer of pain; the hot wind does not touch me. ||1||Pause|| With each and every breath, I sing the praises of the Lord. May I not separate from Him and forget Him even for a moment? ||1|| I admire his lotus feet visualizing the guru. Says Nanak, I do not care about anything else; I have found God the ocean of peace. ||2||18||41|| Saarag, Fifth Master: Guru's teaching tastes sweet to my mind. I am lucky that I became enlightened; I see God in everyone. ||1||Pause|| The supreme Lord, beyond birth, self-existent, is seated in every heart everywhere. I have obtained the sacred God's name; I am a sacrifice to God's lotus feet. ||1|| I anoint my forehead with the dust of the society of saints; it is as if I have bathed at all the shrines. Says Nanak, I am dyed in the deep red colour of His love; the deep love of my Lord shall never fade away. ||2||19||42|| Saarag, Fifth Master: The guru has given me the name of the Lord as my companion. A little bit of God's name enshrined in my mind, and my hunger vanished. ||1||Pause|| The treasure of mercy, master of excellence, my Lord, the ocean of peace is the Lord of all. My hopes rest in You O my Lord; hope in anything else is useless. ||1|| My eyes were satisfied visualizing the guru; he placed his hand on my forehead. Page 1213 Says Nanak, I have found immeasurable peace; my fear of birth and death is gone. ||2||20||43|| Saarag, Fifth Master: You ignorant: why are you going somewhere else? You have the enticing nectar with you; yet you forget it and eat poison. ||1||Pause|| God the Creator is beautiful, wise and incomparable and the architect of destiny, but you have no love for Him. The ignorant is enticed by worldly wealth and being robbed by falsehood. ||1|| The kind God the destroyer of pain has become kind and he is in tune with the saints. I have obtained all treasures in my heart; says Nanak, my light has merged into His light. ||2||21||44|| Saarag, Fifth Master: I have my first love with my beloved God; The word you gave me O guru; I am honoured and adorned by it. ||1||Pause|| I am forgetful, You never forget. I am a sinner; You are the saviour of sinners. I am a lowly tree, You are the sandalwood tree. Please preserve my honour because we live close to each other. ||1|| You are deep and profound, calm and benevolent. What I the poor being am? The kind guru united Nanak with God; and I sleep in peace in my bed. ||2||22||45|| Saarag, Fifth Master: O my mind, blessed and approved is the day; Fruitful and beautiful is that moment; when the guru bestowed me with divine wisdom; ||1||Pause|| Blessed is the time and my husband Lord and blessed are those whom You bestow honour. This body, my home and wealth are Yours; I offer my heart to You; ||1|| Visualizing You for a moment equals peace of millions of kingdoms. When You say to Your servant to sit down close by, the peace I get is unlimited. ||2||23||46|| Saarag, Fifth Master: Now my doubt and pain is gone. I have forsaken all other efforts, and have come to guru's refuge. ||1||Pause|| All my deeds are fulfilled; my sickness of ego is eradicated. Millions of sins are destroyed in an instant by reciting God meeting with the guru. ||1|| My guru brought five servants under control and my mind became stable. It does not come or go; it does not waver, O Nanak, my empire is eternal. ||2||24||47|| Saarag, Fifth Master: Here and hereafter, my God is forever my help. My beloved entices my mind. How do I sing His praises? ||1||Pause|| He plays and caresses me. It is a happy time forever. He cherishes me, as father and mother love their child. ||1|| I cannot survive without Him even for a moment; I never forget Him. Page 1214 Says Nanak; joining the society of saints, I am attuned to God with love. ||2||25||48|| Saarag, Fifth Master: Sing the praises of Your friend and master. Recite God the bestowal of peace and do not hope for anything else. ||1||Pause|| He, who enjoys peace and happiness in His Home; seek His refuge; But if you forsake Him, and serve mortal beings, your honour will dissolve like salt in water. ||1|| I have taken support of my master. I realized this by meeting the guru. Nanak has met God, the treasure of excellence; all dependence on others is gone. ||2||26||49|| Saarag, Fifth Master: I have taken the protection of my God; I do not look up to anyone else. My honour and glory are Yours, O God. ||1||Pause|| God has taken my side and pulled me out of the clutches of corruption. I went and touched guru's feet; he put the medicine of God's sacred name into my mouth. ||1|| How many of Your praises can I say with one mouth O giver to the virtue less. You cut my noose and made me Your own; Nanak found eternal peace. ||2||27||50|| Saarag, Fifth Master: Reciting God, the pain is destroyed. The bestowal of peace became kind and freed me forever. ||1||Pause|| I do not think of anyone other than God; tell me where should I go? Keep me as You please O Lord; You own everything of mine; ||1|| God gave me His Hand and saved me; He has blessed me with eternal life. Says Nanak, my mind is happy that the noose of death is cut. ||2||28||51|| Saarag, Fifth Master: My mind recites Your name all the time. I am Your humble child O father God; bring me up as You wish; ||1||Pause|| When I am hungry, I ask for food; when I am full, I am at peace. I am healthy when I live with You; I become dust when I leave You. ||1|| What power does the slave of Your slave has? The Creator created me. If I do not forget God's name; my life is fulfilled; this is the essence O Nanak. ||2||29||52|| Saarag, Fifth Master: I have driven away the fear and other concern from my mind. I sing the praises of my beloved, kind, playful and loveable God slowly and steadily. ||1||Pause|| I practice guru's teaching by his grace; I do not go anywhere else. I realized the ethical, honourable, concentrating, peaceful and joyous God the love of devotees at my home. ||1|| | enjoy millions of happiness by listening to his words and merge in peace intuitively. He does and makes us to do everything O Nanak He is self existent. ||2||30||53|| Page 1215 Saarag, Fifth Master: Sacred God's name is the support of my mind. I admire him who gave it to me; I humbly bow down to my guru. ||1||Pause|| My thirst is quenched, I am content and I burnt away the poison of lust and anger. This mind does not come and go; it sits where the formless Lord sits. ||1|| One Lord is manifest, hidden and he is in a scary dark place. He exists from the beginning, in the middle and till the end. Nanak says the truth. ||2||31||54|| Saarang, Fifth Master: Without God, I cannot survive, even for an instant. One who finds joy in the Lord, finds total peace. ||1||Pause|| He is my beautiful soul, life and wealth; I get happiness reciting Him. He is all-powerful and with me forever; how can I say His praises? ||1|| His place and glory are sacred; sacred are those who listen and speak of Him. Says Nanak, the dwelling is sacred, in which Your saints live. ||2||32||55|| Saarag, Fifth Master: My tongue says You You You. In mother's womb, You sustained me, You help me in the world as well. ||1||Pause|| You are my father and mother; You are my loving friend and sibling. You are my family, my support. You are the giver of life. ||1|| You are my treasure, You are my wealth. You are my gems and jewels. You are the wish-fulfilling Elysian Tree. Nanak has found You through the guru, now he is satisfied. ||2||33||56|| Saarag, Fifth Master: Wherever I go, I miss my beloved. If one is someone's follower, he will go to his master all the time. ||1||Pause|| He shares his sorrows, his joys and his state of mind with him. He obtains honour and strength and favour from him. ||1|| Some are kings, beautiful, wealthy and have property; some have a father and a mother. Nanak found everything in abundance and his desire is fulfilled. ||2||34||57|| Saarag, Fifth Master: False is intoxication and pride of worldly wealth. Get rid of your fraud and attachment O ignorant; know that God is with you. ||1||Pause|| False are kingdoms, youth, nobility, kings, rulers and princes. False are the fine clothes, perfumes and cleverness, food and drinks. ||1|| O master of the humble! The servant of servants seeks saint's refuge. I humbly and care freely beg to unite with You O Nanak's life. ||2||35||58|| Saarag, Fifth Master: The mortal cannot do anything on his own. He does many deeds, wanders all over and entangles more and more. ||1||Pause|| They are friends for four days; they will not be there in time of need. Page 1216 He is totally involved with those who are of no use to him; ||1|| I am nothing; nothing belongs to me. I have no power or control. O Nanak's God the doer, cause of causes; save me in saint's company. ||2||36||59|| Saarag, Fifth Master: The great enticer keeps enticing; it cannot be stopped. She is the beloved of all mystics and seekers; no one can fend her off. ||1||Pause|| Reciting the six Shaastras and visiting sacred shrines of pilgrimage does not decrease her power. She does not spare even those who worship, draw circles, fast, take vows and do penance. ||1|| The world has fallen into the deep dark pit. O saints, please liberate me; Nanak has been liberated in devotee's company, seeing them even for a moment. ||2||37||60|| Saarag, Fifth Master: What are you going to do by making money? You are puffed up like a bag of air, and your skin is brittle. Your body has grown old and dusty. ||1||Pause|| You move things from here to there, like the hawk dives on the prey. You have forgotten the giver O ignorant; you fill your belly like a traveler in a restaurant. ||1|| You are entangled in the taste of false pleasures and sins; the path which you have to take is very narrow. Says Nanak: realize O childish; your bundle will open soon. ||2||38||61|| Saarag, Fifth Master: Know that the guru is with you. In God's court the most powerful are not honoured but he is; ||1||Pause|| What is the origin of human beings? How they look like? When the soul merged with dirt; then this hard to get body is formed. ||1|| I learned to serve, meditate, penance and the reality from You. Placing His Hand on my forehead, He has cut the chains of Nanak the servant of servants. ||2||39||62|| Saarag, Fifth Master: He blessed his servant with God's name. What can any poor mortal do to him, who has God as his protector? ||1||Pause|| He is the great being and the Leader. He fulfills His servant's deeds. Our Lord the inner-knower destroys all enemies; ||1|| He preserves the honour of his servant and looks after him. From the beginning and for ages, He protects the servant; he is Nanak's God; ||2||40||63|| Saarag, Fifth Master: O Lord, You are my friend, my companion and my life. My mind, wealth, body and soul are all Yours; this body exists by Your support. ||1||Pause|| You have blessed me with all sorts of gifts and honour. O inner knower; You preserve my honour forever. ||1|| Page 1217 The saints who realize You, O Lord; are accepted by You. The fortunate join the company of saints; Nanak praises the saints. ||2||41||64|| Saarag, Fifth Master: Save me, O merciful saint! You are all-powerful cause of causes. You connect the broken. ||1||Pause|| You save the sinners of many lifes; I obtained knowledge in your company. Forgetting God, we wander through countless lifes; so I recite God with every breath. ||1|| Whoever meets God's devotees becomes sacred from sinner. Says Nanak; the fortunate conquers the priceless human life. ||2||42||65|| Saarag, Fifth Master: O my Lord, Your humble servant has come to offer this prayer. Listening to Your name, I am blessed with total peace, bliss and contentment. ||1||Pause|| O treasure of kindness, ocean of peace; Your glory prevails everywhere. O Lord, You enjoy saint's company; You reveal Yourself to them. ||1|| I serve the saints with my eyes and clean their feet with my hair. Nanak finds peace twenty four hours a day seeing the saints; ||2||43||66|| Saarag, Fifth Master: One who is lovingly absorbed in God's name? The fortunate is friendly, kind hearted, content and peaceful. ||1||Pause|| He is free of worldly wealth and eliminates ego. He longs and hopes to see one God and seeks the support of the beloved. ||1|| He is carefree and detached while asleep, awake, standing, sitting and laughing. Says Nanak; God's servants cheat the worldly wealth that cheats the world. ||2||44||67|| Saarag, Fifth Master: Now, no one complains about Lord's humble servant. The guru the transcendent Lord destroys whoever tries to complain. ||1||Pause|| Whoever harbours enmity with the enemyless; loses in God's court. From the beginning, for ages, praising God saves the honour of devotees. ||1|| Taking support of God's lotus feet makes them carefree; all of their concerns are eliminated. Nanak recites God's name through guru's teaching and he is known in the whole world. ||2||45||68|| Saarag, Fifth Master: Lord's humble servant has eliminated his ego. Keep me as You please O Lord. I live by witnessing Your divine power.

||1||Pause|| My worry has vanished through guru's teaching and devotee's company. I look upon friend and foe alike; and I recite God intuitively. ||1|| The inner fire extinguished, I became calm and content listening to divine music and I am delighted. Nanak is truly joyous listening to the sound of divine words. ||2||46||69|| Page 1218 Saarag, Fifth Master: My guru has eliminated my doubt. I admire the guru and I am devoted to Him forever. ||1||Pause|| I recite guru's name day and night and enshrine guru's feet in my mind. I bathe in guru's dust daily and the filth of sins is washed away. ||1|| I continuously serve the perfect guru; I humbly bow to my guru. The perfect guru gave me all the rewards. The guru has bestowed salvation to Nanak. ||2||47||70|| Saarag, Fifth Master: The mortal attains salvation by reciting God's name. His calamities and fears are erased by lovingly attaching to devotee's company. ||1||Pause|| He says God God God and sings God's praises. Abandoning pride, lust, anger and slander, he falls in love with God; ||1|| Worship the kind God and look adorable saying God God. Says Nanak, be the dust of all. Visualize and merge with God saying God God; ||2||48||71|| Saarag, Fifth Master: I admire my perfect guru. He enshrined God's name in my mind by His power and protected me. ||1||Pause|| He made his servant carefree and eliminated all sufferings. So renounce all other efforts, and enshrine Lord's lotus feet in your mind. ||1|| God is one and He is the support of life, my friend and companion; Nanak's Lord is the highest of all; again and again, I humbly bow to Him. ||2||49||72|| Saarag, Fifth Master: Is anyone without God; if so tell me where? The Creator is the bestowal of happiness; recite that God forever. ||1||Pause|| He has strung all beings on His thread; sing the praises of that God. Recite God who gave you everything. Why do you go anywhere else? ||1|| Service to my Lord is rewarding; you obtain the fruit of your choice from Him. Says Nanak, take advantage and profit of it and go home in peace. ||2||50||73|| Saarag, Fifth Master: O my Lord, I have come to Your sanctuary. The doubt of my mind is eliminated since I saw You. ||1||Pause|| You knew my condition even without my speaking. You inspired me to recite Your name. My pains are gone, and I am absorbed in peace and poise. I sing Your praises with joy. ||1|| You took my arm and pulled me out of the dark pit of worldly wealth. Says Nanak, the

guru has cut my bonds, and united me with him, I was separated from him. ||2||51||74|| Page 1219 Saarag, Fifth Master: To realize God's name is soothing. The devotees searched the Vedas, the Puraanas and the Simritees and found it. ||1||Pause|| I wandered around burning in the worlds of Shiva, Brahma and Indra; I became soothed by reciting my master; the pain of suffering and doubt departed. ||1|| Whoever has been saved in the past or present was saved through loving worship of God. This is Nanak's prayer: O God; please let me serve the humble saints. ||2||52||75|| Saarag, Fifth Master; O my tongue, sing the sacred praises of the Lord. Say God God. Listen to God's sermon and say God's name. ||1||Pause|| Collect the jewel, the wealth of God's name in your mind and body with love. Think that the other worship is imaginary; this is the truth; ||1|| God is the bestowal of life, soul and salvation. Attune to Him with love. Says Nanak, go to His refuge; He supports all. ||2||53||76|| Saarag, Fifth Master: I cannot do anything else. I have taken this support, meeting the saints and entered the refuge of the Lord of the world. ||1||Pause|| The five wicked enemies are in the body; they lead the mortal to practice evil and corruption. He desires from the infinite God day and night. He is caught in the net of family life and burning. ||1|| The kind God is the Help of the helpless, the ocean of peace and the destroyer of all pains and fears. Slave Nanak longs for this blessing that he may live, looking at God's feet. ||2||54||77|| Saarag, Fifth Master: Without Lord's name, all other tastes are bland. Sing Gods sacred praises with love and perfect tune. ||1||Pause|| Reciting God obtains eternal peace and all painful deeds are erased. Earn the profit of God's name in devotee's company; load and bring it home; ||1|| He is the highest of high; He has no limit. Nanak cannot express His glories; he is amazed seeing it. ||2||55||78|| Saarag, Fifth Master: The mortal came to hear and read God's sermon. If he forgets God's name and is greedy of other things. His taking birth is useless. ||1||Pause|| O my unconscious mind, become conscious and understand; the saints speak the unspoken speech of the Lord. Earn profit of reciting God's name. Your coming and going will end. ||1|| Efforts, powers and cleverness are yours if You bless me, I recite Your name. Those, who please God, start worshipping and are called God's devotees. ||2||56||79|| Saarag, Fifth Master: Those who deal in

God's name are rich. They earn the wealth of God's name and share with others, contemplating guru's teaching. ||1||Pause|| Page 1220 Abandon deception and become enemyless and see God with you forever. Deal in true wealth, gather the true wealth, and you will never lose. ||1|| Eating and consuming it, it never exhausts; God's treasures are overflowing. Says Nanak; then you go to God's court with honour. ||2||57||80|| Saarag, Fifth Master: O dear God, what I the orphan am? From what source did you create humans? This happens by Your power; ||1||Pause|| O infinite and bestowal of soul and life of all, Your virtues cannot be described? You are the beloved of all, the cherisher of all and the support of all. ||1|| No one knows Your divine wisdom; You created the universe. Please, seat me in the boat of devotees O Nanak, and take me across the terrifying world-ocean. ||2||58||81|| Saarag, Fifth Master: One who comes to God's sanctuary is fortunate. He knows of no other than one God. He has renounced all other efforts. ||1||Pause|| He recites God with mind, body and tongue and obtains peace in devotee's company. He enjoys bliss and pleasure, and savors the unspoken words of the Lord; he merges intuitively into the true Lord. ||1|| Whoever He makes His own by His grace; they speak sacred words. Those who are imbued with God the bestowal of salvation, obtain salvation in devotee's company. ||2||59||82|| Saarag, Fifth Master: Since I went to devotee's refuge; My mind is illuminated with peace and contentment, there is no useless deed left behind. ||1||Pause|| Please be kind and bless me with Your name; this is my request. I forgot other deeds by reciting God's name and earned the real profit; ||1|| I have merged again where I came from; that is the reality. Says Nanak, the guru has eradicated my doubt; my light has merged in supreme Light. ||2||60||83|| Saarag, Fifth Master: O my tongue, sing God's praises. Abandon all other tastes; the taste of God's name is sacred. ||1||Pause|| Enshrine God's lotus feet in the mind and attune to one with love. Become pure in devotee's company and do not take birth again. ||1|| You are the support of my soul and life; You are the home of the homeless. Recite God with each breath and praise Him O Nanak. ||2||61||84|| Saarag, Fifth Master: Worshipping the feet of the Lord of the universe is heaven. Recite God's sacred name and obtain the priceless liberation in devotee's company. ||1||Pause|| O God, please be kind that I may hear with my ears Your sacred sermon. Both sides of my coming and going are complete and I obtained peace and comfort. ||1|| Page 1221 I realized the reality by thinking that worshipping God is the highest worship. Says Nanak, without God's name, all other processes are incomplete. ||2||62||85|| Saarag, Fifth Master: O bestowal the true guru; All sufferings go away visualizing You; I admire Your lotus feet. ||1||Pause|| The supreme Lord is true, the devotees are true and God's name is eternal. So worship the immortal, supreme Lord devotionally and sing His praises. ||1|| The limits of the inaccessible, unfathomable Lord cannot be found; He is the support of all. O Nanak, praise the one, who has no limits and end. ||2||63||86|| Saarag, Fifth Master: Guru's feet are enshrined in my mind. My Lord is omnipresent and lives near all. ||1||Pause|| Breaking my bonds, I am lovingly attuned to God and I am happy with saints. This precious human life became sacred and all my desires are fulfilled. ||1|| O my God, whoever You bless; sings God's praises. He sings God's praises twenty-four hours a day; servant Nanak admires him forever. ||2||64||87|| Saarag, Fifth Master: The life is only worthwhile if you visualize God; O my enticing beloved; be kind and erase the record of my doubt. ||1||Pause|| Peace does not well up by saying or hearing. Nothing can be learned without believing. He, who forgets God and longs for another – his face is blackened; ||1|| One, who is blessed with the wealth of peace of our master, does not believe in any other false image. O Nanak, my mind is fascinated and intoxicated by visualizing God and my desires are fulfilled. ||2||65||88|| Saarag, Fifth Master: O mortal; recite God's name. All sins are eliminated in a moment. It equals, giving millions of awns and sacred bathing. ||1||Pause|| Engaging in other useless deeds is a useless effort; Without God's name any other wisdom is an empty shell. They are freed from the pain of birth and death by reciting the Lord of the world devotionally. ||1|| Your refuge is the perfect ocean of peace O God be kind and bless me with it. Nanak lives by reciting God and his pride is eradicated. ||2||66||89|| Saarag, Fifth Master: He, who loves the origin, is true. He, who recites God with love has attained destiny and lives there; ||1||Pause|| One who deceives and does not earn profit; the ignorant is not true. He abandons profitable business and engages in losing business; he does not recite the beautiful God. ||1|| He is clever, wise, scholar, brave and gives awns. O Nanak, whoever recites God in devotee's company is accepted. ||2||67||90|| Page 1222 Saarag, Fifth Master: God is the life of the humble saints. Instead of evil enjoyments, they enjoy sacred God's name the ocean of peace. ||1||Pause|| They gather the wealth of priceless God's name and enshrine in the mind and body. Imbued with God's love, their minds are dyed deep red and enjoy God's name. ||1|| As the fish is entangled in water, they are entangled in God's name. O Nanak, the saints are like the rain bird; they find peace drinking God's name. ||2||68||91|| Saarag, Fifth Master: Without God's name, the mortal is insane. Whatever they do; they entangle more and more in bonds. ||1||Pause|| Without serving God, one who serves others; the death cuts his life short. When the devil of death kills you; what will happen then? ||1|| Please protect Your slave, O ever kind God; O Nanak, my God is the treasure of Peace; devotee's company is my wealth. ||2||69||92|| Saarag, Fifth Master: My mind and body deal only in God; I sing His praises in devotional worship; the world does not bother me; ||1||Pause|| Listen to God's praises and recite God is the way of devotees. He implants God's lotus feet in his heart; this is his way of worship. ||1|| O kind to the poor God; listen to my prayer and be kind to me; Nanak says God's sacred name from the tongue and admires Him. ||2||70||93|| Saarag, Fifth Master: Those without God's name have low intellect. He does not recite God the master; the blind ignorant suffers terrible pain. ||1||Pause|| He does not love God's name and is attached to other imaginary ways. It does not take much to break that, like the earthen pot that holds water. ||1|| Be kind and give me the joy of Your worship that I get enticed by love. Servant Nanak is at your refuge; I have no one but God. ||2||71||94|| Saarag, Fifth Master: I think of that moment in my mind; When I join the gathering of friendly saints and sing God's praises forever. ||1||Pause|| Without worshipping God, whatever you do will go waste? The perfect God the embodiment of joy tastes sweet to my mind, nothing else; ||1|| Meditation, austere self-discipline and good deeds do not equal devotee's peace of mind. God's lotus feet pierce Nanak's mind; I am absorbed in His feet. ||2||72||95|| Saarag, Fifth

Master: My God the inner knower is always with me. Reciting God's name gives peace and joy here and hereafter. ||1||Pause|| Page 1223 God is my friend and a companion; I sing praises of kind God the Lord. I never forget Him from my mind; the perfect guru united me with Him. ||1|| He, who has all beings in His control; protects His servant by His grace; One who is lovingly attuned to the one, the perfect transcendent Lord O Nanak, is free of all concerns. ||2||73||96|| Saarag, Fifth Master: One who has God's support? All his desires are fulfilled, and no pain afflicts him. ||1||Pause|| The humble who is devotee and servant of God; I live by listening to his praises. I work hard to visualize Him but I only get what I earn; ||1|| I enjoy visualizing Him by guru's grace and no one else. Please bless Nanak with the gift that he lives by washing saint's feet. ||2||74||97|| Saarag, Fifth Master: I live by singing the praises of God. O my kind beloved father; be kind that I do not forget You at all. ||1||Pause|| My mind, body and wealth all are Yours, O my master; there is no other place for me. I live as you keep me; I wear and eat whatever you give; ||1|| I praise devotee's company so much that I will not take birth again. Slave Nanak seeks Your refuge; keep me as You please. ||2||75||98|| Saarag, Fifth Master: O my mind, God's name is the essence of peace. Other affairs of worldly wealth are useless. They are like dirt. ||1||Pause|| The sinner is stuck in the dark pit of miserable hell. He is tired of wandering in many different lifes and keeps doing; ||1|| O purifier of sinners, love of Your devotees, please be kind to the poor. With palms pressed together, Nanak begs for this blessing: O Lord, please save me in the company of devotees. ||2||76||99|| Saarag, Fifth Master: I look adorable by God's grace. The doubt, sickness and ego are all erased, and the three diseases are cured. ||1||Pause|| My thirst quenched, my hopes fulfilled; my sorrow and worry ended. Singing the praises of sacred and immortal God, my mind and body are content. ||1|| The intoxication of lust, anger and greed vanished in devotee's company. God the love of devotees and destroyer of fear is Nanak's mother and father. ||2||77||100|| Saarag, Fifth Master: The whole world is worried without God's name. The dog like desire does not get fulfilled; that is how they are attached to bad and dirty deeds. ||1||Pause|| God cheated them and made them forget God; they take birth time and again. He does not recite God at all; the devil of death will make him suffer. ||1|| O God the destroyer of pain of the poor; be kind. May I be the dust of Your saints. Page 1224 Slave Nanak begs to visualize You; this is the resolve of my mind and body. ||2||78||101|| Saarag, Fifth Master: Without the name of the Lord, the soul is filthy. God has deluded them, they drink poison. ||1||Pause|| They wander in millions of lives in many ways and cannot stay anywhere. They did not surrender to the perfect guru intuitively; the faithless keep coming and going in different life. ||1|| O all-powerful inaccessible and infinite God, please protect me. Slave Nanak seeks Your sanctuary so that he crosses over the terrifying world ocean. ||2||79||102|| Saarag, Fifth Master. Recite and praise God with love. Recite the transcendent God in devotee's company; it is sacred and enjoyable. ||1||Pause|| Reciting one sacred immortal God, the intoxication of worldly wealth vanishes. He is happy and content and infinite divine music plays; he does not suffer again. ||1|| Brahma, Sanak, Sanandan, Sukhdev and Prahlaad sing His praises. Drink the sacred, enticing God's nectar and recite God's amazing name O Nanak. ||2||80||103|| Saarag, Fifth Master: He commits millions of sins. Day and night, he does not get tired of them, and never stops. ||1||Pause|| He carries on his head, a terrible heavy load of sins and corruption. In an instant, he is exposed when the devil of death catches him by the hair. ||1|| He goes through many lifes such as, animal, ghost, camel and donkey. O Nanak, recite God the lord of the universe in devotee's company. nothing will harm you. ||2||81||104|| Saarag, Fifth Master: He is blind! He eats loads of poison. His eyes, ears, body and breath will end in an instant. ||1||Pause|| He fills his belly by robbing the homeless; but the worldly wealth does not go with him; He regrets committing sins but never stops; ||1|| The devil of death arrests the slanderer and hits him on the head. O Nanak, he cuts himself with his dagger, and wounds his mind. ||2||82||105|| Saarag, Fifth Master: The slanderer breaks in the middle. God protects His devotees but those who turn away from Him die. ||1||Pause|| No one listens to him; he has no place to sit; He suffers pain here, and goes to hell hereafter and wanders through many lifes. ||1|| He is known all over the world; he gets what he earns. Nanak sings the praises of carefree Creator in His refuge. ||2||83||106|| Saarag, Fifth

Master: Desire plays in many ways. Page 1225 His desire is not fulfilled by any means, he loses in the end. ||1||Pause|| He does such business that, peace, happiness and contentment do not well up. He does not differentiate between him and others; he burns in lust and anger. ||1|| The world is enveloped by an ocean of pain; O Lord, please save Your slave! Nanak seeks the sanctuary of Your lotus feet; and admires you forever. ||2||84||107|| Saarag, Fifth Master: O sinner, with what lesson did you take? You do not recite God; He gave you the soul and body. ||1||Pause|| He eats drinks and sleeps peacefully but does not recite God. The ignorant cries in the womb of the mother; ||1|| The ignorant intoxicated by useless deeds wanders through many a life. Forgetting God, one suffers countless pains; O Nanak searching God's wisdom obtains peace. ||2||85||108|| Saarng, Fifth Master: O mother, I have taken shelter of God's feet. Visualizing Him my mind got enticed and the ill will washed away. ||1||Pause|| He is unfathomable, incomprehensible, high and immortal. His value cannot be appraised. I am amazed seeing Him in water and land. He is omnipresent. ||1|| Merciful to the meek, my beloved and enticer God is realized meeting the devotee's. Nanak lives by reciting God. The devil of death cannot bother him. ||2||86||109|| Saarag, Fifth Master: O mother, my mind is intoxicated. Visualizing the kind Lord, he is filled with joy and peace and intoxicated with God's love. ||1||Pause|| Singing God's sacred praises I have become pure and will never be filthy again. My mind is attached to God's lotus feet; I have surrendered to infinite Lord. ||1|| He made all his humble servants his own and the divine light is lit. O Nanak, savouring the name of the Lord, I have become detached; I am saved along with my dynasty. ||2||87||110|| Saarag, Fifth Master: O mother, reciting others I will die. Forsaking the Lord of the universe, the giver of souls, the mortal is entangled in worldly wealth. ||1||Pause|| Forgetting God's name they walk on other path and go to hell. They suffer countless punishments and wander from womb to womb. ||1|| They are wealthy, and honourable and merge in God's refuge. By Guru's grace, O Nanak, they conquer the world; they do not come and go again. ||2||88||111|| Saarag, Fifth Master: The Lord has cut down the cheat with an axe. The forest of doubt is burnt away in an instant, by wearing God's name. ||1||Pause|| Lust, anger and slander are driven out in devotee's company. Page 1226 The guru-willed conquers the priceless life; he does not lose it in a gamble. ||1|| Sing God's praises twenty-four hours a day contemplating guru's teaching. Servant Nanak is the slave of Your slaves and bows to you again and again. ||2||89||112|| Saarag, Fifth Master: Granth Sahib the holy book is the place of the transcendent Lord; Singing the praises of the Lord of the universe is the complete divine wisdom. ||1||Pause|| The mystics, seekers and all sages long for Him but only a few are devoted. Whoever God becomes kind to; his deeds are fulfilled. ||1|| One, who has God abiding in the mind, the whole world knows him. May I never forget You, even for a moment O Creator; Nanak begs for this gift. ||2||90||113|| Saarag, Fifth Master: The rain has fallen everywhere. Singing God's praises with joy, the perfect love has grown. ||1||Pause|| He pervades in four corners, ten directions and in water; there is no place without him. O Perfect God, ocean of mercy, You bless all with the gift of soul. ||1|| It is true that there is God; He is realized in devotee's company. True are those humble beings, who believe in Him O Nanak, they have no doubt. ||2||91||114|| Saarag, Fifth Master: O dear Lord of the universe, You are the support of my life. You are my friend, companion, family and support; ||1||Pause|| You placed Your Hand on my forehead; I sing God's praises in devotee's company. By Your grace, I have obtained all rewards; I recite God's name with love. ||1|| The true guru has laid the eternal foundation; it shall never be shaken. O Nanak, when guru became kind; I found the treasure of peace. ||2||92||115|| Saarag, Fifth Master: Only the true load of the name of God stays with you. Singing God's praises he earns the profit and remains detached in the middle of sins. ||1||Pause|| All beings and creatures find contentment, reciting God; they conquer the infinite life and do not take birth again. ||1|| When the Lord of the universe becomes kind; he unites us with His devotees. Nanak found the wealth of God's lotus feet and fell in love with God. ||2||93||116|| Saarag, Fifth Master: O mother, I am watching the amazing play; my mind is enticed by infinite divine music; it has an amazing taste. ||1||Pause|| He is my mother, father and relative. My mind is happy with God. Singing God's praises in devotee's company, my all connections ended. ||1|| I am lovingly attached to His lotus feet; my doubt and fear ended. Servant Nanak has taken the support of one Lord. He shall not wander in reincarnation ever again. ||2||94||117|| Page 1227 Saarag, Fifth Master: O mother, I am intoxicated with Lord's feet. I know none other than the Lord. I have burnt my sense of duality. ||1||Pause|| O kind Lord; please eliminate my desires that are filled with poison. My mind is enticed, thirsty to visualize Him. He pulled me out of hell. ||1|| By the grace of the saints, I have met the Lord, the giver of peace; the noise of ego has been eradicated. Slave Nanak is imbued with God's love; his mind and body have blossomed. ||2||95||118|| Saarag, Fifth Master: The false dealings are finished. Join devotee's company and recite God; this is the reality in the world. ||1||Pause|| Enshrine God's name in the heart and never waver here or hereafter. Fortunately I obtained guru's teaching and obtained salvation. ||1|| The infinite Lord the master of orphans fully pervades water land and in-between. Drink God's sacred nectar O Nanak, other tastes are useless. ||2||96||119|| Saarag, Fifth Master: You do all kinds of deeds and cry. You are intoxicated with useless attachment and never recite God. ||1||Pause|| Those who recite God in devotee's company; their pains are burnt away. Fruitful is the body and blessed is the birth of those who merge with God. ||1|| God's devotees are better than four great blessings, and the eighteen mystic powers. Slave Nanak longs for devotee's dust that he obtains salvation attached to them. ||2||97||120|| Saarag, Fifth Master: God's servants long for His name. My mind and body long for this pleasure, when will I visualize God. ||1||Pause|| You are endless, O God, my supreme Lord; Your wisdom cannot be known. My mind is pierced by the love of Your lotus feet; I have hidden all in my mind. ||1|| God's devotees read Vedas, Puraanas and the Simritees and speak this sermon from their mouth. O Nanak, salvation obtains by reciting God; others are useless stories. ||2||98||121|| Saarag, Fifth Master: A fly! You are just a fly, created by the Lord. Wherever it stinks, you sit there; you enjoy the most toxic stench. ||1||Pause|| You don't stay put anywhere; I have seen this with my eyes. You do not spare anyone except the saints. The Lord of the universe protects Saints. ||1|| You have enticed all beings; no one knows You except the saints. Slave Nanak is imbued with Gods praises. He realizes God through guru's teaching. ||2||99||122|| Saarag, Fifth Master: O mother, my noose of death has been cut. I obtained eternal peace reciting God. I am detached in the middle of household. ||1||Pause|| Page 1228 God made me His won by His grace. Joining saint's company, I sing God's praises; other desires vanished. ||1|| The saint pulled me out of dense forest, and shown me the path; Nanak has found a diamond. Seeing it all sins departed. ||2||100||123|| Saarag, Fifth Master: O mother, I am stuck in the gully of love. I am very thirsty and long to visualize him, none else quenches it. ||1||Pause|| The Lord is my life, honour, spouse, parent, child, relative, wealth and everything. Cursed is the body, bones, the pile of worms and filth, if it knows any other than God. ||1|| The destroyer of pains of the poor has become kind to me, due to previous love. Nanak seeks the refuge of God, the treasure and the ocean of kindness; my love for others has vanished. ||2||101||124|| Saarag, Fifth Master: Reciting God with love is sacred. Those, who recite my master's lotus feet, become His devotees. ||1||Pause|| Thinking of God in the mind washes away the filth of mind. God's support eliminates the useless birth and death cycle. ||1|| Only those rare one, who have pre-ordained destiny obtain it; Sing praises of the Creator O Nanak. This is the truth. ||2||102||125|| Saarag, Fifth Master: The intellect of those, who recite God's name, becomes true. One who forgets God and attaches to others. It is all temporary. ||1||Pause|| Recite God the master in devotee's company, the sins will be destroyed. Enshrining God's lotus feet in the mind, you will not be born or die again. ||1|| He saved me by His grace; His name is my support. O Nanak, recite Him day and night; you will be happy in his court. ||2||103||126|| Saarag, Fifth Master: You shall be honoured in God's court. By singing God's praises in devotee's company, the pride vanishes. ||1||Pause|| By His grace He accepted me and the guru-willed became spiritually wise. Enshrining God in the mind intuitively I obtained eternal peace and joy. ||1|| She who lives close to her husband Lord is ever married and is known in ten directions. She is imbued with the love of her beloved Lord; Nanak praises her. ||2||104||127|| Saarag, Fifth Master: O Lord, I take support of Your lotus feet. I know You, You are my relative O protector Lord of the world. ||1||Pause|| You are mine; I am Yours; You save me here and hereafter. You are endless and infinite O Lord; only a few realize You by guru's grace. ||1|| God the inner-knower knows everything even without saying or talking. Whoever God unites with Him O Nanak, he is honoured in God's court. ||2||105||128|| Page 1229 Saarag, Fifth Master, Chau-Padas, Fifth House: God is one. He is realized by guru's grace. Recite God; other deeds are useless. Pride, attachment and desire do not end; death destroys the world. ||1||Pause|| Eating, drinking, laughing and sleeping, life passes uselessly. He burns wandering in hell and the devil of death takes care of him. ||1|| He cheats and uselessly slanders others and washes his hands after committing sins. He does not realize without the guru; he is filled with ego, attachment and the dark self-pride. ||2|| He is robbed by evil cheating; he does not remember the Creator. The Lord of the universe is hidden and unattached. The mortal is intoxicated with ego. ||3|| God protects His saints by His grace; they have the support of His lotus feet. With his palms pressed together, Nanak has come to the sanctuary of the primal being, the infinite Lord; ||4||1||129|| Saarag, Fifth Master, Sixth House, Partaal: God is one. He is realized by guru's grace. Speak the sacred words; it is a priceless treasure. Why you blow your useless horn? Look and understand! Reciting gurus teaching, one obtains his destiny. Imbued with the love of the Lord, you shall enjoy; ||1||Pause|| The world is a dream. It is imaginary and temporary. O my companion, why are you enticed by false attachment? Enshrine the love of Your beloved in your heart. ||1|| He is total love and affection. God is always kind. Why are you involved with others? Remain involved and enticed by God. When you join the company of devotees; Says Nanak, then you recite God. Now, your association with devil of death ends. ||2||1||130|| Saarag, Fifth Master: You may donate lot of gold; You may donate land. You think and try many ways to purify your mind. When the mind attaches to God's lotus feet; nothing equals it. ||1||Pause|| You may recite the four Vedas with your tongue; and listen to the eighteen Puraanas and the six Shaastras with your ears; Nothing equals to reciting God's name with love. Remain attached to Lord's lotus feet. ||1|| You may observe fast, say evening prayers and contemplate four Vedas. Do good deeds; you may go on pilgrimages everywhere and do not eat. You may cook your food, with rituals of not being touched; You may make many Yogic postures; Burn incense and devotional lamps, but nothing equals God's name. O kind Lord; listen to the request of the humble; my eyes long to visualize You O Nanak, Your name tastes sweet. ||2||2||131|| Saarag, Fifth Master: Say God God God; saying so, God helps you. ||1||Pause|| Page 1230 Touching saint's feet eliminates lust, anger and greed; singing the praise of kind Lord, one obtains the reward of his choice. ||1|| My doubts and blind attachments have vanished and the bonds of worldly wealth broken and realized the perfect enemyless Lord. My Lord became happy and my pain of birth and death ended. Nanak sings God's praises in saint's refuge. ||2||3||132|| Saarag, Fifth Master: Say God God from your mouth and enshrine Him in the mind; ||1||Pause|| Hear Him with your ears, and do devotional worship, these good deeds are obtained by past deeds. Seek devotee's company and forget other recitation. ||1|| Loving Lord's feet forever is the most sacred of all. It eliminates devotee's fear and burns away the sins and sufferings. Those who say; those who listen, obtain salvation and do not take birth again; Saying God God is the essence of all; Nanak says by contemplating. ||2||4||133|| Saarag, Fifth Master: O saint; beg for God's name and forsake everything else. ||1||Pause|| Recite God with love and sing praises of the Lord of the universe. Long for the dust of God's devotees; God will bestow it; ||1|| God's name obtains eternal happiness, peace, comfort and joy. Reciting God the inner-knower eliminates the fear of devil of death. Seeking the refuge of the Lord of the universe eliminates all worldly pain. The devotee's company is the boat that carries across O Nanak, ||2||5||134|| Saarag, Fifth Master: Visualize the guru and sing the praises of the beloved. I escaped from the five thieves, when I fell at devotee's feet. ||1||Pause|| Whatever you see does not go with you; eliminate pride and attachment. Loving God in devotee's company looks adorable. ||1|| I have found God the treasure of virtues; all my hopes have been fulfilled. Nanak's mind is happy; the guru conquered the impregnable fortress. ||2||6||135|| Saarag, Fifth Master: The mind misses God. I search for Him to see His face; ||1||Pause|| Serve the devotees and saints and recite God in the mind. Seeing the joyous and beautiful face, I will attain my destiny. ||1|| I will give up everything and seek God's refuge; O Nanak, I meet and embrace my guru and console with him. ||2||7||136|| Saarag, Fifth Master: This is my condition. Only the kind Lord knows it. ||1||Pause|| I have abandoned my mother and father, and sold myself to the saints. I gave up my social status, birthright and ancestry; I sing God God. ||1|| I have broken away from other people and family; I work only for God. The guru has taught me, O Nanak, to serve only one Lord. ||2||8||137|| Page 1231 Saarag, Fifth Master: You are my beloved enticing Lord of the world. You are in worms, elephants, stones and all beings; You look after them. ||1||Pause|| You are not far away; You are always with all. You are beautiful, the source of nectar. ||1|| You have no caste or social class, no ancestry or family. Says Nanak: O kind God; ||2||9||138|| Saarag, Fifth Master: I enjoy playing with sins; it entices me like the sun and moon. Making useless noise with ankle bells entices everyone except God; ||Pause|| Worldly wealth clings to the three worlds; the false deeds never become true. He does blind deeds like the waves in the ocean. ||1|| God's servant saints are saved and their noose of death is cut. He changes the sinners to sacred; O Nanak recite Him. ||2||10||139||3||13||155 God is one. He is realized by guru's grace. Tune Saarang, Ninth Master: No one helps you except God; who is the mother, father, child or spouse? Who belongs to whom O brother? ||1||Pause|| All the wealth, land and property which you consider your own; When your soul leaves the body, nothing goes with you; why do you cling to it? ||1|| God is kind to the meek and destroyer of fear forever; you never built a relation with Him; Says Nanak, the whole world is imaginary like the dream at night. ||2||1|| Saarang, Ninth Master: O my mind, why are you entangled in bad deeds? No one stays in this world forever. One comes and the other goes. ||1||Pause|| Whose are the body, wealth and property? Who are you in love with? Whatever is seen shall all vanish like the shade of a cloud. ||1|| Abandon ego and go to saint's refuge and you shall be liberated in a moment. O servant Nanak, without worshipping God; there is no peace even in a dream; ||2||2|| Saarang, Ninth Master: O mortal, why are you wasting your life away? Intoxicated by worldly wealth, enticed by poisonous pleasures; you do not go to God's refuge. ||1||Pause|| This whole world is just a dream; why are you enticed by it? Whoever is born has to die; no one lives forever. ||1||

You believe that this temporary body is true; you tie yourself this way. O servant Nanak, he, who worships God with love, is liberated. ||2||3|| Saarang, Fifth Master: I do not sing God's praise with love. Page 1232 I remain under the influence of corruption night and day; I do what I like; ||1||Pause|| I never listened to gurus teaching; I was entangled with other's spouses. I go around slandering others; I was taught, but I never learned. ||1|| How can I say about my deeds; how I wasted my life? Says Nanak, I am filled with faults. I have come to Your sanctuary – please save me, O Lord! ||2||4||3||13||139||4||159|| Tune Saarang, Ashtapadees, First Master, First House: God is one. He is realized by guru's grace. How can I live without God O my mother? Hail to the Lord of the universe. I beg for singing Your praises; I cannot survive without God; ||1||Pause|| The soul bride is thirsty for God and looks for Him the whole night. My mind is imbued with my Lord and master. Only God knows the pain of others. ||1|| I feel serious pain in my body without God; I realized God through guru's teaching. O God; be kind that I remain merged with God. ||2|| O my mind, recite such a recitation that I remain focused on God's feet. Praising my beloved amazes me and I have merged with carefree God intuitively. ||3|| Recite God's name in the mind with true love; It does not decrease and its value cannot be estimated. Everyone is poor without God's name; the guru taught me this. ||4|| The lovers got revived listening to the friends; the enemies died eating poison. It remains same since birth; when I attuned to it then it appealed to me. ||5|| I am absorbed in trance in God's love. I live by singing God's praises. Guru's teaching dyes the renunciate. He is absorbed in trance. ||6|| The pure juice of God's name tastes sweet and realizes the essence of the Lord. You taught me such a lesson that my mind is stuck where you left it. ||7|| Sanak, Sanandan, Brahma and Indra, were imbued with God's worship and realized God; O Nanak, I cannot live for a moment without God. God's name is my honour. ||8||1|| Saarag, First Master: Without the Lord, how can my mind be comforted? The honourable deed eliminates millions of sufferings. Reciting true Lord obtains salvation. ||1||Pause|| Anger is gone, ego and attachment have been burnt away; I am imbued with His ever-fresh love. Other fears are forgotten, I look forward to God. The pure God is with me. ||1||

Forsaking my fickle intellect, I found God, the destroyer of fear; I am lovingly attuned to guru's teaching. Tasting God's sublime essence, my thirst is quenched; God united the fortunate with Him. ||2|| The empty tank has been filled to overflowing. I am truly content by guru's teaching. Page 1233 My mind became carefree intuitively imbued with love of God; God is kind from the beginning and for ages. ||3|| My beloved enticed my mind and I got attuned to Him fortunately. Thinking of God, all sins and sufferings erased and my mind became pure through love. ||4|| God is deep unfathomable ocean full of jewels; there is no other such worship. Contemplating guru's teaching I realized God the destroyer of fear and other concerns. I do not know any other; ||5|| Conquering my mind I obtained high status by totally imbuing with God's love. I do not know any other except God. The guru taught me this. ||6|| God is inaccessible, without a guardian and unborn; I realized him through guru's teaching. Filled to the brim my mind does not waver. The mind conquered the mind. ||7|| By guru's grace, I speak the unspoken; I speak what He makes me speak. O Nanak, my Lord is kind to the humble; I do not know any other. ||8||2|| Saarag, Third Master, Ashtapadees, First House: God is one. He is realized by guru's grace. O my mind, reciting God's name brings honour. I know of none other than God; I obtained salvation reciting God's name. ||1||Pause|| Guru's teaching eradicates any concern and eliminates death by attuning to God with love. The guru-willed realize God the bestowal of peace and merge with Him intuitively. ||1|| Reciting the name of formless God is devotee's food and they wear the honour of worship. They live at home and recite God and obtain honour in God's court. ||2|| The intellect of the self-willed is false; his mind wavers, and it cannot speak the unspoken words. Eternal God's name enshrines in their mind through sacred true sermon. ||3|| Guru's teaching calmed the wavering mind and I recite God intuitively. Those, who are attuned to God with love, are united with the guru forever. ||4|| If the mind is conquered by guru's teaching, obtains salvation by focusing the mind to God's feet. God is the ocean of pure water; one becomes pure by unknowingly bathing in it. ||5|| Those who contemplate guru's teaching get dyed with God's love and eliminate ego and greed. The beloved God the Lord of the soul destroyer of demons abides in their mind; ||6|| The, devotees that please You, serve you imbued with true love. The false world filled with duality does not reach the destiny; it cannot identify vice and virtue. ||7|| When God unites us with Him, then we speak the unspoken sermon through guru's true teaching and sermon. O Nanak, the truthful merge in true God be reciting God's name. ||8||1|| Saarag, Third Master: O my mind, God's name is very sweet. Page 1234 The guru-willed see only one God the destroyer of sins and other concerns of many lifes. ||1||Pause|| Millions of sins are erased, when the true God appeals to the mind. I do not know any other except God; the guru revealed this to me. ||1|| Those, who have priceless love enshrined in the mind, they merge in peace intuitively. Imbued with guru's teaching they are imbued with deep love intuitively. ||2|| The tongue enjoys the taste through guru's teaching and dyes with deep love. The beloved realizes God's name; his mind gets satisfied and peaceful. ||3|| The scholars and sages get tired of studying; the imitators get tired of imitating. I realized God by guru's grace contemplating guru's teaching. ||4|| Guru's true teaching pleases my mind and I am imbued with God's love. My coming and going ended; those who eliminate ego obtain peace serving the guru. ||5|| Through the true teaching the peaceful tune wells up and the mind attunes to the true Lord. The guru-willed enshrines the name of inaccessible and unfathomable Lord in the mind. ||6|| The whole world is contained in one Lord. Only a few realize it. He, who conquers His mind through guru's teaching, realizes God and everything else forever. ||7|| Whoever God blesses, only he realizes; no one else can say anything. O Nanak, those imbued with God's name become detached and are attuned to guru's lesson. ||8||2|| Saarag, Third Master: O my mind, the speech of the Lord is unspoken. Whoever God blesses realizes it; only a few guru-willed know it. ||1||Pause|| God is profound unfathomable, the Ocean of excellence. He is realized through guru's teaching. Mortals do deeds in all sorts of ways in duality, but they are insane without guru's teaching. ||1|| Those who bathe in God's name become pure and never become impure again. The whole world is filthy without God's name and loses honour in love of duality and doubt. ||2|| O renunciate;

what should I recite; I do not know anything. O God, be kind and bless me with your name and be my friend. ||3|| The true Lord is the true giver, the architect of destiny; as He pleases, He links mortals to His name. He realizes God in guru's refuge whom God inspires to realize. ||4|| Seeing the amazing play, still this mind does not miss Him. He keeps coming and going in the world. He, who serves the guru realizes and obtains salvation. ||5|| The guru told me; once you go to God's refuge; you never leave again. They practice truth, self-restraint and good deeds, their coming and going ends. ||6|| The guru-willed who are supported by truth earn truth and become truthful in true court. Page 1235 The self-willed are deluded by duality; they cannot think and realize God. ||7|| God gives and does everything and watches over. O Nanak, whoever God approves, obtains salvation. ||8||3|| Saarag, Fifth Master, Ashtapadees, First House: God is one. He is realized by guru's grace. O Lord of the world, I watch Your wondrous glory. You are the doer, the cause of causes, the Creator and destroyer. You are the sovereign Lord of all. ||1||Pause|| The rulers and nobles and kings shall become beggars. They put up false show. My sovereign king is eternal. Everyone sings His praises. ||1|| Listen to the praises of my Lord King, O saints. I say as much I can. My Lord King, the great giver, is immeasurable. He is the highest of high. ||2|| He has strung the creation by air; He locked the fire in the wood. He placed water and land together, but neither blends with the other. ||3|| Everyone talks about the Lord and yearns for Him with love. First He granted food, and then created the beings. ||4|| He does whatever he wants. He does not consult anyone. The mortals make all sorts of efforts and displays, but He is realized only through true lesson. ||5|| God makes His devotees his own and bestows them with His name. Whoever is disrespectful to Your servants, You sweep them away. ||6|| They are freed joining devotee's company and their sins are destroyed. Seeing them, God becomes kind to others and they swim across the terrifying world ocean. ||7|| I am a little and lowly; You are my great master. Who can talk about Your power? My mind and body are soothed seeing the guru. God's name is my support O Nanak. ||8||1|| Saarag, Fifth Master, Ashtapadees, Sixth House: God is one. He is realized by guru's grace. Listen to the story of the inaccessible and unfathomable God. The congregation of the supreme Lord is amazing! ||1||Pause|| Forever and ever, humbly bow to the true guru. By guru's grace, sing the praises of the infinite Lord. His light shall enlighten your mind. The healing ointment of divine wisdom eliminates ignorance. ||1|| There is no limit to His expanse. His glory is infinite and endless. His many plays cannot be counted. He is not subject to pleasure or pain. ||2|| Many Brahmas write about Him in Vedas. Many Shivas sit in trance. Page 1236 There are many prophets. Many Indras stand at His door.||3|| Many winds, fires and waters are there. Many jewels, oceans filled with butter and milk; Many suns, moons and stars; Many gods and goddesses of many kinds; ||4|| Many earths, many ever milk giving cows; Many miraculous Elysian trees; many Krishna playing the flute; Many skies and underworlds; Many mouths recite the Lord. ||5|| Many Shaastras, Simritees and Puraanas explain God in many ways. Many listeners listen to Lord the treasure. The Lord totally permeates all beings. ||6|| There are many religions and slanderers. Many faces, many mountains of gold. Many thousand-headed snakes, reciting ever-new names of God. They do not know the limits of the supreme Lord; ||7|| Many solar systems, many galaxies are there; Many forms, colours and celestial realms; Many forests, many fruits and roots. He is small and he is large. ||8|| Many ages, days and nights. Much destruction and many creations. Many beings are in His home. Recite God. He is omnipresent. ||9|| His worldly wealth cannot be known. Our sovereign Lord plays many plays. Many sing God's praises in many tunes with love. Many are hidden and revealed in His mind. ||10|| He is above all, and yet He is always with His devotees. Twenty-four hours a day, they sing His praises with love. The infinite joyful divine music plays in many tunes. There is no end or limit of that sublime essence. ||11|| True is the primal being, and true is His place. He is the highest of high, pure and is liberated. He alone knows His work. He pervades each and every heart. The kind Lord is the treasure of kindness O Nanak. Those who recite Him O Nanak, they become content. ||12||1||2||2||3||7|| Saarag, Chhant, Fifth Master: God is one. He is realized by guru's grace. See the giver of fearlessness in all. He pervades all yet hidden. He pervades all completely, like the union of water and waves. He enjoys all hearts. There is no other like Him. Get imbued with God's love devotionally; He is realized in devotee's congregation. O Nanak, I visualize Him like fish in water; I see the carefree bestowal God in all. ||1|| What praises should I sing, and what honour should I offer Him? The perfect Lord is pervading and permeating all places. The perfect enticing Lord adorns each and every heart. When He withdraws, the mortal turns to dust. Page 1237 Joining devotee's company, why you do not worship Him? It is time now; all your property and wealth that you see – none of it will go with you. Says Nanak; say God God. What else praise and honour I can offer to God; ||2|| I ask the saints, what my Lord looks like. I offer my heart to one, who brings me the news of Him. Give me the news of my dear God; where does the beloved live? He the giver of peace is with you and present in the whole universe. He is free from bonds, knows every heart. I cannot say what He is like? Seeing the amazing play my mind is enticed. The humble asks what my master is like? ||3|| By His grace he came to His devotee. Blessed is that heart, which enshrines God's feet in it. Enshrining His feet in the mind in devotee's company eliminates the darkness of ignorance. The heart is enlightened and enjoys that I found God I wanted. Pain is gone, and peace has come to my house. The ultimate intuitive peace prevails. Says Nanak; I have found the perfect Lord. He has come to His humble servant by His grace. ||4||1|| Vaar of Saarang, Fourth Master, To Be Sung To The Tune Of Mehma-Hasna: God is one. He is realized by guru's grace. Hymn, Second Master: The guru is the key to the chains on the feet, mind is a room and the body is the roof. O Nanak, without the guru, the door of the mind cannot open. No one else has the key. ||1|| First Master: He is not won over by music, songs or the Vedas. He is not won over by intuitive wisdom, meditation or Yoga. He is not won over by feeling sad forever. He is not won over by beauty, wealth and pleasure. He is not won over by wandering naked at sacred shrines. He is not won over by giving donations and good deeds. He is not won over by sitting outside in the cold. He is not won over by fighting and dieing in a battle. He is not won over by becoming the dust of others. Your account is written about what your mind did O Nanak! The Lord is won over by reciting His name.

||2|| First Master: You may contemplate eighteen scriptures. You may recite eighteen books of knowledge. Even these cannot find the limits of the Lord. Without God's name, how can anyone obtain salvation? Brahma lived in the lotus of the navel. He did not know the limits of God. O Nanak the guru-willed realizes Him by reciting His name. ||3|| Ladder: The formless God created Himself. He created the drama of the whole world. He created three worldly qualities and induced the enticement of worldly wealth. O Nanak those who obey God's will are saved by guru's grace. O Nanak, the true Lord pervades all; all are absorbed in Him. ||1|| Page 1238 Hymn, Second Master: He creates, and creates the difference as well O Nanak, How can anyone be called bad? When we all have the same master. There is one Lord of all. He watches and assigns all to their task. Some have less, some have more; no one is empty handed. Naked we come, naked we go; in between, we flourish. O Nanak, one who does not understand God's command; what will he do in the next world? ||1|| First Master: He allots food and then he creates the being. When the food ends then He calls them back. He establishes, and disestablishes. He fashions them in various forms. He gives awns to all renunciates that wander around begging. You talk, walk according to pre-ordained destiny, why do you claim your deeds? This is the essence of knowledge. Nanak speaks and proclaims it. Everyone is judged on their deeds; let them say whatever they want? ||2|| Ladder: God created the world this way that the virtues reveal on its own. He says guru's sermon enshrining God in the mind forever. Worldly power and doubt go away and divine light is lit. Those who do good deeds, unite with the primal guru. O Nanak, they merge in God and become peaceful. ||2|| Hymn, Second Master: The merchants go to do business and their fate goes with them. He is ordered to do what is written in his fate and obtains the object. They buy the priceless merchandise and take with them. Some depart making a profit; the others leave losing their principle. No one asks for less; who do we praise? God blesses those who bring their wealth back in full. ||1|| First Master: United are separated and separated are united. The living die and the dead live again. Many became fathers and sons. Many became gurus and devotees. Cannot count what happened before or in future, what

will their caste be and what are they now? They do what is written in their fate; they do what God tells them; the self-willed dies, the guru-willed is saved; O Nanak, it happens by God's grace. ||2|| Ladder: The self-willed wanders in duality enticed by duality. He practices falsehood and deception and tells lies. Love and attachment of children and spouse is all painful. He is tied and killed at death's door and wanders in doubt. The self-willed wastes his life; Nanak loves the Lord. ||3|| Hymn, Second Master: Those who are blessed with your name; they are imbued with Your love. O Nanak, there is only one nectar not two. O Nanak, the nectar is in the mind; it is realized by guru's grace. They drink it with love, those who have such pre-ordained destiny. ||1|| Page 1239 Second Master: Why praise the created being? Praise the one who created him. O Nanak, there is no other giver except One Lord. Praise the Creator, who created the creation. Praise the great giver, who gives sustenance to all. O Nanak, the treasure of the eternal Lord is over-flowing. Praise and honour the one, who has no end or limits. ||2|| Ladder: The name of the Lord is a treasure. Serving it obtains peace. I recite the name of the immaculate Lord, and go home with honour. God's name is the sermon of the guru-willed. He enshrines it in the mind. The bird like intellect comes under control and recites the guru. O Nanak, When God is kind, the devotee attunes to His name with love. ||4|| Hymn, Second Master: What can you say to Him, who knows everything? His order cannot be challenged; He is our supreme Lord and master. Even kings, nobles and commanders obey His command. Whatever pleases Him is a good deed O Nanak. Those who issue orders, have nothing in their hand. When God's order comes, they get up and walk away. Whatever is written in the letter, they act accordingly. They come when they are sent; and go back when called back. ||1|| Second Master: Those, whom the Lord blesses with honour, are the true treasurers. Whoever is given the key, obtains the treasure. God accepts the treasurer with virtues. God blesses those who have support of God's name. ||2|| Ladder: Listening to the name of the sacred God obtains peace. Enshrine it in the mind by listening; only a few devotees realize it. He, who does not forget God while sitting or standing, is truly truthful. His devotees have the support of His name. They obtain peace through His name. O Nanak, God pervades in the mind and body of the guru-willed; ||5|| Hymn, First Master: O Nanak, weigh the weight by balancing the scale with your soul. Nothing equals him. If he can balance it, then he weighs it perfectly. If it is big, then it is heavy to weigh. Other lighthearted speak humbly. The weight of the earth, water and mountains; How can the goldsmith weigh on his scale? He weighs in very lightweights like grams and ounces. O Nanak, when questioned, he answers; the thinking of the ignorant and blind is also blind. The more they say, the more they expose themselves. ||1|| First Master: It is difficult to say and listen; it cannot be said. Some speak guru's teaching everywhere up and down day and night. If there is anything to see, will be seen; but it has no form or caste. The Creator does all deeds. He does it in good and bad places as well. Page 1240 It is difficult to say O Nanak, it cannot be said. ||2|| Ladder: Hearing God's name, the mind is happy. The name brings peace. Hearing God's name, the mind is satisfied, and all pains are eradicated. Hearing God's name, one becomes famous. His name brings honour. God's name bestows honour, status and salvation. The guru-willed recites God's name with love O Nanak. ||6|| Hymn, First Master: Impurity does not come from music or reciting Vedas. Impurity does not come from the phases of the sun and the moon. Impurity does not come from food or bathing. Impurity does not come from raining everywhere. Impurity does not come from the earth or water. Impurity is not absorbed in air. O Nanak, the one without the guru has no virtue. Impurity comes from turning one's face away from God. ||1|| First Master: O Nanak, obtain handful of purities, if someone knows how to obtain it; Handful of purities of divine thinking is for the knowledge seeker, the self-control is for a yogi. Handful of purities of a Brahmin is contentment, giving awns is the handful of purities of the householder. Handful of purities for a king is to administer justice and for a scholar is thinking in the mind. Water cannot clean the mind. It eliminates thirst by drinking. Water is the father of the world and yet everyone drinks it. ||2|| Ladder: Hearing God's name, the mystic powers are obtained and the wealth follows. Hearing the name, obtains treasure of wealth and the fruit of his choice. Hearing the name, contentment comes, and the worldly wealth worships his feet. Hearing the name, contentment and peace well up. God's name is realized by guru's teaching and Nanak sings His praises. ||7|| Hymn, First Master: They are born and die in pain and pain pervades the world. We read and proclaim pain on and on. When the package of pain is opened; there is no happiness in it. In pain, the soul burns; it departs crying in pain. O Nanak, imbued with God's praise, the mind and body are rejuvenated. If you have to kill pain then the medicine is also pain. ||1|| First Master: O Nanak, the world imbued with dust and from dust it turns to dust. Mixing the dust with dust creates the body filled with dust. When the soul is taken out of the body, it becomes dust again. When your account is checked hereafter, it adds ten times more dust. ||2|| Ladder: Hearing the name, one is purified and content. The devil of death does not come close. Hearing the name, one is enlightened and the darkness departs. Hearing the name, one understands him, and earns the profit of God's name. Hearing the name, sins are eradicated, and one obtains pure truth. O Nanak, hearing the name, one becomes happy and the guru-willed recites God's name. ||8|| Hymn, First Master: God is in your home along with other gods. You wash your stone gods and worship them. Page 1241 You offer saffron, sandalwood and flowers. You fall at their feet and console with them. The mortal keeps begging to eat and wear. The blind deeds bring blind punishment. It does not feed the hungry or saves the dead. The blind court administers blind decision. ||1|| First Master: All intuitive understanding, all Yoga, all the Vedas and Puraanas; All actions, all penances, all songs and spiritual wisdom. All intellect, all enlightenment, all sacred shrines and places of worship. All kingdoms, all royal commands, all joys and all delicacies. All mankind, all gods, all Yoga and meditation. All worlds, all realms. All beings of the universe; All function according to God's command and their actions are recorded. O Nanak, there is God. It is true. His congregation and court is also true. ||2|| Ladder: Believing in God's name obtains happiness and salvation. Believing in God's name and enshrining God in the mind obtains honour. Believing in God's name one crosses over the terrifying world-ocean and no obstruction comes his way. Believing in God's name the divine path is revealed and enlightenment obtained. O Nanak, meeting with the guru, one believes in God's name, whoever he blesses; ||9|| Hymn, First Master: He walks all over the world. He meditates standing on one foot. He meditates holding the breath and gets his head shaven and hangs upside down. Whom should he believe and whom should he unite with Him? What can we say O Nanak? Whom does the Creator bless? The ignorant follows his own rules and calls him great. ||1|| First Master I say God God God billions of times. I just keep saying and never stop. I do not get tired, I am not stopped; this is how I keep my mind. O Nanak, this is how I enjoy; saying anything else is a sin. ||2|| Ladder: Believing in God's name the whole dynasty attains salvation. Believing in God's name the congregation who enshrines God in mind obtains salvation. Believing in God's name, those who listen and those who enjoy reciting with tongue obtain salvation. Believing in God's name the pain and hunger of those who enshrine God in the mind vanish. O Nanak, those who meet the guru praise God's name. ||10|| Hymn, First Master: All nights, all days, all lunar dates, all days of the week. All seasons, all months, the earth and everything on it. All waters, all winds, all fires and underworlds. All solar systems and galaxies, all worlds, and the whole universe; I do not know how much power God has! I cannot even imagine? People get tired of saying God, praising God and thinking of God. The poor do not find anything about God. Nanak says they are ignorant. ||1|| First Master: If I see the whole universe with my eyes; I ask the learned, religious scholars, and those who contemplate the Vedas; Page 1242 I ask the gods, men, warriors and the prophets. I have heard of mystics in trance. I go and witness their court. God's name is the highest of all. The carefree God cannot be realized without love. Any other way of thinking and practicing is false. The blind think blindly. O Nanak, to worship God is pre-ordained. Salvation is obtained by His grace. ||2|| Ladder: With faith in God's name, the ill will departs and enlightenment obtains. With faith in God's name, ego and other sicknesses depart. Believing in God's name, the name wells up and intuitive peace obtains. Believing in the name, peace wells up and God enshrines in the mind. O Nanak, God's name is a jewel. The guru-willed recite God. ||11|| Hymn, First Master: If there was any other equal to You. I would talk to him about You. I praise

You in front of You; I am blind but I am called enlightened. How much I say through breathing or guru's teaching; I say intuitively. O Nanak, it is too much to say; it is all Your greatness. ||1|| First Master: How could I serve You when I was not there; what I do when I am born? The Creator does everything and checks it again and again. Whether we keep silent or beg loudly, the bestowal gives it any way. There is one giver and all others are beggars; they beg everywhere. Nanak believes that God lives forever. ||2|| Ladder: With faith in the name, the awareness wells up, realization comes through God's name. With faith in the name, he praises God and obtains peace. With faith in the name, doubts are eradicated and never suffer again. With faith in the name, sing His praises and the sinful thinking is washed away. O Nanak, faith in God's name comes from the perfect guru. Whoever he gives, receives it; ||12|| Hymn, First Master: He reads the Shaastras, the Vedas and the Puraanas. He recites it in ignorance. If he understands, then he will realize God; O Nanak, crying loud attains nothing. ||1|| First Master: When I am Yours, then everything is mine. When I am not, You are there. You are all-powerful, knowing all and strung the world by your power. You send, You recall. You create the creation and check it. O Nanak, there is God. It is true and truth prevails. ||2|| Ladder: The name of the formless Lord is unknowable. How can it be known? The name of the formless Lord is with you; how can you find it O brother? The name of the formless Lord is all-pervading and permeating everywhere. It is realized from the perfect guru; he reveals it in the heart. O Nanak, It happens by His grace, meeting the guru O brother; ||13|| Hymn, First Master: Worship in today's age is like a dog. They eat the dead. They lie and bark; doing so the faith is eliminated. Those who have no honour while living; they will be worse after death. Page 1243 Whatever is pre-ordained, happens, O Nanak, whatever the Creator does, happens. ||1|| First Master: Women have become doves and men have become hunters. Humility, self-control and purity have run away. People eat the uneatable. Humility has left the home, and honour has gone with it. O Nanak, there is only one true God; do not look for any other; ||2|| Ladder: You smear body with ashes, but you are filled black inside. You wear the patched coat, begging bag and wear disguises, but you are still egotistic and proud. You do not recite God. You are entangled in worldly attachment. You are greedy and doubtful inside; you wander like an ignorant. Says Nanak, you do not recite God; you lose the game in a gamble. ||14|| Hymn, First Master: You may be in love with millions and live for thousands of years; what good are these pleasures and enjoyments? Separation to the separated is the poison; they die in a moment. If you eat sweets for hundred years, then eat bitter once; You do not remember the sweet, the bitterness bothers you. The sweet and bitter are both diseases. O Nanak, eating them, you will be ruined in the end. Those who argue; argue uselessly. Only the argumentative go there to argue. ||1|| First Master: They have fine clothes and furniture of various colours. Their houses are painted beautifully. In pleasure and poise, they enjoy themselves. O God; You made them to say so. They eat the bitter, thinking it sweet. The bitter makes them sick. If they receive the sweet later; then their bitterness goes away O mother. O Nanak, the guru-willed obtains that. He, who is predestined to receive; ||2|| Ladder: Those who are filled with the filth of deception may wash the outside. They practice falsehood and deception and it reveals. That which is inside, comes out. It cannot be hidden even if they want to. Attached to falsehood and greed, they take birth again and again. O Nanak, you eat what you sow; God wrote it so; ||15|| Hymn, Second Master: The Vedas bring the stories and legends, and talk about vice and virtue. They give and take and keep talking about going to hell or heaven. High and low, social class and status. The world wanders lost in doubt. The sacred sermon explains the essence. It talks about thinking of divinity. The guru-willed recite and realize through devotional worship. He creates; keeps in His control and watches over by His command. O Nanak, if the ego vanishes then it is approved in his account. ||1|| First Master: The Vedas proclaim vice and virtue; it is the seed of heaven and hell. Whatever is planted grows. You know when you eat it. To praise the great God is divine wisdom. There is God, it is true. Sow the truth, grow the truth; then you will be honoured in God's court. Page 1244 The study of Vedas and divine wisdom is all pre-ordained. O Nanak, without the wealth, no one can buy and take with them. ||2|| Ladder: You can water a bitter neem tree with nectar. You can feed milk to the poisonous snake. The self-willed is like a stone; bathing cannot wet him. Water the bitter plant with nectar; it still bears bitter fruit. O Lord, join devotee's company and your poison will go away. ||16|| Hymn, First Master: Death does not ask the time, the date or the day. Some are loading, some loaded and gone and some are loaded heavily. Some are punished and some are looked after. They have to leave their armies, bands and their beautiful mansions behind. O Nanak, the pile of dust is once again reduced to dust. ||1|| First Master: O Nanak, the body made of dust fell apart and became dust. The soul thief sits inside. It is all false O mortal; ||2|| Ladder: Those who are filled with evil slander; shall have their noses cut and ashamed; They are ugly and always in pain. Their faces are blackened by worldly wealth. They get up in the morning and steal from others; but stay away from God's name. O God; do not join their company; save me O God the Lord. O Nanak, the self-willed act according to their past deeds and suffer. ||17|| Hymn, Fourth Master: Everyone belongs to God; everyone comes from Him. He, who realizes God's command, realizes God. The guru-willed realizes him and no one appears evil to him. O Nanak, the guru-willed recites God's name and becomes content. ||1|| Fourth Master: He is the giver to all; He unites all with Him. O Nanak, those who serve the bestowal unite with Him through guru's teaching and never separate. ||2|| Ladder: The guru-willed becomes peaceful in the mind; God's name wells up inside. He meditates, does penance self-discipline and pilgrimage. It pleases God. Serve the guru, your mind will be purified; you will look adorable singing God's praises. This pleases my dear Lord. He carries the guru-willed across. O Nanak, the guru-willed unite with God and look adorable in His court. ||18|| Hymn, First Master: The wealthy; talks about wealth and goes for more wealth; O Nanak, he is poor the day he forgets God's name. ||1|| First Master: The sunrises and sets and the lifes of all decrease. The mind and body enjoy pleasures. One loses the other wins. Everyone is filled with pride; it does not change by saying. O Nanak, God watches it. When He takes the air out, the body falls down. ||2|| Ladder: True congregation is filled with the treasure of God's name; God is realized there. Page 1245 By guru's grace, the mind is enlightened and darkness is dispelled. Iron transforms into gold, when touched by philosopher's stone. O Nanak, meeting the guru, obtains God's name and recite God's name. Those who have virtues in their fate; they visualize God. ||19|| Hymn, First Master: Worthless is their life, which writes and sell God's name. Their crop is destroyed; where is the place for threshing the grain? Lacking truth and humility, they do not obtain justice in the next world. Wisdom, which leads to arguments, is not called wisdom. Worship the Lord with wisdom and obtain honour. Read wisely and understand; then give awns wisely. Says Nanak, this is the path. Other things are devil. ||1|| Second Master: Whatever he does, so it is called; this is how it is. He should be a saint not an impostor; this is how it should be? Whatever they desire, they receive; O Nanak, they are the image of God. ||2|| Ladder: The guru is the sacred tree and bears the sacred fruit. He, who deserves receives it. It is obtained through guru's teaching. One, who follows guru's will, unites with God. The devil of death cannot rob him because he is enlightened inside. O Nanak, he unites with God by His grace and never rots in the womb again. ||20|| Hymn, First Master: Truth, fast, contentment, bathing at sacred shrines, divine wisdom and concentration; those with kindness as the deity and forgiveness as their rosary, they are above all. Worship process, the loincloth, thinking, the purified kitchen, good deeds and mark on the forehead, love as their food; O Nanak, they are rare. ||1|| Third Master: On the ninth day of full moon, make a vow to speak the truth. He speaks about the lust, anger and desire. On the tenth day, he closes the ten doors; on the eleventh day, know that the Lord is one. On the twelfth day, controls the five thieves and then, O Nanak, the mind pleases. Observe such a fast O religious scholar; why bother with other lessons? ||2|| Ladder: Kings, rulers and monarchs enjoy collecting the poisonous worldly wealth. They fall in love with it and steal more from others. The children and spouse are not trustworthy; why do you love them so much? The worldly wealth cheats you right in front of your eyes. You will be tied and killed at the door of death. It is God's will; ||21|| Hymn, First Master: He sings songs (shabad) but has no knowledge. It is like a hungry Mullah turns his home into a mosque. The useless gets his ears pierced and become a Yogi. Poverty makes him do this; he loses other status. He, who calls him the guru or a spiritual teacher and goes begging; Never touch his feet; He earns and eats and gives a little in awns. O Nanak, he finds the path. ||1|| First Master: Page 1246 They are blind in the mind and talk blind; they do not know the way of worship. The blind in the mind appear to be upside down and ugly. Those who realize what I say, they are wise and adorable. Some do not understand by listening to the Vedas. They do not enjoy the taste. Some have no understanding, intelligence and knowledge. They do not understand anything. O Nanak, those who are proud without any virtue are real donkeys. ||2|| Ladder: To the guru-willed everything is sacred as wealth, property and worldly wealth. They spend it for good cause; they give happiness and obtain happiness. Those who recite God's name, they never run short; The guru-willed realize God and throw away the wealth. O Nanak, the devotees do not think of anything else; they are absorbed in the name of God. ||22|| Hymn, Fourth Master: Those who serve the guru are fortunate. They are lovingly attuned to guru's true teaching. In their household and family, they are absorbed in peace. O Nanak, those imbued with God's name are the true renunciates. Fourth Master: Calculated service is not a service at all, and receives no reward. They do not enjoy guru's teaching and do not love the true Lord. They do not like the guru. The stubborn minded keep coming and going; they take one step forward and go ten back. If he follows guru's will, that is guru's service. He loses his ego and meets the guru; then he absorbs in peace. O Nanak, they never forget God's name and unite with God. ||2|| Ladder: Those called princes and emperors, do not stay forever. Their strong forts and mansions; none of them will go with them. Their gold and fast horses are of no use; so are their clever ideas. Eating the thirty-six-course food, they become bloated with pollution. O Nanak, the self-willed does not know the giver; then he suffers. ||23|| Hymn, Third Master: The scholars and sages got tired of studying, and imitates got tired of wandering all over foreign lands. They do not obtain God's name. They love the duality and suffer serious pain. The blind ignorant serve the three worldly qualities; they deal in worldly wealth. With deception in their hearts, the ignorant read sacred texts to fill their bellies. One who serves the guru finds peace; he eradicates ego from within. O Nanak, reading and counting is only namesake; only those who contemplate realize God. ||1|| Third Master: Naked we come, naked we go. This is by God's order; what can we do? Whoever it belongs to, will take it away; whom do we complain to? The guru-willed obeys God's will and enjoys God's love intuitively. O Nanak, praise the giver of peace forever with your tongue and savor the Lord. ||2|| Page 1247 Ladder: They adorn their body fortress in many ways. The wealthy wear beautiful silk robes of various colours. They hold elegant and beautiful courts, on red and white carpets. But they eat pain and suffer pain, because they are very proud. O Nanak, they do not miss God's name; that will save them in the end. ||24|| Hymn, Third Master: She sleeps in intuitive peace absorbed in guru's teaching. God united her with Him and embraced her. Duality is eradicated with intuitive ease. God's name enshrines in the mind. He, who contemplates will be embraced. O Nanak, those who are destined to meet Him have met Him now. ||1|| Third Master: Those who forget God's name; what other recitation they recite? They are like worms in the filth and they rob others. O Nanak, never forget God's name; all other greed is false. ||2|| Ladder: Those who praise and enshrine God's name in the mind are immortal in the world. They think God in their mind, not any other; every pour of his hair says God God every moment again and again. The birth of the guru-willed is worthwhile. They become pure and filth removes. O Nanak, they recite the immortal and become immortal. ||25|| Hymn, Third Master: Those who forget God's name and do many other deeds O Nanak, they will be caught at the break in like a thief and beaten. ||1|| Fifth Master: Reciting God's name the earth and sky look beautiful. O Nanak, crows eat those without God's name. ||2|| Ladder: Those who recite God's name with love, they reach the destiny. They do not take birth again and never die again. They recite and enjoy God with every breath and morsel of food. The guru-willed are enlightened and God's love never fades away. O Nanak, they are united with God by His grace. ||26|| Hymn, Third Master: As long as the mind is on his own, he is filled with ego and pride. He does not enjoy guru's teaching and does not love God's name. His service is not accepted. He gets stuck and ruined. O Nanak, he, who self-surrenders is a devotee. He obeys guru's will and enshrines guru's teaching in the mind. ||1|| Third Master: The service, recitation and penance that appeal to God are the real service. God blesses him and unites with Him if the mortal eliminates ego. Once united with God, never separates, his soul merges with supreme soul. O Nanak, whoever God blesses, realizes God by guru's grace. ||2|| Ladder: All are held accountable, even the egotistic self-willed. They never recite God's name; devil of death will hit them on the head. Page 1248 They are heavily loaded with sins and filth. The path ahead is difficult and scary; how will they follow it. O Nanak, those protected by the guru are saved enshrining God's name in the mind. ||27|| Hymn, Third Master: Without serving the guru, no one finds peace; they die and reborn turn by turn. They are cheated by false love and useless duality. Some are saved, by guru's grace. Everyone humbly bows in front of them. O Nanak, recite God's name in the mind that bestows salvation. ||1|| Third Master: Enticement of worldly wealth; makes them forget death and God's name. Engaged in worldly affairs, his life wastes away and suffers pain inside. O Nanak, those with pre-ordained destiny serve the guru and obtain peace. ||2|| Ladder: Read the account of God's name, then your account will not be checked. No one will question you, and you will be accepted in God's court forever. The devil of death will surrender to you. He reaches the destiny and his honour is proclaimed. O Nanak, the infinite divine music plays at God's door and he unites with God. ||28|| Hymn, Third Master: If you obey guru's word, it is the essence of happiness. Other concern is eliminated following the guru and obtains salvation O Nanak. ||1|| Third Master: The truth never gets old and God's name does not get dirty; Whoever follows guru's will; will not come again. O Nanak, forgetting God's name both coming and going continue. ||2|| Ladder: The being begs for awns and God gives it intuitively. I am thirsty of visualizing God and seeing Him will fulfill me. I cannot live without seeing Him even for a moment. I will die if I do not see him O my mother. The guru showed God in me. He pervades all places. He wakes up the sleeping O Nanak, and lovingly attunes them to Him. ||29|| Hymn, Third Master: The self-willed cannot say God because they are filled with lust, anger and pride. They do not know the difference between good and bad; they constantly think of corruption. Their account is audited in Gods court and they are declared false. He created the universe and He thinks about it; O Nanak, whom should we tell? God pervades everywhere; ||1|| Third Master: The guru-willed with pre-ordained destiny recite God. O Nanak, I admire those who have God enshrined their mind. ||2|| Ladder: Everyone hopes to live long. They build houses and beautify them for daily enjoyment. They cheat and make all kind of efforts to steal wealth. But the devil of death watches every breath. Those out of synch; their life decreases day by day. Page 1249 O Nanak, they are saved in guru's refuge and guru the God protects them. ||30|| Hymn, Third Master: Reading the scriptures the scholars explain to others for the sake of money. In love of duality, they forget God's name. The self-willed are punished. They do not serve the one who created them, who gives sustenance to all. The noose of death from their necks is not cut. They come and go again and again. The guru comes to meet those, who have the pre-ordained destiny. O Nanak, they recite God's name and merge in true God. ||1|| Third Master: The guru-willed who touch guru's feet serve the truth and deal in truth. O Nanak, those who obey guru's will, merge in truth intuitively. ||2|| Ladder: The self-willed focus on hope and suffer serious pain in hope. The guru-willed become humble and obtain eternal peace. In the midst of their household, they remain detached; they are lovingly attuned to the carefree God. They are not bothered by sorrow or separation obeying God's will. O Nanak, they are attuned to God with love forever and are united with Him in the end. ||31|| Hymn, Third Master: Why keep something that belongs to others? Returning it gives peace. Guru's teaching is found with the guru only; it does not appear anywhere else. The blind finds a jewel; he goes from house to house to sell it. He does not know the value; he does not get even half a shell for it. If he cannot appraise it, he should get it appraised from an appraiser. If he focuses his mind to it, he obtains the true merchandise and obtains the treasure of God's name. They have wealth at home; yet the world is dieing of hunger. They do not realize it without the guru. When guru's soothing teaching enshrines in the mind; then they do not feel sorrow or separation. The object belongs to someone else, but the ignorant is proud of it, and shows his shallow nature. O Nanak, without understanding, no one obtains it; they come and go over and over again. ||1|| Third Master: My mind is happy meeting with my beloved God and all beloved friendly saints. Those who are united with the primal Lord shall never separate again. The Creator has united them with Him. They meet the guru and enshrine his teaching in the mind and all pains are eradicated. I praise God the bestowal of peace forever and enshrine him in the mind. How can the self-willed talk ill of them; who are adorned by guru's true teaching. They have sought refuge at his abode and he preserves their honour. O Nanak, the guru-willed are content and happy in God's court. ||2|| Ladder: Man and a woman are enticed and fall in love. They are happy seeing their children, and spouse. They are attached to worldly wealth. They steal wealth from all over, and feed their family. Page 1250 In the end, enmity and conflict well up, and no one can save them O Nanak, without God's name the false attachments are useless; engrossed in them, they suffer in pain. ||32|| Hymn, Third Master: O guru-willed; God's name is sacred; eating it eliminates all hunger. There is no more greed, if God's name enshrines in the mind. Eating anything other than God's name makes sick. O Nanak, praise and enjoy guru's teaching; he will unite you with him. ||1|| Third Master: Guru's sacred teaching is in the mind, which unites with the beloved God. The world is dark without guru's teaching; enlightenment comes through guru's teaching. The scholars and silent sages get tired of reading; the imitators are tired of washing their body. No one realizes God without guru's teaching; the painful depart crying. O Nanak, He is realized by His grace; you get what you earn. ||2|| Ladder: The man and a woman fall in love and enjoy themselves. All that is seen shall pass away. This is the will of my God. How can anyone remain in this world forever? Can someone find the way? Serving the perfect guru, everything becomes permanent. O Nanak, God blesses them and unites them with him and they merge in His name. ||33|| Hymn, Third Master: Attached to worldly wealth; he forgot the love of the guru the God. The waves of greed take away his wisdom and thinking, and he does not love the true Lord. The guru-willed, who enshrine guru's teaching in the mind, are liberated in God's court. O Nanak, the bestowal unites them with Him by his grace. ||1|| Fourth Master: O Nanak, without Him, we cannot live for a moment. We do not succeed forgetting Him. O my mind; why should you get angry with Him; who worries about you? ||2|| Fourth Master: In the month of Saawan, it rains continuously; recite God's name O guru-willed; all pain, hunger and misfortune end, when it rains heavily. The entire earth is rejuvenated and the grain grows in abundance. The carefree God, invites you by His grace, and approves your service. O saints, recite that God; who saves you in the end. Praising God is the joy of worship; eternal peace enshrines in the mind. The guru-willed who recite God's name, their pain and hunger depart. O Nanak, singing His praises satisfies them and God visualizes them with ease. ||3|| Ladder: The bestowing of the perfect guru increases day by day. Whoever the kind God blesses, cannot be hidden even if he hides. The lotus blossoms in the mind; they lovingly attune to God and become divine intuitively. If anyone tries to equal him gets dust thrown in his head. O Nanak, no one can equal the glory of the perfect true guru. ||34|| Page 1251 Hymn, Third Master: God's rule prevails; clever tricks and arguing does not work there. Give up your ego and fall at his feet and obey His will. The guru-willed cannot be punished by the devil of death because they have eliminated ego. O Nanak, those who attune to truth are the real devotees. ||1|| Third Master: The gift of soul You gave is Your image. Excessive cleverness and ego are mine. He does deeds troubled by greed attachment and ego; he will not escape the cycle of birth and death. O Nanak, the Creator makes us do everything; whatever pleases him is good. ||2|| Ladder, Fifth Master: Eat the truth, wear the truth and take support of the true name. The guru units us with the bestowal God; whoever recites God, they are fortunate. Joining devotee's company they cross over the worldly ocean. O Nanak, praise God and celebrate. ||35|| Hymn, Fifth Master: You look after all beings by your grace. You produce enough of water and food for the down trodden and save them by eliminating pain and poverty. The bestowal heard the prayer and soothed the universe. Take me into Your embrace, and take away all my pain. O Nanak, recite God's name; everything is available in God's house. ||1|| Fifth Master: God commanded and beautiful clouds formed and rained. It grew food for tomorrow and the world is soothed. The mind and body have blossomed, reciting the inaccessible infinite God. O true Creator God; please be kind; He does whatever is needed; Nanak praises Him forever. ||2|| Ladder: The great Lord is inaccessible; His greatness is greater! I enjoyed visualizing Him through guru's teaching and became peaceful. O brother God is all in all. He is the Lord; He controls everyone by His command. O Nanak, God does what He wishes; everything happens by His command. ||36||1|| declaration|| Tune Saarang, Word Of The Devotees. Kabeer Jee: God is one. He is realized by guru's grace. O mortal, why are you so proud of small things? With a few pounds of grain and a few coins in your pocket, you walk crooked. ||1||Pause|| You are known in hundred villages and you are worth two hundred thousand. You power lasts for four days, like the leaves on the trees. ||1|| No one brings this wealth or takes with him. Emperors like Raawan vanished in a moment. ||2|| Page 1252 God's saints who recite God's name become immortal by worshipping. Whoever God blesses join devotee's company; ||3|| Mother, father, spouse, children and wealth, nothing goes with you in the end. Says Kabeer, O ignorant, recite God! The life is going waste. ||4||1|| O God, the world you created does not know Your divine wisdom. I am the humble slave of Your saints. ||1||Pause|| He, who goes laughing returns crying, and the crying returns laughing. What is inhabited becomes deserted, and deserted becomes inhabited. ||1|| The water turns into a desert, the desert turns into a well and the ditch turns into a mountain. He raises the being from earth to sky and drops some from the sky. ||2|| He makes a king from a beggar and a beggar from a king. He changes an idiot to a scholar and a scholar to an idiot. ||3|| He changes a woman to a man and vice versa. Says Kabeer, God is the beloved of devotees. I praise him. ||4||2|| Saarang, The Word Of Naam Dev Jee: God is one. He is realized by guru's grace. O corrupt mind; why do you go to the forest? You are lost and you are being cheated. ||1||Pause|| As the fish lives in water. She does not think of the net and death. She swallows the hook for the taste of tongue. Like a woman is enticed by gold. ||1|| The bee collects honey. Someone comes and takes the honey, and throws dust in its mouth. The cow stores milk for the calf. The milkman comes and ties it by its neck and milks it. ||2|| For the sake of wealth the mortal works hard. He collects wealth and buries it in the ground. He collects a lot but the ignorant does not understand; His wealth remains buried in the ground, while his body turns to dust. ||3|| He burns in lust, anger and desire. He never joins the company of devotees. Says Naam Dev, seek God's shelter; be carefree and recite God; ||4||1|| Why not make a bet with me, O Lord? The master became servant and servant became the master; we play this game. ||1||Pause|| You are the deity, the temple and the worshipper. The wave rises from water and merges again. Everything else is just a talk. ||1|| You sing, You dance and blow the trumpet. Says Naam Dev, You are my master. I am half empty, You are full. ||2||2|| The servant who does not follow anyone else is my image; Visualizing Him for a moment eliminates three day fever. Touching Him saves the sinners. ||1||Pause|| The devotee frees me from bonds; if he ties me up; I cannot escape. Page 1253 Once you tie me up tightly, and then I cannot say anything. ||1|| I am bound by virtue; I am the life of all. My slaves are my life. Says Naam Dev, Those with such a mind, fall in love and are enlightened. ||2||3|| Saarang: God is one. He is realized by guru's grace. O mortal; what did you do after listening to Puraanas? Faithful devotion did not well up, and you did not give awns to the hungry. ||1||Pause|| You did not give up lust, anger and greed. You did not stop slandering others; your service is useless. ||1|| You break in at other's house and fill up your belly. You did those deeds that take you where the sinners go in the next world; ||2|| You never abandoned cruelty and never followed kind path. You did not enjoy devotee's company and did not follow the sacred sermon. ||3||1||6|| O mind, give up the company of sinners. Saarang, Fifth Master, Sur Daas: God is one. He is realized by guru's grace. Godly people live with God. They offer body mind and everything; they are happy and peaceful instantly, like being touched by gust of wind. ||1||Pause|| They became sacred visualizing God; they obtained everything in abundance. They have nothing to do with anything else; seeing the beautiful God enlightens them. ||1|| If one forgets God and wants something else is like a leech stuck to the body of a leper. Says Sur

Daas, God took my hand and took me to the next world. ||2||1||8||
Saarang, Kabeer Jee: God is one. He is realized by guru's grace. Other
than God, who is the support of the mind? Love of mother, father,
sibling, child and spouse, is just an illusion. ||1||Pause|| Build a raft to
the world hereafter; there is no certainty of worldly wealth? Who
knows about this body pot? It will be broken with a slight hit. ||1||
Long for the dust of all beings and obtain the reward of universal
faith. Says Kabeer, listen, O saints: this mind is like the bird, flying in
the forest. ||2||1||9||
Page 1254 Tune Malaar, Chau-Padas, First Master, First House:
*God is one. It is true. He is the Creator. He is carefree. He has
no enemy. He is immortal. He does not take birth. He came into
existence on his own. He is realized by guru's grace.*
He is eating, drinking, laughing and sleeping but forgot death. He is
ruined by forgetting God. His life is useless and he is going to die. ||1||
O mortal, recite God's name; You shall go home with honour. ||1
Pause|| They serve You, they do not give you anything. They do not
stop begging. You are the bestowal of all. You abide in all beings. ||2||
The guru-willed who recite your name obtain the nectar. O mortal;
recite God's name all the time; the filthy will become pure. ||3|| As is
the season, so is the body comfort and the body gets used to it. O
Nanak that season is beautiful, but without God's name, what good is
the season? ||4||1|| Malaar, First Master: I pray to my beloved guru,
that He may unite me with my Husband Lord. Hearing the thunder
my mind is soothed like a peacock and sings His praises, imbued with
love. ||1|| May it rain heavily so that my mind is drenched? The drop
of nectar pleases my mind; the guru drenched me with God's love.
||1||Pause|| The beloved soul bride is content and happy; her mind is
pleased with guru's teaching. She is the happy soul-bride of her
Husband Lord; her mind and body are filled with love. ||2|| Discarding
her demerits, she becomes detached and is married to God forever.
She never suffers separation or sorrow. God has blessed her. ||3|| Her
mind is stable. She does not go or come anymore. She has guru's
support. The guru-willed happy soul bride recites God's name and
merges with God O Nanak. ||4||2|| Malaar, First Master: He is not
truthful and God's name does not satisfy him; he wastes his time in

egotistic deeds. Page 1255 Attached to other's wealth, spouse and slander, he eats poison and suffers. Without following guru's teaching the fear of corruption never goes away. The self-willed talks about wealth and more. Loading the heavy and crushing load, they die, only to be reborn, and waste their lives again. ||1|| When guru's teaching pleases and appeals to the mind. He made many imitating jesters and keeps wandering in different lifes, but when the guru protects him then he realizes the truth. ||1||Pause|| He takes bath at the shrines but does not eliminate anger. God's name does not appeal to him; He abandoned and discarded the priceless jewel since he came in the world. The worms born in the filth merge with the filth. More tastes bring more sickness; contentment is not obtained without the guru. ||2|| The guru-willed serves and sings God's praises and contemplates divinity. The thinking emerges and arguing ends. I admire my guru the God. I am lowly, low intellect and false. You save me through guru's teaching. You liberate me when I search my soul and carry me across O bestowal. ||3|| I sit at a sacred place and sing Your praises; how many of Your praises can I say? The unknown cannot be known O inaccessible, unborn Lord; You are the Master of masters. How can I tell others, what You look like? All are beggars. You are the great giver. The worship less Nanak looks at Your door, if he can enshrine Your name in the mind? ||4||3|| Malaar, First Master: The soul-bride who does not enjoy her husband Lord is shameless and shall wither away. Caught in the noose of previous deed, she is hopeless. Without the guru she is deluded by doubt. ||1|| May it rain heavily? My Husband Lord has come home. I admire my guru, who united me with God. ||1||Pause|| I am always in love with my beloved Lord and enjoy His worship forever. I am liberated visualizing the guru and I enjoy God's worship forever. ||2|| We are yours, the world and universe is yours. I am yours and you are mine. Meeting the guru, I found the formless Lord and I will not take birth again. ||3|| When she is happy to see her beloved Lord; then she is truly adorable. She is truly imbued with the Lord. God's name is her support through guru's teaching. ||4|| The guru removed the bonds and she got liberated. She obtained honour and understanding through guru's teaching. O Nanak, enshrining God's name in the mind the guru-willed is united with God. ||5||4|| First Master, Malaar: To look at other's spouse, wealth, greed and ego are useless poisons. Evil passions, slander of others, lust and anger; give up all these. ||1|| The inaccessible, infinite Lord is sitting inside. He, who follows the jewel of guru's teaching obtains nectar from inside; ||1||Pause|| Page 1256 He sees pleasure and pain, good and bad the same in the world. Reciting God in devotee's company and loving the guru obtains the realization, wisdom and awareness. ||2|| Take benefit of reciting God's name daily through the guru the giver. Whoever God blesses; that guru-willed learns the lesson. ||3|| The body is a mansion, a temple, home of the Lord. He has infused His infinite light in it. O Nanak, inviting into the house, God unites the guru-willed with Him. ||4||5|| Malaar, First Master, Second House: God is one. He is realized by guru's grace. Know that the creation was created through air and water; the heat is hidden inside the body. If you know where the soul comes from? You will be known as a wise scholar. ||1|| We do not know the virtues of the Lord of the universe O mother? Without seeing Him, we cannot say anything about Him. How can anyone speak and describe Him, O mother? ||1||Pause|| The sky on top and the underworld underneath; How can I speak of Him! Tell me? He recites God in the mind instead of saying from the mouth; who knows what is that name? ||2|| Undoubtedly, He is still a mystery? He, who is blessed, realizes it. He enshrines Him in the mind all the time; He merges in the true Lord. ||3|| If someone of high social standing becomes a devotee; what can we say about him? If someone from a low social class becomes a devotee; O Nanak, he shall wear the shoes of honour. ||4||1||6|| Malaar, First Master: The pain of separation is my pain of hunger. Another pain is the attack of the powerful devil of death. Another pain is the disease consuming my body. The ignorant doctor does not give me the medicine. ||1|| The ignorant doctor does not give me the medicine. The pain persists, and the body continues to suffer. Your medicine has no effect on me. O brother. ||1||Pause|| Forgetting the master, the mortal enjoys sensual pleasures; Then the disease inflicts the body. The blind mortal receives his punishment. The ignorant doctor does not give the medicine. ||2|| The value of sandalwood lies in its fragrance. The value of the human lasts till he breaths. When the breathing stops, the body crumbles into dust. After that, no one takes any food. ||3|| The body is golden, and the soul-swan is pure; in that lives the soul the child of God. All pain and disease are eradicated. O Nanak, the mortal is saved through the true name. ||4||2||7|| Malaar, First Master: Lord's name is the antidote of pain of poison. Grind it in the stone of contentment and give awns with your hand; Page 1257 Take it each and every day, and your body shall not wither away. You can kick the devil of death in the end. ||1|| So take such a medicine, O ignorant; by which the useless deeds shall be taken away. ||1||Pause|| Power, wealth and youth are all just shadows; they are like chariots circling around. Neither your body, nor your fame, nor your social status shall go with you. In the next world it is day, while here, it is night. ||2|| Let your pleasures be the firewood, let your greed be the oil. Put the oil on the lust and anger and burn with fire. Some make burnt offerings, hold sacred feasts, and read the Puraanas. Whatever pleases God is acceptable. ||3|| Intense meditation is the paper, and Your Name is the symbol. Those, with pre-ordained destiny obtain it. They are wealthy when they go home; O Nanak, blessed is the mother who gave birth to them. ||4||3||8|| Malaar, First Master: You wear white clothes, and speak sweet words. Your nose is sharp, and your eyes are black. Have you ever seen your Lord O sister? ||1|| I fly and soar into the sky. By Your power, O my all-powerful Lord; I see Him in water, the land, in the mountains, on the river-banks; in all high and low places of interest O brother; ||2|| He fashioned the body, and gave it wings; He gave it great thirst and desire to fly. When He bestows His blessing then I am comforted and consoled. As He makes me see, so I see, O brother; ||3|| Neither this body, nor its wings, shall go with you; It is a fusion of air, water and fire. O Nanak, if it is in the fate; then we recite Him through the guru the teacher. This body shall absorb in the truth. ||4||4||9|| Malaar, Third Master, Chau-Padas, First House: God is one. He is realized by guru's grace. God is the universe; He deludes us in doubt. He creates and watches; He puts us to work as He pleases. Obeying his command is the honour of devotees. ||1|| He knows His will. It is realized by guru's grace. When this power takes over, then we die while living. ||1||Pause|| Brahma, Vishnu and Shiva read the Vedas, explaining and arguing. This three-phased worldly wealth misguides the world; this causes the worry of birth and death. By guru's grace, know one Lord; and the worry of your mind will depart. ||2|| I am meek, ignorant and thoughtless; still You take care of me. Please be kind to me, and make me the slave of Your slaves and I serve You. Please bless me with one treasure that I recite your name day and night. ||3|| Says Nanak, it is realized by guru's grace; know that; the world is like a bubble on water. Page 1258 You shall go back where you came from; the worldly expanse is gone. ||4||1|| Malaar, Third Master: Those who realize God's command unite with Him burning the ego through guru's teaching. They perform true worship day and night; and remain lovingly attuned to God; They see the true Lord through guru's teaching intuitively. ||1|| O my mind, obey God's command and obtain peace. God is pleased by His will. Whoever He blesses, meets no hurdle. ||1||Pause|| The three worldly qualities are the senses that run the world; it is not God's worship or love; No one is ever saved or liberated, by doing deeds in ego. Whatever pleases God happens; we wander according to previous deeds. ||2|| Meeting the guru, the mind becomes humble and God's name enshrines in the mind. Neither you can put a price on it nor say anything about it. He dwells in the fourth state; that is where God lives; ||3|| My Lord is inaccessible and unfathomable. He cannot be priced; You realize Him by guru's grace and follow his teaching. O Nanak, praise God's name; you will be honoured in His court. ||4||2|| Malaar, Third Master: Whoever God blesses; the guru-willed realizes Him. There is no giver except the guru. He blesses by his grace. Peace wells up meeting the guru and the devotee recite God forever. ||1|| O my mind, recite God's sacred name. Obtain God's name meeting with the guru and get absorbed in God's name. ||1||Pause|| The self-willed are separated forever. No one accompanies anyone. Ego is a serious sickness; the devil of death beats the egotistic on the head. Never forsake guru's teaching and devotee's company; recite God forever. ||2|| O God; you are the Creator of all. You create and check it out. He unites some guru-willed with Him bestowing the treasure of worship. You know everything. Who should I complain to? ||3|| God's name is sacred; it is obtained by His grace. Recite God day and night intuitively by guru's grace. O

Nanak, God's name is the treasure. Focus your mind to it. ||4||3|| Malaar, Third Master: I praise the guru, the giver of peace forever. He is truly God. By guru's grace, I obtained the supreme status by His greatness. He sings God's praises all the time and merges in the true Lord. ||1|| O my mind; think of God in the mind; Abandon the false family, ego and evil desire; recite the one that goes with you on departure. ||1||Pause|| True guru is the bestowal of God's name; there is no other such a bestowal. Page 1259 He bestows the satisfying gift to the beings and they merge in God's name. They enjoy God in the mind night and day and absorb in trance intuitively. ||2|| Search your soul through guru's teaching and enshrine true sermon in the mind. My God is unseen; He cannot be seen. The guru-willed speaks the unspoken. When the giver of peace blesses, then we recite God the life of the universe. ||3|| His coming and going ends when the guru-willed recites God intuitively. The mind realizes God in the mind, when mind conquers the mind, the mind absorbs in God. The truthful believes in true Lord and eliminates ego; ||4|| Only one God abides in his mind not anyone else. There is only one sweet and sacred name in the world. It is truly pure. O Nanak, those with pre-ordained destiny obtain God's name; ||5||4|| Malaar, Third Master: All the heavenly celestial singers are saved through God's name contemplating guru's teaching. They eliminate ego and enshrine God in the mind. Whoever He makes to realize, realizes; and unites him with Him. They sing His sermon night and day through guru's teaching and attune to Him with love. ||1|| O my mind, recite God's name all the time. Guru's teaching gives the gift of peace; that stays with you forever. ||1||Pause|| The self-willed never give up the hypocrisy; they suffer in love of duality. Forgetting God's name they are imbued with evil and waste away their life. This opportunity shall not come again; they repent forever. They die and reborn again and again, but they never understand. They rot in filth. ||2|| The guru-willed imbued with God's name obtain salvation contemplating guru's teaching. They are freed from life reciting and enshrining God's name in the mind. Their minds, bodies, thinking and the sermon they recite are all pure. They know only one God not anyone else. ||3|| God does and causes us to do by His grace. My mind and body are imbued with guru's sermon and immersed in His service. The unseen and unreadable Lord dwells within. The guru-willed realize Him. O Nanak, whomever He pleases, gives to him. He makes us do what he wishes. ||4||5|| Malaar, Third Master, Du-Tukas: He finds the door to that house, the palace the sacred place through the guru. The self – pride departs following guru's teaching. ||1|| Those who have God's name inscribed on their foreheads. They recite God's name forever and obtain honour in God's court. ||1||Pause|| They realize the ways of the mind and are attuned to God with love forever. Page 1260 Those imbued with guru's teaching are detached forever and obtain honour in God's court. ||2|| This mind plays under God's command. It wanders around in ten directions in a moment. When God blesses, the guru-willed's mind comes under control. ||3|| Mind only knows how it works; it is realized through guru's teaching. O Nanak, recite God's name forever so that you go across the terrifying world ocean. ||4||6|| Malaar, Third Master: Soul, body and life are all His; He pervades in everybody. I know no other than one God; the guru taught me this. ||1|| O my mind; remain lovingly attuned to God's name. Through guru's teaching; recite the unseen, unfathomable and infinite Creator; ||1||Pause|| Mind and body are pleased, lovingly attuning to God and obtain peace. Enshrining God's name in the mind by guru's grace, the doubt departs. ||2|| When, one does true service through guru's word; he obtains salvation. Only a few among millions realize it; they loving attune to God's name. ||3|| Wherever I look, I see God. I realized this from guru's teaching. I offer mind, body and wealth to him O Nanak and eliminate ego. ||4||7|| Malaar, Third Master: My true Lord the destroyer of suffering is realized through guru's teaching. Imbued with worship, he remains forever detached and obtains honour in God's court. ||1|| O mind, remain absorbed in the Mind. The mind of the guru-willed is pleased with God's name. He lovingly attunes to God. ||1||Pause|| My God is totally inaccessible and unfathomable; He is realized through guru's teaching. Truth and self-discipline come from singing God's praises by lovingly attuning to God. ||2|| He is the true story and guru's teaching; who unites the souls. The frail body lives by breathing; the guru-willed obtains the nectar. ||3|| He creates and puts them to work and the true Lord remains hidden inside. O

Nanak, without God's name no one is worth anything. They obtain honour through God's name. ||4||8|| Malaar, Third Master: The evil mind is heavily loaded with ego and evil attachment. Putting the medicine of guru's teaching in the mouth. God kills the evil ego. ||1|| O my mind; the sickness of ego and attachment is serious; this terrifying world-ocean cannot be crossed; the guru-willed cross over reciting God; ||1||Pause|| The attachment of three worldly qualities and worldly wealth pervade the world. The fourth state is obtained in devotee's company and obtains salvation by God's grace. ||2|| The smell of sandalwood is sublime; but too much indulgence is useless. Page 1261 God's devotees do good deeds. They spread God's praise in the world. ||3|| O Lord; be kind to me that I enshrine God in the mind. Nanak found the perfect guru and recites God's name in the mind. ||4||9|| Malaar, Third Master, Second House: God is one. He is realized by guru's grace. Is this mind a householder, or a renunciate? Is this mind something else and immortal? Is this mind fickle, or detached? Where did this mind get enticed with attachment? ||1|| O scholar; think about this mind; May you not read a lot and carry a heavy load. ||1||Pause|| The Creator created the attachment of the worldly pleasure. He created the universe such a way; it is realized by guru's grace O brother. Remain in God's refuge forever. ||2|| He, who unloads the load of three worldly qualities, is a scholar; He recites God's name all the time. He follows the teachings of the guru. He offers his head to the true guru. He remains forever unattached in the state of salvation. Such a scholar is accepted in God's court. ||3|| He sees one God in all. As he sees one Lord, he knows one Lord. Whoever God blesses, unites with God. He finds eternal peace, here and hereafter. ||4|| Says Nanak, what can anyone do? He, whom God blesses, obtains salvation. He sings God's praises all the time. Then, he does not have to cry about the Shaastras or the Vedas. ||5||1||10|| Malaar, Third Master: The self-willed wanders from life to life. The devil of death disgraces him and kills him. Serving the true guru, the worry of the devil of death is eliminated. He realizes God and obtains the destiny. ||1|| O guru-willed; recite God's name. Lost in duality, you are selling the priceless life for a shell. ||1||Pause|| O God; be kind that the guru-willed falls in love. He enshrines God's worship in the mind with love. Guru's teaching carries us across the terrifying world ocean. In God's court, the truth shows up. ||2|| He performs many rituals but does not go to the guru. Without the guru, many wander lost in worldly pleasure. They are too much attached to ego and false attachment. The self-willed suffers pain in duality. The Creator is inaccessible and infinite. Recite the true Lord through guru's teaching. The carefree honourable God is ever present. Page 1262 O Nanak, the guru-willed merges with God through His name. ||4||2||11||Malaar, Third Master: The salvation is obtained through guru's teaching while living. They remain forever awake in God's worship. They serve the guru, and eradicate their self-conceit. I fall at the feet of such humble beings. ||1|| I live by singing God's praises forever. Guru's teaching tastes very sweet. Reciting God obtains salvation. ||1||Pause|| Attachment to worldly wealth is a whirlwind of ignorance. It entices the self-willed, fools and ignorant. They spend their life doing all kind of deeds. They die and reborn again and again, and receive punishment. ||2|| The guru-willed is attuned to God`s name with love. He does not cling to false greed. Whatever he does, does with intuitive ease. He drinks God`s sublime essence and enjoys it. ||3|| Among millions, only a few understand; God blesses them and bestows honour. Whoever is united with God from destiny, never separates; O Nanak, he recites God`s name. ||4||3||12|| Malaar, Third Master: Everyone speaks the name of God with the tongue. But only by serving the guru the mortal receive God`s name. His bonds are broken and he is liberated in his own home. He lives in a permanent house through guru`s teaching. ||1|| O my mind, why are you sad? In today's age, God`s name is profitable. Recite Him in the mind through guru`s teaching forever. ||1||Pause|| The rain bird cries constantly. She cannot sleep without seeing the beloved. She cannot endure this separation. When she meets the guru, she intuitively meets her beloved. ||2|| One without God`s name dies suffering in pain. He is burnt in the fire of desire and his hunger does not depart. Without luck, God`s name cannot be obtained. He is tired of performing all sorts of rituals. ||3|| The Vedas contemplate the three worldly qualities. He deals in corruption, filth and sins. He dies, only to be reborn; he is ruined over and over. The guru-willed enjoys the fourth state of mind. ||4|| One who has faith in the guru, everyone has faith in him. Through guru's Word, the mind is soothed. Throughout the four ages, that humble being is known to be pure. O Nanak, such a guru-willed is rare. ||5||4||13||9||13||22|| Tune Malaar, Fourth Master, First House, Chau-Padas: God is one. He is realized by guru's grace. He recites God day and night through guru's teaching and his pain is eradicated. The chains of hopes and desires have been cut by God's grace. ||1|| My eyes are attuned to God. My mind is happy seeing the guru; I met the Lord. ||1||Pause|| Page 1263 One who forgets such name of my God? May his family be abused? O God; do not give birth to me in their family. May their mother be a widow! ||2|| O Lord, unite me with the guru the devotee and I enshrine God in the mind. Seeing the guru, the devotee is happy as the child seeing the mother. ||3|| The soul-bride and the Husband Lord live together as one, but the wall of ego has come between them. The perfect guru demolishes the wall of ego; servant Nanak has met God; ||4||1|| Malaar, Fourth Master: People go to the Ganges, the Jamunaa, the Godaavari and the Saraswati; to obtain the dust of the feet of devotees. I am filled with filth of sins; the dust of devotees eliminated my filth. ||1|| They take bath at sixty-eight shrines. The dust of devotee's company flew and fell in my eyes and all my filth of ill will is washed away. ||1||Pause|| The penitents go to Ganges, Bhaageerath and Kaidaar Naath shrines. Krishna grazed cows at Kaashi; his devotees there admire him. ||2|| All shrines established by goddesses are so that they obtain the dust of God's devotees. God's saint meets the guru and applies his dust to the forehead. ||3|| O God; the universe yearns for the dust of the feet of devotees. O Nanak, those with pre-ordained destiny; apply the dust of devotees on their forehead and obtain salvation. ||4||2|| Malaar, Fourth Master: The devotees blessed by God recite God and enjoy; He, who sings God's praises; his hunger and pain goes away. ||1|| O my mind; say God God and obtain salvation. He listens and recites God through guru's teaching and goes across the terrifying world ocean. ||1||Pause|| I deal with that person, who is blessed by God. Meeting with God's servant, peace is obtained and the filth of ill will is washed away. ||2|| God's servant is hungry of God. Singing God's praises satisfies the devotee. God's devotee is like a fish out of water. Forgetting God he dies; ||3||

He, who falls in love, knows it or he knows who enshrines God in the mind. O Nanak, the devotee finds peace visualizing God and his hunger goes away. ||4||3|| Malaar, Fourth Master: All beings that God created; have their fate written on the forehead. God blesses His devotee and enjoins him to worship Him. ||1|| The guru recites and implants God's name in the devotee. Page 1264 O guru's devotees say God; saying God carries across the terrifying world ocean. ||1||Pause|| The devotee, who worships and serves the guru; he pleases my God. Guru's worship is God's worship. God bestows salvation by His grace. ||2|| The blind ignorant are deluded by doubt. He plucks flowers for worship when he wanders. They worship the dead; their effort goes waste. ||3|| He, who realizes God, is the true guru; he tells God's story. Offer food, clothes and other offering to the guru and truly recite him with your mouth and obtain unlimited blessing. ||4|| The guru is the true image of God; he speaks the sacred words. O Nanak, those, who focus their mind to God's feet are fortunate. ||5||4|| Malaar, Fourth Master: Those, who enshrine God's name in the mind, are the true saints. Seeing them, my mind blossoms. I praise them forever. ||1|| O wise people; say God God day and night. Those who enjoy God's love through guru's teaching, their greed and hunger disappear. ||1||Pause|| God's servants and devotees are my companions; meeting them my falsehood ends. As the swan separates milk from water, same way the devotee eliminates the fire of ego. ||2|| Those who do not love God; they are cheats and cheat others. What can anyone give them to eat? They eat what they sow; ||3|| God's devotees have the same signs as God; God abides in his devotees. O Nanak, blessed is the all-seeing guru; he bestows salvation to the slanderers and admirers. ||4||5|| Malaar, Fourth Master: The name of the Lord is inaccessible, unfathomable and sacred; I recite it by His grace. The fortunate devotee found devotee's company and attained salvation in their company. ||1|| My mind is happy forever. I recite God by guru's grace and the doubt of my mind is erased. ||1||Pause|| O God; be kind and unite me with those who sing and recite God's name. I became peaceful seeing him; the pain of sickness of ego departed. ||2|| He, who recites God's name in the mind; his life is fruitful. He attains salvation and bestows salvation to the whole world; his dynasty also obtains salvation. ||3|| You created the universe and kept under Your control. Page 1265 God became kind to Nanak and pulled him from drowning in poison. ||4||6|| Malaar, Fourth Master: Those who do not drink nectar by guru's grace; their hunger and greed do not end. The ignorant self-willed burn in egotistic pride; they suffer pain in ego. They waste away their life in coming and going; they regret when they suffer. They do not miss the one, from whom they are born; their life and food is worthless. ||1|| O mortal the guru-willed; recite God's name. They meet the guru by God's grace and merge in God's name. ||1||Pause|| The life of the self-willed is useless; he comes and goes in shame. The proud drown in lust and anger and they burn in ego. They do not attain divinity or understanding; their intellect worsens. They suffer in the wave of greed. Without the guru, they suffer in terrible pain. They cry when the devil of death arrests them. ||2|| The guru-willed obtain the name of unfathomable God intuitively. The treasure of God's name enshrines inside and I sing God's praises. I am happy all the time and I am attuned to guru's teaching with love. I obtained God's priceless name intuitively by guru's grace. ||3|| God's name enshrines in my mind by guru's grace; this is guru's greatness. I offer my mind and body to everyone and focus my mind to guru's feet. O perfect guru; be kind to me and unite me with you. I am an iron; the guru is the boat, to carry me across O Nanak. ||4||7|| Malaar, Fourth Master, Partaal, Third House: God is one. He is realized by guru's grace. O God; I the humble servant say God God in devotee's company all the time. ||1||Pause|| I deal in and collect Godly wealth; the thieves do not steal it; ||1|| The rain bird and peacock give calls when they hear the cloud thunder. ||2|| Whatever the deer, the fish and the birds sing, they say God not anything else. ||3|| Servant Nanak sings God's praises and the fear of devil of death has ended. ||4||1||8|| Malaar, Fourth Master: The fortunate says God God to find God; if someone shows me the way to God; I will touch his feet. ||1||Pause|| God is my friend and a companion; I am in love with Him. Page 1266 I sing God I say God; I have given up the love of others. ||1|| My beloved God is the enticer of the mind. The detached God is the embodiment of supreme joy. Nanak lives by seeing God; even if I see him for a moment. ||2||2||9||9||13||9||31|| Tune Malaar, Fifth Master,

Chau-Padas, First House: God is one. He is realized by guru's grace. What you think what you imagine and what effort you do? Why he has to worry about anyone; who has the Lord of the universe on his side? ||1|| It rains heavily O companion. The Guest has come into my home. O Lord, treasure of kindness; be kind to poor that I merge with your name. ||1||Pause|| I prepared all sorts of foods in various ways, and all sorts of sweet deserts. I have purified my kitchen; please taste the food O my Lord. ||2|| You destroy the evil and save the friends; you live in this body temple. When my playful beloved came to my home; I found all happiness. ||3|| The society of saints has the full support of the guru; it is pre-ordained; Servant Nanak has found his playful Husband Lord. He shall never suffer in pain. ||4||1|| Malaar, Fifth Master: When baby's food is only milk, it cannot survive without milk. The mother takes care of him and pours milk in his mouth; then he is satisfied and fulfilled. ||1|| I am just a baby; God the great giver is my father. The child is forgetful and makes many mistakes. But he does not go anywhere else. ||1||Pause|| The mind of the poor child is fickle; he touches even snakes and fire. His mother and father embrace him, so he plays in joy. ||2|| What hunger can the child have, O my Lord, when You are his father? You have the treasure of name in your home; he who yearns will get it. ||3|| My kind father has issued this order: give him what the child wants; O Nanak, the child longs to see his father. His feet abide in my heart. ||4||2|| Malaar, Fifth Master: I made every effort and gave up worrying. I started every work at home believing in God. ||1|| I listen and play the beautiful tunes. Sun has risen; I am enjoying visualizing the face of my beloved. ||1||Pause|| I consciously go to the saints and ask. I found my beloved Husband Lord after searching. I worship him and touch his feet. ||2|| Page 1267 When my beloved came to live in my house, I began to sing the songs of joy. My friends and companions are happy; God united me with the perfect guru. ||3|| My friends and companions are happy; the guru has completed my deeds. Says Nanak; I have met my Husband, the giver of peace. He never leaves me and goes away. ||4||3|| Malaar, Fifth Master: From a king to a worm, and from a worm to the lord of gods, they do evil deeds to fill their bellies. They renounce God the ocean of mercy, and worship some other; they are thieves and killers of the soul. ||1|| Forgetting the Lord, they suffer in sorrow and die. They wander in many lifes and cannot stay anywhere. ||1||Pause|| They abandon the master and think of some other; they are ignorant, stupid, idiot like a donkey. How can they cross over the ocean in a paper boat? It is the ignorant way to say; ||2|| Shiva, Brahma, angels and demons, all burn in the fire of death; Nanak seeks the refuge of Your lotus feet O God; you do not neglect me. ||3||4|| Tune Malaar, Fifth Master, Du-Padas, First House: God is one. He is realized by guru's grace. My God is detached and free of desire. I cannot survive without Him, even for an instant. I am in love with Him. ||1||Pause|| I miss God in saint's company and I woke up by saint's grace. Hearing the teachings, my mind has become pure. I sing God's praises in love. ||1|| The saint's became my friends by surrendering my mind to them and they became kind to the fortunate. I cannot say how much happiness I obtained? Servant Nanak obtained the dust of the devotees. ||2||1||5|| Malaar, Fifth Master: O mother, please unite me with my beloved. All my friends sleep in peace those who have their beloved living at home. ||1||Pause|| I am worthless; God is kind forever. I am unworthy; what good am I? I try to match those who are imbued with their beloved; it is my stubborn ego. ||1|| I became humble and sought the refuge of the guru the bestowal of peace; He eliminated all my pain in a moment O Nanak, I spend the night in peace. ||2||2||6|| Malaar, Fifth Master: Rain down, O beloved cloud; do not delay. Rain down O beloved the support of my mind, so that I am happy in my mind forever. ||1||Pause|| I am your property O master; why do you forget me from your mind? Page 1268 I am Your maid servant; I have no honour without my husband Lord. ||1|| When my Lord heard my prayer; He hurried to shower me with His grace. Says Nanak, I am married and obtained honour, nobility and good character. ||2||3||7|| Malaar, Fifth Master: Reciting the name of the true beloved Lord. The pains and sorrows of the terrifying world-ocean are dispelled, by enshrining the image of the guru in the heart. ||1||Pause|| The enemies killed and evil disappeared since I came to God's refuge. The saviour saved me by giving His hand and I obtained the wealth of God's name. ||1|| By His grace He eliminated all my sins and bestowed the pure name on me. O Nanak, the treasure of virtue enshrines in my mind; I shall never again suffer in pain. ||2||4||8|| Malaar, Fifth Master: O my beloved God the love of my life. O kind God be kind and bestow me with love and worship; ||1||Pause|| I recite Your feet O beloved and your hope in the mind; I request the saints that I yearn to visualize God. ||1|| O God; visualize me so that visualizing You my birth and death end. O my God, be kind and bestow Nanak the wealth of your name. ||2||5||9|| Malaar, Fifth Master: Now, I am in tune with my beloved. Reciting God the Lord, I obtained happiness; the cloud of peace has rained. ||1||Pause|| I have obtained the treasure of God's name. I do not forget Him even for a moment. My future has awakened, meeting with the helpful saints. ||1|| Peace has welled up; all pain has been dispelled by lovingly attuning to the supreme Lord. Nanak recites His feet and has crossed over the difficult world ocean. ||2||6||10|| Malaar, Fifth Master: The clouds have rained down all over the world. My beloved God became kind and I obtained peace and joy. ||1||Pause|| My sorrows are erased; my thirsts are quenched by reciting the supreme Lord in the mind. My birth and death have ended in devotee's company and I do not wander anymore. ||1|| My mind and body are imbued with God's name and I am imbued to His lotus feet. God has made Nanak His Own; slave Nanak has entered His refuge. ||2||7||11|| Malaar, Fifth Master: Separated from the Lord, how can anyone survive? My mind yearns to meet Him so that I enjoy the essence of His lotus feet. ||1||Pause|| Those who are thirsty for You, O my beloved, are not separated from You. Those who forget my beloved Lord are dead and are dying. ||1|| Page 1269 The Lord of the universe abides in my mind and body; I see Him close by; O Nanak, He pervades in all and the whole world. ||2||8||12|| Malaar, Fifth Master: Tell me, whom worshipping God has not carried across? The bird, the fish, the deer, and the pig obtained salvation in devotee's company. ||1||Pause|| The families of gods, demons, titans, celestial singers and human beings are carried across the ocean. Whoever worships in devotee's company; their pain is eliminated. ||1|| They gave up the lust, anger and sins. Poor Nanak recites the merciful God and admires Him. ||2||9||13|| Malaar, Fifth Master: Today, I sit in God's shop. I discus the wealth of God's name with customers; I will not follow the path of devil of death. God saved me by his grace and the doubtful door of my mind has opened. I have found a rich banker and I took profit of the wealth of His feet. ||1|| I sought the refuse of the sacred immortal God; He picked and eliminated my sins. Slave Nanak's sorrow and suffering have ended. He will not go through the pot of life again. ||2||10||14|| Malaar, Fifth Master: In many ways, attachment to worldly wealth leads to ruin. There are only a few complete worshippers among millions for ages; ||1||Pause|| They wander here and there; finally their body and wealth belong to others. They cheat hiding from the people; but they do not know the one inside them. ||1|| They take birth as deer, bird, fish and other lowly species. Says Nanak; O God, carry me the rock across, that I may enjoy peace in devotee's company. ||2||11||15|| Malaar, Fifth Master: The cruel and evil died after taking poison, O mother. God saved them by His grace, because they belong to Him. ||1||Pause|| The inner-knower abides in all; then why worry O brother? God my support is always with me. He never leaves; He is omnipresent. ||1|| He is the master of orphans and destroyer of pains; He attaches us to Him. O Lord, Your slaves live by Your support; Nanak is at Your refuge. ||2||12||16|| Malaar, Fifth Master: O my mind; recite God's feet. My mind is enticed by the thirst of visualizing God; May I have the wings to fly to meet God; ||1||Pause|| I found the way by searching; now I serve the devotees. By the grace of my master I drink the sublime nectar. ||1|| I came to His refuge begging that I am burning; please be kind to me; Please give Your Hand to slave Nanak and make him your own. ||2||13||17|| Page 1270 Malaar, Fifth Master: It is God's nature to love His devotees. He destroys the slanderers, crushing them under the feet. His glory prevails. ||1||Pause|| His is admired in the whole world. He is kind to the beings. He embraces His servants and nothing harms them. ||1|| My master made me His; I found peace by eliminating the fear of doubt. Lord's slaves enjoy ultimate joy O Nanak, they believe Him. ||2||14||18|| Tune Malaar, Fifth Master, Chau-Padas, Second House: God is one. He is realized by guru's grace. The guru-willed sees God's creation. The guru-willed knows that the universe is run by three worldly qualities. The guru-willed hears and contemplates the scriptures. Without the perfect guru, there is pitch dark; ||1|| O my mind, saying guru guru obtains eternal peace. Enshrine guru's the God's lesson in the mind and recite God with every breath and morsel of food. ||1||Pause|| I praise guru's feet. Night and day, I continuously sing the praises of the guru. I take bath in the dust of guru's feet. I am honoured in the true court of the Lord. ||2|| The guru is the boat, to carry me across the terrifying world-ocean. Meeting the guru, I shall not be born again. That humble being who serves the guru has the pre-ordained destiny written on his forehead. ||3|| The guru is my life; the guru is my support. The guru is my way of life; the guru is my family. The guru is my master; I seek the sanctuary of the true guru. O Nanak, guru is God; His value cannot be estimated. ||4||1||19|| Malaar, Fifth Master: I enshrine God's feet in my heart; By His grace, God has united me with Him. God unites His servant with Him. His worth cannot be expressed. ||1|| Please be kind to me, O perfect giver of peace. I miss You by Your grace. I am imbued with Your love twenty-four hours a day. ||1||Pause|| Singing and listening is all by Your will. One who understands Your command; merges with You. I live by reciting Your name. Without You, there is no place for me. ||2|| Pain and pleasure come by God's will. He blesses by His will and punishes by His will. The Creator is the master of both sides. I admire Your divine power. ||3|| You alone know Your value. You alone understand, You speak and listen. Those who please You are Your devotees. Page 1271 Nanak admires them forever. ||4||2||20|| Malaar, Fifth Master: The transcendent Lord has become kind; the nectar rains heavily. All beings are satisfied; their affairs are perfectly resolved. ||1|| O my mind, recite God's name forever. It is obtained by serving the perfect guru; it stays with you here and after. ||1||Pause|| He is the destroyer of pain and fear. He takes care of His beings. The saviour Lord is kind forever. I admire Him forever. ||2|| The Creator has eliminated death. O my mind; recite Him forever. He protects all beings by His grace. Sing the praises of the Lord all the time; ||3|| He is the only Creator. Lord's devotees know His power; He preserves the honour of His name. Nanak speaks as the Lord inspires him to speak. ||4||3||21|| Malaar, Fifth Master: All treasures are found in the sanctuary of the guru. Honour is obtained in the true court of the Lord. Doubt, fear, pain and suffering are taken away; by singing God's praises in devotee's company; ||1|| O my mind, praise the perfect guru. Recite the treasure of God's name day and night and obtain the fruit of your choice. ||1||Pause|| No one is as great as the true guru. Guru is the supreme Lord, the transcendent God. He saves us from the pain of death and birth; we will not taste the poison of worldly wealth again. ||2|| Guru's glory cannot be described. Guru is the transcendent Lord. It is true. True is His self-discipline and true are all His actions. The mind that loves the guru becomes pure. ||3|| Perfect guru is found by luck. By eliminating the lust, anger and greed from your mind; By His grace, I enshrined His sacred feet in my mind; Nanak offers this true prayer to God; ||4||4||22|| Tune Malaar, Fifth Master, Partaal, Third House: God is one. He is realized by guru's grace. Pleasing the guru, I have fallen in love with my kind beloved Lord. I have worn my entire make up; and renounced all corruption; my wandering mind has become stable. ||1||Pause|| O my mind, give up your ego and join the company of devotees. The divine music plays loudly and the song bird sings God God and she looks adorable; ||1|| O beloved; visualizing You is glorious beyond imagination; so is to visualize Your saints; Reciting Your name carries across the terrifying world ocean. Say God God God like a rosary. Page 1272 I turn my mind to the company of God's companions. O servant Nanak, my beloved is my friend. ||2||1||23|| Malaar, Fifth Master: My mind wanders through the dense forest. It walks with eagerness and love; longing to meet God; ||1||Pause|| The three pronged worldly wealth is ahead of me. Who I tell my pain to? ||1|| I tried everything else, but nothing eliminates my pain. O Nanak, go to devotee's refuge and sing the praises of the Lord of the universe in their company. ||2||2||24|| Malaar, Fifth Master: The glory of my beloved is adorable. The celestial singers and angels sing His praises in love and joy. ||1||Pause|| They sing His praises in many melodious tunes and in many forms. ||1|| Throughout the mountains, trees, deserts, oceans and galaxies, my beloved abides in everyone and everywhere. O Nanak, those who obtain God's essence in devotee's company; their thinking becomes pure. ||2||3||25|| Malaar, Fifth Master: O mortal, love the guru and enshrine his lotus feet in the mind. ||1||Pause|| Seeing him is fruitful and my sins are erased. My mind has become pure and enlightened. ||1|| I am wonderstruck, stunned and amazed. Reciting God's name millions of sins are eradicated. I fall at His feet and touch my forehead to guru's feet. You You You, O God. Your devotees take Your support. Servant Nanak has come to the door of Your sanctuary. ||2||4||26|| Malaar, Fifth Master: It rains heavily all over by God's will; Bless me with total bliss and good fortune. ||1||Pause|| My mind blossoms in saint's company, like the earth after rainfall. ||1|| The peacock loves the thunder of clouds. The rain bird's mind is drawn to the raindrop. So is my mind enticed by the Lord? I have renounced the cheat the worldly wealth. Joining the saints, Nanak is awakened. ||2||5||27|| Malaar, Fifth Master: Sing forever the praises of the Lord of the world. Enshrine Lord's name in your mind. ||1||Pause|| Forsake your pride, abandon your ego and join devotee's company. O friend, recite God and the pain will depart. ||1|| The supreme Lord has become merciful; Corrupt entanglements have ended. Touching the feet of devotees. Nanak sings forever the praises of the Lord of the world. ||2||6||28|| Malaar, Fifth Master: The embodiment of the Lord of the universe roars like thunder. Singing His praises brings peace and joy. ||1||Pause|| The world ocean is crossed over in God's refuge and divine music plays. ||1|| The mind of the thirsty traveler's focuses to the pool and drinks sacred water. O God; be kind and visualize to servant Nanak by Your grace. ||2||7||29|| Page 1273 Malaar, Fifth Master: O Lord of the universe, O Lord of the world, O kind beloved; ||1||Pause|| O master of life of orphans, friend of humble; please eliminate my pain. ||1|| O all-powerful, inaccessible, perfect Lord, please be kind to me; ||2|| Please, carry Nanak across the terrible, deep dark worldly well. ||3||8||30|| Malaar, First Master, Ashtapadees, First House: God is one. He is realized by guru's grace. The duck does not want to sleep. She cannot sleep without seeing the beloved. She sees the beloved at sunrise and bows down and touches his feet. ||1|| She loves the beloved friend. She is so thirsty that she cannot survive without him even for a moment. ||1||Pause|| The lotus blossoms in the pool with the sunray in the sky intuitively. I am in so much love with my beloved that my soul has merged in his soul. ||2|| The rain bird cries beloved, beloved without water. It cries helplessly. It thunders and rains all over but his thirst does not quench without water. ||3|| The fish is born in water and lives in water; she enjoys the pain and pleasure of past deeds. She cannot survive without water even for a moment; her life and death depends on water. ||4|| The soul-bride is separated from her Husband Lord, who lives away; she shows her love through guru's teaching. She gathers virtues, and enshrines God in her heart. Imbued with devotion, she is happy. ||5|| Everyone cries, beloved! Beloved! She, who pleases the guru, meets the beloved. Our beloved is always with us truly. He unites with us by His grace. ||6|| The soul is in everyone and soul is God; it abides in everyone. By guru's grace, He is revealed in the heart; I intuitively merge with Him. ||7|| O God the Lord of the world the bestowal of peace; resolve Your affairs. Nanak found God in the heart by guru's grace and the burning fire extinguished. ||8||1|| Malaar, First Master: I serve the guru and remain awake; I have no one but God. I cannot stay here with all efforts; I will melt like glass in the fire. ||1|| Tell me; why are you so proud of your body and wealth? It does not take long to vanish; such a world is stuck in ego and pride. ||1||Pause|| Hail to the Lord of the universe, God, our saviour; He judges and saves us. All that exists belongs to You. No one else is equal to You. ||2|| Creating all beings you put them under your control such a way that You only are the cure of it. He is the protector of the orphans like me. He is the destroyer of death and birth, doubt and fear. ||3|| Page 1274 This world is a fortress of paper, imbued with colour form and clever tricks. A drop of water or a gust of wind destroys its honour in a moment and dies. ||4|| It is like a tree on the bank of a river, or a snake living in the house. When the river changes course, where is the tree and what happens when the snake bites; ||5|| Guru's word, wisdom and contemplation are the medicine. Guru's teaching burns away the sins. The mind and body are soothed; I obtained truth through God's unique worship. ||6|| All that exists begs of You; You are kind to all beings. I seek Your refuge; please save my honour and unite me with God O Lord of the world. ||7|| He is blind and cannot see, yet he acts like a hunter. If he meets the guru, then he realizes and understands and enshrines the divine wisdom in the mind. ||8|| Without the truth, the body is false and worthless; I asked my guru. O Nanak, God revealed Himself to me. The world is a dream without Him. ||9||2|| Malaar, First Master: The rain bird and the fish find peace in water; the deer enjoys the sound; ||1|| The rain bird chirps in the night, O my mother. ||1||Pause|| O my beloved, my love for You shall never end, if it pleases you. ||2|| Sleep is gone, bodies ego is tired and true lesson merged in the mind. ||3|| I am hungry and fly tree to tree and drink God's name intuitively. ||4|| My eyes are focused; mind cries and my thirst quenched seeing Him. ||5|| Doing makeup without the husband Lord gives fever; wearing clothes do not appeal to the body. ||6|| I cannot live even for a moment without my beloved; I cannot sleep without meeting him. ||7|| Her Husband Lord is nearby, but the ignorant does not know; the guru has revealed God to her. ||8|| She meets Him with ease and finds peace; guru's teaching quenches her thirst. ||9|| Says Nanak, my mind is pleased with You O God; I cannot imagine what it is worth? ||10||3|| Malaar, First Master, Ashtapadees, Second House: God is one. He is realized by guru's grace. The earth is upside down and yet filled with water. The mountain is high, yet the bottom is in the underworld. The ocean is soothed through guru's teaching. The path of liberation is found by eliminating ego. ||1|| I am blind; I see by the light of God's name. I take support of God's name and walk by guru's secret love. ||1||Pause|| Page 1275 I found the way through guru's teaching. With guru's support, one realizes the true powerful God. God's name is eternal and realized through beautiful sermon. If it pleases You then I find Your door; ||2|| Flying high or sitting down, I am lovingly focused on one Lord. God's name is my resolve through guru's teaching. There is no deep ocean, no high mountain ranges. The place I live; there is no path or a traveller. ||3|| You know where You live; it is very difficult to find that place. No one understands without the guru; the whole world is buried under thorny branches. They make lot of effort and cry but God's name is not realized without guru. God's name liberates in a moment through guru's teaching. ||4|| Some are ignorant, blind, stupid and ignorant. Some take support of God's name through guru's love. True sermon is sweet and the nectar pours out of it. Whoever drinks it obtains salvation. ||5|| Believe in God's name in your mind lovingly through true sermon by guru's grace; When it rains, the earth is rejuvenated. God abides in all. The evil-minded sows the salty land; this is the sign of those without the guru. Without the guru, there is pitch dark; they drown without water. ||6|| Whatever happens; happens by God's will. That which is pre-ordained cannot be erased. Bound by Lord's command, the mortal does his deeds. He is imbued with guru's teaching and merges with God. ||7|| Your command prevails in four directions O God; Your name prevails in four directions and the underworld. Guru's teaching prevails in all and what you earn is obtained by luck. Birth and death hang over the head along with hunger, sleep and death. O Nanak, obtain the pleasing God's name by God's grace. ||8||1||4|| Malaar, First Master: You do not understand the essence of death and liberation. You are sitting on the edge; better follow guru's teaching. ||1|| You stork; how were you caught in the net? You did not remember in your heart the unseen Lord; ||1||Pause|| For your one life, you consume many lives. You were supposed to swim in the water; instead you drowned in it; ||2|| You have tormented all beings. When you are caught then you repent; ||3|| When the heavy noose is placed around your neck; You may spread your wings, but you cannot fly. ||4|| You were pecking the flavour O self-willed ignorant. You can be freed from the net by contemplating the virtues of divine wisdom. ||5|| Serving the guru, the net of devil of death breaks; Enshrining guru's teaching in the mind. ||6|| Guru's teaching is the essence of all. Enshrine God's name in the mind; ||7|| The enjoyment you enjoyed will give pain ahead. O Nanak, there is no liberation without the true name. ||8||2||5|| Malaar, Third Master, Ashtapadees, First House: Page 1276 God is one. He is realized by guru's grace. If it is in your fate, you meet the guru. He cannot be obtained without luck. He meets the guru, and transforms into gold, if it is Lord's will. ||1|| O my mind; focus on God's name. God is realized through the guru and merge with God. ||1||Pause|| Spiritual wisdom wells up through the guru, then this worry goes away. God is realized through the guru and the person does not go through the womb again. ||2|| By guru's grace, the mortal dies while living and lives by practicing guru's teaching. He, who eliminates ego, obtains salvation. ||3|| By guru's grace, the mortal enshrines God in the mind and eliminates worldly pride from inside. He eats the uneatable, and obtains the discriminating intellect; he unites with the perfect primal being. ||4|| The world is innocently cheated and departs by losing the principle. Obtain the profit of devotee's company; it is realized by luck. ||5|| No one obtains it without the guru; think about it; the fortunate finds the guru and go across the terrifying world ocean. ||6|| God's name is His support and saying God God is his resolve. O God; be kind and unite me with the guru that I attain salvation. ||7|| The pre-ordained destiny written on the forehead by God cannot be erased. O Nanak, those who obey God's will become perfect. ||8||1|| Malaar, Third Master: The world deals in Veda's sermon and contemplates three worldly qualities. Without the name, it suffers punishment by the devil of death and keeps taking birth and dies again and again. Meeting with the guru, they are liberated, and obtain salvation. ||1|| O mind, immerse yourself in service to the true guru. By good fortune, the mortal finds the perfect guru, they recite God's name. ||1||Pause|| God created the universe by His will and looks after it; Lord made the mind pure by His will and I fell in love with God. I met the guru by God's will the saviour of life. ||2|| Admirable is the true sermon; only a few guru-willed realize it. Praise the Lord; no one is as great as He. God blesses and unites with Him; you only get what you earn. ||3|| The true guru is expert and reveals the supreme Lord. The nectar rains down and the mind is satisfied, and lovingly attunes to God. Reciting God's name everything becomes green; it never withers or dries. ||4|| Page 1277 Without the guru, no one finds the Lord; check it out; One finds the guru by God's grace intuitively. The self-willed is deluded by doubt; Godly wealth cannot be obtained without good luck. ||5|| Everyone is lead by three worldly qualities; they read and contemplate. They cannot obtain salvation and reach the destiny. The bonds do not break without the guru and God's name does not well up in the mind. ||6|| The scholars and silent sages got tired of reading and discussing Vedas. They do not miss God's name and do not find the destiny. They are ruined by corruption and the devil of death does not spare them. ||7|| Everyone longs for God's name but it cannot be obtained without luck. By God's grace one meets the guru and God's name enshrines in the mind. O Nanak, the honour obtains through God's name and merges with God. ||8||2|| Malaar, Third Master, Ashtapadees, Second House: God is one. He is realized by guru's grace. When God blesses then he puts the devotee to guru's work. His pains are taken away, and Lord's name dwells in the mind. True wisdom comes by focusing one's mind on the true Lord. Listen to guru's sermon through his teaching. ||1|| O my mind; serve God the true treasure. Godly wealth is obtained by guru's grace, then one focus on him forever. ||1||Pause|| The soul-bride who adorns herself without her Husband Lord; She is called ill mannered and is ruined. This is the useless character of the self-willed. She does many deeds but forgets God's name. ||2|| The guru-willed bride is beautifully adorned. She enshrines her husband Lord in the mind through guru's teaching. She realizes one God, and subdues her ego. That soul-bride is admirable. ||3|| Without the guru, the giver, no one finds the Lord. The greedy self-willed are enticed by duality. Only a few spiritually wise realize this; Without meeting the guru, liberation is not obtained. ||4|| Everyone tells the stories hearing from others. Without controlling the mind, worship cannot be performed. Obtaining divine knowledge the lotus blossoms. God's name dwells in their mind. ||5|| Everybody worships in ego. Peace is not obtained till the mind agrees. They hearsay and tell others yet want the credit for it. His worship goes waste and his life is a total waste. ||6|| Those who please God are the real devotees. They are attuned to God's name day and night. They see God nearby through God's name. Page 1278 God is realized through guru's teaching. ||7|| God blesses and bestows love. The world is suffering from the terrible disease of ego. By guru's grace, this disease is cured. O Nanak, the truthful merges in truth. ||8||1||3||5||8|| Tune Malaar, Chhant, Fifth Master: God is one. He is realized by guru's grace. My beloved God is the giver of love and worship. Your devotees are attuned to You with love. They are attuned to You with love and never forget You even for a moment. The Lord of the world, the treasure of virtue and glory is always with you. My mind is enticed by His feet and I am attuned to His name with love. O Nanak, my beloved is forever kind; only a few realize Him out of millions; ||1|| O beloved, Your divine wisdom is inaccessible and infinite. You save even the worst sinners. My Lord is the purifier of sinners, the love of His devotees and the ocean of mercy; Recite God the inner-knower freely in devotee's company forever. They wander in millions of lifes but obtain salvation only by reciting God's name. Nanak is thirsty for visualizing the beloved God; please look after him. ||2|| My mind is absorbed in the lotus feet of the Lord. O God, You are the water; Your humble servants are the fish. O God, You are water and the fish. There is no difference. Take me by the arm and bless me with Your name. My mind agrees by Your grace. Recite kind to the poor God, the lord of the world and the universe with love. Nanak, the lowly and helpless, seeks your refuge; be kind and accept him. ||3|| He unites us with Him. Our sovereign Lord is the destroyer of doubt. I met the amazing Lord the inner-knower my beloved, the treasure of virtue; I obtained extreme happiness and peace by praising the virtuous Lord of the universe daily. I am happy in His Company; I obtained the pre-ordained destiny. Prays Nanak, I seek their refuge, who recite God; ||4||1|| Vaar Of Malaar, First Master, Sung To The Tune Of Rana Kailaash And Malda: God is one. He is realized by guru's grace. Hymn, Third Master: Meeting the guru, my mind is happy, like the land with rain. Everything becomes lush green; the pools and ponds are filled to overflowing. The inner self is imbued with the deep red colour of love of God. The heart-lotus blossoms and the mind becomes true and content through guru's teaching. Page 1279 The self-willed is on the wrong side. He can see it by God's grace. He is caught in the trap like the deer; the death hovers over his head. Hunger, thirst and slander are evil; lust and anger are horrible. You cannot see with these eyes, till you contemplate guru's teaching. When it pleases You, the eyes become content; the entanglements go away. Serving the guru, his capital is preserved. The guru is the ladder to climb the boat. O Nanak, the true realizes the truth; true God is found in true mind. ||1|| First Master: There is one path and one door. The guru is the ladder to reach there. O Nanak, God is beautiful; all peace obtains through true name. ||2|| Ladder: He created Himself and realized Himself. Separating the sky and the earth, He has spread His canopy. He supports the sky without the pillars; He is realized through guru's teaching. Creating the sun and the moon, He infused His light into them. He created the night and the day by His amazing play. He created the shrines to bathe and religion to contemplate on special occasions. There is no other equal to You; how can we speak and describe You? You sit on eternal throne; all others come and go in reincarnation. ||1|| Hymn, First Master: O Nanak, when it rains in the month of Saawan, all four corners are happy; The snake, the deer, the fish and the wealthy; all enjoy. ||1|| First Master: O Nanak, when it rains in the month of Saawan, four suffer the pain of separation: The cow's calves, the poor, the travelers and the servants; ||2|| Ladder: You are true, O true Lord; You dispense true justice. Like a lotus, You hide and sit in trance; Brahma is called great, but even he did not know Your limits. You have no father or mother; who gave birth to You? You have no form or feature. You transcend all social classes. You have no hunger or thirst; You are satisfied and satiated. You dwell in the guru and realized through his teaching. Believing in truth, one merges in truth. ||2|| Hymn, First Master: The doctor was called; he held my arm and felt my pulse. The ignorant doctor does not know; that the pain is in the heart. ||1|| Second Master: O doctor; you are a real doctor only if you diagnose the disease. Prescribe such a medicine that eliminates the sickness. Give the medicine that eliminates the sickness and peace wells up. O Nanak, you are a real doctor only if you eliminate your disease. ||2|| Ladder: Brahma, Vishnu, Shiva and the deities were created. Brahma was given the Vedas, and he put people to worship; Ten prophets came including the king Raam. According to His will, they killed the demons. Shiva serves Him, but cannot find His limits. He established His throne on the principles of truth. He puts the world to work and He hides. Page 1280 You are told to do good deeds from above. ||3|| Hymn, Second Master: The month of Saawan (rainy season) has come, O friend; think of your Husband Lord. O Nanak, the divorcee loves others; she dies crying. ||1|| Second Master: The month of Saawan has come, O friend; the rain clouds have come; O Nanak, the happily married dwell in peace; they love the husband Lord. ||2|| Ladder: He staged a wrestling bout and arranged the arena for wrestlers. The guru-willed entered the arena with pomp and show. The false and ignorant self-willed are defeated badly. God wrestles and defeats them. He staged this play. One God is the Lord of all; know that O guru-willed? He writes your fate without pen and ink. He is realized in devotee's congregation, where His praises are sung forever. O Nanak, praise God through guru's teaching and realize Him; ||4|| Hymn, Third Master: The cloud comes in droves and is changing colour. What do I know; how my beloved Lord is pleased? The soul brides that are sincere are imbued with His love. O Nanak, those without love do not find peace. ||1|| Third Master: The cloud comes in droves and rains heavily. O Nanak, the soul-bride, whose mind is not attached to her Husband Lord, suffers in pain. ||2|| Ladder: One Lord created both sides and pervades on both sides. He created the sermon of Vedas and put arguments in it. Attachment and detachment are the two sides of it. Religion is the guide between the two. The self-willed are worthless and false. They definitely lose in God's court. Those who follow guru's teachings are brave; they have conquered lust and anger. God abides in the mind; he is realized through guru's teaching. The devotees who recite Your name lovingly are pleasing to You O Lord; I admire those who serve their true guru. ||5|| Hymn, Third Master: The cloud comes in droves and rains down for a long time. O Nanak, she, who follows her Lord's will, is happy forever. ||1|| Third Master: Why are you standing and looking around? This cloud has nothing in his control; The One who sent the cloud; enshrine him in the mind; Whoever He blesses; enshrines Him in the mind. O Nanak, without God's grace, they cry and weep and wail. ||2|| Ladder: Serve the Lord forever; He does everything in no time; He created the universe; He creates and destroys in an instant. He created the world by His power and thinks about it; O self-willed; they will ask for your account and punish you severely. Page 1281 The account of the guru-willed is settled with honour; God praises him. No one can reach there; no one hears anyone's cries. The guru is your friend there; he will save you in the end. These beings shall not serve anyone else but guru the God. ||6|| Hymn, Third Master: O rain bird, the one whom you call, everyone longs for Him. It will rain by His grace and the forests and fields will blossom. He is realized by guru's grace; only a few realize Him. Recite Him while sitting or standing and obtain eternal peace. O Nanak, the nectar rains down forever. God gives to the guru-willed. ||1|| Third Master: When the people of the world suffer; they pray sincerely. True Lord listens intently and gives comfort with ease. He commands the god of rain to rain heavily. The grain grows in abundance; its value cannot be described. O Nanak, praise God's name; who gives food to all. Eating that brings peace and the mortal never suffers again. ||2|| Ladder: O God, You are the truest of the true. You unite the truthful with You. Those caught in duality are on the other side; the false cannot unite with God even if they want. You unite, and separate. You display Your creative power. Attachment brings the sorrow and separation; they get what they earn. I admire those, who lovingly attune to God's feet. They are like the lotus, which remains detached, floating on water. Those who eliminate ego are peaceful and adorable. Those, who merge with God; have no sorrow of separation; ||7|| Hymn, Third Master: O Nanak, praise the Lord; everything is in His power. Serve Him, O mortals; there is no other than Him. God abides in the mind of the guru-willed, and he is at peace, forever. He never worries; all worries are eliminated from inside. Whatever happens, happens naturally; no one has any say in it. When the true Lord abides in the mind, the mind's desires are fulfilled. O Nanak, God listens to their words, whose accounts are settled? ||1|| Third Master: The nectar rains all the time; those who can realize; realize it. The guru-willed; who realize; they enshrine the sacred God in the mind. They drink Lord's nectar, and remain forever imbued with it and eliminate self-pride and greed. God's name is the nectar; it rains by His grace. O Nanak, the guru-willed visualize God the Lord of the soul. ||2|| Page 1282 Ladder: How can the unweighable be weighed? It cannot be obtained without weighing. Think of it through guru's teaching and merge in the virtuous. He will weigh Himself and unite us with Him. His value cannot be estimated; nothing can be said about Him. I praise my guru, who made us realize the truth. The world is being robbed of nectar; the self-willed does not realize. Without the name, nothing goes with you. He wastes his life, and departs. Those who remain awake through guru's lesson guard their house; the evil cannot do anything to them. Hymn, Third Master: O rain bird, do not cry and feel thirsty; obey God's command. O Nanak, obeying God's order the thirst quenches; His blessing increases four folds. ||1|| Third Master: O rain bird, you live in water and wander like water in water. You do not know the essence of water, so you cry; it rains in water and land in ten directions; no place is without it. Those, who are thirsty even after that much rain, are unlucky; O Nanak, the guru-willed who enshrine God in the mind realize it. ||2|| Ladder: The Yogic masters, celibates, mystics and spiritual teachers – none of them has found the limits of God. The guru-willed recites Your name and merges with You. He was happy in the darkness of thirty-six ages. You created the scary water and the bubble; You created the infinite, endless and inaccessible. You created the fire of hunger and thirst. Death hangs over the heads of the people of the world in love of duality. The saviour saves those who realize Him through guru's teaching. ||9|| Hymn, Third Master: This rain falls all over intuitively. Those trees become green, which remain immersed in God. O Nanak, by His grace, there is peace; the pain of these creatures goes away. ||1|| Third Master: The lightning flashes in the middle of dark night and the rain fall heavily. Food and wealth are produced in abundance when it rains by God's will. Consuming it, the minds are satisfied, and the beings follow the right path. This wealth is God's play. Sometimes it comes, and sometimes it goes. God's name is the wealth of divine people; they remain absorbed in it forever. O Nanak, whoever He blesses, obtains this wealth. ||2|| Ladder: He does, and causes all to do; whom can I complain to? He makes us do deeds and asks for the account as well. Whatever pleases Him happens. Only a fool issues commands. We are freed by His grace; He is the forgiver. He sees and hears everything; He gives food to all. He abides in all and checks everybody's account. Page 1283 The guru-willed searches him and falls in love with the true God. O Nanak, who else can we ask? He is the great giver. ||10|| Hymn, Third Master: This world is a rain bird; let no one have any doubt; This rain bird is an animal; it has no understanding at all. God's name is the nectar; drinking it the thirst goes away. O Nanak, the guru-willed who drink the nectar are not thirsty again. ||1|| Third Master: Malaar is a soothing tune; peace wells up reciting God; The nectar falls on the whole world if God blesses; From this rain, all creatures find food and the earth looks adorable. O Nanak, this world is all water; everything came from water. By guru's grace, a rare few realize the Lord; those humble beings are liberated forever. ||2|| Ladder: O kind God; You alone are worry free. You are everything; who else is of any account? False is the pride of man. True is Your greatness. You created the creation and the coming and going. He, who serves the guru, is judged to be somebody. If the ego departs; there is nothing like it; the self-willed is lost in the darkness of emotional attachment, like a man lost in the wild. A tiny bit of God's name eliminates billions of sins. ||11|| Hymn, Third Master: O rain bird, you do not know God's palace; pray to see His palace. When one speaks too much, it is not accepted. God is a great giver; you can obtain whatever you want. Not only the poor rain bird, but the thirst of the whole world quenches. ||1|| Third Master: The rain bird called truthfully and peacefully in the middle of the night; this water is my soul; I cannot survive without it. This water is obtained through guru's teaching and ego is eliminated. O Nanak, the one I cannot live without; the guru united me with him; ||2|| Ladder: There are countless worlds and underworlds; I cannot even count. You are the Creator, the Lord of the universe; You create and destroy it. The millions of species are born of You. Some are called kings, emperors and nobles. Some are called bankers, they collect wealth; they lose their honour in duality. Some are givers, and some are beggars; God is the master of all. Without God's name, they wander around scared. False does not last, O Nanak, whatever God does, happens. ||12|| Hymn, Third Master: O rain bird, the virtuous soul-bride obtains the destiny; the virtueless does not; O guru-willed; God abides in you and is always present. When God blesses by His grace, there is no more crying; O Nanak, those imbued with God's name merge with God through guru's teaching. ||1|| Page 1284 Third Master: The rain bird prays: O Lord, be kind and bless me with a gift of life. May my thirst never quench without water and I die. You are the giver of peace, O Infinite Lord; and the giver of treasure of virtue. O Nanak, bless the guru-willed and be my friend in the end. ||2|| Ladder: He created the world and contemplates their merits and demerits. Three worldly qualities are entanglements; it does not let one follow guru's teaching. Forsaking virtues, they practice evil; they shall be punished in God's court. They lose their life in the gamble; why did they come into the world? Those who conquer their mind through guru's teaching; love God's name forever. Those who enshrine the true, invisible and infinite Lord in their hearts? O Lord, You are the treasure of virtues; we are without virtues. Whoever He blesses realizes God contemplating guru's teaching. ||13|| Hymn, Fifth Master: The faithless; who forget God's name; cannot spend the night in peace; O Nanak, days and nights become peaceful by singing God's praises. ||1|| Fifth Master: All sorts of jewels and gems, diamonds and rubies are found by churning. O Nanak, those who obey God's will; look adorable in His court. ||2|| Ladder: Serving the true guru, I realized the true Lord. The service you did for the guru reveals in the end. The devil of death cannot rob when the true Lord protects. Lighting the lamp of guru's teachings, my mind is lit. The self-willed are false without the name, they wander around like demons. They are animals wrapped in flesh; they are filthy inside. True Lord pervades all; He is realized through guru's teaching. O Nanak, God's name is a treasure; the perfect guru revealed it to me. ||14|| Hymn, Third Master: The rain bird realizes God's Command with intuitive ease through the guru. The cloud rains heavily by God's grace. The cries and wailings of the rain bird end and peace wells up inside. O Nanak, praise God; who gives food to all beings. ||1|| Third Master: O rain bird, what you are thirsty for; drinking that eliminates the thirst; You wander in love of duality; you cannot obtain the sacred water; When God blesses with His grace, then the mortal meets the guru easily. O Nanak, the sacred water is obtained from the guru and he attains peace. ||2|| Ladder: Some go and sit in the forest, and do not answer any call. Some bathe in icy cold water in the middle of winter. Some rub ashes on their bodies, and never wash the dirt. Some look scary with matted hair. They bring dishonour to their family and ancestry. Page 1285 Some wander naked day and night and never sleep. Some burn their limbs in fire and ruin themselves. Without God's name, the body is reduced to ashes; what can I say? Those who serve the guru look adorable in God's court. ||15|| Hymn, Third Master: The rain bird gave a call at the sacred time; his call is heard in God's court. The order is issued to the clouds, to rain by His grace. I praise those, who enshrine truth in the mind. O Nanak, through God's name, all blossom through guru's teaching. ||1|| Third Master: O rain bird, your thirst will not quench this way; you may call hundred times. By God's grace, the true guru is found; by His grace, love wells up. O Nanak, when the Lord abides in the mind, the evil deeds leave. ||2|| Ladder:

Some Jains waste their time in the wilderness; they are ruined from destiny. They do not say God from the mouth or bathe at a shrine. They pull out their hair with their hands, instead of shaving. They remain filthy day and night; guru's teaching does not appeal to them. They have no status, honour or good deeds; they waste away their lives. Their minds are false and impure; they eat the false. Nobody obtains good character without guru's teaching. The guru-willed merges with the true Lord. ||16|| Hymn, Third Master: In the month of Saawan, the bride enjoys contemplating guru's teaching. O Nanak, she is happily married forever through guru's unlimited love. ||1|| Third Master: She, without virtues burns in the month of Saawan; she loves duality. O Nanak, she does not appreciate the value of her Husband Lord; all her decorations are worthless. ||2|| Ladder: The true, unseen, mysterious God is not won over by stubbornness. Some sing lovely tunes, but the Lord is not pleased by tunes. Some dance to the beat, but the beat is not a worship. Some do not eat; what can be done to these ignorant? How can the mind find peace if you have a lot of desire. Rituals tie some; they bury themselves to death. In this world, take advantage of God's name and drink nectar. The beloved guru-willed collect sacred offering for God's worship. ||17|| Hymn, Third Master: The guru-willed who sing the tune of love, their mind and body are soothed. They realize truly the true God through guru's teaching. Enshrining true God in the mind, the mind body and thinking become true. With true worship inside, they are automatically blessed with honour. It is pitch dark in today's age. The self-willed have no way to go, O Nanak, the guru-willed who realize God are fortunate. ||1|| Third Master: It rains by God's grace and joy wells up in people's mind. I praise the one, by whose command the clouds bring rain. Page 1286 The guru-willed recite guru's teaching and sing God's praises. O Nanak, those imbued with God's name become pure and merge in truth with ease. ||2|| Ladder: Serving the perfect guru, I have found the perfect Lord. Reciting Him with perfect luck, I enshrined the perfect God in the mind through guru's teaching. Contemplating God's divine wisdom the filth washes away. Believing God to be a pool at sacred shrine, my mind took bath in it. One who dies by guru's teaching conquering his mind; blessed is his mother.

The truthful truly came to the court of the true Lord. No one can question him, who is pleasing to God. O Nanak, praising the true Lord is pre-ordained; ||18|| Hymn, Third Master: Those who offer ceremonial turban of honour are ignorant; those who receive are shameless. The mouse cannot enter its hole with a basket tied around its waist. Those who give medicine die and those who receive it also die. O Nanak, no one knows God's command, where shall we go and merge. The spring crop and fall crop is the name of God; the autumn harvest is the true name. I received pardon from Lord's court. There are so many courts of the world, and many come and go there. There are many beggars begging, so many die begging. ||1|| First Master: The elephant eats a hundred pounds of butter and jagry and five hundred pounds of grain. He belches branches, grunts and blows dust around, he regrets when he stops breathing. The blind and dishonoured die insane. Submitting to the Lord, one becomes pleasing to Him; The sparrow eats only half a grain then it flies through the sky and chirps. She, who pleases God, is honourable if she says God God. The powerful tiger kills hundreds of deer; many others eat the left over. He is so powerful that he does not enter the den but regrets when breathing stops. Who the blind impresses with a roar? He is not pleasing to his Lord. The moth loves the milkweed plant; it eats sitting on the branches. He, who pleases God is honourable, if he says God God. O Nanak, the world lasts for four days; enjoying pleasure brings pain. Many, talk about it but no one can stop enjoying. The fly dies stuck in the sweets. O Lord, death does not approach those whom You protect. They go across the terrifying world-ocean. ||2|| Ladder: You are inaccessible and unfathomable invisible and infinite O Lord; You are the giver, all others are beggars. You alone are the great giver. Those who serve You find peace, contemplating through guru's teaching. Some love the worldly wealth by Your will. Praise God through guru's teaching with love. Without love, there is no worship. Without the guru, love does not well up. You are God; everyone serves You. This is the prayer of a humble minstrel. Please bless me with the gift of contentment, that I may receive the true name as my support. ||19|| Page 1287 Hymn, First Master: Through the night and the day the time ticks on. The body wears away and turns to straw. All are involved and entangled in worldly entanglements. The mortal has mistakenly renounced the way of service. The blind ignorant is caught in conflict, bothered and bewildered. Those who weep after he dies; can they bring him back? Without realization, nothing can be understood. They cry the dead and die crying; O Nanak, this is the will of the Lord. Those who do not remember God, die. ||1|| First Master: Love dies, and affection dies, hatred and the enmity die. The colour fades, and beauty vanishes; the body suffers and rots. Where did he come from? Where did he go? Was he or not? The self-willed talk and enjoy. O Nanak, without the true name, he is disgraced from tip to toe. ||2|| Ladder: God's sacred name gives peace forever and helps in the end. Without the guru, the world is insane. It does not know the essence of God's name. Those who serve the guru are accepted. Their light merges in supreme Light. That servant who enshrines God's will in his mind is just like his Master. Tell me, who found peace following his will? The blind act blindly. No one is fulfilled by evil deeds. The hunger of the ignorant does not extinguish. Attached to duality, they are ruined; without the guru, there is no realization. Those who serve the guru find peace; He blesses them by His will. ||20|| Hymn, First Master: Modesty and righteousness both, O Nanak, are qualities of those who are blessed with true wealth. Do not call that wealth friendly, which gets you beaten over the head. Those who possess the real wealth are called the beggars. But those, who have your name dwelling in their mind, are a bundle of virtues. ||1|| First Master: If you acquire the worldly wealth through pain, you feel pain when it leaves. O Nanak, without the true name, hunger is never satisfied. Beauty does not satisfy hunger; wherever I look, I see hunger. As many as are the pleasures of the body; they give that much pain. ||2|| First Master: Acting blindly, the mind becomes blind. The blind mind makes the body blind. Nothing happens by plastering, when the stonewall cracks. The dam has burst. There is no boat. There is no raft and no one helps. O Nanak, they drown without true name and take many with them. ||3|| First Master: With plenty of gold and silver, he is the emperor of emperors. He has thousands of armies, marching bands and spearmen, the emperor of thousands of horsemen. Where he has to cross over; there is unfathomable ocean of fire. The other shore cannot be seen; only the cries can be heard there. O Nanak, then you know what kind of emperor he is; ||4|| Ladder: Some have chains around their necks in bondage with Lord. They are released from bonds truly by realizing the true Lord. Page 1288 He receives what he earned and written in his fate. It is true. Everything happens by His command; you know if you go there. God who carries you across the world ocean is realized through guru's teaching. Thieves, cheats and gamblers are pressed like seeds in the oil mill. Slanderers and gossipers are handcuffed. The guru-willed absorbs in the true Lord, and is honoured in God's court. ||21|| Hymn, Second Master: The beggar is called a king and the ignorant is called the scholar. The blind man is known as a seer; this is how people talk. The troublemaker is called a leader, and the liar is seated with honour. O Nanak the guru-willed; know that this is justice in today's age. ||1|| First Master: Deer, falcons and government officials are known to be trained and clever. When the trap is set, they trap their own kind; they find no place to rest hereafter. He is learned and wise, and he, who practices God's name, is a scholar. First, the tree puts down its roots, and then it spreads out its shade above. The kings, tigers, government officials and dogs; they go and awaken the sleeping people to harass them. The public servants inflict wounds with their nails. The dogs lick the blood that spills. But where all beings are judged; those who violated people's trust; their noses will be cut and fall down and disgraced; ||2|| Ladder: He creates the world, and takes care of it. Without God's fear the doubt is not dispelled and love does not well up for God's name. Love wells up through the guru, and the devotee obtain salvation. The God fearing obtains contentment and the soul merges with infinite soul. Contemplating guru's teaching the God fearing cross over the world ocean. The God fearing realizes the carefree God. He has no limit or end. The self-willed do not know the essence of fear; they burn in greed and cry. O Nanak, enshrining God's name in the mind obtains peace. ||22|| Hymn, First Master: Beauty and lust are friends; hunger and taste are tied together. Greed mingles with wealth and the drowsy sleeps in the bed. The angry barks and bothers him, the poor blindly pursues useless deeds. O Nanak, silence is better; filth gets in the mouth without God's name.

||1|| First Master: Royal power, wealth, beauty, social status and youth are the five thieves. These thieves have plundered the world; they do not spare anyone; those who fall at the guru's feet rob these thieves. O Nanak, without good fortune, many more are robbed. ||2|| Ladder: The educated are called to account for their actions. Without God's name, they are judged false and punished. Their path becomes difficult, and the streets are blocked. The true carefree God is realized through guru's teaching and obtains contentment. The Lord is deep and profound and unfathomable; He cannot be found; nobody is freed without the guru and they are punched in the face. Reciting God's name they go home with honour. Know that; He gives food and breathing by His command. ||23|| Page 1289 Hymn, First Master: Living beings are formed of air, water and fire. What is pain and pleasure to them? There are God's courtiers in this world, the underworld and the sky. Some live long lifes, while others suffer and die. Some give and consume, and never fall short; the others beg forever. He creates and destroys millions in an instant. He has noose in everybody's nose; He breaks it by His grace. He has no colour or features; He is invisible and without account. How can we describe or know Him; it is true. He does and describes everything and He is beyond description. Hearing the story of the indescribable; obtains wealth, intelligence, perfection, spiritual wisdom and eternal peace; ||1|| First Master: He who lives long establishes his name and dynasty. One who worships God becomes eternal. Where has he come from, and where will he go? Remaining dead while yet alive, he is accepted. Whoever understands Lord's command, realizes the reality. This is known by guru's grace. O Nanak, know this: that you have to realize the existing God. Those without ego or self-conceit are not consigned to reincarnation. ||2|| Ladder: Read God's name and praise; other intelligent ideas are false. Without dealing in truth, life is worthless. God has no end or limit; no one can find it; the world is enveloped by the darkness of egotistic pride. It does not like the truth. Those who depart forgetting God's name shall be roasted in the frying pan. They pour oil in the burning fire of duality. They come in the world and wander aimlessly. They worry when they go. O Nanak, imbued with truth, the mortals merge in truth. ||24|| Hymn, First Master: First, the

mortal is conceived in the flesh, and then he lives in the flesh. When he takes birth, his mouth, flesh; his bones, skin and body are flesh. He comes out of the womb of flesh, and takes a mouthful of flesh at the breast. His mouth is flesh, his tongue is flesh; his breath is in the flesh. He grows up and is married, and brings his wife of flesh into his home. Flesh is produced from flesh; all relatives are made of flesh. When he meets the guru; he understands everything obeying God's command. No one can free himself O Nanak, it happens through guru's teaching. ||1|| First Master: The ignorant argue about flesh, they do not know but they talk about divine wisdom and meditation. What is meat, and what is called vegetables? What leads to sin? The gods killed rhinoceros; they burned butter and offered feasts to the saints. They renounce meat and pinch their noses when sitting near the meat, but eat human at night. They pinch their nose to show to others; they do not know the divine wisdom or meditation. O Nanak, what can we say to the blind? He does not understand what I say. He, who does blind deeds; he does not have those eyes in the mind. They are born from the blood of their mothers and fathers, but they do not eat fish or meat. Page 1290 But when men and women meet in the night, they come together in the flesh. We are conceived and born from flesh; we are pots of flesh. He does not think of divine wisdom or meditation; but he is called a scholar; O master, the meat from outside is bad and the one from home is good. All beings are created from flesh and the soul lives in flesh. Who have a blind guru, they eat the uneatable; they reject the eatable; We are conceived and born from flesh; we are pots of flesh; He does not know of divine wisdom or meditation; but he is called a scholar; Meat is allowed in the Puraanas, the Bible and the Quran. Throughout the four ages, meat has been used. It is featured and used in sacred feasts and marriages; Women, men, kings and emperors are born from meat. If you see them going to hell, then do not accept gifts from them. The giver goes to hell, the receiver goes to heaven; what a justice? You do not understand, but you preach others. O scholar, you are ignorant wise indeed. O scholar, you do not know where meat originated? Corn, sugarcane and cotton are produced from water. The three worlds came from water. I say that water is good and bad in many ways. Says humble Nanak that giving up so many tastes you became detached; ||2|| Ladder: What can I say with only one tongue? No one can find your limits. Those who contemplate true guru's teaching, merge with You. Some wander in saffron robes, but without the guru, no one finds God. They get tired of wandering in foreign lands, but You hide in them. Guru's teaching is a diamond; his touch enlightens. He realizes himself and merges with truth through guru's teaching. Those who create the bazaars, wander in coming and going in the bazaar. Those who love God become immortal by praising God. ||25|| Hymn, First Master: O Nanak, the worldly wealth is a tree of deeds. It yields both sacred and poisonous fruits. The Creator does all deeds; we eat the fruits we sow; ||1|| Second Master: O Nanak, burn worldly greatness in the fire. These burnt offerings have caused mortals to forget God's name. None of these go with you in the end. ||2|| Ladder: He judges everyone; His command prevails. Justice is in Your Hands, O Lord; You are pleasing to my mind. The mortal is tied by death and led away; no one can rescue him. The old, the tyrant, dances carried on the shoulders. So climb aboard guru's boat and the true Lord will rescue you; the fire of desire burns like an oven, consuming mortals night and day. Like trapped birds; the mortal pecks at the grain; he is freed by God's order. Whatever the Creator does, happens; falsehood shall end. ||26|| Page 1291 Hymn, First Master: The all knowing guru the primal being shows us our home inside; The divine music plays there through guru's teaching and that is the truth; Worlds and realms, underworlds, solar systems and galaxies are amazingly revealed. The string instruments and the harps play; the true throne of the Lord is there. Listen to the music in the home of peace. The mind enters in intuitive trance; contemplating the unspoken speech, the desires of mind vanish. The upside down heart lotus is reversed and filled with nectar. This mind does not wander anymore. It does not forget the divine recitation and merges with God forever. The five guru-willed friends get together and live in divine home. Nanak is the slave of those who contemplate guru's teaching and reach home; ||1|| First Master: The extravagant glamour of the world will end. My twisted mind does not believe that it will end up in a grave. I am the lowest of low; You are the great river O God; Please, give me one thing;

other poisonous things do no please me. You filled this fragile body with the water of life, O Lord, by Your creative power. You are powerful by Your grace. Nanak is a dog in Your court, intoxicates more and more, all the time. Reciting God's name cools down the worldly fire. ||2|| New Ladder, Fifth Master: His wonderful play is all pervading; it is wonderful and amazing! The guru-willed realizes the transcendent Lord, the supreme God. All my useless deeds vanished through guru's teaching. I became free from bad deeds and obtained salvation in devotee's company. I enjoy everything by reciting the bestowal God. I have become known in the world by His grace. He unites us with Him by His grace; I admire Him. O Nanak, He unites us with Him if He pleases. ||27|| Hymn, First Master: Blessed is the paper, the pen, the inkpot and the ink. Blessed is the writer, O Nanak, who writes the true name. ||1|| First Master: You are the wood plank, the pen and the writing written on it. Speak of the one Lord, O Nanak, why any other? ||2|| Ladder: You are all pervading; You created the creation. Without You, there is no other at all; You are pervading everywhere. Only You know Your divine wisdom. Only You can estimate Your worth. You are invisible, imperceptible and inaccessible. You are revealed through guru's teachings. There is ignorance, suffering and doubt in me; guru's wisdom eliminates all. He unites us with Him by His blessing and we recite His name. You are the Creator, the inaccessible primal Lord; You are omnipresent. They do what You make them do; Nanak sings Your praises. ||28||1|| Sudh|| Page 1292 Tune Malaar, word of The Devotee Naam Dev Jee: God is one. He is realized by guru's grace. Serve the pure sovereign Lord of the world who has no ancestry; Please bless me with the gift of worship, the humble saints beg for. ||1||Pause|| His Home is filled with fine heavenly paintings that fill the seven worlds alike. In His Home, the virgin Lakshmi (worldly wealth) dwells. The moon and the sun are His two lamps; poor devil of death plays his play and levies taxes on all. Such is my sovereign Lord, the supreme Lord of all. ||1|| In His house, the four-faced Brahma, the cosmic potter lives. He created the entire universe. In His House, the devoted Shiva, the guru of the world, lives; he imparts spiritual wisdom to explain the essence of reality. Sin, virtue and the recorder of deeds are the standard-bearers at His door; The justice of destiny and destruction is the guard at His door. Such is the supreme sovereign Lord of the world. || 2|| In His Home are the heavenly heralds, celestial singers, saints and poor minstrels, who sing sweetly. All dressed in different clothes and entice all in His arena singing beautiful songs. The wind waves the fan over Him; The worldly power that conquers the world is His servant. The shell of the earth is His fireplace. Such is the sovereign Lord of the universe; ||3|| In His home, the celestial turtle is the bed-frame, woven with the strings of the thousand-headed snake. His gardeners are the eighteen loads of vegetation; millions of clouds are His water-carriers. River Ganges flows out of His sweat. The seven seas are His water-pitchers. All worldly beings are His household utensils. Such is the sovereign Lord King of the universe. ||4|| In His home are Arjuna, Dhroo, Prahlaad, Ambreek, Naarad, Bheesham, the mystics, the learned, the ninety-two heavenly heralds and celestial singers. All the creatures of the world are in His house. God pervades all. Prays Naam Dev and seeks His protection. All the devotees are His banner and insignia. ||5||1|| Malaar: Please do not forget me O Lord; Please do not forget me, O Lord. ||1||Pause|| My family has this doubt and all are angry with me. Calling me low-caste and untouchable, they beat me and drove me out; what should I do O beloved Lord? ||1|| If You liberate me after death; the burnt charcoals do not know about salvation. These scholars, call me low cast and say that you will be dishonoured. ||2|| You are called kind and compassionate; You are all-powerful and unrivalled. The Lord turned the temple around to face Naam Dev; He turned His back on the scholars. ||3||2|| Page 1293 Malaar, the word of The Devotee Ravi Daas Jee: God is one. He is realized by guru's grace. O humble towns people, I am just a shoemaker. I recite God the lord of the universe in my mind. ||1||Pause|| Even if wine is made from the water of the Ganges, the saints do not drink it. This wine, and any other polluted water which mixes with the Ganges, is not separate from it. ||1|| The palmyra tree juice is impure as it is written in papers. But if devotional prayers are written on paper made from its leaves, people bow in respect and worship it. ||2|| It is my occupation to prepare and cut leather; each day, I carry the carcasses out of the city. Now, the important Brahmins of the city

bow down before me; Ravi Daas, Your slave, seeks the sanctuary of Your name. ||3||1|| Malaar: Those humble beings that recite God's lotus feet – no one equals them. God is one; He became many in many forms. He pervades all. ||Pause|| He who sings God's praises and does not praise anyone else. He is a low caste seamster. He is seen in Vyaas and Sanak; the glory of God's name prevail the seven continents. ||1|| He whose family used to kill cows at the festivals of Eid and Bakareed, who is worshipped by elders, martyrs and spiritual teachers, Like father like son; so is Kabeer known in the universe. ||2|| All his family members go around Banaras removing the dead cattle The honourable Brahmins pray to Ravi Daas, the slave of Lord's slaves. ||3||2|| Malaar: God is one. He is realized by guru's grace. What type of worship will unite me with my beloved? The salvation is obtained in devotee's company. ||Pause|| How long shall I wash these dirty clothes? How long shall I remain asleep? ||1|| Whatever I was attached to, has perished. The shop of false merchandise has closed down. ||2|| Says Ravi Daas, when the account is audited; whatever the mortal has done is revealed; ||3||1||3||
Page 1294Tune Kaanraa, Chau-Padas, Fourth Master, First House:
God is one. It is true. He is the Creator. He is carefree. He has no enemy. He is immortal. He does not take birth. He came into existence on His own. He is realized by guru's grace.
Meeting with the devotees, my mind has blossomed. I praise the devotees. I obtained salvation joining their company. ||1||Pause|| O Lord, be kind that I touch the feet of Your devotees. Blessed are the devotees, who realized God; the sinners obtained salvation in devotees company. ||1|| My mind wanders all over; meeting with devotees it came under control. As the fisherman spreads his net over water and catches fish. ||2|| God's saints are noble. Meeting with the saints, filth is washed away. All the sins and ego are washed away, like soap washes dirty clothes. ||3|| God wrote the fate on the forehead. I enshrined guru's feet in my mind. I realized God, the destroyer of poverty and pain; servant Nanak is saved through God's name. ||4||1|| Kaanraa, Fourth Master: My mind is the dust of the feet of the saints. I listen to God's sermon in congregation; my new unwashed mind is dyed by God's love. ||1||Pause|| I am thoughtless

and unconscious; I do not know God's state and extent. My guru has made me thoughtful and conscious. God, kind to the poor made me His own and my mind recites God's name. ||1|| Meeting with Lord's beloved saints, I will cut my heart, and offer it to them. Meeting with God's saints, I meet God; this sinner has been sanctified. ||2|| God's servants are proclaimed sacred in the world; meeting them the stone hearted melt. Page 1295 I cannot describe the glory of God's devotees. God made them sacred. ||3|| O Lord, You are the great merchant's banker; you loan money to us traders. O God, be kind to Nanak that he loads God's priceless treasure and takes away. ||4||2|| Kaanraa, Fourth Master: O mind, recite God and you will be enlightened. Meet with Godly saints and fall in love with them; you will be detached while living in the household. ||1||Pause|| I recite God in my mind and the Lord became kind to me. My mind became happy forever and I became hopeful of realizing God by reciting. ||1|| I am in love with God. I love Him with every breath and morsel of food I take. My sins were burnt away in an instant; the noose of worldly wealth broke. ||2|| I am a worm! What can I do? I am an ignorant fool, but God has saved me. I am an unworthy heavy stone, but I swam across the world ocean in devotee's company. ||3|| The entire universe God created is all above me; I am the lowest and corrupt. The guru eliminated my sins in his company and he united me with God O Nanak. ||4||3|| Kaanraa, Fourth Master: O my mind, recite God through guru's word. God the Lord of the world became kind to me. My ill will and duality went away. ||1||Pause|| God shows up in many forms and He is hidden in everybody. Meeting reveals God with God's saints and the hidden sins are found. ||1|| The saints who enshrine God in the mind are honoured everywhere. Meeting with God's saints, I met God, like the calf meets the cow. ||2|| The Lord abides in His saints; God's servants are sacred. They enshrine God's smell in the mind and other smells are erased. ||3|| You hire Your own servants and protect them by Your grace. Godly brothers are Nanak's mother father and relatives. ||4||4|| Kaanraa, Fourth Master: O my mind, recite God's name in the mind. Enshrining God in the mind the devotee has surrounded the fortress of worldly wealth and conquered the fortress through guru's teaching. ||1||Pause|| The people wander all over in doubt; they are enticed by the love of children and spouse. Like the shade of a tree, your body shall vanish in a moment. ||1|| My sacred beloved devotees are my life; meeting with them I believe in God. Reciting Him with love reveals the immortal God inside. ||2|| Page 1296 Godly saints are sacred; meeting them the mind gets dyed with love. God's love never fades. The devotee realizes God by loving God. ||3|| I am a sinner; I committed many sins. The guru has cut my sins in pieces. The guru gave me the medicine of God's name and sinner Nanak became sacred. ||4||5|| Kaanraa, Fourth Master: O my mind, recite the name of God the Lord of the universe. I was caught in the whirlpool of poisonous sins. The guru gave His Hand and pulled me out. ||1||Pause|| O my fearless true Lord, please save me. I am a heavy sinner like a stone. I am enticed by lust, anger, greed and corruption; I am carried across like the iron attached to wood. ||1|| You are the great primal being, the inaccessible and unfathomable Lord; I search for You, but cannot find You. You are the farthest of all O infinite Lord; You know Yourself, O Lord of the universe. ||2|| I recited the name of the unseen and unfathomable Lord in devotee's company and found the path. I listened to God's sermon in devotee's company and realized the unrealized God by reciting. ||3|| My God is the Lord of the world, the Lord of the universe and Lord of creation. Please save me; Servant Nanak is the slave of slaves of Your slaves. O God, please be kind and keep me with Your devotees. ||4||6|| Kaanraa, Fourth Master, Partaal, Fifth House: God is one. He is realized by guru's grace. O mind, recite God the Lord of the world. The Lord is the jewel, the diamond and the ruby. O guru-willed; mint your mind in God's mint. O Lord, please be kind to me. ||1||Pause|| O God; Your virtues are inaccessible and unfathomable; how can my one poor tongue describe them? O my beloved God; I say God God God. O God; You only know Your untold story. I am content saying God God. ||1|| O Lord you are my friend, my life my beloved God; my mind and body say God God. God's name is my wealth and property. The lucky bride is married forever singing God's praises through guru's teaching. Servant Nanak praises her and he is content reciting God: ||2||1||7|| Kaanraa, Fourth Master: Sing the praises of God the Lord of the universe. Let my one tongue become two million; With all of them, I recite God through guru's teaching. O Lord, please be kind to me. ||1||Pause|| O my master God; be kind and put me to serve You; may I keep reciting God the Lord of the world. Your humble servants, who recite God, are sacred. I praise them forever. ||1|| Page 1297 O God, You are the greatest and the highest; You do what pleases You. Servant Nanak drinks the nectar through guru's teachings. Blessed are the servants and the guru. I praise the guru. ||2||2||8|| Kaanraa, Fourth Master: O mind, say God God God. He has no form or feature; He is great! Join devotee's company and recite God. You are fortunate and it will be written in your fate. ||1||Pause|| The house where God's praise is sung; joy wells up there by reciting God; Sing praises of beloved God's name through guru's teaching. Says the guru that peace wells up by reciting God; ||1|| O kind Creator God; You created the universe. Everyone says God God God; Servant Nanak seeks Your refuge; please bless him to recite God. ||2||3||9|| Kaanraa, Fourth Master: I kiss the feet of the true guru. Meeting Him, the path to the Lord becomes smooth and easy. I lovingly recite God and gulp down the essence. The Lord has written this destiny on my forehead. ||1||Pause|| The mystics, the seekers and yogis with their matted hair perform a great deal of the six rituals. God is not realized by wearing religious robes; God's worship is obtained in devotee's congregation through guru's teaching and saint's mind opens up. ||1|| O my Lord, You do not owe to anyone, you are beyond imagination. You abide water land and everywhere, You and only You. You know and understand entire systems O Nanak's God. You abide in everybody. ||2||4||10|| Kaanraa, Fourth Master: O mind, recite God the Lord of the universe. The Lord is inaccessible and unfathomable. He is realized through guru's teaching. Whatever is written in your destiny comes to pass. ||1||Pause|| Collecting the evil worldly wealth the mind thinks of evil. But reciting God in devotee's company meeting the guru O devotee finds peace. As the iron becomes gold by touching with philosopher's stone, same way the sinner becomes sacred through guru's teaching in devotee's company. ||1|| As iron attached to wood floats; same way the sinner attains salvation in devotee's company through guru's teaching O devotee. There are four social classes, and four ways of worship. Whoever met Guru Nanak, was carried across along with his dynasty. ||2||5||11|| Kaanraa, Fourth Master: Sing the praises of the Lord; Singing His praises, sins are washed away. Learn through guru's teachings and listen to His praises with your ears. The Lord will be kind to you. ||1||Pause|| Page 1298 Your humble servants focus their mind and recite God. Those devotees obtain peace by reciting the treasure of God's name. The devotees join together and praise the guru the God. ||1|| Those who have You in the mind O master, obtain peace and swim across the world ocean. They are Your real devotees. O Nanak's God; please make me to serve You. You are my God; ||2||6||12|| Kaanraa, Fifth Master, Second House: God is one. He is realized by guru's grace. Sing the praises of the Lord of the world, the treasure of mercy. True guru is the destroyer of pain, giver of peace; meeting Him, one is totally fulfilled. ||1||Pause|| Recite His name; He is the support of the mind. Millions of sinners are carried across in an instant. ||1|| Whoever misses his guru? Shall not suffer pain even in a dreams; ||2|| Whoever is protected by the guru? That person enjoys reciting God's name with his tongue. ||3|| Says Nanak, the guru is Kind to me. Here and hereafter, I will be happy. ||4||1|| Kaanraa, Fifth Master: I worship and adore You, O my Lord and master; I say God with every breath while standing, sitting, sleeping and awake. ||1||Pause|| God's name enshrines in his mind. Whomever does God bless? ||1|| He becomes peaceful; by surrendering to God through guru's teaching; ||2|| they become wise and blessed with all powers; Whom, the guru blesses with the lesson of God's name. ||3|| Says Nanak, I admire those, who obtain God's name in today's age; ||4||2|| Kaanraa, Fifth Master: Sing the praises of God, O my tongue. Humbly bow to the saints, over and over; the feet of the Lord of the universe abide there. ||1||Pause|| Making all kind of efforts, one cannot reach the destiny. When God becomes kind then they say God God. ||1|| The body is not purified by millions of rituals. They obtain divine wisdom in the mind in devotee's company. ||2|| Greed does not vanish enjoying many pleasures of worldly wealth. Saying God God they obtain eternal peace. ||3|| When the supreme Lord becomes kind; Says Nanak, then one is freed from worldly entanglements. ||4||3|| Kaanraa, Fifth

Master: Pray for such a blessing from the Lord of the universe: That, you serve the saints in devotee's company and obtain salvation reciting God; ||1||Pause|| Worship the feet of the Lord and seek His sanctuary. Be happy in whatever God does. ||1|| This precious human body becomes fruitful; Page 1299 Whoever God blesses; ||2|| The place of ignorance, doubt and pain are destroyed; Whoever enshrines guru's feet in the mind. ||3|| Recite God in devotee's company with love. Says Nanak, you shall realize the perfect Lord. ||4||4|| Kaanraa, Fifth Master: Worship is the life of devotees. Their bodies and minds are intoxicated with God; He unites them with Him. ||1||Pause|| The singer sings songs; But those who enshrine in the mind obtain salvation. ||1|| Those who serve food enjoy the flavour. But those who eat are satisfied. ||2|| People disguise themselves with all sorts of costumes; in the end, they are what they were. ||3|| Speaking and talking are all just entanglements. O slave Nanak, the truth is the essence of all. ||4||5|| Kaanraa, Fifth Master: Your humble servant listens to Your Praises and enjoy. ||1||Pause|| Listening to God's praises their mind enlightens; they see God everywhere. ||1|| You are the farthest from all, the highest of all, profound, unfathomable and unreachable. ||2|| You are united with Your devotees, through and through; You have lifted Your veil for Your humble servants. ||3|| By guru's grace, Nanak sings Your praises in intuitive trance. ||4||6|| Kaanraa, Fifth Master: God came to the saints to bestow salvation to them. ||1||Pause|| I became sacred by seeing him and by saying God God. ||1|| Taking the medicine of God's name my sickness is erased and I became pure. ||2|| I became stable, and live in peaceful place. I shall never again wander anywhere. ||3|| By the grace of saints everyone obtains salvation. The worldly wealth does not touch them. ||4||7|| Kaanraa, Fifth Master: I have forgotten my jealousy of others; since I joined the company of devotees; ||1||Pause|| No one is my enemy or stranger; I get along with everyone. ||1|| Whatever God does, I accept it. I obtained this realization from devotees. ||2|| God abides in all; Nanak is joyous seeing it. ||3||8|| Kaanraa, Fifth Master: O my Lord, You alone are my support. You are my honour and glory and support; I seek Your refuge. ||1||Pause|| You are my Hope, and faith. I recite and enshrine Your name in the mind; You are my power;

I am content with You; whatever You say I do; ||1|| I find peace by Your kindness and grace; be kind that I swim across the terrifying world ocean. Reciting God I obtained the supreme gift and became carefree; Nanak has placed his head on saint's feet. ||2||9|| Page 1300 Kaanraa, Fifth Master: I have focused my mind to saint's feet in their refuge. I heard and saw in a dream that the guru taught me to recite God's name; ||1||Pause|| Power, youth and wealth do not bring satisfaction; people chase after them forever. I have found peace and my thirsty desires have been quenched and obtained peace singing His praises. ||1|| Without understanding, they are like animals; they are enticed by false attachment and bothered by worldly wealth. His chain of death is cut in devotee's company and Nanak has merged in peace. ||2||10|| Kaanraa, Fifth Master: Sing the praises of Lord's feet in your heart. Reciting God all the time, one becomes soothed and peaceful. ||1||Pause|| All your hopes are fulfilled and the pain of millions of lifes goes away. ||1|| Joining devotee's company you will obtain the benefit of giving awns and many other good deeds. Sorrow and suffering shall be erased; O Nanak, and you will not die again. ||2||11|| Kaanraa, Fifth Master, Third House: God is one. He is realized by guru's grace. Speak and discus God's divine wisdom with saints; they are God's perfect light and obtain honour reciting God. ||1||Pause|| Reciting God in devotee's company the trouble of coming and going ends; Attuning to God with love the sinners become sacred in a moment. ||1|| Whoever speaks and listens to God's praises; their ill will departs. Their deeds are completed and desires fulfilled O Nanak. ||2||1||12|| Kaanraa, Fifth Master: The treasure of God's name is obtained in devotee's company. He is the companion and support of the soul. ||1||Pause|| Continuously bathing in the dust of the feet of the saints, the sins of countless different lifes are washed away. ||1|| The sermon of the humble saints is sacred. Reciting it the mortal obtains salvation; ||2||2||13|| Kaanraa, Fifth Master: O devotee, sing God's praises. Mind, body, wealth and the breath of life, belong to God. Reciting God the pain goes away. ||1||Pause|| Why are you entangled in this and that? Focus your mind on one; ||1|| The place of the saints is most sacred; recite God in their company. ||2|| O Nanak, I gave up everything and came to Your refuge. Please unite me with You. ||3||3||14|| Kaanraa, Fifth Master: I sit in trance and enjoy seeing my beloved God. ||1||Pause|| He is the image of joy, peace and contentment. There is no other like Him. ||1|| Saying God once, millions of sins are erased. ||2|| Page 1301 Singing God's praises the pain goes away and the mind becomes peaceful. ||3|| O Nanak, imbued with God's love, drink the sacred nectar. ||4||4||15|| Kaanraa, Fifth Master: O friends, O saints, come to me. ||1||Pause|| Singing the praises of the Lord with joy, the sins will be erased. ||1|| Touch your forehead to the feet of the saints; your dark house shall be illuminated. ||2|| The heart lotus blossoms by saint's grace; and he sees the Lord of the universe close by and recites his name. ||3|| He met the saint by God's grace and he admires him forever. ||4||5||16|| Kaanraa, Fifth Master: I seek the sanctuary of Your lotus feet, O Lord of the world. Please wash away my false attachment and pride and save me by cutting my chains. ||1||Pause|| I am drowning in the world-ocean. Reciting God the ocean of jewels obtains salvation. ||1|| O Lord; Your name is soothing. God, my lord and master, is perfect. ||2|| He is the destroyer of pain of the poor and bestowal of salvation. God the treasure of kindness is the saviour of the sinners. ||3|| I have suffered the pain of millions of different lifes. Nanak is at peace that the guru has implanted God's name in him. ||4||6||17|| Kaanraa, Fifth Master: Blessed is the love, which attunes to Lord's feet. The fortunate has realized the benefit of millions of meditation and penance. ||1||Pause|| I am Your helpless servant and slave; I have given up all other support. The darkness of doubt is cut reciting God and I am asleep while awake receiving the medicine of divine wisdom. ||1|| You are unfathomable and the greatest O master; please be kind O ocean of jewels. Nanak, the beggar, begs for God's name; he rests his forehead on God's feet. ||2||7||18|| Kaanraa, Fifth Master: I am filthy, stonehearted, deceitful and obsessed with lust. Please carry me across, as You wish, O my Lord and master. ||1||Pause|| You are all-powerful and potent to grant refuge. You save us by Your power. ||1|| Chanting and deep meditation, penance and austere self-discipline, fasting and purification; salvation does not attain by any of these means. O God; please take me out of the deep dark ditch by Your grace. ||2||8||19|| Kaanraa, Fifth Master, Fourth House: God is one. He is realized by guru's grace. I pay my regards to the Lord of all. I admire such a guru, who has obtained salvation and guides me to it. ||1||Pause|| No matter how many praises of Him I sing, there is no end to it. They are in millions; is there anyone who can think so? ||1|| Page 1302 I am wonder-struck and amazed, dyed in the deep red colour of my beloved. Says Nanak, the saints enjoy this sublime essence, like the mute enjoys the sweet; ||2||1||20|| Kaanraa, Fifth Master: The saints do not know any other but God. They look upon high and low all equally; they recite God and honour Him in the mind. ||1||Pause|| God the ocean of happiness abides in all, the destroyer of fear and my life. I am enlightened, and doubt dispelled, when the guru whispered His lesson in my ear. ||1|| He knows all previous and present deeds, the ocean of mercy. Twenty-four hours a day Nanak sings His praises, and begs for the gift of the Lord. ||2||2||21|| Kaanraa, Fifth Master: Many speak and talk about God. But One who understands the reality of worship is rare; ||1||Pause|| He has no pain but all happiness and he sees one and only one God. He does not think bad but good all the time; he does not lose but wins all. ||1|| He is never sad; he is always happy; he always gives, does not take anything. Says Nanak; God's servant realizes God. God does not come or go. ||2||3||22|| Kaanraa, Fifth Master: May I not forget the love from my mind? My body and mind are intoxicated with him; the enticer entices me O my mother. ||1||Pause|| Whoever I tell my state of mind; they all are hindrance. The worldly wealth has cast the net in many ways. Caught in it cannot be freed. ||1|| Wandering all over, slave Nanak has come to the sanctuary of saints. The bonds of ignorance, doubt, attachment to worldly wealth are cut and he embraced me. ||2||4||23|| Kaanraa, Fifth Master: I am filled with happiness, pleasure and joy. I sing and recite God's name. God's name is the support of my life. ||1||Pause|| I obtain divine wisdom through God's name; I bathe in God's name; God's name fulfills my deeds. Admiration and honour is obtained through God's name. God's name carries us across the terrifying world ocean. ||1|| I have obtained the unfathomable treasure, the priceless gem in guru's refuge. Says Nanak, God became kind; I became intoxicated in my mind and visualized God. ||2||5||24|| Kaanraa, Fifth Master: My beloved friend, my Lord and master, is near. He sees and hears everything; He is with everyone. You are here for a short time – why do you do evil deeds? ||1||Pause|| Other than God's name, whatever you are entangled with; nothing belongs to you. Hereafter, everything is revealed to you; but here, you are enticed by the darkness of doubt. ||1|| People are entangled with children spouse and worldly wealth; and forgot the bestowal. Page 1303 Says Nanak, I have faith in one. My guru is the destroyer of bonds. ||2||6||25|| Kaanraa, Fifth Master: the wicked army of corruption overwhelms Your saint. I take your support, believe in you and I have come to your refuge. ||1||Pause|| My sins of many lifes have been eliminated by seeing you. I am enlightened and filled with joy. I am intuitively absorbed in trance. ||1|| Who says that You cannot do anything? You are infinite and all-powerful. Nanak enjoys your love, beauty and joy by reciting Your name. ||2||7||26|| Kaanraa, Fifth Master: reciting God saves the drowning being. The pain of false attachment, doubt and suffering is erased. ||1||Pause|| I worship guru's feet day and night. Wherever I look, I see Your sanctuary. ||1|| By the grace of saints, I sing the praises of the Lord. Meeting with the guru, Nanak has found peace. ||2||8||27|| Kaanraa, Fifth Master: Reciting God's name attains peace in the mind. Singing God's praises in devotee's company. ||1||Pause|| O God, be kind and enshrine in my mind. I touch my forehead to the feet of the saints. ||1|| O my mind, recite the supreme Lord; O Nanak, the guru-willed listens to God's praises. ||2||9||28|| Kaanraa, Fifth Master: O my mind; touch the feet of God with love. Saying God satisfies my tongue. My eyes are content visualizing God. ||1||Pause|| My ears are filled with the praise of my beloved; all my sins and faults are erased. My feet follow the Godly path of peace. He is with me in the company of saints. ||1|| I have sought the sanctuary of perfect immortal God; I am tired of doing other things. O Nanak, He made me his own by his grace. I shall not die in the terrifying world ocean. Kaanraa, Fifth Master: He cheats, deceives, steals, ignorant and loud mouth. He dies again and again. ||1||Pause|| Intoxicated with ego, imbued with other tastes, he does not love the beloved; he wanders through many lifes. ||1|| He does many menial deeds intoxicated with worldly wealth and burns with anger. O merciful Lord of the world, embodiment of compassion, protector of the poor. O Nanak, seek his refuge and obtain salvation; ||2||11||30|| Kaanraa, Fifth Master: God is the bestowal of soul life and honour. Forgetting the Lord, all is lost. ||1||Pause|| Forsaking God, attached to others; he gave up the nectar and fell to the ground. Loving the taste of evil deeds O ignorant; how can you find happiness? ||1|| Page 1304 He is bothered by lust, anger and greed; that is cause of taking birth time and again. But I have come to the refuge of the purifier of sinners. O Nanak, know that I shall be saved. ||2||12||31|| Kaanraa, Fifth Master: I long to visualize God; I have found the jewel by searching. My worry is eliminated. ||1||Pause|| Enshrining His lotus feet in my heart. Pain and wickedness have been dispelled. ||1|| The Lord of the universe is my kingdom, wealth and family. I got the benefit of devotee's company O Nanak, I will not die again. ||2||13||32|| Kaanraa, Fifth Master, Fifth House: God is one. He is realized by guru's grace. Worship God, by reciting His name. Seek the refuge of the true guru. You will find the unfathomable Lord. Conquer the world by guru's grace. ||1||Pause|| I searched other type of worship many ways; whatever appeals to God is the real worship. This body-puppet is made of clay; what is it doing? O God, whomever You take by the arm and show the path; realizes You. ||1|| I do not know of any other support; O Lord, You are my only Hope and support. What prayer the poor can offer? God abides in every heart. My mind is thirsty for the feet of God. Your servant Nanak says: I admire You forever. ||2||1||33|| Kaanraa, Fifth Master, Sixth House: God is one. He is realized by guru's grace. Your Name, O my beloved, is the saviour of the world. God's name is the priceless treasure. One who is imbued with the love of the incomparably beautiful Lord is joyful. O mind, why do you cling to emotional attachments? With your eyes, see the devotees of God. He, who has it written in the fate, obtains it. ||1||Pause|| I serve at the feet of God's devotees and saints. I long for the dust of their feet, which purifies and sanctifies. It washes away the filth as much as bathing at sixty-eight shrines. With each and every breath I recite His name and never turn away from it. Out of your thousands and millions, nothing shall go with you. Only God's name helps in the end. ||1|| Enshrine God in the mind. Abandon the love of everything else. What praises of You can I say O my beloved? I cannot describe even one of Your virtues. My mind is very thirsty for visualizing You and meeting Nanak Dev the guru of the World. ||2||1||34|| Page 1305 Kaanraa, Fifth Master: Is there any way to visualize God; ||1||Pause|| I hope and thirsty for visualizing You, my heart yearns for You. ||1|| The meek and humble saints are thirsty for God like fish for water. I am the dust of the feet of Lord's saints. I offer my heart to them. God has become kind to me. O Nanak, God is realized by eliminating pride and emotional attachment; ||2||2||35|| Kaanraa, Fifth Master: The playful Lord imbues all with His love. From an ant to an elephant, He is permeating and pervading all. ||1||Pause|| Some go on fasts, make vows, and take pilgrimages to sacred shrines on river Ganges. They stand naked in water, enduring hunger and poverty. They sit cross-legged, perform worship services and do good deeds. They apply religious symbols to their bodies, and ceremonial marks to their limbs. God cannot be realized without the true congregation. ||1|| They stubbornly practice ritualistic postures, standing on their heads. They are troubled by the sickness of ego and it does not go away. They burn in the fire of lust, anger and greed. He is liberated, O Nanak, whose true guru is good. ||2||3||36|| Kaanraa, Fifth Master, Seventh House: God is one. He is realized by guru's grace. My thirst has been quenched, meeting with devotees. The five thieves ran away, and I am in peace singing God's praises with love to visualize Him. ||1||Pause|| Whatever God did to me; how can I do that to Him? I admire You in my mind forever. ||1|| First, I fall at the feet of the saints; then I recite His name with love. O God, where is that place, where You think about all Your beings? Countless slaves sing Your praises. He, who pleases You realizes You. Servant Nanak remains absorbed in his Lord. You, You, You alone O Lord; ||2||1||37|| Kaanraa, Fifth Master, Eighth House: God is one. He is realized by guru's grace. Give up your pride, ego. The kind beloved God watches it. O mind, become the dust of His feet. ||1||Pause|| Through the lesson of Lord's saints, obtain divine wisdom and meditation of the Lord of the world. ||1|| Sing the praises of the Lord of the universe, kind to the poor and beloved Lord lovingly attuning to His feet; O kind God; be kind to me. Nanak begs for the gift of God's name. I have abandoned emotional attachment, doubt and all egotistic pride. ||2||1||38|| Kaanraa, Fifth Master: Saying God meeting the guru, the filth is burnt away; there is no other way. ||1||Pause|| Page 1306 Making pilgrimages to sacred rivers, observing the six rituals, wearing matted and tangled hair, performing fire sacrifices and carrying ceremonial walking sticks; none of these are of any use. ||1|| All sorts of efforts, austerities, wanderings and telling various stories; none of these will find the destiny; I have contemplated everything O Nanak, peace obtains only by reciting God's name. ||2||2||39|| Kaanraa, Fifth Master, Ninth House: God is one. He is realized by guru's grace. The purifier of sinners, love of His devotees, the destroyer of fear. He carries us across the world ocean. ||1||Pause|| My eyes are satisfied, visualizing him and enjoying by listening to his praises. ||1|| He is the bestowal of life and master of orphans; I the poor seek His refuge. My hope fulfilled, pain ended by taking shelter at God's feet. ||2||1||40|| Kaanraa, Fifth Master: I seek refuge of the feet of my kind Lord; I do not go anywhere else. It is the inherent nature of our Lord to purify the sinners. Salvation obtains reciting God. ||1||Pause|| The world is a swamp of the ocean of wickedness and corruption. The blind sinner is blinded by emotional attachment and pride. The entanglements of worldly wealth bewilder him. O God; be kind and take me out of it. O Lord of the universe; save me; ||1|| He is the master of orphans, the support of the saints, and the destroyer of millions of sins. My mind thirsts for visualizing Him. God is the perfect treasure of virtue. O Nanak, sing the praises of the kind and compassionate Lord of the world. ||2||2||41|| Kaanraa, Fifth Master: I admire Him again and again forever. That was the moment of peace, the night I enjoyed with my beloved; ||1||Pause|| Mansions of gold, silk and beds; O sisters, I have no love for these. ||1|| Other than God's name I have forsaken the pearls, jewels and countless pleasures, O Nanak I am at peace to eat dry food, sleep on the hard floor in the company of my beloved. ||2||3||42|| Kaanraa, Fifth Master: Give up your ego, and turn your face to God. Yearn to say God God in your mind. My beloved is my love. ||1||Pause|| Eliminate the company of five enemies and enjoy the beautiful bed at home and peace in the yard. ||1|| God does not come or go. He lives in the body; realizing Him the inverted lotus blossoms. The pain of ego is eliminated. Nanak sings the praises of God the bundle of virtues. ||2||4||43|| Kaanraa, Fifth Master, Ninth House: This is why you should recite God. The Vedas and the saints say that the path is difficult. You are intoxicated with emotional attachment and the fever of ego. ||Pause|| Those who are imbued and intoxicated with worldly wealth suffer the pain of emotional attachment. ||1|| Whoever God blesses, obtains salvation by reciting God's name. O Nanak, by saint's grace the emotional attachment, fear and doubt are dispelled; ||2||5||44|| Page 1307 Kaanraa, Fifth Master, Tenth House: God is one. He is realized by guru's grace. Bless me with such a gift O saint that I admire you. I am enticed by pride, I live close to and trapped by five thieves; may I live in the refuge of devotees; please eliminate my company of demons. ||1||Pause|| I am tired of wandering through millions of lifes. I have fallen at God's door. ||1|| The Lord of the universe has become Kind to me. He has blessed me with God's name. This precious human life has become fruitful O Nanak, I am carried across the terrifying world-ocean. ||2||1||45|| Kaanraa, Fifth Master, Eleventh House: God is one. He is realized by guru's grace. He came to me, His own Way. I know nothing, and I see nothing. I have met God through innocent faith, and obtained peace. ||1||Pause|| By pre destined fortune I met the company of devotees. I do not go anywhere; I dwell in my own home. God, the treasure of virtue, has been revealed in this body. ||1|| I have fallen in love with His feet; I have abandoned everything else. He is all pervading in all high and low places of interest. Nanak sings God's praises with love. ||2||1||46|| Kaanraa, Fifth Master: It is hard to meet the Lord of the universe, my master. The immeasurable, inaccessible and unfathomable God pervade all. ||1||Pause|| He is not realized by saying, by clever tricks and devices. ||1|| I try every means but He is realized by His grace. God is kind and compassionate, the treasure of mercy. Servant Nanak is the dust of the feet of the saints. ||2||2||47|| Kaanraa, Fifth Master: O mother, I say God God God. Without God, there is no other at all. I miss His lotus feet with every breath, night and day. ||1||Pause|| He loves me and made me His Own; my union with Him shall never break. He is my life, mind, wealth and everything. God the treasure of virtue gives me peace.

||1|| Here and hereafter, God pervades all perfectly; He is realized in the mind. In the sanctuary of the saints, I am carried across; O Nanak, the terrible pain has been taken away. ||2||3||48|| Kaanraa, Fifth Master: God's humble servant is in love with Him. You are my beloved friend; everything is in Your home. ||1||Pause|| I beg for honour, strength, wealth, property and children. ||1|| You are the way of liberation, enjoyment, the perfect Lord of supreme joy, the transcendent treasure. Page 1308 Loving God obtains contentment; Nanak admires Him forever. ||2||4||49|| Kaanraa, Fifth Master: The debaters debate and argue with their arguments. The Yogis and meditators, religious and spiritual teachers roam and ramble, wandering all over the earth. ||1||Pause|| They are egotistic, self-centred and egotistic, ignorant, stupid, idiotic and insane. Wherever they wander, death is always with them forever. ||1|| Give up your pride and stubborn ego; death is always close by. Says Nanak; Listen O ignorant, recite God. The life goes waste without reciting God. ||2||5||50||12||62|| Kaanraa, Ashtapadees, Fourth Master, First House: God is one. He is realized by guru's grace. Reciting God obtains peace, O my mind. More you recite more peace you get, serving the true guru, you will merge with him. ||1||Pause|| The devotees long for God every moment; they find peace reciting his name. The taste of other pleasures is eradicated. Nothing pleases them, except His name. ||1|| God seems sweet through guru's teaching; the guru makes them say sweet words. Guru's sermon is the sermon of primal Lord; you will be attached to the sermon. ||2|| My mind is satisfied listening to guru's sermon; I go home drenched with it. Infinite divine music plays there and the stream of nectar trickles down. ||3|| He sings God's name all the time and his mind has merged in God's name through guru's teaching. He enjoys listening to God's name and gets satisfied doing so. ||4|| People wear gold bracelets and all sorts of fancy clothes. Without God's name all taste bland. They die to be reborn again. ||5|| The veil of worldly wealth is heavy; you will keep circling in the house wearing it. The sins weigh heavy; carrying it you cannot swim across the terrifying world ocean. ||6|| Let the fear of God's separation be the boat; guru's teaching will carry you across. Surrender and recite God's name and merge with Him. ||7|| Attached

to ignorance, people are asleep. The guru will awaken them through divine wisdom. O Nanak, by His will, He makes us walk as He pleases. ||8||1|| Kaanraa, Fourth Master: O mind, recite God; you will swim across the world ocean. Whoever recites God obtains salvation, like Dhroo and Prahlaad. ||1||Pause|| Page 1309 O dear God, be kind and attach me to Your name. Please be kind and unite me with the true guru and I recite Your name. ||1|| Filth attached from many a life is washed away meeting devotee's company. As iron floats attached to wood, same way attaching to guru's teaching obtains salvation. ||2|| Join the company of saints and enjoy the sublime essence of God's name. The egotistic acts without the congregation; he takes out water and puts mud in. ||3|| God protects His devotees; they enjoy God's sublime essence. They obtain honour reciting God's name and merge with true guru's teaching. ||4|| Bow forever in respect to humble devotees; being humble obtains the reward. Those wicked that slander God's devotees are destroyed like Harnaakhash. ||5|| Brahma, the son of the lotus, and Vyaas, the son of the fish, practiced austere penance and worshipped. Worshipping God's devotees eliminates wandering in doubt. ||6|| Do not be fooled by high and low social class. King Janak touched Sukhdev's feet and worshipped. Although he threw his leftover on Janak's head. his mind did not waver at all. ||7|| Janak sat on his throne and applied the dust of sage's dust to his forehead. O God, be kind to Nanak that I become the servant of servants. ||8||2|| Kaanraa, Fourth Master: O mind, follow guru's teachings, and joyfully sing God's praises. If I have millions of tongues, I will recite God millions of times with each tongue. ||1||Pause|| The serpent king recited God with thousand tongues, still did not find His limits. You are beyond comprehension. The mind stabilizes through guru's teaching. ||1|| Those who recite You are sacred. Reciting God obtains happiness. Bidar, the son of a servant girl, was an untouchable, but Krishna embraced him. ||2|| Wood is produced from water; it floats in water. God looks after His devotees by His natural instinct. ||3|| I am heavy like a stone, or a piece of iron. I will swim across attached to guru's company. As Kabeer the weaver obtained salvation in the congregation. He was pleasing to the saints. ||4|| Recite God while standing or sitting or walking. True guru is the word; the word is the true guru, who teaches the path of liberation. ||5|| I have become accustomed to recite God with every breath; may I be able to recite God without breathing also. By guru's grace, ego is eliminated, and I recite God through guru's teaching. ||6|| Page 1310 True guru is the giver of life to the beings. He does not appeal to the unfortunate. This opportunity shall not come again; they will repent by His grace. ||7|| If anyone seeks good for himself, he should fall and touch guru's feet. O God, be kind to Nanak that he applies guru's dust to his forehead. ||8||3|| Kaanraa, Fourth Master: O mind, be attuned to His love, and sing. The fear and love of God makes one pure through guru's teaching. ||1||Pause|| Imbued with God's love one becomes detached and God comes close to him. If I obtain his dust, I will live by it. May God bless me with it? ||1|| People are attached to greed and duality. Brand new mind cannot be dyed by God's love. But their lives are transformed through guru's teaching. They get imbued meeting with the primal guru. ||2|| There are ten senses; they wander guided by three worldly qualities. They cannot stabilize even for a moment. They are controlled by coming in contact with the true guru and obtain salvation. ||3|| God abides in all and all will merge with Him. He is one but in many forms, all follow the same rule. ||4|| The guru-willed knows one and only one God. The guru-willed recites Him. The guru-willed goes and meets him in His palace and plays the divine music. ||5|| God created all beings of the universe; He blesses the guru-willed with honour. Without meeting the guru, no one obtains the destiny. They suffer in coming and going. ||6|| O my beloved, I am separated from you for many lifes; please unite me with the guru by Your grace. Meeting the true guru, I found absolute peace; my filthy intellect blossomed. ||7|| O Lord, the life of the world, be kind and attach me to Your name lovingly. Nanak is the guru, the true guru; may I meet him in his refuge. ||8||4|| Kaanraa, Fourth Master: O mind, follow guru's teaching. As the iron rod controls the wild elephant; reciting guru's teaching controls same way my mind. ||1||Pause|| The mind wanders all over; it is controlled by the guru and attunes to God lovingly. The true guru implants his teaching in the mind and the nectar of God's name trickles in the mouth. ||1|| The snakes are poisonous; guru's teaching is the antidote; put it in your mouth. The poisonous worldly wealth does not come close to him. He shuns the poison and attunes to God with love. ||2|| The dog like greed is strong in the body village. The guru drives it away in a moment. Truth, contentment and faith dwell in God's town; God's praise is sung there. ||3|| Page 1311 The beings are sunk in enticing emotional attachment. The guru lifts them and saves them from sinking. They come to his refuge crying and the guru pulls them out by giving his hand. ||4|| The worldly play is like a dream. Everyone plays it. Earn the profit of God's name and take it to God's court. ||5|| They act in ego, and make others to act in ego. They collect the blackness of sins. When death comes, they suffer in pain; they eat what they sowed. ||6|| O saints, gather the wealth of God's name; take it with you and obtain honour. So eat and spend. God gives plentiful. God's gifts never fall short. ||7|| The wealth of God's name is hidden in the mind; you will find it in guru's refuge. O Nanak, God has blessed him and removed pain and poverty, He has merged with God. ||8||5|| Kaanraa, Fourth Master: O mind, seek the sanctuary of the true guru, and recite God. Iron is transformed into gold by touching philosopher's stone. It becomes the same. ||1||Pause|| True guru, the great primal being, is philosopher's stone. Whoever touches him reaps the reward. As Prahlaad was saved by guru's teachings, the guru protects the honour of His servant. ||1|| Word of the true guru is noble. Through guru's word, the nectar is obtained. As Ambreek obtained the state of immortality by reciting true guru's word; ||2|| True guru's refuge appeals to my mind. I recite God believing it sacred. True guru has become kind to the humble and showed God's path. ||3|| Those who enter true guru's refuge are protected. God protects them. If someone aims an arrow at Lord's servant, it will turn around and hit him back. ||4|| Those who bathe in God's sacred Pool are honoured in God's court. Recite God through guru's teaching and God will meet and embrace you. ||5|| God is realized by listening to the teachings and reciting by guru's grace. God's servant becomes God's image by worshipping God. ||6|| The faithless does not follow the true guru. God misguides the faithless. The waves of greed are like packs of dogs. The poison of worldly wealth sticks to the skeleton. ||7|| God's name is the saviour of the world; recite God's name in devotee's company. O my God; send Nanak to devotee's company and unite him with You. ||8||6|| Chhakaa 1. Page 1312 Kaanraa, Chhant, Fifth Master: God is one. He is realized by guru's grace. Those who recite God obtain salvation. Making every effort for worldly wealth is of no use. Blessed are the fortunate that recite God. They reap the reward. They remain awake in true congregation and lovingly attune to one God. Give up emotional attachment and ego; touch devotee's feet and obtain salvation. Prays Nanak to seek Lord's refuge and visualize Him. ||1|| Join the company of devotees and recite God. Sing God's praises lovingly. Sing His praises with love and drink the nectar; birth and death cycle will end. Recite God's name in devotee's company; you shall not suffer again. O bestowal the architect of destiny; be kind so that I serve the saints. Nanak begs for the dust of devotees to visualize God and merge with Him. ||2|| All beings, recite God. It brings the merit of all efforts of meditation, penance and self-discipline. Recite the inner knower master daily. Your life will become fruitful. Those who sing and recite the Lord of the universe daily; their coming into the world is approved. The wealth of meditation, penance self-discipline of formless God the Lord of the universe goes with you. Prays Nanak, please be kind and bestow me with the jewel of God's name in my lap. ||3|| His wondrous and amazing plays are blissful; Please be kind that I obtain the supreme joy. I realized God the bestowal of happiness and the desire of my mind are fulfilled. Admirations pour in; I intuitively absorb in God. I shall never cry in pain. He embraced me close to him and I obtained peace; all useless sins are eliminated. Prays Nanak; I have met my Lord, the primal Lord, and the embodiment of joy. ||4||1|| Vaar Of Kaanraa, Fourth Master, Sung To The Tune Of Vaar Of Musa: God is one. He is realized by guru's grace. Hymn, Fourth Master: God's name is a priceless treasure, enshrine Him in your mind through guru's teaching. Become the slave of God's slaves, and conquer ego and corruption. You shall win this treasure of life and never lose. Blessed and fortunate are those, O Nanak, who savor the sublime essence of the Lord through guru's teachings. ||1|| Fourth Master: I say God, God, God. The Lord of the universe is the treasure of virtue. Recite

God through guru's teaching and obtain honour in God's court. Page 1313 Saying God God you shall be happy and famous. O Nanak, guru is God the Lord of the universe; meeting Him obtains God's name. ||2|| Ladder: You are the mystic and the seeker; You are the way of worship of Yogi's. You are the taster of tastes; You are the enjoyer of pleasures. You are all pervading; whatever You do happens. Blessed is the congregation of the true guru. Joining them I recite God's name. Everyone; say God God; saying God all sins are eliminated. ||1|| Hymn Fourth Master: God's name is God; only a few guru-willed obtain it. It eliminates ego and emotional attachment and washes away the evil; O Nanak, those with pre-ordained destiny sing God's praises. ||1|| Fourth Master: God is kind; whatever he does happens. God pervades all; there is no one as great as God. Whatever pleases God happens; whatever he does happens. No one can appraise His value; God is endless. O Nanak the guru-willed praise God, your mind and body will be soothed. ||2|| Ladder: You are the light of all, the life of the world; You imbue everyone with love. O my beloved; all worship you; You are true, the true primal formless God. One God is the giver; the whole world is the beggar. All beg from Him. You are the servant, and the master. You appeal to the mind through guru's teaching. O all people; say God the bestowal of salvation; Reciting Him obtains the fruit of choice. ||2|| Hymn, Fourth Master: O my mind, recite God's name and obtain honour in God's court. You shall obtain the fruits of your choice by concentrating through guru's teaching. All your sins shall be erased and your ego and pride will vanish. The heart-lotus of the guru-willed blossoms seeing God in every soul; O God, be kind that servant Nanak recites Your name. ||1|| Fourth Master: Reciting God's name is sacred; reciting His name eliminates the sufferings. God dwells in the mind of those with pre-ordained destiny. Those who follow true guru's will; their poverty and pain disappear. No one finds God on his own; check it out; Servant Nanak is the slave of the slave of those who fall at the feet of the true guru. ||2|| Ladder: Page 1314 You pervade in all high and low places O Creator; You created everything. You created the entire universe, in many ways forms and shapes. Your light, lights up every soul. It is realized through guru's teaching. Whoever You are kind to, meet the true guru. He teaches the guru-willed to recite God. O people; all of you say God God; saying God eliminates pain and poverty. ||3|| Hymn, Fourth Master: God's name is sacred; enshrine it in the mind; God pervades in devotee's company; He is realized through guru's teaching. Recite God in the mind; it drives away the poison of ego. Those who do not recite God's name; they lose their life in a gamble. The kind guru guides you to recite God; enshrine God's name in the mind. O servant Nanak; they are happy in true Lord's court. ||1|| Fourth Master: Singing God's praises is sacred; it is the essence in today's age. His praises come through guru's teachings. Wear the necklace of Lord's name. Those who recite God are fortunate; God entrusts them with His treasure. Doing deeds without God's name in ego will ruin you. You may bathe and scrub an elephant. He will still throw dust on his head. O true guru; please unite me with God so that God enshrines in my mind. Those guru-willed who listen and believe in God; servant Nanak salutes them. ||2|| Ladder : God's name is the priceless merchandise. God is our Lord the master. God set the play in motion and He plays it and the whole world trades as well. Your Light is in every soul O Creator; Your creation is true. All those who recite You through guru's teaching are successful O God; Let everyone say God the lord of the world the life of the world; It takes us all, across the terrifying world ocean. ||4|| Hymn, Fourth Master: I have only one tongue O God; Your virtues are infinite and unfathomable. O God; how I the child recite Your name; You are great, unapproachable and immeasurable. O God, bless me with that sublime wisdom, that I fall at true guru's feet. O God, unite me with true congregation so that I the sinner go across with them. O Lord, please bless servant Nanak and unite him with You. O Lord, be kind and listen to my prayer, that a sinner, worm like me can go across. ||1|| Fourth Master: O Lord, the life of the world, be kind and unite me with the true guru. I am happy to serve the guru; the Lord has become kind to me. Page 1315 All my hopes and desires are forgotten; worldly entanglements have disappeared from my mind. The honourable guru, taught me God's name through his teaching and I am content. Servant Nanak has earned the inexhaustible wealth; God's name is his wealth and property. ||2|| Ladder: O Lord, You are the greatest and highest of all. Those who recite the infinite God; they are rejuvenated by reciting Him. Those who sing and listen to Your praises, O Lord; their sins are erased. Knowing, beings like You O God through guru`s teaching, the intellect of the fortunate becomes sacred. Let everyone recite God, true from the beginning for ages and true forever; Servant Nanak is the servant of His servants. ||5|| Hymn, Fourth Master: O my God the life of the world. I recite God through guru`s lesson. God is unapproachable, inaccessible and unfathomable; I realized the carefree God. The Lord is pervading each and every heart; He is unlimited. God enjoys all pleasures; He is the husband of Lakshmi (worldly wealth). God created the entire universe and all beings, He gives awns to all. O kind God; please give awns to Your saints; they are begging. O God of servant Nanak, please come and meet me; I sing the songs of your praises. ||1|| Fourth Master: God and the name of my beloved, is enshrined in my mind and body. All hopes of the guru-willed are fulfilled; servant Nanak is satisfied hearing His name. ||2|| Ladder: God`s sublime name is energizing and rejuvenating. O pure formless God; The worldly wealth serves the feet of those who recite God day and night. God looks after all beings and lives close to them. Those, whom the Lord inspires, realize Him; God the true guru is pleased with them. Let everyone sing the praise of the Lord of the universe; singing His praises they realize His virtues. ||6|| Hymn, Fourth Master: O mind, recite God even in sleep; you will merge with God in intuitive trance. Servant Nanak's mind longs for God. May the kind guru unite me with God O mother? ||1|| Fourth Master: I am in love with one God and only God is in my mind. Servant Nanak takes the support of one God; salvation and honour obtains through Him. ||2|| Ladder: The fortunate plays divine music playing five instruments through guru`s teaching. I realized God the root of joy. The lord of the universe reveals through guru`s teaching. God is the same from the beginning, for ages, recite Him through guru`s teaching. O kind God, bless me with Your gift and preserve the honour of your devotee. Page 1316 Praise the true guru; meeting Him, God covers all faults; ||7|| Hymn, Fourth Master: The sacred pool of worship is filled to the brim and overflowing. Those who obey the true guru, O servant Nanak, are fortunate. ||1|| Fourth Master: God`s names are many; God`s virtues cannot be described. God is inaccessible and unfathomable. How can God`s humble servant realize Him! Reciting and singing God`s name the devotee cannot know His value at all. O servant Nanak, God is inaccessible; please unite and attach me to your lap. ||2|| Ladder: God is inaccessible and unfathomable. How will I visualize You O God? If He is a material object, then I could describe Him, but He has no form or feature. Whoever He inspires; understands and realizes Him. The true congregation is guru`s school where God`s virtues are learned. Blessed is the tongue, and the teacher, the true guru; meeting Him God`s account is written. ||8|| Hymn, Fourth Master: God`s name is the nectar; recite God through true guru`s love. God`s name is sacred; reciting and hearing God, the pain goes away. Those with pre-ordained destiny recite God`s name. Those, who have God`s name enshrined in the mind; they are honoured in God`s court. O Nanak, they are happy, who listen to God`s name with love. ||1|| Fourth Master: God`s name is a priceless treasure; the guru-willed obtain it. Those with pre-ordained destiny, meet the true guru. Their bodies and minds are soothed; peace comes to dwell in their minds. O Nanak, enjoy saying God; all pain and poverty will be eliminated. Ladder: I admire those who have visualized my beloved God forever. Those with pre-ordained destiny meet the true guru. I recite the inaccessible Lord through guru`s teaching. He has no form or feature. Those who recite the inaccessible God merge with God and become one. Let everyone say God the Lord of men and obtain the benefit of worshipping God; ||9|| Hymn, Fourth Master: Recite God`s name and merge with Him reciting. God abides in all; God played this play with love. God the love of the world lives close by. He is revealed through guru`s teaching. Page 1317 Those, who have God`s love written in their destiny, realize God the master. Servant Nanak recites God`s name through guru`s teaching in the mind with love. ||1|| Fourth Master: O fortunate, find the beloved God and enshrine in the mind. The perfect guru reveals Him O Nanak, by lovingly attuning to Him. ||2|| Ladder: Blessed and fruitful is the moment, when serving God pleases the mind. O my guru brothers, tell me God`s unspoken story. How can I attain Him? How can I see Him? My Lord is all knowing and all seeing. God reveals Himself through guru`s teaching reciting His name. Nanak admires those who recite God the bestowal of salvation. ||10|| Hymn, Fourth Master: My eyes are imbued with God`s love. The guru gave the medicine of divine wisdom. I have found my beloved God; servant Nanak is intuitively absorbed in peace. ||1|| Fourth Master: The guru-willed is filled with peace enshrining God`s name in the mind and body. He thinks and reads God`s name; he remains lovingly attuned to God`s name. He obtains the treasure of God`s name and his worry is gone away. Meeting with the true guru, God`s name wells up; all hunger and thirst depart. O Nanak, one who is imbued with God`s name gathers the name. ||2|| Ladder: You created the world, and You control it. You defeat some self-willed and unite some with the guru to win. God`s name is sacred; the fortunate recite Him through guru`s teaching. All pain and poverty are taken away, when the guru bestows God's name. Let everyone serve the enticer of the mind and the world; He created and controls the world. ||11|| Hymn, Fourth Master: The disease of ego is in the mind; the self-willed evil is deluded by doubt. O Nanak, meeting the true guru the devotee and friend cure the disease. ||1|| Fourth Master: My mind and body are honoured, when I see the Lord with my eyes. O Nanak, may I meet God, I live by hearing His words. ||2|| Ladder: The Creator is the Lord of the world, the master of the universe, the infinite primal immeasurable being. O my guru's followers; recite God`s name; God is sacred and His name is priceless. Those who recite Him in their hearts, day and night, definitely realize Him. The fortunate find the congregation through true guru`s word. Let everyone recite God the Lord of men; reciting Him the conflict with devil of death ends. ||12|| Hymn, Fourth Master: God`s humble servant recites God and an ignorant shoots an arrow at him. O Nanak, God`s servant is saved and the arrow kills the one who shot the arrow. ||1|| Page 1318 Fourth Master: My eyes are enticed by God`s love. They recite God`s name and see God. If they see anyone else O Nanak, I will take my eyes out. ||2|| Ladder: The infinite Lord totally permeates water and land. He takes care of all beings; whatever He does happens. Mother, father, children, sibling and friends; no one is without Him. He pervades everyone; but only a few recite Him. Let all recite praises of the Lord of the world, He pervade everywhere. ||13|| Hymn, Fourth Master: The guru-willed meet those friends, who have realized God through love. O servant Nanak, praise God`s name and go to God`s court raising arms with joy. ||1|| Fourth Master: O God; You are the bestowal of all; all beings are your. All recite Your name; bless me with a gift O beloved. The gifts are in bestowal's hand; he showers it to the world. The grain crop grows in the field intuitively, contemplating God`s name. Servant Nanak begs for the gift of the support of God`s name. ||2|| Ladder: Reciting God the ocean of peace fulfills the desires of mind. Recite God`s feet through guru`s teachings the ocean of jewels. Joining devotee's company obtains salvation and the account of devil of death gets torn. Conquer the treasure of human life reciting the detached God. Let everyone seek guru`s refuge and the scars of sufferings will erase. ||14|| Hymn, Fourth Master: I am searching for my beloved; but he is with me. O servant Nanak, the unseen is not seen. but He is revealed to the guru-willed. ||1|| Fourth Master: O Nanak, I am in love with the true Lord. I cannot survive without Him. Meeting the true guru, the perfect Lord is found reciting God with love. ||2|| Ladder: Some sing, some listen, and some speak and preach. The filth of many life's is eliminated; you obtain the reward of your choice. Singing God`s praises, the coming and going ends. They save themselves, their companions and their dynasty as well. Servant Nanak admires those, who are pleasing to God. ||15||1|| declaration|| Tune Kaanraa, the word Of Naam Dev Jee: God is one. He is realized by guru`s grace. Such is the sovereign Lord, the inner-knower; Like seeing your face in the mirror; ||1||Pause|| He dwells in each and every heart; no stain or stigma sticks to Him. He is free from bonds. He does not go and cannot be seen as well. ||1|| As you see the reflection of your face in water; so is Naamaa's master the Lord. ||2||1||

Page 1319 Tune Kalyaan Fourth Master

God is one. It is true. He is the Creator. He is carefree. He has no enemy. He is immortal. He does not take birth. He came into existence on His own. He is realized by guru`s grace.

Tune Kalyaan, Fourth Master: O God, no one can find Your limits by reciting Your name. I am a child. You look after me. You are great primal being, my mother and father. ||1||Pause|| God's names are unlimited; God is beyond comprehension O Lord. The learned and the spiritual people think a lot but cannot find His value at all. ||1|| They sing praises of the Lord of the universe forever. They cannot find His limits. You are immeasurable, unweighable, and infinite, O Lord; Your depth cannot be found no matter how much any one recites. ||2|| Your humble servant praises and sings Your praises O God the Lord of the world. You are the ocean and I am Your fish. I cannot fathom You. ||3|| Please be Kind to Your servant O Lord; please bless me to recite Your name. I am a blind ignorant; Your name is my support. Servant Nanak has realized God. ||4||1|| Kalyaan, Fourth Master: God's devotee sings God's praises and smiles. He worships God through guru's teaching. God writes it in his fate. ||1||Pause|| He serves and recites God day and night enshrining God in the mind. Everyone sings God's praises in the world by applying grounded sandalwood to the forehead. ||1|| God's devotee lovingly attunes to God and the faithless follow him. The slanderer follows his previous deeds. He touches the snake and gets stung. ||2|| O Lord; you are the protector of your devotees. You protect them in all ages. What happened to the demon by doing evil deeds? He is destroyed doing so. ||3|| All beings created by God are swallowed by death. God protects His servants; servant Nanak seeks His refuge. ||4||2|| Kalyaan, Fourth Master: Page 1320 O my mind, recite God the Lord of the world. Recite God through guru's teaching, all sins and pains will be erased. ||1||Pause|| I have only one tongue; I cannot sing Your praises. Please bless me with many tongues to recite. Again and again, all sing Your praises; they cannot describe your virtues. ||1|| I am deeply in love with God my master; I long to visualize God. You are the great giver of all beings; You know my state of mind. ||2|| If someone shows me the way to God! Tell me; what should I give him? I will surrender my body and mind to him, if someone unites me with God. ||3|| God's virtues and praises are many; How many I the humble can describe; My intellect is under Your control O Nanak's Lord; You are all-powerful. ||4||3|| Kalyaan, Fourth Master:

O my mind, recite God's virtues which are said to be inexpressible. Good deeds are the way to attain salvation. The servant follows it around. ||1||Pause|| God's devotee, who recites God's name has it written on his forehead. The court, where God asks for your account; reciting God frees you there; ||1|| My sins are from many lifes; the pain of filth of ego is attached to it. The guru bathes us in Godly water by his grace and all sins are eliminated. ||2|| God the Lord enshrines in devotee's mind; the devotee recites God's name. When the end comes, God's name protects then and there. ||3|| O God; your devotees in the world sing Your praises and recite Your name. O God, You are the saviour of servant Nanak; I am a stone, please save me from sinking. ||4||4|| Kalyaan, Fourth Master: God knows what is in my mind. If someone slanders God's servant. God does not listen what he says. ||1||Pause|| Give up everything else, and serve the imperishable God; our Lord and master, is the highest of all. Death cannot rob if you serve God; death comes and falls at his feet. ||1|| Whoever God protects; he whispers wisdom in his ears. No one can equal them; whose worship God accepts. ||2|| Watch God's amazing play. He finds out the genuine and counterfeit in an instant. God's devotee obtains wealth and understands and enjoys. The counterfeit regrets; ||3|| O God the bestowal. You are all powerful. I beg for one gift from You. O God, bless servant Nanak, that my mind dwells at God's feet forever. ||4||5|| Page 1321 Kalyaan, Fourth Master: O God, treasure of mercy, please bless me, that I sing God's praises. I always hope O God, when will you take me in Your embrace? ||1||Pause|| I am foolish and ignorant child O father, please teach me! Your child makes mistakes again and again, but still, You are pleased with him, O father of the universe. ||1|| Whatever You give me, O Lord; that is what I receive. There is no other place where I can go. ||2|| Those devotees who are pleasing to the Lord. Lord is pleasing to them. Their light merges in the light; the lights merge together. ||3|| The Lord becomes kind and He lovingly attunes me to Him. Servant Nanak seeks the refuge of His door; He will protect my honour. ||4||6|| Chhakaa 1. Kalyaan Bhopaalee, Fourth Master: God is one. He is realized by guru's grace. The supreme Lord, transcendent Lord and master, is the destroyer of pain; All Your devotees beg of You O

Ocean of peace; You carry us across the terrifying world-ocean; You are the Wish-fulfilling jewel. ||1||Pause|| O merciful to the meek, Lord of the world, support of the earth, inner-knower, searcher of hearts, Lord of the universe. Those who recite God become carefree. Through guru's teachings, they recite God the liberator Lord. ||1|| Those who come to the sanctuary at the feet of the Lord of the universe; they cross over the terrifying world-ocean. Lord preserves the honour of His humble devotees O servant Nanak, Lord showers them with His grace. ||2||1||7|| Tune Kalyaan, Fifth Master, First House: God is one. He is realized by guru's grace. Please grant me this blessing: May the bumblebee enjoy again and again the Honey of Your lotus feet. ||1||Pause|| I am not concerned with any other water. Please bless this rain bird with a drop of Your water O Lord. ||1|| I am not content without meeting You; Nanak longs to visualize You O Lord; ||2||1|| Kalyaan, Fifth Master: This beggar begs and begs for Your name. You are the support of all, the master of all, and the giver of peace to all. ||1||Pause|| They beg for many things but they receive what pleases You. ||1|| Fruitful is to visualize You and sing Your praises by meeting You. O Nanak, the reality meets the reality. He is enlightened like a diamond touching a diamond. ||2||2|| Page 1322 Kalyaan, Fifth Master: The glory of my beloved! His glory is ever new and always pleases my mind. ||1||Pause|| Brahma, Shiva, the mystics, the sages and Indra beg for worshipping and praising Him. ||1|| Yogis, spiritual teachers, meditators and the thousand-headed serpent all recite with love. Says Nanak, I admire the saints; who always dwell with God. ||2||3|| Kalyaan, Fifth Master, Second House: God is one. He is realized by guru's grace. Recite and respect God in your mind. To see and to listen to His sermon gives peace to my body and soul. ||1||Pause|| You pervade here, there, ten directions, the mountains and the blade of grass. ||1|| Wherever I look, I see the Lord, the supreme Lord the primal being. Doubt and fear are eliminated in devotee's company O Nanak with divine wisdom. ||2||1||4|| Kalyaan, Fifth Master: Enjoy by listening and reading the virtues of God. The sages speak and listen to God's sermon in devotee's company. ||1||Pause|| Reciting God's name obtains spiritual wisdom, meditation, honour and giving donations, and destroys the sins. ||1|| The way of worship, divine wisdom, devotion and knowledge comes through guru's teaching the essence of discriminating intellect and uninterrupted recitation and penance. Through and through, he merges in His light O Nanak. He shall never again suffer pain and punishment. ||2||2||5|| Kalyaan, Fifth Master: What should I do, and how should I do it? Should I focus on meditation, wisdom or scriptures? How can I endure this unendurable state? ||1||Pause|| Vishnu, Shiva, the Siddhas, the sages and Indra; whose refuge should I seek? ||1|| Some become kings, some long for heaven; only a few among millions obtain salvation. Says Nanak, I have attained the sublime essence of God's name touching devotee's feet. ||2||3||6|| Kalyaan, Fifth Master: The kind Lord of life, primal Lord is my friend. God saves me from entering the womb for life and the net of death in today's age and He eliminates my sufferings. ||1||Pause|| I obtained your name and seek Your refuge. The kind Lord is my support. ||1|| You are the Hope of the helpless, and the poor. Your name, O my Lord is the lesson of the mind. ||2|| I know of nothing except You O God. You are recognized throughout the ages. ||3|| God enshrines in my mind day and night. The Lord of the universe is Nanak's support. ||4||4||7|| Kalyaan, Fifth Master: Recite God from your mind and body. The perfect guru is pleased. I obtained eternal peace and happiness. ||1||Pause|| All affairs are resolved singing the praises of the Lord of the world. I recite God in devotee's company and the pain of death ran away. ||1|| O My God; be kind that I serve You day and night. Page 1323 Slave Nanak seeks the refuge of God, the perfect, primal being. ||2||5||8|| Kalyaan, Fifth Master: My God is the inner-knower. O perfect transcendent Lord; be kind and bless me with Your symbol of eternal true guru's teaching. ||1||Pause|| O Lord, no one is as powerful as God; You are my hope and strength. You are the giver to all beings, O Lord; I eat and wear what You give. ||1|| Intuitive understanding, wisdom and cleverness, glory and beauty, pleasure, wealth and honour; All comforts, bliss, happiness and salvation, O Nanak, are realized by reciting God's name. ||2||6||9|| Kalyaan, Fifth Master: The sanctuary of Lord's feet bestows salvation. God's name is the purifier of sinners. ||1||Pause|| Whoever recites God without any doubt; devil of death does not kill him. ||1|| The way to liberation and all sorts of peace do not come close to God's worship. Slave Nanak longs for visualizing God, and he shall never again wander in different lifes. ||2||||7||10|| Kalyaan, Fourth Master, Ashtapadees: God is one. He is realized by guru's grace. O God; my mind gets drenched by listening to God's name. God's name is sacred and sweet; drink it through guru's teaching intuitively. ||1||Pause|| As fire exists in wood and it comes out by constantly churning the wood. God's name pervades all souls; it is realized through guru's teaching. ||1|| There are nine doors, they all taste bland; the nectar trickles down at tenth door. O beloved, be kind and bless me with guru's teaching that I drink the nectar. ||2|| The body-village is sacred; God's sublime essence is traded in it. The priceless gems and jewels are obtained by serving the true guru. ||3|| The true guru the Lord is beyond comprehension. It is the ocean full of worship. Please be kind to the poor swan and pour a drop of Your name in my mouth. ||4|| My beloved is dyed in deep red colour. The guru dyes the mind by his grace. Those imbued with God's love drink the sublime essence daily. ||5|| If you take gold out of seven continents and oceans and keep in front of them; God's humble servants do not long for it; they long for the path to divinity. ||6|| The faithless beings remain hungry forever; they continuously cry in hunger. They travel millions of miles in love and search of wealth. ||7|| The humble servants of God are sacred. What praise can we offer them? Page 1324 Nothing else can equal the glory of Lord's name; please bless servant Nanak with Your grace. ||8||1|| Kalyaan, Fourth Master: O Lord, the guru is a philosopher's stone. Touching it makes one philosopher's stone. I was unworthy, useless, completely bland. Meeting the guru I became philosopher's stone. ||1||Pause|| Everyone longs for paradise, liberation and heaven. God's humble servants do not long for salvation. They are satisfied visualizing God. ||1|| Emotional attachment of worldly wealth is very powerful. This attachment is a black stain, which sticks. The humble servants of my Lord are unattached and liberated, like the feathers of a duck do not get wet. ||2|| Due to fragrance the sandalwood tree is encircled by snakes; how can anyone get to the sandalwood? The guru draws the mighty sword of wisdom and drinks the nectar by slashing the poison. ||3|| You may gather other worship material; the fire burns it in a moment. The faithless commits serious sins; the sins burn away meeting God's devotees. ||4|| Those who have nectar enshrined in them are sacred God's devotees. The mortal visualizes God by the touch of God's humble devotees. ||5|| The thread of the faithless is entangled badly; how can he weave it? The company of a faithless is like the entangle thread; do not accompany them; ||6|| True guru's congregation is sacred; recite God in devotee's company. The gems, jewels and precious stones are inside; by guru's grace, they are found. ||7|| My Lord is the greatest of all. How can I meet Him? O Nanak, the perfect guru unites the humble being with God perfectly. ||8||2|| Kalyaan, Fourth Master: O God; I say God God. God's devotees are sacred; one enjoys God's love meeting with His devotees. ||1||Pause|| The minds of all beings of the world waver forever. O God, be kind and unite them with Your devotees the pillars, to support the world. ||1|| The earth beneath us comes on top of us; instead you shall lie in devotee's feet. You shall become the most sacred and the entire universe shall be under your feet. ||2|| The soul of the guru-willed is sacred and divine; all others are full of worldly power. The white teeth come out by guru's teaching; then chew God's essence and enjoy the taste. ||3|| By the grace of God's name. I met the guru, God's devotee. Reciting God's name earnestly. God bestows with the honour of the entire universe. ||4|| God enshrines in the mind of devotees; they cannot live without visualizing Him. Like the fish loves water, it dies without water instantly. ||5|| Page 1325 The unfortunate do not get to drink the dust of God's devotees. The burning fire of greed does not extinguish; they suffer the punishment of the justice of destiny. ||6|| You may visit sacred shrines, observe fasts and offer sacred feasts, give generously and waste away the body in melting snow. God's name is unweighable; it is realized through guru's teachings; nothing else equals it. ||7|| O God, You alone know Your virtues. Servant Nanak seeks Your sanctuary. You are the ocean and I am Your fish. Please be kind, and keep me with You. ||8||3|| Kalyaan, Fourth Master: O God; I worship You by saying God God. I offer my mind and body to him, if I can realize divine wisdom through guru's teaching. ||1||Pause|| God's name is the tree, His virtues the branches. I pick daily and worship

God; the soul is God; God is the soul. Worship Him with love. ||1||
The discriminating intellect is the most sacred in the world, think
and drink the nectar. Obtain the priceless treasure through guru's
teaching; surrender your mind to guru. ||2|| God is a priceless
diamond; diamond enlightens the diamond by touching. The mind is
the jeweller; it appraises the diamond through guru's teaching. ||3||
The devotees in saint's company go high like a vine attached to a
tree. The mortal who enjoys the fragrance of God's name is the
sacred of all. ||4|| He does sacred deeds all the time and new branches
sprout up daily. The guru taught me the flower and fruit of faith
through divine wisdom; it permeates the world with fragrance. ||5||
God is one; One God enshrines in my mind; I see one God in all.
One God pervades all; all should touch His feet. ||6|| People look like
criminals without God's name; they rub and wear down their noses.
The faithless are proud persons; their living without God's name is
worthless. ||7|| As long as you breathe, you should hurry to God's
refuge. O God, be kind to Nanak that I wash the feet of Your devotees.
||8||4|| Kalyaan, Fourth Master: O Lord, I wash the feet of devotees.
May my sins be burnt away in an instant; O Lord, be kind to Nanak.
||1||Pause|| The poor humble beggars stand begging at Your door.
They yearn for Your blessing. I have come to Your refuge begging;
please bless me with Your name through guru's teaching. ||1|| I am
filled with lust and anger. I fight against them daily. Please be kind
and save me by driving them out by guru's grace. ||2|| I am filled with
the fire of great sins; soothe me with the icy water of guru's teaching.
Page 1326 My mind and body become peaceful; the sickness goes
away and I sleep in peace. ||3|| Like the rays of sun spread everywhere,
God pervades each and every heart. Devotees obtain the nectar
meeting devotees; they drink the essence sitting at home. ||4|| The
humble being is in love with the guru, like the chakvi (duck) loves to
see the sun. She keeps watching the whole night; she drinks nectar
when the sun rises. ||5|| The faithless is greedy like a dog. He is filled
with the filth of evil deeds. He talks a lot for self-interest. How can he
be trusted? ||6|| Seek refuge in devotee's company and find God's
essence by churning. They do good deeds talk good virtues; God
blesses the devotee saints. ||7|| You are inaccessible, Kind and

compassionate, and the great giver, please shower us with Your kindness, and save us. One God the life of all looks after everyone O Nanak, ||8||5|| Kalyaan, Fourth Master: O Lord, please make me the slave of Your slaves. As long as I live, may I drink the dust of Your devotees? ||1||Pause|| Shiva, Naarad, the thousand-headed snake and sages long for the dust of Your devotees. All the worlds and realms where your devotees put their feet are sanctified. ||1|| Forget worrying about people talk and pride; live in devotee's company. The fear of justice of destiny eliminates and God pulls you out from drowning in sins. ||2|| Some are dead, some half dead through doubt. All rejuvenate meeting with God's devotees. So do not delay even for an instant, go and fall at devotee's feet. ||3|| The praise of God's name the priceless jewel is kept with his devotees by God. Whoever follows guru's teaching truthfully; He takes out the jewel and gives to him. ||4|| Listen, O my brotherly saints. The guru calls loudly with raised arms; if you long for everlasting peace for your soul then go to guru's refuge. ||5|| If you are fortunate, then you recite God's name through guru's teaching. You swim across the evil worldly pleasure by drinking God's sublime essence. ||6|| Those who long for worldly wealth keenly, they rot stuck in it. The path of ignorance is dark and difficult; it is loaded with ego. ||7|| O Nanak, say God God God; saying God obtains salvation. Meeting the true guru, one recites God's name and absorbs in it. Chhakaa 1. ||8||6||

Page 1327 *God is one. It is true. He is the Creator. He is carefree. He has no enemy. He is immortal. He does not take birth. He came into existence on His own. He is realized by guru's grace.*
Bibhaas, First Master, Chau-Padas, First House: Your name carries us across; Your Name brings respect and worship. Your name is the ornament; the intellect is the mixing spoon. Your name brings honour to everyone's name. Without Your name, no one is ever respected. ||1|| All other clever tricks are just for show. Whoever God blesses; his affairs are resolved. ||1||Pause|| Your name is my strength; Your name is my justice. Your name is my army; Your name is my king. Your name brings honour, glory and approval. By Your grace, one is blessed with the banner of good deeds. ||2|| Your name brings intuitive peace; Your name brings praise. Your name is the nectar, which cleans out

the poison. Through Your name, peace abides in the mind. Without God's name, they are tied and taken to the village of death. ||3|| Man is involved with his wife, boat, home, land and country; He enjoys wearing fine clothes; But when the call comes, he cannot delay. O Nanak, in the end, the false turns out to be false. ||4||1|| Parbhaatee, First Master: Your name is the gem, and Your grace is the light. Your light enlightens. Darkness fills the dark, and everything is lost. ||1|| This whole world is useless. Your name is the cure; everything else is false, O infinite Creator Lord. ||1||Pause|| You may put the whole universe on one side of the scale. O my beloved, Your worth cannot be estimated even if you put everything else on the scale. ||2|| Page 1328 Pain brings pleasure and pleasure brings pain. The mouth which praises You; what hunger can that mouth suffer? ||3|| O Nanak, you alone are ignorant; rest of the world is great. The body in which God's name does not well up; that body is useless. ||4||2|| Parbhaatee, First Master: The reason, Brahma spoke the Vedas and Shiva renounced the worldly wealth; the reason the mystics became renunciates; the goddesses did not find the cure; ||1|| O elder; speaking the truth with truthful mouth obtains salvation. Enemy and pain do not come close; if someone realizes divine wisdom. ||1||Pause|| Fire, water and air created the world; all three are the slaves of God's name. He who does not recite God's name is a thief; He is known millions of miles away. ||2|| If someone does one good deed and feels proud of it in the mind! The Lord bestows many virtues and goodness; He does not regret. ||3|| Those who praise You gather the wealth in their laps; this is Nanak's wealth. Whoever shows respect to them is not summoned by the devil of death. ||4||3|| Parbhaatee, First Master: One who has no beauty, no social status, no mouth and no flesh? The formless God is realized meeting the guru enshrining His name in the mind. ||1|| O detached Yogi, contemplate the reality; So that you do not come into the world again; ||1||Pause|| One who does not do good deeds or have faith or wears a sacred rosary; Listening to divine wisdom obtains the understanding through the protector guru. ||2|| One, who does not observe any fasts, does not make religious vows or recites; He does not worry about salvation; he obeys the command of the true guru. ||3|| He who has trained his mind; is not hopeful, or hopeless; He meets the Supreme Being O Nanak, and he obtains divine wisdom. ||4||4|| Parbhaatee, First Master: What he says is approved in the court of the Lord. He looks upon poison and nectar as the same. ||1|| What can I say? You are permeating and pervading all. Whatever happens; happens by Your will. ||1||Pause|| Divine light shines and egotistic pride is dispelled. The true guru bestows the sacred name. ||2|| That person is accepted in today's age. He is honoured in God's court. ||3|| Speaking and listening about the unknown, he goes home. Mere words of mouth do nothing O Nanak, they are burnt away. ||4||5|| Parbhaatee, First Master: One who bathes in the nectar of divine wisdom; obtains the reward of bathing at sixty-eight shrines. Guru's teachings are the gems and jewels; the devotee who searches finds it. ||1|| There is no sacred shrine equal to the guru. Guru is the ocean of contentment. ||1||Pause|| Page 1329 Guru is the river, its water is forever pure; bathing in it eliminates the filth of evil. Meeting the guru is a perfect bath. Bathing there the animals and ghosts become gods. ||2|| He is imbued with God's love from top to bottom. Such a guru is like sandalwood. Its fragrance bestows fragrance to the vegetation. Touch his feet lovingly forever. ||3|| The fragrance wells up in the guru-willed and he goes to God's house. O Nanak, the guru-willed merges in truth and obtains salvation. ||4||6|| Parbhaatee, First Master: He contemplates wisdom by guru's grace and obtains honour by reading. Within the self, the self is revealed when one is blessed by God's sacred name. ||1|| O Creator, You are my host. I beg for one blessing from You: please bless me with Your name. ||1||Pause|| The five wandering thieves are captured and held, and the pride of the mind is eliminated. Evil seeing and evil thinking have departed; such is the divine wisdom. ||2|| Please bless me with the rice of truth and self-restraint, the wheat of compassion, and the leaf of rice as the enlightenment. Make milk the good deeds, butter the contentment. I beg for such a gift. ||3|| Let forgiveness and patience be my milk-cow, and the calf drinks milk intuitively. I beg for the clothes of modesty; may Nanak keep singing God's praises. ||4||7|| Parbhaatee, First Master: No one stops from coming; why should anyone stop from going? From whom, he is born; he only knows and merges with Him again; ||1|| You are admirable; so is your will.

Whatever You do happens, no one else can do anything. ||1||Pause|| As the buckets on the chain of the wheel well rotate; one empties and the other fills. Same is the play of the master He does as He pleases. ||2|| Following the path of divinity, one's mind is reverted and enlightens. O divine master; think in your mind; who is householder and who is renunciate? ||3|| Whoever you hope from, return it back to him and obtain salvation. We come from Him; surrendering to Him, O Nanak, whether householder or a renunciate, both are accepted. ||4||8|| Parbhaatee, First Master: I admire the one, who ties the evil will in a bundle. He does not know the difference between vice and virtue, he wanders around uselessly. ||1|| Say the true name of the Creator. Then, you shall never again have to come into this world. ||1||Pause|| The Creator transforms the high into the low, and makes the lowly into kings. Those who know the all-knowing Lord are approved as perfect in this world. ||2|| You go to guide the one, who is lost; Page 1330 The Creator plays all the games; only a few understand this. ||3|| Recite God's name in the morning through guru's teaching; forget the worldly love. Prays Nanak, the slave of God's slaves: the world loses, and he wins. ||4||9|| Parbhaatee, First Master: The mind chases after the worldly wealth; the mind is a bird flying in the sky. The thieves are driven away by guru's teaching and the body-village is admired. O Lord, when You save someone, he is saved; his capital is safe and sound. ||1|| Such a jewel of God's name is my treasure; Please bless me with guru's teachings; I will touch Your feet. ||1||Pause|| The mind is a worshipper and enjoyer; mind is an ignorant fool. The mind is the giver, the mind is the beggar; the mind is the great guru, the Creator. Killing the five thieves obtains peace; such is the divine wisdom. ||2|| One Lord is said to be in each and every heart, but no one can see Him. The false are cast upside-down into the womb; without the name, they lose their honour. If You unite me, I unite with You; it is by Your grace. ||3|| God does not ask about social class or birth; He takes you to the true home. Whatever type of deeds you do; that is your social class and status. The pains of death and birth are eradicated; O Nanak, salvation obtains through God's name. ||4||10|| Parbhaatee, First Master: He is awake and happy, but he is being plundered – he is blind! The noose is around his neck, and yet, his head is busy with worldly affairs. In hope, he comes and with desire, he leaves. The strings of his life are tangled; he is helpless. ||1|| Lord of awareness, the Lord of life is awake and aware. He is the ocean of peace the treasure of nectar. ||1||Pause|| He does not understand what he is told; he is blind; he does not see; yet he does evil deeds. The beloved transcendent Lord showers His love; honour obtains by what you do? ||2|| His life decreases day by day but he increases his love for worldly wealth. He drowns without the guru as long as he is caught in duality. ||3|| Day and night, God watches over His beings; pain and pleasure come by previous deeds. The unfortunate begs for the awns of truth, please bless Nanak with this honour. ||4||11|| Parbhaatee, First Master: If I remain quiet, the world calls me an ignorant. If I talk too much, I miss out on Your love. My mistakes and faults will be judged in Your court. Without Your name, how can I maintain good conduct? ||1|| Such is the falsehood which is plundering the world. The slanderer slanders me, but I love him. ||1||Pause|| He, who is slandered; knows the way; through guru's teaching, he is stamped and sealed in God's court. The Creator of name knows the inner state of mind. Whoever He blesses; knows the way. ||2|| I am filthy; the true Lord is pure. Calling great does not make great. The self-willed openly eats the dangerous poison. But the guru-willed is imbued with true name. ||3|| I am blind, deaf, foolish and ignorant; Page 1331 The lowest of the low, the worst of the worse. I am poor, but I am in love with God's name. This is the essence of wealth; all else is poison and ashes. ||4|| I pay no attention to slander and praise; I contemplate guru's teaching. I celebrate the one who blesses me with it. Whoever You bless, O Lord, is blessed with status and honour. Says Nanak; I say what He makes me say. ||5||12|| Parbhaatee, First Master: Eating too much increases filth; wearing fancy clothes is a disgrace. Talking too much starts arguments. Without God's Name, everything is poison. ||1|| O elder, my mind is caught in such a wicked net; Riding the waves of the storm, it will be enlightened by intuitive wisdom. ||1||Pause|| They eat poison, speak poison and do poisonous deeds. They are tied and killed at the door of death; God's name will free them. ||2|| They go as they come; whatever they do is recorded. The self-willed loses his capital, and is punished in the court of the Lord. ||3|| The world is false. Truth is pure. It is realized through guru's teaching. Those who have God's spiritual wisdom inside are rare. ||4|| They endure the unendurable, they are immortal and joyful. O Nanak, the fish is in love with water; keep me with love if it pleases You. ||5||13|| Parbhaatee, First Master: Songs, sounds, pleasures and clever tricks; Joy, love and the power to command; Wearing clothes and food have no place in the consciousness. True intuitive peace comes by enshrining God's name in the mind. ||1|| What do I know about what God does or makes us do? Nothing pleases me without God's name. ||1||Pause|| Yoga, thrills, delicious flavours and joy; wisdom, truth and love all come from worshipping the Lord of the universe. My occupation is to praise the Lord. I recite God the Lord of all in my mind. ||2|| I have lovingly enshrined the love of my beloved in my heart. The master of the poor is the Lord of all. He blesses with the gift of His name and longing for it. Contemplating the reality my mind is satisfied. ||3|| What power do I have to speak the unspoken? I worship God by His grace. You live in me and my ego and possessiveness disappears. Who else shall I serve; there is none else for me to worship. ||4|| Guru's teaching is enjoyable and very sweet. I see such a nectar inside. Those who taste it attain the state of perfection. O Nanak, they are satisfied, and their bodies are at peace. ||5||14|| Parbhaatee First Master I realized Him inside through guru's teaching; there is no other who can dye me; He watches and takes care of all beings forever; He is the ruler of all. ||1|| My God is dyed in the most beautiful and glorious colour. My beloved is kind to the poor and enticing; He is dyed with tasty red colour of love. ||1||Pause|| I fetch nectar from the worldly well and drink it. He who created the creation knows the way; the guru-willed realizes it contemplating divine wisdom. ||2|| Page 1332 The rays of light spread out, and the heart-lotus joyfully blossoms; the sun enlightens the moon. I have conquered the demon of death and destroyed the desires of the mind. I realized God by guru's grace. ||3|| I am dyed in the deep red colour of love. I am not dyed with any other colour. Nanak sings His praises with love; He pervades all. ||4||15|| Parbhaatee, First Master: The Yogis have twelve schools, the renunciates have ten. The Kapadia Yogis wander around with their hair hanging all over; but without guru's teaching the noose of death hangs around their neck. ||1|| Those who are imbued with guru's teaching are the real renunciates. They beg for awns in their mind attuning to God with love. ||1||Pause|| The scholar reads and argues, and then he does his intuitive deeds. Nothing is realized without realization; the self-willed suffers separation from God. ||2|| Those who obtain guru's teaching are truthful and pure; they are honoured in God's court. They are imbued with the jewel of God's name forever and merge in truth. ||3|| Good deeds, faith, purification, self-discipline, meditation, penance and going to pilgrimage; all are enshrined in guru's teaching. O Nanak, uniting with the true guru, suffering, sin and death run away. ||4||16|| Parbhaatee, First Master: Be the dust of the saints in devotee's company and sing God's praise; you will swim across the world ocean. What can the poor devil of death do to those, who have God in their mind? ||1|| May I be burnt alive without God's name? Reciting God like the rosary, the guru-willed enjoys in the mind. ||1||Pause|| Those who follow guru's teaching are truly peaceful; how can I praise them? The guru-willed seeks and finds the gems, jewels, diamonds, rubies and treasures. ||2|| Focusing On guru's teachings realizes wisdom and meditation. He remains absorbed in the primal, immaculate, independent and carefree God; ||3|| The seven oceans are filled with pure water and the upside down boat floats in it. The guru-willed controls the wandering mind and merges in peace. ||4|| The guru-willed who realizes himself is a householder, as well as a renunciate; Says Nanak, my mind follows guru's teachings not anyone else; ||5||17|| Tune Parbhaatee, Third Master, Chau-Padas: God is one. He is realized by guru's grace. Only a rare guru-willed understand by absorbing in guru's teaching. Those imbued with God's name are at peace forever. They lovingly attune to truth. ||1|| Page 1333 O my brother; recite God's name. The mind stabilizes by guru's grace and is satisfied by enjoying God's name. ||1||Pause|| Worship God all the time, this is the benefit of this age O brother. Focusing the mind to the true name the person becomes pure and filth does not attach to him. ||2|| True guru has revealed the adornment of peace; God's name is a great honour. His treasures are inexhaustible; it never runs short. Serve God forever O brother. ||3|| Whoever God blesses; He enshrines in their mind. O Nanak, recite God's name forever; the true guru reveals it. ||4||1|| Parbhaatee, Third Master: O God, forgive the virtueless and unite with You by Your grace. You are endless; no one can find Your limits. You are realized through guru's teaching. ||1|| O dear Lord, I praise You. I offer my mind and body to You. May I live in Your refuge forever? ||1||Pause|| O Lord; keep me as You please; honour me by blessing with Your name. Through the perfect guru, God's will is revealed and merges in peace forever. ||2|| It is Your worship if it pleases You; You unite us with You by your grace. Eternal peace obtains by Your will; the guru extinguishes the fire of greed. ||3|| Whatever You do; happens O Creator. No one else can do anything. O Nanak, there is no bestowal as great as reciting Your name; it is obtained from the perfect guru. ||4||2|| Parbhaatee, Third Master: The guru-willed who praises God realizes God. Realizing guru's teachings the doubt of duality is erased. ||1|| O dear Lord, You are my one and only one. I recite and admire You; realization is obtained by Your grace. ||1||Pause|| The guru-willed who admire You obtain the taste the essence of sweet nectar. It tastes sweet forever never bland, contemplating through guru's teaching. ||2|| He, who makes it taste sweet, knows it; I praise Him. Praising God the bestowal of happiness forever, eliminates ego. ||3|| My true guru is forever the giver. I receive whatever fruit I desire. O Nanak, honour obtains through God's name realized through guru's teaching. ||4||3|| Parbhaatee, Third Master: Those who enter Your refuge O dear Lord, are saved by Your grace; I cannot think of anyone as great as You. There was none, there will be none. ||1|| O dear Lord, I shall remain in Your sanctuary forever. O Lord; keep me as You please by Your grace. ||1||Pause|| O dear Lord, You look after those who seek Your sanctuary. Page 1334 O dear Lord, whoever You protect by Your grace; the devil of death cannot rob him. ||2|| True is Your refuge, O dear Lord; it never diminishes or goes away. Those who abandon God and attach to duality shall continue to die and reborn. ||3|| Those who seek Your sanctuary O Lord; shall never be hungry for anything. O Nanak, praise God's name forever and merge in Him through guru's teaching. ||4||4|| Parbhaatee, Third Master: O guru-willed, recite God as long as you live. The mind becomes pure through guru's teaching and pride of mind ends. Those who merge in God's name; their taking birth is fruitful. ||1|| O my mind; listen to the teachings of the guru. God's name bestows happiness forever by drinking God's sublime juice intuitively. ||1||Pause|| Those who realize their origin merge in it intuitively and obtain peace. The lotus blossoms through guru's teaching and obtains peace with ease. One God abides in all; only a few realize it. ||2|| The mind becomes pure through guru's teaching and realizes the essence of nectar. Enshrining God's name in the mind forever, the mind conquers the mind. I admire my guru forever, who realizes God the Lord of soul. ||3|| Those who do not serve the guru, they waste away this human life. When God blesses, He unites us with the true guru, and we become content intuitively. O Nanak, the fortunate recites God's name and obtains honour. ||4||5|| Parbhaatee, Third Master: God plays the play by creating many species in many ways in the universe. He creates and tests for quality and then feeds all beings. ||1|| God pervades all in all ages. God pervades in everyone; He reveals to the guru-willed reciting His name. ||1||Pause|| God's name fully pervades in all in today's age. The jewel of God's name is revealed in the hearts of those who seek guru's refuge. ||2|| Through guru's teaching the five senses are controlled; forgiveness and contentment obtains. Blessed is God's devotee who sings God's praises in love and detachment. ||3|| If someone turns his face away from the guru, and does not enshrine guru's words in his mind! He may perform all sorts of rituals and accumulate wealth. Whatever he does goes to hell. ||4|| God pervades all; realized through guru's teaching. Everything originates from Him. O Nanak, God unites the guru-willed and absorbs him with Him. ||5||6|| Parbhaatee, Third Master: O my mind, praise your guru. Page 1335 Those with good fortune written in their fate, sing God's praises. ||1||Pause|| God bestows the nectar of God's name for food to them. Out of millions, only a few receive it. Only those who are blessed by God receive it; ||1|| Whoever enshrines guru's feet in his mind? Their pain and ignorance is eliminated. The true Lord unites him with Himself. ||2|| So, fall in love with guru's sermon. Here and hereafter, this is your only support. The Creator bestows it. ||3|| One whom the Lord inspires to obey His will; He is a wise and knowledgeable devotee.

Nanak admires Him forever. ||4||7||17||7||24|| Parbhaatee, Fourth Master, Bibhaas: God is one. He is realized by guru's grace. Sing God's praises through guru's teaching intuitively enshrining God's name in the mind with love. I drink God's nectar through guru's teaching; I admire God's name. ||1|| God the life of the world is my life. Sacred God appeals to my mind. The guru whispered His lesson in my ear. ||1||Pause|| Come, O brotherly saints: let us join together and recite God's name. Please bless me with God's gift that I understand the process of realizing God. ||2|| God abides in true congregation; sing God's praises in the congregation. I found the congregation with good luck. I realized God by meeting the guru. ||3|| I sing the praises of the inaccessible God. Singing His praises amazes me. The guru became kind to servant Nanak and bestowed him with God's name. ||4||1|| Parbhaatee, Fourth Master: The guru-willed says God with sunrise and talks about God the whole night. I yearn for God and I search for God. ||1|| My mind is the dust of the feet of God's devotees. Guru has implanted God's sweet name in me. I dust guru's feet with my hair. ||1||Pause|| Day and night are dark for the faithless; he is caught in the net of worldly attachment. God does not enshrine in his mind at all. He is in debt up to the hair of his head. ||2|| Joining the true congregation, I obtained wisdom and understanding; and I am freed from the net of false attachment. God's name tastes sweet to me. The guru made me happy through his teaching. ||3|| I am a child; guru is unfathomable Lord of the world. He looks after me by His grace. I am drowning in the ocean of poison; O God, guru, Lord of the world, please save Your child, Nanak. ||4||2|| Parbhaatee, Fourth Master: God became kind to me for a moment and I sing His praises with love. Page 1336 Those guru-willed who sing or listen to God's praise obtain salvation and enjoy it. ||1|| The sublime essence of the name of the Lord is enshrined in my mind. The guru-willed obtains the cool water of God's name and drinks it to the full. ||1||Pause|| Those who are imbued with God's love in the mind; the mark of purity is written on their forehead. They are famous and admired in the entire world like the moon among the stars. ||2|| Those who do not enshrine God's name in the mind; their all affairs are not resolved. They may adorn and decorate their bodies, but without

God's name, they look like their noses have been cut. ||3|| The sovereign Lord pervades all and looks after all equally. God became kind to servant Nanak and he recites God at home. ||4||3|| Parbhaatee, Fourth Master: The inaccessible God became kind and I say God God from my mouth by His grace. I recite God the purifier of sinners and all my sins and pains ended. ||1|| O mind, say God God the all-pervading God. I sing the praises of God, merciful to the meek, destroyer of pain. I obtained priceless God's name through guru's teaching. ||1||Pause|| God abides in the body; God is pleasing to my mind through guru's teaching. God is revealed in the body pool. I realized God in my body temple. ||2|| Those who wander in the wilderness of doubt; the faithless ignorant are robbed. As the deer has musk in his body, but he wanders from bush to bush to find; ||3|| You are great and unfathomable; Your divine wisdom is beyond comprehension; please teach me divine wisdom that I realize God. The guru has placed His Hand on servant Nanak's head; he fell in love with God's name. ||4||4|| Parbhaatee, Fourth Master: I am in love with God's name; I recite the name of great God. Guru's teaching is pleasing to my mind by God's grace. ||1|| O my mind, recite God's name a little bit. The perfect guru blessed me with Godly gift; God's name dwells in my mind. ||1||Pause||. God abides in the temple of my body; reciting God obtains honour by His grace. turning towards God. ||2|| Here and hereafter, God's servants become content; the guru-willed become happy turning towards God. ||2||They are attuned to the carefree God; they have enshrined God in the mind. God erases millions of their sins and sufferings in an instant. ||3|| Your servants are known through You O God; it shows on their faces. God abides in His devotees O servant Nanak; God and His devotees are the same. ||4||5|| Page 1337 Parbhaatee, Fourth Master: True guru has implanted God's name in me; I live and die by reciting God. Blessed is the perfect true guru; He reached out and took me from drowning in poison. ||1|| O mind, recite God's name, worthy of reciting. God cannot be found by any other means. He is found through the perfect guru. ||1||Pause|| Recite God's name with love through guru's teaching and enjoy drinking it. The lowly iron becomes gold in devotee's company enshrining God the guru in the mind. ||2|| They are enticed by the poisonous love of children and spouse. The saints do not serve them. They are self-willed filled with ashes. ||3|| O God, You alone know Your virtues; I got tired and seek Your refuge. Keep me as You please O master. Servant Nanak is Your servant. ||4||6|| Chhakaa 1. Parbhaatee, Bibhaas, Partaal, Fourth Master: God is one. He is realized by guru's grace. O mind, recite the treasure of God's name. You shall be honoured in God's court. Those who recite God, obtain salvation. ||1||Pause|| O mind: listen to God's name intently. Listen, O mind: singing God's praises is as good as bathing at sixty-eight shrines. Listen, O mind: the guru-willed obtains honour. ||1|| O mind, recite the primal God the transcendent great Lord. Millions of sins shall be destroyed in an instant. O Nanak, realizing God; ||2||1||7|| Parbhaatee, Fifth Master, Bibhaas: God is one. He is realized by guru's grace. The Lord created the mind and the body. He created it from five elements and infused soul in it. He made the earth its bed, and water to use. Do not forget Him for a moment. Serve the Lord of the world. ||1|| O mind, serve the true guru, and obtain salvation. If you remain unaffected by sorrow and joy, you shall find the Lord of life. ||1||Pause|| He enjoys wearing clothes and other pleasures. He made your mother, father and all relatives. He provides food to all, in water and on land, O friend. So serve the Lord, forever. ||2|| He helps where there is no one else. He washes away millions of sins in an instant. He bestows His gifts, and never regrets. He bestows once and never calls again. ||3|| Page 1338 By pre-ordained destiny, I have searched and found God. God the lord of the world lives in devotee's company. Meeting with the guru, I have come to Your door. O Lord, please visualize to servant Nanak. ||4||1|| Parbhaatee, Fifth Master: Serving God is the honour for the devotees. Their lust, anger and greed are erased. Your name is the treasure of Your humble servant. They sing Your praises with love to visualize You. ||1|| O God; You bless us to worship You. You free them by cutting the chains. ||1||Pause|| Those humble beings, who are imbued with God's love They find peace in God's congregation. Those, who enjoy the taste; they only know. They are amazed in the mind by visualizing. ||2|| They are at peace; they are sacred of all. In whose mind, dwells God; they are eternal; they do not come and go in reincarnation. Night and day, they sing God's praises. ||3|| All shall bow down to them in respect. In whose minds enshrines the formless Lord? Be kind to me O Lord the master. May serving these humble beings save Nanak? ||4||2|| Parbhaatee, Fifth Master: Singing His praises, the mind becomes happy. Recite God twenty-four hours a day; reciting him the sins go away. I fall at the feet of that guru. ||1|| O beloved saints, please bless me with wisdom; I recite God's name that I may obtain liberation. ||1||Pause|| The guru has shown me the straight path; I have abandoned everything else. I am in love with God's name. I admire the guru forever. Through that guru I recite God; ||2|| Guru carries those beings across, and saves them from drowning. By his grace, they are not enticed by worldly wealth; in this world and the next, they are looked after by the guru. I admire that guru forever. ||3|| From the most ignorant, I have been made spiritually wise; through the unspoken speech of the perfect guru; the divine guru, O Nanak, is the supreme Lord. By good fortune, I serve the Lord. ||4||3|| Parbhaatee, Fifth Master: He made me recite His name and all pains are erased and happiness obtained. By His grace he made me to serve Him; all my evil deeds ended. ||1|| I am only a child; I seek God's refuge. Erasing my faults, God made me His. My guru, the Lord of the world saved me. ||1||Pause|| My sicknesses and sins were erased in an instant, when the Lord of the world became kind. I recite God the bestowal of salvation with each breath. I admire my true guru. ||2|| My Lord is inaccessible, unfathomable and infinite. His limits cannot be found. We earn the profit, and become wealthy by reciting our God. ||3|| Page 1339 I recite and sing praises of the supreme Lord twenty-four hours a day forever. Says Nanak, my desires have been fulfilled; I have found my guru, the supreme Lord. ||4||4|| Parbhaatee, Fifth Master: Reciting God's name, the sins go away. Guru has blessed me with the wealth of the true name. God's servants are admired in God's court; Serving Him, the devotees look adorable. ||1|| O my brothers, recite God's name. All sickness and sin shall be erased; the darkness of ignorance will depart from the mind. ||1||Pause|| Guru has saved me from death and rebirth, O friend; I am in love with God's name. The suffering of millions of lives is gone; whatever pleases Him is good. ||2|| I praise my guru forever. By His grace, I recite God's name. The fortunate find such a guru. Meeting Him, one is lovingly attuned to the Lord. ||3|| Please be kind O supreme Lord and master; the inner-knower of all beings; Twenty-four hours a day, I am lovingly attuned to Him. Servant Nanak has come to the sanctuary of God. ||4||5|| Parbhaatee, Fifth Master: By His kindness, God has made me His own. He has blessed me with reciting God's name. Twenty-four hours a day, I sing the praises of the Lord of the universe. Fear is erased, and all worry has been removed. ||1|| I have been saved, touching the feet of the true guru. Whatever the guru says is good and sweet to me. I have renounced the intellectual wisdom of my mind. ||1||Pause|| God abides in my mind and body. There are no conflicts, pains or obstacles. God is with my soul forever. Filth is washed away by the love of God's name. ||2|| I am in love with the lotus feet of the Lord. Lust, anger and ego have been eliminated. Now, I know the way to realize God. Through devotional worship, my mind is pleased and believes in God. ||3|| Listen, O friends, saints, my peaceful companions. The jewel of God's name is unfathomable and immeasurable: Sing the praises of God the treasure of virtues; Says Nanak, the fortunate find Him; ||4||6|| Parbhaatee, Fifth Master: They are wealthy, and they are the true merchants; they have faith in God's name and they are honoured in God's court. ||1|| Recite God's name in the mind O friend; the perfect guru is found by good luck through perfect and pure way. ||1||Pause|| They earn the profit and are admired. By the grace of the saints, they sing the praises of the Lord. ||2|| Their lives are fruitful and their birth is approved; they enjoy God's love by guru's grace. ||3|| Lust, anger and ego have vanished. O Nanak, the guru-willed is carried across the world ocean. ||4||7|| Parbhaatee, Fifth Master: Guru is perfect, and perfect is his power. Page 1340 Guru's teaching is eternal and forever. In whose mind guru's sermon abides; their pain and sufferings go away. ||1|| Imbued with God's love, they sing the praises of God. They are liberated, bathing in the dust of the feet of devotees. ||1||Pause|| By guru's grace, they are carried across the world ocean. Their concern of doubt and other useless deeds go away. Guru's feet abide in their minds and bodies. The carefree devotees seek God's refuge. ||2|| They are blessed with happiness, pleasure and peace. Enemy and pain do not approach them. The perfect guru makes them His own, and protects them. Reciting God's name, the sins and sufferings are erased. ||3|| The saints, spiritual companions and followers become content. The perfect guru leads them to meet God. The painful noose of death and rebirth is cut. Says Nanak, the guru covers their sins; ||4||8|| Parbhaatee, Fifth Master: The perfect true guru has bestowed me with God's name. I enjoy bliss, happiness, liberation and eternal peace. All my affairs have been resolved. ||1||Pause|| The lotus feet of the guru abide in my mind. The pain of sufferings doubt and other false deeds is dispelled. ||1|| Get up in the morning and sing God's sermon. Twenty-four hours a day, recite God O mortal. ||2|| God abides inside and out everywhere. Wherever I go, He is always with me and helps me. ||3|| With my palms pressed together, I offer my prayer. O Nanak, I recite and sing God's praises. ||4||9|| Parbhaatee, Fifth Master: The supreme Lord is wise and all knowing. The fortunate finds the perfect guru and I praise to visualize Him. ||1||Pause|| Guru's teaching has cut my sins and bestowed happiness. I have become worthy of reciting God's name. I am enlightened in devotee's company. God's lotus feet abide in my mind. ||1|| He who created me protects me. God is perfect, the master of the master less. He, upon whom He showers His kindness. His deeds and character are perfect. ||2|| They sing the praises of ever fresh God continuously. They do not wander in millions of different lifes. Here and hereafter, they worship Lord's feet. They are happy in God's court. ||3|| The person, upon whose forehead the guru places His Hand; is rare among millions; He sees the perfect God fully in water and Land. The dust of the feet of such a humble being saves Nanak. ||4||10|| Parbhaatee, Fifth Master: I praise my perfect guru. By his grace, I recite God. ||1||Pause|| Listening to the sacred sermon, my mind has become content. My entanglements of evil deeds have ended. ||1|| I am in love with guru's true teaching. I remember my God in my mind. ||2|| Reciting His name I am enlightened. Page 1341 God abides in my mind through guru's teaching. ||3|| The guru is all-powerful and kind forever. Reciting God, Nanak has become content. ||4||11|| Parbhaatee, Fifth Master: Saying guru guru obtains eternal happiness. God, kind to the poor became kind and inspired me to recite His name. ||1||Pause|| Joining the society of saints, I am enlightened. Saying God God, my hopes are fulfilled. ||1|| I am blessed with total salvation, and my mind is filled with peace. I sing the praises of the Lord O Nanak, by guru's grace. ||2||12|| Parbhaatee, Fifth Master, Second House, Bibhaas: God is one. He is realized by guru's grace. There is no other place of rest; Not at all without Lord's name; there is total success and salvation; all my deeds are fulfilled. ||1|| I recite God's name all the time. Falling in love with God erases lust, anger and ego. ||1||Pause|| Reciting God's name the pain goes away; God sustains us in His refuge. Those with pre-ordained destiny surrender to the true guru and the devil of death does not bother them; ||2|| Recite God day and night and eliminate doubt from your mind. One, with perfect destiny realizes God in devotee's company. ||3|| The sins of countless lifetimes are erased, and God protects them. He is our mother, father, friend and sibling; O servant Nanak, recite God. ||4||1||13|| Parbhaatee, Fifth Master, Bibhaas, Partaal: God is one. He is realized by guru's grace. Say God God God. Conflict, suffering, greed and emotional attachment and the fever of ego shall be eliminated. ||1||Pause|| Renounce your pride and fall at saint's feet; your mind becomes sacred and sins erased. ||1|| Nanak, the child, does not know anything. God the protector is my mother and father. ||2||1||14|| Parbhaatee, Fifth Master: I have taken the support of Lord's lotus feet. You are the highest of all O Lord; You are master of all. ||1||Pause|| He is the support of life, the destroyer of pain and the giver of discriminating understanding. ||1|| So bow down in respect to the saviour Lord, worship and adore one God. Bathing in the dust of the feet of the saints, Nanak is blessed with many comforts. ||2||2||15|| Page 1342 Parbhaatee, Ashtapadees, First Master, Bibhaas: God is one. He is realized by guru's grace. The insanity of duality drives the mind insane. In false greed, life is wasting away. Duality clings to the mind; it cannot be stopped. True guru saves us by implanting God's name in the heart. ||1|| Without controlling the mind, the worldly wealth cannot be eliminated. He, who created everything, knows all. One is carried across the terrifying world ocean contemplating guru's teaching. ||1||Pause|| The proud kings gather wealth. But this beloved wealth does not go with them. The enticement of worldly wealth has many colours. Other than God's name, there is no friend or a companion. ||2|| He sees the others the way he thinks. As is his thinking, so is his state of mind. According to one's previous actions, one focuses his mind; seeking the advice of the true guru, one goes home in peace. ||3|| Singing and listening to music the mind is caught by the love of duality. He is filled with corruption and suffers serious pain. Meeting with the true guru, he obtains realization. He remains lovingly attuned to the true name. ||4|| Through guru's true teaching, he practices truth. He sings God's praises through the true sermon. He lives in his home and attains immortal status. Then, he obtains honour in God's court. ||5|| Without serving the guru, there is no worship; Even though one may make all sorts of efforts; Ego and possessiveness is erased through guru's teaching. God's pure name dwells in his mind. ||6|| In this world, practicing guru's teaching is the essence of worship. Without guru's teaching, everything else is the darkness of false attachment. Through guru's teaching, enshrine God's name in the mind. Realization comes through guru's teaching and obtains salvation. ||7|| There is no other who does anything and looks after. True Lord is infinite and incomparably beautiful. Reciting God obtains salvation. O Nanak, only a few search and find Him. ||8||1|| Parbhaatee, First Master: Emotional attachment to worldly wealth is spread over the entire world. Seeing a beautiful woman the lustful man is enticed. His love for his children and gold steadily increases. He sees everything as his own, except God. ||1|| Recite such a recitation like the rosary. That eliminates pain and pleasure and attains special devotional worship. ||1||Pause|| O treasure of virtues, Your limits cannot be found. Through guru's true teachings I am absorbed in You. You created the coming and going in life. Those who enshrine the true Lord in the mind are the true devotees. ||2|| Contemplating divine wisdom and meditation of God obtains salvation. No one realizes without meeting the true guru. Lord's light fills the sacred pools of all beings. I admire peace giving beautiful face. ||3|| Through guru's teachings, one achieves loving devotional worship. Guru's teaching burns away the ego from within. Page 1343 The wandering mind is controlled from wandering and held in place. Enshrining the true name in the mind; ||4|| The amazing happiness obtains first; to those who follow guru's teaching and attune to God with love. Seeing this, the fire in water is extinguished. Those who are fortunate, realize it. ||5|| Serving the true guru, doubt is dispelled. They remain awake forever attuning to the true Lord with love. They know One God and no other. Serving the giver of peace, they become pure. ||6|| Selfless service and intuitive awareness come by contemplating guru's teaching. Reciting God, penance and self-discipline obtains by eradicating ego. One becomes liberated from life by listening to guru's teaching. Living a truthful life, one finds true peace. ||7|| Giver of peace is the eradicator of pain. I cannot think of serving any other. I offer my body, mind and wealth to God. Says Nanak; I have tasted the supreme, sublime essence of God. ||8||2|| Parbhaatee, First Master: You may practice divinity acquiring veins, and breathing control. Without the true guru, you will not understand anything; deluded by doubt you shall drown and die. The blind are filled with filth; they may wash and wash, but the inner filth does not go away. Without God's name, everything is useless; like the magician who deceives through illusions. ||1|| The merits of the six religious rituals are obtained through the name of formless God. O Lord, You are the ocean of virtues; I am virtueless. ||1||Pause|| Running around chasing the worldly wealth is an evil-minded useless act. The ignorant boasts about him; He does not understand anything. The self-willed is enticed by worldly wealth; his words are useless and empty. The ritual cleansings of the sinner are fraudulent; his rituals and decorations are useless. ||2|| False thinking of mind creates useless disputes. The false are filled with ego; they do not enjoy Godly taste. Doing anything other than God's name tastes bland. The company of evil is destructive. Their words and living are useless. ||3|| Do not be deluded by doubt; do not invite your own death. Serve the true guru, and you shall be at peace forever. Without the true guru, no one is liberated. They come and go in reincarnation; they die, only to be reborn again. ||4|| This body wanders, caught in the three worldly qualities. It is troubled by sorrow and suffering. So serve the one who has no mother or father. Desire and self-pride shall depart from within. ||5|| Wherever I look, I see Him. Without meeting the true guru, no one is liberated. Enshrine true God in your heart; this is the essence of all. All other hypocrite actions and worship are useless. ||6|| By eliminating duality, one can understand guru's teaching. Realize one God inside out. This is the real wisdom, the essence of guru's teaching. Ashes fall on the heads of those attached to duality. ||7|| To praise God through guru's teachings is the excellent action. In the society of saints, contemplate the glories of God and divine wisdom. Whoever conquers his mind is in the state of being dead while yet alive. O Nanak, God is realized by His grace. ||8||3|| Page 1344 Parbhaatee, First Master, (southern language): Seeing Ahalyaa the wife of Gautam the seer! Indra was enticed. His body was inflicted by thousands of boils, then he regretted. ||1|| O brother, no one should make a mistake knowingly. Whoever God misguides forgets Him. Whom He inspires to understand, understands Him. ||1||Pause|| Like the king Harichand was disgracefully sold for less than the price of a paper. If he knew the mistakes he made, he would have done good deeds and not sold in the market. ||2|| God disguised in the form of a dwarf, and asked for two and half steps of land. If king Bal had recognized Him, why should he be cheated and sent to the underworld. ||3|| Vyaas had told him not to read the sealed letter; but king Janmeja read it. He offered eighteen feasts by killing animals but his sins could not be erased. ||4|| I do not know the account; I obey God's order and say this intuitively. No matter what happens, I will praise God. It is all Your greatness, O God! ||5|| The guru-willed remains detached; filth never attaches to him. He remains forever in God's sanctuary. The ignorant self-willed does not think ahead; he regrets when he suffers pain. ||6|| The Creator who created this creation acts, and causes all to act. O Lord, the pride does not depart from the soul. The egotistic die stuck in it. ||7|| God created everyone forgetful, but he does not forget. O Nanak, salvation obtains reciting God's name by guru's grace. ||8||4|| Parbhaatee, First Master: Recite, listen and take support of God's name. Worthless entanglements are erased and gone. The self-willed caught in duality, loses his honour. I have no one other than God's name. ||1|| Listen, O blind, ignorant, idiotic mind. Aren't you ashamed of coming and going? You will drown without the guru again and again. ||1||Pause|| This mind is ruined by its attachment to worldly wealth. It is written by God's command from destiny; what can we say? Only a few, guru-willed understand this. Salvation is not obtained without reciting God's name. ||2|| People wander lost in millions of different lifes. Without knowing the guru, they are hanged by the devil of death. This mind, from one moment to the next, goes from heavens to the underworld. The guru-willed are freed by reciting God's name. ||3|| When God sends His summons, there is no delaying. When one dies in by guru's teaching, lives in peace. No one understands without guru's teaching. God does everything and makes us do as well. ||4|| Singing God's praises the conflict is eliminated. Through the perfect true guru, one absorbs in true God. This wobbling mind is stabilized; He does truthful deeds. ||5|| He, who is impure inside; how can he become pure. Only a few wash it with guru's teaching and become pure. Only a few guru-willed practice truth; their coming and going in different lifes ends; ||6|| Page 1345 They eat and drink with love and enjoy peace. Company of God's devotees bestows salvation. They speak the truth, and lovingly inspire others to speak as well. Guru's teaching is the essence of all. ||7|| Singing God's praises is a good deed, faith and worship. Lust and anger are burnt in the fire. They enjoy God's sublime taste and their minds are drenched with it. Prays Nanak, there is no other at all. ||8||5|| Parbhaatee, First Master: Reciting God's name in the mind is the real worship. Contemplate guru's teaching not anything else. ||1|| One God is pervading all places. I do not see any other; whom should I worship? ||1||Pause|| I offer my mind, body and soul to You. Keep me as You please; this is my prayer. ||2|| The tongue which recites God with love is truthful. Following guru's teachings, one is saved in the sanctuary of God. ||3|| My God created good deeds and faith. Honour of reciting God's name is pre-ordained and written on the forehead. ||4|| The four great blessings are under the control of the true guru. When the first three are realized, then the fourth is bestowed. ||5|| The true guru bestows the contemplation of salvation. Realize the state of divinity and become honoured. ||6|| Their minds and bodies are soothed; the guru imparts this understanding. Who can estimate the value of those whom God blesses with honour? ||7|| Says Nanak, the guru has imparted this understanding; No one obtains salvation without God's name. ||8||6|| Parbhaatee, First Master: Some are blessed from destiny; the perfect guru has fashioned the true creation.

Those imbued with God's love are imbued truly; their pain ends and obtains honour. ||1|| False are the clever tricks of the evil-minded. They shall disappear in no time at all. ||1||Pause|| Pain and suffering afflict the self-willed. The pain of the self-willed does not depart. The guru-willed realizes God the bestowal of happiness. He unites those with Him who seek His refuge. ||2|| The self-willed cannot do devotional worship; they are insane and rot in ego. This mind flies in an instant from sky to the underworld, till he follows guru's teaching. ||3|| The world is hungry and thirsty; without the true guru, it is not satisfied. Merging intuitively in God, obtains peace and one goes to God's court with honour. ||4|| God knows and bestows everything in His court through guru's pure sermon. He is aware and contemplates truth; He knows the state of salvation. ||5|| He mixed the waves of water, the fire and the air and created the world. He blessed these elements with such power, and kept them under His control. ||6|| Such people are rare in the world; He appraises and puts them in His treasury. They are beyond caste and colour, and eliminate the greed. ||7|| Attuned to God's name they become pure; their pain of ego and filth is eliminated. Nanak washes the feet of those guru-willed, who love the true Lord. ||8||7|| Page 1346 Parbhaatee, Third Master, Bibhaas: God is one. He is realized by guru's grace. See by guru's grace, that the temple of God is in you. Search God's temple through guru's teaching reciting God's name. ||1|| O my mind, attuning to guru's teaching imbues with God's love. Truly worshipping the true God's temple, thinking becomes true. ||1||Pause|| This body is God's temple in which the jewel of spiritual wisdom is revealed. The self-willed do not know at all; human body is not God's temple. ||2|| Dear Lord created the temple of the Lord. He adorns it by His will. All act according to their pre-ordained destiny; no one can erase it. ||3|| Contemplating guru's teaching obtains peace, loving the true name. God's temple is adorned by guru's teaching; it is an infinite golden fortress. ||4|| This world is the temple of the Lord; without the guru, there is pitch dark. The blind and ignorant self-willed worship in love of duality; ||5|| Where the account is audited, the body and caste do not go there. Those attuned to truth are saved; those in love of duality are miserable. ||6|| The treasure of God's name is in God's temple. The ignorant fools do not realize it. It is realized by guru's grace by enshrining God in the mind. ||7|| Those attuned to guru's teaching with love realize guru's sermon. Those attuned and absorbed in God's name become sacred and pure. ||8|| God's temple is God's shop; which is adorned by guru's teaching. The merchandise of God's name is in it; the guru-willed lovingly purchase it. ||9|| The mind inside God's temple is like dirty iron; it is enticed by duality. Touching the philosopher's stone the iron becomes priceless gold. ||10|| God abides in the temple of God. He is pervading all. O Nanak, the guru-willed deals in the merchandise of truth. ||11||1|| Parbhaatee, Third Master: Those who remain awake in God's love eliminate the filth of ego. They remain awake forever, and protect their homes and drive away the five thieves. ||1|| O my mind the guru-willed; recite God's name. O mind, do the deeds, which lead to the path to realize God. ||1||Pause|| The divine tune wells up O guru-willed; it eliminates the pain of ego. God abides in the mind by reciting God's name and one sings God's praises intuitively. ||2|| Those who follow guru's teachings are happy; they enshrine God in the mind. Here and hereafter, they find absolute peace; they attain salvation enshrining God in the mind. ||3|| Page 1347 In ego, one cannot remain awake, and God's worship is not accepted. The self-willed find no place in God's court; they do deeds in love of duality. ||4|| Cursed are the food and clothes of those who are in love with duality. The worms of filth love the filth; they die to be reborn and are ruined. ||5|| I admire those who meet the true guru. I shall join their company and merge in true Lord. ||6|| By perfect destiny, the guru is found. He cannot be found by any other efforts. Contentment wells up through the true guru. Guru's teaching burns away the ego. ||7|| O my mind, hurry to the sanctuary of the Lord; He is capable to do everything. O Nanak, never forget God's name. Whatever He does, happens. ||8||2||7||2||9|| Bibhaas, Parbhaatee, Fifth Master, Ashtapadees: God is one. He is realized by guru's grace. Mother, father, siblings, children and spouse Involved with them, people eat the food and enjoy. The mind is entangled in sweet emotional attachment. Those who seek God's virtues are the support of my life. ||1|| My one Lord is the Inner-Knower. He alone is my support and protection. My great Lord is the master of all. ||1||Pause|| I have broken my ties to that deceitful serpent. The guru has told me that it is false and fraudulent. It looks sweet, but it tastes bitter when you eat. My mind is satisfied with God's sacred name. ||2|| I do not like greed and emotional attachment. The kind guru has rescued me from them. These cheats have cheated many homes. The kind guru has saved me. ||3|| I have no dealings with lust and anger. I listen to guru's teachings. Wherever I look, I see the wicked ones. My guru, the Lord of the world, has saved me from them. ||4|| I have divorced the ten senses. Guru has told me that these pleasures are the cause of corruption. Those who associate with them go to hell. The guru has saved me. I am lovingly attuned to the Lord. ||5|| I have given up listening to my ego. The guru has told me that it is ignorant and stubborn. This ego is homeless; it shall never find a home. The guru has saved me; I am lovingly attuned to the Lord. ||6|| I have become enemy of these people. We both cannot live together in one home. Holding the hem of guru's robe, I have come to God. Please be fair with me O all-knowing Lord. ||7|| God smiled and said that he has passed the judgment. He made all the demons perform service for me. You are my master; this home belongs to You. Says Nanak, the guru did the justice. ||8||1|| Parbhaatee, Fifth Master: Page 1348 He is filled with anger and ego. He performs worship service with great pomp and ceremony. He takes bath and applies sacred marks on the body. This way the inner filth does not depart. ||1|| No one has ever found God this way. He looks like a devotee but is enticed by worldly wealth. ||1||Pause|| They commit sins, under the influence of the five thieves. They bathe at sacred shrines, and claim that everything is washed off. They commit sins again without any fear. The sinners are arrested and taken to the city of death. ||2|| They put ankle-bells on the ankles and dance with it. They are corrupt inside and wander insane like demons. By destroying its hole, the snake is not killed. God, who created you, knows everything. ||3|| You worship fire and wear saffron coloured robes. Stung by misfortune, you abandon your home. Leaving your own country, you wander in foreign lands. But you bring the five wicked thieves with you. ||4|| You make holes in your ears, and steal crumbs. You beg from door to door, but you fail to be satisfied. You have abandoned your wife, now you eye other women. God is not found by wearing religious robes; you are utterly miserable! ||5|| He does not speak; he became quiet. But he is filled with desire; he wanders in reincarnation. Abstaining from food, his body suffers in pain. He does not realize God's command; he is bothered by false attachment. ||6|| Without the true guru, no one has attained divinity. Go ahead and ask all the Vedas and the Simritees. The self-willed do useless deeds. They are like a house of sand, which cannot stand. ||7|| Whoever God is kind to. They carry guru's teaching in the lap. There are only a few saints among millions. O Nanak, with him, we are carried across. ||8|| If one has such good destiny, then he visualizes God. He saves himself, and carries across his family as well. ||1||second pause ||2|| Parbhaatee, Fifth Master: Reciting God, all sins are erased. The accounts held by the justice of destiny are torn up. Joining the company of devotees, obtains the taste of reciting God. God enshrines in my mind. ||1|| I find peace saying God God. Your slaves seek the sanctuary of Your feet. ||1||Pause|| The cycle of reincarnation is ended, and darkness is dispelled. The guru has revealed the door to liberation. My mind and body are forever imbued with loving devotion to the Lord. I realize God when He inspires me to realize. ||2|| He dwells in each and every heart. Without Him, there is no one at all. Enmity, conflict, fear and doubt have been eliminated. God, the soul of pure goodness did the good deed. ||3|| He has rescued me from the most dangerous waves. Separated from Him for countless lifes, I am united with Him again. Reciting God's name obtains all rewards of meditation, penance and self-discipline. My Lord has blessed me with His grace. ||4|| Bliss, peace and salvation are found there. Page 1349 Where the servants of the Lord of the world abide; God, the Lord of the world, is pleased and satisfied with me. My birth from many ghosts like life is erased. ||5|| He offers burnt feasts, does intense meditations and worship services He takes millions of cleansing baths at sacred shrines. Enshrine God's lotus feet in the mind for a moment; Recite the Lord of the universe and all deeds will be fulfilled. ||6|| God's place is the highest of all. Lord's humble servants intuitively focus their mind on Him. I long for the dust of the slaves of Lord's slaves. My beloved God has all powers. ||7|| My beloved Lord is my mother and father;

He is always near me. O my friend and companion, You are my trusted support. God takes His slaves by the hand, and makes them His own. Nanak lives by singing Your praises O Lord; ||8||3||2||7||12|| Bibhaas, Parbhaatee, The Word Of Devotee Kabeer Jee: God is one. He is realized by guru's grace. My doubt of death and rebirth has run away. I am in peace through God's love. ||1|| Divine light has dawned, and darkness has been dispelled. I have found the jewel the God by contemplating. ||1||Pause|| Pain runs far away from that place where there is happiness. The jewel is hidden in the mind and is found by lovingly attuning to God. ||2|| Whatever happens, happens by Your will. Whoever understands this, merges in peace. ||3|| Says Kabeer, my sins have been eliminated. My mind has merged in the Lord the life of the world. ||4||1|| Parbhaatee: If God lives only in the mosque, then whom does the rest of the world belong? According to the Hindus, God lives in the idols, but there is no truth in either of these claims. ||1|| O Allah, O Raam, I live by Your name; Please be kind to me, O master. ||1||Pause|| God of the Hindus lives in the south and God of the Muslims lives in the west. Search your soul; that is where God lives; ||2|| The Brahmins observe twenty-four fasts during the year, and the Muslims fast for a month during the month of Ramadaan. They set eleven months aside, and claim that priceless treasure is obtained in one month. ||3|| What is the use of bathing at Orissa? Why do the Muslims bow their heads in the mosque? If he is corrupt in the mind and recites Namaaz. What is the use of going to Hajj at Mecca? ||4|| You created all men and women. All are Your form. Kabeer is the child of God, Allah, Raam. All gurus and divine people are mine. ||5|| Says Kabeer, listen, O men and women: seek God's refuge. Recite God's name O mortal and you shall obtain salvation. ||6||2|| Parbhaatee: First, Allah created the light, then all beings. They all belong to Him. From one light, the entire universe welled up. So who is good and who is bad? ||1|| Page 1350 O people, O brothers; do not be deluded by doubt. God is in beings and beings are in God; God abides everywhere. ||1||Pause|| The clay is the same, but the maker has made it in various ways. There is nothing wrong with the pot and the potter. ||2|| One true Lord abides in all. Everything happens by His will. Whoever realizes His command, realizes God.

He is the real man. ||3|| God is unseen; He cannot be seen. The guru gave me the sweet jagry. Says Kabeer, doubt is gone and I have realized the formless God of all. ||4||3|| Parbhaatee: Do not say that the Vedas, the Bible and the Quran are false. Those who do not contemplate them are false. You say that one God is in all, so why do you kill chickens? ||1|| O Mullah, tell me: is this God's justice? The doubts of your mind have not been dispelled. ||1||Pause|| You catch the living, bring it home and kill its body; you have killed only the clay. The soul has gone into immortal state. Tell me, what sacred killing You did? ||2|| What is the purification by washing the face and bowing down in the mosque? Your heart is corrupt and you say Namaaz; what good is to go Hajj to Kaabaa? ||3|| You are impure; you do not understand the pure Lord. You do not know His mystery. Says Kabeer, you have missed out on paradise; you are going to hell. ||4||4|| Parbhaatee: Hear my prayer O Lord; You are the king, the primal, all-pervading master. The mystics did not find your limit; then they sought Your refuge. ||1|| Take the lamp worship service of the formless Lord and worship the guru O brother; Standing at His door, Brahma studies the Vedas, but he cannot find the mystery. ||1||Pause|| Make oil the essence, God's name the wick and light the lamp and illuminate the body. Remain awake with the light of the Lord of the world and realize Him. ||2|| Then play the divine music with five instruments in God's refuge. Kabeer, Your slave, performs this worship O formless bestowal of salvation. ||3||5|| Parbhaatee, the word Of devotee Naam Dev Jee: God is one. He is realized by guru's grace. The mind alone knows the state of mind; what can I say to the all Knowing God. I recite the inner knower God; why should I be afraid? ||1|| My mind is pierced by the love of the Lord of the world. My God is pervading everywhere. ||1||Pause|| The mind is the shop, the mind is the town, and the mind is the shopkeeper. The mind hides in various forms, wandering all across the world. ||2|| This mind is imbued with guru's teaching, duality is changed into peace. Page 1351 He is the command and the commander. The carefree Lord looks at all alike. ||3|| The devotee who intently recites God; his sermon is eternal. Says Naam Dev; I have found the Lord, the life of the world, in my heart. ||4||1|| Parbhaatee: He existed from the beginning, for ages; no one can find

His limits. God is omnipresent, abides in all; this is how He is described? ||1|| When the Lord of the universe is realized the divine music plays. My Lord is the embodiment of happiness. ||1||Pause|| The beautiful fragrance of sandalwood emanates from the sandalwood tree; that fragrance gives peace. God, the primal source of everything; is like the sandalwood tree; He transforms the trees into fragrant of sandalwood. ||2|| You are philosopher's stone, and I am iron; I became gold touching You. You are kind, the gem and the jewel. Naam Dev is absorbed in true Lord. ||3||2|| Parbhaatee: The primal Lord has staged this play. God is hidden in each and every heart. ||1|| No one knows the Light the soul. Whatever I do, is known to You O Lord. ||1||Pause|| Just as the pitcher is made from clay; everything is made by the beloved divine Creator. ||2|| The actions become the fate of the soul. Whatever God does, does on his own. ||3|| Prays Naam Dev, whatever this soul wants, it obtains. He becomes immortal and goes to God's home. ||4||3|| Parbhaatee, the word of devotee Baynee Jee: God is one. He is realized by guru's grace. You rub your body with sandalwood oil, and place basil leaves on your forehead. But you carry a knife in your heart. You look like a cheat; pretending to meditate, you pose like a crane. Seeing God's devotee you run away and die. ||1|| You pray for hours to God. But your look is evil, and your nights are wasted in conflict. ||1||Pause|| You perform daily cleansing rituals; You wear two loincloth, perform religious rituals and eat milk pudding. But in your heart, you have drawn out a sword. You routinely steal the property of others. ||2|| You worship the stone idol, and paint ceremonial marks of Ganesh. You remain awake throughout the night, pretending to worship God. You dance, but think evil in the mind. You eye other's women. Your dance is faithless. ||3|| You sit on a deerskin, and wear a sacred rosary. You put the sacred mark on your forehead. You wear the rosary beads of Shiva around your neck, but you are filled with falsehood. You are a wicked man; You do not recite God's name. ||4|| Those who do not contemplate the essence of the soul; their religious actions are hollow and false. Says Baynee; recite God O guru-willed. Without the true guru, you cannot find the way to God; ||5||1|| Page 1352

God is one. It is true. He is the Creator. He is carefree. He has no enemy. He is immortal. He does not take birth. He came into existence on His own. He is realized by guru's grace.

Tune Jaijaavantee, Ninth Master: Recite God, this will help you in the end. Give up worldly wealth and take shelter in God's refuge. Remember that the worldly pleasures are false; the whole show is false. ||1||Pause|| Know that the wealth is like a dream; then why are you proud of it? The empires of the earth are like walls of sand. ||1|| Servant Nanak speaks the truth that your body will perish. Moment by moment yesterday has passed. Today is passing as well. ||2||1|| Jaijaavantee, Ninth Master: Recite God; the life is slipping away. Why am I telling you again and again You ignorant? Why don't you understand? It does not take long to melt like hails. ||1||Pause|| So give up all doubts and recite the name of the Lord of the universe. Only this will go with you in the end. ||1|| Forget the poisonous sins of corruption, and enshrine God's praise in the mind; Servant Nanak proclaims that this opportunity is slipping away. ||2||2|| Jaijaavantee, Ninth Master: O mortal, what your condition will be? In this world, you have not listened to Lord's name. You are totally engrossed in corruption and sin; you have not changed your mind at all. ||1||Pause|| You are born as a human being; yet you do not recite God at all. For enjoyment, you are slave to your woman; you have chains tied to your feet. ||1|| Servant Nanak proclaims that the expanse of this world is just a dream. Why do not you recite God? Worldly wealth is His slave. 2||3|| Jaijaavantee, Ninth Master: Your life is uselessly slipping away. Night and day, you listen to the Puraanas; O ignorant you do not understand them; Death has arrived; now where will you run? ||1||Pause|| Page 1353 You believed that this body was permanent, but it shall turn to dust. Why don't you recite God's name o shameless ignorant? ||1|| Enshrine God's worship in the mind and eliminate the pride from the mind. Says Servant Nanak; this is the way to live in the world. ||2||4||

God is one. It is true. He is the Creator. He is carefree. He has no enemy. He is immortal. He does not take birth. He came into existence on His own. He is realized by guru's grace.

Hymn Sehskritee, First Master: You study the scriptures; you say prayers and contemplate; You worship idols and sit like a crane, pretending to meditate. You speak lies but talk sweet. You recite your daily prayers three times a day. You wear a rosary around your neck, and apply sacred mark is on your forehead. You wear two loincloths, and keep your head covered. Those who know the way to Godliness; Know that all these rituals are useless. Says Nanak, recite God intently; without the true guru, no one finds the way. ||1|| The mortal's life is fruitless, if he does not recite God. By guru's grace only, they cross over the world-ocean. The Creator, the cause of causes, is all-powerful. Says Nanak, after deliberations; the creation is under Creator's control; He created the creation. ||2|| Guru's teaching is yoga, divine wisdom and Vedas to Brahmin. Guru's teaching is bravery for the Khshatriya and is service to others to low caste. Guru's teaching is the essence of all, if anyone knows the mystery. Nanak is the slave of the formless God; ||3|| God is the Lord of all gods. The soul is God. God is the inner knower if anyone knows it. Nanak is the slave of the formless God; ||4|| Hymn Sehskritee, Fifth Master:

God is one. It is true. He is the Creator. He is carefree. He has no enemy. He is immortal. He does not take birth. He came in to existence on His own. He is realized by guru's grace.

Where is the mother, father the son and where is spouse's intuitive love. Where are the brother friend companion and relative; what is family attachment? Who is restlessly attached to beauty? It disappears in front of your eyes. Only God remains with you O Nanak, long for the sacred name in your mind; ||1|| Page 1354 Cursed is love of parents, friends and relatives. Cursed is the love and enjoyment of spouse and children. Cursed is attachment to household affairs. Only loving attachment to the company of devotee's gives peace O Nanak, ||2|| The body is false; its strength decreases and ends. It grows old but the attachment to worldly wealth increases. Too much desire and the home are not forever. The justice of destiny counts your breath. Attachment to the hard to obtain body takes it into the dark deep ditch. God is the only support at that time; this is true O Nanak. O God, Lord of the universe and the world, please be kind; ||3|| This fragile body-fortress is made up of water, plastered with blood and wrapped in skin. It lives in a fort, which has nine gates, where it can walk down the steps to the bottom for water and it has no pillars. The ignorant does not recite the name of the Lord of the universe. He thinks that he is immortal. This precious body is saved in the sanctuary of devotees O Nanak, by saying God God God. ||4|| O adorable, sacred, virtuous, perfect, powerful and kind Lord! Profound and unfathomable, lofty and exalted, all-knowing and infinite Lord; O love of Your devotees, Your feet are the sanctuary of peace. O master of the master less, Nanak seeks Your refuge. ||5|| Seeing the deer, the hunter aims his weapons. But if the Lord of the world, O Nanak, protects one no one can harm him. ||6|| He may be surrounded on all four sides by servants and powerful warriors. He may live in a lofty palace difficult to reach, and never thinks of death. But when the Order comes from the primal Lord O Nanak, even an ant can take away his life. ||7|| He is imbued and attuned to guru's teaching and is kind; he sings God's praises in today's age. In this way, one's inner doubts and emotional attachments are dispelled. God is pervading and permeating all places. Enshrining and reciting His name with the tongue visualize sacred God. O Nanak, recite the beloved God by saying God God God. ||8|| Beauty, sight, sun, moon and the stars in the sky will fade way. Earth, mountains and forests will fade away. One's spouse, children, siblings and loved friends will fade away. Gold and jewels and the worldly wealth will fade away. Only the eternal, unchanging Lord does not fade away. O Nanak, the humble saints are stable forever. ||9|| Do not delay in practicing faith but delay in committing sins. Recite God's name and give up greed. In saint's refuge the sins depart and faith wells up. O Nanak, with whom the Lord is pleased and satisfied. ||10|| The ignorant is dying in emotional attachment; he is engrossed in pursuits of pleasure with his wife. Youth beauty and golden earrings. Wonderful mansions, beautiful clothes; this is how he is troubled by worldly wealth. O sacred Lord; Nanak humbly bows to You in saint's refuge; ||11|| If there is birth, there is death. If there is pleasure, there is pain. If there is enjoyment, then there is disease. If there is high, there is low. If there is small, there is large. Page 1355 If there is power, there is pride. If there is pride, there will be a fall. Engrossed in worldly ways, one is ruined.

Recite God in devotee's company O Nanak, worshipping God makes immortal. ||12|| By the grace of God, one obtains divine wisdom. The intellect blossoms and one becomes peaceful. The senses are brought under control, and pride is abandoned. The heart is soothed by reciting God and obtains divine wisdom O saints. God is visualized and taking birth ends. O Nanak, the divine music plays with musical instruments. ||13|| The Vedas preach and recount God's Glories; people hear them in various ways. The kind Lord implants spiritual wisdom inside. Nanak begs for the gift of God's name; guru the Lord of the world bestows it. ||14|| Do not worry about your mother, father and siblings. Do not worry what the others say. Do not worry about spouse, children and friends. God created the worldly wealth. One God is Kind O Nanak. He is the cherisher and nurturer of all beings. ||15|| Wealth is temporary; conscious is temporary; hopes of all sorts are temporary. Emotional attachment, ego, doubt and worldly wealth are all useless. He goes through the womb for birth again and again but the ignorant does not recite God. O Lord of the universe; be kind that sinner Nanak obtains salvation in devotee's company. ||16|| You may fall from the mountain into the underworld and burn in the fire; You are swept away in the high waves of water; the pain and worry of household is the cause of birth and death. Many other efforts do not help O Nanak. The words of God's devotees are the pillars of life. ||17|| Serious pain, countless deaths and births, poverty and terrible deeds; All are destroyed by reciting God's name O Nanak, as fire destroys the wood. ||18|| Reciting God the darkness is illuminated. Singing God's praises destroys the sins. Enshrining God in the heart and doing good deeds scares the enemies. Successfully visualizing God, birth and death are eliminated and peace obtains. O Nanak, God gives refuge to the beloved saints and blesses them. ||19|| Those who were left behind by despair; the Lord brings them to the front and fulfills their desire. He makes the poor rich, and cures the illnesses of the ill. He blesses His devotees with devotion to recite His name and praise Him. O Nanak, those who serve the guru find the supreme Lord the great giver ||20|| He gives support to the unsupported. Name of God is the wealth of the poor. Lord of the universe is the master of orphans; the beautiful-haired Lord is the power of the weak. God is kind to all; He is sacred and unchanging; He is the friend of the poor. The all-knowing, perfect, primal Lord the love of His devotees is kind. Page 1356 The supreme Lord, the transcendent, luminous Lord, dwells in each and every heart. Nanak begs for this blessing from the merciful Lord, that he may never forget Him; ||21|| I have no power; I do not serve You, I do not love You, O supreme Lord. By Your grace, Nanak recites the kind God the guru. ||22|| God feeds and sustains all living beings; He blesses them with gifts of peace and fine clothes. He created the jewel of human life, with all its intelligent ideas. By His grace, mortals abide in peace and joy. O Nanak, say God God God. The mortal is freed from the attachment of the world. ||23|| The kings are enjoying the blessings of good deeds of their past life. Those cruel minded who kill people O Nanak, shall suffer in pain for a long time. ||24|| Even their reciting God the Lord of the universe goes waste. The healthy become sick, those who do not recite God, by God's grace. ||25|| To sing God's praises is a good deed in this human body. O Nanak, drinking the nectar of God's name never fulfills the saints. ||26|| The saints are tolerant and good-natured. Friends and enemies are the same to them. O Nanak, all kind of food is same to them; slander or even someone draws a sword to kill them is also same. ||27|| They pay no attention to dishonour or disrespect. They are not bothered by gossip; the miseries of the world do not touch them. Those who recite God's name in devotees company O Nanak, they live in peace. ||28|| Army of devotees the invincible warriors are protected by the Humility armour. Their weapons are the praises of God; guru's teaching is their shield. Their way to find God's path is their riding horses, chariots and elephants. They fearlessly walk through the armies of their enemies singing God's praises. They conquer the entire world, O Nanak, and control the five thieves. ||29|| The mirage of the abode of celestial singers is temporary like the shade of a tree. Emotional attachment to family is false, so recite God O Nanak. ||30|| I do not possess the treasure of the wisdom of Vedas, nor do I possess the merits of the praises of God's name. I do not have a beautiful voice to sing jewelled melodies; I am not clever, wise or shrewd. By destiny and hard work, the worldly wealth is obtained. O Nanak. The ignorant becomes a scholar in devotee's company. ||31|| Recite God with the rosary of the mind. God's love is the highest reward. O beloved saint; those who say sacred hymns obtain salvation and joy. ||32|| That mortal who is without guru's teaching; useless and cursed is his life. He is like a dog, pig, donkey, crow and a snake; ||33|| Whoever worships God's lotus feet, and enshrines His name in the heart; Page 1357 Sing God's praises in devotees company O Nanak, you will not face the devil of death. ||34|| Wealth beauty heaven and kingdom are not difficult to obtain. Foods delicacies and fine clothes are not difficult to obtain. Children, friends, siblings and relatives are not difficult to obtain. The pleasures of woman are not difficult to obtain. Knowledge wisdom cleverness and tricks are not difficult to obtain. Only difficult to obtain is God's name O Nanak. It is obtained by God's grace, in devotee's company. ||35|| Wherever I look, I see God, whether this world, paradise, death land or the underworld. The Lord of the universe is omnipresent; O Nanak, no blame or stain sticks to Him. ||36|| Poison is transformed into nectar, and enemies into friends and companions. Pain is changed into pleasure, and the fearful become fearless. Those who have no place to rest, find peace reciting kind God's the guru's name O Nanak. ||37|| They are most peaceful among peaceful and sacred among sacred. The Creator does everything O Nanak, no blame or stain sticks to Him. ||38|| The moon is not so cool nor is the white sandalwood tree. The winter season is not cool; O Nanak, only God's devotees are cool. ||39|| Saying God God intently is the essence of all. Those who have divine wisdom see pain and pleasure the same; they are pure and enemyless. They are kind to all beings; they have overpowered the five thieves. They take singing God's praise as their food; they remain untouched by worldly wealth like the lotus in water. They teach friends and foes alike, the worship of God with love. They do not listen to slander, renouncing ego, they become the dust of all. Whoever has these six qualities, O Nanak, is called God's devotee a friend. ||40|| The goat enjoys eating fruits and roots, but if it lives near a tiger, it is scared. This is the condition of the world, O Nanak; it is afflicted by pleasure and pain. ||41|| It is filled with fraud, accusations, millions of diseases, sins and filth of evil; Doubt, emotional attachment, pride, dishonour and intoxication of worldly wealth bother all. They wander in birth and death cycle and hell; they cannot attain salvation by any means. O Nanak, reciting the name of the Lord of the world in devotee's company is purifying. They continuously sing the praises of the Lord of the universe all the time. ||42|| Reciting the name of the transcendent Lord in His refuge bestows salvation. God is all-powerful cause of causes. Perfect God gives the perfect gifts. He gives hope to the hopeless. He is the source of all riches. O Nanak, singing the praise of God obtains the priceless treasure, all beg for it. ||43|| The most difficult place becomes easy, and the worst pain turns into pleasure. Evil words, differences and doubts are destroyed and faithless become good people. They become stable, whether happy or sad; their fear departs and they become fearless. Page 1358 The forest becomes a big city; such are the merits of faith by God's grace. Say God God in devotee's company O Nanak, in the refuge of the lotus feet of the merciful Lord. ||44|| O invincible brave warrior; You destroy the most powerful armies. You entice heavenly heralds, celestial singers, gods, mortals, beasts and birds. Nanak bows humbly to God, who does everything. He seeks the refuge of the Lord of the world. ||45|| O lust, you lead the mortals to hell and they wander in many different lifes. You cheat the mind of everyone in the universe; You destroy meditation, penance and virtue. You give a little bit of pleasure; make people unstable; you pervade the high and low. Your fear is dispelled in devotee's company in God's refuge O Nanak, ||46|| O anger, you are the root of conflict; sympathy never wells up in you. You take the corrupt, sinful beings in your power, and make them dance like monkeys. Associating with you, mortals are punished by the devil of death in many ways. O destroyer of pain of the poor, kind Lord; Nanak prays for You to protect all beings from anger. ||47|| O greed, you cling to even the great ones, assaulting them with countless waves. You cause them to run around in many ways; make them waver in many ways. You have no respect for friends, ideals, relations, mother or father. You make them do what they should not do. You make them eat what they should not eat. You make them do what they should not do. I have come to Your refuge O my Lord; save Nanak through divine wisdom O Lord of humans. ||48|| O ego; you are the root of birth death arrogance and sin. You forsake friends, and hold tight to enemies. You spread worldly wealth many ways. They get tired of coming and going and suffer many pains and pleasures. You lead them to wander lost in the terrible wilderness; you lead them to contract the most horrible, incurable diseases. The only doctor is the supreme Lord, the transcendent Lord. Nanak recites God. ||49|| O Lord of the universe, master of life, treasure of mercy, guru of the world; O destroyer of fever of the world, king Lord, please take away all my pain. O merciful Lord, potent to give sanctuary, master of the meek, please be kind to me. Whether his body is healthy or sick; Nanak recites Your name O Lord. ||50|| I have come to the refuge of God's lotus feet and I sing His praises. The terrifying world ocean is crossed over in devotee's company O Nanak. ||51|| The supreme Lord protects my head and forehead; the transcendent Lord protects my hands and body. God, my Lord saves my soul; the Lord of the universe saves my wealth at His feet. The kind guru protects me from everything, and destroys my fear and suffering. God the love of His devotees, the Master of orphans; Nanak has entered the sanctuary of the imperishable primal Lord. ||52|| His power supports the sky, and locks fire in the wood. His power supports the moon, the sun and the stars, and infuses soul and life in the body. Page 1359 His power provides nourishment in mother's womb and saves from terrible diseases. His power holds the ocean O Nanak, the waves cannot destroy it. ||53|| Lord of the world is supreme and beautiful; reciting Him is the life of all. In the society of saints, O Nanak, the path of God's worship is found. ||54|| The mosquito pierces the stone; the ant crosses the mud; The cripple crosses the ocean, and the blind sees in the darkness; O Nanak, recite God the Lord of the universe in devotee's company. ||55|| Like a Brahmin without a sacred mark on his forehead, or a king without the power of command; A warrior without weapons, so is God's devotee without faith. ||56|| God has no conch-shell, no religious mark, no wooden heavy weapon and no blue skin. His form is amazing. He is beyond birth. The Vedas say that He has no limit. The Lord of the universe is the highest, greatest and infinite. The immortal God abides in devotee's mind. The pure fortunate find Him O Nanak, ||57|| The world lives in the jungle of relatives like dogs, jackals and donkeys. Intoxication of false attachment is difficult; the five unconquered thieves lurk there. The mortals wander lost in love and emotional attachment, the net of ego is sharp and difficult. The ocean of fire is terrifying and impassable. You cannot cross over to the other side. O Nanak, recite the Lord of the world in devotee's company; salvation obtains in God's refuge by His grace. When the Lord of the universe grants His grace, all illnesses are cured. O Nanak, sing God's praises in devotee's company in the refuge of the perfect transcendent Lord. ||59|| The mortal is beautiful and speaks sweet words, but harbours enmity in the heart. He pretends to bow in worship, but he is false. Beware of him, O friendly saints. ||60|| The thoughtless ignorant does not know that his life decreases every day. His beautiful body is wearing away; the maid of death will engulf him. He is engrossed in family play; placing his hopes in useless pleasures. He is tired of wandering in countless lifes. Nanak seeks the refuge of the kind Lord. ||61|| O tongue, you love to enjoy the sweet delicacies. You kill the true, and love the enemy; this is your true character. O God the Lord of the world and the universe; ||62|| Those who are proud, and intoxicated with the pleasures of sex; Assert their power over others; they do not worship God's lotus feet; their life is worthless like a straw. O ant; you destroy the elephant by reciting God the Lord of the universe. Nanak bows in humble worship, countless times, over and over again. ||63|| The blade of grass becomes a mountain, and the salty land becomes green. The drowning swims across, and the empty is filled to the brim. Millions of suns illuminate the darkness; prays Nanak, when the guru, the Lord, becomes kind. ||64|| Page 1360 He, who does Godly deeds obtains salvation in the company of a scholar. Those who are imbued with the worldly affairs O Nanak, their life is fruitless. ||65|| They steal from others, do evil deeds; everyone says that they do everything for themselves. They are driven by greed and worldly wealth and they act like pigs. ||66|| Those intoxicated by God's lotus feet, are carried across the terrifying world ocean. Many sins are destroyed and doubts erased in devotee's company O Nanak, ||67||4|| Fifth Master, Gaathaa (God's praise): God is one. He is realized by guru's grace. Camphor, flowers and perfume become contaminated, by touching the filthy body. O Nanak, the ignorant is proud of his foul-smelling marrow, blood and bones. ||1|| Even if the mortal could become as small as an atom, and shoot through the sky, continents and other realms like an arrow O Nanak, the enticing eyes cannot save it without the company of devotees. ||2|| Know for sure that death will come; whatever is seen is false. Singing God's praises in devotee's company goes with you O Nanak. ||3|| The worldly wealth entices the mind of guru brothers, friends and relatives. Reciting the Lord of the world in devotee's company finds peaceful place O Nanak. ||4|| The lowly Neem tree, growing near the sandalwood tree, and becomes like the sandalwood tree. The bamboo tree, growing near it, does not pick up its fragrance; it is too proud. ||5|| Listening and singing God's praises in devotee's company, destroys the pride. The five enemies are killed, O Nanak, by shooting an arrow by the Lord. ||6|| Words of devotee's are the path of peace. They are obtained by good deeds. Singing God's praises eliminates the birth and death O Nanak. ||7|| When the leaves wither and fall, they cannot be attached to the branch again. Without God's name O Nanak, gives pain that lasts through the whole life day and night. ||8|| The fortunate find the love of devotee's company. The world ocean does, not trouble whoever sings the praises of God's name O Nanak. ||9|| Only a few realize the true praises of the profound and infinite God; They forsake worldly pleasures and recite God in devotee's company O Nanak, ||10|| Devotee's sacred words eliminate millions of sins. Reciting God's lotus feet bestows salvation to the whole family O Nanak. ||11|| That temple is beautiful and friendly, where God's praises are sung. Reciting God obtains salvation O Nanak. The fortunate obtain it. ||12|| I have found the Lord, my best friend. He will never break my heart. Who has the eternal Lord as a friend? Nanak has made Him the friend of his soul. ||13|| One's bad reputation is erased by a true son; by reciting guru's teaching in the mind; Page 1361 The beloved Lord is untouched and pure. O Nanak, He carries us across the world-ocean. ||14|| Reciting the Lord of the universe one forgets the fear of death. They live by reciting God's name. God is found in the company of devotees. O Nanak, by pre-ordained destiny written by God. ||15|| The snake charmer, by his charm, neutralizes the poison and leaves the snake without fangs.

Same way, the saints remove suffering; O Nanak, they are found by good luck. ||16|| God is all pervading; He gives sanctuary to all living beings. The mind is touched by His love, O Nanak, Visualizing Him by guru's grace; ||17|| My mind is pierced through by Lord's lotus feet. I am blessed with total happiness. Nanak sings His praises due to pre-ordained destiny on the forehead. ||18|| Singing His praises in devotee's company obtains salvation. They never take birth in the world again. ||19|| People contemplate the Vedas, Puraanas and Shaastras. They enshrine God's name in the mind. Everyone in their family obtains salvation. The fortunate Nanak obtains salvation. ||20|| Reciting the name of the Lord of the universe the whole family obtains salvation. O Nanak, in devotee's company the fortunate realizes God. ||21|| Abandon all your evil habits, and practice faith. Those with pre-ordained destiny find devotee's company O Nanak. ||22|| God was, is, and shall always be. He creates and destroys all. Know that the devotees are true due to love O Nanak, ||23|| The mortal is engrossed in sweet words and temporary pleasures which shall fade away. They are troubled by sickness sorrow and separation. They do not find peace even in a dream. ||24|| Tune Phunhay, Fifth Master: God is one. He is realized by guru's grace. With pen in Hand, the inaccessible Lord writes the mortal's destiny on his forehead. He the beautiful Lord is involved with everyone. I cannot describe Your praise from my mouth. Nanak is fascinated by visualizing You and admires You. ||1|| Sitting in the society of saints, I sing Your praises. I offer all my ornaments and my soul as well. With hope and yearning for Him, I have made the bed for my husband. O Lord; with a good fortune written on the forehead, one finds the beloved. ||2|| O my companion, I have prepared everything: make up, garlands and betel-leaves. I decorated myself with the sixteen decorations, and applied the mascara to my eyes. If my Husband Lord comes home, then I obtain everything. O Lord! Without my husband, all these adornments are useless. ||3|| Very fortunate is she, in whose home the Husband Lord abides. She is totally adorned and decorated; she is a happy soul-bride. I sleep worry free; the hopes of my mind have been fulfilled. O Lord! When my husband came into my home, I obtained everything. ||4|| Page 1362 I hope that all my hopes will be fulfilled.

When the true guru becomes kind, then I realize the perfect Lord. My body has many faults; I am covered with faults and demerits. O Lord! When the true guru becomes kind, then the mind stabilizes. ||5|| Says Nanak, I recite infinitely the infinite Lord. This world-ocean is difficult to cross; the true guru has carried me across. My coming and going in life ended, when I met the perfect Lord. O Lord! I have obtained the nectar of God's name from the true guru. ||6|| The lotus is in my hand; peace dwells in my yard. O my companion, the jewel is around my neck; seeing it, the pain ran away. I live with the Lord of the world, and obtain all of His happiness. O Lord; wealth, mystic power and the nine treasures are in His Hand. ||7|| Those men who go out to enjoy other men's women shall be ashamed. Those who steal the wealth of others; how can their guilt be hidden? Singing God's praises, one becomes sacred and the whole dynasty is liberated. O Lord! Those who listen to God's sermon become sacred. ||8|| The sky above looks lovely, and the earth below is beautiful. Lightning flashes in the ten directions; which entices me. I keep searching for my beloved in foreign lands; how will I find him? O Lord! If it is in my fate. I will visualize him. ||9|| I have seen all places, but none can be compared with You. O Lord of destiny; if you say then I will adorn you. Ramdaspur is prosperous, well populated, and beautiful. O Lord! Bathing in Raam Daas's pool of knowledge, the sins are washed away, O Nanak. ||10|| The rain bird thinks in its mind. It longs for the beloved one. It longs for that, on which its life depends. It wanders depressed, from forest to forest, for the sake of a drop of water. O Lord! Same way, God's devotee begs for God's name; Nanak admires him. ||11|| The mind of the beloved is beyond comprehension; its mystery cannot be found. If the merchant is full of virtues, then he will know the reality. When the mind merges with mind then it is dyed with deep love. O Lord! When the fickle thieves are killed, the true wealth is obtained. ||12|| I was standing in a dream; why didn't I cover myself? Seeing the handsome sitting with ease, my mind is fascinated. I am searching for His path – tell me, where can I find Him? O Lord! Tell me how I can find my beloved, O my companion. ||13|| The eyes which do not see the devotee, those eyes are miserable. The ears, that do not hear his, sound; plug those ears; the tongue that does not recite God's name; May it be cut in pieces. O Lord! When one forgets the king the Lord of the universe, grows old day by day. ||14|| The wings of the bumblebee are caught in the intoxicating fragrant petals of the lotus. With its limbs entangled in the petals, it loses its senses. Page 1363 Is there any such friend, who can untie this difficult knot? O Nanak, one supreme Lord of the earth reunites the separated. ||15|| I run around in all directions, searching for the love of God. The five evil enemies are tormenting me; how can I destroy them? Shoot them with the sharp arrows of reciting the name of God. O Lord! The way to kill these terrible enemies is obtained from the perfect guru. ||16|| True guru has blessed me with the gift which shall never be exhausted. Eating and consuming it, all guru-willed are emancipated. God blessed me with the treasure of sacred name. O Nanak, recite it forever, you will never die. ||17|| Wherever God's devotee goes is a beautiful place. All comforts are obtained, reciting Lord's name. People praise them but the slanderers are stuck and die. Says Nanak, O friend, reciting God's name you shall be happy. ||18|| The mortal never serves the immaculate Lord, the purifier of sinners. The mortal wastes away his life in false pleasures. How long can this go on? Why do you take such pleasure, looking at this mirage? O Lord! I admire those who are honoured in God's court. ||19|| The ignorant does many ignorant deeds; Ignorant body smells rotten, and turns to dust. He wanders lost in the darkness of pride, and never thinks of dieing. O Lord! Why do you believe that seeing the mirage is true? ||20|| When someone's time comes; who can save him? How long can the doctor go on, suggesting various therapies? You ignorant, remember one God; it will help you. O Lord! Without God's name the body will become dust and destroyed. ||21|| Drink the medicine of the incomparable, priceless name. The saints get together and eat and give it to everyone. He, who is blessed, receives it. O Lord! I admire those who enjoy God's love. ||22|| The doctors get together and discus the cure. The medicines are effective, when God stands in their middle. The deeds they do become their destiny. O Lord! Pains, diseases and sins all vanish from their bodies. ||23|| Chaubolas, Fifth Master: God is one. He is realized by guru's grace; if someone is hit by the love like Samman; there is no poor like Raawan, whose head was cut. ||1|| My body is drenched with love; there is no gap in between us. God's lotus feet pierce my mind. He is realized with love intuitively. ||2|| Page 1364 He wandered in oceans, mountains, forest and all over the world. Moosan was in love and that is all he did. ||3|| Moosan was lit by love which enlightened the sky. He was enticed by love like the bumblebee is caught in the lotus flower. ||4|| Meditation, penance, self-discipline, pleasure, pain, honour, respect and pride; Moosan had given up all for a little bit of love. ||5|| Moosan did not know the reality that the world is robbed by death. He who is not pierced by love is entangled in worldly deeds. ||6|| When someone's home and property are burnt he loves, then he suffers pain. Moosan could only be robbed if he forgot the primal kind Lord. ||7|| Whoever enjoys the taste of God's love, remembers His lotus feet in his mind. O Nanak, the lovers of God do not go anywhere else. ||8|| Climbing thousands of steep hills, the fickle mind becomes miserable. Look at the humble, lowly mud; the beautiful lotus grows in it. ||9|| My Lord has lotus-eyes adorned with mascara, beautiful body and happy face. His master intoxicated Moosan. He was torn into pieces. ||10|| He was intoxicated with love; he was not worried about his body. God is revealed in the whole world; O Nanak, the lowly moth burns in flame. ||11|| Hymns Of Devotee Kabeer Jee: God is one. He is realized by guru's grace. Kabeer; my rosary is my tongue, which recites God. From the beginning, throughout the ages, God's devotees live in peace. ||1|| Kabeer; everyone laughs at my caste. I admire this caste that recites the Creator. ||2|| Kabeer, why do you waver? Why does your soul waver? God is the master of all peace; drink the sublime essence of God's name. ||3|| Kabeer, earrings made of gold and studded with jewels. Their ears look like burnt twigs, if God's name is not in the mind. ||4|| Kabeer, rare is such a person, who remains dead while yet alive. Care freely sings God's praises; he sees God wherever he looks. ||5|| Kabeer, the day I died; joy prevailed behind me. I realized my God and the companions recite God. ||6|| Kabeer; I am the worst of all. Everyone else is good. Whoever thinks that way is a friend of mine. ||7|| Kabeer; it came to me in various forms and disguises. My guru saved me, and guided them as well. ||8|| Kabeer; kill only that, which shall bring peace when killed; everyone calls you good; no one thinks that you are bad. ||9|| Kabeer; the night is dark, and men go about doing their dark deeds. Page 1365 They take the noose and go around, but God already killed them. ||10|| Kabeer; the sandalwood tree is said to be good, though it is surrounded by weeds. Those who dwell near the sandalwood tree, become like the sandalwood tree. ||11|| Kabeer; the bamboo is drowned in its pride. No one should drown like this. Bamboo also dwells near the sandalwood tree, but it does not take up its fragrance. ||12|| Kabeer; the mortal loses his conduct for the sake of the world; the world does not go with him in the end. The ignorant hit his foot with an axe. ||13|| Kabeer; wherever I go, I see strange things everywhere. But without the devotees of the Lord, they seem wandering in the wild to me. ||14|| Kabeer; the huts of saints are good. May the characterless village burn down; the mansion, where Gods name is not recited; may it burn down. ||15|| Kabeer; why cry at the death of a saint? He is going back to his home. Cry for the faithless that is sold from store to store. ||16|| Kabeer; the faithless is like a piece of garlic. Even if you eat it sitting in a corner, it becomes obvious to everyone. ||17|| Kabeer; worldly wealth moves around, mixed by wind. The saints eat the butter, while the world drinks the buttermilk. ||18|| Kabeer; the worldly wealth moves around with the speed of wind? Whoever churns eats the butter; there will be more to do so. ||19|| Kabeer; worldly wealth is a thief, which breaks in and robs the store. Only Kabeer is not robbed; he has cut her into twelve pieces. ||20|| Kabeer; peace does not come in this world by making lots of friends. Those who keep their mind focused on one God find eternal peace. ||21|| Kabeer; the world is afraid of death; I like it. The complete happiness is obtained only after death. ||22|| Once you obtain divine treasure, do not tell anyone O kabeer; There is no market, no appraiser, no customer, and no price. ||23|| Kabeer; be in love with that, whose master is God. What good are the scholars, kings and landlords? ||24|| Kabeer; when you are in love with the one, the other duality departs. You may have long hair, or you may shave your head bald. ||25|| Kabeer; the world is a room filled with black soot; the blind fall in it. I praise those who fall in it and escape. ||26|| Kabeer; this body shall perish; save it, if you can. Those who had millions went bare feet.

||27|| Kabeer; this body shall perish; what path you are on; either join the company of devotees, or sing the praises of God. ||28|| Kabeer; the whole world keeps dieing, but they do not know how to die. Page 1366 They should die such a death that they die no more. ||29|| Kabeer; it is difficult to obtain this human life; it does not happen again and again. It is like, when the fruit ripen and fall down it cannot be re-attached to the branch. ||30|| Kabeer; you are Kabeer; your name means great. God the jewel is obtained only after leaving the body. ||31|| Kabeer; do not talk nonsense; nothing happens by your doing. Whatever the kind Lord does, cannot be erased by anyone. ||32|| Kabeer; the false cannot pass the test of the Lord. He alone can pass God's test; who remains dead while yet alive. ||33|| Kabeer; some wear clean clothes, and chew betel leaves and betel nuts. Without God's name, they are arrested and taken to the city of death. ||34|| Kabeer; the boat is old, and it has thousands of holes. Those who are light, get across, those who carry the weight on their heads, drown. ||35|| Kabeer; the bones burn like wood and the hair burns like straw. Seeing the world burning like this, Kabeer has become sad. ||36|| Kabeer; do not be proud; you are bones wrapped in skin. Those who rode horses and sat under the canopies, were buried under the ground; ||37|| Kabeer; do not be proud of your high mansions. Today or tomorrow, you shall lie on the ground, and grass will grow above you. ||38|| Kabeer; do not be proud, and do not laugh at the poor. Your boat is still out at sea; who knows what will happen? ||39|| Kabeer; do not be proud, looking at your beautiful body. Today or tomorrow, you will have to leave it, like the snake shedding its skin. ||40|| Kabeer; if you must rob, then rob God's name; it is to be robbed. You will repent later, when the soul leaves the body. ||41|| Kabeer; there is no one born as such, who burns his own home; Burns his five sons and remains lovingly attuned to the Lord. ||42|| Kabeer; some sell sons, some sell daughters. Enter into partnership with Kabeer and deal with the Lord. ||43|| Kabeer; let me remind you this, let there be no doubt? The pleasures you enjoyed in the past; you must eat their fruits now; ||44|| Kabeer; at first, I thought learning was good; then I thought worship was better. I shall never abandon God's worship, even if people slander me. ||45|| Kabeer; how can people slander me?

They have no divine wisdom? Kabeer recites God. He gave up other deeds. ||46|| Kabeer; the skirt of the stranger caught fire from all directions. The cloth burned to ashes but the fire but did not touch the sacred thread. ||47|| Kabeer; the cloth burnt and reduced to ashes, and the begging bowl broken in pieces. The poor Yogi played his game; only ashes remain on his seat. ||48|| Page 1367 Kabeer; the fish is in the shallow water; the fisherman has cast his net. You will not escape from this pond; think about returning to the ocean. ||49|| Kabeer; do not leave the ocean, even if it is very salty. If you poke around searching from puddle to puddle, no one will call you smart. ||50|| Kabeer; those who have no guru are washed away. No one can help them. Be poor and humble; it happens what the Creator does. ||51|| Kabeer; even the dog of a devotee is good, while the mother of the faithless is bad. The dog hears the praises of Lord's name, while the other commits sins. ||52|| Kabeer; the deer is weak, and the pool is lush with green vegetation. Thousands of hunters are chasing after one soul; how long can it escape death? ||53|| Kabeer; some make their homes on the banks of Ganges, and drink pure water. Without God's worship, they are not liberated. Kabeer proclaims this. ||54|| Kabeer; my mind has become pure, like the water of Ganges. The Lord follows me around, calling, Kabeer! Kabeer! ||55|| Kabeer; tumeric is yellow, and lime is white. You shall meet the beloved Lord, only when both colours are lost. ||56|| Kabeer; tumeric has lost its yellow colour, and no trace of lime's whiteness remains. I admire this love that eliminates social class and status, colour and ancestry. ||57|| Kabeer; the door of liberation is very narrow, less than the width of a mustard seed. Your mind is larger than an elephant; how will it pass through? ||58|| Kabeer; if I meet such a true guru, who kindly blesses me with the gift; Then the door of liberation will be wide open, and I will easily pass through. ||59|| Kabeer; I have no hut or hovel, no house or village. I hope that God will ask who I am. I have no social status or name. ||60|| Kabeer; I want to die; may I die at Lord's door. I hope that the Lord does not ask, "Who is lying at my door?"||61|| Kabeer; I have not done anything; I shall not do anything; my body cannot do anything. I do not know what the Lord has done, but everyone says "Kabeer; Kabeer."||62|| Kabeer; if someone utters the name of the Lord in a dream; I would make my skin into shoes for his feet. ||63|| Kabeer; we are puppets of clay, but called the human being. We are guests here for a few days, but we occupy so much space. ||64|| Kabeer; I have made myself into henna, and I grind myself into powder. O my Husband Lord, You did not ask me; You never applied me to Your feet. ||65|| Kabeer; that door, through which people keep coming and going; there is no stopping. How can I leave such a door; where people keep going through? ||66|| Kabeer; I was drowning, but the waves of virtue saved me in an instant. Page 1368 When I saw that my boat was rotten, I immediately got out. ||67|| Kabeer; the sinner does not like God's worship; he does not appreciate worship. The fly forsakes sandalwood and goes where there is filth. Kabeer; the doctor is dead, and the patient is dead; the whole world is dead. Only Kabeer is not dead; there is no one to mourn for him. ||69|| Kabeer; I have not recited God; I developed such a habit. The body is a wooden pot; it cannot be put back on the fire second time. ||70|| Kabeer; it so happened that I did whatever I wanted. Why should I be afraid of death? I have the saving omen in my hand. ||71|| Kabeer; the mortals suck the sugar cane, for juice. They do not work for virtues. No one calls the sinner a good person. ||72|| Kabeer; the pitcher is full of water; it will break, today or tomorrow. Those who do not remember their guru shall be robbed on the way. ||73|| Kabeer; I am Lord's dog; Moti is my name. He has a chain around my neck; I go where he pulls me; ||74|| Kabeer; why do you show other people your rosary beads? You do not miss God in the mind; what use is the rosary? ||75|| Kabeer; the poison of separation from God abides in my mind; it does not respond to any cure. One who is separated from the Lord does not live; if he does, he goes insane. ||76|| Kabeer; the philosopher's stone and sandalwood have the same fragrance. Whatever touches them becomes sacred? Iron becomes gold, and wood becomes fragrant. ||77|| Kabeer; death's club is terrible; it cannot be endured. I have met with a devotee; he has attached me to him. ||78|| Kabeer; the doctor says that he is good; I have the medicine with me. But it belongs to God; He takes them away whenever He wishes. ||79|| Kabeer; take your drum and beat it for ten days. Life is like people meeting on a boat on a river; they shall not meet again.

||80|| Kabeer; if I could make the seven seas into ink and make all vegetation the pen; The earth the paper, even then, I cannot write the praises of God. ||81|| Kabeer; what can me the lowly weaver do? God lives in my mind. Kabeer and God embrace each other; and all entanglements ended. ||82|| Kabeer; is there anyone, who burns his house? Kills five sons and remains lovingly attached to God? ||83|| Kabeer; will anyone burn his body? The blind people do not know, although Kabeer continues to say loudly. ||84|| Kabeer; the woman to be burned alive cries; listen, O brother the cremator. All people have gone; it is only you and I."||85|| Page 1369 Kabeer; the mind has become a bird; it flies all over in ten directions. According to the company it keeps, so are the fruits it eats. ||86|| Kabeer; Who I was searching for; found Him at home; You have become the same, whom you were saying someone else. ||87|| Kabeer; I have been ruined by bad company; like the banana plant near the thorny bush. The banana swings and the bush cut the leaves. Do not accompany the faithless? ||88|| Kabeer; the mortal travels to destination carry other's load on the head. He is not afraid of his own load; the road ahead is difficult and treacherous. ||89|| Kabeer; the wood burning in the forest cries. "Do not fall in the hands of the blacksmith, he will burn you twice. ||90|| Kabeer; one died then two died. When two died, then four were dead. When four died, six were dead, four males and two females. ||91|| Kabeer; I have searched all over the world, but I did not find a place to rest. Those who do not miss God's name; why they wander lost further? ||92|| Kabeer; Keep devotee's company; it will help you in the end. Do not associate with the faithless; they will destroy you. ||93|| Kabeer; I miss God in the world; because God abides in the world. Those who do not recite God's name; why did they take birth? ||94|| Kabeer; place your hopes in the Lord; other hopes lead to despair. Those who do not recite God; they go to hell. ||95|| Kabeer made many friends and disciples, but he has not made God his friend. He set out to meet God, but his mind stopped in the middle. ||96|| Kabeer; what can the poor creature do, if the Lord does not help him? Whatever branch he steps on breaks and collapses. ||97|| Kabeer; those who preach others; sand falls in their mouths. They keep their eyes on other's property, while their own farm is being eaten up. ||98||

Kabeer; remain in the company of a devotee; eat his coarse and burnt food. Whatever happens, let it happen; do not accompany the faithless. ||99|| Kabeer; the love doubles daily in devotee's company. The faithless is like a black blanket, which does not become white by washing. ||100|| Kabeer; you have not shaved your mind, why do you shave your head? Whatever is done is done by the mind; it is useless to shave the head. ||101|| Kabeer; do not abandon God; if your body and wealth goes; so be it; My mind is pierced by God's lotus feet; I am absorbed in the name of the Lord. ||102|| Kabeer; all the strings of the instrument I played are broken. What can the poor instrument do, when the player has departed? ||103|| Kabeer; shave the head of the mother of the guru, who does not eliminate your doubt; Page 1370 He is drowning in the four Vedas; he drowns his disciples as well. ||104|| Kabeer; whatever sins he committed, he kept under the cover of his bed. When the justice of destiny questions; all are revealed by itself. ||105|| Kabeer; you forgot God's name and you raised a large family. You kept working for them; but none of your brothers and relatives remains. ||106|| Kabeer; those who give up reciting God's name and practice staying awake at night; They shall be born as snakes that eat their own offspring. ||107|| Kabeer; abandoning God's name, the maid keeps fast for Ahoy goddess. She shall be born as a donkey, to carry heavy burdens. ||108|| Kabeer; it is the smartest wisdom, to recite God in the mind. He plays on the hanging stage; if he falls there is no place to save him. ||109|| Kabeer; blessed is that mouth, which says God God God. Not only his body but also the whole village will become sacred. ||110|| Kabeer; that family is good, in which Lord's slave is born. But the family in which the Lord's slave is not born is useless like weeds. ||111|| Kabeer; some keep horses, elephants and carriages, and thousands of banner waving; Begging is better than these comforts, where one spends the day reciting God. ||112|| Kabeer; I have wandered all over the world, carrying the drum on my shoulder. No one belongs to anyone else; I have looked and studied it carefully. ||113|| The pearls are scattered on the road; the blind man comes along. Without the light of the Lord of the universe, the world just passes by. ||114|| Kabeer's family has drowned, since the birth of this handsome son. He has given up reciting God and brings home the wealth. ||115|| Kabeer; when you go to meet a devotee; do not take anyone with you; Do not turn back – keep on going. Whatever happens; let it be; ||116|| Kabeer; do not tie yourself with chains like the rest of the world. As is the salt in the flour, so is this beautiful body in the world. ||117|| Kabeer; the soul-swan flew away, the body is being buried, and still he makes gestures. Even then, the mortal does not give up the cruel look in his eyes. ||118|| Kabeer: I see You with my eyes and listen to your name with my ears O God; I say your name with my tongue and enshrine Your lotus feet in my mind. ||119|| Kabeer; I am free from heaven and hell by guru's grace. From beginning to end, I live in the joy of the Lord's lotus feet. ||120|| Kabeer; I cannot imagine and describe the happiness I get at God's lotus feet. It does not look good to say; I just admire by seeing. ||121|| Kabeer; how can I describe what I have seen? No one will believe my words. God is as He is; I sing His praises with joy. ||122|| Page 1371 Kabeer; the goose feeds and remembers her chicks. Like the chicks to the goose; so is the attachment of the worldly wealth. ||123|| Kabeer; the sky is overcast with clouds; the ponds and lakes are overflowing with water. Like the rain bird, some remain thirsty – what is their condition? ||124|| Kabeer; the chakvi duck is separated from her love through the night, but in the morning, she meets him again. Those who are separated from God do not meet Him in the day, or the night. ||125|| Kabeer: O conch shell, remain in the ocean. If you are separated from it, you will be blown at sunrise from temple to temple. ||126|| Kabeer; what are you doing sleeping? Wake up and cry in fear and pain. Those who live in the grave – how can they sleep in peace? ||127|| Kabeer; what are you doing sleeping? Get up and recite God. One day you shall sleep with your legs outstretched forever. ||128|| Kabeer; what are you doing sleeping? Wake up, and sit; attach yourself to the one, from whom you have been separated. ||129|| Kabeer; do not leave the society of the saints; follow their path. Seeing them, you will be sanctified; recite God's name meeting with them. ||130|| Kabeer; do not associate with the faithless, run far away from them. If you touch a vessel stained with soot, some of the soot will stick to you. ||131|| Kabeer; you have not recited God, and now old age has overtaken you. Now the door of your mansion is on fire, how can anyone pull you out? ||132|| Kabeer; the Creator does whatever He pleases. There is none other than Him; He alone is the Creator of all. ||133|| Kabeer; the fruit trees are bearing fruit, and the mangoes are becoming ripe. They will reach the owner, only if the crows do not eat them first. ||134|| Kabeer; some buy idols and worship them; they go to pilgrimage with stubborn mind; They look at one another, and wear religious robes, but they are deluded and lost. ||135|| Kabeer; some call a stone idol the God and they worship it. Those who believe it will drown in the midstream. ||136|| Kabeer; the paper is the four legged bed; rituals are the ink of mind. The stone idols have drowned the world, and the religious scholars, robbed them on the way. ||137|| Kabeer; what you were to do tomorrow, do it today; what was to be done today do it now. Nothing can be done later when the death hovers over the head. ||138|| Kabeer; I have seen a person, who is like a washed tar. He seems clever and virtuous, but he has no intellect and is impure. ||139|| Kabeer; the devil of death respects my intellect. I recite God, who created this devil of death. ||140|| Kabeer has become musk and his followers have become the bumblebees. Page 1372 More they worship Kabeer; more they merge with God. ||141|| Kabeer; he is caught in the family affairs but he recites God from the mouth. He went to the justice of destiny with pomp and show. ||142|| Kabeer; a pig is better than the faithless; the pig keeps its place clean. Poor faithless died; nobody talks about him. ||143|| Kabeer; the mortal gathers wealth, penny by penny, and collects millions. He does not keep anything on departure; they even take away his loincloth also. ||144|| Kabeer; what good is to become a devotee of Vishnu, and recite rosary four times? On the outside, he looks like pure gold, but inside, he is filled with filth. ||145|| Kabeer; be a pebble stone lying on the road by giving up ego. Such a humble slave shall meet the Lord. ||146|| Kabeer; what good is the pebble; which gives pain to the walking by. O Lord, Your servant should be like dirt on the earth. ||147|| Kabeer; what good is the dust, which blows and sticks to the body. God's servant should be such, as water in water. ||148|| Kabeer; what good is water which becomes cold and hot. God's servant should just like God: ||149|| With gold and women in a lofty palace and the flag unfurls on top. The bumblebee is better than him; it sings God's praises in saint's company. ||150|| Kabeer; the wilderness is better than a palace if Lord's devotees live there. Those without God' love; better go to the city of death for me. ||151|| Kabeer; between the Ganges and Jamunaa Rivers, there is a place of contentment. Kabeer has made his home there. The sages and mortals search for the way to go there. ||152|| Kabeer; whatever branches the tree bears, will remain the same till end. What to say of a diamond, millions of jewels do not match that. ||153|| Kabeer; I saw a strange thing. A diamond being sold in a store; without the right buyer; it was sold for a penny. ||154|| Kabeer; where there is divine wisdom, there is faith; where there is falsehood, there is sin. Where there is greed, there is death. Where there is forgiveness, there is God; ||155|| Kabeer; what good is it to give up wealth, if the mortal does not give up pride? Even the sages and seers are destroyed by pride; pride eats up everything. ||156|| Kabeer; I met the true guru; He aimed one arrow of his teaching. As soon as it struck me, I fell to the ground with a hole in my heart. ||157|| Kabeer; what can the true guru do, when there is fault in the devotees? The blind is not affected by it; it is like blowing into the bamboo. ||158|| Kabeer; the wife of the king has all sorts of horses, elephants and carriages. Page 1373 But she is not equal to the water-carrier of God's humble servant. ||159|| Kabeer; why do you slander the dancer woman? Why do you honour the slave of the Lord? Because one wears a makeup for bad deeds, while the other recites God. ||160|| Kabeer; with the support of Lord's support, I have become stable. Kabeer trades pearls near Lake Mansarovar. ||161|| Kabeer; God is the pearl and His devotee is the jeweller; he has set up a shop. As soon as an appraiser is found, the price of the jewel is set. ||162|| Kabeer; you recite God when you need something; you should recite Him forever. You shall live in the city of immortality, and God shall restore the wealth you lost. ||163|| Kabeer; it is good to serve both; one the saint the other the God. God is the bestowal of liberation; the saint inspires us to recite His name. ||164|| Kabeer; the crowds follow the path which the religious scholars follow. There is a difficult hill on the way to God; Kabeer has climbed it. ||165|| Kabeer; the mortal dies for world's sake, so that his dynasty flourishes. Whose family is disgraced when he is placed on the funeral pyre? ||166|| Kabeer; O ignorant you will drown worrying about what other people think. You know that whatever happens to your neighbours, will also happen to you. ||167|| Kabeer; the bumblebee is better than him; it tastes from flower to flower. She does not claim like people brag about their vast empire and power. ||168|| Kabeer; those who brag, shall burn. Those who do not brag remain carefree. Those, who do not claim anything; think of king Indra and a poor alike; ||169|| Kabeer; the pool is filled surrounded by beautiful boundary, but no one can drink the water. By good fortune, you have found it; Kabeer drinks it with hands full. ||170|| Kabeer; just as the stars disappear at dawn, so shall this body disappear. Only these two letters do not disappear that Kabeer enshrines in his heart. ||171|| Kabeer; the wooden house is burning on all sides. The religious scholars are burnt to death, but the ignorant ran away. ||172|| Kabeer; give up your skepticism; let your papers wash away. Remember fifty-two letters of alphabet and focus your mind to God's feet. ||173|| Kabeer; the saint does not give up his saintly nature; he may meet millions of evil. Like the sandalwood tree does not give up soothing affect even if it is encircled by snakes. ||174|| Kabeer; my mind is soothed; I have realized divine wisdom. The fire, which has burnt the world, is like the stomach of a person. ||175|| Kabeer; no one knows the play of the Creator. Either he knows or the beloved devotees of His court. ||176|| Kabeer; it is good that twilight has dawned; all directions are forgotten. Page 1374 The hailstones have melted into water, and flowed into the ocean. ||177|| Kabeer; the body became a pile of dust, collected and packed together. It is a show, which lasts for only a few days, and then dust returns to dust. ||178|| Kabeer; bodies are like the rising and setting of the sun and the moon. Without meeting the guru, the Lord of the universe, it is reduced to dust again. ||179|| Where there is carefree God, there is no fear; where there is concern, God is not there. Kabeer speaks after thinking careful; listen O saints, in your minds. ||180|| Kabeer; those who do not know anything, sleep in peace. But I have understood the riddle; I am faced with all sorts of troubles. ||181|| Kabeer; those who are beaten cry a lot; but the cries of separation are different. Struck by the mystery of God, Kabeer fell on the spot; ||182|| Kabeer; the stroke of a spear is easy to bear; it takes away the breath. But one who bears the stroke of guru's teaching; is my guru, I am his devotee. ||183|| Kabeer: O Mullah, why do you climb to the top of the minaret? God is not deaf. For whose sake you give a loud call, is in your heart. ||184|| O elder without contentment, why do you go on Hajj to Kaabaa. Kabeer; he who does not recite God whole-heartedly; How can he realize his Lord? ||185|| Kabeer; worship God; reciting God all pains go away. God reveals in the mind and the burning fire extinguishes reciting God's name. ||186|| Kabeer; to use force is a crime, even if you call it earned (halaal). When your account is called in God's court; what will happen then? ||187|| Kabeer; the dinner of beans and rice is excellent, if it is flavoured with the nectar of salt. Who will get his throat cut for the sake of food? ||188|| Kabeer; when one is touched by the guru, he will know; his worldly attachment and the fever of the body go away. He is not burned by pleasure or pain, and he merges with God. ||189|| Kabeer; there is a difference in saying God; there is a secret in it. Everyone says same word God; same word God creates wonders; ||190|| Kabeer; everyone says God (Raam). There is distinction in saying. One is known by all and adorned by all, but the other one merges in one. ||191|| Kabeer; the houses, where God's devotee is not served; that house is like a cremation ground; the ghosts live there. ||192|| Kabeer; I have become mute, insane and deaf. I am crippled – the true guru has pierced me with his arrow. ||193|| Kabeer; the brave true guru shot me with his arrow. As soon as it struck me, I fell to the ground, with a hole in my heart. ||194|| Kabeer; the pure drop of water falls from the sky, to the dirty ground. Page 1375 Believe that everything is burned to ashes without devotee's congregation. ||195|| Kabeer; the pure drop of water falls from the sky, and mixes with dust. Millions of intelligent people tried and failed; it cannot be separated. ||196|| Kabeer; I was going on a pilgrimage to Mecca, and God met me on the way. He scolded me and asked. Who told you that I live only there? ||197|| Kabeer; I went on hajj to Kaabaa many times? O Lord, what is the fault with me? You do not speak to me from Your mouth. ||198|| Kabeer; those who kill by force and say that they worked for it and call it kosher. When the Lord calls their account, they will know what happens; ||199|| Kabeer;

to use force is a crime; God will call you to account. When your account is called, you will be slapped on the face. ||200|| Kabeer; it is easy to pay your account, if your heart is pure. In the true court of the Lord, no one will help you. ||201|| Kabeer: You made both earth and the sky free of all; the six Shaastras and the eighty-four mystics are filled with doubt. ||202|| Kabeer; nothing is mine in me. Whatever there is; is Yours, O Lord. If I offer to You what is already Yours, what does it cost me? ||203|| Kabeer; saying You, You, Kabeer became You. I have no ego left in me. When the difference between others and me is erased, then wherever I look, I see You. ||204|| Kabeer; those who think of evil and entertain false hopes. None of their desires shall be fulfilled; they shall depart in despair. ||205|| Kabeer; whoever recites God is happy in the world. One, who is protected by the Creator, shall never waver, here or hereafter. ||206|| Kabeer; I was being crushed like sesame seeds in the oil-press, the true guru saved me. My pre-ordained primal destiny has been revealed. ||207|| Kabeer; I spent the day pondering; the interest is increasing day by day. Neither I recited God nor the letter got torn and the time of death has come. ||208|| Fifth Master: Kabeer; the mortal is a barking dog, chasing after a corpse. I met the true guru due to pre-ordained destiny and he got me freed. ||209|| Fifth Master: Kabeer; the thieves have occupied the land of God's devotees. The land is not affected by their weight but they got the benefit. ||210|| Fifth Master: Kabeer; for the sake of rice the husk gets beaten with a mallet; When people sit in evil company, the justice of destiny asks questions. ||211|| Friend Trilochan says, O Naam Dev; you are enticed by wealth. Why are you printing designs on the sheets, and not focusing your mind to God; ||212|| Naam Dev answers, O Trilochan, say God from the mouth; Page 1376 Work with your hands and feet and keep your mind focused to the formless God. ||213|| Fifth Master: Kabeer; no one belongs to me, and I belong to no one. He, who created the creation; I shall merge with Him. ||214|| Kabeer; the flour has fallen into the mud; nothing came in my hands. That which was eaten while it was being ground! I only got that much. ||215|| Kabeer; the mind knows everything; knowing that it still makes mistakes. What good is a lamp in one's hand, if he falls into the well? ||216|| Kabeer; I am in love with the all-knowing Lord;

the ignorant people want to stop it. How could I ever break with the one, who owns my soul and life? ||217|| Kabeer; why kill yourself for love of decorations of your home and mansion? In the end, only six feet, or a little more, shall be your lot. ||218|| Kabeer; whatever I wish, does not happen. What can I do by thinking? The Lord does whatever He wishes; I may not be thinking about it; ||219|| Third Master: God makes the mortals anxious, and He takes the anxiety away as well. O Nanak, praise the one, who takes care of all. ||220|| Fifth Master: Kabeer; he does not miss God but wanders around engrossed in greed. He died committing sins and his life ended in an instant. ||221|| Kabeer; the body is like an uncured clay pot, only uncured clay. If you wish to keep it safe recite God; otherwise, it will break. ||222|| Kabeer; say the name of the beautifully haired Lord; do not sleep unaware. Recite His name night and day; the Lord will eventually hear your cries. ||223|| Kabeer; the body is a thick forest, and the mind is an intoxicated elephant. The controlling rod is jewel of spiritual wisdom, and the rare saint is the rider. ||224|| Kabeer; Lord's name is the jewel, and the mouth is the pouch; open the pouch in front of an appraiser. Some right customer will come and will buy it at a high price. ||225|| Kabeer; the mortal does not know Lord's name, but he has raised a large family. He died doing his deeds, it made no sound outside. ||226|| Kabeer; in the blink of an eye, moment by moment, life is passing by. The mortal does not give up his worldly entanglements; devil of death comes by beating the drum. ||227|| Kabeer; the Lord is the tree, and the separation is the fruit. The devotee is the shade, who has given up useless conflict. ||228|| Kabeer; plant the seeds of such a plant, which bears fruit throughout the twelve months; It gives cool shade and lot of fruit; the birds enjoy it with love. ||229|| Kabeer; the bestowal is the tree; kindness is the fruit which blesses the beings. When the birds go to other lands, the tree still bears the fruitful fruit. ||230|| Kabeer; obtaining devotee's company is pre-ordained written on the forehead. Page 1377 He obtains the treasure of liberation, and the difficult road is not blocked. ||231|| Kabeer; one moment, half a moment, or half of that. Discussing with God's devotees is beneficial. ||232|| Kabeer; those who consume marijuana, fish and wine; Even if they go to pilgrimages, keep fast and or recite a word, they will all go to hell. ||233|| Kabeer; keep your eyes down, and enshrine the beloved in the mind. Enjoy all pleasures with the beloved and never show it to anyone; ||234|| Twenty-four hours a day, my soul continues to look to You, O Lord. Why should I keep my eyes down? When I see my beloved in everyone; ||235|| Listen, O my friend: my soul dwells in my beloved, and my beloved dwells in my soul. I do not know the soul or the beloved; whether it is soul or God in my body? ||236|| Kabeer; the Brahmin is the guru of the world, but not the guru of God's devotees. He rots and dies entangled in the four Vedas. ||237|| The Lord is like sugar, scattered in the sand; it cannot be picked by hand. Says Kabeer; the guru told me the truth: become an ant, and eat it. ||238|| Kabeer; if you desire to play the game of love, then cut your head, and make it into a ball. Play and play till you get out of control; then whatever happens, let it be; ||239|| Kabeer; if you desire to play the game of love, play it with someone with commitment. Pressing the unripe mustard seeds produces neither oil nor the waste. ||240|| Searching, the mortal stumbles like a blind person, and does not recognize the saint. Says Naam Dev, how can one realize God without devotee's company? ||241|| Forsaking the diamond the God, the mortals put their hopes in something else. Those people will go to hell; Ravi Daas speaks the truth. ||242|| Kabeer; if you live the householder's life, practice faith; otherwise, you better become a renunciate. If the renunciate performs rituals; he is really unlucky. ||243|| Hymns Of Sheikh Fareed Jee: God is one. He is realized by guru's grace. The day of the bride's wedding is pre-ordained. On that day, he who is called the devil of death comes and shows his face. He shakes the bones and takes away the life. That pre-ordained time of marriage cannot be changed. Explain this to your soul. The soul is the bride, and death is the groom. He will marry her and take her away. After the body sends her away with its own hands, whom will it embrace? The bridge is narrower than a hair; ears cannot hear walking sound on it? Fareed; the call has come; be careful; don't get robbed. ||1|| Fareed; it is difficult to follow the saint's path. I follow the worldly path. Page 1378 I tied and picked up the bundle, but where can I take it? ||2|| I know nothing; I understand nothing. The world is a smouldering fire. My Lord did good thing otherwise I will also be burnt. ||3|| Fareed; if I knew that sesame seeds are less, then I will pick it in the hand careful. If I had known that my Husband Lord was young and innocent, I would not have been so arrogant. ||4|| If I knew that my robe would come loose, I would have tied a tighter knot. I have found none as great as You O Lord; I searched and saw the whole world. ||5|| Fareed; if you are kind enough; please do not write black essay. Look in your yard humbly instead. ||6|| Fareed; do not turn around and strike those who strike you with their fists. Kiss their feet, when they go to your home. ||7|| Fareed; when there was time for you to earn you were in love with the world. Death has a strong footing; when the load is full, it takes away. ||8|| See, Fareed; what happened: your beard has become grey. Your end is near and the youth is behind. ||9|| See, Fareed; what happened: sugar has become poison. Without my Lord, whom can I tell my pain to? ||10|| Fareed; my eyes have become weak, and my ears have become hard of hearing. The body's crop has become ripe and changed colour. ||11|| Fareed; those who did not recite God when their hair was black; only a few do when they turn grey; So, be in love with the Lord, so that your colour may ever remain new. ||12|| Third Master: Fareed; whether one's hair is black or grey, God is always there to recite if anyone wants. Love does not well up if someone tries. This cup of love belongs to the Lord; he gives to whomever he wishes. ||13|| Fareed; those eyes which have enticed the world. I have seen those eyes. Once, they could not endure even a bit of mascara; now, the birds hatch chicks there. ||14|| Fareed; they shouted and yelled, and constantly gave advice. When the devil of death takes them away. How can they turn their mind around? ||15|| Fareed; become like tall grass and fall on the path, If you long for the Lord of all. One will cut you down, and another will trample you under the feet; then, you shall enter the court of the Lord. ||16|| Fareed; do not slander the dirt; noting is as great as dirt. When we are alive, it is under our feet, and when we die, it is on top. ||17|| Fareed; when there is greed, what love has to do there; when there is greed, love is false. How long can one remain in a grass hut? It will be destroyed by rain. ||18|| Fareed; why do you wander from jungle to jungle by pushing the thorny brush aside? God abides in the mind; what are you searching in the forest?

||19|| Fareed; with these small legs, I crossed deserts and mountains. But today O Fareed; my water jug seems hundreds of miles away. ||20|| Fareed; the nights are long, and my body aches. Page 1379 Cursed are the lives of those who place their hopes in others. ||21|| Fareed; if I was there when my friend came, I would offer my life to him. Now my flesh is burning red on the hot coals. ||22|| Fareed; the farmer plants acacia trees, and wishes for grapes. He is spinning wool, but he wishes to wear silk. ||23|| Fareed; the path is muddy, and the house of my beloved is far away. If I go, my blanket will get wet, if I do not, then my love ends. ||24|| My blanket is soaked with the downpour of Lord's rain. I am going to meet my friend, so that my love does not end. ||25|| Fareed; I was worried that my turban might become dirty. My thoughtless soul does not realize that one day, dust will eat my head as well. ||26|| Fareed: jagry, sugar, molasses, honey and buffalo's milk. All these things are sweet, but they are not equal to God. ||27|| Fareed; my chapati is hard like wood, but it eliminates my hunger. Those who eat buttered chapati will suffer in terrible pain. ||28|| Eat dry hard chapati without any side dish and drink cold water. Fareed; if you see someone else's buttered chapati, do not envy him. ||29|| This night, I did not sleep with my Husband Lord; my body is aching. Go, and ask the discarded bride; how she passes her night. ||30|| She finds no place of rest in her father-in-law's home, and in her parent's home. Her Husband Lord does not care for her; what sort of happy soul-bride is she? ||31|| In her father-in-law's home and in her parent's home, she belongs to her inaccessible and unfathomable husband Lord; O Nanak, she is the happy soul-bride, who is pleasing to her carefree Lord. ||32|| Bathing, washing and decorating herself, she comes and sleeps without worry. Fareed; she still smells like asafetida; the fragrance of musk is gone. ||33|| I am not afraid of losing my youth, as long as I do not lose the love of my Husband Lord. Fareed; many youths, without love, have withered and dried. ||34|| Fareed; anxiety is my bed, pain is my mattress, and the pain of separation is my quilt. This is my life, O my true Lord; see it. ||35|| Many talk about separation, but your separation is the real separation O Lord. Fareed; the body, which does not feel the pain of separation; is like a graveyard; ||36|| Fareed; these are poisonous sprouts coated

with sugar. Some die planting them and some harvest cook and destroy them. ||37|| Fareed; spent four days wandering and four days sleeping; God will call for your account, and ask you why you came into this world? ||38|| Fareed; go to the place where people get together and look at the gong; this sinless is being beaten; imagine what will happen to us sinful; ||39|| Each and every hour, it is beaten; it is punished every day. This beautiful body is like the gong; it passes the night in pain. ||40|| Page 1380 Sheikh Fareed has grown old, and his body has begun to tremble. Even if he could live for hundred years, his body will eventually turn to dust. ||41|| Fareed begs, O Lord, do not make me sit at another's door. If You keep me this way; better take the life out of my body; ||42|| With the axe on his shoulder, a bucket on his head, the blacksmith goes to forest to cut wood. Fareed; I long for my Lord; you long only for the charcoal. ||43|| Fareed; some have food for future and some do not even have salt. When they go beyond this world, it shall be seen, who is punished. ||44|| Drums beaten in their honour, canopies above their heads, and bugles to announce their coming. They have gone to sleep in the cemetery, buried like orphans. ||45|| Fareed; those who built houses, mansions and lofty buildings, are also gone. They made false deals; they are lying in the graves. ||46|| Fareed; there are many seems on the patched coat, but there are no seems on the soul. The elders and their disciples have all departed, when their turn came. ||47|| Fareed; two lights are still lit; the messenger of death has arrived. He conquered the fortress and robbed the body and extinguished the lamps. ||48|| Fareed; look at what has happened to the cotton and the sesame seed; The sugar cane and paper, the clay pots all burnt with charcoal. This is the punishment for those who do evil deeds. ||49|| Fareed; you carry the prayer mat on the shoulder, wear black robe. Your heart is like scissors but you talk sweet. Outwardly, you look enlightened but your heart is dark as night. ||50|| Fareed; not even a drop of blood will come out, if someone cuts his body. Those bodies which are imbued with God; those bodies contain no blood. ||51|| Third Master: This body is all blood; without blood, this body could not exist. Those who are imbued with their Lord; do not have the blood of greed in them. When the body becomes thin for fear of God; the greedy blood goes away from inside. As metal is purified by fire, same way the love of God removes the filthy evil residue. O Nanak, those humble beings are beautiful, who are imbued with Lord's love. ||52|| Fareed; seek that sacred pool, in which the genuine merchandise is found. Why bother to search in the pond? Your hand will only sink in the mud. ||53|| Fareed; when she is young, she does not enjoy her Husband. When she grows old she dies. Lying in the grave, the soul-bride cries, "I did not meet You, my Lord!"||54|| Fareed; your hair and beard and moustaches have turned grey. O my thoughtless and insane mind, what pleasures you are enjoying? ||55|| Fareed; how long can you run on the rooftop? Wake up for your beloved; the days, which were allotted to, you are numbered, and they are passing by. ||56|| Fareed; houses, mansions and balconies; do not fall in love with these. They will put unweighed dirt on you when you die; no one will be your friend. ||57|| Fareed; do not focus on mansions and wealth; focus your mind on death. Page 1381 Remember that place where you have to go. ||58|| Fareed; those deeds which do not bring merit – forget about those deeds. Otherwise, you shall be ashamed in the court of the Lord. ||59|| Fareed; serve your Lord and Master; dispel the doubts of your heart. God's devotees are peaceful like trees. ||60|| Fareed; my clothes are black, and my outlook is black. I wander around full of sins, and yet people call me God's devotee. ||61|| The crop which is burnt will not bloom, even if it is soaked in water. Fareed; she who is forsaken by her Husband Lord, grieves and laments. ||62|| When she is unmarried, she is full of desire; when she is married, the troubles begin. Fareed; this is the only regret, otherwise she will remain unmarried. ||63|| The swans have landed in a pond in the salty land. They dip their bills, but do not drink; they fly away, still thirsty. ||64|| The swans fly away and land in the crops. People go to chase them. The thoughtless people do not know that the swans do not eat grains. ||65|| The birds which lived in the pools have gone away. Fareed; the filled pool shall also empty; only the lotus flowers shall remain. ||66|| Fareed; a stone will be your pillow, and the earth will be your bed. The worms shall eat your flesh. Countless ages will pass, and you will still be lying on one side. ||67|| Fareed; your beautiful body shall break apart, and the subtle thread of breath shall be snapped. In which house will the devil of death go today? ||68|| Fareed; your beautiful body shall break apart, and the subtle thread of the breath shall be snapped. Those friends who were a burden on the earth; why should they come back today? ||69|| Fareed: why you do not recite Namaaz; this is not a good way of life. You never come to the mosque for your five daily prayers. ||70|| Fareed; get up and cleanse yourself and recite the morning Namaaz. The head, which does not bow to the Lord – chop off that head. ||71|| That head which does not bow to the Lord – what is to be done with that head? Put it in the furnace instead of firewood. ||72|| Fareed; where are your mother and father, who gave birth to you? They have left you, but you did not understand yet? ||73|| Fareed; flatten your mind; smooth out the hills and valleys. Hereafter, the fire of hell shall not touch you. ||74|| Fifth Master: Fareed; the Creator is in the creation, and the creation is in God. Whom can we call bad? When there is none without Him. ||75|| Fareed; the day the umbilical cord was cut, the neck should have been cut instead; I would not have so many troubles, or suffer so many hardships. ||76|| My teeth, feet, eyes and ears have stopped working. My body cries, "Those whom I knew have left!"||77|| Fareed; answer bad with goodness; do not be angry in the mind. Page 1382 Your body shall not suffer from any disease, and you shall obtain everything. ||78|| Fareed; we the birds are the guests in the beautiful worldly garden. The morning has come. Get ready to leave! ||79|| Fareed; musk is released at night. Those who are sleeping do not get it. Those who are sleeping; how can they receive it? ||80|| Fareed; I thought that I was in pain; the whole world is in pain! When I climbed high and saw the same fire in each and every home. ||81|| Fifth Master: Fareed; in the midst of this beautiful earth, there is a garden of thorns. Those beings who are blessed by the divine teacher, do not suffer a scratch. ||82|| Fifth Master: Fareed; life is adorable with the beautiful body. There are only a few who love their beloved Lord. ||83|| O river, do not destroy your banks; you too will be asked to give your account. The river flows; in whatever direction the Lord orders. ||84|| Fareed; the day passes painfully; the night is spent in pain. The boatman stands and shouts, "The boat is caught in the waves!"||85|| The river flows on; it loves to eat into its banks. What can the waves do to the boat, if the boatman remains alert? ||86|| Fareed; there are many who say they are friends; I searched and I did not find even one. I am burning for the sake of those beloved ones. ||87|| Fareed; this body is always crying. Who can stand this constant pain? I have plugged my ears; I don't care how much wind is blowing. ||88|| Fareed; God's dates have ripened, and rivers of honey flow. With each passing day, your life is decreasing. ||89|| Fareed; my withered body has become a skeleton; the crows are pecking at my palms. Still, God has not come to help; this is the fate of a man. ||90|| The crows have searched my skeleton, and eaten all my flesh. Please do not touch these eyes; I hope to see my Lord. ||91|| O crow, do not peck at my skeleton; if you have landed; fly away. Do not eat the flesh from the skeleton, in which my Husband Lord abides. ||92|| Fareed; the poor grave calls, O homeless; come back to your home. You have to come to me; do not be afraid of death."||93|| These eyes have seen a great many leave. Fareed; people worry about them, and I am worried about me. ||94|| God says, if you reform yourself, you shall meet Him, meeting Him you shall be at peace. O Fareed; if you become mine, the whole world will be yours."||95|| How long can the tree remain implanted on the riverbank? Fareed; how long can water be kept in an uncured clay pot? ||96|| Fareed; the mansions are vacant; those who lived in them are buried underground. Page 1383 Those humble souls lie in graves. O elder, pray to God; you will have to depart, today or tomorrow. ||97|| Fareed; the shore of death looks like the river-bank; Beyond that is the burning hell, from there the cries and shrieks are heard. Some understand this completely, while others wander around carelessly. The deeds you do in this world; are revealed in God's court. ||98|| Fareed; a crane perches on the riverbank, playing joyfully; While it is playing, a hawk suddenly pounces on it. When the Hawk of God attacks, playful sport is forgotten. God did what was not expected or even thought of; ||99|| This two hundred pound body is nourished by water and food. The mortal comes into the world with high hopes. The devil of death comes destroying all the doors. They tie you up in front of your beloved ones and brothers. See; the man is going carried on the shoulders of four men. Fareed; the good deeds you did in the world were useful in God's court.

||100|| Fareed; I admire those birds that live in the forest. They peck at the roots and live on the ground, and do not forget God; ||101|| Fareed; the season changed, the woods shake and the leaves drop from the trees. I searched the four corners, but I did not find any place to rest. ||102|| Fareed; I have torn my clothes; now I wear only a blanket. I wear only those clothes, which will lead me to meet my Lord. ||103|| Third Master: Why do you tear apart your fine clothes, and wear a blanket? O Nanak, you will realize God sitting at home if you cleanse your mind. ||104|| Fifth Master: Fareed; those who are proud of their greatness, wealth and youth; they go empty hand like the rain washes away the sand doons. ||105|| Fareed; the faces of those, who forget Lord's Name, are scary. They suffer terrible pain here, and hereafter they find no place to rest. ||106|| Fareed; if you do not remain awake in the early hours; you are dead while yet alive. Although you have forgotten God, God has not forgotten you. ||107|| Fifth Master: Fareed; my Husband Lord is full of joy; He is completely carefree. To be imbued with the Lord is the most truthful deed. ||108|| Fifth Master: Fareed; look at pleasure and pain alike; eradicate corruption from your heart. Accept God's will; then you shall find His court. ||109|| Fifth Master: Fareed; the world dances as it is made to dance, and you dance with it. Whoever God cares for, does not dance. ||110|| Fifth Master: Fareed; the heart is imbued with this world; the world is of no use to it at all. Page 1384 It is difficult to obtain devotee's honour. Only those with perfect destiny obtain it. ||111|| The first watch of the night brings flowers, and the last watch brings fruit. Those who remain awake, receive the gifts from the Lord. ||112|| The gifts are from our Lord; who can force Him to bestow on them? Some are awake, and do not receive it, yet He awakens some from sleep to bless them. ||113|| You search for your Husband Lord; you must have some fault in you. Those who are known as happy soul-brides do not look to others. ||114|| Make the bow, and arrow tip of contentment. With the arrow of patience, the Creator will not let you miss the target. ||115|| Those who are filled with patience; in this way, they burn their bodies. They are close to the Lord, but they do not tell anyone. ||116|| Let patience be your purpose in life; implant this in you. This way, you will become a great river; you will not

break into tiny streams. ||117|| Fareed; it is difficult to follow the divine path; buttered bread is easy to eat. Only a few follow the way of the saints. ||118|| My body is hot like an oven; my bones are burning like firewood. If my feet get tired, I walk on my head if I can meet my beloved. ||119|| Do not heat up your body like an oven, and do not burn your bones like firewood; what mischief did your feet and head do? God lives inside; ||120|| I search for my friend, but my friend is with me. O Nanak, the unseen Lord cannot be seen; He is revealed to the guru-willed. ||121|| Seeing the swans swimming, the cranes became excited. The poor cranes drowned and died, with their heads down and feet up. ||122|| I thought him a great swan, so I joined with him. If I had known that he was a crane, I would have never associated with him. ||123|| Whether swan, or crane, whoever God blesses? If it pleases God O Nanak, He changes a crow into a swan. ||124|| There is only one bird in the lake, but there are fifty trappers. This body is caught in the waves of desire. O true God, You are my only hope! ||125|| What is that word, what is that virtue, and what is that magic mantra? How I decorate myself so that I can entice my husband Lord? ||126|| Humility is the word, forgiveness is the virtue, and sweet words are the magic mantra. Wear these three robes, O sister, and you will entice your Husband Lord. ||127|| Be like a child in spite of being intelligent. Be humble in spite of being powerful. When there is nothing to share, and then share you with others. Such a person is God's devotee. ||128|| Do not say harsh words; God abides in all. Do not break anyone's heart; these are all priceless jewels. ||129|| The minds of all are like precious jewels; to harm them is not good; If you hope for your beloved, then do not break anyone's heart. ||130||Page 1385.

God is one. It is true. He is the Creator. He is carefree. He has no enemy. He is immortal. He does not take birth. He came into existence on His own. He is realized by guru's grace.

Swaiyas From The Mouth Of The honourable Fifth Master: O primal Lord, You are the Creator, the cause of all causes. You are all pervading and abide in everyone. You pervade the world; who can know Your wisdom? You protect all; You are our Lord. O my imperishable and formless Lord, You came into being on Your own. You are one and

Only one; no one else is like You. O Lord, there is no end to Your creation. Who can contemplate You? You are the father of the world, the support of all life. Your devotees are at Your door, O God; they are just like You. How can servant Nanak describe You with only one tongue? I admire You forever. ||1|| Streams of nectar flow; Your Treasures are unweighable and overflowing in abundance. You are the farthest of the far, infinite and incomparably beautiful. You do whatever You please; You do not listen to others. You create and destroy in a moment. No one else is equal to You; Your light is pure. Millions of sins are eradicated by reciting Your name. Your devotees are at Your door O God; they are just like You. How can servant Nanak describe You with only one tongue? I admire You forever. ||2|| You created the universe from You; You abide in all yet are detached from all. O Lord, there is no end to Your virtues; all beings are Yours. You are the giver of all, the one invisible Lord. Page 1386 He came into existence on His own. He is seen in the whole universe. He has no colour, form, mouth or moustache. Your devotees are at Your door, O God; they are just like You. How can servant Nanak describe You with only one tongue? I admire You forever. ||3|| You are the treasure of all virtues; no one can know your value. Your place is the highest of all. My mind, wealth and life belong to You. The world is strung on one thread. What praises can I give to You? You are the greatest of the great. Who can know Your mystery? O unfathomable, infinite, divine Lord, Your power is unstoppable. O God, You are the support of all. Your devotees are at Your door, O God; they are just like You. How can servant Nanak describe You with only one tongue? I admire You forever. ||4|| O formless formed, undeceivable, perfect and imperishable Lord; O blissful, unlimited, beautiful, immaculate and blossoming Lord: Many sing Your praises, but no one can find Your limits. Whoever You are kind to; unites with You. Blessed are those, to whom God has been kind. O Nanak, whoever meets God the guru; his birth and death is eliminated. ||5|| I say; there is God and it is true. There is no other like Him. He is the primal being. Reciting God's sacred name the mind obtains eternal peace. Those who taste it with their tongue get fulfilled. Whoever God is kind to, enjoy the love of devotee's congregation. Whoever meets God the guru; his dynasty is liberated O Nanak. ||6|| True is His congregation and His court. True Lord made it so. Sitting on His throne of truth, He administers true justice. True Lord created the universe. He is infallible, and does not make mistakes. His name is the jewel and infinite; it is priceless. It cannot be priced. Whoever the Lord of the universe is kind to; obtain eternal peace. O Nanak, whoever meets God the guru, does not take birth again; ||7|| What is Yoga, what is the spiritual wisdom and meditation, how can I praise Him? The mystics, the seekers and millions of gods did not know a tiny bit of His value. Brahma, Sanak, or the thousand-headed serpent king cannot find the limits of His virtues. The incomprehensible cannot be comprehended; He fully pervades all. Whose noose of death is cut by the kind God; they worship Him. O Nanak, those who meet with God the guru; they are liberated here and hereafter. ||8|| I am a beggar; I seek the sanctuary of God, the giver of gifts. Please bless me with the dust of saint's feet that I swim across the terrifying world ocean holding their feet. Please listen to my prayer, if it pleases You, O my Lord: Page 1387 My mind yearns to visualize You. This mind is stabilized by devotional worship. The lamp is lit in the darkness; all are saved in today's age through faith in one name. The guru the supreme God is revealed in all the worlds. O servant Nanak. ||9|| Swaiyas from the mouth Of the honourable fifth master; God is one. He is realized by guru's grace. This transitory body is bound by false attachments. I am ignorant, stonehearted, filthy and unwise. My mind wanders and wobbles, it does not stabilize. It does not know the divine wisdom of the supreme Lord. I am intoxicated with youth, beauty and wealth. I am horrible and egotistic. The wealth and women of others, arguments and slander, are sweet and dear to my soul. I try to hide my bad deeds, but God, the inner-knower, watches and hears all. I have no humility, faith, compassion or purity, but I seek Your sanctuary, O giver of life. O all-powerful Lord the cause of causes. Save Nanak O Lord his master; ||1|| I sing His praises in the refuge of my beloved the enticer, to eliminate my sins. The all-powerful Lord is the boat capable of carrying us across; He saves us all. O my unconscious mind; miss Him in the true congregation. Why are you wandering around, enticed by the darkness of doubt? Recite God's name with your tongue for an hour, a moment, even an instant. You do worthless deeds for shallow pleasures; why do you want to suffer for millions of lifes? Recite God's name O Nanak, through saint's teachings and get imbued with God's love. ||2|| The little sperm is planted in the body-field of the mother, and the human body, so difficult to obtain, is formed. He eats and drinks, and enjoys pleasures; his pains are taken away, and his suffering is gone. He is given the understanding to recognize mother, father, siblings and relatives. He grows day by day, and the horrible old age comes closer and closer. You worthless, petty worm of worldly wealth; recite God for a moment. O Kind God, be kind to Nanak and eliminate his doubt. ||3|| O mind, you mouse living in a mouse hole; you are very proud, and do ignorant deeds. You are intoxicated by worldly wealth and wander like an owl. You are in extreme love with your children, spouse, friends and relatives. You have planted the seeds of ego, and the false attachment is sprouting. You pass your life making sinful mistakes. The cat of death, with his mouth wide-open, is watching you. She is hungry and will be satisfied by eating you. O Nanak, recite God the Lord of the world in devotee's company; know that the world is a dream. ||4|| Page 1388 Neither body, nor house, nor worldly love last forever. How long will you be proud of worldly wealth? Neither crown, nor canopy, nor the fan waving servants last forever. You do not think that your life is going by; the chariots, horses, elephants and royal throne will disappear in a moment and you will go naked. Neither warrior, nor hero, nor king or ruler lasts forever; see this with your eyes. Neither fortress, nor shelter, nor treasure will save you; you do evil deeds, you shall depart empty-handed. Friends, children, spouses and companions; none of them last forever; they change like the shade of a tree. God is the perfect primal being, kind to the poor; recite the inaccessible and infinite God every moment. O Lord my master, servant Nanak seeks Your refuge; please be kind and save him; ||5|| I spent my life in pride, begging and robbing others for the love of wealth. I have kept it hidden from my friends, relatives, companions, children and siblings. I ran around practicing falsehood, burning up my body and growing old. I gave up good deeds, faith, self-discipline, purity and religious vows; I associated with the fickle worldly wealth. Beasts, birds, trees and reptiles; I wandered through many lifes in many ways. I did not recite God's name even for a moment, O master of orphans the Lord of all. Food, drink and the sweet tasty dishes became totally bitter at the last moment. O Nanak, salvation obtains in saint's refuge; all those intoxicated with wealth lost it and departed. ||6|| Brahma, Shiva, the powerful and the sages, all sing God's praises with love. Indra and Vishnu search for God wandering on earth and sky again and again. The mystics, human beings, gods and demons, cannot find even a little bit of His mystery. Worshipping God lovingly, God's devotees visualize God and merge with Him. Those who forsake Him and beg from others; their mouths, teeth and tongue wear away; O my ignorant mind, recite God the bestowal of happiness; servant Nanak says so. ||7|| He is enticed by worldly wealth and deluded by the dark doubt and false attachment. He is so proud that he does not contain in the sky; his belly is filled with filthy worms and bones. He wanders in ten directions for sinful deeds; he robs others, he is robbed by ignorance. His youth passes away, the illnesses and old age has taken over; he will be punished by the devil of death and die. He suffers the pain of hell for many lifes; he rots in the pit of pain and condemnation. O Nanak, those whom the saint blesses with grace; worship and obtain salvation. ||8|| All virtues and the reward of all deeds are obtained; all my hopes are fulfilled. The medicine of guru`s lesson is a magic charm. It cures all pains and illnesses. Page 1389 Lust, anger, ego, jealousy and desire are eliminated by reciting God`s name. Enshrining God`s lotus feet in the mind bestows as much as bathing at shrines, giving awns, ascetic worship and truthful deeds. The Lord is my beloved friend, companion and relative. God is the food of the soul the support of life. I have taken the shelter of all-powerful Lord; slave Nanak praises Him forever. ||9|| Weapons cannot cut the joy of love of God`s lotus feet. Ropes cannot tie the person whose mind is pierced by visualizing God. Fire cannot burn that person who is attached to the dust of the feet of God`s devotees. Water cannot drown that person whose feet walk on God's path. O Nanak, diseases, faults, sinful mistakes and emotional attachment are pierced by the arrow of God`s name. ||1||10|| People make lot of efforts; they contemplate the various aspects of six Shaastras. They wander at sacred shrines applying ashes to the body and braiding their hair. They all suffer pain without reciting God, entangled in love like a parrot in the cage. They perform worship ceremonies, draw ritualistic marks on their bodies, cook their own food fanatically, and adorn themselves in many ways. ||2||11||20|| Swaiyas in Praise Of The First Master: God is one. He is realized by guru's grace. Reciting the primal Lord the bestowal of blessings in the mind; Saint Sahar always explains. Enshrining God's lotus feet in the mind. Then, I sing praises of the sacred guru, Guru Nanak. ||1|| I sing praises of the sacred guru the ocean of peace the destroyer of evil through guru's teaching. The serious, the profound understanding, ocean of wisdom, the Yogis and wandering hermits sing His praises. Indra and devotees like Prahlaad, who knew the joy of soul, sing his praises. Poet Kal sings the praises of Guru Nanak, who enjoyed the kingdom of worship. ||2|| King Janak and Shiva who knew the way of worship sing guru's praises with love. Sanak, the mystics, devotees, the sages and mortals sing the praises of the undeceivable guru the God. Dhoma the seer and Dhroo sing His praises and obtain the joy of worship. Kal the poet sings the praises of Guru Nanak, who enjoyed the kingdom of worship. ||3|| Kapilaad and the other Yogis sing guru's praises. He is the incarnation of infinite Lord. Parasraam the son of Jamdagan sings his praises, Raam Chander took away his axe and power. Udho, Akrur and Bidar sing his praises, who knew God, the soul of all. Kal the poet sings the praises of Guru Nanak, who enjoyed the kingdom of worship. ||4|| Page 1390 The four castes and the six Shaastras sing and likes of Brahma sing guru's praises. The thousand-tongued serpent sings His praises with lovingly attuning to him. The detached Shiva who knew the way of worship also sings guru's praises. Poet Kal sings the praises of Guru Nanak, who enjoyed the kingdom of worship. ||5|| He enjoyed the kingdom of worship enshrining the enemyless God in the mind. The whole world is saved by reciting God's name and swims across the world ocean. Sanak and Janak and the others sing guru's praises in all ages. Blessed and fruitful is the birth of the guru in the world. Even in the underworld, his music plays says poet Kal. O guru Nanak, reciting God's name with love you enjoyed the kingdom of worship.

||6|| In the first age (satyug); You cheated king Bal taking the form of a dwarf. In the second age (Traytaa) You were called Raam of the Raghu dynasty. In the third age (Dwaapur) You were Krishna; You did a good deed by killing Kans. You restored Ugarsain's kingdom, and You blessed Your humble devotees with love. In todays age (kalyug). You are known as guru Nanak, guru Angad and Amar Daas. The throne of the honourable guru is eternal and immovable. God set it this way. ||7|| His praises are sung by the devotees Ravi Daas, Jai Dev and Trilochan. The devotees Naam Dev and Kabeer praised Him forever seeing in their eyes. The devotee Baynee sings His praises intuitively and enjoys divine love. Without guru's teaching, yoga and meditation etc are not possible. Sukhdev, Preekhyat and saint Gautam sing guru's praises; Poet Kal, the ever-fresh praises of Guru Nanak is spread throughout the world. ||8|| Devotee Shyash – Naag sings guru's praises in the underworld. Shiva, the Yogis, celibates and the wandering hermits sing guru's praises forever. Vyaas the sage, who wrote the Vedas and grammar, sings guru's praise. Brahma who takes care of the entire universe sings guru's praises. God pervades the entire universe; He sees manifest and unmanifest the same Says Kal; Guru Nanak enjoyed the same contentment and mastery of worship. ||9|| The nine masters of Yoga sing His praises; blessed is the guru, who is merged in God. Maandhaataa, who called himself the ruler of the world, sings His praises. King Bal who lives in the seventh underworld sings His praises. King Bharthari, lived with the guru all the time and sang his praises. Doorbaasaa, King Paruro and Angra sing the praises of Guru Nanak. Poet Kal says, the praises of Guru Nanak intuitively that permeate in everyone. ||10|| Page 1391 Swaiyas In praise of the second master; God is one. He is realized by guru's grace. Blessed is the primal Lord, the Creator, and all-powerful cause of causes. Blessed is the true guru Nanak, who placed His hand on Your forehead. He placed His hand on Your forehead, then the nectar began to rain down; the gods and human beings, heavenly heralds and sages were drenched with its fragrance. You control the scary death and save the five-element body of all. You conquer the world in guru's refuge; You play the game riding the chariot of divine wisdom and protect us O formless God. Kal Sahaar sings the praises

of Lehnaa the guru, who pervades throughout the seven continents; He touched the Lord, and became guru of the world. ||1|| The stream of nectar from His eyes washes away the filth of sins; the sight of His door dispels the darkness of ignorance. Whoever serves the difficult task of the essence of guru`s teaching; that being crosses over the terrifying world ocean and becomes sin free. True Congregation, is the essence of contentment, contemplate guru`s teaching and remain awake and humble and imbued with God`s love forever. Kal Sahaar, sings the praises of Lehnaa the guru, who pervades throughout the seven continents; He touched the Lord, and became guru of the World. ||2|| You recited the infinite God and became totally pure; you are the support of mystics, seekers and the wise. You are the incarnation of King Janak. Guru`s teaching the essence of the world remains sacred and like lotus in the water. Like the Elysian tree, You cure all illnesses and take away the sufferings of the world. The three-phased soul is lovingly attuned to You. Kal Sahaar sings the praises of Lehnaa the guru who pervades throughout the seven continents; He touched the Lord, and became guru of the world. ||3|| You served and obeyed the guru and obtained honour and divine wisdom doing utmost worship. You visualized God and obtained the inner wisdom, which is accepted by the guru. Focus on the unmoving Lord and Your thinking will become pure; wear the armour of peace and give up worldly power. Kal Sahaar sings the praises of Lehnaa the guru, who pervades throughout the seven continents; He touched the Lord, and became guru of the world. ||4|| By his grace the ego departs and all evil sins are destroyed. Through the most powerful brave guru`s teaching, the lust and anger depart. He controls the false attachment; the seekers seek the refuge of the caretaker. You gather the joyful love of the soul by saying the sacred words that change the mind. The true guru puts the mark of guruship on the forehead and he is carried across. The lion guru of the world, the son of Pheru, is guru Angad; Lehnaa enjoys the kingdom of worship. ||5|| Page 1392 Your mind remains lovingly attuned to the Lord forever; You do whatever you desire. Like the tree loaded with fruit, You bow in humility and contemplate purity. You realize this reality, that God is all pervading, unseen and amazing. You are full of contentment; the ray of sacred sermon shines in your body. You are the certified guru; you are truthful and content. Kal proclaims; whoever meets Lehnaa meets God. ||6|| My mind believes that you are divine and unfathomable. The filth of your body has been eradicated and you drink the nectar. You have been enlightened and Godly power is infused in you forever. O true guru, You are intuitively and completely absorbed in trance; You are open minded the destroyer of poverty; seeing You, sins get scared. Kal lovingly and peacefully sings the praises of Lehnaa with his tongue. ||7|| God's name, is the medicine, support, meditation and eternal peace; God's name is our adorable resolve. Kal is imbued with the love of God's name that gives fragrance to gods and mortals. Whoever obtains God's name from the guru; is known as truthful in the world. Visualizing the guru gives the reward of bathing at sixty-eight shrines. ||8|| True name is the cleansing bath at a sacred shrine, true food and true love. The truthful look adorable speaking the truth. True name is obtained through guru's teaching; true name spreads fragrance in the true congregation. Poet Kal says the praises of the one whose self-discipline and fast is God's name. Seeing the face of the guru, the life becomes truthful and fruitful. ||9|| When You bestow Your glance of grace, You eradicate all wickedness, sin and filth. Says Bal that it controls lust, anger, greed and emotional attachment; Your mind is filled with peace forever; You eliminate the suffering of the world. Guru is the river of the nine treasures that washes away the dirt of our lives. So speaks Tal: serve the guru, day and night, with intuitive love and affection. Seeing guru's face the pain of birth and death is eliminated. ||10|| Swaiyas In praise of the third master: God is one. He is realized by guru's grace. Recite the true primal being; His one name is undeceivable. He carries His devotees across the terrifying world-ocean; recite that supreme name. Reciting that name, Nanak established Lehnaa as the guru and with all divine powers. Says poet Kal: singing God's praises devotee Amar Daas is known in the world. His praises shine throughout the world like the rays of sun, and the branches of the fragrant tree. In the north, south, east and west, people speak of you with admiration. Page 1393 The guru-willed is blessed; by reciting God's name his fortune is reversed as if the river Ganges flows to the west. Same undeceivable name that carries the devotees across the terrifying world ocean dawned to guru Amar Daas; ||1|| The gods and heavenly heralds, the mystics and seekers recite the same name. The stars and the realms of the world, and devotees like Naaraad and Prahlaad recite the same name. The moon and the sun recite the same name; it has saved even mountain ranges. Same undeceivable name that carries the devotees across the terrifying world ocean dawned to guru Amar Daas. ||2|| Reciting the same name, Shiva the master of nine schools of divine knowledge and Sanak etc obtained salvation. The eighty-four mystics and the learned like Ambreek were carried across the terrifying world ocean. It has erased the sins of Udho, Akroor, Trilochan, Naam Dev and Kabeer in today's age. Same undeceivable name that carries the devotees across the terrifying world ocean dawned to guru Amar Daas. ||3|| Millions of angles, celibates, and ascetics recite and enshrine the same name in the mind. Bhisham Pitamah, the son of Ganges recited the same name and enjoyed God's sacred feet in the mind. Reciting the same through great guru's teaching, the congregation obtains salvation. Same undeceivable name that carries the devotees across the terrifying world ocean dawned to guru Amar Daas. ||4|| God's name is like the ray of sun that enlightens the world and like the branches of the Elysian tree that bears fruit the year around. His praises are sung in all four directions of the world. Life is fruitful, when the name of God enshrines in the heart. The angels, beings, heavenly heralds, celestial singers and the six schools of philosophy yearn for God's name. The son of Tej Bhaan of the Bhalla family is noble and famous; with his palms pressed together, Kal worships him. The same name that destroys devotee's fear of the world ocean; you obtained O Amar Daas guru. ||5|| Millions of god's, seekers, mystics, mortals and He who created the entire universe recite the same name. Whoever recites God's name in trance sees the sorrows and pleasures the same. God's name is the highest of all; God's devotees recite it lovingly. The Creator O guru Amar Daas bestows same priceless name to you. ||6|| He is the true brave, peaceful and powerful intuitively; he is realized in devotee's congregation. He is without an enemy. Patience is His symbol since the beginning of time, planted on the bridge to heaven. Saints meet their beloved guru, who unites them with God. Serving the true guru, they find peace; Guru Amar Daas has given them this ability. ||7|| God's name is His cleansing bath, food He eats joyfully. He speaks sweet words reciting God's name. Blessed is he who serves the true guru. By his grace he realizes the inaccessible God. Enshrining God's name in the mind the whole dynasty is liberated. Page 1394 Says Kal: fruitful is the life of one who meets with guru Amar Daas and enlightens. ||8|| On His right hand is the lotus; and supernatural divine powers; On His left are worldly powers, which fascinate the universe. Those who have God abiding in the mind; they only know the taste. He recites God's name from the mouth; guru Amar Daas is dyed with love. On His forehead is the symbol of truth; with his palms pressed together, Kal recites him. Whoever meets the guru, the certified true guru, has all his desires fulfilled. ||9|| Praiseworthy are the feet which follow the path of guru Amar Daas. Praiseworthy are the hands, which touch the feet of guru Amar Daas. Praiseworthy is the tongue, which sings the praises of guru Amar Daas. Praiseworthy are the eyes that see the face of guru Amar Daas. Praiseworthy are the ears, which hear the praises of guru Amar Daas. Praiseworthy is the soul in which dwells guru Amar Daas, the father of the world. Praiseworthy is the head that bows forever in front of guru Amar Daas says Jaalap. ||1||10|| They do not suffer pain or hunger, and they cannot be called poor. They do not feel sorrow, and their limits cannot be found. They do not serve anyone else; they give gifts to hundreds and thousands. They sit on beautiful carpets; they create and destroy at will. They find peace in this world, and live fearlessly among their enemies. Says Jaalap that they are praise worthy; with whom guru Amar Daas is happy; ||2||11|| You studied God single-mindedly and realized God. You see one God, speak of one God. You believe in one God not any other. You dream about one God and are definitely absorbed in one God. At the age of seventy-one, You are still strong. People describe God in many ways; but still He is one in the end. Says Jaalap: O guru Amar Daas, You long for and believe in one God; ||3||12|| The realization that Jai Dev and Naam dev obtained; The realization that Trilochan and devotee Kabeer obtained; Through which Rukmaangad constantly recited God O brother; Amreek and Prahlaad obtained divine knowledge in the refuge of the Lord of the universe. Says Jal, you gave up greed, anger and desire and obtained the same knowledge. Guru Amar Daas is God's devotee; seeing his face obtains salvation. ||4||13|| Meeting with guru Amar Daas, the earthly sins are eliminated. The mystics and seekers get satisfaction meeting with guru Amar Daas. Meeting with guru Amar Daas lovingly ends the journey of life. Meeting with guru Amar Daas, one becomes fearless and coming and going ends. Page 1395 O mortal, realizing one God the duality goes away; and the person becomes divine. Says Jaalap: the countless treasures are obtained by seeing guru Amar Daas. ||5||14|| Guru Nanak recited the true name of the Creator, and implanted in the mind. Through Him, Lehnaa became guru Angad, by lovingly attuning to His feet. Guru Amar Daas of that dynasty is the home of hope. How can I praise his virtues? His virtues are unknowable and unfathomable. I do not know the limits of His virtues. The Creator, the architect of destiny, has made Him a boat to carry all His generations and congregation across the world ocean. Says Keerat: O guru Amar Daas, please protect me I seek your refuge. ||1||15|| God came in the world in the form of a guru. The formless Lord illuminated the realms of the world by His light. He is fully all pervading; He is seen through the light of guru's teaching. Whoever collects the essence of his teachings shall be absorbed in God's feet. Lehnaa, who became guru Angad, and guru Amar Daas, have been reincarnated into the pure house of guru Nanak. Guru Amar Daas is our saviour; I seek your refuge from life to life. ||2||16|| Guru's devotees obtain all meditation asceticism, truth, contentment by seeing the guru. Whoever seeks His sanctuary is saved; his account is cleared in the city of death. His heart is totally filled with loving devotion; he recites God in the mind. Guru is the river of pearls; in a moment, he carries the drowning ones across. He was reincarnated in guru Nanak's dynasty; he praises the virtues of God. Those who serve guru Amar Daas; their pain and poverty go away. ||3||17|| I think and pray in my mind, yet I cannot say in words. You worry about all. I realize you in devotee's company. I think of you and obey your command and serve you O Lord; when the guru looks at you kindly, then he puts the fruit of God's name in your mouth. The unfathomable and unseen primal Lord the cause of causes; I say what he tells me. O guru Amar Daas, doer of deeds, cause of causes; keep me as you please. ||4||18|| Words Of Bhikhaa: Contemplating wisdom and reciting God, the guru merges in the reality. In reality the true Lord is realized by lovingly attuning to him. By controlling lust, and anger and controlling the wandering mind; then he lives in God's place; obeying his order and contemplating he realizes God. In today's age God the Creator created everything and He knows it. Says Bhikhaa: I met the guru. Seeing him I fell in love and became peaceful. ||1||19|| I have been searching for the saints; I have seen many so called spiritual people. The renunciates, ascetics and sweet talking Pandits; I wandered around for a year, but no one touched my soul. Page 1396 I listened to their preaching, but I was not happy with their code of conduct. They forgot God's name and attached to something else; how can I praise them? Says Bhikhaa: O God; unite me with the guru; then I will live the way You want; ||2||20|| I sit in trance at my place of worship wearing the armour of divine wisdom. Holding bow and arrow of faith, the devotee fights with devotion and humility. Through the fear of eternal God the guru stuck his spear in my mind through his teaching. He destroyed lust, anger, greed, emotional attachment and five evil thieves. Guru Amar Daas, the son of Tej Bhaan, of the noble Bhalla family, blessed by guru Nanak, is the master of kings. Says Sall the truth; O guru Amar Daas, you have conquered the army of evil, fighting the battle this way. ||1||21|| The rain drops from the clouds; countless flowers bloom on the earth in spring. Who can know the limits of the rays of sun and moon, the waves of the ocean and the Ganges? Says poet Bhal; he who sings guru's praises obtains the wisdom and intellect of Shiva. O guru Amar Daas, Your Virtues are great; Your praises belong only to You. ||1||22|| Swaiyas In Praise of The Fourth Master: God is one. He is realized by guru's grace. Recite the formless God single-mindedly. By guru's grace, sing the praises of the Lord forever. Singing His praises, the mind becomes enlightened. True guru fulfills the hopes of His humble servant. Serving the true guru, the supreme status is obtained. By reciting the immortal formless God; Meeting with Him, one escapes poverty. Kal Sahaar sings His praises. Sing the praises of the pure wise guru; to whom God's sacred name dawned. He served the true guru and obtained the essence of his teaching by enshrining God's name in the mind. He recites and savors God's name, he trades and longs for the essence of pool of nectar. Says poet Kal: guru Raam Daas, the son of Har Daas, fills up the empty pools. ||1|| The stream of nectar flows and the immortal status is obtained by drinking it; the pool is forever overflowing with nectar. Those saints who have served God previously drink this nectar, and bathe in it; God eliminated their fear, and blessed them with fearlessness. They obtained salvation through guru's teaching. Says poet Kal: guru Raam Daas, the son of Har Daas, fills up the empty pools. ||2|| True guru's understanding is deep and profound. In true congregation the soul gets dyed with deep red colour of love. The lotus of His mind woke up, illuminated with intuitive wisdom and realized the formless God in his home. Page 1397 The kind true guru has implanted God's name in me. By His grace, I controlled the five senses. Says poet kal: Guru Raam Daas, the son of Har Daas, fills up the empty pools; ||3|| The mind got attached to the carefree God intuitively and touched by the touchstone in his home. By the grace of the true guru, He attained the supreme status; He is overflowing with the treasures of loving devotion. He was freed from birth and fear of death by attuning his mind to the ocean of contentment. Says poet Kal; guru Raam Daas, the son of Har Daas, fills up the empty pools. ||4|| He fills up the empty pools; He has enshrined the infinite God in His heart. He realized the destroyer of sufferings contemplating divine wisdom in the mind. He yearns for God's love forever; He knows the joyful taste of His love. By the grace of the true guru, He intuitively enjoys the love. By the grace of guru Nanak, and the sublime teachings of guru Angad, guru Amar Daas played the immortal play. Says poet Kal; O guru Raam Daas, You have attained the state of immortality. ||5|| You abide in the pool of contentment; You enjoy the nectar and enlighten with it. Meeting with You, peace wells up, and sins run away. You have attained the ocean of peace, and You never leave Godly path. The armour of self-restraint, truth, contentment and humility can never be pierced. The Creator certified the true guru, and the world blows the trumpet of his praises. Says poet Kal; O guru Raam Daas, You have attained the supreme state of immortality. ||6|| O certified true guru;

You have conquered the world reciting one God in the mind. Blessed is the true guru Amar Daas, who implanted God's name in your mind. God's name is a priceless treasure; wealth and mysticism are his slaves. He obtained the ocean of peace by surrendering to the immortal God. Guru is the primal God. Attaching to him and reciting God's name the devotee obtains salvation. Says poet Kal; O guru Raam Daas, You have obtained the wealth of Lord's love. ||7|| The flow of loving devotion and primal love does not stop. True guru's teaching is unfathomable; it flows like a stream and intoxicates. Wisdom is His mother, contentment is His father; He is absorbed in the ocean of peace. God does not take birth and came into existence on his own; guru's teaching carries us across and realizes God. The unseen, unfathomable and infinite God is realized by enshrining guru's teaching in the mind. Says poet Kal; O guru Raam Daas, You have realized God the saviour of the world. ||8|| He is the saviour of the world, the priceless treasure and saviour of his devotees. A drop of God's sacred name eliminates the poison of sins. The tree of intuitive peace bears the fruit of sacred divine wisdom. He is realized by guru's grace; blessed and fortunate are those who realize Him. They are liberated through guru's teaching; guru's teaching touches their mind. Says poet Kal; O guru Raam Daas, You carry the insignia of guru's teaching. ||9|| Page 1398 Make the bed of faith, bed cover of peace, canopy of contentment and armour of humility. Recite God's name through guru's teaching and enlighten the companions with it. O unborn God, you abide with the Bhalla guru. Says poet Kal; O guru Raam Daas, You abide in the sacred pool of peace. ||10|| Whoever guru is happy with; he enshrines God in the mind. Whoever guru is happy with; his sins go away. Whoever guru is happy with; his pride and ego are eliminated. Whoever guru is happy with; obtain salvation following guru's teaching. Those who are accepted by the guru; their taking birth in the world is fruitful. Says poet kal; in the refuge of the honourable guru, one obtains joy of salvation. ||11|| Guru has pitched the tent; under it, people from all ages are gathered. He carries the spear of intuition, and support of God's name; it fulfills the devotees. Guru Nanak, guru Angad and guru Amar Daas, merged with God through worship. O guru Raam Daas, You know the taste of kingdom of worship. ||12|| He, who is enlightened sits on the chariot of divine wisdom like Janak. He gathers truth and contentment, and fills up the empty pool. He speaks the unspoken speech of the eternal city. Whoever God blesses, obtains it. O guru Raam Daas, Your sovereign rule, like that of Janak, is Yours alone. ||13|| He who recites the true guru's name single-mindedly; why should he suffer pain of sins? Whoever the guru bestows with a glance of grace a little bit, contemplates guru's teaching and eliminates lust and anger. Guru is the giver to all beings; He speaks the divine wisdom of the unfathomable Lord, and contemplates God day and night. He never sleeps, even for an instant. Seeing Him, poverty vanishes, and the guru willed obtains the treasure of God's name; He washes away the filth of sins through divine wisdom. He recites true guru's name single-mindedly; he does not suffer pain or sins. ||1|| Faith and good deeds are obtained from the perfect guru. The mystics, seekers, devotees, sages, mortals, gods and heroes long to serve him; they attune to him through guru's teaching. Who can know Your limits O carefree formless God? You only can explain the unspoken speech. Reciting God through guru's teaching eliminates worldly doubt, eliminates birth and death and the punishment of devil of death. O ignorant man; think in your mind; recite God all the time and obtain faith and good deeds through the true guru. ||2|| I praise the true guru and the true name. What praises and service can I offer to You? I recite your name with my tongue with love forever. Think Him in the mind intuitively; do not think of anyone else. Enshrine the name of the infinite God in the mind through guru's teaching. Page 1399 Says poet Nal; like touching the philosopher's stone, glass becomes gold, and the sandalwood tree imparts its fragrance to other trees; reciting God's name liberates all. Seeing His door eliminates lust and anger. I praise true guru's name. ||3|| Guru Raam Daas was blessed with the throne of divine wisdom. First, Nanak the moon was born to enlighten and bestow happiness to the world; He blessed guru Angad with the treasure of divine wisdom, and the unspoken words; He controlled the five demons and thirst of the devil of death. True and honourable guru Amar Daas preserved honour in today's age. Seeing His lotus feet, sin and evil are destroyed. When His mind was totally satisfied in every way, He was totally pleased; then he bestowed on guru Raam Daas the throne of divine wisdom. ||4|| Radd: He established the earth, the sky, the air, the water, the oceans, fire and food. He created the moon, the stars and the sun, night and day and mountains; he blessed the trees with flowers and fruits. He created gods, human beings and the seven seas; He established the universe. Guru Amar Daas was blessed with the same true name and was enlightened. ||1||5|| Glass is transformed into gold, listening to guru's teaching. Poison is transformed into nectar, reciting the name of the true guru. Iron becomes diamond when the true guru bestows his blessing Stones are transformed into emeralds, when the mortal contemplates guru's teaching. The true guru transforms ordinary wood into sandalwood, eradicating the pain of poverty. Whoever touches the feet of the true guru; the animal and ghosts change into gods and men. ||2||6|| One who has the guru on his side; how could he be proud of his wealth? One who has the guru on his side; what would millions of supporters do for him? One who has the guru on his side does not depend on others for spiritual wisdom and meditation. One who has the guru on his side contemplates guru's teachings, and abides in truth. The servant poet prays to him, who says guru guru all the time. Whoever enshrines the name of the guru in his heart gets rid of both birth and death. ||3||7|| Without the guru, there is utter darkness; without the guru, realization does not come. Without the guru, there is no awareness or success or liberation. Say guru guru and truly contemplate the guru; say guru guru O my mind. Say guru guru and become sacred saying guru; your all sins will be erased. Speak guru, see guru, say guru guru; poet Nalh says that guru is truly God. Those who do not see the guru, do not make him their guru; their coming in the world is useless. ||4||8|| Say guru guru O my mind; Page 1400 All-powerful guru carries those across in today's age; who get in trance by listening to guru's teaching. He, who intuitively contemplates God; God abides close to him and destroys his pains and bestows happiness. He recites the perfect God in the mind and seeing his face the sins are destroyed. If you long for wisdom, wealth, mystic power; then say guru guru O my mind. ||5||9|| Seeing the face of the guru obtains real happiness. The thirst and yearning to drink the nectar is fulfilled by intuitively meeting the guru. My mind was wandering in ten directions and now it has become perfectly stable and recites God and enjoys. Goindwal is the city of God, built on the bank of the Beas river. The pain of many years has disappeared seeing guru's face and obtained eternal happiness. ||6||10|| All-powerful guru placed His hand on my head. Guru was kind, and blessed me with God's name. Looking at His feet, my sins are erased. He, who listens to God's name regularly day and night; the devil of death is afraid of him. Says God's slave: whoever longs for the world guru; meet guru Raam Daas and transform by his touch. Guru Raam Daas realized the true God. All-powerful guru placed His hand on His head. ||7||11|| Now, please preserve the honour of Your humble bhaat slave. God saved the honour of devotee Prahlaad, when he tore Harnaakhash apart with his claws. Then, he preserved Dropadi's honour; when her clothes were removed from her, she was blessed with more and more clothes. Sudaamaa was saved from misfortune; a prostitute recited God, her deeds were fulfilled. O honourable true guru, if it pleases You, saves the honour of Your slave bhaat in today's age. ||8||12|| Jholnaa: O mortal say guru guru guru. Say God enshrining his name in the mind; say God and believe in it; You will obtain His love by saying God; give up other paths and say God lovingly. Enshrine guru's word in the mind and control the five senses; you will be liberated and honoured in God's court. If you long for happiness here and hereafter; say guru guru O mortal. ||1||13|| Say guru guru truly and believe in it. Know that, God is the treasure of excellence. Enshrine Him in your mind all the time enshrining guru's word in the mind. Then, cleanse yourself in the pure and unfathomable water of the guru; O guru's followers and saints; cross over the world Ocean through the true love of God's name. Recite the carefree formless God forever lovingly through guru's teaching and worship God with love and joy. O ignorant mind, give up your doubts; say guru guru. ||2||14|| Page 1401 Saying guru guru realizes God. Guru is an ocean, profound, infinite and unfathomable. Lovingly attuned to God's name obtains the jewels, diamonds and emeralds. Then the guru makes us fragrant and fruitful, and His touch transforms us into gold. Reciting guru's teaching washes the filth of evil deeds away. The stream of nectar flows constantly from His door. The saints and followers bathe in the pure pool of guru's divine wisdom. Enshrine the bestowal of salvation God's name in the mind; say guru guru and realize God. ||3||15|| O my mind; say guru guru guru. Serving Him, Shiva, mystics, seekers, angels, demons and millions of gods obtained salvation. Listen to guru's word with your ears. Then, those saints who say guru guru are liberated. Prahlaad obtained salvation meeting the saint guru. Naarad and Sanak obtained liberation by saying God; recite God's name and you will be saved and give up other enjoyments. The servant prays and recites his name. Say guru guru O my mind; ||4||16||29|| The honourable supreme guru showers His kindness on all; He blessed Dhroo in first age (Sat Yug). He saved the devotee Prahlaad. Placing the lotus of His Hand on his forehead; the unseen form of God cannot be seen. All mystics and seekers seek his refuge. Enshrining guru's word in the mind truly. Obtains salvation for this human body; Guru is the boat, guru is the boatman. Without the guru, no one can cross over. By guru's grace, God is realized. Without the guru, no one is liberated. Guru Nanak lived close to the Creator. He established Lehnaa as guru, and enlightened the world. Lehnaa established the path of faith. He passed on to guru Amar Daas, of Bhalla family. Then, He established the great Raam Daas of the Sodhi family. He was blessed with the inexhaustible treasure of God's name. He was blessed with the treasure of God's name; throughout the four ages, serving the guru is rewarding. Those who bow at his feet and seek His refuge obtain peace; they are blessed with supreme joy by saying guru guru. Guru's Body is the embodiment of the supreme Lord the master and primal being; that feeds and cherishes all. Serve the true guru. His wisdom cannot be comprehended; He is Guru Raam Daas the bestowal of salvation. ||1|| The devotees recite his sacred words of sermon with amazing happiness. Seeing guru's face obtains eternal happiness and fulfillment in the world. Seeing guru's sacred face is rewarding in the world. His touch bestows salvation. Even sinful people conquer the realm of death, if they are imbued with God's love. He is certified, like the handsome Ram Chander in the house of Dasrath of the Raghu dynasty. Even the sages seek his refuge. Page 1402 Serve the true guru; He is beyond description. That is guru Raam Daas the bestowal of salvation. ||2|| The world is the ocean of fire; God's name is the raft the guru put in your mouth. The cycle of birth and death in this world ends by realizing God. Those humble beings who realize Him, obtain a high status. They eliminate worldly wealth, emotional attachment, greed, lust and anger. Their doubt of others eliminated. They obtained divine vision the cause of causes. Serve the true guru; He is beyond description. That is guru Raam Daas the bestowal of salvation. ||3|| Guru's greatness is manifest forever in each and every heart. His humble servants sing his praises. Some read, listen and sing Him, taking bath early in the morning. After taking bath they worship the guru with clear mind. Touching philosopher's stone, their bodies are transformed into gold by focusing their mind to the divine light. Master of the universe, the life of the world pervades water and land; he is seen in many forms. Serve the true guru; He is beyond description. That is guru Raam Daas the bestowal of salvation. ||4|| Those who realize the eternal, unchanging word of God, like Dhroo, are saved from death. They cross over the terrifying world-ocean in an instant; Lord created the world like a bubble of water. Their stars rise in devotee's company and they are extremely happy through guru's word. The honourable guru is the highest of all. Serve him with love intuitively. ||5|| I praise my guru I say Waahay Guru, guru guru, God God. You have lotus like eyes, you talk sweet. You enjoy the company of millions of friends and companions. Mother Yashoda invites You O Krishna to eat rice and yoghurt. Seeing your amazing face everyone is enticed; you stutter when you talk. The ankle bells make tinkling sound when you play. Death's pen and command are in Your hand. Tell me, who can erase it? Shiva and Brahma yearn to enshrine Your divine wisdom in their hearts. You are the true Lord from the beginning and forever; guru guru God God O Waahay guru; ||1||6|| God's name is the most sacred place with realization and intellect. You are formless and infinite O God. You abide in pure devotee's mind. You disguised and killed Harnaakas with your claws. You carry a conch, a circle on the body, divine symbol on the palm, you cheated Bal, you are beyond comprehension. No one can explain you O God; You are true primal Lord from the beginning and forever. Guru Guru God God O Waahay guru; ||2||7|| You wear yellow robe, with teeth like jasmine flowers; You live with your beloved, you wear a rosary and crown adorned with peacock feathers. Page 1403 You have no advisors, You are patient and have faith; You are unseen and unfathomable. You staged the play of the universe and enjoy it. You are beyond description. You are omnipresent. You disguise in the form of a mystic and you are the emperor of emperors. You are true primal Lord from the beginning and forever. Guru guru God God O Waahay guru||3||8|| True Guru, guru guru God God Waahay guru the Lord of the universe. You cheated the most powerful king Bal. You bless Your devotees O child prince Krishna; the thunder of your army and the beat of drums echo across the universe. Reciting God eliminates evil deeds and the whole world becomes happy. You are the Lord of the universe, God of gods and that of a thousand headed serpent. He took birth in the form of fish, tortoise and wild boar. You played ball and enjoyed on the banks of river Jamuna. Enshrining Your name in the mind and eliminating useless deeds says Gayand; true guru true guru the Lord of the universe. ||4||9|| The supreme guru, supreme guru is really the God. Obey guru's word; believe it and treasure it; recite guru's teaching day and night. You will obtain salvation and the highest status. Renounce lust, anger, greed and attachment; give up deceiving others. Cut the noose of ego, and be imbued in devotee's company. Eliminate attachment of body, home, spouse, and the pleasures of this world. Serve forever at His lotus feet, and firmly implant these teachings inside. Enshrine the essence of God's name in the mind; give up useless deeds from the mind O Gayand. O honourable guru guru God God waahay guru. ||5||10|| Your servants are totally fulfilled, throughout the ages; O Waahay guru (God); it is all Your blessing. O formless Lord, You are eternal and will be forever; no one can say how long You have been there. You created countless Brahmas and Vishnus; they were intoxicated with emotional attachment. You created millions of species of beings, and provide them with food. Your servants are totally fulfilled, throughout the ages; O Waahay guru, it is Your entire blessing. ||1||11|| I admire saying Waaho! Waaho! Great! Great is the play of God! He laughs, He thinks; He illuminates the sun and the moon. He is water, the earth and its support. He abides in each and every heart. He is male and female; He is the pawns and the game of chess. O guru-willed; praise God in devotee's company. That is the true praise. ||2||12|| You created this big play of the great game. O Waahay guru, this is all Your doing. You are pervading the water, land, skies and the underworld. Your Words are sweeter than nectar. Brahmas and Shivas respect and obey You. O destroyer of death, formless Lord, I beg of You. Page 1404 By guru's grace, good deeds are done attaching the mind to true congregation. You have formed and created this play, this great game. O Waahay guru, this is all Your making. ||3||13||42|| The Lord is inaccessible, infinite, eternal and primal; no one knows His origin. Shiva and Brahma meditate on Him; the Vedas describe Him again and again. God is formless, enemyless; there is no one like Him. He creates and destroys – He is all-powerful; God is the boat to carry all across. He created the world in various forms; servant Matura sings His praises. There is God. It is true. He is the Creator. He abides in guru Raam Daas's mind. ||1|| I am holding tight to the powerful guru; in order to improve my thinking and intellect. His symbol of faith flies proudly forever, to defend against the waves of sin. Servant Matura speaks the truth O God, there is nothing else I can say. In today's age God's name is a big ship to take us across the terrifying world ocean. ||2|| The saints imbued with His love sing His praises in true congregation. God the Lord of the earth started the faithful path. He follows it lovingly and does not leave it. Says Matura: fortunate are those who follow it and reap the reward. Those who focus their mind to guru's feet; the justice of destiny does not bother them. ||3|| The sacred name fills their mind through the wave of guru's teaching before the dawn. He is deep and profound, unfathomable and very large and full of jewels forever. The honourable saints do amazing things. Their fear of death and their painful account is erased. In today's age, see guru's face the ocean of peace to eliminate the sins. ||4|| The sages focus their mind to him. People wander around in all four ages but only a few obtain divine wisdom. In the hymns of the Vedas, Brahma sings His praises; Shiva the sage sings his praises on Kailash Mountain. The yogis, celibates, mystics, seekers, many with matted hair and renunciates wander all over searching for Him. True guru blessed guru Raam Daas with God's name by his grace. ||5|| He focuses His mind inside; and illuminates the universe by His divine power. Seeing his face the wandering, doubt and pain disappear; peace and contentment well up. The devotees and followers long for him like the bumblebee for the fragrance of flowers. The knowledgeable guru established the Eternal throne of truth, in guru Raam Daas. ||6|| Page 1405 He saved the world which was intoxicated with worldly wealth by bestowing the sacred name by his power. The praiseworthy guru is blessed with eternal peace, wealth and prosperity; the mystic powers do not leave his company. The gifts of the powerful Lord are great; the servant devotee speaks the truth. He does not care about anyone, upon whose head the guru puts his hand. ||7||49|| He is totally pervading the universe. In the entire world, He did not create another like Him. He came into being on his own. The angels, human beings and demons have not found His limits. The angels, demons and human beings have not found His limits; the heavenly heralds and celestial singers wander searching for Him. God is eternal, imperishable, unmoving and unchanging, unborn, self-existent, primal being and infinite; He is all-powerful cause of causes; all beings recite his name. O honourable guru Raam Daas; You are admired in the entire world and you obtained the supreme status. ||1|| Nanak, the true guru, worshipped God single-mindedly; He surrendered His body, mind and wealth to the Lord of the universe. The infinite Lord enshrined His own image in guru Angad. And enshrined the infinite wisdom in his mind; Guru Amar Daas controlled the Creator by praising Him. O honourable Raam Daas, You are admired in the entire world and you obtained the supreme status. ||2|| Naarad, Dhroo, Prahlaad and Sudaamaa are God's devotees from previous lifes. Ambreek, Jai Dev, Trilochan, Naam Dev and Kabeer also; they were born in today's age and their admiration spread all over the world. O honourable guru Raam Daas, You are admired in the entire world and you obtained the supreme status. ||3|| Those who recite you with love; their lust and anger are erased. Those who intently recite You, their pain and poverty ends in a moment. Those who visualize you and touched by you, sing your praises like bhatt Balh. O honourable guru Raam Daas, You are admired in the entire world and you obtained the supreme status. ||4|| Those who recite the true guru, the darkness from their eyes are removed in an instant. Those who recite the true guru in the mind, their love for God's name increases day by day. Those who recite the true guru; the burning fire of their mind is eliminated. Those who recite the true guru; they obtain mystic powers wealth and all treasures. Says bhaat Balh; praise guru Raam Daas in devotee's company. O mortals; recite the true guru; meeting with him God is realized. ||5||54|| Those who obtain the supreme status practicing guru's teaching; serve them and do not leave their refuge. From that diamond the divine light is obtained which destroys the darkness pain and poverty. Page 1406 Says poet Keerat; those who attach to saint's feet; their lust, anger and the thirst of devil of death are eliminated. As Nanak was with Angad forever; so was guru Amar Daas with guru Raam Daas. ||1|| Whoever serves the true guru obtains the treasure; he lives at God's feet night and day. In his company eternal love wells up; as the fragrance wells up in the company of sandalwood tree. Dhroo, Prahlaad, Kabeer and Trilochan recited God's name and were enlightened. Seeing Him, the mind becomes happy; that is guru Raam Daas, says saint Kal Sahaar. ||2|| Guru Nanak realized the formless God reciting His name; he worshipped Him with love. Then he merged with guru Angad like water in the ocean; and he laid the foundation through guru's teaching. The story of guru Amar Daas is beyond telling. It cannot be told. Guru Raam Daas of the Sodhi family was given the honour to bestow salvation to all; ||3|| I am full of faults; I have no virtue. I eat poison forsaking the nectar. I am deluded by worldly wealth, emotional attachment and doubt. I am in love with my son and spouse. I heard that the most sacred path is guru's company; meeting with him the fear of devil of death gets eliminated. Keerat the poet offers this prayer: O guru Raam Daas; keep me in your refuge; ||4||58|| He is out of control under the influence of false attachment. The lust caught him by the hair and threw him away. He is torn apart by anger, extreme greed and insulting others. In life and death, with palms pressed together, obey his order whatever it may be; He brought the terrifying world-ocean under His control and carried across the followers with joy. He sits on the throne of truth, with the canopy above His Head; He enjoys the worship and all pleasures by his power. Says devotee Salh; O guru Raam Daas, Your kingdom and army are invincible. ||1|| You are the true guru, throughout the four ages; You are the transcendent Lord. The angels, beings, seekers, mystics, and followers serve you all the way. You are from the beginning, without parents, for ages; Your power supports the universe. You are inaccessible; You are the protector of Vedas. You have conquered the age and death. Guru Amar Daas is permanently established; you carry all across the world ocean. O guru Raam Daas, the destroyer of sins; poet Salh seeks your refuge. ||2||60|| Swaiyas In praise of the fifth master: God is one. He is realized by guru's grace. Recite the primal, permanent and immortal Lord. Reciting him the filth of ill will goes away. I enshrine the lotus feet of the true guru in my heart. Page 1407 Guru Arjan intuitively contemplates contentment. He was born in the House of guru Raam Daas; And all hopes were fulfilled. From birth, He realized God through guru's teachings. With palms pressed together, Kal the poet speaks his praises. God brought him into the world, to practice the divine worship. He was enlightened through guru's teaching and enshrined God on his tongue. Attached to guru Nanak, guru Angad and guru Amar Daas, He attained the supreme status. In the house of guru Raam Daas, God's devotee, guru Arjun was born. ||1|| The fortunate intuitively enshrined guru's teaching in the mind. His jewel mind was content and the guru taught him to recite God's name. The inaccessible and unfathomable, supreme Lord is revealed through the true guru. In the house of guru Raam Daas, guru Arjun has come as God's image. ||2|| The eternal rule of king Janak has been established, and the first age has returned. His mind has accepted guru's teaching and he realized the unrealized. Guru Nanak laid the foundation of truth; He is merged with true guru. In the house of guru Raam Daas, guru Arjun has come as the image of infinite God. ||3|| The sovereign Lord staged this amazing play; contentment and pure intellect was infused in him by the true guru. Says poet Kal; he sings the praises of unborn and self existing God. Guru Nanak blessed guru Angad, and guru Angad blessed guru Amar Daas with the treasure. Guru Raam Daas blessed guru Arjun, with the touch of philosopher's stone, and was certified. ||4|| O guru Arjun, You are eternal, invaluable, unborn, self-existing God; You are the destroyer of fear, the dispeller of pain, infinite and carefree; You have seen the unseen; destroyed the doubt and worry and bestowal of peace and soothing. Self-existent, perfect primal God the Creator has taken birth. First, guru Nanak, then guru Angad and guru Amar Daas, true guru abides in true guru`s teachings. Blessed is guru Raam Daas, the philosopher's stone, who transformed guru Arjun into the guru. ||5|| He is proclaimed all over the world; He remains united with God intuitively. The fortunate met the perfect guru and was attuned to God with love and took the weight of the earth. He is the destroyer of fear, the pain of others. Kal Sahaar sings his praises. In Sodhi family, son of guru Raam Daas, God`s pre-ordained devotee Arjun is born. |6|| He is the pillar of faith, filled with guru`s teaching and destroyer of sins of others. Through the essence of guru`s teaching, he is kind like God and destroyer of ego. He is bestowed with supreme divine wisdom by the true guru and he loves it. He is truthfully filled with God`s name and his treasure never empties. O son of guru Raam Daas, You have pitched the canopy of contentment in the world. Says poet Kal; you have enjoyed the kingdom of worship. ||7|| Page 1408 You enjoyed the love of carefree God. You among millions have seen the unseen God. Through the true guru, You have obtained the state of the inaccessible, unfathomable, profound Lord. Through the guru, You are certified and approved; You enjoy the kingdom of worship. Blessed is the guru, who has filled to brim, the pools which were empty. Through the certificate of guruship, You endure the unendurable; You are immersed in the pool of contentment. Says poet Kal; you have obtained the contentment of divine worship. ||8|| Nectar drips from Your tongue, you bless others, O incomprehensible and infinite divine hero. O guru, your teaching eliminates ego. You have conquered the five thieves, and obtained the eternal contentment. The world obtains salvation reciting God`s name by enshrining the true guru in the mind. Says poet Kal that you have lit the lamp of divine wisdom of Janak; ||9|| Sorathe; Guru Arjun is the certified primal being; like Arjuna, He never leaves the battlefield. God`s name is his spear adorned by guru`s teaching. ||1|| God's name is the boat, the bridge to cross over the terrifying world-ocean. You are in love with the true guru; attached to God`s name, You have saved the world. ||2|| God`s name the saviour of the world is obtained from the honourable true guru. Now, I am not concerned with anything else; I am fulfilled at your door. ||3||12|| Guru Nanak is the embodiment of God. From Him, came guru Angad; His essence was absorbed into the essence. Guru Angad showered His grace and established Amar Daas as the true guru. Guru Amar Daas blessed guru Raam Daas with the umbrella of divine wisdom. Says Matura the sacred words, by seeing the face of guru Raam Daas; With your eyes, see the certified primal being guru Arjun, the fifth guru. ||1|| He is the true guru, full of truth and contentment. From the very beginning, the primal being has written this destiny on His forehead. Divine Light shines; his divine power pervades the entire world. With philosopher's touch of the guru; he became the guru. Says Matura: enshrine his picture in the mind and be at his service all the time. In today's age guru Arjun is the ship to carry the world across the world ocean. ||2|| The world knows him and begs of him; his fragrance merges in those who recite God`s name with love day and night. He is completely unattached, and imbued with love of the transcendent lord; He is free of desire, but he is a family man. He is in love with infinite God; any other taste other than God is useless. Matura's God pervades all; the devotee's realize God by loving guru Arjun. ||3|| Page 1409 All the gods, sages, Indra, Shiva and Yogis have not found God's limits. Even Brahma who created the Vedas, says; do not forget God`s name even for a moment. Matura's God is kind to the poor; he bestows contentment to the universe in devotee's company. Guru Raam Daas lit guru's Light in guru Arjun to save the world. ||4|| In the great darkness of this world, God revealed Himself, incarnated as guru Arjun. Says Matura; those who drink God`s sacred name; their millions of pains are erased. O my mind; do not leave this path; I do not know any different; Perfect God has come in the mind of guru Arjun. ||5|| Till it was not written on my forehead; I wandered all over. I was drowning in the horrible world-ocean of this age; the reward of my deeds can never be erased. Matura speaks the truth; God created the prophet to liberate the world. Whoever recites guru Arjun Dev; shall not suffer the pain of going through the womb. ||6|| In the ocean of this dark age; it is revealed; reciting God`s name bestows salvation.

Pain and poverty are taken away from those; in whose heart the saint abides. He is the pure form of the infinite Lord; there is no other except him. Whoever recites him intently becomes like him. He is totally pervading the earth, the sky and the entire universe. Says Mathuraa: there is no difference between God and guru; guru Arjun is the true image of God. ||7||19|| The stream of God's name flows like the Ganges, invincible and unstoppable. The congregation of devotees bathes in it; they read the Puraanaas and sing Brahma's Vedas daily. The invincible fan waves over His head; he says God's name from his mouth. Transcendent Lord has placed the royal canopy over the head of guru Arjun. Guru Nanak, guru Angad, guru Amar Daas and guru Raam Daas met and went to God. Says Harbans; the whole world sings his praises; who says that the guru has died? |1|| By God's will, guru Raam Daas went to the city of God. God offered him His throne and seated him on it. The angels and gods celebrated him by singing his praises. The demons ran away; their sins made them shiver. Those who worshipped guru Raam Daas; their pains were eliminated. He gave the royal canopy and throne to guru Arjun, and went home. ||2||21||9||11||10||10||22||60||143|| Page 1410

God is one. It is true. He is the Creator. He is carefree. He has no enemy. He is immortal. He does not take birth. He came into existence on his own. He is realized by guru's grace.

Hymns of tune of Vaar and others. First Master: O proud, youthful, self-centred and out of control bride. How can you be respectful to your mother in law if you are not humble? O sister, those painted mansions built as high as mountains. I have seen them fall O bride do not be proud? ||1|| O bride with deer-like eyes, listen to the words of infinite wisdom. First, check the merchandise, and then buy it. Do not associate with evil but honour and celebrate the friends. O blind; contemplate the ways by which you meet the beloved one. Surrender mind and body to the beloved; this is the essence of happiness. Do not fall in love with one who is destined to leave. O Nanak, I admire those who understand this. ||2|| If you wish to swim across the water, then ask those who swim through the waves. Those who have survived these treacherous waves are wise. ||3|| The storm rages and the rain floods the land; thousands of waves rise and surge. If you cry for true guru's help; believe in him and the boat will not sink; ||4|| O Nanak, what has happened to the world? There is no guide or friend. There is no love, even among brothers and relatives. For the sake of the world, people have lost their faith. ||5|| They cry and weep all over. They cry, beat their chest and pull their hair; but if they recite God's name; they will be absorbed in it. O Nanak, I admire them ||6|| O my mind, do not waver or wander; take the straight path. The fear of scary tiger is behind you, and the pool of fire ahead. My mind is doubtful, but I cannot see any other way; O Nanak, the guru-willed are saved in the company of beloved God. ||7|| The fear is killed by killing the mind by those who are blessed by the true guru. One who realizes him, meets with God, and never dies again. Page 1411 By his one glance of grace you will be content and your hands will not get dirty in mud. O Nanak, the guru-willed are saved; guru is the true embankment of the ocean. ||8|| If you want to put out the fire, then find water; without the guru, the ocean of water is not found. You will continue to wander in different lifes; no matter how many good deeds you do? If you follow true guru's will; the devil of death will not tax you. O Nanak, the pure immortal status is obtained, and guru will unite you with God. ||9|| The crow rubs and washes itself in the mud puddle. Its mind and body are polluted and its beak is filled with filth and it stinks. The swan in the pool associated with the crow, does not know that it was evil. Such is the love of the faithless; it is realized through love O wise man; So proclaim the victory of the society of saints, and do good deeds O guru-willed. O Nanak, the guru is a sacred shrine on the riverbank; bathe in it and become pure. ||10|| What reward can you get if you do not worship and love God? Wearing clothes and eating food is useless, if the mind is filled with the love of duality. Seeing and hearing is false, if one tells lies. O Nanak, praise God's name; everything else is coming and going in ego. ||11|| Saints are few and far between in the world; ||12|| O Nanak, one who is struck by the Lord dies instantaneously; the power to live is lost. If someone dies by such a stroke, then he is accepted. He, who is struck by the Lord; after such a stroke, he is approved. The arrow of love, shot by the all-knowing Lord, cannot be pulled out. ||13|| Who can wash the unbaked clay pot? Joining the five elements together, the Lord made a false cover. When it pleases Him, He makes the pot perfectly. The supreme light shines, and the divine music plays; ||14|| Those who are totally blind in their mind? Do not have the integrity to keep their word. With their blind minds, and their upside-down heart-lotus, they look totally ugly. Some know how to speak and understand what they are told. They are wise and adorable. Some do not know the sound, spiritual wisdom or the joy of singing. They do not understand good and bad. Some have no idea of perfection, wisdom or understanding; they know nothing about the mystery of the word. O Nanak, those are the real donkeys; who are proud without having any virtue. ||15|| He is a Brahmin, who knows God. He recites God and practices austerity and good deeds. He keeps faith in humility and contentment. Breaking his bonds, he is liberated. Such a Brahmin is worthy of worship. ||16|| He is a true warrior, who fights and performs good deeds. He uses his body to give awns; He understands his farm, and plants the seeds of generosity. Such a warrior is accepted in the court of the Lord. Whoever practices greed, possessiveness and falsehood? He receives the fruit of his doing. ||17|| Do not heat your body like a furnace, or burn your bones like firewood. What is wrong with your head and feet? See your Husband Lord Inside; ||18|| Page 1412 God abides in all; there is nobody without God; O Nanak, the guru-willed who realize God; are the happy soul brides. ||19|| If you desire to play this game of love; Then put your head on your palm and come to my street. When you put your feet on this path; You may lose your head but never turn back. ||20|| False is the friendship with the false and greedy. False breeds false; the ignorant does not know death; where does he go after death? ||21|| Without divine wisdom, the people worship ignorance. They deal in the darkness of love of duality. ||22|| Without the guru, there is no divine wisdom; without faith there is no meditation. Without truth, there is no credit; without capital, there is no balance. ||23|| The mortals are sent into the world; then, they get up and depart. There is no joy in this. ||24|| Raam Chander was sad in his mind; still he assembled his army and forces. The army of monkeys was at his service; his mind and body became eager for war. Raawan took away his wife Sita, and his brother Lachhman died of a curse. O Nanak, the Creator is the doer of all; He creates and destroys and looks after all; ||25|| In his mind, Raam Chander mourned for Sita and Lachhman. Then, he remembered Hanuman the monkey, who came to him. The misguided demon did not understand that God is the doer of all deeds. O Nanak, God has no concern with anything; God does not erase your deeds. ||26|| The city of Lahore suffered terrible destruction for four hours. ||27|| Third Master: The city of Lahore is a pool of nectar, the home of praise. ||28|| First Master: What are the signs of a prosperous person? His stores of food never run out. Prosperity dwells in his home, with the sounds of girls and women. All the women of his home shout and cry over useless things. Whatever he takes, does not give back. He earns more and more and suffers. ||29|| O lotus, your leaves were green, and your flowers golden. What pain has burnt you, your body is black? O Nanak, my body is battered. I have not received that water which I love. Seeing it, my body blossomed I was blessed with a deep beautiful colour. ||30|| No one lives long enough to accomplish all he wishes. Only the spiritually wise live forever; they are honoured for their intuitive awareness. Bit by bit, life passes by uselessly. O Nanak, whom should we complain? Death takes one away without asking; ||31|| Do not blame the Lord; when someone grows old, his intellect leaves him as well. The blind man talks and babbles, and then falls in the ditch. ||32|| All that, the perfect Lord does is perfect; there is no less or more. O Nanak, if the guru-willed knows this; he merges in perfect God. ||33|| Page 1413 Hymn, Third Master: God is one. He is realized by guru's grace. Do not call them God's devotees; who have doubt in the mind; they impart the similar faith, as them O Nanak. ||1|| One who begs for the supreme status of the formless God? O Nanak, only a few receive awns of such food; ||2|| If I was a religious scholar, or an astrologer, I read four Vedas with my mouth. I was known in the entire universe through the deeds I did. ||3|| If a Brahmin kills a cow or a female child, and accepts the offerings of an evil person; He is cursed with leprosy; he is forever filled with egotistic pride. One, who forgets God's name O Nanak, is covered by countless sins. Burn all other wise ideas but keep the essence of divine wisdom. ||4|| No one can erase that what is written on one's forehead from above. O Nanak, whatever is written happens; whoever is blessed realizes it. ||5|| Those who forget God's name in love of false greed; they are filled with enticing worldly wealth and fire of greed. They are not left with vine or a pumpkin; they are robbed by the worldly wealth. The self-willed is tied and taken away; like a dog he cannot not mix with cattle herd; God misleads the misguided. He unites them in His union also. O Nanak, the guru-willed is freed if he follows true guru's will. ||6|| If you want to praise anyone; praise the praiseworthy God. O Nanak, only God's door is true; stay away from all other doors. ||7|| O Nanak, wherever I go, I find the true Lord. Wherever I look, I see One Lord. He reveals to the guru-willed. ||8|| Guru's teaching is the destroyer of pain; if anyone enshrines in the mind. By guru's grace, it enshrines in the mind; you get what you plant; ||9|| O Nanak, acting in ego, countless are wasted away to death. Those who meet the true guru are saved through guru's indescribable teaching. ||10|| Those who serve the true guru single-mindedly; I touch their feet. God enshrines in the mind through guru's teaching and the hunger for wealth goes away. The beings are pure and happy, who are absorbed in God's name. O Nanak, other empires are false; those imbued with God's name are real emperors. ||11|| As wife worships the husband at home and adores him with love. She prepares and offers him all sorts of sweet delicacies and dishes of all flavours. Same way God's devotees admire God's sermon focusing their mind to God's name. They offer their mind, body and wealth to the guru, and sell their heads to Him. God's devotees long for God's worship with love and God unites them with Him and fulfills their desire. Page 1414 God is carefree; He is satisfied without eating. Whoever follows guru's will; gets fulfilled by singing God's praises. Blessed are they in today's age; who follow guru's will. ||12|| Those who do not serve the true guru, and do not enshrine guru's teaching in the mind; Cursed are their lifes. Why did they come in the world? Following guru's teachings, love wells up and they fall in love with God. God's name obtains by pre-ordained destiny O Nanak, and they cross the world ocean. ||13|| The world is deluded by the attachment of worldly wealth; their home is being robbed and they do not know it. The self-willed is blind in the world; his mind is robbed by lust and anger. With the sword of spiritual wisdom, kill the five demons and remain awake through guru's teachings. The jewel of God's name is revealed, their mind and body are purified. Those without God's name wander around with noses cut and cry without God's name. O Nanak, whatever God wrote from destiny; no one can erase it. ||14|| The guru-willed earn the wealth of God's name through guru's teaching. They receive the wealth of God's name; their treasures are overflowing. They sing God's praises and speak God's virtues; there is no limit to His creation. O Nanak, the Creator does everything and looks after as well. ||15|| The guru-willed is content and his mind ascends to tenth divine gate. No one is sleepy or hungry there; they dwell in peace reciting God's sacred name. O Nanak, pain and pleasure do not afflict anyone, where God's light shines. ||16|| All have come, wearing the robes of lust and anger. Some are born, some pass away. They come and go by God's order. Their comings and goings in different lifes does not end; they are attached to duality. They wander tied by deeds; nothing can be done to them. ||17|| Whoever God is kind to; they meet the true guru. Meeting with the true guru, their fate is turned around; they remain dead while still alive, with intuitive peace. O Nanak, those imbued with God's worship merge with God reciting His name. ||18|| The intellect of the self-willed is fickle; he is very tricky and clever inside. Whatever he has done, and whatever he does, is useless. Nothing gets accepted. Those who do good deeds and give awns; all go to the court of justice of destiny. Without the true guru, the devil of death does not leave him alone; he is ruined by the love of duality. Youth slips away imperceptibly, old age comes, and he dies. The mortal is caught in love and emotional attachment to children and spouse, but none of them will help him in the end. Whoever serves the true guru finds peace; God's name comes to dwell in their mind. O Nanak, those who are absorbed in God's name are really fortunate. ||19|| The self-willed do not recite God's name; without God's name they cry in pain. Page 1415 They do not worship the supreme Lord; how can they find peace in duality? They are filled with the filth of ego; even guru's teaching cannot wash it away. O Nanak, those without God's name die filthy; their valuable life is lost. ||20|| The self-willed are deaf and blind; they are filled with the fire of ego. They have no understanding of guru's sermon; guru's teaching does not illuminate them. They do not know their inner being, and they have no faith in guru's word. Spiritually wise are filled with guru's teaching; they are attuned to God with love and are happy forever. God saves the honour of the spiritually wise. I admire them forever Servant Nanak is the slave of those guru-willed who serve the Lord. ||21|| Worldly wealth is a poisonous snake. It has encircled the world and put venom in it, O mother! The antidote to the venom is God's name; the guru puts it in the mouth through his teaching. Those with pre-ordained destiny, meet the true guru. Meeting the true guru, they become pure; their poison of ego goes away. The faces of the guru-willed are happy and they are honoured in God's court. Servant Nanak admires them forever, who follow guru's will. ||22|| True guru, the primal being, is enemyless. He recites God in the mind with love. Whoever creates enmity with the enemyless; he burns his own house. He is filled with anger and ego. He burns forever and suffers. They tell lies and bark like dogs; they eat poison in love of duality. They wander for poisonous worldly wealth. They go door to door and lose honour. It is like the son of a prostitute; he does not know the name of his father. They do not recite God's name. The Creator ruins them. God showers kindness on the guru-willed; He unites the separated devotees with Him. Servant Nanak admires them; who touch true guru's feet. ||23|| Those attached to God's name are saved; those without God's name go to the city of death. O Nanak, without God's name, there is no peace; they regret in coming and going. ||24|| When anxiety and wanderings come to an end, the mind becomes happy. By guru's grace, the soul-bride understands, and she sleeps without worry. Those with pre-ordained destiny surrender to guru the Lord of the universe. O Nanak, they merge in peace and realize God the bestowal of eternal happiness. ||25|| They serve the guru contemplating guru's teaching. They follow guru's will and enshrine God's name in the mind. They are honoured here and hereafter and they deal in God's name. The guru-willed are always recognized in God's true court. They buy truth, spend truth and they love the true beloved Lord in the mind. The devil of death does not approach them; the Creator blesses them. Page 1416 O Nanak, those imbued with God's name are rich, rest of the world is poor. ||26|| God's name is the support of God's servants. Without His name, there is no place of rest. God's name enshrines in the mind through guru's teaching and intuitively merges in peace; the fortunate recite God's name and are in love forever. Servant Nanak begs for the dust of their feet; and admires them forever. ||27|| Millions of species burn in greed and cry; The attachment of worldly wealth is all over; it does not go with you on departure. Without God, peace does not well up; who do we complain to? The fortunate meet the true guru and realize God by thinking. The fire of greed is extinguished O Nanak, enshrining God in the heart. ||28|| We commit many sins; there is no limit to it. O Lord, please be kind and save me; I am a great sinner and a criminal. O dear Lord, if You check my account, my turn will never come; only You can forgive and unite me with you. The kind guru united me with God by eliminating all my sins and useless deeds. Servant Nanak admires and celebrates those, who recite God's name. ||29|| Those who were separated and reunite with God; unite through true guru's love. The guru-willed escape the cycle of birth and death, reciting God's name. Joining the devotees of guru's congregation, the diamonds and jewels are obtained. O Nanak, the guru-willed find the priceless jewel. ||30|| The self-willed do not recite God's name; their life and living is worthless. God, who gives us to eat and wear; why should we not enshrine Him in the mind and sing His praises. This mind does not contemplate guru's teaching; how can it live in its home? The self-willed discarded brides are ruined in coming and going. Reciting God's name is the eternal marriage. The jewel is written on the forehead. Enshrining God's name in the heart, the lotus of mind blooms; I admire those who serve their true guru. O Nanak, those who have God's name enshrined in the heart are happy faces ||31|| Those who die with guru's teaching are saved; without guru's teaching salvation is not obtained. They wear religious robes and perform all sorts of rituals. They are ruined by duality. O Nanak, without the true guru, God's name is not obtained, they may think forever. ||32|| God's name is the greatest and highest of all. No one can reach there; they may think forever. They do not become pure by self-discipline; many wander in such disguises. They climb guru's ladder; it is pre-ordained. God enshrines in the mind if he contemplates guru's teaching. Page 1417 O Nanak, if he dies by guru's teaching, then the mind accepts and the thinking becomes true. ||33|| Emotional attachment of worldly wealth is the ocean of suffering; the terrifying world ocean cannot be crossed over. Screaming, "mine, mine, they rot and die; they pass their life in ego. The self-willed are neither this side nor the other side; they rot in the middle. They act as they are pre-destined; they cannot do anything. The jewel of divine wisdom wells up in the mind through guru's teaching and intuitively realizes God. O Nanak, the fortunate embarks true guru's boat and carries across the terrifying world ocean. ||34|| Without the true guru, there is no giver who can bestow Lord's name. By guru's grace, God's name dwells in the mind and remains enshrined forever. The fire of desire is extinguished, and satisfaction obtained loving God's name. O Nanak, God is realized by His grace. ||35|| Without guru's teaching the world is so insane, that it cannot be described. Those protected by God are saved; they attune to God through guru's teaching. O Nanak, the Creator who created the creation knows everything. ||36|| They perform burnt offerings and the Pandits get tired of reading the Puranaas. The false attachment of the worldly wealth does not end; they keep coming and going in ego. Meeting with the true guru, the filth is washed away by reciting the all-knowing God. Servant Nanak is forever a sacrifice to those who serve the Lord. ||37|| They long for the attachment of worldly wealth; they have great hope and useless greed. The self-willed cannot stabilize. They die and disappear in an instant. They meet the true guru with good fortune and they eliminate ego and useless deeds. They find peace reciting God's name O Nanak, contemplating guru's teaching. ||38|| Without the true guru, there is no devotional worship, and love of God's name does not well up. Servant Nanak recites God's name through the love of the guru. ||39|| Do not trust greedy people, stay away from them; they drag you in such a place where no one can reach and help you. Whoever associates with the self-willed; will have a black mark put on his face. The faces of the greedy are blackened and they waste away their lives. O Lord, unite me with true congregation; so that God's name enshrines in my mind. The filth of many births is erased O Nanak, by singing God's praises. ||40|| Whatever is pre-written by the Creator cannot be erased. Body and soul are all His. The sovereign Lord King cherishes all. The gossipers and slanderers remain hungry and die; they cannot hold on to anything. Outwardly, they do good deeds, but they are hypocrites; they practice deception in the mind. Whatever is planted in the body farm; shall grow and stand before them in the end. Page 1418 Nanak offers this prayer: O God, please be kind and unite me with You. ||41|| My mind does not know about coming and going nor does it know about God's court. He is wrapped in emotional attachment of worldly wealth and filled with ignorance. The sleeping person wakes up, when he is hit on the head by a heavy club. The guru-willed who raises his hands and recites God; reaches the door of salvation; O Nanak, they save themselves, and all their relatives are carried across as well. ||42|| Whoever dies with guru's teaching is known to be dead. By guru's grace, he is satisfied reciting God's name. He is recognized in God's court through guru's teaching. Without guru's teaching, everyone is dead. The self-willed dies; his life is wasted. He does not recite God's name and suffers in the end. O Nanak, whatever the Creator does, comes to pass. ||43|| The guru-willed who understand the divine wisdom inside do not get old. They sing God's praises in the mind with peace and contentment forever. They dwell forever in peace and have discriminating intellect. They see pain and pleasure alike. They see one Lord; realize one Lord, the supreme Lord in all. ||44|| The self-willed is like a child or an old person; they do not think of God inside. They do deeds in ego and all go to the court of justice of destiny. The guru-willed are healthy and pure intuitively through guru's teaching. They are not touched by filth at all if they follow guru's will. The impurity of the self-willed does not wash, even if they wash hundred times. O Nanak, the guru-willed are united with God and merge with God the guru. ||45|| How can someone do bad things, and still live with himself? By his anger, he burns himself. The insane self-willed rubs his nose and struggles with worries and stubborn deeds; the guru-willed understands everything. O Nanak, the guru-willed struggles with his mind. ||46|| Those who do not serve the true guru, and do not contemplate guru's teaching. They are not human beings, call them ignorant animals. They have no spiritual wisdom or thinking. They cannot love God.

The self willed die in evil deeds; they die and reborn, again and again. The living meets the living; he enshrines God the life of the world in the mind. O Nanak, the guru-willed look adorable in true God's court. ||47|| God created this body the God's temple and He lives in it. Following guru's teachings, I have realized God burning away the enticement of worldly wealth. Everything is God's temple; the treasure is realized by reciting God's name. Blessed is that guru-willed happy soul-bride, O Nanak, who realizes God by searching. The fortunate search the body fort and find God in the heart. ||48|| The self-willed wander in ten directions; they are filled with desire and greed. Page 1419 Their attachment to worldly wealth does not end; they die, only to be reborn again. Serving the true guru, peace is found; the useless greed disappears. The pain of death and birth is eliminated O Nanak, contemplating guru's teaching. ||49|| O my mind recite God's name; you will be honoured in God's court. All your sins and crimes will be erased; the pride and ego will depart. The heart-lotus of the guru-willed blossoms, realizing God the soul of all; O God, please be kind that servant Nanak recites Your name. ||50|| The desire of wealth is realized by working for the true guru O brother; By surrendering the body and mind and obeying his command O brother. I sit where He asks me to sit, O brother; I go where He sends me; There is no other wealth as great as God's true name O brother; I sing true God's praises forever and live with him forever. So wear the good deeds and virtues O brother; you eat what you plant. How can I praise Him, O brother? I admire visualizing Him. Great is the greatness of the true guru, O brother; you get it if it is pre-ordained. Some do not know how to obey God's order; they wander deluded by duality. They find no place of rest in the congregation O brother; they find no place to sit. O Nanak: they obey God's command that have earned God's name from destiny. I admire them whole-heartedly forever O brother; ||51|| Those beards are true, which touch the feet of the true guru. They serve their guru all the time and are happy forever. O Nanak, their faces look adorable in true God's court. ||52|| True are the faces and the beards of those who speak the truth and live the truth. Enshrining God's name in the mind they merge in the true guru the God. True is their capital, and true is their wealth; they obtain the high status. They hear the truth, they believe in truth; they act and work in truth. They go to the true court and merge with the true God. O Nanak, without the true guru, the true Lord is not found. The self-willed are lost and depart. ||53|| The rain bird cries for beloved water! She is in love with the treasure of raindrop. Meeting with the guru, the soothing water is obtained, and all the pain leaves. Its thirst quenches, peace wells up; and the cries end. O Nanak, the guru-willed becomes peaceful enshrining God's name in the mind. ||54|| O Rain bird, you are truly happy and attuned to the true Lord. Your word shall be accepted and approved, if you speak as a guru-willed. Contemplating guru's teaching quenches the thirst by obeying God's will. Page 1420 It rains heavily in all four corners and falls drop by drop intuitively. Everything grows from water and the thirst does not quench without water. O Nanak, whoever drinks Godly water, shall never feel hungry again. ||55|| O rain bird, chirp with contentment through guru's teaching intuitively. Everything is with you; true guru will show you. If you realize your-self, you meet the beloved and the rain pours. Drop by drop, the nectar rains down continuously; the thirst and hunger are erased. Then there is no crying; you shall merge with the supreme Lord. O Nanak, the happy soul-brides sleep in peace; they merge with true name. ||56|| God sent it from destiny by His command. It rains continuously with bubbles by His grace. The rain bird becomes peaceful in the body and mind, when raindrop falls in its mouth. Plenty of grain grows and wealth increases and the lands look adorable. People worship God night and day through guru's teaching and realize God. True Lord blesses them, by his kindness and will. O brides, sing God's praises through guru's teaching and merge with true God. Decorate yourself with God's fear and attune to God lovingly. O Nanak, God's name abides in the mind by reciting, and frees you in God's court. ||57|| O rain bird if you fly the whole earth and fly high in the sky; But meeting the true guru obtains the water; that eliminates thirst and hunger. Soul and body all belong to Him; everything is His. He knows everything, without saying; to whom should we offer our prayers? O Nanak, God abides in everybody; He is realized through guru's teaching. ||58|| O Nanak, those who serve the true guru; it is spring season for them. God showers His kindness and every mind and body blossoms; the entire world becomes green. ||59|| It is always spring through guru's teaching; that rejuvenates the mind and body. O Nanak, do not forget God's name; He created everything. ||60|| O Nanak, it is spring season for those; who have God dwelling in the mind. When God showers His grace, the mind and body blossom, and whole world turns lush green. ||61|| In the early morning, whose name should we recite? Recite the name of God; who creates and destroys everything. ||62|| You are the well wheel saying you you and speak the good words. God is always with you; why do you cry so loud? I admire God; who created everything and loves it. Give up your ego, then you shall meet your Husband Lord; believe it. Speaking bland in ego, no one understands the ways of God. The forests and fields, and the entire universe recite You day and night forever. Nobody realizes God without the true guru; many tried in vain. Page 1421 God casts His glance of grace, then He embellishes us. O Nanak, the guru-willed who recite God; their coming in the world is worthwhile. ||63|| God's worship is not wearing saffron coloured or dirty clothes. O Nanak, God is worshipped sitting home through true guru's teaching. ||64|| You may wander in all four corners and read four Vedas in all four ages. O Nanak, if you meet with the true guru, then God enshrines in the mind and obtains salvation. O Nanak, God's command rules; your mind might wander misled by flickering mind. If you make friends with the self-willed O friend, whom can you ask for peace? Make friends with the guru-willed, and focus your mind to the true guru; the root cause of birth and death ends, and you shall find peace, O friend. ||66|| The Lord guides the lost, whoever He bestows his blessing to; O Nanak, those without His grace, cry and cry. ||67|| Hymn, Fourth Master: God is one. He is realized by guru's grace. Fortunate are married forever; those who realize God the Lord. Divine light shines inside O Nanak, they absorb in God's name. ||1|| The true guru the primal being is admirable, who knows God and guides to realize God. Meeting Him, thirst is quenched, and the body and mind are soothed. The true guru the primal being is admirable; he has true realization. Admirable is the enemyless true guru; who accepts admiration and slanders the same.

Admirable is the all-knowing true guru; who contemplates divine wisdom inside. Admirable is the formless true guru; there is no limit to His creation. Admirable is the true guru, who implants the truth in all; O Nanak, admirable is the true guru; who blesses us with God's name. ||2|| The guru-willed sing God's true song reciting the name of the lord of the universe. He recites God's name all the time and enjoys reciting; The fortunate realize God the source of perfect happiness. O Nanak, by reciting God's name; there shall be no hindrance to mind or body. ||3|| I am in love with my beloved; how can I meet my dear friend? I seek that friend, who truly takes care of all. True guru is my friend; if I meet Him, I will offer this mind to Him. He has shown me my beloved Lord, my friend, the Creator. O Nanak, I was searching for my beloved; the true guru showed Him in me. ||4|| I stand by the side of the road, waiting for You; O my friend, I hope that You will come. If someone would come today and unite me with my beloved; Page 1422 I will offer my body to him lovingly, if someone unites me with my beloved. O Nanak, when God is kind then one meets the perfect guru. ||5|| I am filled with ego and longing for wealth; it is all false; it goes the way it comes. If you do not obey guru's teaching; then the terrifying world ocean cannot be crossed. Whoever is blessed by God; follows guru's will. Seeing the true guru is fruitful; you can receive the reward of your choice. I touch the feet of those who believe and obey the true guru. Nanak is the slave of those, who night and day remain lovingly attuned to God. ||6|| Those who are in love with their beloved – how can they find satisfaction without seeing him? O Nanak, the guru-willed meets Him intuitively and enjoys. ||7|| Those who are in love with their beloved – how can they live without Him? When they see their Husband Lord, O Nanak, they are rejuvenated. ||8|| Those guru-willed who are filled with love for You O my true beloved; O Nanak, they remain immersed in the Lord's love, night and day. ||9|| The love of the guru-willed is true; through it, the true beloved is realized. Night and day, they are happy O Nanak, and merge in peace. ||10|| True love and affection are obtained from the perfect guru. It never breaks, O Nanak, if one sings the praises of the Lord. ||11|| How can those who have true love in them, live without their Husband Lord? The Lord unites the guru-willed with Him O Nanak, those separated for a long time. ||12|| You grant Your grace to those whom You bless with love and affection. O Lord, please bless Nanak with God's name and unite the beggar with you. ||13|| The guru-willed laughs and cries; whatever the guru-willed does is the real worship. Whoever becomes guru-willed contemplates the Lord. The guru-willed O Nanak crosses over to the other shore. ||14|| Those who have the treasure of God's name inside; they contemplate guru's sermon. Their faces are always happy in the court of the true Lord. If God blesses them, they never forget God whether standing or sitting. O Nanak, once united, the guru-willed never separate from God; if He unites them. ||15|| To work for the guru, or a spiritual teacher, is difficult, but it brings real peace. Whoever God casts His glance of grace to; they fall in love with Him. Serving the true guru, the mortal crosses over the terrifying world-ocean; He obtains the reward of choice, with clear contemplation and discriminating intellect inside. O Nanak, meeting the true guru, meets God; the destroyer of all sins. ||16|| The self-willed may perform service, but attaching his mind to duality. The emotional attachment to children, spouse and relatives increases the attachment to worldly wealth. When his account is called in God's court; no one can save him. Page 1423 Without God's name, everything is painful. Attachment to worldly wealth gives pain. O Nanak, the guru-willed realizes God and the enticing worldly wealth departs. ||17|| The guru-willed obeys the order of the beloved Lord and obtains peace through it. Obeying God's order, he recites God and merges with God through God's command. Obeying God's command is, taking a vow, fast, cleansing ritual, and self – discipline. And he obtains the reward of his choice. She, who realizes God's command, is married forever; she serves the true guru with love. O Nanak, whoever God blesses, unites them with Him by his command. ||18|| The ignorant self-willed do not realize His order; they continuously act in ego. By keeping fasts, vows, purities, self-discipline and ceremonial worship, they still cannot get rid of their hypocrisy and doubt. Inside they are impure, enticed by worldly wealth; they are like elephants, who throws dirt on the body right after bath. They do not remember the Creator who created them. Without thinking of Him, they cannot find peace. O

Nanak, the primal Creator played the game such a way that all act, as they are pre programmed. ||19|| The guru-willed realizes and his mind satisfies. Night and day, he serves the Lord, and absorbs in Him. Everyone worships the true guru inside and all come to see the true guru. Obeying the guru contemplates the supreme wisdom; meeting him eliminates the hunger and thirst. I praise my guru forever, who unites us with God. O Nanak, those who come and fall at guru's feet are blessed with truthful deeds. ||20|| The beloved who I love is with me. I wander inside and outside, but I always keep Him enshrined in my heart. ||21|| Those who recite God attaching to the true guru lovingly; they get rid of pain, hunger, and the illness of ego. They become sin free lovingly attuning to God. They sing His praises, and speak His praises; they sing his praises in sleep. O Nanak, through the perfect guru, they realize God and merge in peace. ||22|| The self-willed are emotionally attached to worldly wealth; they cannot love God's name. They practice falsehood, gather falsehood, and eat falsehood. They gather the poisonous worldly wealth and property! It becomes dirt in the end. They perform religious rituals of purity and self-discipline, but they are filled with greed, evil and corruption. O Nanak, whatever the self-willed earns is not accepted; he suffers pain in God's court. ||23|| Of all tunes, that is the best through which God enshrines in the mind. Tunes and singing is all true; its value cannot be expressed. Without tune and singing, God's command cannot be understood. O Nanak, those who understand God's command obtain the wealth; it is realized through the true guru. Everything happens by His will. ||24|| Page 1424 The nectar of God's name is in the true guru; that is the real nectar. Follow guru's true teachings, recite God's name through guru's teaching. Guru's sermon is the essence of nectar; it enshrines in the mind of the guru-willed. The lotus blossoms in the heart; and one's light merges in the supreme Light. O Nanak, those with pre-ordained destiny meet the true guru. ||25|| The self-willed is burning with the fire of greed and his hunger does not vanish. Emotional attachments to family are false; they remain engrossed in falsehood. Night and day, they are troubled by anxiety; bound by anxiety, they depart. Their coming and going does not end; they do their deeds in ego. They are saved in guru's refuge and he frees them

O Nanak. ||26|| The true guru recites God the primal being in devotee's company through love. Those, who join the congregation and serve the true guru – the guru unites them with God. The world is a terrifying ocean. Guru's boat carries them across reciting God's name. Guru's followers obey his will and the perfect guru carries them across. O God; bless me with the dust of the feet of guru's followers that I the sinner obtain salvation. Those with pre-ordained destiny written on their foreheads by God, meet the guru O Nanak. He drives away the devil of death and frees them in God's court. Blessed are guru's devotees; the honourable God unites them with Him. ||27|| The perfect guru implanted God's name in me; it dispelled my doubts from within. Reciting God's name and singing God's praise; he enlightens and shows the path. Conquering my ego, I am lovingly attuned to God; enshrining His name in the mind. Following guru's teaching the devil of death cannot rob and you merge in true name. The Creator pervades all; whoever he pleases, blesses them with His name. Servant Nanak lives by reciting His name; he will die without God's name in a moment. ||28|| The evil self-willed are sick with ego and wander lost in doubt. O Nanak, meeting the true guru and a devotee friend, the sickness is cured. ||29|| Say God God following guru's teaching. Attracted by God's love, day and night, the body-robe is imbued with God's love. I cannot find primal being like God. I have searched the entire world. The true guru has implanted God's name in me; my mind does not waver anymore. Servant Nanak is the slave of the Lord, the slave of the slaves of the true guru. ||30|| Page 1425. Hymn, Fifth Master: God is one. He is realized by guru's grace. Those who do not turn away from God are imbued with Him and realize Him. They are falsely detached; those who do not know to detach fall down; ||1|| Without my master, I will burn my silk clothes in the fire. O Nanak I will enjoy rolling in Your dust. ||2|| Recite God's name with love and detach through guru's teaching. I conquered five passions and the tune of detachment is rewarded O Nanak. ||3|| You are the only one for me and there are millions like me standing at Your door. O scholar, your life is useless if you forget the one who created you. ||4|| Drink such nectar in the early morning that never loses its taste. O Nanak, sing the praises of God's name, which is honoured, in God's court. ||5|| Whoever is protected by God, no one can kill him. The treasure of God's name is in the mind; it is the essence of all virtues. Take the support of the immortal God and enshrine Him in the mind. Imbued with the infinite God's love; no one can take it away. The guru-willed sings God's praise and obtains peace and contentment. O Nanak, they enshrine the treasure of God's name in their hearts. ||6|| Whatever he does, accept it as good; it eliminates the love of duality. God attaches you to Him by His grace. O God; please guide me that my doubt goes away. Whatever is written in your fate that is what you do? Everything is under His control; there is no other place like it. Nanak is at peace and bliss accepting the will of God. ||7|| Those who recite the perfect guru are content; O Nanak, reciting God's name all deeds are fulfilled. The sinners commit sins and cry. O Nanak, the justice of destiny churns like a churning stick. ||9|| O friend, reciting God's name conquers the priceless life. O Nanak, such a faith wells up and the body becomes sacred. ||10|| I am stuck in an evil place; the ill advice appears good to me. O Nanak, only the fortunate is saved. ||11|| They are imbued with love, with their Lord and sleep in peace. They feel the pain of separation from Lord twenty-four hours a day. ||12|| Millions are asleep, in the false illusion of worldly wealth. O Nanak, those who recite God's name with their tongue remain awake. ||13|| Seeing the mirage, the people are confused and deluded. Those who recite the true Lord; they are adorable in the mind and body O Nanak. ||14|| All-powerful supreme Lord, infinite primal being saves the sinners. Page 1426 Those, whom He saves, recite the Creator. ||15|| Forsake duality and evil ways; focus your mind on one Lord. In love of duality, O Nanak, the mortals are washed away. ||16|| The traders trade in three pronged market. Those who load the true merchandise are the true traders. ||17|| The ignorant does not know the path of love; she is confused and lost. O Nanak, forgetting God, they fall in a dark pit of hell. ||18|| They do not forget the worldly wealth from the mind and beg for more and more. They do not remember God. It is not in their fate O Nanak. ||19|| It never falls short as long as God is kind to them. O Nanak, guru's teaching is an inexhaustible treasure; it never falls short by eating and spending. ||20|| If I find the feathers on sale;

I will buy it for the correct price. I will attach them to my body, fly around and find my friend. ||21|| My friend the true supreme Lord is emperor of emperors. The company you sit in, you should have faith in it. God is one. He is realized by guru's grace. Hymns of Ninth Master: If you do not sing the praises of God, your life is a waste. Says Nanak, recite God O mind, as the fish misses water. ||1|| Why are you engrossed in sins? You do not feel the pain of separation from God. Says Nanak, recite God O mind, so that you are not caught in the noose of death. ||2|| Your have spent your youth taking care of your body. Says Nanak, recite God O mind; the life is passing by. ||3|| You have become old, and you do not understand that death is near. Says Nanak, O ignorant being, why do not you recite God? ||4|| Your wealth, spouse and all the possessions which you claim as your own; Nothing goes with you O Nanak, believe it; ||5|| He is the saviour of sinners and guardian of orphans. Says Nanak, realize Him, who is always with you. ||6|| He gave you body and wealth; yet you do not love Him. Says Nanak, O poor ignorant man; why do you waver now? ||7|| He, who gave you body wealth property and beautiful place to live; Says Nanak, listen O mind: why don't you recite God? ||8|| God is the giver of peace and comfort. There is no other; Says Nanak, listen O mind: reciting Him obtains salvation. ||9|| Page 1427 Reciting Him obtains salvation; worship Him, He is your friend; Says Nanak, listen O mind: your life is passing by! ||10|| Your body is made up of the five elements; know this O wise and clever man. O Nanak, merge with Him from whom you are born; ||11|| God pervades in every soul; the saints proclaim and tell everyone. Says Nanak, recite Him O mind and go across the terrifying world ocean. ||12|| One who is not touched by pleasure, pain, greed and egotistic pride? Says Nanak, listen O mind: he is the image of God. ||13|| One, who is beyond praise and slander, and looks at gold and iron alike; Says Nanak, listen O mind: he has attained salvation. ||14|| He is not affected by pleasure or pain; he looks at friend and foe alike, says Nanak, listen O mind: he has attained salvation. ||15|| He does not scare anyone, and he is not afraid of anyone. Says Nanak, listen O mind: call him a divine person. ||16|| He who gives up all sins and becomes detached from the world; Says Nanak, listen O mind: good luck is written on his forehead. ||17|| One who renounces worldly wealth and is detached from everything; Says Nanak, listen O mind: God lives in his heart. ||18|| That mortal, who forsakes ego, realizes the Creator Lord; Says Nanak, that person is liberated; O mind, believe it true. ||19|| Enshrining God's name in the mind, fear and evil will go away. O Nanak, he who recites God day and night; his deeds are rewarded. ||20|| Sing God's praises with tongue and listen God's name with ears. Says Nanak, listen O man: you shall not have to go to the place of death. ||21|| The mortal who renounces possessiveness, greed, emotional attachment and ego; Says Nanak, he saves himself and others as well. ||22|| Know that the world is like a dream. None of this is true, O Nanak, without God. ||23|| Night and day, for the sake of worldly wealth, your mind wavers all the time; O Nanak, there are only a few who keep God in the mind. ||24|| As the bubbles in the water well up and disappear again; that is how the creation is created listen O friend. ||25|| The mortal does not remember anything intoxicated and blinded by worldly wealth. Says Nanak, without reciting God; he falls in the trap of the devil of death. ||26|| If you yearn for eternal peace, then seek the sanctuary of the Lord. Says Nanak, listen O mind: this human body is difficult to obtain. ||27|| For the sake of worldly wealth the fools and ignorant wander all over; Says Nanak, without worshipping God, the life passes away uselessly. ||28|| The mortal who recites God day and night; know that he is the image of God; Page 1428 There is no difference between God and His devotee O Nanak, believe it; ||29|| The mind is entangled in worldly wealth and forgot the name of the Lord of the universe. Says Nanak, without worshipping God; what good is the life? ||30|| The mortal does not think of God; he is blinded by the wine of worldly wealth. Says Nanak, without worshipping God; he is caught in the noose of death. ||31|| In good times, there are many friends; there is no friend in bad times. Says Nanak, recite God; he will help you in the end. ||32|| Mortals wander through countless lifes; their fear of death never ends. Says Nanak, recite God and you shall realize the carefree God. I have tried so many ways, but the pride of my mind has not been erased. Nanak is caught in evil-mindedness, O God; please save me! ||34|| Childhood, youth and old age, are the three stages of life. Says Nanak, without worshipping God; all are useless. ||35|| You did not do what you were supposed to do; you are caught in the trap of greed. O Nanak, the time is gone by; why are you crying now, you blind ignorant? ||36|| The mind is absorbed in worldly wealth. It cannot escape my friend! O Nanak, it is like a shadow which does not leave the ground. ||37|| The man wishes for something, but something different happens. He thinks of cheating others O Nanak, but the noose of death catches him. ||38|| He makes lots of efforts for happiness but nothing for sorrow. Says Nanak, listen O mind: whatever pleases God comes to pass. ||39|| The world wanders around begging, but God is the giver of all. Says Nanak, O my mind; recite him so that your deed is fulfilled. ||40|| Why do you take pride in falsehood? Know that the world is like a dream. None of this is yours; Nanak says it to you. ||41|| You are proud of your body; it shall perish in a moment, my friend! The mortal who sings God's praise conquers the world; ||42|| Those who recite God are liberated; know that; There is no difference between him and God; believe it O Nanak. ||43|| The person, who does not worship God in his mind; O Nanak, know that his body is like a pig, or a dog. ||44|| A dog never leaves the home of his master. O Nanak, recite God this way single-mindedly. ||45|| Those who make pilgrimages to shrines observe fasts and give awns and then feel proud of it; O Nanak, it goes waste like the elephant taking bath. ||46|| The head shakes, the feet stagger, and the eyes cannot see. Says Nanak, this is your condition. Even then you do not enjoy reciting God. ||47|| Page 1429 I have looked around the world; but no one belongs to anyone else. O Nanak, only God's worship is eternal; keep Him in the mind; ||48|| The worldly creation is all false; know this O friend. Says Nanak, it is like a wall of sand; it shall not last. ||49|| Raam Chander is gone; so is Raawan who had a large family; Says Nanak, nothing is forever; the world is like a dream. ||50|| You should worry only if it happens, which was not supposed to happen. This is the way of the world, O Nanak, nothing is permanent. ||51|| Whoever is born has to die today or tomorrow. O Nanak, sing God's praises and give up all worldly entanglements. ||52|| Dohraa: My strength is gone, and I am caught in bonds; I cannot do anything. Says Nanak; now, God is my support;

He will help me, as He did to the elephant. ||53|| If you have strength the bonds are broken and everything can be done. O Nanak: everything is in Your hand O Lord; please help me now. ||54|| My friends and companions have all left me; no one remains with me. Says Nanak, in this tragedy, God alone is my support. ||55|| God's name remains; the devotee remains; the guru, the Lord of the universe, remains. Says Nanak, those who recite guru's word are rare. ||56|| Enshrine God's name in the soul; nothing equals it. Reciting Him, the calamities are erased and God is visualized. ||57||1|| Seal of approval Fifth Master: There are three things put on the platter; truth contentment and knowledge. In that is the sacred name of God; He is the support of all. One who eats and digests it; he is liberated. This can never be forgotten once enshrined in the soul. The world is spiritually ignorant; falling at guru's feet liberates it! The world is God's creation O Nanak. ||1|| Hymn fifth Master. I do not know Your creation. I just worship You; I am unworthy – I have no virtue. You have taken pity on me. You took pity on me and blessed me; I met the true guru, my friend. O Nanak, if I am blessed with God's name, my mind and body will blossom. ||1|| Rosary of tunes; God is one. He is realized by guru's grace. There is one tune (God). The whole world sings His praise in classical Tunes in the group of five; The first major tune is Tune Bhairao (Devotee's tune). Page 1430 It sings the praise of God in a group of five including other sub tunes. First sub tune in the group is Bhairavee, and Bilaavalee; Your praises are sung in melodious tunes. Then comes the turn of other truthful tunes; these are the five tunes of major tune Bhairao. All five sing Your praises joyfully in godly tunes. Singing your praises in beautiful tunes full of melody. ||1|| Tunes Lalat and Bilaaval – each have their own melody. Everyone is the son of Bhairav (God). Sings your praise in devotion! ||1|| The second major tune is Maalakausak (Acquired knowledge) also sing Your praises in the group of five tunes! Gondakaree and Dev Gandhaaree sing Your praises in loud voice. Including Dhanaasaree and maal Tune in the group of Maalakausak; Maaroo Tune is the devotional tune of Maiwar sung emotionally in the group. The devotional singers sing their best. Every one is the son of Maalakausak (God). ||1|| Then comes Hindol (joy) sing Your praises in the group of five. They sing in harmony to the best of their ability. ||1|| Then, comes Taylangee the music of gods; it is sung with the best attire including saffron on forehead. The universe blooms and becomes green O brother; here also Your praises are sung in the group of five tunes. The singers come well dressed wearing mascara, scent of sandalwood on the forehead and wearing the sacred thread. The whole atmosphere fills with joy; they sing Your praises in tune Basant with musical instruments. God pervades in every one. Then comes the turn of Deepak (enlightenment) ||1|| Todee Tune is sung with lot of zest in the group of five tunes. Goojree Tune is sung with musical instruments in the group major Tune Deepak. ||1|| The ugly the beautiful and the devotees of God; all are the children of the same flower The God. Tune Gauraa, Kaanaraa and Kaylaanaa; all are the son of Deepak (God). ||1|| All join and sing Siree Tune (tune to honour God) that also is sung in the group of five. Bairaaree is the tune of Karnaatka. The Aasaavaree is sung in a simple tune. Then follows Tune Sindhavee; It is also the part of the group of tune siree Tune. ||1|| Deep tune Tune Saarag is sung in deep devotion and Tune Gond is serious. Everyone is the son of Siree Tune (God) whether named Gund, Kumbh or Hameer. ||1|| The sixth major tune is Maygh Tune. (tune of guru`s grace) Also sung in the group of five tunes! The tunes Sorath, Gond, and Malaar are part of Mayagh Tune. Including Aasaa that is sung in slow rhythm in the head; All sung in devotion loudly and form the part of the group of five the Maygh Tune. ||1|| The salty land, jungles, the religious shrines, the land of warriors and the land of rivers; everywhere the devotees and the prophets sing Your praises. Those are the names of the sons of God the Maygh Tune. ||1|| Six major tunes have been sung including the sub tunes totalling thirty in Your admiration. One more added later. All are the sons of the Creator of music (God) whether eighteen, ten or twenty. ||1||1||